The Best Book of Microsoft Works for the PC

2nd Edition

RELATED TITLES

The Best Book of WordPerfect® 5.1
Vincent Alfieri, Revised by Ralph Blodgett

The Best Book of: WordStar® (Features Release 5.0)
Vincent Alfieri

The Best Book of Microsoft Word 5
Kate Miller Barnes

The First Book of WordPerfect® 5.1
Kate Barnes

The Best Book of: dBASE IV™
Joseph-David Carrabis

The First Book of Microsoft® Word 5
Brent D. Heslop and David Angell

The First Book of Paradox® 3
Jonathan Kamin

The First Book of PC Tools® Deluxe
Gordon McComb

The First Book of Quicken
Gordon McComb

The Best Book of DESQ™View
Jack Nimersheim

The First Book of ProComm Plus
Jack Nimersheim

The Best Book of: DOS
Alan Simpson

The Best Book of: Lotus® 1-2-3®, Third Edition, Release 2.2
Alan Simpson

The First Book of Lotus® 1-2-3®, Release 2.2
Alan Simpson and Paul Lichtman

The Best Book of Microsoft® Word for Windows
Richard Swadley

The Best Book of Professional Write and File
Douglas J. Wolf

The Best Book of *Microsoft Works for the PC*

2nd Edition

Ruth K. Witkin

HOWARD W. SAMS & COMPANY

A Division of Macmillan, Inc.

11711 North College, Suite 141, Carmel, IN 46032 USA

SECOND EDITION
FIRST PRINTING—1990

International Standard Book Number: 0-672-22710-X
Library of Congress Catalog Card Number: 89-90-60522

Acquisitions Editor: *James S. Hill and Scott Arant*
Development Editor: *Jim Rounds and Scott Arant*
Manuscript and Production Editor: *reVisions Plus, Inc.*
Editorial Coordinator: *Amy Perry*
Illustrator: *Don Clemons*
Production Coordinator: *Becky Imel*
Cover Art: *DGS&D Advertising, Inc.*
Cover Photography: *Cassell Productions, Inc.*
Indexer: *Hilary Adams*
Production: *Brad Chinn, Sally Copenhaver, Tami Hughes, William Hurley, Jodi Jensen, Jennifer Matthews, Joe Ramon, Dennis Sheehan, Bruce Steed, Mary Beth Wakefield, Nora Westlake*

Printed in the United States of America

To Burt, Karen, and David, with love.

Overview

Contents

P A R T

one

Getting Acquainted with Works 1

P A R T

The Spreadsheet 41

P A R T

three

The Database 167

P A R T

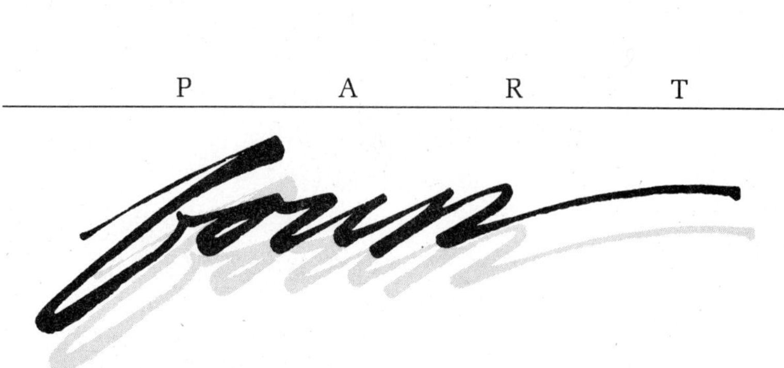

The Word Processor 273

P A R T

Five

P A R T

Six

Works Fireworks 391

Introduction

Works is an all-in-one spreadsheet, database, word processing, and communications package.

Welcome to the world of Microsoft Works, and what a dazzling world it is. Works combines the four most important applications—spreadsheet, database management, word processing, and communications—in one easy-to-use package. Works is integrated, so you can switch from one application to another with lightning speed, copy between applications with little effort, and mix text and graphics with remarkable results. Integration also means consistency in commands, keystrokes, and screen layouts, which makes it easy to apply what you learn in one application to all the others. After only a short time, you're bound to be surprised at how even the new things take on a familiar ring.

The Works spreadsheet works with numbers. It lets you develop budgets, prepare financial forecasts, calculate loan payments, track everyday operations, and explore "what if" scenarios to gauge the dollar impact of what you're thinking about doing before you actually do it. When you rework those numbers, Works recalculates instantly. A powerful charting feature lets you turn those spreadsheet numbers into graphs enhanced with text.

The database is a vast filing system. It gives you a place to store and organize the details that abound: facts and figures, names and addresses, inventory and invoices, then sort, select, and switch them around—and, even better, find them in record time. The database's reporting feature lets you produce polished, professional reports including summaries and statistics.

The word processor handles words from memos to manuscripts. It lets you enter, edit, and format text, explore your creativity in every way, check spelling, and then print documents with dash. The merge feature makes it easy to pull data from the database to print personalized form letters and mailing labels.

The communications application and a modem (an electronic conversion device) gives you access to other personal computers and a wide range of electronic information services including bulletin boards and commercial databases.

Works provides a calculator, alarm clock, and telephone dialer.

Works also provides a built-in calculator, alarm clock, and telephone dialer—handy accessories you'll use every day.

Threading through all these applications and accessories is the macro feature. Macros let you perform a whole series of tasks with only a keystroke or two, speeding and smoothing your work with Works.

A file is a collection of related information.

Even more, you can have as many as eight windows open on screen at one time and display a different spreadsheet, database, word processor, or communications file in each of them.

About This Book

If you're new to Works, this book will get you up and running in the shortest possible time. If you're already working well with Works, you'll find shortcuts and techniques that can help you work even better. Everything is written in plain English, not computerese, so you don't need any programming, technical, or computer background to understand it.

The book is organized into seven parts. The first part, *Getting Acquainted with Works*, deals with elements common to the Works program, including menus, commands, the mouse, windows, and macros.

The next four parts—*The Spreadsheet, The Database, The Word-Processor*, and *Works and the Outside World (Communications)*—cover each Works application individually. Each section starts with concepts followed by a workout chapter that lets you try your hand at a practical example. Each step is explained before you take it, and numerous illustrations keep you on course to a successful conclusion. The Communications part doesn't contain a workout example.

Part Six, aptly called *Works Fireworks*, describes how to merge files created in different applications and again provides a workout example. The last part, *Putting Works To Work*, is filled with practical examples that sharpen your skills and let you experience the fun of working with macros.

The book ends with a comprehensive glossary. If you aren't familiar with any of the terms mentioned in the book, chances are you'll find a definition in the glossary.

Read concepts first or jump right in. The choice is yours.

Some people prefer to learn concepts first, while others find it easier to tackle a program after some hands-on experience. This book accommodates both approaches. You can read through the concepts or jump right in with a workout. The workout explains everything you need to know at that point. Whichever way you choose to go, be patient with yourself. Don't expect everything to sink in at the first keystroke or the first reading. That's rare for anyone, even you.

The System Used in This Book

Because system configurations differ, it's always interesting to know what kind of equipment was used to develop the material you're reading and working with.

I developed the hands-on examples on my Tandy 4000SX, which has a 16 MHz Intel 80386SX microprocessor, one megabyte of memory, one 5.25-inch drive, one 3.5-inch drive, and an 80-megabyte SCSI hard disk. It's running under MS-DOS version 3.30. I produced the figures, including screen dumps and charts, on my Tandy LP-1000 laser printer in HP LaserJet+ mode.

You don't have to match this configuration (or even come close) to create every example in this book. You will, however, need Microsoft Works version 2.0. Earlier versions are simply not in step with the step-by-step instructions.

Rules of the Game

Rules of the game, called *conventions*, explain how the author presents information and instructions. Here are the conventions that apply to this book:

Computer font and boldface. Words, phrases, and messages that Works displays on the screen appear in computer font in this book to distinguish them from the surrounding text. For example, the screen message that describes the Move command—`Moves selection to another location`—appears in computer font. Text and numbers that you type—for example, type **FX** or type **2**—appear in boldface.

Uppercase. Filenames and the names of special calculating functions, such as SUM, are shown in uppercase letters for the same reason—to make them stand out from the surrounding text in this book. It doesn't matter if you type filenames, function names, or anything else, for that matter, in uppercase or lowercase.

A dialog box gives or asks for more information.

Cursors. A cursor is a moveable highlight that shows where action can take place on the screen. Works has two cursors that appear in different areas. To distinguish one from the other, the cursor in the workspace is called the *cursor*. The cursor that appears in dialog boxes is called the *blinker*.

Arrow-Marked Keys. Certain computer keyboards have arrows instead of keynames imprinted on keys. Shift is the key with a thick arrow pointing up, Tab has opposing arrows, Enter shows a broken arrow pointing left, and Backspace shows a straight arrow pointing left. The text refers to these keys by their keynames, not arrows.

*Arrow keys are also called **direction keys**.*

Arrow Keys. The Arrow keys that move the cursor are referred to in the text as Left Arrow, Up Arrow, Right Arrow, and Down Arrow. These keys are usually clustered at the right side of the keyboard, often in or near the numbers keypad. Arrow keys are not the same as arrow-marked keys. You'll find the differences between them easy to discern once you get started.

Key Combinations. When you see a two-key combination such as Shift+F1 in the text, hold down the first key (Shift) and press the second key (F1). With three-key combinations such as Ctrl+Shift+F8, hold down the first two keys (Control and Shift) and press the third key (F8). If you hold down both keys in a two-key combination or all three keys in a three-key combination, they won't work. The use of these keys will become clearer as you go through each application.

Icons. Small graphic images, called *icons*, appear at appropriate places throughout the book. Like roadsigns, these icons alert you to something special coming up. Watch for them!

This icon marks a *tip* to help you master the fine points.

This icon shows a neat trick—a super tip for power users.

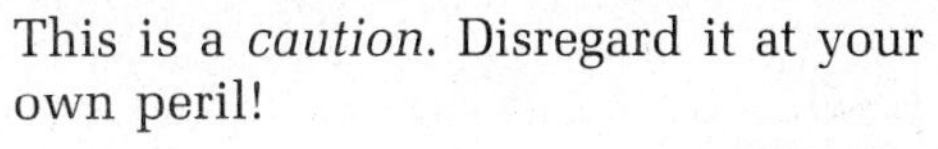
This is a *caution*. Disregard it at your own peril!

This icon marks a preview of the skill sharpeners present in the hands-on chapters.

This icon marks a macro that speeds and simplifies your work with Works.

The Disks That Run Works

The Works program and Learning Works tutorial are stored on 5.25-inch floppy disks and 3.5-inch minidisks. Which size you use depends on the type of disk drive available on your computer.

Before you do anything else, make a copy of each of the original disks. Keep the originals in a safe place and work only with the copies. (You should use the copies even when you install Works on a hard disk.)

You'll also need several blank, formatted data disks to hold the files you create. This applies to floppy disk, minidisk, and hard disk users.

Copy and format instructions are in your DOS manual and the Works manual.

You'll find copy and format instructions in your computer's DOS (Disk Operating System) manual and in the Works manual (see *Disks* in the *Files, Windows, & Accessories* section). You can use some DOS commands, including COPY and FORMAT, without leaving Works. These commands—called Copy Disk and Format Disk—are accessible via the File Management command in the File menu.

Backing Up Your Work

Disks are reasonably hardy, but they can be damaged by heat, dust, magnetism, spills, and careless handling. It's imperative that you keep the very latest version of your work on a backup data disk. Floppy disk and minidisk users should keep two copies of each data disk—a working master and a backup. Hard disk users usually find that one backup data disk is sufficient, although two backups can be comforting if disaster strikes.

Before you turn off your computer, even for a short while, be sure to back up every file that you've changed even slightly. No excuses.

Understanding Works Backup Files

Works can play an important part in protecting your work. Assume you created and saved a file and then made changes to it. When you save it again, you can tell Works not to overwrite the earlier version, but keep it as a backup file instead. If you later change your mind about the changes, you can easily bring back the backup version.

In the Works directory, Works assigns an extension beginning with the letter B (for Backup), so you can distinguish it from the active file. For example, BUDGET.WKS is the current budget spreadsheet, while BUDGET.BKS is its backup.

Backup files take up room on a disk. When you're sure you have no further use for the backup, delete it in DOS or Works.

Printing Works

Works supports many makes and models of dot-matrix, daisy wheel, and laser printers. The instructions in the hands-on chapters assume you're working with a dot-matrix printer. Dot-matrix printers have the ability to mix font sizes and styles on the same page (as in the examples in Chapters 15 and 25) and print charts. The fonts Works makes available to you depend on the capability of your printer.

You can print the examples with a laser or a daisy wheel printer, of course. Some laser printers can produce only one font per page, but most will print the examples beautifully. If you're using a daisy wheel printer, you'll be able to print everything but the charts, and you will be unable to mix fonts on a page.

You'll find detailed printer information in the Works manual.

Running the Setup Program

It takes only a few minutes to get Works and your computer humming in perfect harmony. Simply use the Setup program to copy the Works files to a hard disk system or make a working copy of Works for a minidisk (3.5-inch) or floppy disk (5.25-inch) system. During Setup, you need to tell Works about your printer, video card, monitor, and mouse (if you intend to use one).

Working with a Hard Disk System

To set up Works on a hard disk:

1. Turn on your computer if it's not already turned on.
2. Insert your backup copy of the Works Setup/Utilities disk in drive A or B, whichever is appropriate.
3. At the DOS prompt (usually `C:>`), type **A:SETUP** or **B:SETUP**, as appropriate, and press Enter. (The letter refers to the current drive—the one where your computer looks for information it needs to process your instructions.) Follow the instructions that appear on the screen.

Printer drivers and video drivers are stored in compressed form on the Works disks (extension `.CPR` for Compressed Printer or `.CVD` for Compressed Video Driver). You can only bring a driver into the Works program via the Setup steps, which decompresses the driver and makes it usable to Works. So, if you get a new printer or new video system, run the Setup program again.

Working with a Minidisk or Floppy Disk System

To set up Works on a minidisk or floppy disk system:

1. Insert your DOS disk in drive A and turn on your computer if it's not already turned on.
2. When the DOS prompt appears, replace the DOS disk in drive A with your backup copy of the Works Setup/Utilities disk.
3. At the DOS prompt (usually `A:>`), type **A:SETUP**, and press Enter. (The letter refers to the current drive—the one where your computer looks for information it needs to process your instructions.) Follow the instructions that appear on the screen.

The prompt lets you know your computer is ready to accept instructions.

Loading Works

A few simple steps get Works up and running. Follow the instructions below under "Working with a Hard Disk System" or "Working with a Minidisk or Floppy Disk System." It doesn't matter if you use uppercase or lowercase.

Working with a Hard Disk System

1. Turn on your computer if it's not already turned on. The DOS prompt appears on your screen.
2. At the DOS prompt, change to the directory into which you copied Works (normally WORKS). Using your directory name, type **CD DIRECTORYNAME** and press Enter.
3. When the DOS prompt reappears, type **WORKS** and press Enter.

Loading Works with a Batch File

The easy way to load Works from a hard disk is with a batch file you've written. A batch file is a list of DOS commands you want DOS to perform one after the other. The exact syntax of the batch file depends on how you direct the file traffic in DOS. For example, my Works batch file (named *W.BAT*) looks like this:

```
ECHO OFF
CD C:\WORKS
WORKS
CD\
TYPE RUTH.MNU
```

These commands automate the manual steps described earlier. I only have to type a simple **W** at the DOS prompt to load the Works program. Here's how it works:

ECHO OFF turns off the display of batch file commands.

CD C:\WORKS gives the path name to the Works subdirectory. (CD is the DOS command for *Change Directory*.)

WORKS gives the name of the program to load.

CD\ gives the path to the root directory after I quit Works.

TYPE RUTH.MNU brings up the natty root directory menu I created as an ANSI file.

Batch files are a fascinating subject unto themselves. They're particularly relevant for hard disk users. You can learn more about batch files and pathnames in your DOS manual and computer-related publications. Virtually every issue has something about it.

Loading Works and a Works File at the Same Time

If you work with the same file almost all of the time, you can save keystrokes by opening that file when you load Works. At the DOS prompt or in a batch file, you can enter a command line argument that takes one of these forms:

`WORKS FILENAME.EXT`—Opens the specified file (in place of FILENAME.EXT) when loading Works

`WORKS FILENAME.EXT FILENAME.EXT`—Opens all specified files when loading Works

`WORKS B:DIRECTORYNAME\FILENAME.EXT`—Opens the specified file in the specified directory when loading Works

You can open as many as eight files in this way.

Working with a Minidisk or Floppy Disk System

1. Insert the DOS disk in drive A and turn on the computer if it's not already turned on.
2. At the DOS prompt, replace the DOS disk in drive A with your working copy of the Works Program disk. This is the working copy created during the Setup steps.
3. If your computer has a second disk drive, insert a blank formatted disk in drive B. Works will store your work on this disk.
4. At the DOS prompt, type **WORKS** and press Enter.

The Gateway to Works

Commands tell Works what to do.

Whichever route you take—hard disk, minidisk, or floppy disk—you're now greeted by the File menu, the gateway to Works shown in

Figure I-1. It's here that you tell Works to create a new file, open an existing file, save a file, close a file, and do other exciting things you'll learn about shortly.

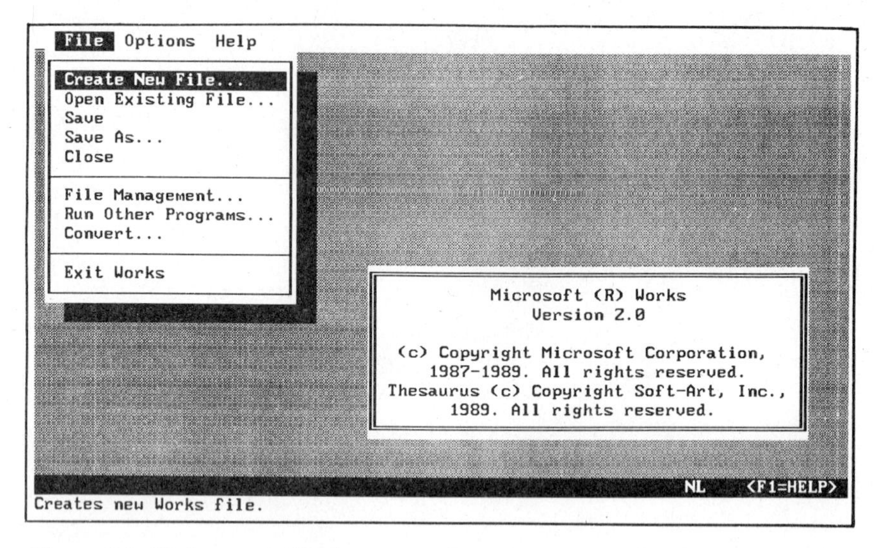

Figure I-1. Welcome to Works screen showing commands in the File menu

Choosing the `Create New File` command brings up the New File dialog box shown in Figure I-2, which lists each Works application. A

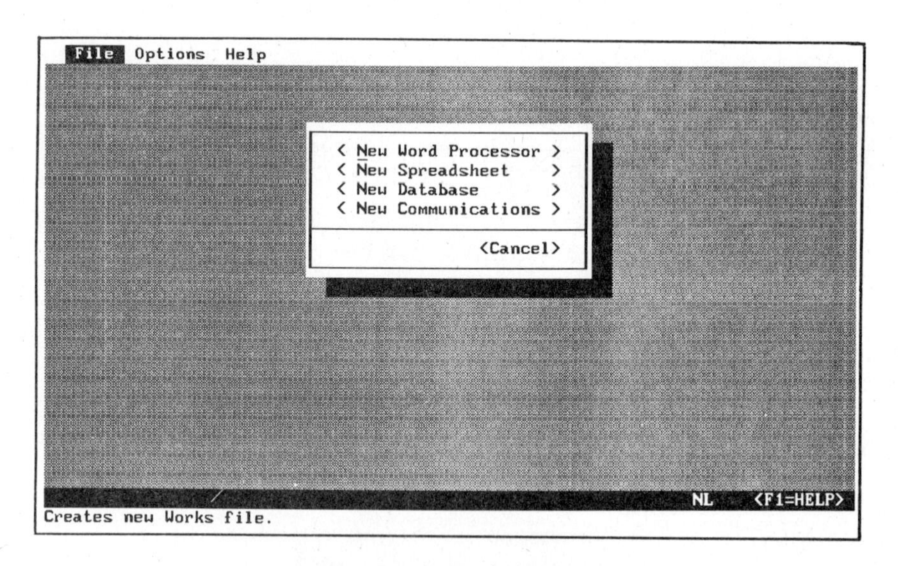

Figure I-2. The Works New File dialog box

dialog box is the place where you and Works engage in a dialogue, getting and giving information.

Here, Works asks what type of new file you want to create, with the blinker in the `New Word Processor` line. If you want to work with the word processor, you type **W** or press Enter. If you want something else, you type the first letter of the application: **S** for Spreadsheet, **D** for Database, or **C** for Communications.

In Chapter 1, you'll find out what happens after you choose an application.

The dazzle is just beginning.

Trademarks

All terms mentioned in this book that are known to be trademarks or service marks are listed below. In addition, terms suspected of being trademarks or service marks have been appropriately capitalized. Howard W. Sams & Company cannot attest to the accuracy of this information. Use of a term in this book should not be regarded as affecting the validity of any trademark or service mark.

Microsoft and Microsoft Word are registered trademarks of Microsoft Corporation.

WordPerfect is a registered trademark of WordPerfect Corporation.

DisplayWrite is a trademark of International Business Machines Corporation.

MultiMate is a registered trademark of MicroPro International Corporation.

Acknowledgments

Bouquets to Burt Witkin for being an all-around good guy. Burt's the kind of person who, without fanfare, simply does what has to be done. Thanks also to Champagne the Cat for being there during those long days and nights at the computer.

My everlasting gratitude to Roy Harper of Microsoft Corporation, my buddy at the other end of the phone. When it comes to Works, Roy knows just about everything.

My appreciation to Michael Jerzewski, Jeffrey Mehler, and John Perkett of Radio Shack for going that extra mile. Many thanks to Carole Grabinski of Microsoft Corporation for listening and helping, and to the brothers Vaglica—Sal and Anthony—for keeping my computers humming.

This is my fourth time around with the talented professionals at Howard W. Sams—and it just keeps getting better every time. I want to give special thanks to Jim Hill, Scott Arant, development coordinator Amy Perry, who did such a great job on my last book and now on this one, and other valued members of the editorial and production teams.

Many thanks to copy editor Katherine Murray and her associate Carrie Torres Marshall for their contributions to this book.

Ruth K. Witkin
Long Island, New York

P A R T

Getting Acquainted with Works

The Works Environment

Screens are the framework for your activities.

The Works environment is filled with screens in which you perform activities. Because Works is an integrated program, these screens bear a close family resemblance, regardless of which application you use. Let's suppose you choose the spreadsheet at the New File dialog box, bringing up the spreadsheet screen shown in Figure 1-1.

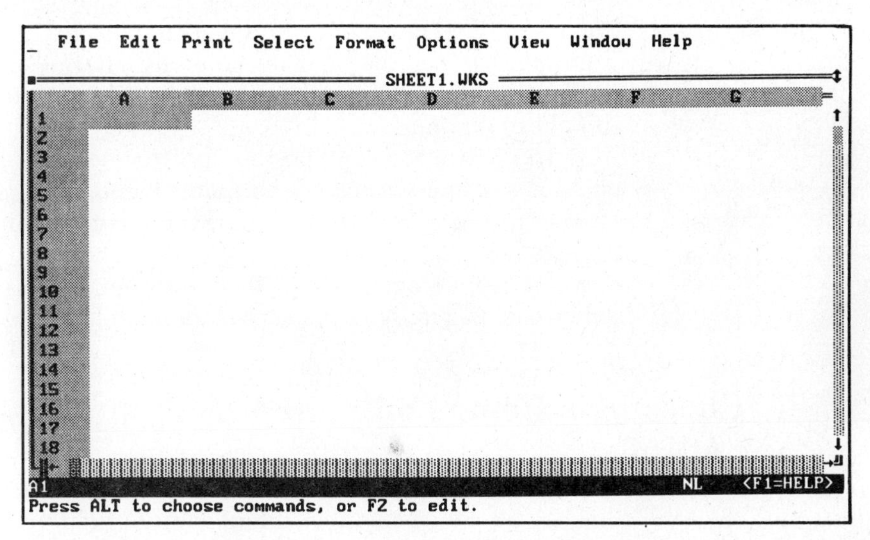

Figure 1-1. The spreadsheet screen showing menus across the top

The menu line at the top of the screen shows the activities you can perform on a spreadsheet:

```
File Edit Print Select Format Options View Window Help
```

The database and word processing applications present the same menus, with only the View menu missing in the word processor. Though the activities in each menu are different in each application, this kind of consistency throughout the Works program makes it easy to transfer the techniques of working with menus from one application to another. (The communications application has many of the same menus, as well as others from which to choose. These menus are discussed in the communications chapter.)

Choosing a Menu

The menu bar is turned off when you first see the screen. Pressing Alt turns it on.

Works assumes you'll want to enter information in a file before using any commands, so the menu bar is inactive when you first see the screen. *Inactive* means that menu names appear without showing one letter in each name in bold (actually, in high-intensity white) or in color, depending on the screen mode selected in the Options menu's Works Settings command. Pressing the Alt key turns on the menus. You then can see the bold (or colored) letter, often the first letter of the menu name. For example, the **F** in **File** and the **E** in **Edit** appear in bold or color.

To open a menu, type the bold (or colored) letter. Works then changes the appearance of the menu name from normal video (dark letters on a light background) to reverse video (light letters on a dark background). This identifies a menu as the active menu and pulls down a list of commands. The top command appears in reverse video, identifying it as the active command.

Choosing a Command

Figure 1-2 shows the commands in the spreadsheet's Edit menu. In this menu, you can move or copy information from one place to another, erase information entirely, or name certain cells, among other things. Like the menus, each command contains a bold or colored letter.

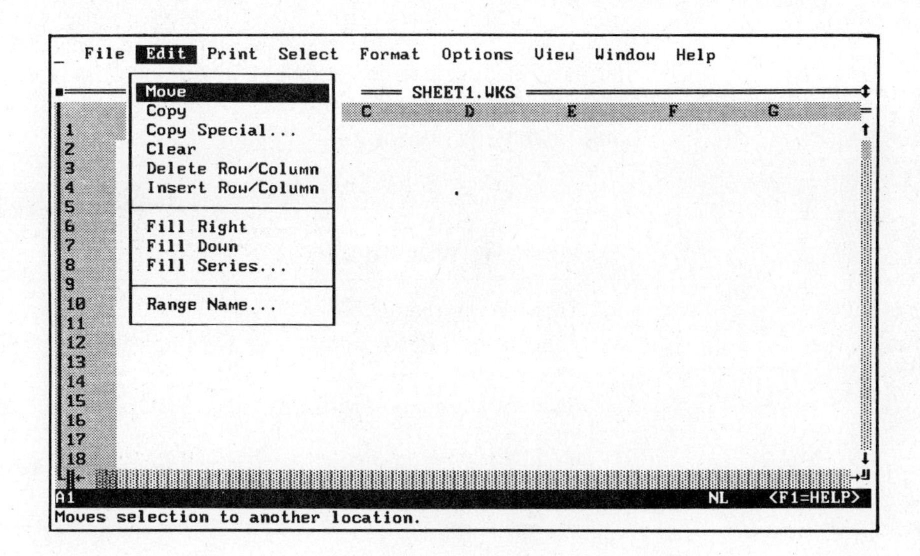

Figure 1-2. Commands in the spreadsheet's Edit menu

Light letters on a dark background (reverse video) identify the active menu or active command.

The active command—Move—is in reverse video. You can choose the active command by pressing Enter or by typing the bold (or colored) letter, in this case **M.** If you're like most people, you're more likely to remember the letter M than the fact that Move is the active command, so make it a habit to choose a command by typing the bold letter instead of pressing Enter.

Many commands have shortcut keys that let you choose a command without going through a menu. These keys are described in the applications chapters.

Learning the names of menus and commands is a matter of working with them. In the early stages, you may have to think twice to remember which menu contains which command. That's only natural. If you're searching for a particular command and find yourself opening and closing menus, you can open one menu and browse through the others by pressing the Right Arrow or Left Arrow keys. It isn't necessary to close one menu before opening another.

If you're not sure which command does what, you can browse through each command in an open menu by pressing the Up Arrow or Down Arrow keys. As each command is activated (that is, shown in reverse video), Works displays a one-line description of the command on the message line. For example, with the Move command, you see `Moves selection to another location.`

Table 1-1 summarizes the action of the keys that work the menus and commands in every Works application. You may find it handy to keep a copy of this and other keystroke summaries in this book near your computer.

Table 1-1. Keys that work the menus and commands

What You Want To Do	Keystroke
Turn Works menus on or off	Alt
Select a pull-down menu (with menus turned on)	Bold or colored letter
Select a command (with a menu open)	Bold or colored letter
Cycle through the other menus (with a menu open)	Right or Left Arrow
Browse through the commands (with a menu open)	Up or Down Arrow
Carry out a command	Enter
Turn off menus or cancel a command	Escape

When Commands Are Dimmed

Sometimes you'll open a menu and see one or more command names dimmed—that is, shown in low intensity or in blue, depending on your screen configuration. This means that the command isn't available, either because it has no bearing on that particular file or because you haven't identified information needed by the command.

For example, if you haven't inserted a page break in a spreadsheet, Works dims the Delete Page Break command in the spreadsheet's Print menu. Or, if you didn't select a number in a record, Works dims the format and style choices in the database's Format command. Another possibility is that you didn't enter footnotes in a document, so Works dims the Show Footnotes command in the word processor's Options menu. It makes sense. According to Works, if you don't need it, there's no point in offering.

All commands dimmed usually means an incompleted action.

At times you'll find just about every command in a menu dimmed. This can be a perplexing moment. Chances are, you opened the menu before completing your last action. Look first at the entry/edit line immediately below the menus, which shows what you're typing or the information already in a cell. If you see text and a blinking underline or a blinking underline alone, you know that you've forgotten to enter something you typed. Also look at the line immediately above the message line at the bottom of the screen. If you see MOVE or COPY, you know you're in the midst of another action. To get things back to normal, press Escape to close the open menu. Next either press Enter to confirm your previous action or press Escape once or twice to cancel it, and then choose the menu again.

Working in a Dialog Box

Three dots after a command lead to a dialog box.

Works carries out a command only when you tell it to, using information you supply. Some commands, such as the Edit menu's Clear command, are carried out as soon as you identify what you want to clear and press Enter. Other commands need more information. In these cases, Works shows the command name (such as Copy Special, Fill Series, and Range Name in Figure 1-2) followed by three dots, called an ellipsis. Think of the ellipsis as meaning *more...*

When you choose a command with an ellipsis, Works brings up a dialog box where you can enter more information or make other choices. Dialog boxes all look different from each other, but they all have common elements. Figure 1-3 shows the Print dialog box in the spreadsheet's Print menu and the Open Existing File dialog box in the File menu.

Your dialogue with a dialog box takes these forms:

A. **Check box**. A check box lets you turn an option on or off. In the Print dialog box, for example, you can turn on the Print row and column labels check box to have Works print row numbers down the left side of the spreadsheet and column letters across the top. An X inside the brackets means that the option is turned on. If you leave the check box empty (turned off), Works prints the spreadsheet without these labels.

   In some check boxes, such as Print specific pages and Print to file in Figure 1-3, Works dims the sub-box (Pages and File name) until you check off the check box.

   A dash in a check box means that you've selected more than one item. You can turn on the check box containing the dash or leave it alone. If you leave it alone, Works retains the selection.

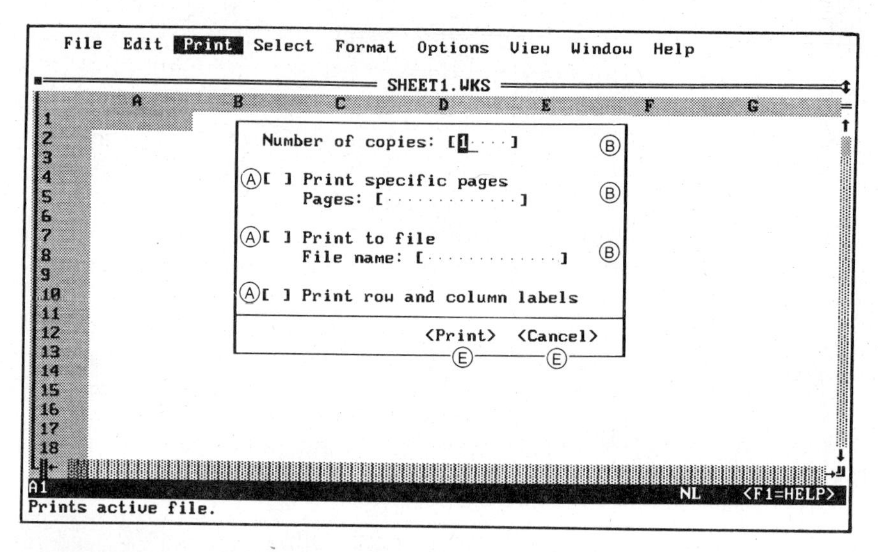

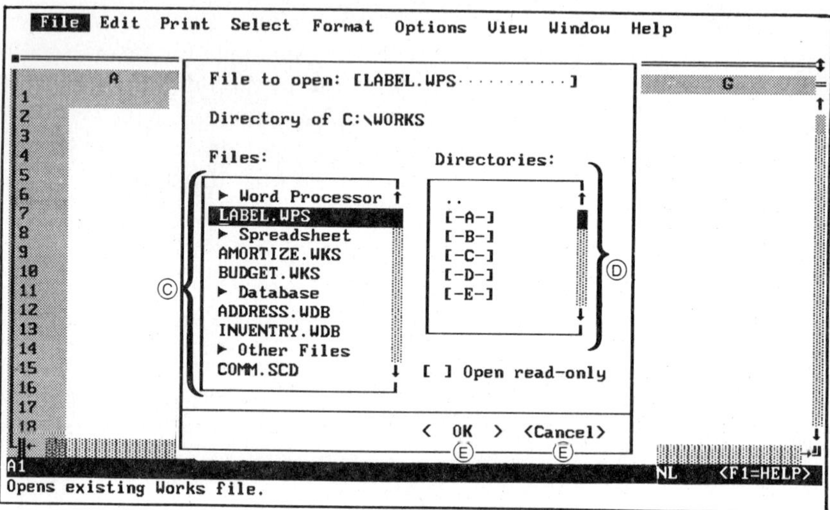

Figure 1-3. The Print and Open Existing File dialog boxes in the Works spreadsheet

If you change your mind about changing anything, pressing Escape closes the dialog box.

B. **Fill-in box**. You can type text or a number in a fill-in box. Works often proposes a number but leaves the text up to you. For example, in the Number of copies fill-in box, Works proposes to print one copy. You can accept this or overtype it with another number. In the File name box, which is empty now, Works expects text.

C. **List box**. A list box presents a list of such items as files, fonts, or formats. For example, you can list the files on the current drive in the Files list box. The fastest way to move to an item in a list box is to type the first letter in its name, which moves the blinker to the first item starting with that letter. Then either type the same letter or use Down Arrow as many times as needed to move to your item.

D. **Option box**. An option box offers several options from which you can choose. For example, in the Open Existing File dialog box you can load an existing file stored on the current drive or have Works list the files in subdirectories stored on a different drive (A through E). A mark beside an option shows the selected item. You can select only one option at a time.

E. **Command button**. Those who work with a mouse can click on an <OK> or <Cancel> button to carry out or cancel a command. Users without a mouse simply press Enter to carry out the command and Escape to cancel it.

Works has other buttons in other menus, such as *Topic* and *Lessons* in the Help menu's Help Index command and *Print* in the Print menu's Print command, that you can access by clicking on them with a mouse or typing the bold (or colored) letter in the button name.

Table 1-2 lists the keys that work the dialog boxes. You can move around a dialog box by holding down Alt, which turns on the bold letters, and typing the bold letter of your choice, or you can use the Tab key to move from box to box. Unless the boxes you want are one after the other, the Alt+bold letter method is faster.

Table 1-2. Keys that work the dialog boxes

What You Want To Do	Keystroke
Turn on bold letters	Alt
Select a field	Alt+Bold Letter
Move clockwise from field to field	Tab
Move counter-clockwise from field to field	Shift+Tab
Move left or right in a fill-in box	Left or Right Arrow
Delete a character in a fill-in box	Backspace or Delete

(*continued*)

Table 1-2. *(continued)*

What You Want To Do	Keystroke
Select an item in a list box	Up or Down Arrow or first letter of item
Select the last item in a list box	End
Select the first item in a list box	Home
Scroll down by page in a list box	Page Down
Scroll up by page in a list box	Page Up
Select an item in an option box	Up or Down Arrow
Select/unselect a check box	Alt+Bold Letter
Select/unselect with cursor on check box	Spacebar
Carry out a selection	Enter
Cancel a selection	Escape
Close dialog box	Escape

The Select-Do Concept

Most of the time, you must select before you can do.

Certain commands act on cells, while others act on the entire spreadsheet. For example, when you copy information from one cell to another, you're working with cells; when you store a file on disk, you're working with the spreadsheet. With a cell command, you *select* information to work on first, and then *do* the command. Hence the important Select-Do concept, which applies throughout the Works program.

Figure 1-4 shows a sales summary spreadsheet. The numbers at the left are row numbers and the letters across the top are column letters (you'll find out more about the spreadsheet screen in Chapter 3). Each intersection of a row number and column letter forms a cell. Cash sales are in cells B5 to B10 and charge sales are in cells C5 to C10.

Suppose you want to clear (that is, erase or blank) the numbers in those cells. Clearing cells is the province of the Edit menu's Clear command. You must first *select* the cells to clear by placing the cursor on B5, pressing F8 to extend the selection, and pressing Arrow keys until the cells from B5 to C1 are highlighted. You can now *do* the Clear command: Press Alt to activate the menu bar, E to open the Edit menu, E to choose the Clear command, and Enter to confirm the command. Works then erases the numbers in the selected cells.

```
           A                   B            C                  D
1                       DAILY SALES SUMMARY
2    =====================================================================
3    Department          Cash Sales   Charge Sales              Total
4    ---------------------------------------------------------------------
5    Housewares             $296.60        $433.78            $730.38
6    Paint                  $176.54         $98.70            $275.24
7    Plumbing               $156.68        $366.83            $523.51
8    Electrical              $84.75        $234.67            $319.42
9    Lighting               $137.42        $421.40            $558.82
10   Heat/Air                $76.20        $734.85            $811.05
11                        ---------      ---------          ---------
12          Totals          $928.19      $2,290.23          $3,218.42
```

Figure 1-4. A small spreadsheet showing cells B5 to B10 and C5 to C10 selected

Select-Do, like a one-two punch, is a potent combination. Keep it in mind and you can avoid the annoyance of starting a command only to realize that you haven't selected the cells yet. If you're working with a command that acts on the entire spreadsheet, you don't have to select anything first.

Using a Mouse

Although this book gives the keystrokes needed to perform actions, you can always use either the mouse or the keyboard. Both methods produce the same results.

Using a mouse is another way to choose menus and commands, work the dialog boxes, move around the screen, enter information in a file, and select information. Instead of typing letters or pressing direction keys, you can have the mouse do it. Every key on the keyboard is still available for manual entry and movement, even when the mouse is active.

To use a mouse with Works, you must install the mouse software on your DOS disk or hard disk during the Works setup. To connect the mouse to your computer, follow the installation instructions that came with your mouse.

In text mode, the pointer is a rectangle; in graphics mode, an arrow.

When you activate the mouse, a mouse pointer appears on screen as either a small rectangle or an arrow, depending on the screen mode you specified during setup or the one you selected in the Options menu's Works Settings command.

Mouse Activities

The mouse is a plastic device with two buttons on top and a ball below. Pressing one or both of the buttons—known as clicking, double-clicking, and dragging—produces different results, depending on the action you're taking. You'll find that you use the left button most often.

The ball controls the movement of the mouse pointer on screen. When you slide the mouse across a desktop or other flat surface, your computer translates the rotation of the ball into direction and distance. If you run out of room to move the mouse, you can lift it and put it down elsewhere without changing the location of the pointer.

The Mouse Screen

Special symbols along the screen perimeter give the mouse user free run of the screen. Figure 1-5 identifies these symbols.

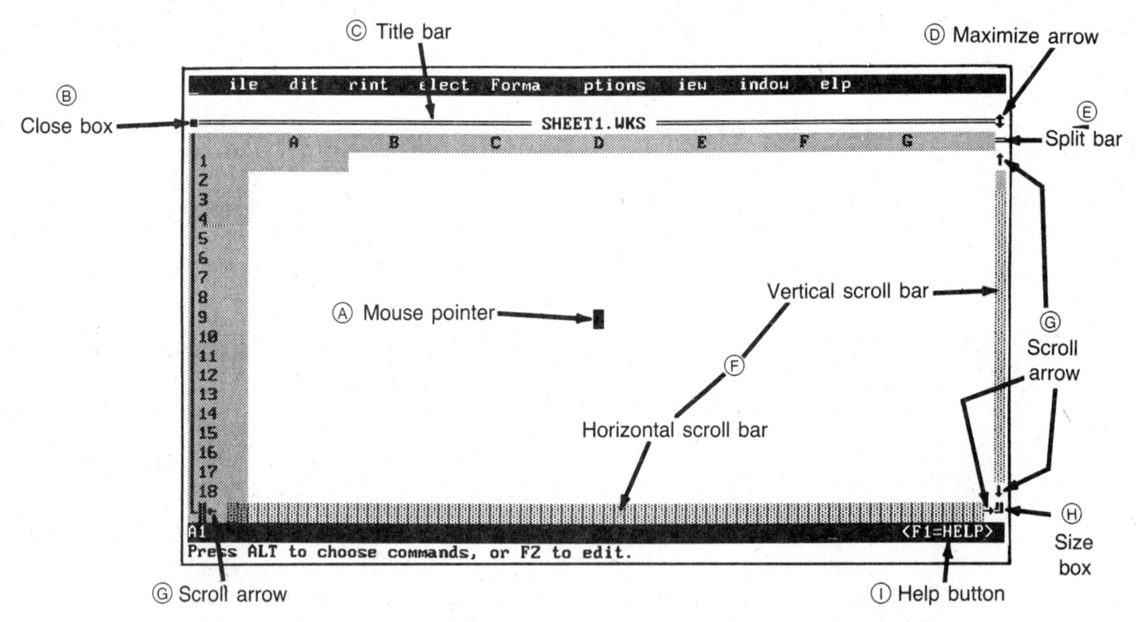

Figure 1-5. The spreadsheet screen with points of interest for mouse users

The following list highlights each of these items:

A. In the middle of the screen is the *mouse pointer*, where the small rectangle indicates text mode.
B. At the left end of the title line is the *close box*. Clicking the mouse here closes the file.
C. Across the top of the screen is the *title bar*. Dragging the mouse down pushes the window down.
D. At the right end of the title line is the *maximize arrow*. Clicking the mouse here restores the window to the full size of the screen.
E. Directly below the maximize arrow is the *split bar*. Dragging the mouse down from this point splits the window into two parts so you can see distant parts of a file at the same time.
F. At the right edge of the work area and directly below the work area are *scroll bars*. Each scroll bar contains a black rectangle that shows the relative location of the cursor within the file. Dragging the black rectangle lets you move the mouse in large increments.
G. Above and below the vertical scroll bar is a *scroll arrow*. Clicking the mouse here scrolls the cursor by line or row, depending on the application. Before and after the horizontal scroll bar are other *scroll arrows*. Clicking here scrolls the cursor by character or column.
H. To the right of the second horizontal scroll arrow is the *size box*. Dragging the mouse here lets you change the size of the window.
I. Below the horizontal scroll bar is the *help button*. Clicking here brings up help information.

Mouse Exercises

Here's what you might call aerobics for a healthy mouse.

When you have the Works spreadsheet on your screen, you can become familiar with mouse activities by doing the following short exercises:

1. To move the cursor to the mouse pointer, place the mouse pointer somewhere on the screen (not at the same place as the cursor) and click the left mouse button. *Clicking* means that you press and quickly release the button.

2. To select an area of the screen, position the pointer in the lower part of the screen, hold down the left button, and move the mouse up. As you do, Works highlights each cell touched by the cursor. This process is called *dragging*. In essence, the mouse pointer is dragging the cursor.
3. To collapse the selection, leave the mouse pointer in the highlighted area and click both buttons.
4. To move the cursor one screenful to the right, place the pointer to the right of the black rectangle on the horizontal scroll bar and click the left button.
5. To jump one screenful down, place the pointer below the black rectangle on the vertical scroll bar and click the left button.
6. To see the calculator, place the pointer on the Options menu and click the left button. Works pulls down the menu. Now place the pointer on the `Calculator` command and click the left button. Works brings up the calculator.
7. To get help on a specific topic—for instance, how to use the calculator—place the pointer on `<F1=HELP>` in the lower right corner of the screen and click the left button. To return to the calculator, place the cursor on `<Cancel>` and click the left button. To remove the calculator from the screen, place the pointer on `<Cancel>` and click the left button again.
8. To open the Help menu, as seen in Figure 1-5, click with the left button on the Help menu, and then click on the Help Index command. Now move the pointer to `Choosing Commands` and click the left button to select the topic. To display the help information, leave the pointer where it is and double-click the topic—that is, press the left button twice in rapid succession. Now return to the spreadsheet by clicking on `<Cancel>` again.
9. To open the Edit menu, click on the Edit menu. To close the menu without selecting a command, place the pointer anywhere outside the menu and click the left button.
10. To close the spreadsheet file, place the pointer on the rectangle (called the *close box*) at the very beginning of the double line before the spreadsheet name and click the left button.

Though the mouse behaves somewhat differently in the word processor and database applications, the basic principles are the same. The Works manual describes mouse movements for each application in detail. If you intend to use a mouse, be sure to read it.

Working with Windows

One file can take up the entire screen or several files can share the screen.

Whether you're working with one or several files, windows are an important part of every Works session. Windows display files on the screen—in fact, as many as eight different files can be displayed on the screen at one time, each in its own window. For instance, you can keep a spreadsheet budget on screen along with a memo relating to the budget, as well as a database list of customers and a mailing label layout, switching smoothly between them to make changes.

Windows can overlap, as shown in Figure 1-6, or they can be arranged side-by-side, as shown in Figure 1-7. In an overlapping situation, the file in the active window (here, the budget) appears in front of all other windows on screen; in a side-by-side arrangement, the active window (here, the label layout) is the one Works loads into the upper-left slot.

In both cases, the file in the active window contains the cursor, allowing you to work on that file as if it were the only one on screen. Active files display normal colors with border lines and scroll bars, while nonactive files appear in stark black-and-white. The menu bar, status line, and message line always correspond to the active file, changing only when you make another file active.

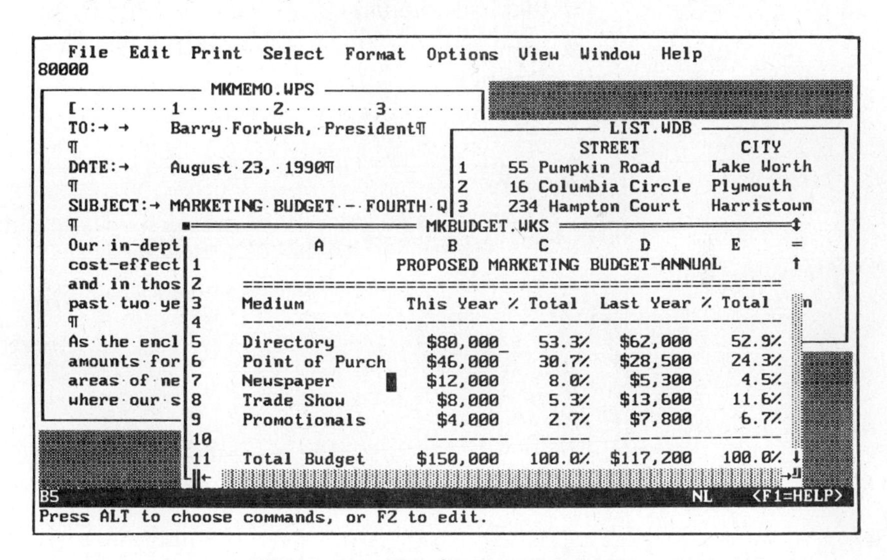

Figure 1-6. Overlapping windows

You can even move a window so that part of it is off screen, as long as the upper-left corner remains on screen.

Whichever arrangement you choose to work with, you can use the Windows menu shown in Figure 1-8 and its commands to

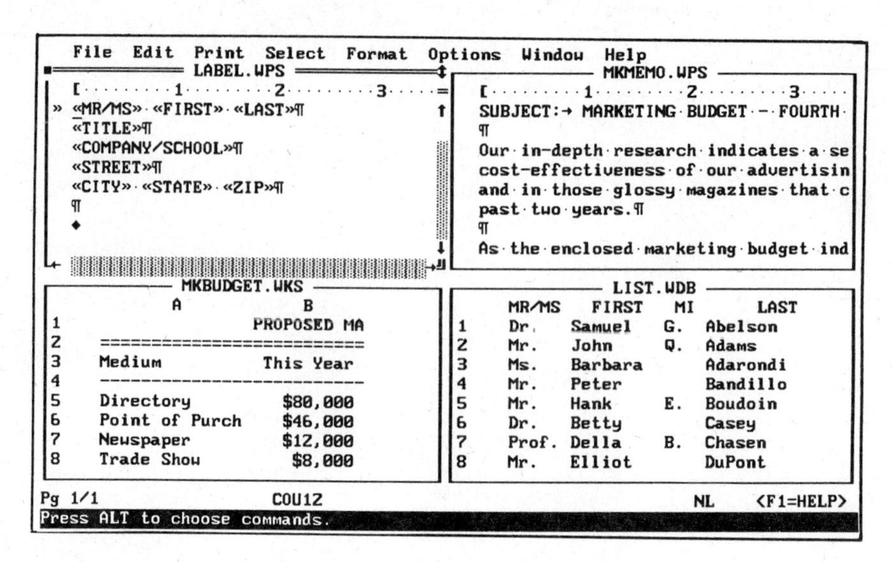

Figure 1-7. Side-by-side windows

- Move windows from one place on the screen to another (Move).
- Reduce or enlarge the size of a window (Size).
- Increase a smaller window to full screen size in one step (Maximize).

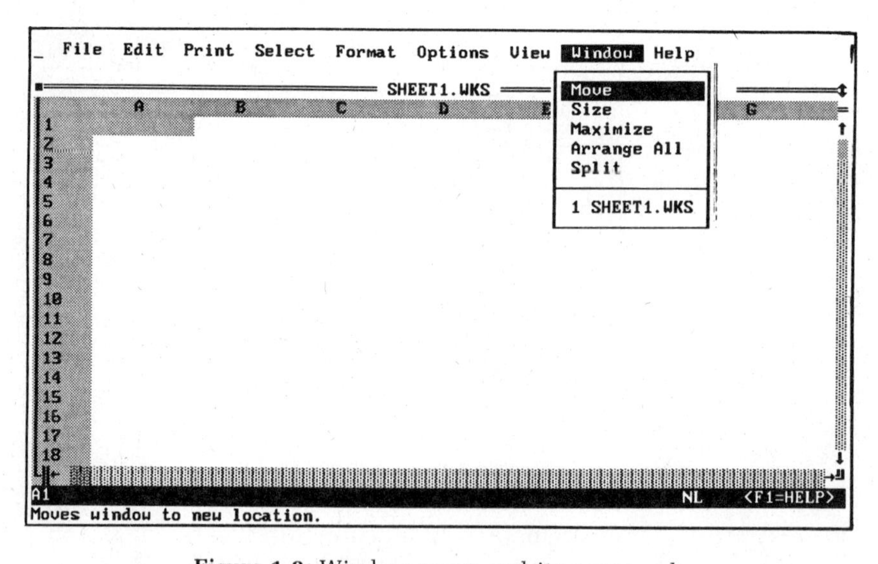

Figure 1-8. Window menu and its commands

- Have Works arrange open files in side-by-side windows (Arrange All).
- Split a window into two panes (word processor) or four panes (spreadsheet and database) so you can view distant parts of the same file at the same time (Split).

The overlapping arrangement in Figure 1-6 was the result of a fair degree of window manipulation using the Move and Size commands. The side-by-side arrangement in Figure 1-7 was a matter of simply choosing the Arrange All command. This time, Works did all the work.

You can switch between open files with lightning speed, particularly when using a mouse. Simply click on the file to make the window active. Without a mouse, press Ctrl+F6 to move the cursor to the next window or Ctrl+Shift+F6 to move the cursor to the previous window. If you prefer, press Alt and type **W** to open the Window menu, and then type the number of the file you want to activate.

Works Accessories

The Options menu offers three handy-dandy desk accessories you'll use over and over again: a calculator, alarm clock, and telephone dialer.

The Calculator

The calculator shown in Figure 1-9 works like that old familiar handheld calculator, but with some special bells and whistles.

You can use one of three methods to do calculations:

1. Press number keys and arithmetic operators and symbols on the keyboard.
2. Click the numbers, operators, and symbols on screen with the mouse.
3. Use the arrow keys to move the cursor to the numbers, operators, and symbols on the screen, pressing Enter after each one.

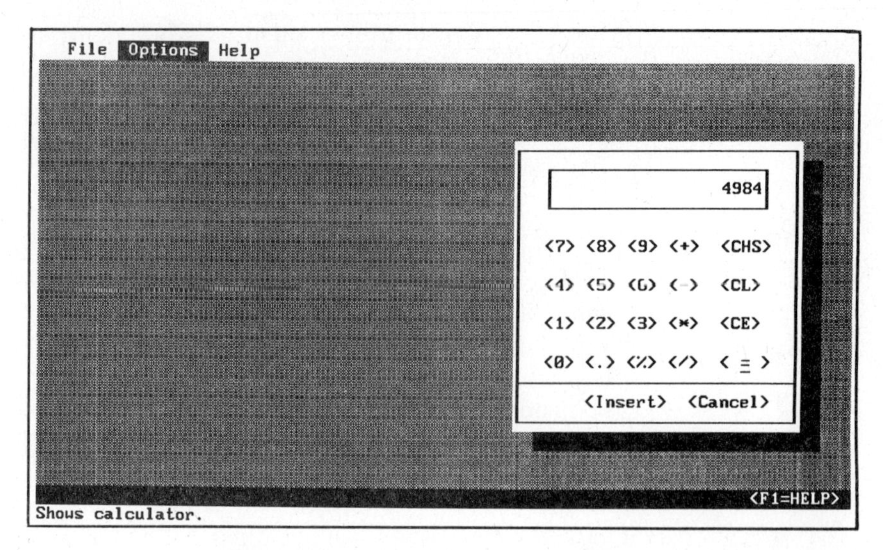

Figure 1-9. Quick and handy calculator

Clearly, methods 1 and 2 are the fastest way to get results.

Like a hand-held calculator, the Works calculator has keys that let you change the sign of the displayed number (CHS, change sign), clear everything (CL, clear), or clear only the last entry (CE, clear entry). Works retains the last number calculated during the current session, even if you close the calculator and go on to other things.

You can copy a calculated number from the calculator to a file and from a file to the calculator.

Inserting a calculated number directly into a word processor, spreadsheet, or database file is a breeze. First display the file and put the cursor where you want the number inserted, and then bring up the calculator, enter the calculation, and press Alt+I.

Copying a number from the calculator into a file is just as easy. First select the number you want to copy from the file, and then choose the Edit menu's Copy command. Bring up the calculator, and Works shows your number in the calculator window.

The Alarm Clock

If you tend to get caught up in your Works work and become oblivious of the outside world, the alarm clock gets you going to places you're supposed to be.

Though the Works alarm clock uses the same philosophy and works in many of the same ways as your everyday noncomputerized

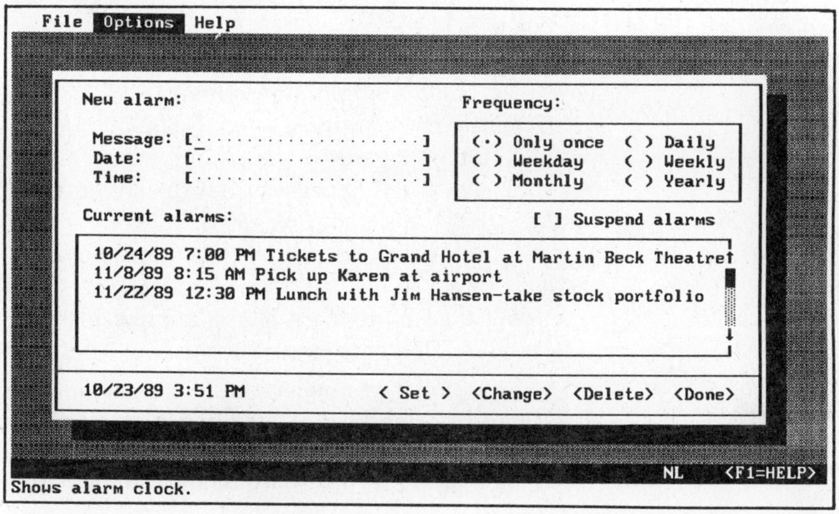

```
File  Options  Help

New alarm:                                        Frequency:

 Message: [_.......................]             (•) Only once   ( ) Daily
 Date:    [........................]             ( ) Weekday     ( ) Weekly
 Time:    [........................]             ( ) Monthly     ( ) Yearly

Current alarms:                                  [ ] Suspend alarms

 10/24/89 7:00 PM Tickets to Grand Hotel at Martin Beck Theatre
 11/8/89 8:15 AM Pick up Karen at airport
 11/22/89 12:30 PM Lunch with Jim Hansen-take stock portfolio

10/23/89 3:51 PM                 < Set >  <Change>  <Delete>  <Done>

                                                      NL    <F1=HELP>
Shows alarm clock.
```

Figure 1-10. Alarm clock settings

alarm clock, there are vast differences. Figure 1-10 shows the alarm clock settings.

Alarms can go off once and only once if you want them to, every day, only on weekdays, once a week, monthly, or yearly. You may never miss another date again!

You can set alarms to go off at specific times and dates as well as enter a reminder of why you set the alarm. Your reminder can be as many as 60 characters long. When it seems like you've run out of input room in the Message field, Works slides what you've already typed under the left bracket and pulls out more room from under the right bracket.

You can type the date in these formats: 2/23/90, Feb 23, 1990, or February 23, 1990. Available time formats are 4:30 PM, 16:30, and 4:30.

As you enter alarm dates and times, Works arranges them chronologically in the `Current alarms` box. Though you can see only five alarms listed there, you can enter more. Works deletes alarms that have already been issued, allowing others to come into view.

You can set the alarm frequency, change and delete alarms yourself, and even prevent them from going off without deleting them. As alarms come due, Works sounds a beep and displays the date, time, and message, giving you the choice of shutting off the alarm, resetting it, or having it go off again in 10 minutes.

If Works isn't running when an alarm is scheduled to go off, the alarm sounds and the reminder appears the next time you start the program.

The Telephone Dialer

Works can dial a telephone number in a word processor, spreadsheet, or database file. Suppose you have a database of customers that includes a contact name and phone number. Simply select a number from that field, tell Works to dial the number, and then pick up your phone when the person answers.

There are certain prerequisites to enjoying this feature:

When you create a file containing phone numbers, enter the codes needed for automatic dialing.

1. You must be using a Hayes compatible modem that can operate at a data transmission rate of at least 1200 baud.
2. The number you select must contain any special codes you would normally dial—for instance, 1 before the area code for a long-distance number, 9 before the number for an outside line, or a comma to tell the modem to pause during dialing.
3. The communications settings—Modem port (COM1 or COM2) and Dial type (tone or pulse)—in the Options menu's Works Settings command must match your own system.

With these items out of the way, open the file containing the number you want to dial and select the number. Then choose Dial This Number in the Options menu. Works dials the number and asks you to pick up your telephone and press Enter. If the call doesn't go through, or if you cancel the call before the person on the other end picks up, Works returns you to your file.

Help at Your Fingertips

You can get help on more than 220 topics and tasks from anywhere within Works.

When you're exploring new territory, it helps to have a good road map on hand, and the Works on screen help instructions are precisely that. If you lose your way or want more details on the terrain, all you need do is press F1 to get task-related help, Shift+F1 to view the Works tutorial, or Alt+H to pull down the Help menu shown in Figure 1-11, where you can access either the Help Index shown in Figure 1-12 or the tutorial.

If you're working with a floppy disk system or didn't copy the help information or tutorial to your hard disk during setup, Works prompts you to insert the proper disk.

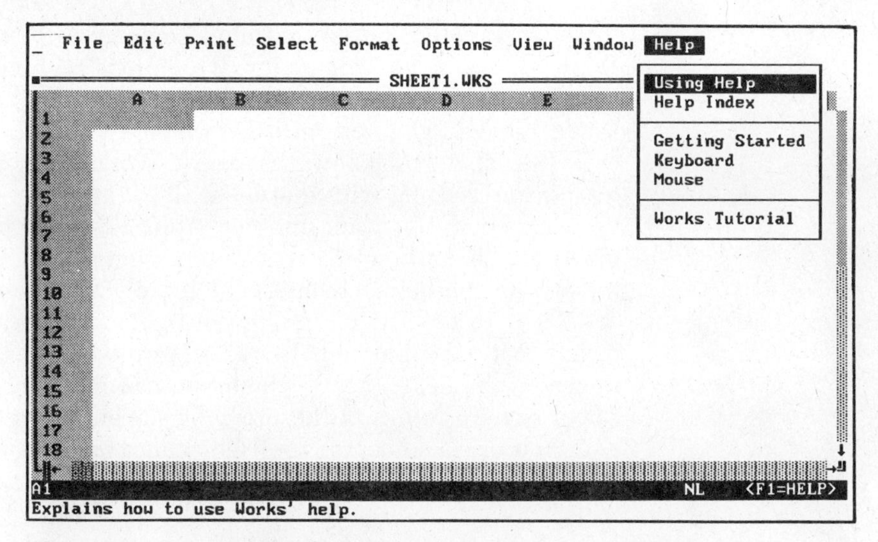

Figure 1-11. Commands in the Help menu

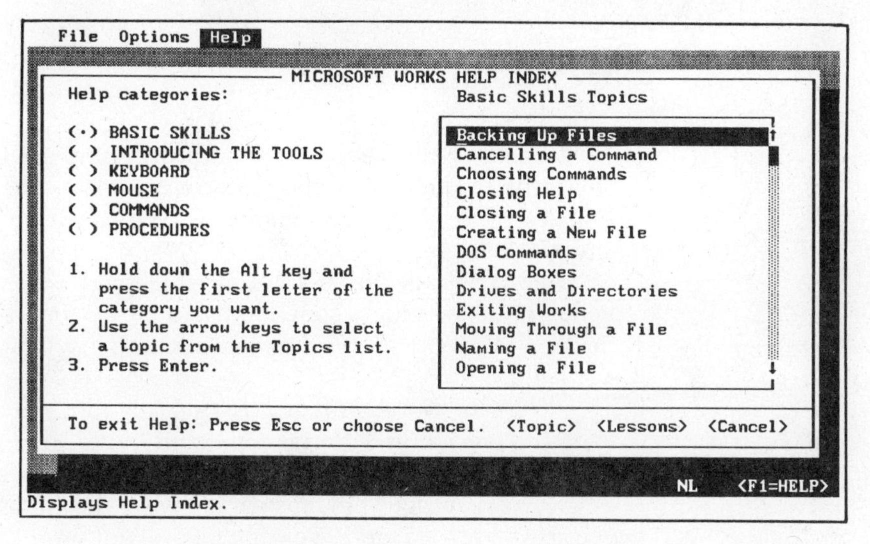

Figure 1-12. Help Index, which lists all available Help topics

The Help Screen

Pressing F1 brings up a Help screen that explains the command or dialog box you're currently using. If no Help screen exists on that topic, or if you're not executing a command or other common task, Works displays the Help Index, which lists all help topics.

You can browse through the topics by pressing the Up Arrow, Down Arrow, PgUp, or PgDn keys or by typing the first letter of the topic name, if you know the name. Works then jumps to the first topic name starting with that letter. If that topic is the one you want, press Enter. If you want another topic, use the Down Arrow key to move to the topic and press Enter. Works then replaces the Help Index with the help screen for the topic you've selected.

Two rectangles in the lower right corner of the topic screen means that the topic ends there. An arrow means that the topic continues on the next screen, which you can reach by pressing the Page Down key. To return to the previous screen, press the Page Up key.

You can also access the Help Index by opening the Help menu or by choosing the Index button in the Help screen you access with F1.

Mouse users can get immediate help by clicking on **<F1=HELP>** in the bottom right corner of the screen.

The Works Tutorial

The Learning Works tutorial offers on-line training on over 50 topics and tasks.

Holding down Shift and pressing F1 brings up a tutorial lesson on the command or dialog box you're currently using. These lessons provide practice sessions and summaries as well as easy-to-take explanations and glorious graphics.

If you press Shift+F1 and no lesson exists on that topic or you're not executing a command or other common task, Works either displays a menu of tutorial lessons or tells you that no lesson is available.

You can work through the tutorial from the very beginning by choosing the Works Tutorial command in the Help menu or by choosing the Lesson button in the Help screen you access with F1.

After you get your answer or view the tutorial, Works returns you to where you were working before you left off.

If you're using the communications application and your computer is connected to another computer, press Alt and then F1 to get help or Alt and then Shift+F1 to view the tutorial.

About Macros

Macros are like player pianos. Snap in a song roll, flip the switch, and invisible fingers hit all the right keys. The difference is that macro song rolls perform not songs but a whole series of actions, and the switch is a key on your keyboard.

Macros make things happen in the blink of an eye.

You create a macro by storing keystrokes under a key of your choosing. If you store the letters of your name under function key F10, for example, every time you press F10, the macro will type out your name. Macros can open menus, choose commands, enter text and numbers, move the cursor from place to place, and do hundreds of other tasks in the blink of an eye.

Macros are meant for tasks you perform often or repeatedly. If you type the same closing in every letter, a macro can type it for you. If you display numbers as dollar amounts in virtually all of your spreadsheets, a macro can format them for you. If you regularly sort customers in your database by ZIP code, and then select records for special mailings, a macro can do that for you. Macros save time, eliminate typing errors, and keep keyboard drudgery down to a minimum.

The subject of macros is long and detailed. If you're just getting started with Works, you may want to skim through this chapter now and return to it after you get experience in the step-by-step chapters that feature macros.

A Macros Overview

Your work with macros revolves around two macro menus. When you hold down Alt and type a slash (that is, press Alt+/), Works brings up the macro options menu shown in Figure 2-1. These options let you take the following actions:

- Define the series of keystrokes in your macro (Record Macro).
- Flip the switch—the playback key—that runs the macro (PlayMacro).
- Restore the playback key of a previously-created macro to its original purpose (Skip Macro).
- Get rid of an unneeded macro (Delete Macros).
- Assign a different playback key and macro name (Change Key & Title).
- Turn off all macro actions for a while (Turn Macros Off).

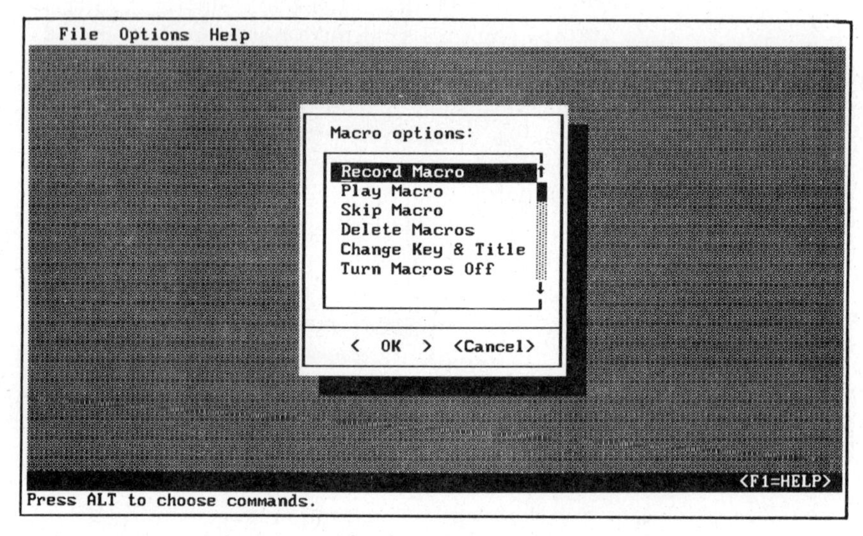

Figure 2-1. The first macro options menu

If you press Alt+/ during the recording process, Works brings up the other macro menu shown in Figure 2-2. Here, you can take these actions:

- Turn off recording after completing a macro (End Recording).
- Cancel a macro before its end (Cancel Recording).

- Restore the playback key of a macro to its original purpose so you can use the key without running the macro (Skip Macro).
- Insert one of three types of pauses: timed (Pause), fixed input (Fixed Input), or variable input (Variable Input).
- Nest one macro within another (Nested Input). More about pauses and nesting shortly.

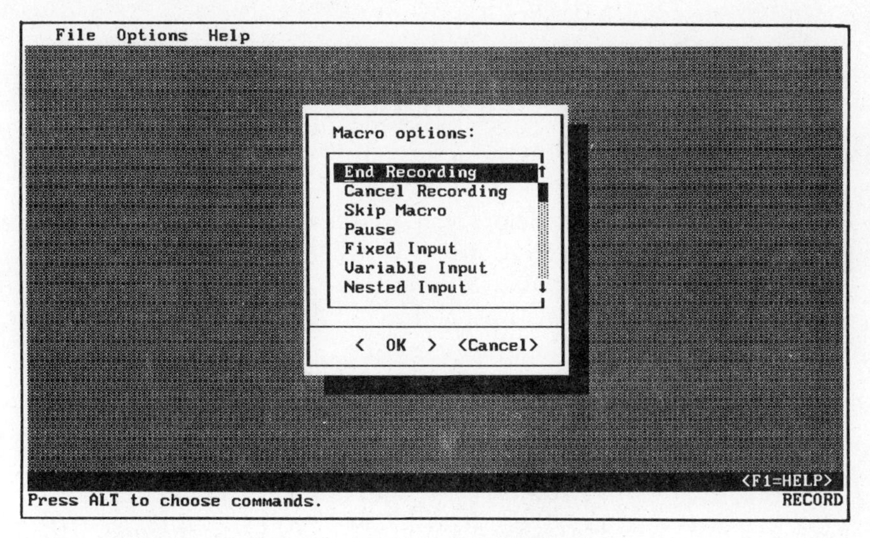

Figure 2-2. The second (and last) macro options menu

You select macro options in the same way that you select any other Works option. If the highlight is on the one you want, press Enter. If you want another option, type its first letter and press Enter.

Creating a Macro

You can either record your keystrokes or write a macro from scratch.

Works offers two ways to create a macro: recording and writing. When you record, you perform each task, hitting keys and typing characters, while Works stores your keystrokes in a special file called MACROS.INI. When you write a macro, you type the names of keystrokes and other elements directly into the MACROS.INI file without actually going through the tasks. For speed and ease, recording is the clear winner.

How Recording Works

The macro recording process has many fine points. Understand the basic scenario first:

1. You turn on recording.
2. You assign a playback key.
3. You hit the keys that perform the actions, in essence "teaching" the macro what to do later on its own.
4. You turn off recording.

Pressing Alt+/ and then Enter starts the macro recording process.

Before you start recording a macro, be sure to set up the file exactly as it will be when the macro runs, and place the cursor where you want the macro to begin when you run it. To start recording, press Alt+/ and hit Enter to choose Record Macro. Works now brings up the playback screen shown in Figure 2-3.

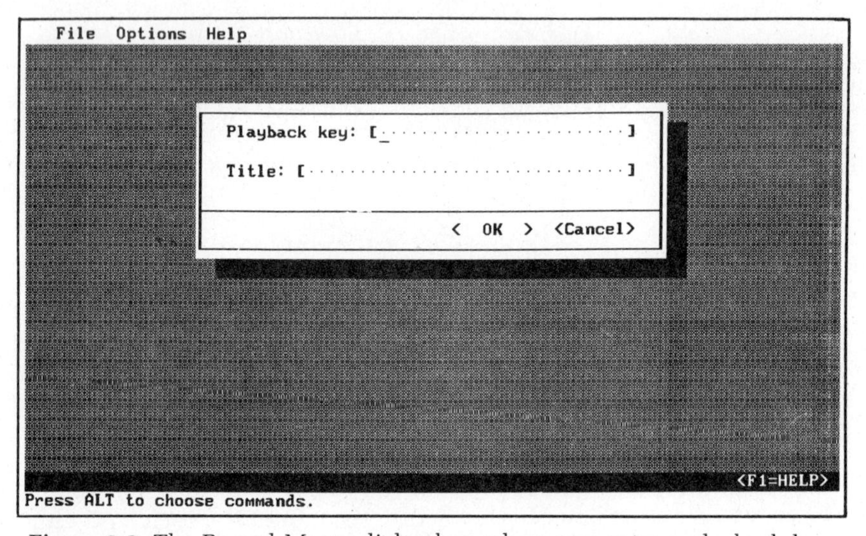

Figure 2-3. The Record Macro dialog box where you enter a playback key and macro title

A macro description can be up to 30 characters long.

Press the key or key combination you'll later use to replay the macro—for instance, F12 or Ctrl+W. Works displays the keyname of the pressed key in the Playback key field, showing it enclosed in angle brackets. You then tab to the Title field and enter a description of the macro's purpose—for instance, SET VARIABLE COLUMN WIDTHS. Although

Works doesn't insist that you enter a description, you'll find it vital in recalling what a macro does.

Works, tracking your actions since you started recording, stores the playback key and macro description in MACROS.INI.

It's a good idea to include the application in the macro description—for instance, SS for spreadsheet, DB for database, WP for word processor, or ALL for all of them. This way you know at a glance which macros are available for the work you're doing.

Keystroke recording begins. To define the macro's actions, you open menus and choose commands, type text and numbers, and move the cursor as if nothing special was going on. As a reminder that it is, the message line displays the word RECORD.

As you hit the keys, Works captures your keystrokes, assigning them to the playback key you designated earlier. Works records all of your keystrokes, even those hit in error. This is usually not serious. You can correct the situation as you're recording and later edit the extraneous keystrokes out of the macro.

When you finish, you can turn off recording in one of two ways: Either press Alt+/ to bring up the second macro menu containing the End Recording option or, even faster, press Alt+- (minus sign) to stop recording instantly.

Macro recording is a civilized, well thought-out process but it may take a few attempts (particularly when everything is so new) to get a macro to behave exactly as it should. Be easy on yourself. Even old hands have times when they must do things over and over.

Writing a Macro

Having easy access to MACROS.INI lets you write a new macro from scratch or edit an existing one.

Writing a macro from scratch puts the entire burden on you. Before you can get started, you need to be thoroughly familiar with macro syntax and how Works shows elements in a macro definition. This involves a good deal of planning, patience, and perseverance to get everything right with as few rewrites as possible.

Writing takes place directly in the MACROS.INI file. You open the file and type in all of the elements including the playback key and description. Works stores a recorded macro automatically but not a written one, so you then close MACROS.INI (using the File menu's Close command) and save it.

You cannot run any macros while MACROS.INI is open, which means that you can't use a macro already written to help write a new macro. You can, however, copy and modify an existing macro to create a new one.

Assigning a Playback Key

The key that you assign for playback can be almost any key or key combination on your keyboard. Works uses many of the function keys and the Alt, Ctrl, and Shift keys in combination with other keys for it's own commands, so it's best to search out an unused key (there are a few in each application) or one you won't use often in your daily work.

If there are conflicts in key usage—that is, a key that you use for occasional Works activities is also assigned to a macro—you can resolve it in two ways.

1. Use the `Skip Macro` option available in both macro menus to ignore the macro and temporarily restore the key's original purpose. For instance, if you've assigned F3 as a playback key in the spreadsheet and now want the macro to move information (the purview of the F3 key), select `Skip Macro` before pressing F3.
2. Suspend all macro actions by choosing `Turn Macros Off`, available in the first macro menu. When you've turned off macros, this option changes to `Turn Macro On`, which you can select when you're ready to resume normal macro operations.

Examples of Playback Keys

Works reserves F1 to summon the Help screen and Shift+F1 to start the Tutorial.

The table in 2-1 shows playback keys in angle brackets, the way Works displays them in macro definitions. These are the results on my computer, which may be different than yours. The key in the second column represents the group in the first column. Where the key isn't available for playback (as with F1 and SHIFT+F1—the Help/Tutorial keys), the table shows NA (Not Available).

Table 2-1. Examples of playback keys

Group	Representative of group	Used alone	With SHIFT	With CTRL	With ALT
Function keys	F1	NA	NA	<ctrlf1>	<altf1>
Function keys	F2	<f2>	<shift2>	<ctrlf2>	<altf2>
Alphabetic keys	a	<a>	<A>	<ctrla>	<alta>
Numeric keys-standard	1	1	!	<ctrl1>	<alt1>
Numeric keys-keypad	1	<k1>	K	<ctrlend>	<altk1>

Group	Representative of group	Used alone	With SHIFT	With CTRL	With ALT
Symbol keys-standard	!	NA	!	<ctrl1>	<alt1>
Symbol keys-keypad	*	<k*>	<shiftk*>	<ctrlk*>	<altk*>
Punctuation keys	,	,	<	<ctrl,>	<alt,>
Enter key	NA	NA	NA	<ctrlenter>	<altenter>
Spacebar		<space>	<shiftspace>	<ctrlspace>	<altspace>
Delete key		<delete>	<shiftdelete>	<ctrldelete>	<altdelete>
Insert key		<insert>	<shiftinsert>	<ctrlinsert>	<altinsert>
Arrow keys-keypad	Left Arrow	<k4>	NA	<ctrlleft>	NA

Before you delve deeply into macros, it's a good idea to check out your keyboard and make a chart like the one in Table 2-1. To do this, press Alt+/ to display the macro menu, and confirm Record Macros. In the Playback key field, press a key and jot down the result. If the key isn't available, Works will leave the playback field empty. Keep hitting keys alone and in combination with Shift, Ctrl, and Alt, jotting down the results for future reference.

Pressing Backspace or Delete to erase the prior keyname from the Playbackkey field only displays the keynames for Backspace and Delete! Simply overtype one keystroke with another. If something's amiss during this time, press Escape to bow out gracefully, and then pick up from where you left off.

Refer to the Works manual for a complete list of keys and keynames available for playback keys.

Running the Macro

Running a macro is a matter of pressing the playback key. Before doing that, however, position the cursor or blinker at the proper starting point. The macro then goes along its merry way replaying keystrokes in the same order you entered them. If you included any playback keys of other macros, it types those also in the same order. To cancel a macro in mid-run, press Alt+/ and choose Cancel Recording.

But what if you don't remember the playback key? Works has an easy solution. When you forget which key does what, selecting the Play Macro option in the first macro menu (Alt+/, type **P**, and hit Enter) brings up a list of macro descriptions and playback keys such as the one in Figure 2-4, which lists the macros you'll soon be creating in the hands-on chapters.

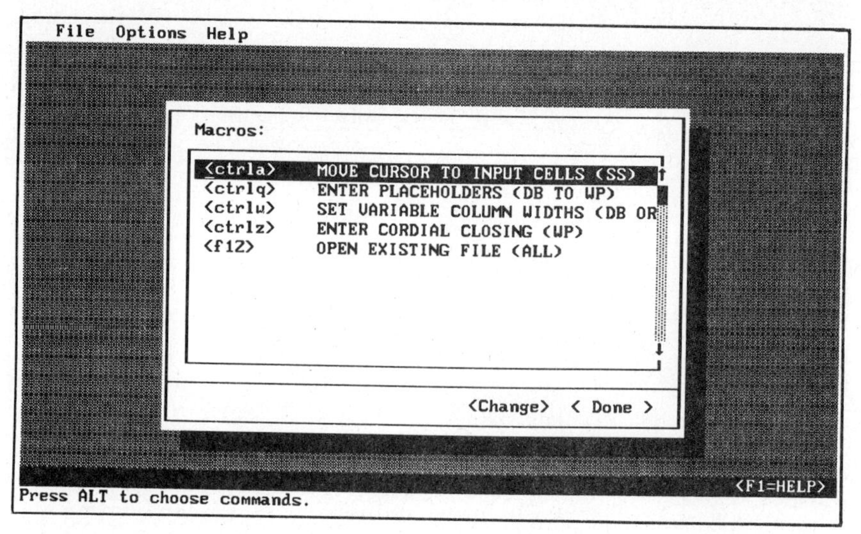

Figure 2-4. The Play Macro screen showing playback keys and titles of macros created in this book

Move the blinker to the macro you want, hit Enter, and the macro is off and running.

A Macro Example

Macros can be a few to several thousand characters long. My all-time favorite contains only four keystrokes: Alt, letter F, letter O, and Tab. When I press F12, my playback key, the macro opens the `Open Existing File` menu and tabs into the `Files` list so I can select a file. Here's the macro definition, shown in Figure 2-5 in a word processor screen:

```
<begdef><f12><menu>FO<tab><enddef>
```

This definition may resemble Sanscrit at the moment. Taking each element one at a time makes it easy to understand.

- Works generates `<begdef>` to indicate the beginning of the macro definition.
- Element `<f12>` is clearly the playback key.
- Element `<menu>` results from hitting the Alt key to activate the menus.
- Element `FO` chooses the `Open Existing File` command in the `File` menu.

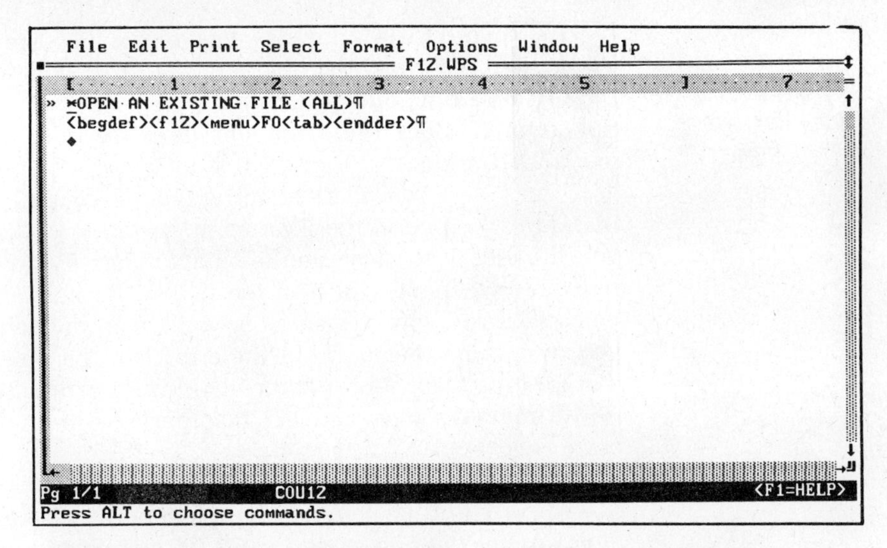

Figure 2-5. The macro definition of the Open Existing File macro, as seen in a word processor screen

- Element `<tab>` jumps the blinker into the `Files` list box.
- Works generates `<enddef>` to indicate the end of the macro definition.

This macro saves only a few keystrokes each time I use it. Multiplied by the number of times I open files, the long-term saving is astronomical.

Creating the Example

When you're ready to take the plunge into macros, here's how to record this simple, invaluable file-open macro:

1. Hold down Alt and type a slash (/) to bring up the first macro menu.
2. Press Enter to confirm `Record Macro`. Works asks which key to record.
3. Press F12 to assign it for recording and playback. If your keyboard doesn't have an F12 key, chances are it doesn't have an F11 key either. F10, unused in the word processor, is a good alternate. Otherwise, press your choice of a playback key.
4. Press Tab to jump to the Title field. To describe the macro's purpose, type **OPEN EXISTING FILE (ALL)** and press Enter.

The word RECORD now appears on the message line, meaning that Works will record everything you type from this point on.

When you're recording a macro, Works records every keystroke—even wrong ones.

A brief time-out: If you make an error, you can only correct it, not undo it. Both the error and its correction become part of the macro definition.

Let's say you inadvertently type **E**, opening the Edit menu, instead of **F** to open the File menu. Instantly realizing your mistake, you hit Escape to close the Edit menu. The *E* and Escape keystrokes will play whenever you run the macro. Because macro actions happen so quickly, chances are you won't even notice it. But if it bothers you, you can either edit out the error later or cancel the macro now (Alt+/, type **C** for Cancel Recording, hit Return), and then start again.

Time-out's over and the recorder is still running, so hit these keys:

- Type **F** and **O**. You can type letters in uppercase or lowercase. I prefer uppercase, so I can spot menus and commands quickly. Works now displays the Files dialog box.
- Press Tab to move the blinker into the Files list. This is as far as you want the macro to go.
- Press Alt+/ to activate the second macro menu. This time, hit Return to confirm End Recording.
- Now run the macro by hitting your playback key. Either select a file to open or press Escape to close the Files box. That's all there is to it.

The recording process is a good deal simpler than it sounds. What you end up with this time is a macro that is truly remarkable. Like Napoleon, it's short, powerful, and gets places fast.

Macro Maintenance

Working with macros means more than recording and running them. It also means viewing, editing, copying, switching, and deleting them. These activities take place either in MACROS.INI or in the first macros menu.

You can work in MACROS.INI just as in any other word processor file.

Works creates MACROS.INI when you record your first macro, storing the macro as text. Each time you record a new macro, Works stores it in MACROS.INI. When you want to edit an existing macro or write a new macro from scratch, you can open MACROS.INI as a full-fledged word processor file and work with the macro definitions there exactly as you would in any other document. Works suspends all macro actions while MACROS.INI is open, so remember to close the file before moving on to your next Works activity.

Figure 2-6 shows a MACROS.INI file, here listing descriptions and definitions of macros you create in this book. In addition to bracketing certain elements and defining keystrokes in its own special way, Works inserts an asterisk before each description to separate one macro from another. The asterisk appears even if you omit a description when you first create a macro.

```
File  Edit  Print  Select  Format  Options  Window  Help
======================== MACROS.INI ========================
[·······1·······2·······3·······4·······5·······]·······7····
» *MOVE·CURSOR·TO·INPUT·CELLS·(SS)¶
<begdef><ctrla><menu>SG<vfld><enter>¶
<vfld><xdown><vfld><xdown><xdown><xdown><xdown><xdown><vfld>
<xdown><vfld><xdown><vfld><xdown><vfld><xdown><xdown><xdown>
<xdown><xdown><vfld><xup><xup><xup><xup><xup><xup><xup><xup>
<xup><xup><xup><xup><xup><xup><enddef>¶
*ENTER·PLACEHOLDERS·(DB·TO·WP)¶
<begdef><ctrlq><menu>EF<xdown><tab><enddef>¶
*SET·VARIABLE·COLUMN·WIDTHS·(DB·OR·SS)¶
<begdef><ctrlw><menu>TW<vfld><enter>¶
<xright><pause·0:00:02.0><ctrlw><enddef>¶
*ENTER·CORDIAL·CLOSING·(WP)¶
<begdef><ctrlz><tab><tab><tab><tab><tab><tab><tab>Cordially,
<enter>¶
<enter>¶
<enter>¶
<enter>¶
<enter>¶
<enter>¶
<tab><tab><tab><tab><tab><tab><tab>William·C.·Conroy<enter>¶
<tab><tab><tab><tab><tab><tab><tab>President·and·
Publisher<enddef>¶
*OPEN·EXISTING·FILE·(ALL)¶
<begdef><f12><menu>FO<tab><enddef>¶
◆
Pg 1/1                COU12                          <F1=HELP>
Press ALT to choose commands.
```

Figure 2-6. The macros in this book in the MACROS.INI file. The word processor screen is artificially elongated to show them all

Editing a Macro

Macros always do what you tell them to do, which may not always be what you want them to do. If your macro takes an unintended tack during playback, correct it in the MACROS.INI file. You can edit-in missing elements, delete doomed ones, and even insert more actions in a macro if you want them.

You can also change the macro's playback key and description in MACROS.INI. The result is the same as choosing the Change Key & Title option in the first macro menu. Because both Change Key & Title and MACROS.INI get information from the same source, any change in one is reflected in the other.

After editing is a good time to print MACROS.INI so you'll have a hardcopy reference of what all your macros look like.

When you close MACROS.INI, Works asks if you want to save the changes. Answer Yes and the task is done.

Recycling a Macro

If you create one macro and need another one that's similar, it's not necessary to start from scratch. Open the MACROS.INI file and use the Edit menu's Copy command to copy the entire macro. Then modify the copy, including typing in a new description and key assignment. Save MACROS.INI, and you have a spanking new macro with little effort.

Switching Macros

You can have an unlimited number of macros—for example, one group that you use in the spreadsheet, another group in the word processor, still another in the database, and yet another in communications. This means that you're likely to end up with duplicate playback keys. For instance, F11 may store an adding macro for the spreadsheet, a boldfacing macro for the word processor, and a copying macro for the database.

Works won't let you have more than one macro file—MACROS.INI is it—but you can switch macros in and out. For example, when you're ready to start working on a monthly report after doing a budget spreadsheet, switch your budget macros out of MACROS.INI and into a word processor file, and then switch your report macros from its word processor file to MACROS.INI. You can even create macros to do the switching for you.

Deleting Macros

Deleting a macro that outlives its usefulness is a simple matter of choosing `Delete Macros` from the first macro menu. Works then brings up a list of macros in a screen similar to the one in Figure 2-4. When you place the blinker on the doomed macro and hit Enter, it disappears—permanently. Once done, there's no way to undo, so exercise caution.

You can also delete macros directly from MACROS.INI by using the Edit menu's Delete command or the Backspace or Delete key. The advantage to this approach is that you can get a last-minute reprieve if you change your mind before saving the file. Simply reload MACROS.INI and you'll find the once-deleted macro still in it.

Because `Delete Macros` and MACROS.INI get their information from the same source, any deletion in one is reflected in the other.

Macro Bells and Whistles

Macros can do much more than start, run their course, and stop. They can, for example, pause during playback to await keyboard input, run other macros, and replay themselves without prompting. You insert these actions by pressing Alt+/ while recording a macro, then choosing one of the options in the second macro menu.

Fixed-Input Pause Macros

Your input at a pause during playback can be fixed (the same number of characters every time) or variable (a different number of characters every time). This determines the type of pause to insert in the macro.

Pausing macros stop during their run to await input from the keyboard. This input can be of fixed or variable length. Suppose you intend to type in a year—1990, for instance—at the pause. Because years always contain four digits, you insert a fixed-input pause.

To insert a fixed-input pause, begin recording a new macro, assigning a playback key and title. Here's how to continue:

- At the point where you want the pause, press Alt+/ to bring up the second macro menu.
- Select `Fixed Input` and hit Enter.
- Specify the input length by typing a typical entry, for example, 1990. It can just as easily be 1111—that is, any four characters. Works counts the number of keystrokes, ignoring what you type.
- Press Alt+/ again. Works now asks you to confirm the end of input, so hit Enter.
- Continue recording the macro. To end recording, press Alt+/ and hit Return.

During playback, when the macro detects a fixed-input pause, it stops and displays `FIXINPUT` on the message line. When you type the last of the specified number of keystrokes, the macro continues its run. There's no need to press Enter.

In a macro definition, Works shows a fixed-input pause as `<ffld>` and a number. In the case of the four-digit year, for instance, it displays `<ffld 4>`.

Variable-Input Pause Macros

When you know you'll be typing any number of keystrokes at a pause, insert a variable-input pause in the macro. Suppose you want

The difference between a fixed-input pause and a variable-input pause is that Works presses Enter after you type a fixed number of keystrokes and you press Enter after the last of a variable number of keystrokes.

your macro to change column widths in the database. Columns can be from 0 to 79 characters wide. Since you'll be typing either a 1-digit or 2-digit number, you want the macro to wait until you tell it to resume.

Begin recording a new macro, assigning a playback key and title. Here's how to continue:

- At the point where you want the variable-input pause to occur, press Alt+/ to bring up the second macro menu.
- Select `Variable Input` and press Enter. You now see **VARINPUT** (variable input) on the message line.
- The length of the input is irrelevant, so don't even bother to type an entry. Press Enter to enter the entry you didn't type. Works doesn't know the difference. You now see **RECORD** on the message line.
- Continue recording the macro. To end recording, press Alt+/ and hit Return.

When the macro detects a variable-input pause during playback, it stops and displays **VARINPUT** on the message line. It then waits patiently while you enter any number of keystrokes and press Enter, which tells it to resume its run.

In a macro definition, Works shows a variable-input pause as `<vfld>`. You can experience a variable-input pause macro in Chapter 21.

Timed-Pause Macros

Timed pauses cause macros to wait a specified amount of time during playback.

When you tell it to, a macro will pause during playback for a specified length of time, which can be as short as a tenth of a second to as long as several days. Say your macro needs a dollar amount that will be available as soon as certain calculations take place on your spreadsheet. These calculations take a little less than than three minutes to complete, so you insert a three-minute pause in your macro.

When you want to insert a timed pause, begin recording a new macro, assigning a playback key and title. Here's how to continue:

- At the point where you want the timed pause to occur, press Alt+/ to bring up the second macro menu.
- Select **Pause** and hit Enter. Works asks you to specify the time delay in this form: `hh:mm:ss.t` (*h* hours, *m* minutes, *s* seconds, and *t* tenths of seconds). You can also use these short forms:

.5 for a 5/10 of a second delay

10. for a 10 second delay

1:00 for a 1 minute delay

1:30:00 for a one-and-one-half hour delay

- After typing the time delay, press Enter and continue recording the macro.

During playback, when the macro detects a timed pause, it suspends action, displays PAUSE on the message line, waits for the specified amount of time to elapse, and then resumes running. You can interrupt the pause by pressing any key.

In a macro definition, Works shows a timed pause of three minutes as <pause 3.00>.

Nested-Input Macros

Nesting one macro within another tells the macro to pause during playback and await your input. Works assigns this input to a playback key you specify, creating it as a separate macro. When you press Enter, the macro continues its run, replaying your input whenever it finds the nested playback key. Your initial input isn't recorded as part of the nested macro because you're likely to type something different each time you run the macro.

Assume someone new is working on your spreadsheet. Wanting to make your macros as helpful as possible, you insert statements like Enter the current balance. You follow this with <nest ctrla>—the nest command and playback key. The number that the user types, say 23456, becomes the temporary definition of ctrla. You can have the macro later display Please confirm that the current balance is 23456 by inserting ctrla in the macro where you want the number to appear.

Looping Macros

Pressing Alt+/ stops a looping macro.

A looping macro replays itself until you tell it to stop. Suppose you want to enter field names in the database. You can create a macro that moves the cursor to the next field, waits for you to type the field name, enters the name, and then moves the cursor to the next field and waits again, repeating this pattern over and over.

To create a looping macro, begin recording a new macro as usual, assigning a playback key and title. Then follow these steps:

- Enter the keystrokes and commands that define the macro's tasks.
- When you've completed the macro, press the macro's playback key—the same one you pressed when you started recording. Works is tracking your actions and now advises `You have created a looping macro.`
- Press Enter to tack the macro's playback key to the end of the macro. This also ends recording.

At playback, when the macro comes to the end of its run and detects its own playback key, it loops around to the beginning and starts again. Chances are, you can stop the looping action by pressing Alt+/. If not, you'll find the following Tip particularly relevant.

Things happen fast in a looping macro, so it's a good idea to insert a timed pause, however brief, before the playback key at the end. This gives you the chance to stop the looping action exactly when you want to. With some of the faster computers, a timed pause is imperative. Otherwise, you'll keep going around in an endless circle.

Linked (Subroutine) Macros

Macros can contain the playback keys of other macros, enabling one macro to trigger the actions of another. When Works detects the playback key of another macro in a macro that's running, it makes a detour and runs the other. When it finishes, it returns to the first macro and continues running there.

This arrangement works well when you need the same macro routine in several macros or several times in one macro. Instead of typing the same thing over and over, simply create a separate macro and insert its keyname wherever you want to run its routine.

Table 2-2 summarizes the keystrokes that perform macro functions, aside from the macro menus. In Part Seven, "Putting Works to Work," you'll experience the wonderful things that macros can do.

Table 2-2. Keys that perform macro functions

What You Want To Do	Keystroke	Macro Menu (1) or (2) Option Equivalent
Open the macro menu	Alt+/ (slash)	
Select a macro option (with macro menu open)	Enter or bold letter	
Skip a macro	à (accent grave)	(1) Skip Macro
Insert fixed input pause	Ctrl+] (bracket)	(2) Fixed Input
Insert variable input pause	Ctrl+ – (minus sign)	(2) Variable Input
Stop macro recording	Alt+ – (minus sign)	(2) End Recording
Carry out the command	Enter	
Cancel the command	Escape	

P A R T

The Spreadsheet

Spreadsheet Essentials

Electronic spreadsheets let you explore "what if" scenarios.

Imagine doing complex calculations in fractions of a second and knowing those calculations are correct, changing dozens of numbers and getting new results instantly, and printing reports that are number perfect. Imagine no more dog-eared ledgers, stubby pencils, worn-out erasers, desktop calculators, and paper tapes. Utopia, you say? Not at all. Merely the dazzle of the electronic spreadsheet.

Electronic spreadsheets blaze new paths in the way you work with numbers. Like their handwritten counterparts, they let you plan a budget or a balance sheet, calculate payback on a loan or an investment, keep track of income and expenses, project sales and cash flow, and perform countless other activities dealing with numbers. Unlike their handwritten counterparts, they let you explore "what if" scenarios with lightning speed.

"What ifs" are the tough choices you face in keeping business and personal matters on a sound financial footing. Let's say you project a sales increase of 20 percent in the next six months. What if sales increase only 10 or 15 percent? Or suppose you expect to pay 8.7 percent interest for a car loan. What if you must pay 11 or 12 percent? Suppose you plan to give your employees a 7 percent raise this year. What if you give them a 5 percent or 9 percent raise instead? All you do is enter one number to test the waters, then a different number to test that effect. With a spreadsheet, you can test to your heart's content and see the immediate impact on the bottom line.

Getting Acquainted with the Spreadsheet

This chapter discusses the essential "whys" and "hows" of the Works spreadsheet. It describes the spreadsheet screen, how to move the cursor around the screen, shortcut keys, and the kinds of information you can enter in cells, with a special spotlight on formulas.

You can get a good idea of how the spreadsheet works by reading the text and referring to the illustrations. You don't have to keep Works on screen all the time. However, you may find it helpful to have Works up and running at certain times, particularly while you read about the spreadsheet screen.

When you're ready to work with Works, fire up your computer and follow the instructions in "Loading Works" in the Introduction to this book. At the Works gateway, type **NS** (Create New File/New Spreadsheet) to create a new spreadsheet file.

The Spreadsheet Screen

Your first view of the spreadsheet screen can be an eye-opening experience. There it is—a large, empty area surrounded by letters, numbers, and words, as shown in Figure 3-1. Understanding what happens on the screen is essential to creating efficient, working spreadsheets, so this section describes what each element tells you and explains how you will work with it.

You can see only part of a spreadsheet through the window.

A. The empty area is your *workspace*. It is a window to your computer's memory through which you view and manage a spreadsheet. Large as it may seem to you now, you're looking at only a small portion of the whole. The actual spreadsheet is a rectangular grid 256 columns across and 4096 rows down—more than 7,500 times larger than the area visible on-screen. Because the spreadsheet is so vast, you can see only a portion of it at one time, much as you can see only a portion of a scene through the viewfinder of a camera. By moving the Works window (your viewfinder), you can see and work on the entire spreadsheet one screenful at a time.

B. The vertical line at the left edge is the *window border*, which separates the window from the screen.

C. The numbers 1 through 18 down the left side of the screen identify the *rows* visible at this time. Imagine a horizontal line between one row number and the next.

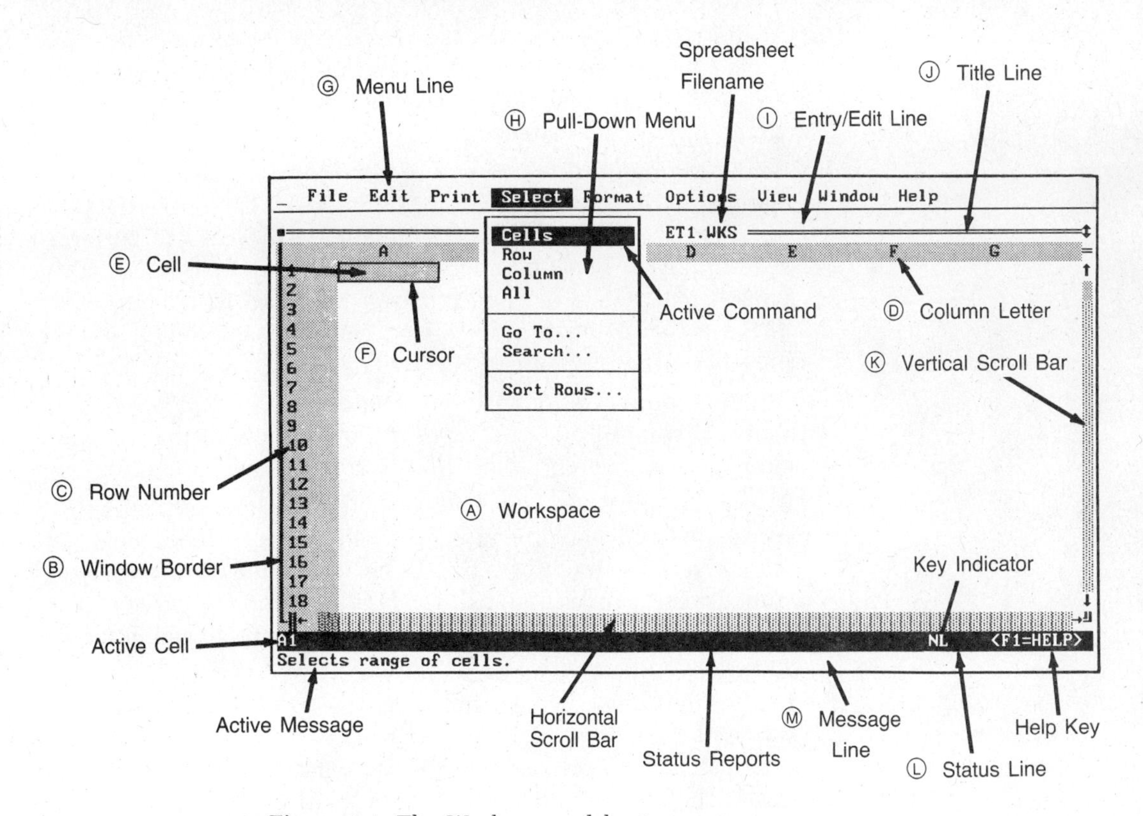

Figure 3-1. The Works spreadsheet screen

D. The letters A through G across the upper part of the screen identify the *columns* visible at this time. Imagine a vertical line between one column letter and the next.

The intersection of a column and row forms a cell.

E. The rectangle formed by the intersection of the imaginary column and row lines is a *cell*. Works refers to a cell by a column letter and row number. A1 is the cell at the intersection of column A and row 1, and D12 is a cell at the intersection of column D and row 12. Cells are used to store numbers, text, and formulas. The Works spreadsheet contains over one million cells.

F. The rectangular highlight in the workspace is the *cursor*. The cursor identifies the active cell, the one that can accept the information you type. You can make any cell active by using the direction keys to move the cursor to it. If you have a mouse installed, the cursor shares the workspace with the mouse pointer—either a small rectangle or an arrow, depending on screen mode.

G. At the top of the screen is the *menu line* containing the spreadsheet menus: File, Edit, Print, Select, Format, Options, View, Window, and Help. The menus let you create and maintain your spreadsheet.

H. Below the menu line is a *pull-down menu* listing the commands in the Select menu: Cells, Row, Column, All, Go To, Search, and Sort Rows. Commands tell Works to perform specific tasks. The first command—Cells—appears in reverse video (light letters on a dark background), which identifies it as the active command. Each time you choose a menu, Works presents a list of commands.

I. Directly below the menu line is the *entry/edit line* where Works displays what you type or the contents of the cell your cursor is on. The entry/edit line is empty now.

J. Below the entry/edit line is the *title line*, which contains the spreadsheet filename. You use this filename to load, store, and otherwise keep track of a file. Until you name the new spreadsheet, Works assigns the standard filename—**SHEET1.WKS**. The extension **.WKS** stands for worksheet, another name for a spreadsheet.

K. At the right edge of the window is the *vertical scroll bar* that shows the location of the cursor relative to all rows on the spreadsheet. A *horizontal scroll bar* below the workspace shows the cursor's location relative to all columns.

Mouse users can zip along to distant parts of the spreadsheet by gliding the scroll box along a scroll bar.

Each scroll bar contains a *scroll box* that moves along the scroll bar as you move the cursor, showing which part of the file is currently on screen. For instance, when the cursor is on A2048, the scroll box is in the middle of the vertical scroll bar. With the cursor on EA2048, the scroll box is in the middle of both the vertical and horizontal scroll bars.

L. Directly below the horizontal scroll bar is the *status line*. The left end of the status line shows the location of the active cell. The cursor is always on A1 when you open a new spreadsheet, so the cell indicator shows A1. During recalculation and when you save or print, Works replaces this indicator with percentages showing how much of the spreadsheet has already been processed. The right end shows the key to press (F1) to get immediate on-screen help. Mouse users can click on this element to get help.

Works reserves the area between the cell indicator and Help key for status reports on your activities, such as **EXTEND** (when you're selecting more cells), **COPY** (when you're copying cell contents), or **SPLIT** (when you're splitting the window screen into panes). It also shows when certain keys are active (`NL` is Num Lock and `CL` is Caps Lock).

M. Below the status line is the *message line* where Works describes the active command or prompts your next action. The Cells command is active, so the message line displays `Selects range of cells.`

Around the perimeter of the screen are click-on symbols and other mouse elements described in Chapter 1.

Moving the Cursor

Table 3-1 shows the keys that move the cursor around the spreadsheet. You can have the cursor take small steps one cell at a time, jump by blocks of cells, make huge leaps through an entire file, or move in special ways in a selected area. If you're practicing on your computer, be aware that some of the following keystrokes work only if you have information in the cells.

Table 3-1. Keys that move the cursor

What You Want To Do	Keystroke
Move left one cell	Left Arrow
Move right one cell	Right Arrow
Move up one cell	Up Arrow
Move down one cell	Down Arrow
Move left one block	Ctrl+Left Arrow
Move right one block	Ctrl+Right Arrow
Move up one block	Ctrl+Up Arrow
Move down one block	Ctrl+Down Arrow
Move left one screen	Ctrl+Page Up
Move right one screen	Ctrl+Page Down
Move up one screen	Page Up
Move down one screen	Page Down
Move to left of screen	Home
Move to right of screen	End
Move to beginning cell (A1)	Ctrl+Home
Move to ending cell in active area	Ctrl+End

(continued)

Table 3-1. *(continued)*

In Area Selected with Shift+Arrow or Shift+F8 (when more than one column is selected)

What You Want To Do	Keystroke
Move down by cell to end of selected column, then to top cell in next selected column, and so on	Enter
Move up by cell to top of selected column, then to bottom cell in previous selected column, and so on	Shift+Enter
Move down by cell, then left to right in selected columns	Tab
Move up by cell, then left to right in selected columns	Shift+Tab

Move One Cell

Pressing the Up, Down, Left, or Right Arrow keys moves the cursor one cell in the direction of the arrow. When you hold down an arrow key, the cursor moves rapidly. The arrow keys (also called *direction* or *movement keys*) are usually located in the right of the keyboard.

Move One Block

Holding down the Ctrl (Control) key and pressing an arrow key jumps the cursor to the first or last cell in a block of contiguous cells containing information. After Works runs out of filled blocks, it zips the cursor to the farthest cell on the spreadsheet in the direction of the arrow.

For example, holding down Ctrl while you press Down Arrow ultimately brings the cursor to row 4096, the bottommost row; Ctrl+Right Arrow brings the cursor to column IV, the rightmost (256th) column.

If the row or column is empty, pressing Ctrl and an arrow key moves the cursor directly to the farthest cell.

Move One Screen

Pressing Page Up or Page Down moves the cursor up or down one screen at a time, while Ctrl and Page Up or Page Down move the cursor left or right one screen. When you hold down these keys, the cursor jumps to the same position in the next screen and in succeeding screens. The Home key moves the cursor to the leftmost cell on the current screen, and End moves it to the rightmost cell.

Move One File

Holding down Ctrl and pressing Home jumps the cursor to A1, the cell in the upper left corner (the beginning cell) of the active spreadsheet. Holding down Ctrl and pressing End moves the cursor to the cell in the lower right corner (the ending cell) of the active spreadsheet. The active spreadsheet is the rectangular area that contains information. The ending cell is determined by the intersection of the rightmost and bottommost filled cell in the active area, even though the ending cell itself may not contain any information.

Move to a Specific Place

Two commands in the Select menu move the cursor in special ways: the Go To command sends the cursor to a specific cell, while the Search command sends the cursor to a specific piece of information.

Confining the Cursor to a Selected Area

The cursor moves in special ways in a confined area.

One of the neat things you can do in the Works spreadsheet is confine cursor movement to a selected area. This is helpful when you're entering information in a large but limited area. Your keystroke after typing each entry controls the direction in which the cursor moves. The only caveat is that you select the area with the Shift+Arrow keys.

Suppose you select rows 5 to 12 in columns B, C, and D, as shown in Figure 3-2. You are entering numbers, and the cursor is on

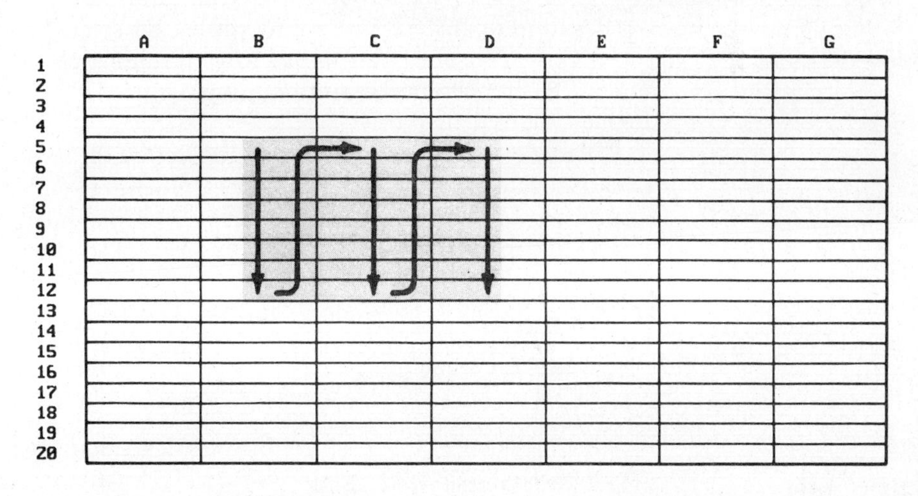

Figure 3-2. Cursor movements in a selected area

B5. Each time you type a number and press Enter, the cursor moves one cell down. When it gets to B12, the bottom cell in the selected area, the cursor scoots up to C5, the top cell in the next selected column. Subsequent Enter keystrokes move the cursor down column C. After C12, pressing Enter sends the cursor up to D5, which continues in this manner in the selected area in a top to bottom zig-zag.

Other keystrokes cause zig-zags in different directions. Shift+Enter moves the cursor in a bottom to top zig-zag, Tab moves the cursor down in a left to right zig-zag; and Shift+Tab moves the cursor up in a left to right zig-zag. Works' zig-zag capability can be a real time-saver when you have a heavy load of entries. Try it.

Shortcut and Selection Keys

Shortcut keys bypass the menus, speeding your work with Works.

When you work with commands, the typical procedure is to open a menu first, then select a command. Works makes things easier than that. In many cases, Works provides shortcut keys that let you bypass the menus entirely. These keys are called *shortcut keys*.

By now you know all about F1, the key that summons immediate help. F1 is a shortcut key that circumvents the Help menu's array of commands. Instead of opening the Help menu and selecting a command, you simply press F1. Other menus and commands have shortcut keys too. For instance, pressing F5 brings up the `Go to` dialog box just as if you opened the Select menu and selected the Go To command. Hit F3 and you can move selected information without going anywhere near the Edit menu's Move command. And so it goes.

Shortcut keys also let you select information for commands to work with. For instance, pressing Shift+F8 selects an entire column, while Ctrl+F8 selects an entire row. It's not necessary to move the cursor to the beginning and ending cells. These kinds of conveniences abound in Works.

Table 3-2 shows the shortcut and selection keys that speed your spreadsheet work. The function keys (imprinted with the letter F and a number) are located at the left end of the keyboard on some computers and in the top row on others.

Table 3-2. Spreadsheet actions and the keystrokes that perform them

What You Want To Do	Keystroke	Command Equivalent
Get help	F1	Help/Help Index
Access tutorial	Shift+F1	Help/Works Tutorial

What You Want To Do	Keystroke	Command Equivalent
Enter or exit edit mode	F2	
Move information	F3	Edit/Move
Copy information	Shift + F3	Edit/Copy
Define absolute cell reference in formula (insert $ sign)	F4	
Go to next named range	Shift + F5	Select/Go To
Go to a specific cell	F5	Select/Go To
Go to next window pane	F6	
Go to previous window pane	Shift + F6	
Go to next window	Ctrl + F6	
Go to previous window	Ctrl + Shift + F6	
Repeat last search immediately	F7	
Repeat last copy command immediately	Shift + F7	
Extend selection	F8 then Arrow (also Shift + Arrow)	
Select a column	Shift + F8	Select/Column
Select a row	Ctrl + F8	Select/Row
Select entire spreadsheet	Ctrl + Shift + F8	Select/All
Calculate formulas	F9	Options/Calculate Now
Enter formula results only, not formula	F9 then Enter	
From chart screen, return to spreadsheet screen	F10	View/Spreadsheet
Display active chart	Shift + F10	View/Chart
Collapse current selection	Escape or Arrow	
Turn off extend action	Escape	

(*continued*)

Table 3-2. (*continued*)

What You Want To Do	Keystroke	Command Equivalent
Enter into a range (select cells, type info, press Ctrl+Enter)	Ctrl+Enter	
Enter current date	Ctrl+; (semicolon)	
Enter current time	Ctrl+Shift+;	(semicolon)
Copy contents of cell above (with formula, copy result only)	Ctrl+'	(apostrophe)
Move clockwise to next unlocked cell (protection on)	Tab	
Move counter-clockwise to next unlocked cell (protection on)	Shift+Tab	
Erase contents of a cell (with cursor on cell)	Backspace then Enter	Edit/Clear

Entering Numbers

Works considers anything that looks or acts like a number to be a number. Numbers can consist of numerals 0 to 9, numerals and other characters (decimal point, minus sign, dollar or percent sign, parentheses, or the letter E [for scientific notation], and dates and times, which Works stores as numbers. Numbers can take these forms:

−456
(456)
4,567
1.75
5 7/8 or 5.875
876E-2
55%
$1.50
6/21/90
June 21, 1990

Slashes (6/21/90) tell Works a date is a value. Hyphens (6-21-90) make it text.

The format of the cell determines the appearance of the number. Until you change it, the General command shows numbers as precisely as possible in an integer, decimal fraction, or exponential format. You can use the Format menu to replace the General format with a Fixed, Currency (Dollar or other), Comma, Exponential, Percent, True/False, or Time/Date format. Except for True/False and Time/Date, which are different kinds of values, these formats allow 0 to 7 decimal places. Typing certain elements with a number changes the cell format. For example, entering $1.50, a number with a dollar sign, gives the cell the Dollar format; entering 15%, a number with a percent sign, gives the cell the Percent format.

When you have many numbers to enter, typing them plain, then formatting the cells as a group can save keystrokes. With only a few numbers, it's often more efficient to type the dollar or percent signs and save the format step.

To enter a number, place the cursor on the selected cell and type the number. As you type, the number appears on the entry/edit line below the menu line and at the cursor's location. When you finish typing, either press Enter or move the cursor to another cell. Moving the cursor serves the same purpose as pressing Enter. The number then appears in the selected cell. Works aligns a number in the right of the cell. You can center or left-align it with the Format menu's Style command.

Number Overflows

If the number you enter is too small or too large for the cell, Works converts it into scientific notation. For example, if you type 1234567890 (a 10-digit number) into a cell 10 characters wide, Works displays it as `1.235E+09`. Why is a 10-digit number too large for a 10-character cell? Good question. Works reserves a space at the right end of the cell for either a close parenthesis (which appears in a negative number in Dollar or Comma format) or a percent sign.

Date and Time Numbers

Works can figure out the elapsed days between dates and elapsed hours between times.

You can enter dates and times in cells and use them in calculations. Works reformats the cell to show them as dates and times but stores them as numbers.

Date Numbers

The Works calendar starts with January 1, 1900 and ends with June 3, 2079. January 1, 1900 is number 1; January 2, 1900 is number 2; and so on to June 3, 2079, which is number 65534. If you use a date outside this range, Works considers it text.

You can enter a date in long form (June 21, 1990; June 1990; June 21; or June) or short form (6/21/90 or 6/21 or 6/90), then use the dates in a calculation. For example, subtract 6/21/89 from 10/19/90 and you get 485, the number of elapsed days. Conversely, you can enter a number, say 33045, in a cell and use the Format menu's Time/Date command to convert it into the date 6/21/90.

Time Numbers

The Works clock begins with 12:00:00 PM and ends with 11:59:59 PM. When you enter times in 24-hour form (15:30:00 or 15:30) or 12-hour form (3:30 PM or 3PM), you can use them in a calculation to get the elapsed hours and minutes between two times.

Assume you consulted with a client from 1:30 PM to 3:10 PM. When you enter these times on the spreadsheet and subtract one from the other, Works calculates an elapsed time of 1 hour and 40 minutes. Use the Format menu's Time/Date command to format the formula cell to show hours and minutes.

Entering Text

Text can take different forms and can even look like a value.

Works treats as text anything it can't interpret as a number or formula. Text is typically used at the beginning of rows to describe what's in the cells to the right and at the tops of columns to describe what's in the cells below, just as on a paper spreadsheet. Text can take these forms:

Cash Disbursements

121-17-0562

1600 Pennsylvania Avenue

(516) 555-1212

#172

6-21-88 =(hyphens instead of slashes make this date text)

234 567 =(the space between the 4 and 5 makes this number text)

"= = = = = = = = = = = = (quotes turn the equal signs into text)

"June 21, 1931 = (quotes turn the date into text)

Typing leading quotation marks turns into text an entry that might otherwise be considered a value. For example, you can create lines across a spreadsheet with a series of equal signs or minus signs (which Works normally recognizes as numerical values) by typing quotation marks first. The quotes appear only before the text on the entry/edit line, not in the cell.

Enter text in the same way as numbers—by placing the cursor on the cell, typing the text, and either pressing Enter or moving the cursor to another cell afterward. Works aligns text in the left of the cell. Alignment contributes to the readability of a spreadsheet. You can center or right-align text with the Format menu's Style command.

About Formulas

Formulas are the shining stars of a spreadsheet.

Formulas express the mathematical relationship between numbers and give a spreadsheet real power. Whenever you rework any numbers, the formulas recalculate and produce new results. You signal Works that you're entering a formula by first typing an equal sign. Here's what formulas look like:

```
=1+1
=A10-A22
=SUM(DD22:DD33)
=(RATE+.5)/12
```

The Variables in a Formula

Formulas contain numbers, operators, and functions, all of which are called *variables* because they vary from formula to formula. Variables can be

- A number or anything that evaluates to a number, such as a reference to a cell location (A10) or a named cell (RATE) that contains a number or a formula that yields a number, or a number you supply (.5).

- Functions, which have names like IF and SUM. These are calculations and routines built into the Works program. You'll find explanations and examples of functions in Chapter 4.
- Arithmetic operators that tell Works the kind of calculation to perform. These operators are ’ (exponentiation), * (multiplication), / (division), + (addition), – (subtraction), and % (percentage).
- Comparison operators that compare the numbers in an IF formula and arrive at a true or false conclusion. These operators are = (equal to), <> (not equal to), < (less than), > (greater than), <= (less than or equal to), and >= (greater than or equal to).
- Logical operators: ~ (not), | (or), and & (and).
- Special duty operators: : (colon range operator) and $ (absolute reference).

The use of these operators will become clear to you as you learn more about Works formulas. They are all assembled in Table 3-3.

Table 3-3. Spreadsheet operators and symbols

Character Typed	Operation Performed
Arithmetic Operators:	
^	Exponentiation
*	Multiplication
/	Division
+	Addition
–	Subtraction
Comparison Operators:	
=	Equal to
<>	Not equal to
<	Less than
>	Greater than
<=	Less than or equal to
<=	Greater than or equal to
Logical Operators:	
&	And
~	Not
|	Or

Character Typed	Operation Performed
Other Operators and Symbols:	
:	Range
%	Percentage
"	Start of text
=	Start of a formula (also + or −)
$	Absolute reference
?	Wildcard (replaces single character)
*	Wildcard (replaces multiple characters)

A Formula Example

An equal sign typically signals the start of a formula, but you can use a plus or minus sign instead.

Figure 3-3 shows an income and expense spreadsheet. The formula in B8 subtracts the expenses in B6 from the gross income in B5 to produce net income. Because the cursor is on B8, you can see **=B5-B6** on the entry line in the upper left corner. Cells B5 and B6 are cell references. The equal sign before the formula signals Works that this entry is a formula, not text or a number. (You can also use a plus or minus sign instead of an equal sign.)

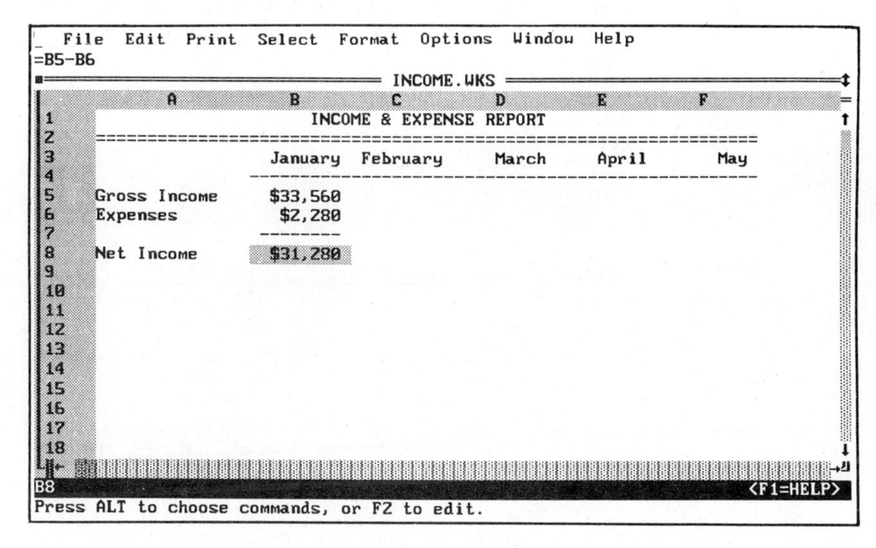

Figure 3-3. Income and expense spreadsheet with a subtraction formula in B8

If you change either or both of the numbers in B5 and B6, the formula in B8 calculates a new result. If other formulas refer to any of those cells, their results change too, all of which makes the effort you put into creating a spreadsheet eminently worthwhile.

Cell References

Cell references in a formula can be relative or absolute. The difference is important only if you copy the formula.

Spreadsheets often need the same formula in several cells. Consider the spreadsheet in Figure 3-4, which now shows income and expenses for January, February, and March. The formula in B8 that calculates net income in January can calculate net income in February, March, April, and May as well. That's because the relation of the cells to the formula—gross income three cells above and expenses two cells above—remain constant. You don't have to build a new formula each month. You can enter the formula once, and then copy it to all other cells that need it.

```
  File  Edit  Print  Select  Format  Options  Window  Help
=C5-C6
                               INCOME.WKS
         A              B          C          D          E          F
1                        INCOME & EXPENSE REPORT
2   ===============================================================
3                     January   February     March      April       May
4   ---------------------------------------------------------------
5   Gross Income      $33,560    $29,560    $39,100
6   Expenses           $2,280     $1,660     $1,990
7                    --------   --------   --------   --------   --------
8   Net Income        $31,280    $27,900    $37,110         $0         $0
9
10
11
12
13
14
15
16
17
18
C8                                                              <F1=HELP>
Press ALT to choose commands, or F2 to edit.
```

Figure 3-4. Income and expense spreadsheet illustrating relative cell references

And here's where the concept of relative and absolute references enters the picture.

Relative and absolute references tell a formula where to find the cells it needs to work with. The difference between these references is important only when you copy a formula from one location to another. A *relative reference* refers to a different cell, depending on where the formula is copied. An *absolute reference* always refers to the same cell, no matter where the formula is copied. This concept is sometimes difficult to grasp, but it's critical that you understand it if you are to create hard-working spreadsheets that produce accurate results.

Relative References

Relative references always refer to different cells.

References in a formula are more often relative than absolute. Relative references view cell relationships in terms of direction (left, right, above, below) and distance (number of rows and columns away) from the formula cell. It's like saying "go two blocks up and one block over." When you establish a cell reference as relative, the pattern doesn't deviate. Wherever you copy that formula containing that relative reference, the formula will still look for the cell that is "two blocks up and one block over" in relation to itself.

Relative references can look like a cell location (such as AA22), a named cell (such as SALES), or a range of cells (such as AA22:AB31).

In Figure 3-3, the formula in B8 uses cells B5 and B6 as relative references. In Figure 3-4, the formula in B8 is copied to C8, D8, E8, and F8, where it performs the same calculation, subtracting the value in the cell two cells above from the value in the cell three cells above. Because the cell references are relative, Works adjusts the cell locations in the copied formulas to reflect the new locations. The formula in C8 works with C5 and C6, the formula in D8 works with D5 and D6, and so on.

Absolute References

Absolute references always refer to the same cell.

An absolute reference is a target for a formula. It's like directing the formula to a specific place, say 798 Works Street. Wherever you copy that formula, it will still look for whatever is in the cell at 798 Works Street.

Because relative references are far more common than absolute, Works always assumes you're working with a relative reference. You indicate otherwise by inserting a dollar sign ($) in the reference you want to make absolute.

An interest rate can be an ideal candidate for absolute reference status because it's often a unique type of value on a spreadsheet. Suppose you're creating a loan amortization schedule. Several formulas refer to the interest rate in cell C4. To be sure each formula continues to refer to C4 no matter where you copy it, you press the F4 key with your cursor on C4. Works then embeds dollar signs in the cell reference, which appears as **$C$4** in the formula. If you give C4 the name of RATE, **$RATE** appears instead.

Mixed References

Mixed references are useful to build spreadsheets that resemble multiplication tables.

You will sometimes want to mix your references so that either the column or row is relative or absolute. For example, a relative column and absolute row would look like C$4 and an absolute column and relative row would look like $C4.

A range of cells can also be a mixed reference—for example, $C$4:D10, which defines a range whose upper left cell ($C$4) is absolute and whose lower right cell (D10) is relative.

You can type a mixed reference into a formula or use the F4 key to insert it. Just be sure the cursor is on the referenced cell before pressing F4.

The F4 key has a talent you're sure to like. Holding down F4 cycles through combinations of references in this order: relative column/relative row, absolute column/absolute row, relative column/absolute row, and absolute column/relative row. All you do is press Enter when the right combination appears on the entry line and Works drops the reference into the formula.

When you copy a formula that contains a mixed reference, the absolute reference remains fixed and the relative reference varies.

How Works Calculates a Formula

To build a formula correctly—and get the correct results—you must know how Works calculates it. Works follows standard algebraic rules, evaluating equations as it finds them, from left to right, the values in the innermost set of parentheses first, and operators in their order of precedence.

Operator Order of Evaluation

Operators are evaluated in the following order:

- Exponentiation (^) has the highest priority and is calculated first, followed by a negative value (for example, −5) or a positive value (for example, +5), which share second spot.
- Multiplication (*) and division (/) share third place, and addition (+) and subtraction (−) share fourth place. You can remember the sequence of these operators the way my algebra teacher taught me, by thinking of "**M**y **D**ear **A**unt **S**arah" (**MDAS**).

My Dear Aunt Sarah helps build a formula.

- The comparison operators share fifth place: Equal to (=), not equal to (<>), less than (<), greater than (>), less than or equal to (<=), and greater than or equal to (>=).
- The NOT operator (~) takes sixth place, while the OR (|) and AND (&) operators bring up the rear. These operators perform logical duties with the IF function.

If a formula has more than one of the same operator or more than one operator with the same order of evaluation, Works evaluates them from left to right.

A Calculation Example

To get the flavor of how Works evaluates a formula, consider the following diverse elements:

```
=12+6*(26-3)^2/8
```

Here's how Works handles it: (26-3) is calculated first because it is in parentheses. The result, 23, is raised to the power of 2. That result, 529, is multiplied by 6. That result, 3174, is divided by 8 to get 396.75, to which 12 is added. The answer, 408.75, is displayed in the formula cell. All of this happens in a fraction of a second.

Building and Entering a Formula

Always start with the cursor on the cell that receives the formula. If other (contiguous) cells need the same formula, press F8, and select the cells with an arrow key. Type an equal sign (or a plus or minus sign) to signal Works that you're building a formula. If you omit the sign, Works will receive the formula as text, not a value.

You may be tempted to type in the cell locations, but move the cursor to them instead. It's easier and more accurate than typing. Type only the operators and symbols, numbers you supply, and any function names. To turn a relative reference into an absolute reference, press F4 with the cursor on the cell or type a dollar sign before a cell name.

If you mistype anything, press Backspace to back up the cursor and erase. Though Works is forgiving and usually closes up spaces in a formula, it's good practice not to leave any spaces.

When the formula is complete, press Enter to enter it in a selected cell or Ctrl+Enter to enter it in a group of contiguous selected cells. If you run into a snag before you complete the formula, press the Escape key and start over.

And If Your Formula Won't Work

Ideas to get you through those times when your formula acts up.

No matter how carefully you plan, no matter how meticulously you enter a formula, there will be times when you're convinced your formula has a mind of its own—and that mind is on something else, not on what you're doing. So, you end up with a wrong answer, an error message, or that ultimate indignity—a formula Works won't accept unless you revise it. It happens to all of us. Most problems are easy to solve, but some require a bit of sleuthing. Here are some approaches to try.

Sorry, Wrong Number

If your formula is producing the wrong answer, look at construction and concept:

- Start with the obvious, such as wrong operators and mistyped numbers.
- Be sure the formula refers to the proper cells, including any named cells.
- If you copied the formula, compare the absolute and relative cell references in the original and copied versions. Be sure that any absolute reference has a dollar sign ($) before it.
- Examine the function argument for anomalies. For example, you can get distorted results if you inadvertently include blank single cells with the AVG and COUNT functions.
- Look carefully at the order of calculation. Check for parentheses around calculations that you want Works to handle first. Review the precedence of arithmetic operators.
- Consider the concept and what you want your formula to do. Rethinking and reworking the logic behind the formula can get you going in the right direction.
- Reduce a long and complicated formula to its simplest form. If possible, break the formula into parts and have Works calculate each part separately.

It's often worthwhile to substitute simple numbers when testing a formula's workings. This can be helpful in at least two ways: it gives you an idea of how far away your answer is from the correct answer and makes it easier to spot incremental patterns and orders of magnitude, both of which can be important clues.

Error Messages and Other Red Flags

If something other than wrong answers is wrong with your formula, Works lets you know about it in several ways.

Cell Messages

When you ask a formula to do something it cannot do, such as divide by zero or work with a cell reference you've deleted, Works displays ERR (error) in the formula cell. When information your formula needs isn't available yet, it displays N/A (not available) instead.

Error messages have a way of propagating like the weeds of summer, so you may sometimes see ERR or N/A in several cells. Stay calm. This doesn't necessarily mean you have a slew of problem formulas. One problem formula can spawn a host of error messages simply because other formulas refer to it. When you correct the problem, chances are good that the other messages will disappear.

Status Line Messages

Another type of error message shows up on the status line. If your formula refers to itself (for example, a formula in A1 referring to A1) or a chain of formulas depend on each other's values (for example, A1 depends on B1, which depends on C1, which depends on A1), you have a circular reference. To alert you to this sticky situation, Works displays CIRC on the status line. Examine each formula and its relationship to other formulas until you find the circular reference, then eliminate it.

When you want to examine all of the formulas on screen, you can press Alt and type **OF** (Options/Show Formulas). Works then doubles the width of the columns and displays the formulas. If long formulas are truncated, either place your cursor on the formula cell and look at the formula on the entry/edit line or increase the column width until you can see it in its entirety. If the formula is longer than the maximum column width (79 characters), place your cursor on the formula cell, press F2, and Works will display the end of the formula.

In a large spreadsheet packed with text and numbers but only a few formulas, you can use the Select menu's Search command to locate the formulas quickly. With the formula version on-screen, enter an equal sign in the `Search for` field. Works will zip the cursor to either a formula or to a line you created with equal signs. Press F7 to find the next equal sign (formula or line) and continue in this way until you check all formulas. When you want to restore the spreadsheet, press Alt and type **OF** again.

On-Screen Messages

Works' on-screen error messages pinpoint the source of the problem.

Works dutifully tracks your keystrokes while you build a formula. If you overlook a needed element, Works immediately alerts you with an on-screen error message. For example, if you omit an arithmetic operator, you'll see `Missing operator` in the center of the screen. Because Works won't let you continue until you supply the missing element, simply type the operator and move on.

Works also displays an on-screen error message when you try to enter an incomplete or improper formula. For example, if you omit an argument in an IF formula, you'll see `Wrong number of arguments`. Or if you use the letter O instead of a zero, you'll see `Illegal reference or wrong operand type`.

In most cases, you can correct the formula without starting from scratch, so resist the temptation to press Escape when you see a message. Instead, press Enter calmly. The error message disappears and you now see the formula on the entry/edit line with a highlight in the problem area. Use the Left Arrow key to back up the highlight without erasing anything, type in the information the formula needs, delete what it doesn't need, and press Enter again.

Editing a Problem Formula

Editing a problem formula already in its cell is a simple process. With your cursor on the cell, press F2. This places the formula on the entry/edit line with the blinker immediately after the last character. If your formula is very long, you'll see only the last part at this time. Use the following keys to move the blinker to the problem area:

- Backspace moves the blinker to the left, erasing characters as it goes.
- Left Arrow and Right Arrow move the blinker left or right without erasing anything.
- Home moves the blinker to the first character in the formula.

- End moves the blinker after the last character in the formula.
- Delete deletes the character at the blinker.

Type in the correct information, including cell locations. When you complete the editing, press Enter. If you turned off automatic recalculation, press F9 to calculate the corrected formula.

Number Signs

Sometimes you'll see ####### (number signs) in a cell containing a formula or a formatted number. This only means that the cell is too narrow to show the number completely. To avoid misleading you with a truncated number, Works enters number signs instead.

Simply widen the column or change the format to display fewer characters. For example, replace the dollar format with a fixed format, which eliminates the 1-character dollar sign, or remove any decimal places.

Planning Your Spreadsheet

Spreadsheets are never etched in stone. You can make changes whenever creative lightning strikes, but changes do take time and many can be avoided by careful planning. Before you even turn on your computer, know where you're heading and the best way to get there. Mapping the route on paper may be your best bet, at least at the beginning. This doesn't mean that you have to write down all the numbers, titles, and other details, but you should have a pretty good idea of the purpose and structure of the spreadsheet, the kinds of headings and titles you want to use, what the numbers mean and how they should look, and the relationships between numbers, so you can plan the formulas.

In the next chapter, you learn about all of the Works functions and how they add power and personality to formulas.

About Functions

Functions make it easy to do mathematical and other types of operations in the spreadsheet and database.

Functions are shortcuts built into the Works program. They let you build formulas that perform common and complex calculations, extract information from cells, and select from among several possible answers.

Like a "black box," each function contains exotic innards designed to achieve a specific purpose. Works has 57 "black boxes" that make it just as easy to calculate standard deviation or internal rate of return, for example, as to add a list of numbers.

The Form of a Function

Functions consist of a function name and an argument the function works on. The function name tells Works the kind of operation to perform—for example, SUM to add numbers, AVG to average numbers, and STD to calculate standard deviation.

The argument typically consists of variables enclosed in parentheses. A variable can be a number, a formula that produces a number, a cell containing a number or formula, or a range of cells containing numbers or formulas. Some functions need only one variable in the argument, while others need several. A few functions, such as PI and TRUE, need no variables, but the parentheses still remain.

A Function Example

How do functions work? Consider the spreadsheet in Figure 4-1 for a company that sells linens and supplies to restaurants. Say you want to add all sales amounts in column B. You could do it by adding the value in each cell like this:

```
=B5+B6+B7+B8+B9+B10+B11+B12+B13
```

```
                    A                          B         C
1         RESTAURANT SALES IN JANUARY
2    ======================================
3    Customer                              Amount
4    --------------------------------------
5    Bugles & Trumpets Eatery                $528
6    Corner Deli                              $87
7    Houlihan's Bar & Grill                  $175
8    The Shady Nook Cafe                     $431
9    Rick's Casablanca Cafe                  $222
10   Boccaccio Ristorante                  $1,200
11   Down Mexico Way                          $45
12   General Tsao's                          $876
13   Puppet On A String Diner                $497
14                                      ----------
15                Total                    $4,061
```

Figure 4-1. A restaurant sales spreadsheet illustrating the SUM function

But that's clumsy and old-fashioned. Instead, you can enter a sleek SUM formula in B15 that does the same thing and looks like this:

```
=SUM(B5:B13)
```

A colon separates the first and last cells in a range of cells.

The equal sign, which tells Works you're about to enter a formula, is followed by the function name and a set of parentheses that encloses references to cells containing the numbers. All you need to do is enter the location of the first and last cells in the group (called a *range*) separated by a colon (the range operator). This tells Works to work on the entire range, in this case SUM the numbers in cells B5 to B13.

Works lets you name cells, which makes it even easier to build formulas. If you name B5 *BUGLES* and B13 *PUPPET*, you can use plain English words instead of cell references. This formula does the same thing:

```
=SUM(BUGLES:PUPPET)
```

Formulas often mix and match variables, as in the following:

```
=MIN(8.75%,RATE,E14,$B$6,C12*7)
```

This formula uses the MIN (minimum) function to extract the smallest number from these variables: 8.75% (a percentage that you supply), RATE (a named cell), E14 (a relative reference), $B$6 (an absolute reference), and C12*7 (a formula). Commas separate variables in the list.

The Functions Directory

The following directory covers all of Works' functions for the spreadsheet and database. The function name appears in uppercase to distinguish it from the surrounding text. Typing it in lowercase works equally well.

The directory shows functions in alphabetical order. For quick reference, Table 4-1 lists the functions by function.

Table 4-1. Works functions listed by function

Arithmetic Functions

ABS(Value)
AVG(List)
EXP(Value)
INT(Value)
LN(Value)
LOG(Value)
MAX(List)
MIN(List)
MOD(Numerator,Denominator)
PI()
ROUND(Value,NumberOfPlaces)
SQRT(Value)
SUM(List)

Trigonometric Functions

ACOS(CosineOfAngle)
ASIN(SineOfAngle)
ATAN(TangentOfAngle)
ATAN2(X-Coordinate,Y-Coordinate)
COS(AngleInRadians)
SIN(AngleInRadians)
TAN(AngleInRadians)

(continued)

Table 4-1. (*continued*)

Financial Functions

CTERM(Rate,FutureValue,PresentValue)
FV(Payment,Rate,Term)
IRR(Guess,Range)
NPV(Rate,Range)
PMT(Principal,Rate,Term)
PV(Payment,Rate,Term)
RATE(FutureValue,PresentValue,Term)
TERM(Payment,Rate,FutureValue)

Logical Functions

FALSE()
IF(Test,ValueIfTrue,ValueIfFalse)
ISERR(Value)
ISNA(Value)
TRUE()
AND is handled by the ampersand (&)
NOT is handled by the tilde (~)
OR is handled by the vertical line (|)

Date and Time Functions

DATE(Year,Month,Day)
DAY(DateNumber)
HOUR(TimeNumber)
MINUTE(TimeNumber)
MONTH(DateNumber)
NOW()
SECOND(TimeNumber)
TIME(Hour,Minute,Second)
YEAR(DateNumber)

Search Functions

CHOOSE(IndexValue,List)
HLOOKUP(LookupValue,LookupTable,RowNumber)
INDEX(Range,Column,Row)
VLOOKUP(LookupValue,LookupTable,ColumnNumber)

Other Functions

COLS(Range)
COUNT(List)
DDB(Cost,Salvage,Life,Period)
ERR()
NA()

Other Functions *(continued)*

RAND()
ROWS(Range)
SLN(Cost,Salvage,Life)
STD(List)
SYD(Cost,Salvage,Life,Period)
VAR(List)

Proper syntax is vitally important to formula success, so each description shows examples of function construction and arguments. By all means jump right in and try them out. Keep in mind, though, that formulas work with numbers. To get the proper result, be sure to enter a number in any cell referred to by the formula.

ABS(Value)

ABS produces the absolute value of the argument. An absolute value is a number without a plus or a minus sign. For example:

`=ABS(-56)` produces 56, not -56

`=ABS(C6-370)` where C6 contains 55, produces 315, not -315

ACOS(CosineOfAngle)

ACOS computes the arccosine of a number, expressed in radians. The number must be in the range from -1 through 1. The resulting angle ranges from 0 radians (0 degrees) through π radians (180 degrees). For example:

`=ACOS(-0.5)` produces 2.094 (radians), the angle whose cosine is -0.5

To convert angles from radians to degrees, multiply radians by 180/PI(). For example:

`=ACOS(-0.5)*180/PI()` produces 120 (degrees)

ASIN(SineOfAngle)

ASIN computes the arcsine of a number, expressed in radians. The number must be in the range from -1 through 1. The resulting angle ranges from -π/2 radians(-90 degrees) through π/2 radians (90 degrees). For example,

`=ASIN(-0.5)` produces -0.523 (radians), the angle whose cosine is -0.5

To convert angles from radians to degrees, multiply radians by 180/PI(). For example:

`=ASIN(-0.5)*180/PI()` produces -30 (degrees)

ATAN(TangentOfAngle)

ATAN computes the arctangent of a number, expressed in radians. There are no restrictions on the input number. The resulting angle ranges from -π/2 radians (-90 degrees) through π/2 radians (90 degrees). For example,

`=ATAN(4)` produces 1.326 (radians), the angle whose tangent is 4

ATAN2(X-Coordinate,Y-Coordinate)

ATAN2 computes the arctangent of an angle defined by X and Y coordinates. The arctangent is an angle in radians determined by the point described by the coordinates. The resulting angle ranges from -π radians to, but not including, π radians. For example:

`=ATAN2(1,1)` produces 0.785 (π/4 radians)

If both X coordinate and Y coordinate equals 0, ATAN2 produces error message `ERR`.

AVG(List)

AVG adds the values in a list and divides the result by a count of the values to produce the average. The list can contain numbers, cell references, range references, or formulas. AVG counts a blank cell in a single cell reference as zero, ignores a blank cell in a range reference, and counts text in either reference as zero. For example:

`=AVG(1,5,6,5,5)` produces 4.4

`=AVG(SALES)` produces the average of the values in the range of cells named SALES, ignoring any blank cells in the range but counting text cells as zero

Other variations in syntax include:

`=AVG(D5:D15,F15)`

`=AVG(B5,$B$9,C10)`

CHOOSE(IndexValue,List)

CHOOSE uses an index value to select a value from a list. If the index value is 0, CHOOSE selects the first value in the list. If the index value is 1, CHOOSE selects the second value, and so on. Assuming A1 contains the number 2, the formula

`=CHOOSE(A1,5,10,E5,BB22)` selects the value in E5

If the index value is less than 0 or greater than the number of values in the list, CHOOSE produces the error message `ERR`.

COLS(Range) and ROWS(Range)

COLS produces the number of columns in a specified range, and ROWS produces the number of rows. For example:

`=COLS(B5:E6)` produces 4

`=ROWS(B5:E6)` produces 2

If you name the range B5:E6 TABLE, then

`=COLS(TABLE)` produces 4

`=ROWS(TABLE)` produces 2

COS(AngleInRadians)

SIN(AngleInRadians)

TAN(AngleInRadians)

These functions calculate the ratio of the relevant triangle sides when the argument is entered as an angle in radians. COS calculates the cosine of an angle, SIN calculates the sine of an angle, and TAN calculates the tangent of an angle. For example:

`=COS(1.047)` produces 0.5 (ratio)

`=SIN(1.047)` produces 0.866 (ratio)

To convert angles from degrees to radians, multiply degrees by PI()/180. For example:

`=TAN(45*PI()/180)` produces 1 (ratio)

COUNT(List)

COUNT counts the items in a list, including cells that contain a number, a formula, text, and error values ERR and N/A. COUNT counts a blank cell in a single cell reference and ignores a blank cell in a range reference. Examples:

`=COUNT(14,7,9,1,6)` produces 5

Where you use a range reference in the spreadsheet, use a field name in the database.

`=COUNT(D2:D10,F11)` where two cells in range D2:D10 are blank, produces 8

`=COUNT(SALARIES)` produces a count of filled cells in the range named SALARIES

CTERM(Rate,FutureValue,PresentValue)

CTERM calculates the number of compound periods needed for an investment earning a periodic interest rate to grow from a present value to a future value. Rate represents an annual compound period. To compute monthly compound periods, divide the annual rate by 12.

Suppose you deposit $5,000 in a savings account with an annual interest rate of 8.75%, compounded monthly. To find out how long it will take to double your investment, you enter

`=CTERM(8.75%/12,10000,5000)`

The answer is 95.41 months, or about 8 years.

DATE(Year,Month,Day)

DATE converts the year, month, and day to a date number. The date number is an integer from 0 to 65534 corresponding to the dates from January 1, 1900, to June 3, 2079. January 1, 1900, is date number 1, January 2, 1900, is date number 2, and so on through June 3, 2079, which is date number 65534. For example:

`=DATE(1900,1,1)` produces 1

`=DATE(2079,6,3)` produces 65534

To show a date number as a date, choose the Format menu's Time/Date command.

The year, month, and day must be in the valid range—that is, a year from 1900 to 2079 (or, alternately, a number from 0 to 179), a month from 1 to 12, and a day from 1 to 31. If you use an invalid date such as DATE(2988,2,28), Works displays the error message ERR in the formula cell.

Combining the MOD and DATE functions produces a number corresponding to the day of the week. In most computer programs, Sunday is 1, Monday is 2, Wednesday is 3, and so on through Saturday, which is 7. The formula

```
=MOD(DATE(90,7,4),7)
```

produces 4, the number corresponding to Wednesday, the day of the week for July 4, 1990

You can use DATE to perform other types of calculations. For example:

`=DATE(90,6,21)-DATE(31,6,21)` produces 21550, the elapsed days.

Using dates in this form:

`=.6/21/88.-.6/21/31.` produces the same result

The apostrophe before and after these dates prevents Works from interpreting the slash as the division operator.

Suppose that A1 contains 3, a number representing the third quarter of the year. The formula

`=DATE(90,A1*3+1,1)` produces 33147, the date number corresponding to 10/1/90, the first day of the fourth quarter

`=DATE(88,A1*3+1,1)-DATE(88,A1*3-2,1)` produces 92, the number of days in this quarter

DAY(DateNumber)

MONTH(DateNumber)

YEAR(DateNumber)

Each of these date functions produces an integer corresponding to the date number in parentheses. DAY produces a number from 1 to 31,

MONTH a number from 1 to 12, and YEAR a number from 1900 to 2079 (or, alternately, from 0 to 179). For example:

`=DAY(3456)` produces 17

`=DAY(.6/21/88.)` produces 21

`=MONTH(23456)` produces 3

`=YEAR(36990)` produces 101, the year corresponding to 2001

Valid serial numbers are in the range from 1 to 65534, which corresponds to dates January 1, 1900, through June 3, 2079. January 1, 1900, is date number 1; January 2, 1900, is date number 2; through June 3, 2079, which is date number 65534.

DDB(Cost,Salvage,Life,Period)

DDB uses the double declining method to determine the depreciation allowance on an asset at a specified period of time. Cost is the amount you paid for the asset. Salvage is the amount you expect to receive when you sell the asset at the end of its life. *Life* is the number of periods (usually measured in years) you expect to use the asset. *Period* is the time period for which you want to find the depreciation allowance.

You can name cells, and then use the name in formulas.

Let's suppose you buy a printing press for $36,000. You expect it to last 10 years, after which you can likely sell it for $4,000. Figure 4-2 shows your spreadsheet. After naming these cells: B3 is COST, B4 is SALVAGE, and B5 is LIFE, you enter the following formula in B9:

```
=DDB($COST,$SALVAGE,$LIFE,A9)
```

	A	B	C
1	DOUBLE DECLINING BALANCE	DEPRECIATION	
2	========================	============	
3	Original Cost of Asset	36,000.00	Cost
4	Salvage Value	4,000.00	Salvage
5	Life in Years	10	Life
6			
7	Year	Allowance	
8	----	---------	
9	1	7,200.00	
10	2	5,760.00	
11	3	4,608.00	
12	4	3,686.40	
13	5	2,949.12	
14	6	2,359.30	
15	7	1,887.44	
16	8	1,509.95	
17	9	1,207.96	
18	10	831.84	

Figure 4-2. A depreciation allowances spreadsheet illustrating the DDB (double declining balance) function

The $ sign makes each named cell an absolute reference, which ensures that the formula will refer to the proper cells when you copy it into B10 through B18. A9 remains a relative reference because each copied formula must refer to the cell to the left for the depreciation year.

Now, say you want to calculate the DDB allowance for the seventh year only, without setting up a spreadsheet. You can enter

```
=DDB(36000,4000,10,7)
```

and get the answer 1887.44. To compare DDB results with other depreciation methods, refer to the SLN and SYD functions.

ERR()

ERR displays the error message ERR in a cell. It is often combined with the IF function to force a cell to display ERR when an error condition exists. For example, you can enter the formula

```
=IF(A1=0,ERR(),A1)
```

in B22. If the formula in A1 produces a zero, the formula in B22 alerts you by entering ERR in its cell. Otherwise, the formula in B22 copies the amount in A1.

EXP(Value)

EXP calculates the natural logarithm's base value *[e]* (2.7182818 . . .) raised to the power of the value in parentheses. For example:

`=EXP(1)` produces 2.7182818 (the value of *[e]*)

`=EXP(3)` produces 20.085537

Use the exponentiation operator (^) to compute the powers of other bases. EXP is the inverse of the function LN.

FALSE()

TRUE()

FALSE and TRUE produce the logical values 0 and 1, respectively. These functions are often used with the IF function to test the workings of a formula. For example, TRUE and FALSE serve as the ValueIfTrue and ValueIfFalse statements in this formula:

```
=IF(COSTS>455,TRUE(),FALSE())
```

If the cell named COSTS contains a number greater than 455, the ValueIfTrue statement enters 1 in the formula cell. If COSTS contains a number less than or equal to 455, the ValueIfFalse statement enters a 0. When your formula is working properly, replace TRUE() and FALSE() with the actual variables.

FV(Payment,Rate,Term)

FV calculates the future value of an investment based on a number of equal payments at a periodic interest rate for a specified term. FV assumes that the first payment occurs at the end of the first period.

Say you plan to deposit $5,000 each year into an account that earns 8.25 percent interest, compounded annually. You want to know how much money will be in the account at the end of five years. You enter

```
FV(5000,8.25%,5)
```

in a cell formatted for dollars with two decimal places and get the answer $29,479.58.

HLOOKUP(LookupValue,LookupTable,RowNumber)

VLOOKUP(LookupValue,LookupTable,ColumnNumber)

HLOOKUP (horizontal lookup) and VLOOKUP (vertical lookup) search for a lookup value in a lookup table and retrieve the value from the corresponding cell. You can arrange information in a lookup table vertically (more rows than columns), horizontally (more columns than rows), or as a square (equal number of columns and rows).

Figure 4-3 shows a stockroom report containing a horizontal lookup table in columns B through G in rows 15 through 17. This spreadsheet contains two lookup formulas, one retrieves the quantity and the other the cost. Cell B6 contains the following formula:

```
=HLOOKUP(A6,$B$15:$G$16,1)
```

HLOOKUP searches row 15 (the top row of the table) until it finds the largest number less than or equal to the lookup value in A6. It then moves one row down (the number of rows in the argument) to get the corresponding value. The other lookup formula, in C6, is

```
=HLOOKUP(A6,$B$15:$G$17,2)
```

This time, HLOOKUP moves down 2 rows to get the value. Both formulas are copied into the cells below them in rows 7 through 9.

```
          A          B         C           D          E          F          G
1              WORLD OF SYNTHESIZERS
2                STOCKROOM REPORT
3    ======================================
4    Part         Qty      Cost    Stock Value
5    --------------------------------------
6    7777         57      $120.00  $6,840.00
7    7995         23       $16.80    $386.40
8    7008         134       $5.75    $770.50
9    7897         12       $79.97    $959.64
10
11
12
13   HORIZONTAL LOOKUP TABLE
14   ==========================================================================
15   Part          7008      7234        7777       7897       7990       7995
16   Qty            134        18          57         12          2         23
17   Cost          5.75    203.75      120.00      79.97      75.50      16.80
```

Figure 4-3. A stockroom report featuring a horizontal lookup table

Figure 4-4 shows the same stockroom report, this one containing a vertical lookup table in columns F through H, rows 14 through 19, and two lookup formulas. Cell B6 now contains the following formula:

```
=VLOOKUP(A6,$F$14:$H$19,1)
```

```
          A          B         C           D      E     F        G        H
1              WORLD OF SYNTHESIZERS
2                STOCKROOM REPORT
3    ======================================
4    Part        Stock     Cost    Stock Value
5    --------------------------------------
6    7777         57      $120.00  $6,840.00
7    7995         23       $16.80    $386.40
8    7008         134       $5.75    $770.50
9    7897         12       $79.97    $959.64
10                                          | VERTICAL LOOKUP TABLE
11                                          | ========================
12                                          |   Part     Stock     Cost
13                                          | ------------------------
14                                          |   7008      134      5.75
15                                          |   7234       18    203.75
16                                          |   7777       57    120.00
17                                          |   7897       12     79.97
18                                          |   7990        2     75.50
19                                          |   7995       23     16.80
```

Figure 4-4. A stockroom report featuring a vertical lookup table

VLOOKUP searches column F (the left column of the table) until it finds the largest number less than or equal to the lookup value in

A6. It then moves one column to the right (the number of columns in the argument) to get the corresponding value.

The other lookup formula, in C6, is

```
=VLOOKUP(A6,$F$14:$H$19,2)
```

It, too, searches the table, then moves two columns to the right to get the corresponding value. Both formulas are copied into the cells below.

The boundaries of the lookup table are defined by absolute references because copied formulas must continue to refer to the table regardless of the cells into which they are copied.

If the column or row number in the formula is negative or is greater than or equal to the number of rows or columns in the table, Works produces the error message [ERR].

When you create a lookup table, be sure to follow the cardinal rule: Enter the numbers in the top row or left column of the table in ascending order.

To tie up some loose ends: A formula in D6 multiplies the amount in C6 by the amount in B6. In Figure 4-4, the vertical line that separates the lookup table from the rest of the spreadsheet is centered in a 3-character column E. Lines like this enhance the legibility of a spreadsheet.

HOUR(TimeNumber)

MINUTE(TimeNumber)

SECOND(TimeNumber)

These time functions produce an integer corresponding to the specified time number. HOUR produces an integer from 0 to 23, and MINUTE and SECOND produce an integer from 0 to 59. Because the time number for a unit of time smaller than a day is a decimal fraction from 0 to 0.999 (corresponding to times 12:00:00 AM through 11:59:59 PM), HOUR, MINUTE, and SECOND use only the fractional part of the time number you specify. For example:

`=HOUR(.9)` produces 21

`=HOUR(.18:45:30.)` produces 18

Combining time functions converts the time into a serial number, then into an integer. If the current time is 7:45:30, then

```
=MINUTE(NOW()) produces 45
=SECOND(TIME(7,45,30)) produces 30
```

IF(Test,ValueIfTrue,ValueIfFalse)

IF is a logical function that determines if a test is true (correct) or false (not correct). Based on the test results, IF uses one of its two alternative statements—ValueIfTrue or ValueIfFalse—to produce the answer.

Assume you're working on the commission report shown in Figure 4-5. Your company pays a 10 percent commission only on sales exceeding $5,000. You enter the following formula in C5:

```
=IF(B5>5000,10%*(B5-5000),0)
```

	A	B	C	D
1	OCTOBER COMMISSION REPORT			
2	==			
3	Salesperson	Sales	Commission	
4	--			
5	David W. Clark	$8,607	$360.70	
6	John O'Hara	$5,500	$50.00	
7	Susan Stafford	$7,822	$282.20	
8	Al B. Good	$4,550	$0.00	
9	Donald Chen	$8,275	$327.50	
10	Barbara Shimaya	$5,000	$0.00	

Figure 4-5. A commission report illustrating the IF function

The Test is `B5>5000`, the ValueIfTrue statement is `0.1*(B5-5000)`, and the ValueIfFalse argument is `0`. The symbol `>` is the logic operator for *greater than*, and `0.1` is the way Works shows the 10 percent you typed into the formula. The formula is saying: *If* the sales amount in B5 is greater than 5000, then use the ValueIfTrue statement to calculate a 10 percent commission on anything over 5000; otherwise, use the ValueIfFalse statement to show no commission.

The location of parentheses is important to a formula's calculations.

The parentheses around B5-5000 plays an important part in producing the correct answer. The ValueIfTrue statement performs two calculations: it subtracts 5000 from sales and multiplies the result by 10 percent. Without the parentheses, the formula would take 10 percent of the amount in B5, then subtract 5000, producing a wrong answer. The result in C5 is $360.70. Copied into C6 through C10, the formula calculates the other sales commissions.

IF can be combined with logical symbols to compare more than one condition in the test argument. The tilde (~) is the NOT operator;

the vertical line (|) is the OR operator; and the ampersand (&) is the AND operator.

For example, the following formula uses the OR operator to compare three tests:

```
=IF(A12>50|B14=100|C7<25,TRUE(),FALSE())
```

If any one of the three tests is true, the formula produces the number 1. If every test is false, the formula produces a zero.

INDEX(Range,Column,Row)

INDEX extracts the value at the intersection of a column and row in a range of cells. The column and row number must be a value or a reference to a cell containing a value.

Figure 4-6 shows a commission schedule consisting of four columns and three rows—the range of B7:E9, named COMMTABLE for ease of use. In an INDEX table, the leftmost column is column 0 and the top row is row 0. Therefore, column B is column 0, column C is column 1, and so on. Row 7 is row 0, row 8 is row 1, and so on. The formula

```
=INDEX($COMMTABLE,2,1)
```

in B12 extracts 1.8 percent—the value in the cell at the intersection of column 2 and row 1 of the table. The absolute range name ensures that the formula will continue to refer to the table regardless of where you copy it.

	A	B	C	D	E
1					
2					
3			COMMISSION SCHEDULE		
4		======	======	======	======
5		Sales	Year 1	Year 2	Year 3
6		------	------	------	------
7		$10,000	1.0%	1.2%	1.7%
8		$15,000	1.5%	1.8%	2.4%
9		$20,000	1.7%	2.5%	2.8%
10					
11					
12		1.8%			

Figure 4-6. A commission table used by the INDEX function

If the column or row number is negative or is greater than or equal to the number of columns or rows in the table, the formula produces the error message **ERR**.

INT(Value)

INT produces the integer part of the value in parentheses. It removes the decimal portion of the value without rounding to the nearest integer. For example:

`=INT(1.99)` produces 1

`=INT(-1.99)` produces -1

Use the ROUND function to round the value to the nearest integer.

IRR(Guess,Range)

IRR calculates the internal rate of return of an investment based on the series of cash flows (inflows and outflows) in the range. Internal rate of return is the interest rate that equates the present value of the expected future cash flow to the initial outlay of funds, making the net present value equal to zero.

Your guess tells Works where to begin. Try numbers between 0 and 1 until you get a percentage, not ERR. (ERR means that the formula can't produce an answer accurate to 0.0000001 within 20 iterations.) Then, guess again.

Assume you decide to invest in a franchise operation. Figure 4-7 shows your spreadsheet. You plan to make an initial investment of $85,000 and two further payments of $12,500. You expect to receive payments of $60,000, $41,000, and $28,000. You enter the cash flows in B3 to B9, typing the outflows as a minus number (for example, -85000).

The value in the first cell in the range must be a negative cash flow.

You then format B3 to B9 to show dollar amounts with no decimal places, and B12, the formula cell, to show a percentage with one decimal place.

You enter the formula:

```
=IRR(B11,B3:B9)
```

in B12. After a few tries, you type .1 in B11, your guess cell, and IRR calculates a 15.8% internal rate of return.

A neat technique makes working with this function easier. Keep your guess in a separate cell instead of in the formula and you won't have to edit the formula repeatedly.

```
              A                         B              C          D
1    INTERNAL RATE OF RETURN
2    ===========================
3    Cash Flow 1              ($85,000)
4    Cash Flow 2               $60,000
5    Cash Flow 3              ($12,500)
6    Cash Flow 4               $41,000
7    Cash Flow 5               $28,500
8    Cash Flow 6              ($12,500)
9    Cash Flow 7               $15,000
10
11   Guess                          0.1
12   IRR                          15.8%
```

Figure 4-7. A cash flow spreadsheet illustrating the IRR (internal rate of return) function

ISERR(Value)

ISERR produces the logical value 1 (True) if the value in parentheses is ERR. Otherwise, it produces the logical value 0 (False). ISERR is often combined with the IF function to test for error conditions.

Consider the formula

```
=IF(ISERR(RATIO),0,RATIO)
```

If the cell named RATIO contains ERR, the ValueIfTrue statement enters a 0 in the formula cell. If RATIO doesn't contain ERR, the ValueIfFalse statement copies the amount from the cell named RATIO.

ISNA(Value)

ISNA produces the logical value 1 (True) if the cell reference in parentheses contains N/A (not available). Otherwise, it produces the logical value 0 (False). ISNA is a handy way to test for N/A values on your spreadsheet.

Say you have a cell named BALANCE. If the balance isn't available yet, you enter the function NA() in the BALANCE cell, which Works translates into N/A. Therefore:

=ISNA(BALANCE) produces 1

If you leave the BALANCE cell empty—without NA() in it—the formula produces 0.

Now, suppose you combine ISNA with the IF function. You enter the formula

```
=IF(ISNA(BALANCE),0,BALANCE)
```

If the balance cell produces N/A, the ValueIfTrue statement produces 0 in the formula cell. Otherwise, the ValueIfFalse statement copies the amount from the BALANCE cell.

LN(Value)

LN computes the natural logarithm of a value to the base *e*. The value must be a positive number. For example:

=LN(2.7182818) produces 1

LN is the inverse of the function EXP.

LOG(Value)

LOG computes the base 10 logarithm of the value specified. The value must be a positive number. For example:

=LOG(100) produces 2

=LOG(150) produces 2.1760913

=LOG(1000) produces 3

LOG is the inverse of exponentiation.

MAX(List)

MIN(List)

MAX extracts the largest value in a list, and MIN extracts the smallest value. The list can contain numbers, cell references, range references, or formulas. MAX and MIN treat a blank cell in a single cell reference as zero and ignore a blank cell in a range reference. They treat text in either a single cell or a range reference as zero. For example:

=MAX(B2,C5,C7:C10) extracts the largest value in the cells in the list

=MIN(SALARIES) extracts the smallest value in the cells named SALARIES

=10%*MAX(25000-SALES,COST) produces 10 percent of either 25000 minus SALES or the value of COST, whichever is more

MINUTE(TimeNumber)
See HOUR.

MOD(Numerator,Denominator)

MOD calculates the remainder (modulus) of a numerator divided by a denominator. The remainder has the same sign as the numerator. For example:

`=MOD(65,9)` produces 2 (65 divided by 9 = 7 with 2 remaining)

If B6 contains 12 and C3 contains 7, the formula

`=MOD(B6,C3)` produces 5 (12 divided by 7 = 1 with 5 remaining)

To illustrate the sign characteristics:

`=MOD(-3,2)` produces -1
`=MOD(3,-2)` produces 1

If the denominator is zero, MOD produces the error message `ERR`.

MONTH(DateNumber)

See DAY.

NA()

NA, which means not available, is useful for keeping track of values that have not yet been entered. Suppose you are shopping for a loan. You don't know what the interest rate will be, so you type

```
=NA()
```

in the interest rate cell. Works then displays `N/A` in the rate cell and in every other cell that refers to the rate cell until you enter the rate.

NOW()

NOW produces the date and time number for the current date and time, based on your input at the DOS prompt at startup or the date and time kept by your computer's automatic clock. This number, which is updated at every recalculation, has an integer part (date number) and a decimal fraction (timenumber).

Pretend it's now June 21, 1990, at 4:20:45 in the afternoon. Enter =NOW() and Works produces 33045. From the Time/Date Cells command in the Format menu, you select [i[Month, Day, Year]r]. In the short form, Works produces 6/21/90 or, in the long form (with the width of the cell increased), Jun 21, 1990.

To see how the time formats work, enter

```
=NOW()
```

in another cell, and select [i[Hour, Minute, Second]r]. Works now produces 16:20:45 in the 24-hour format or 4:20:45PM in the 12-hour format.

NPV(Rate,Range)

NPV determines the net present value of a series of future cash flows. Because of the time difference, future dollars aren't equivalent to present dollars so they are discounted at a specified interest rate. The range contains the stream of cash (even or uneven payments) that will be received at future intervals. The range can be a number, a single cell, or a range of cells in a single row or column.

Suppose you plan to invest $55,000 in one of two projects from which you require a 12.5 percent rate of return. Figure 4-8 shows your spreadsheet. You expect Project A to yield a steady $18,500 after taxes each year for 5 years. You enter the cash flows in B8 through B12 and the following formula in B15:

```
=NPV(B12,B6:10)
```

	A	B	C	D
1	NET PRESENT VALUE			
2	================	==========	==========	
3		Project A	Project B	
4		-----------	-----------	
5	Investment	$55,000	$55,000	
6				
7	Cash Flows:			
8	Year 1	$18,500	$27,000	
9	Year 2	$18,500	$22,000	
10	Year 3	$18,500	$16,000	
11	Year 4	$18,500	$9,000	
12	Year 5	$18,500	$2,000	
13				
14	Rate of Return	12.5%	12.5%	
15	Net Present Value	$65,871	$59,349	

Figure 4-8. An investment spreadsheet illustrating the NPV (net present value) function

Instantly, the formula calculates the expected cash flows to a present value of $65,871. You expect Project B to yield a series of uneven cash flows, which you enter in C8 through C12. When you copy the formula from B15 to C15, NPV calculates the cash flows in Project B to a present value of $59,349.

Cells B14 and C14 are formatted to show the rate as a percentage with one decimal place (you can enter it as .125 or 12.5%). Keeping the rate in a separate cell lets you easily test different rates without having to edit the formula.

PI()

PI() produces the number 3.14159265358979, which approximates the mathematical constant π. For example:

`=PI()*2` produces 6.28218530717959

The circumference of a circle equals 2 times pi times the radius. If the radius is 6 inches,

`=PI()*2*6` yields approximately 37.7 inches

PMT(Principal,Rate,Term)

PMT calculates equal payments on a loan or an investment, given the principal, interest rate, and term. The rate is an annual percentage, and the term is in years. To get a monthly rate, divide the annual rate by 12. To get monthly payments, multiply the term by 12.

For example, you plan to borrow $50,000 for a five-year period, with an annual payback rate of 12.5 percent. To find out how much you have to repay each month, you enter the formula

```
=PMT(50000,12.5%/12,5*12)
```

In a cell formatted for dollars with 2 decimal places, the answer is $1,124.90. You can see PMT in action in the car loan spreadsheet in Chapter 22.

PV(Payment,Rate,Term)

You can enter a percentage amount in a formula as a percentage or as a decimal.

PV calculates the present value of a series of equal payments earning a fixed rate of interest for a given term. Works assumes the first payment occurs at the end of the first period.

Suppose you are to inherit $5,500 at the end of each year for the next five years. You estimate an annual inflation rate of eight percent during that period. You enter the formula

```
=PV(5500,8%,5)
```

and PV calculates the value your inheritance as $21,959.91 in today's dollars.

RAND()

RAND generates random numbers from 0 to 1 (not including 1). Entering

```
=RAND()
```

in a cell generates a random number every time Works recalculates the spreadsheet. For example, in a cell formatted for two decimal places, RAND() may produce 0.87 one time, 0.39 the next, and 0.55 the time after that. The RAND function is useful for simulating business models.

RATE(FutureValue,PresentValue,Term)

RATE calculates the periodic interest rate needed for an investment entered in present dollars to grow to a specified number of future dollars during a given term.

Suppose you're considering investing $255,000 in a condominium with the expectation of selling it for $545,000 in five years. You enter

```
=RATE(545000,255000,5)
```

in a cell formatted for percentage with one decimal place and Works calculates an annual rate of return of 16.4 percent.

ROUND(Value,NumberOfPlaces)

ROUND rounds the value in parentheses to the specified number of places to the left or right of the decimal point. For example:

`=ROUND(3.1416,3)` produces 3.142

Either the value or the number of places can be a cell reference. The number of places can range from -14 to 14.

If the number of places is 0, ROUND rounds to an integer. For example:

`=ROUND(3.1416,0)` produces 3

If the number of places is negative, ROUND rounds the integer portion of the number. With -1 as the number of places, the integer rounds up at 5 or more and rounds down at less than 5. For example:

`=ROUND(25,-1)` produces 30

`=ROUND(3.1416,-1)` produces 0

With -2 as the number of places, the integer rounds up at 50 or more and rounds down at less than 50. For example:

`=ROUND(50,-2)` produces 100

`=ROUND(49,-2)` produces 0

ROWS(Range)

See COLS.

SECOND(TimeNumber)

See HOUR.

SIN(AngleInRadians)

See COS.

SLN(Cost,Salvage,Life)

SLN uses the straight line method to determine the depreciation allowance on an asset for any given period. Cost is the amount you paid for the asset. Salvage is the amount you expect to receive when you sell the asset at the end of its life. Life is the number of periods (usually measured in years) you expect to use the asset.

Suppose you buy a printing press for $36,000. You expect it to last 10 years, after which you can likely sell it for $4,000. Figure 4-9 shows your spreadsheet with these cells named: B3 is COST, B4 is SALVAGE, and B5 is LIFE. You enter the following formula in B6:

`=SLN(COST,SALVAGE,LIFE,A9)`

	A	B	C
1	STRAIGHT LINE DEPRECIATION		
2	====================================		
3	Original Cost of Asset	36,000.00	Cost
4	Salvage Value	4,000.00	Salvage
5	Life in Years	10	Life
6	Allowance per Year	3,200.00	

Figure 4-9. A depreciation allowances spreadsheet illustrating the SLN (straight line) function

The formula calculates a depreciation allowance of $3,200.00 during each year of the term. To compare SLN results with other depreciation methods, refer to the DDB and SYD functions.

SQRT(Value)

SQRT produces the square root of a value. Examples:

`=SQRT(576)` produces 24

`=SQRT(SUM(4,3,7,6,5))` produces 5

`=SQRT(ABS(-4)+1)` produces 2.236068

If the value is negative, Works produces the error message **ERR.**

STD(List)

STD calculates the population standard deviation of the values in a list—that is, how far away these values are from their average. The list can consist of numbers, single cells, and ranges of cells. STD treats a blank cell in a single cell reference as zero, ignores a blank cell in a range reference, and ignores text in both references. Examples:

`=STD(1,2,3,3,6)` produces 1.6733201

`=STD(SALARIES)` and `=STD(B7:B16)`

produce the standard deviation of the values in those ranges

SUM(List)

SUM adds all the values in a list. The list can contain numbers, cell references, range references, or formulas. SUM treats a blank cell in a single cell reference as zero, ignores a blank cell in a range reference, and ignores text in both references.

Examples:

`=SUM(51,36,25,24,15)` produces 151

`=SUM(22,E6,D6:D16)` adds the values in that list

`=SUM(RECEIPTS)` adds the values in the cells named RECEIPTS

SYD(Cost,Salvage,Life,Period)

SYD uses the sum-of-the-years' digits method to determine the depreciation allowance on an asset over a specific period of time. Cost is the amount you paid for the asset. Salvage is the amount you expect to receive when you sell the asset at the end of its life. Life is the number of periods (usually measured in years) you expect to use the asset.

Suppose you buy a printing press for $36,000. You expect it to last 10 years, after which you can likely sell it for $4,000. Figure 4-10 shows your spreadsheet with these cells named: B3 is COST, B4 is SALVAGE, and B5 is LIFE. You enter the following formula in B6:

```
=SYD($COST,$SALVAGE,$LIFE,A9)
```

```
                  A                            B            C
1    SUM-OF-THE-YEARS'-DIGITS DEPRECIATION
2    ====================================
3    Original Cost of Asset            36,000.00  Cost
4    Salvage Value                      4,000.00  Salvage
5    Life in Years                            10  Life
6
7                 Year                 Allowance
8                 ----                 ---------
9                   1                   5,818.18
10                  2                   5,236.36
11                  3                   4,654.55
12                  4                   4,072.73
13                  5                   3,490.91
14                  6                   2,909.09
15                  7                   2,327.27
16                  8                   1,745.45
17                  9                   1,163.64
18                 10                     581.82
```

Figure 4-10. A depreciation allowances spreadsheet illustrating the SYD (sum-of-the-years' digits) function

Pressing F4 with the cursor on the cell while you build a formula makes the cell reference absolute.

The formula calculates a depreciation allowance of 5,818.18 in the first year. The $ signs make the named cell references absolute, so the formula continues to refer to the correct cells when you copy it into B10 through B18. If you want the depreciation allowance for the first year only, the formula

```
=SYD(36000,4000,10,1)
```

produces the same answer. To compare SYD results with other depreciation methods, refer to the DDB and SLN functions.

TAN(AngleInRadians)

See COS.

TERM(Payment,Rate,FutureValue)

TERM determines the number of periods needed for a series of equal payments earning a periodic interest rate to grow to a given future value. The rate is based on an annual compound period. To compute monthly compound periods, divide the annual interest rate by 12.

Always keep time elements in a formula on an equal basis— for example, monthly interest rate for monthly payments.

Say you deposit $350 each month in an account earning 8.75% interest compounded monthly. To find out how long it will take to accumulate $15,000, you enter

```
=TERM(350,8.75%/12,15000)
```

The answer is 37.42 months, or about 3 years.

TIME(Hour,Minute,Second)

TIME converts the hour, minute, and second in parentheses into a time number. The time number is a fraction ranging from 0.0 through 0.999, corresponding to times from 0:00:00 (12:00:00 PM) through 23:59:59 (11:59:59 PM). Hour is generally a number from 0 through 23, while Minute and Second are generally numbers from 0 through 59. For example:

`=TIME(6,0,0)` produces 0.25 (one-quarter of a day)

`=TIME(15,45,0)+TIME(9,45,0)` produces 1.0625 (a bit more than one full day)

TRUE()

See FALSE.

VAR(List)

VAR calculates the variance of the numbers in a list. The list can contain numbers, cell references, range references, or formulas. VAR treats a blank cell in a single cell reference as zero, ignores a blank cell in a range reference, and treats text in both references as zero. For example, the formula

```
=VAR(A10:A16,B29)
```

determines the variance in the values in cells A10 through A16 and cell B29.

VLOOKUP(LookupValue,Range,RowNumber)

See HLOOKUP.

YEAR(DateNumber)

See DAY.

In the next chapter, you put many of these principles to work when you create your first spreadsheet.

Spreadsheet Workout: Advertising Budget

A simple budget lets you try out a variety of important spreadsheet techniques.

Learning new concepts is always easier with some solid hands-on experience, so Figure 5-1 presents your first Works spreadsheet, a simple, straightforward advertising budget that allocates spending in five media categories. Column and row indicators generated by the Print command make it easy to compare your results with mine.

```
ADBUDGET-page 2                                          6/21/90 1:30 PM

             A                B            C            D            E
1                      COMPARATIVE ADVERTISING BUDGET
2    ================================================================
3    Medium          This Year      % Total    Last Year      % Total
4    ----------------------------------------------------------------
5    Newspaper         $34,000        42.0%      $28,500        43.1%
6    Television        $12,000        14.8%      $13,600        20.5%
7    Radio              $8,000         9.9%       $4,300         6.5%
8    Direct Mail       $23,000        28.4%      $12,000        18.1%
9    Magazine           $4,000         4.9%       $7,800        11.8%
10                    --------     --------     --------     --------
11   Total Budget      $81,000       100.0%      $66,200       100.0%
```

Figure 5-1. An advertising budget spreadsheet that shows media allocations for two years

In this chapter, you change column widths, enter lines, enter and format text and numbers, create formulas, name cells to use in formulas, define the page layout including margins and first page number, create a header that prints the filename, date, and time, and preview and print the spreadsheet. What a way to start!

Keystrokes and Other Matters

The instructions guide you each step of the way, giving keystrokes and cursor movements that relate to each task. In some actions, you need to *press* the Alt key and in others *hold down* the Alt key. There's only a slight semantic difference between pressing and holding down a key, but it makes a big difference in the way Works works.

- When you see such instructions as *Press Alt and type TW (Format/Width)*, press and release Alt before you type the letters. Alt activates the menu line, and the letters choose a menu and a command.
- With instructions such as *Hold down Alt and type E (to move to Left Margin)*, press the Alt key and, without releasing Alt, type the letter. The letter leads you to a field in a dialog box.

Unless the instructions say otherwise, use the Arrow keys (Left, Right, Up, and Down) to move the cursor. Keep an eye on the cell indicator in the left of the status line to be sure the cursor is on the correct cell before you take the next action.

If you run into a snag, press the Escape key to cancel what you're doing. Then pick up where you left off.

'Nuff said. It's time for action.

Creating a New Spreadsheet

Load Works as described in the Introduction to this book. At the File menu, the gateway to Works, type **NS** (Create New File/New Spreadsheet). Works brings up a new spreadsheet with the standard filename `SHEET1.WKS`. Let's make your spreadsheet look like the one in Figure 5-2.

Adjusting the Column Widths

Widening columns gives entries room to stretch.

When you start a new spreadsheet, each column is 10 characters wide. To give the media titles the room they need, make column A wider. Your cursor is on A1.

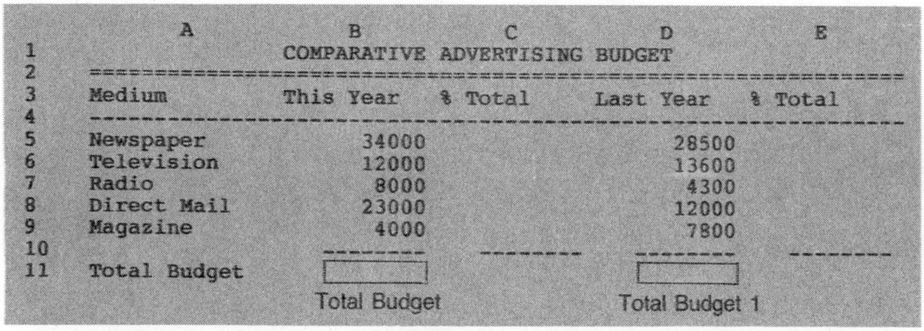

```
            A               B           C           D           E
1                     COMPARATIVE ADVERTISING BUDGET
2   ==========================================================================
3   Medium          This Year    % Total     Last Year    % Total
4   --------------------------------------------------------------------------
5   Newspaper            34000                   28500
6   Television           12000                   13600
7   Radio                 8000                    4300
8   Direct Mail          23000                   12000
9   Magazine              4000                    7800
10                    --------    --------    --------    --------
11  Total Budget      [        ]              [        ]
                    Total Budget             Total Budget 1
```

Figure 5-2. Titles, lines, numbers, and named cell locations in the advertising budget

- Press Alt and type **TW** (Format/Width). Works displays the `Width` dialog field showing the current width of column A—10 characters.
- Type **15** (the new width) and press Enter.

The entries in columns B through E can also use more room, so widen these columns to 12 characters. Place the cursor on B1.

- Press F8 (to extend the selection).
- Press Right Arrow three times (to select B1 through E1). Check the cell indicator on the status line, which should now show `B1:E1`.
- Press Alt and type **TW** (Format/Width).
- Type **12** and press Enter.

Entering the Lines

Lines make a spreadsheet easy to read and more pleasing to the eye. Use an equal sign to enter a double line across row 2. Because Works recognizes the sign as a value, typing quotation marks first signals Works that you're using the sign as text. The quotation marks don't appear in the cell. Place the cursor on A2.

- Type quotation marks and 15 equal signs (the width of the cell).

As you type, Works shows the equal signs in A2 and on the entry/edit line below the menus and at the cursor's location. After you type the last equal sign, move the cursor to B2.

Here's a neat little shortcut you want to know about.

Now enter a double line in cells B2 through E2. Works provides a quick and easy way to enter the same information in several contiguous cells at the same time. Select the cells, type the entry, and then use Ctrl+Enter instead of Enter alone. Your cursor is on B2.

- Press F8 (to extend the selection).
- Press Right Arrow three times (to select B2 through E2).
- These cells are 12 characters wide, so type quotation marks and 12 equal signs.
- Hold down Ctrl and press Enter. Presto. Each cell is filled with equal signs.

Now use a minus sign in the same way to enter the single line in row 4. Place the cursor on A4.

- Type quotation marks and 15 minus signs. Move the cursor to B4.
- Press F8 (to extend the selection).
- Press the Right Arrow three times (to select B4 through E4).
- Type quotation marks and 12 minus signs.
- Hold down Ctrl and press Enter.

Each of the short lines in B10 through E10 separates a list of items from its total. To avoid an unsightly overhang before and after the numbers, indent the line with spaces and stop it one character shy of the full column width. You can enter these lines simultaneously, just as before. Place the cursor on B10.

- Press F8 (to extend the selection).
- Press the Right Arrow three times (to select B10 through E10).
- Press the Spacebar three times (this works the same as typing quotation marks), and type 8 minus signs.
- Hold down Ctrl and press Enter.

Entering the Titles

Typing and moving the cursor saves pressing Enter every time.

The next step is to enter the titles shown in Figure 5-2. Instead of pressing Enter after you type each title, move the cursor to the next cell needing a title. When you move the cursor, Works enters the title you just typed in its cell. If you make a typo, press the Backspace key (not an Arrow key) to back up the cursor. Now place the cursor on B1.

- Type **COMPARATIVE ADVERTISING BUDGET** (in uppercase).

As you type, Works displays the title in two places: On the entry/edit line in its entirety and in B1, hiding earlier letters to allow room for more letters. Move the cursor to A3 and Works enters the title in B1, spilling it into C1 and D1.

- Type **Medium** (in upper and lowercase) and move the cursor to A5.
- Type **Newspaper** and move the cursor to A6.
- Type **Television** and move the cursor to A7.

Referring to Figure 5-2, enter the rest of the titles in A7 through A9, then the ones in A11 and B3 through E3 in the same way. After you type the last title (`% Total` in E3), press Enter.

Aligning the Titles

To better align titles with the numbers soon to be entered in the cells below them, right-align all titles in row 3 except `Medium`. Leave the cursor on E3.

- Press F8 (to extend the selection).
- Press Left Arrow three times (to select B3 through E3).
- Press Alt and type **TS** (Format/Style). You now see the `Style` dialog box containing alignment, emphasis, and protection boxes. You selected more than one cell, so the dialog box appears in a neutral condition with some boxes empty and others containing a dash.
- Type **R** (to move to `Right`) and press Enter. All the titles now shift to the right.

Entering the Numbers

Next, enter the numbers shown in Figure 5-2. You enter numbers in the same way as titles—by typing a number and moving the cursor to the next cell that needs a number. When you format the numbers in the next step, Works will enter dollar signs and commas, so you only have to type the number now. Place the cursor on B5.

- Type **34000** and move the cursor to B6.
- Type **12000** and move the cursor to B7.
- Type **8000** and move the cursor to B8.

Referring to Figure 5-2, enter the rest of the numbers in column B, then move the cursor to D5 and enter the numbers in column D. After you type the last number (**7800** in D9), press Enter.

Formatting the Numbers

All of the numbers are dollar amounts, so give them and the column total in D11 the Dollar format. Leave the cursor on D9.

- Hold down Shift and press F8 (to select column D). It doesn't matter that titles, lines, and empty cells are included in the selection.
- Press Alt and type **TU** (Format/Currency). In the `Decimals` dialog box, Works proposes 2 decimal places, which you can accept or replace with your own number.
- Decimal places are unnecessary, so type **0** and press Enter. Works now shows the numbers as dollars and embeds commas in the thousands place.

Format the numbers in column B in the same way. Place the cursor on B9.

- Hold down Shift and press F8 (to select column B).
- Press Alt and type **TU** (Format/Currency).
- Type **0** and press Enter.

The cells in column C will soon hold formulas. Format them to show formula results as percentages with one decimal place. Place the cursor on C9.

- Hold down Shift and press F8 (to select column C).
- Press Alt and type **TP** (Format/Percent). Again, Works proposes 2 decimals.
- Type **1** (the number of decimals) and press Enter.

Now do the same in column E. Place the cursor on E9.

- Hold down Shift and press F8 (to select column E).
- Press Alt and type **TP** (Format/Percent).
- Type **1** and press Enter.

Naming the Cells

Naming lets you refer to cells in plain English. You can name single cells as well as ranges of cells.

Works lets you name cells, and then use these names as cell references in formulas. This makes the formula easy to enter and highly readable. Several formulas need the total in B11 for their calculations, so name it. Place the cursor on B11.

- Press Alt and type **EN** (Edit/Range Name).

Works brings up the `Name` dialog box and proposes `Total Budget` (the title in A11, the closest text) as the name for B11. This is fine, so press Enter. Though no change is apparent on screen, B11 is now known as `Total Budget`.

Cell D11 is another candidate for naming because some formulas use the total in that cell. Since B11 is already named `Total Budget`, name D11 `Total Budget1`. Place the cursor on D11.

- Press Alt and type **EN** (Edit/Range Name).

Works proposes the line in D10 (the closest text) as the name for D11. Clearly, that will not do.

- Type **Total Budget1** and press Enter. Again, the screen is unchanged.

To see both names and the cells they refer to, leave the cursor on D11.

- Press Alt and type **EN** (Edit/Range Name). Everything looks fine, so press Escape (not Enter) to return to the spreadsheet.

Saving the Spreadsheet

A filename can contain up to eight characters plus a decimal point and three-character extension.

This is a good time to save the spreadsheet and give it the filename ADBUDGET. Leave the cursor on D11.

- Press Alt and type **FA** (File/Save As).

Works brings up the `Save as` dialog box so you can type a filename and, if needed, a drive or directory. If you're saving to the current drive, simply type the filename. Otherwise, type the drive or directory before the filename, for example A:ADBUDGET.

- Type **ADBUDGET** and press Enter.

Works quickly appends the extension `.WKS` for Worksheet. As the file is being saved, the cell indicator on the status line shows the percentage already processed. When the cell location reappears, Works is ready for your next action.

Entering the Formulas

Formulas are mathematical equations that use numbers on the spreadsheet and other elements to produce new numbers. This spreadsheet contains three formulas whose locations are shown in Figure 5-3. You enter formulas in the unshaded cells containing zero or `ERR` and copy them to the shaded cells at the same time.

First read the explanation of how the formula works, then follow the step-by-step instructions. Keep an eye on the status line to make sure the cursor is on the correct cell before taking your next action. If you run into a snag, press Escape and start again.

```
           A                  B            C              D           E
1                       COMPARATIVE ADVERTISING BUDGET
2   ===========================================================================
3   Medium             This Year      % Total     Last Year      % Total
4   ---------------------------------------------------------------------------
5   Newspaper                            ERR ②                        ERR ③
6   Television                           ERR                          ERR
7   Radio                                ERR                          ERR
8   Direct Mail                          ERR                          ERR
9   Magazine                             ERR                          ERR
10                     --------      --------      --------      --------
11  Total Budget             $0 ①        ERR            $0           ERR
```

Figure 5-3. The formula locations in the advertising budget spreadsheet

Formula 1: Total Budget =SUM(B4:B10)

The range operator, a colon, represents all cells between the first and last in the range.

Formula 1 adds the budget amounts (B5 through B9) to produce the total budget in B11. It uses the SUM function to handle the cells as a range so you don't have to add each one individually (that is, B5+B6+B7+B8+B9). The colon is the range operator. It represents all cells between the first and the last cell in the range.

The formula includes the lines in B4 and B10, which expands the actual cell range. With this technique, you can later insert rows anywhere between rows 4 and 10, and Works will adjust the formula to include the new entries.

Formula 1 can do the same calculation in columns C, D, and E because they all have the same relative layout as column B. Because both cell references are relative, you can create the formula once, enter it in all four cells in row 11 at the same time, and expect each formula to use the proper cells for its calculations. All of this will make more sense after you do it. Place the cursor on B11.

- Press F8 (to extend the selection). You can now see **EXT** on the status line.
- Press End (to select B11 through E11).
- Type =**SUM(** and press Up Arrow to move the cursor to the line in B10.
- Press F8 (to extend the selection) and press Up Arrow 6 times to move the cursor to the line in B4. You should now see =SUM(B4:B10 on the status line and in B11.
- Type a close parenthesis. The cursor jumps back to B11.
- Hold down Ctrl and press Enter.

Each time you type a character, the cursor returns to the formula cell.

The formula results are: **$81,000** in B11, **$66,200** in D11, and **0.0%** in C11 and E11. Looking good.

Formula 2: Percent of This Year's Total =B5/$Total Budget

Formula 2 divides the amount in B5 (the cell to its immediate left) by the amount in B11 (the cell named Total Budget). The result reflects each medium as a percentage of the total budget.

Cell references start out as relative. A dollar sign tells Works a cell reference is absolute.

Formula 2 behaves the same way in each cell, dividing the amount in the cell to its immediate left by the total budget in B11. Therefore, the cell to the left is a relative reference and the cell named `Total Budget` is an absolute reference. Works considers every cell reference to be relative unless you make it absolute with a dollar sign ($). Place the cursor on C5.

- Press F8 (to extend the selection).
- Press Down Arrow four times (to select C5 through C9).
- Type an equal sign and press Left Arrow (to enter B5 in the formula).
- Type a slash (/, the division operator). The cursor jumps back to C5. Now move it to B11. Works shows `=B5/Total Budget` on the entry/edit line and `Total Budget` in C5.
- Press F4 (to make Total Budget absolute). Works inserts $ before `Total Budget`.
- Hold down Ctrl and press Enter.

Percentages appear in C5 through C9 on cue. The formula in C11 dutifully adds them and produces `100.0%`.

Formula 3: Percent of Last Year's Total =D5/$Total Budget1

Formula 3 works with last year's numbers as Formula 2 does with this year's. This time, it uses the amount in D11 (the cell named Total Budget1) to produce the percentages. Place the cursor on E5.

- Press F8 (to extend the selection).
- Press Down Arrow four times (to select E5 through E9).
- Type an equal sign and press Left Arrow (to enter D5 in the formula).
- Type a slash (the cursor jumps back to E5) and move the cursor to D11. Works shows `=D5/Total Budget1` on the entry/edit line and `otalBudget1` in E5.
- Press F4 (to make Total Budget1 absolute). Works insert $ before `Total Budget1`.
- Hold down Ctrl and press Enter.

You now have all the percentages, which completes the spreadsheet. Press Escape to collapse the selection.

Now save the spreadsheet with the formulas. Leave the cursor where it is. Press Alt and type **FS** (File/Save).

Previewing the Spreadsheet

In a Preview version, Works miniaturizes things in proportion, showing margins, headers, footers, and page breaks at their proper locations and text scaled down to the specified font size.

After you enter everything on a spreadsheet is a good time to see how it will look on paper at the standard print settings. This can help you decide if you need to change any settings. You can print the spreadsheet, of course. Even easier, you can preview it on screen. Leave the cursor where it is.

- Press Alt and type **PV** (Print/Preview). You now see the `Preview` dialog box containing the same settings as the `Print` dialog box.
- To get the effect of printing row and column labels, hold down Alt, type **L**, and press Enter. Works brings up the spreadsheet showing columns A through D.
- With your Num Lock key turned off, press the Page Down key. Here's column E. Well, that's not exactly what we had in mind. There's work to be done. Press Escape to return to the spreadsheet.

Defining the Page Layout

This advertising budget spreadsheet is 68 characters wide including the 5 characters Works needs for row numbers and a space down the left side. A header at the top of the page, as shown in Figure 5-1, will add a professional touch. Reducing the standard margins and using 12-point type can get it to fit on one sheet of 8-by-11-inch paper.

Creating a Header

First, create a header to identify and date stamp the budget. My date and time are June 21, 1990 at 1:30 in the afternoon. Your date and time will be what you typed at DOS startup or the date and time kept by your computer's clock/calendar. It doesn't matter that it's different than mine.

- Hold down Alt and type **PH** (Print/Headers & Footers). Works brings up the `Headers & Footer` dialog box with the blinker in the `Header` field.

- To tell Works what to print and where, type:

&LADBUDGET-page &P&R&D &T (Be sure to leave a space after **page** and after **D**.)

Before pressing Enter, take a good look at what you typed in the `Header` field. Here's what each element means:

&L	left-align what follows
ADBUDGET-page	print this text
&P	print a page number
&R	right-align what follows
&D	print the date
&T	print the time

Now press Enter.

Setting the Print Margins

Reducing the left and right margins allows the entire spreadsheet to print on one page. Leave the cursor where it is.

- Press Alt and type **PM** (Print/Page Setup & Margins). You now see the `Page Setup & Margins` dialog box where all margin settings are made.
- Hold down Alt and type **E** (to move to `Left margin`).
- Type **.5** (the new left margin) and press Tab (to move to `Right margin`).
- Type **.5** (the new right margin). Don't press Enter yet.

Changing the Page Width

When you print, the header will right-align according to the page width setting, which is now 8 inches. Because the spreadsheet is 7.8 inches wide (spreadsheet and row numbers, 6.8 inches; right and left margins, one inch), this creates an unsightly jog. To produce a smooth right edge, all you need do is match the page width to the spreadsheet width.

- Hold down Alt and type **W** (to move to `Page width`).
- Type **7.8** (the new page width). You're not quite finished, so don't press Enter yet.

Defining the First Page Number

Note to hard disk users: To store a file on a backup disk in drive A (or B), press Alt and type **FA**. *Press Left Arrow to jump the blinker to the first character in the filename. Type* **A:** *(or* **B:***) and press Enter.*

Let's pretend this spreadsheet is meant to appear on the second page of a report. Change the first page number so the spreadsheet page is in proper numerical sequence.

- Press Tab (to move to `1st page number`).
- Type **2** (the new first page number). All other print settings are fine, so press Enter.

Now let's save the spreadsheet again: Leave the cursor where it is. Press Alt and type **FS**.

Previewing and Printing the Spreadsheet

Preview the budget again to see the effect of these changes. Leave the cursor where it is.

- Press Alt and type **PV** (Print/Preview). You still have the labels box checked off, so press Enter. That's more like it. All columns fit on one page and the spacing within the header and at the right side is perfect.

If you specified more than one printer, press Escape now. Press Alt, type **PS** *(Print/Printer Setup) and choose your printer. Then Preview again and type* **P**.

You can print directly from Preview, so turn on your printer. Assuming you specified one text printer during the Works setup steps, all you need do is tell Works to print by typing **P**.

The printer whirs and here's your spreadsheet looking, as promised, like the completed one in Figure 5-1 and the one you previewed on screen.

In Chapter 7, you'll transform this budget into a pie and bar chart. You'll want everything then exactly as it is now. But if you just can't wait to try things out, save this budget under another name first: Press Alt, type **FA** (File/Save As) and give it another name. Experiment with that one.

Now get ready for a tour of the spreadsheet menus, which you embark on in the next chapter.

Exploring the Spreadsheet Menus

The heady experience of creating your first spreadsheet is bound to raise as many questions as it answers. Now that you know so much, you undoubtedly want to know more. Works is a powerful program and there is indeed a great deal more to know, so in this chapter you explore all the spreadsheet menus and commands.

To make it easy to maneuver the menus, Works keeps related commands in the same menu whenever possible. An ellipsis (. . .) after a command name means that choosing these commands produces a dialog box, where you can make further choices.

Common Menus and Commands

Several spreadsheet menus and commands are used in the same or in a similar fashion in the database and word processor. If the spreadsheet is your first exposure to Works, much of what you learn now is easily transferred to the other applications. Here's an overview of the Works menus:

- All three applications have a File menu, Window menu, and Help menu with identical commands. There are minor variations in how these commands are used in the word processor.
- Five commands in the Print menu (Print, Page Setup & Margins, Headers & Footers, Preview, and Printer Setup) are identical in all applications. Other print commands are specific to the application.

- Four commands in the Options menu (Works Settings, Calculator, Alarm Clock, and Dial This Number) are identical in all applications. Other options commands are specific to the application.
- Each application has an Edit, Select, Format, and Options menu. Most commands in these menus differ between applications.
- The spreadsheet and database have a View menu that lets you display information differently—as a chart in the spreadsheet and in one of two screen layouts in the database.

The communications application has a File, Window, and Help menu with the same commands as the other three applications, plus menus and commands that differ.

And now, onto the spreadsheet menus.

The File Menu

A file is a collection of related information.

Works stores your spreadsheets, documents, and databases in files. In the spreadsheet, files consist of titles, numbers, and formulas; in a document, words and numbers; and in a database, records containing names, numbers, and formulas.

The File menu is the traffic manager for files. It lets you create new files, open and close existing files, save and name files, use DOS (Disk Operating System) commands without leaving Works, run other programs from Works, and quit the Works program. All commands in the File menu are the same in every application.

Create New File . . .

When you choose the Create New File command, Works presents the dialog box where you can open a new word processor, spreadsheet, database, or communications file.

Instead of starting from scratch each time, you can use a template file to get a headstart.

If you've already created and saved a template file in that application (see the Save As command), Works opens the template file instead. A template file contains your standard settings.

Open Existing File . . .

The Open Existing File command lets you open a file you've already created. The `File to open` dialog box lists the names of all files in the current directory and provides access to other drives and directories. Double dots in the `Directories` box take you to the next higher directory.

Works lists files alphabetically by type—Word Processor, Spreadsheet, Database, Communications, and Other Files. The fastest way to select a file from this list is to type the first letter of the filename. You can have as many as eight files open at a time, and then use the Window menu to switch quickly from one to another or to show several files on screen at one time.

If you want to list the filenames of only one type of file, use the asterisk wildcard in the File to open box. For instance, type *.WKS to list only spreadsheet files, *.WDB for database files, *.WPS for word processor files, and *.WCM for communications files. The asterisk stands for any number of characters in the same position.

If your computer is part of a network, you can open the file as a read-only file. This allows more than one person to see the file but not make any changes.

Save and Save As . . .

The Save and Save As commands store an open file on disk. Any work you've done since you last saved the file is stored only in computer memory. If something unexpected happens (power outage, electric cord pulled out of socket, and so on), that unsaved work is lost.

The Save command saves a file to the current drive, replacing any prior version if it exists. Works doesn't ask you to confirm the replacement. It just goes ahead and does it. If you save a new file with the Save command, Works responds as if you had chosen the Save As command.

The Save As command lets you save a new file and give it a filename. If you don't type an extension, Works tacks one on based on file type: .WPS for word processor, .WKS for spreadsheet, .WDB for database, and .WCM for communications.

If you type a drive letter and colon first (for instance, **A:FILENAME**) or drive letter and subdirectory first (for instance, B:\WDATA\FILENAME), you can save the file under the same filename but to a different drive or directory. When you use Save As to save to another drive or directory, Works asks you to confirm replacement of an existing file.

The Save As command is loaded with other goodies. For starters, it lets you make a backup copy of a file after you save and name it the first time. If you check the Make backup copy box, work on the file, and save your changes, Works saves the current version as the active file and the prior version as a backup file with a new extension—.BKS for spreadsheet, .BDM for database, .BPS for word processor, and .BCM for communications.

Before you start experimenting with a spreadsheet and doing all those glorious things you're sure will enhance it, turn on the Make backup copy box. If the experiment fails, use the File menu's File Management command, the Rename File option, to rename the backup version (but not with the same name as the active file) and give it the .WKS extension. You don't have to open the backup file first. Then use the Delete File option in the File Management command to delete the noble failure.

You can also use the Save As command to save a file as a text (ASCII) file with or without formatting. ASCII (which stands for American Standard Code for Information Interchange) lets you convert a file so it can be read by other spreadsheet, database, and word processor programs.

But that's not all. The Save as template check box lets you create a master file (aka template)—for instance, a monthly budget with titles, formats, formulas, and print settings but no entries. Each time you create a new spreadsheet file, Works brings up the master budget awaiting your entries. If you turn off the budget's template status, Works brings up a virgin file instead. You can also turn off or turn on template status in the Options menu's Works Settings command.

Close

Before Works closes a changed file it asks for permission to save it.

The Close command removes an open file from computer memory and clears it from the screen. When you finish work on a file or you want to open another file but already have eight files open, the Close command makes room for others.

File Management . . .

Your computer's disk operating system (DOS) provides commands that make working with files and functions easier. You can do such tasks as copy, delete, and rename files, create or remove a directory, copy or format a disk, and set your computer's date and time. The File Management command lets you access these DOS commands without leaving Works. When you're ready to return to Works, type *Exit* (not Works).

Run Other Programs . . .

The Run Other Programs command lets you launch applications programs without leaving Works. This gives you direct access to other commonly used software as well as to DOS commands, such as CHKDSK, EDLIN, and TREE, that are unavailable in the File Management command. You can choose the programs that appear on the launcher menu. As with File Management, type Exit (not Works) to return to Works.

Convert . . .

You can use Works spreadsheet files in Lotus 1-2-3 (and vice versa) without going through this conversion process. Exchanging with other spreadsheet programs often requires an ASCII file convert.

Convert lets you convert a file created in another word processing program, such as Microsoft Word, WordPerfect, DisplayWrite, and MultiMate, to Works file format with most if not all formatting intact. You then can open and use the converted file just as you would any Works document. You can also do the reverse—convert a Works file to another word processor file format. Pressing Escape during a file conversion cancels the conversion.

Exit Works . . .

When you Exit, Works saves information about your work, your printer, and any changes you made using the Works Settings command in a file called WORKS.INI. It uses this information the next time you start Works.

The Exit command is a safe and sure way out of the Works program. If you just turn off the computer in midstream, everything in computer memory is lost. Instead, Works gently prods you to save each changed or new, unsaved file, giving you one last chance to rescue your work from oblivion.

The Edit Menu

No matter how much work you put into a spreadsheet and how well it performs, there's often a little something you can do to make it better. The Edit menu, with its Move, Copy, Clear, Delete, Insert, Fill, and Name commands, is clearly the tinkerer's delight.

Move

Select the information to move before pressing F3.

The Move command moves whatever is in a cell—both content and format—to another part of the spreadsheet. Moved information disappears from its original location and reappears at its destination. This information can be in one cell, several cells, or in rows and columns of cells. Pressing the shortcut key F3 gets you moving without going through the Move command. During a move, Works displays the word MOVE on the status line.

When you move information from cell to cell, Works overwrites anything in the destination cells. When you move entire rows or columns of information, Works inserts (not overwrites) the moved row or column at the destination, shifting any columns to the right of the inserted column further to the right and shifting any rows below the inserted row further down. This saves you the bother of inserting a new column or row first.

Copy, Fill Right, and Fill Down

These Copy and Fill commands let you copy the content and format of cells. Copied information remains in its original location and also appears at its destination.

Select the information to copy before pressing Shift+F3.

The Copy command copies information to noncontiguous cells on the spreadsheet and to other open Works files. You can use shortcut key Shift+F3 to copy without going through the Copy command and Shift+F7 to immediately repeat the last Copy command. During a copy, Works displays the word COPY on the status line.

The Fill Right command copies to contiguous cells to the right of the source cell. The Fill Down command copies to contiguous cells below the source cell. Select the source cell and the cells you want to fill before choosing Fill Right or Fill Down.

Copy Special . . .

Because the information at each end is different, Copy Special is not, in the strict sense of the term, a copy command. It does, however, perform these special tasks admirably well:

1. Adds the values in selected cells to the values in other cells.
2. Subtracts the values in selected cells from the values in other cells.
3. Converts a formula to its value; that is, it replaces the formula with the formula result.
4. Without converting the formula, copies the formula results, but not the formula, to another cell.

Fill Series . . .

The Fill Series command is one of those little gems you wonder how you ever did without. Effortlessly, it fills any number of cells with a series of numbers, dates, days, months, or years in increments of your choice. The starting value must be a number or date you enter in a cell, not a number or date generated by a formula.

The starting value can also be a month, as shown in Figure 6-1. Here, entering Jan in B2, selecting eleven more cells to the right of B2, and then telling the Fill Series command to enter a series of months in one-month increments (Step by: 1) produces an entire year's worth of column headings from Jan through Dec.

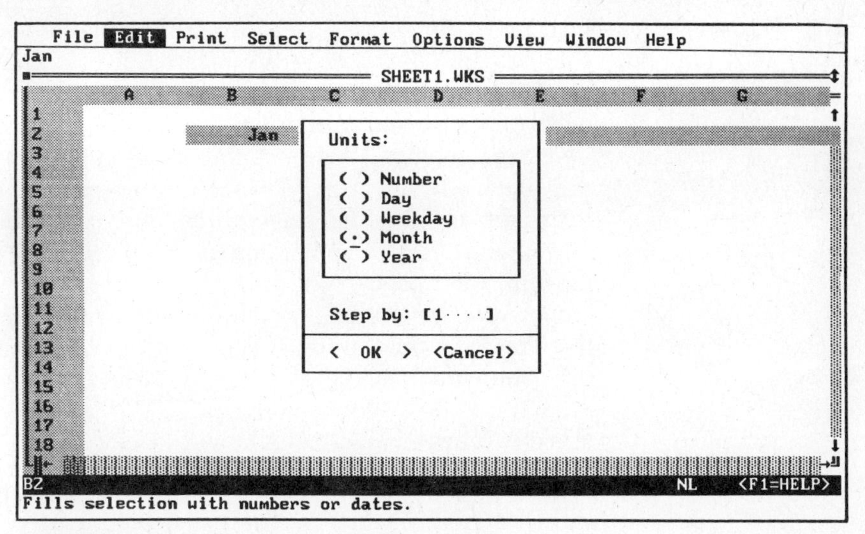

Figure 6-1. The Fill Series command prepares to enter a series of months across row 2

Clear

The Clear command clears or "erases" the information in cells. This leaves the cell empty and the format intact. Clear works with a single cell, a block of cells, or rows or columns of cells.

The quick way to clear a single cell without going through the Clear command is to place the cursor on the cell, and then press Backspace and Enter.

Delete Row/Column and Insert Row/Column

These Delete and Insert commands let you delete and insert columns and rows. Unlike Clear, which erases only the contents of columns and rows, Delete removes entire columns and rows, including their contents and formats.

Delete is straightforward. Simply place the cursor on any cell in the doomed column or row, choose the Delete command and Column or Row option. Poof, it's gone, and the remaining columns or rows close the gap. To delete more than one row or column, use F8 to select contiguous cells before starting the command.

Check carefully before deleting a column or row to make sure it doesn't contain a cell reference needed by a formula. If you do delete a cell to which a formula refers, Works waves a red flag by displaying the error message ERR in the formula cell.

Works inserts rows above the cursor's location. To insert one row, place the cursor directly below the insertion and choose the

Insert command and Row option. Inserting more than one row is a bit trickier. Before choosing the Insert Row command, place the cursor on the cell directly below the insertion and select as many more cells below as you want new rows.

Here's how to insert more than one row at a time.

For instance, to insert four rows, place the cursor on the cell directly below where you want the insert to start. Use F8 to extend the selection, and then select three more cells below the cursor. When you choose the Insert command's Row option, Works parts the way for four new rows.

Works inserts columns to the left of the cursor. Therefore, place the cursor in the column to the right of the insertion before starting the command.

Range Name . . .

The Range Name command is one of the shining stars of a spreadsheet. It lets you give single cells, blocks of cells, and columns or rows of cells plain English names, which you then can use to create easy-to-understand formulas. You can also use a name instead of a cell location to select cells for copying, moving, clearing, or printing. The **Name** dialog box lists named cells, which you can change or delete at any time.

This command has another important capability. When you want to document a complex spreadsheet, you can have Works print a list of cell names and locations right on the spreadsheet. You'll learn how to do this in Chapter 22.

The Print Menu

Works gives you a great deal of control over how a printed spreadsheet looks. You can specify, among other things, margins, pages to print, print area, size and style of characters, page size, page numbers, page breaks, and the content and alignment of headers and footers. Each selection is handled within the Works program itself. You don't have to go near your printer until the big moment arrives —and then only to turn it on.

Print . . .

You can hardcopy that part of the spreadsheet that appears on screen without going through the Print command. The

The Print command tells Works how many copies to print, which pages to print if you're not printing every page, whether to send the spreadsheet to the printer or to a disk file, and whether to print row and column labels (row numbers and column letters).

keys that do this on many computers are Print Screen (PrtSc) or Shift+Print.

To print certain pages only, turn on the Print specific pages box, which undims the Pages field. Type the page numbers in the Pages field. Separate single pages with commas (for instance, **3,5,9,10** tells Works to print pages 3, 5, 9, and 10) and a range of pages with a colon or dash (for instance, **4:6** or **4-6** tells Works to print pages 4, 5, and 6).

Page Setup & Margins . . .

Figure 6-2 shows the standard margin and page settings in the Page Setup & Margins command. Margins (Top, Bottom, Left, and Right) tell Works when to start and stop printing on a page. One-inch top and bottom margins are fine for most spreadsheets, but you may want to reduce the standard left and right margins to print more columns across.

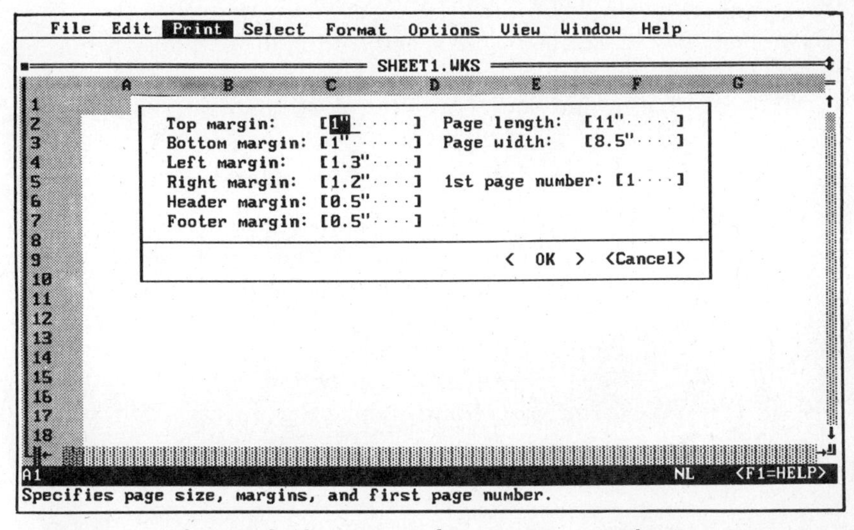

Figure 6-2. The standard margin and page settings in the Page Setup & Margins command

Header and footer margins control the distance between the top of a page to the top of a header and the bottom of a page to the bottom of a footer. Header and footer margins should always be smaller than the regular top and bottom margins.

The page length and page width settings tell Works the size of the paper you'll be using to print your spreadsheet. Works prints as many rows as the page length and top and bottom margin settings allow, printing any leftover rows on second and subsequent pages. It prints as many columns as the page width and the left and right margin settings allow, printing any leftover columns on second and subsequent pages.

If your printer can print sideways (check your printer manual), you can give your spreadsheet a landscape orientation, which allows more columns across a page but less rows down. Simply reverse the page length and width settings. For example, for 8.5-inch by 11-inch paper, enter **8.5** in the page length field and **11** in the page width field.

If you use a page number in a header or footer, you can tell Works what you want the first page number to be.

Preview . . .

The Preview command shows on screen how your spreadsheet will look on paper. In this miniature version, Works shows margins, headers, footers, and page breaks in their proper locations and scales text to show the specified size. You can print from Preview by typing **P**.

Set Print Area

An area selected for printing can be as small as one cell.

Unless you specify otherwise, Works prints all the information on your spreadsheet. If you want to print a specific area, select the area, choose the Set Print Area command, and then use the Print command to print the area.

Insert Page Break and Delete Page Break

When your spreadsheet is wider than can fit on a page, Works breaks it into pages. The Insert Page Break command lets you determine where page breaks occur, making it easy to split an oversize spreadsheet into logically related sections. You can create a horizontal page break between rows or a vertical page break between columns.

Works uses the symbol » to show a page break on screen. The row or column displaying the page break symbol becomes the first row or column on the next printed page. You can remove a page break that outlives its usefulness with the Delete Page Break command.

Headers & Footers

The Headers & Footers command lets you create headers and footers on your spreadsheets. A header is text that prints at the top of each page and a footer is text that prints at the bottom. Headers usually contain such things as a filename, page number, date, or time. Footers usually contain a page number. You can have a header, footer, both, or neither.

You can find the header and footer codes in Table 14-6 in Chapter 14.

Figure 6-3 shows the dialog box where you enter text and special codes that control alignment and enter such things as filename and date in a header or footer. The standard alignment centers header and footer text, which you can right-justify or left-justify by using the alignment codes.

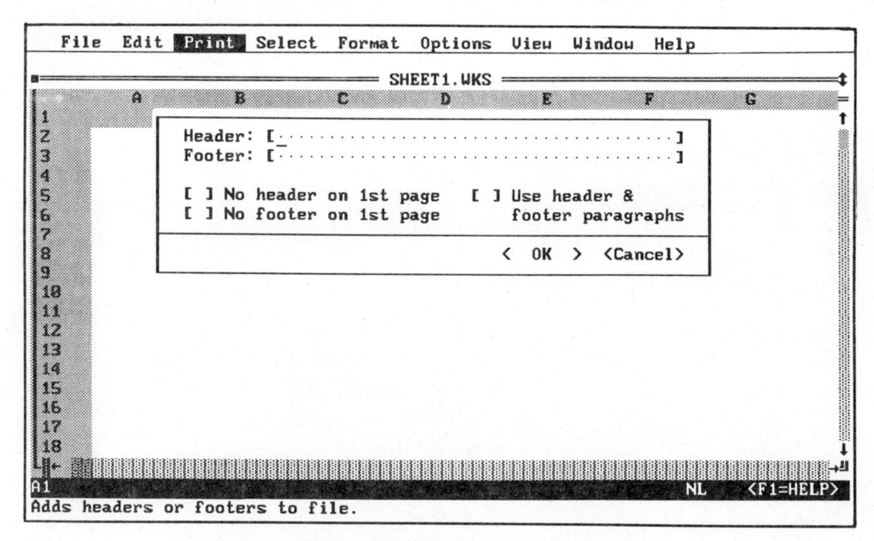

Figure 6-3. Header and footer dialog box

Headers print one-half inch from the top of the paper, while footers print one-half inch from the bottom. You can change these settings in the Page Setup & Margins command to print higher or lower on the page.

You can print a header or footer on every page but the first by checking the No header (or No footer) on 1st page box. This works well when the first page is a title page. You can turn off a spreadsheet header or footer only by deleting the text. The Use header and footer paragraphs box is dimmed, meaning it's not available in the spreadsheet.

Printer Setup . . .

If you specified more than one printer during the Works setup steps, the Printer Setup command lets you choose which printer to use to print your report. If you specified one printer only, Works uses that printer.

If you want to add or replace printer drivers, be aware that drivers on the Works Setup disk are stored in compressed form (.CPR extension). To use these drivers, you must go through the Works setup steps so Works can decompress the driver. Drivers stored on the Supplemental Printer disks have a .PRD extension. You can simply copy these drivers directly into the Works subdirectory.

With printers that print graphics, the Graphics list in the dialog box offers a choice of print resolutions (fineness of line) expressed in dots per inch (dpi). Works uses the resolution setting only for printing charts, not text.

This command also lets you change page feed from continuous to manual, which is useful when you want to feed single sheets to the printer. It also gives you the choice of which communication port to connect to your printer.

The Select Menu

The commands in the Select menu let you select areas on the spreadsheet, move the cursor to specific cells, and locate specific information. Shortcut keys make it easy to sidestep most of the commands in this menu. The advantage to having a Select menu is that you may not always remember the shortcut key.

Selecting tells your next command which cells to work with.

Cells

The Cells command lets you select a block of cells for your next command to work with. With the cursor on the first cell selected, start the Cells command, and then move the cursor to the last cell you want selected. Pressing F8 instead of going through the Cells command is faster and saves keystrokes.

Row and Column

The Row and Column commands let you select a row or column. Using Ctrl+F8 to select a row and Shift+F8 to select a column is faster than going through the command. If you want to select several rows or columns, select one row or column first, press F8 to extend the selection, and then move the cursor to the others.

All

The All command selects the entire spreadsheet. This is useful, for example, when you want to give every cell the same format. It's faster to simply press Ctrl+Shift+F8 first.

Go To . . .

The Go To command quickly moves the cursor to a specific cell location. You can do it quicker by using the shortcut key F5. When you press F5, Works displays the Go to dialog box with a place to type in the location of the cell and a list of named cells. After you type the cell location or select the cell name, Works sends the cursor to the specified cell.

Search . . .

The Search command searches cells for the text, number, or formula you specify, starting at the cursor position and cycling around. Works routinely searches by rows, but it can also search by columns if you tell it to. Works ignores hidden columns in its search.

In a row search, Works searches the current row, and then continues downward, searching each row until it gets to the last filled row. It then cycles back to the first row and starts downward again. In a column search, Works searches the current column and then continues to the right, searching each column until it gets to the last filled column. It then cycles back to the first column and starts rightward again. If you select an area before starting the search, Works searches only that area.

When Works finds the searched-for item, it parks the cursor on that cell. Pressing F7 sends Works searching for the next occurrence of the search item.

When you don't know the exact spelling, it's wildcards to the rescue!

Works provides two wildcards—question mark (?) and asterisk (*)—to help find entries that are similar but not the same. A wildcard represents characters in the search item.

- The question mark represents a single character in the same position. Say you don't know if a name is spelled Smith or Smyth. Enter `Sm?th` in the `Search for` box and Works will find either name.
- The asterisk represents multiple characters in the same position. For instance, if you don't know if it's Smith or Smydie, enter Sm* in the `Search for` box, and Works finds the name.

In a spreadsheet loaded with text, numbers, and formulas, you can find the formulas quickly by first using the Options menu's Show Formulas command to display formulas, and then typing an equal sign in the `Search for` box.

Sort Rows . . .

Sorting arranges rows on the spreadsheet based on the contents of selected cells. For instance, if you select A6 through A12, Works sorts rows 6 through 12 based on the contents of A6 through A12. Works can sort on cells in one, two, or three columns and arrange the rows in ascending or descending order.

The Format Menu

Formats determine how numbers and text look in their cells.

The commands in the Format menu, shown in Figure 6-4, control how Works displays text and numbers on screen and in print. Works provides standard formats—General for numbers and left-justified for text—which you can replace in any or all cells. Each number format allows 0 to 7 decimal places. Works routinely proposes two decimal places.

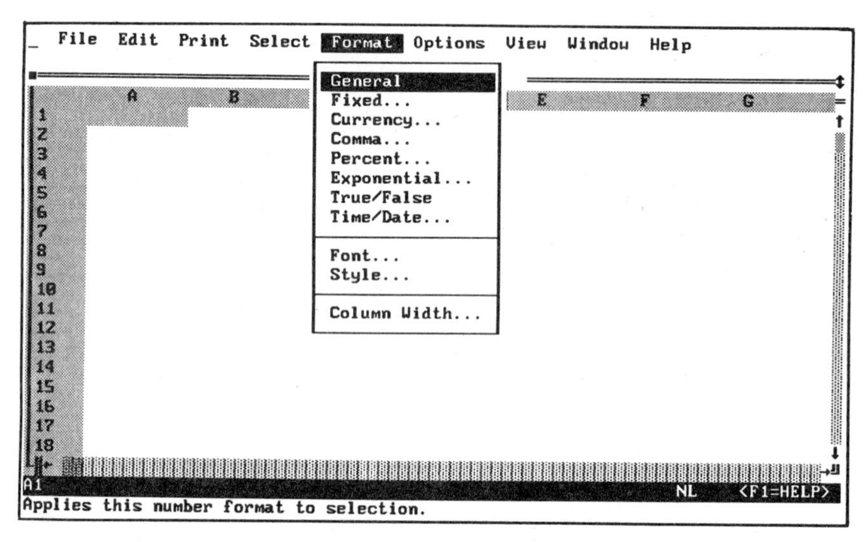

Figure 6-4. Commands in the spreadsheet's Format menu

General

Works initially gives numbers the General format, showing each number as an integer (567), decimal fraction (5.67), or, if the number is too large or too small to fit into the cell, in scientific notation (5.68E+11). Negative numbers have a leading minus sign.

You can enter a fraction, such as **2/5**, in a cell just by typing it in. If you want Works to convert the fraction to its decimal counterpart, type a whole number first. For example, enter **0 2/5** in a cell, and Works converts it to .4; enter **12 5/8** and Works converts it to 12.625. This feature is useful if you work with stock prices.

If a formula's result is too long to be displayed completely, Works displays ##### in the cell.

Fixed . . ., Comma . . ., and Percent . . .

The Fixed command shows numbers with a fixed number of decimal places and no commas. The Comma command embeds a comma every third place. The Percent command multiplies the number by 100 and adds a percent sign. Negative numbers in a Fixed or Percent format have a leading minus sign. Negative numbers in a Comma format are enclosed in parentheses.

Currency . . .

The Currency command shows numbers according to the country selected during the Works setup steps or the Country setting in the Options menu's Works Settings command. With USA selected, numbers appear with a leading dollar sign and an embedded comma every third place. Negative numbers are enclosed in parentheses.

Exponential . . .

The Exponential command displays numbers in scientific notation, which is handy when you need to display very large or very small numbers. For example, the number 1234567890 with 2 decimal places becomes 1.23E+09. Negative numbers have a leading minus sign.

True/False

The True/False command causes cells to display the logical values TRUE or FALSE in place of a number. A cell that contains a zero displays FALSE, and a cell that contains a number other than zero displays TRUE.

Time/Date . . .

The Time/Date command displays a number in date or time format. You can show a date in long or short form as month, day, and year; month and year; month and day; or month only. The long forms are Jan 31, 1991, Jan 1991, Jan 31, and Jan. The short forms are 1/31/91, 1/91, and 1/31.

If you want to see months fully spelled out (January instead of Jan), take an Aussie holiday. In the Options menu's Works Settings command, choose Australia in the Country box. You'll still get dollars as currency, but you'll also get 31 January, 1991 in the month, day, and year form.

You can show time in hours, minutes, and seconds or in hours and minutes, based on a 24-hour or 12-hour clock. The forms in the 12-hour version are 2:30:00 PM, 2:30 PM, and 2 PM; in the 24-hour version, 14:30:00 and 14:30.

Font . . .

A spreadsheet can have only one font.

The Font command lists font types and sizes available on your printer. A font is a family of characters in a distinctive design. Font size, measured in points, expresses how large your printed characters will be. A point is about 1/72 of an inch. The larger the point size, the larger the character.

Works selects a font type and size for you, which you can easily change to something else. It's a good idea to print a small spreadsheet in each font type and size available on your printer so you know your choices.

The Style command aligns, enhances, locks, and unlocks entries in cells. The General, or standard, alignment left-aligns text, right-aligns numbers, and centers ERR (error) messages. You can left-justify, right-justify, or center these entries, as well as print them in bold, italic, underline, or a combination of styles. Works displays enhanced entries on screen either in high intensity or as they print on paper, depending on screen mode selected (Text or Graphics) in the Works Settings command.

Right-justified text and numbers stop one character short of the right edge of the cell. This aligns them nicely when the text is at the head of a column with numbers in the cells below.

The Works cell protection scheme allows you to lock cells to prevent accidental change. Protection is handled in part by the Style command. The turned-on Locked box in the dialog box enables the protection. You need only toggle the Protect command in the Options menu to lock every cell.

It's a good idea to disable the lock on cells whose contents you want to change regularly before you turn on protection in the Options menu.

Width . . .

You can see only 75 characters on screen, but you can print columns 79 characters wide.

The Width command lets you change the width of a column from the standard 10 characters to anything from 0 through 79 characters. You can apply these widths to every column on the spreadsheet or to selected columns only. You need to select only one cell in the column before you choose the Width command to apply the new width to the entire column.

Reducing a column to 0 characters hides it on screen and in a printed report. Hidden columns can hold intermediate and other calculations best left unshown. Use the Select menu's Go To command to get to a hidden column, and then use the Width command to unhide it.

The Options Menu

The first four commands in the Options menu—Works Settings, Calculator, Alarm Clock, and Dial This Number—are the same and work the same in all applications. They let you customize the window display, select settings that affect the entire Works program, and access the desk accessories. Chapter 1, "The Works Environment," covers the desk accessories in more detail.

Other commands in this menu keep titles on screen, protect the contents of cells, show the formulas that produce values in cells, and determine the frequency of calculation.

Works Settings . . .

Works stores your settings in the WORKS.INI file, so you need to make your changes only once.

The Works Settings command lets you change the current settings in the Works program. Many of these settings reflect your response to questions about your hardware configuration during Works setup. Works now gives you the chance to change your mind.

Figure 6-5 shows the variety of settings in this command's dialog box. It's here that you can:

- Select the subset of another country. Countries have different standards. Your choice can affect page size, currency symbol, and date and time format.
- Redefine the unit of measure from inches to centimeters, pitches, or points.
- Choose the screen colors. Your options depend on the capabilities of the video card selected during the Works setup steps.
- Choose the screen mode, again a function of your video card. The screen mode controls the way character styles and the mouse pointer appear on screen. In text mode, Works shows enhanced characters (bold, underline, and italic) in different colors. In graphics mode, it's WYSIWYG (What You See Is What You Get), with Works showing characters on screen similar to the way they look on paper.

- Increase the number of lines displayed on the screen, again depending on the video card used. With my configuration, I can replace the standard 25-line screen with a 43-line screen, which compresses an open file vertically. Using Window commands to move and position, this gives me one file across the top half of the screen and another across the bottom half. This way, I can see far more of each file than ordinarily possible. I wouldn't want a 43-line screen as a steady diet, but it serves me well on special occasions.
- Apply or deny template status. When you save a file in the File menu's Save As command and make it a template, Works turns on the check box for that application in the `Use templates`

for box. Erasing the check mark removes template status, while checking off an application applies template status. The last file opened in that application becomes the designated template.

- Specify the communications port to which your modem is connected.
- Specify whether your telephone has tone or pulse dialing.
- View your Works version and serial number.

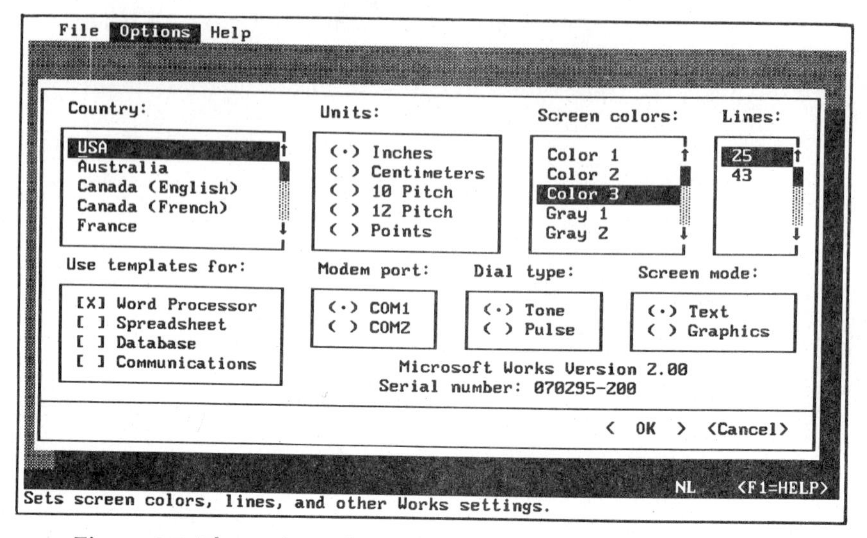

Figure 6-5. The variety of options in the Works Settings command

Calculator . . .

The Calculator command displays a screen calculator that works a lot like a hand-held calculator. It performs simple calculations that you can transfer into a word processor, spreadsheet, or database file.

Alarm Clock . . .

The Alarm Clock command displays a screen where you can enter appointment dates, times, and reminders. At the appointed time, your computer beeps and displays the reminder. If your computer is turned off when the appointed time arrives, Works flashes the reminder the next time you start up.

Dial This Number

With a Hayes-compatible modem hooked up to your computer, you can have Works dial a phone number in your spreadsheet, database, or word processor file.

Freeze Titles (Unfreeze Titles)

The Freeze Titles command anchors column and row titles in place as you scroll through a large spreadsheet. Works freezes all columns to the left of the cursor and all rows above the cursor.

Though you can't move the cursor into frozen rows or columns, you can use the Select menu's Go To command to select a duplicate of a cell or range in the frozen area. Any changes you make remain after you unfreeze.

The Freeze Titles command is a toggle. When titles are frozen, the command name switches to Unfreeze Titles. Use this command to restore the spreadsheet to its original condition.

Show Formulas

Formulas are the underpinnings of your spreadsheet. Not only is it a good idea to keep a hardcopy formula printout, it also helps to see formulas on screen when you need to troubleshoot. Turning on the Show Formulas command displays the formulas, while turning it off restores the spreadsheet exactly as it was.

Protect Data

When you're working on a spreadsheet, it's all too easy to overtype a formula with something else. Locking prevents this kind of unhappy accident. Locking is in a ready state but not enabled until you choose the Protect command, which then locks every filled cell.

Though cells containing formulas—particularly intricate ones—are prime candidates for protection, it can be a bother to have all text and numbers locked too. Before you choose the Protect command, select the cells whose contents you plan to change regularly and unlock them in the Format menu's Style command.

Manual Calculation and Calculate Now

Works displays **CALC** *on the status line when manual recalculation is on.*

Works recalculates the spreadsheet each time you enter a number or a formula. Recalculation is quick, but it can take longer and longer as you enter more information. Continuing to work interrupts recalculation. Works will wait until you stop, and then resume recalculating. You can turn off automatic recalculation with the Manual Calculation command and have Works calculate only when you tell it to, which is merely a matter of pressing the F9 key.

To return the spreadsheet to automatic recalculation, choose the Calculate Now command. When Works knows the spreadsheet needs to be calculated, **CALC** appears on the status line.

You can also use the Calculate Now command to enter only the result of a formula, not the formula itself. To do this, create the formula as usual, but instead of pressing Enter to enter it in the cell, press F9 and then Enter.

The View Menu

The commands in the View menu let you show spreadsheet information as a chart. You'll learn more about these commands in Chapter 8, "Exploring the Chart Menus." Here's a summary:

Spreadsheet	Switches from the chart screen to the spreadsheet screen. Pressing F10 in the chart screen does it faster.
New Chart	After you select a series, displays a new bar chart based on that series. Pressing Escape then takes you to the chart screen.
Charts . . .	Brings up a list of charts you can name, rename, delete, or copy.
Chart List	Lets you activate an existing chart. Pressing Shift+F10 displays the active chart.

The Window Menu

All commands in the Window menu are the same in every application. They let you view and work on as many as eight different files at a time, each in its own window. You can determine the size, position, and arrangement of the windows. The shortcut keys Ctrl+F6 switch to the next window, and Shift+Control+F6 switch to the previous window.

Chapter 1, "The Works Environment," covers the Move, Size, Maximize, and Arrange All commands in more detail.

Move

The Move command lets you move a window anywhere on screen and even off screen, as long as the upper left corner remains on screen.

Size

The Size command lets you reduce or enlarge the size of a window.

Maximize

The Maximize command lets you increase a window you reduced with the Size command so that it fills the entire screen again.

Arrange All

The Arrange All command places open files in side-by-side windows.

Split

The Split command divides the window into panes through which you can view and work on different areas of the spreadsheet. You can create two side-by-side panes, two top-and-bottom panes, or four panes, making panes the same or different sizes in each type of split. Be sure to press Enter after you split the window into panes.

Use the F6 key to move the cursor to the next pane and Shift+F6 to move to the previous pane.

Open Files

Each time you open a file, Works adds it to the list in the Window menu. If you have only one window open, you can display a file from this list by simply typing its number. That file then replaces the one that was on screen.

When you finish work on a file, close it with the File menu's Close command. The file disappears from computer memory, leaving room for the next file you want to open.

The Help Menu

When you have questions about Works, you can interrupt your work temporarily to get answers and instruction from commands in the Help menu, and then return to where you left off before asking for help. All commands in the Help menu are the same in every application. Chapter 1, "The Works Environment," covers the Help commands in more detail.

Using Help

This command explains how to go about getting help.

Help Index

Pressing F1 brings up a Help screen on the task you're currently engaged in. If no Help screen exists for that task, Works displays a Help Index listing all help topics. You can also view the index by choosing the Help Index command in the Help menu or by selecting the Index button in the Help screen you access with F1.

Works Tutorial

Pressing Shift+F1 presents the Works tutorial. You can also view the tutorial by choosing the Works Tutorial command or by selecting the Lesson button in the Help screen that you access with F1.

Getting Started

The Getting Started command brings up an explanation of how to use Works with the type of file (spreadsheet, database, word processor, or communications) now on screen.

Keyboard and Mouse

The Keyboard command brings up a comprehensive list of keystrokes that run the Works program. The Mouse command explains how to get around with the mouse.

What Was That Number?

Works and numbers are inseparable companions—not only the numbers you enter in a spreadsheet but the numbers you need to work with files, such as how many files you can keep open at one time and how many characters you can use in a filename. When you need to answer these and other *how many?* questions, you may not always remember where to find them. To help you in your day-to-day work with Works, the numbers pertaining to the spreadsheet are assembled in Table 6-1.

Table 6-1. Useful spreadsheet numbers

Parameter	Number
Files open at one time	1 to 8
Length of a filename	1 to 8 characters plus 3-character extension (any character except * ? / . , ; [] + = \ : | < > space)
Maximum length of command in Run Other Programs dialog box	124 characters
Maximum number of ranges to print in Print dialog box	10
Maximum number of columns	256 (A to Z, then AA through AZ, then BA through BZ, and so on to IA through IV)

Parameter	Number
Maximum number of rows	4096
Total available cells	1,048,576 (use depends on RAM)
Standard column width	10 characters
Available column widths	0 to 79 characters (screen can only display 75 characters)
Maximum user characters on 80-character screen	75 (four spaces needed for row numbers, plus one space between last digit of row number and first user-available space)
Number of fonts per spreadsheet	1
Maximum length of a formula	254 characters
Length of cell name in a displayed list	1 to 15 characters
Available window panes	2 or 4
Available decimal places	0 to 7
Built-in functions	57
Standard print settings:	
*Top and bottom margins	1 inch
*Left margin	1.3 inches
*Right margin	1.2 inches
*Page length	11 inches
*Page width	8.5 inches
*Header and footer margins	0.5 inches

Chart Workout: Pie and Bar Charts

Charts help get your points across in reports and pack a special punch in presentations.

If "one picture is worth a thousand words," then one chart is surely worth a thousand numbers. A chart lets you present facts in a form that's easier to understand and interpret than mere facts alone.

Works gets facts from your spreadsheet numbers, using them to create pie charts, bar charts, line charts, hi-lo-close charts, and scatter charts. Bar charts can be standard bar, stacked bar, or 100% bar. Line charts can be standard line or area line. You can also create mixed line and bar charts and charts with two different scales.

Switching between chart formats—for example, from a pie chart to a bar chart to a line chart—is a breeze with Works. All you do is identify the part of the spreadsheet you want to chart, specify the format, and Works designs the chart. Then specify another to see which works best. You can try formats to your heart's content until you find the one that best presents the facts.

This chapter gets you off to a flying start with charting techniques and concepts. You learn how to depict information in the advertising budget spreadsheet as a pie chart and a bar chart. In the process, you speed-chart the pie chart, add titles and subtitles, select fonts, create a border, and name the chart. You then create a bar chart from the pie chart, adding a Y-series, gridlines, titles, and legends. You save and print both charts. Whew!

Keystrokes and Other Matters

The instructions guide you each step of the way, giving keystrokes and cursor movements relating to each task. As you did when you created the spreadsheet, be sure to observe the distinction between pressing and holding down a key.

- With instructions such as *Press Alt and type TW (Format/ Width)*, press and release Alt before you type the letters.
- With *Hold down Alt and type N (to move to Name)*, press the Alt key, and without releasing Alt, type the letter.

Unless the instructions say otherwise, use the Arrow keys (Left, Right, Up, and Down) to move the cursor.

Creating a Pie Chart

A spreadsheet can have as many as eight chart formats. Each time you update the charted information, Works updates the associated charts.

Figure 7-1 shows the advertising budget you created in the spreadsheet workout as a pie chart. Pie charts can represent only one group of numbers, so it shows this year's media allocations only. The chart titles are from column A in the spreadsheet and the amounts from column B (refer to your spreadsheet printout or Figure 5-1).

Chart elements (Menu/Command):
A Title (Data/Titles)
B Title font (Format/Title Font)
C Subtitle (Data/Titles)
D Subtitle font (Format/Other Font)
E Border (Options/Show Border)
F Pie format (Format/Pie)
G Data point
H Category name

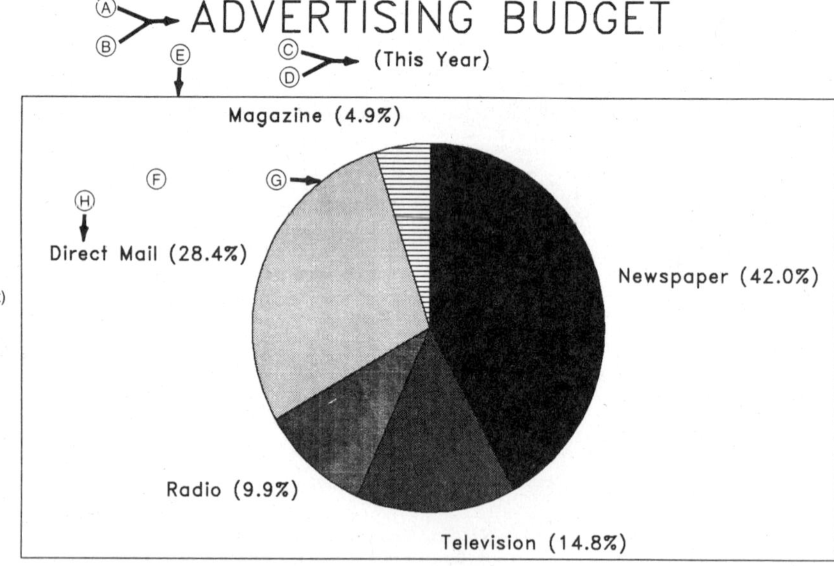

Figure 7-1. This year's advertising budget spreadsheet as a pie chart. The slices are the Y-series. Each slice is a data point.

Slices in the pie are called a Y-series, which refers to the Y-axis in bar or line charts. In those charts, the Y-axis is a fixed line perpendicular to the X-axis, or base line. Even though a pie chart doesn't have a Y-axis, the numbers are still called a Y-series.

Spreadsheet cells B5 through B9 provide the numbers in the Y-series. Each number, or slice in the pie, is a data point. Works adds the numbers, calculates each one as a percent of the total, and determines the size of each slice. It doesn't need the percentages calculated by the spreadsheet formulas. Works figures everything out by itself.

Loading the Budget Spreadsheet

If you already have the advertising budget (ADBUDGET.WKS) on screen, skip to the next section, "Speed Charting a Pie Chart."

If you're starting a new session, load Works as described in the Introduction to this book. At the New File screen, load the advertising budget.

- Type **O** (Open Existing File) and press Enter. You now see the Open Existing File dialog box with the blinker in the File to open field.
- Press Tab (to move the blinker into the Files box).
- Type **A** (to move the blinker to the first filename that starts with the letter A).
- If this is ADBUDGET.WKS, press Enter. Otherwise, type **A** as many times as needed to reach ADBUDGET.WKS (it appears in reverse video), and press Enter. You now have the advertising budget on screen.

Specifying the Printer

Your printer driver has the chart printer driver built into it.

Works needs to know which printer to use to print your chart. If you specified only one printer during Works setup or you want to stay with the printer you used for the budget, skip to the next section, "Speed Charting a Pie Chart." If you specified more than one printer and want to change to another one, leave the cursor where it is.

- Press Alt and type **PS** (Print/Printer Setup).

Move the blinker to the printer, tab to the Model list and specify the model, and then tab to the Graphics list and specify dpi (dots per inch). When you're satisfied that all settings are correct, press Enter.

Speed Charting a Pie Chart

A dandy little process called *speed charting* takes information in spreadsheet cells and converts it into a chart in only one step. All you do is identify what to chart (in this case, the media titles in column A and their corresponding numbers in column B). Place the cursor on A5.

- Press F8 (to extend the selection).
- Move the cursor down to A9, and then right to column B (to select A5 through B9).

Now tell Works you want to chart this information.

- Press Alt and type **VN** (View/New Chart). Works instantly produces a bar chart. You'll see the bar chart again later in this chapter.
- Press Escape (to return to the spreadsheet).

You're now in the chart screen, which has distinctive chart menus and the word CHART on the status line. Use the selected data as a pie chart. (In the following steps, it doesn't matter where the cursor is located.)

- Press Alt and type **TP** (Format/Pie).

Though it seems too quick and easy, you've already accomplished a great deal. To see how much, tell Works to draw the pie chart.

- Hold down Shift and press F10 (the shortcut key for the active chart in View/Chart).

Chart titles initially appear in your computer's screen font. You can have Works display the fonts the chart will have when printed.

Works does as it's told, using the numbers in column B to form pie slices and the titles in column A to label them. So far so good, but there's work to be done. Press Escape to return to the spreadsheet.

Adding Titles and Subtitles

Now enter a title and subtitle so that anyone viewing this chart knows what it represents.

- Press Alt and type **DT** (Data/Titles). You now see the `Titles` dialog box with the blinker in the `Chart title` field.
- Type **ADVERTISING BUDGET** (all in uppercase).
- Press Tab (to move to `Subtitle`).
- Type **(This Year)** (in upper and lowercase) and press Enter.
- To view the chart again, hold down Shift and press F10. You can see the improvement. Now press Escape.

Selecting a Title Font

A large title will surely add pizazz to the printed chart. Works initially lists the fonts available for screen display. Tell it to list the fonts available on your printer instead.

- Press Alt and type **OP** (Options/List Printer Formats). You can now select the printer font.
- Press Alt and type **TF** (Format/Title Font).

Works supplies 16 special fonts used only for printing chart text. They're stored on your Works disk with the extension .RFT (raster font) or .SFT (strokefont). All printers that Works supports that are able to print charts can print these fonts.

Works shows the `Title Font` dialog box containing the special fonts. A 36-point font called Bold Modern B produced the chart title in Figure 7-1. The blinker is in the `Fonts` box.

- Type **B** twice (to choose `Bold Modern B`).
- Press Tab (to move to the `Sizes` box).
- Type **3** as many times as necessary to get the number 36 in reverse video. Press Enter.

Selecting a Subtitle Font

Now choose a subtitle font compatible in style and proportion to the title font.

- Press Alt and type **TO** (Format/Other Font).

Works shows the Other Font dialog box containing the special fonts. The subtitle in Figure 7-1 was produced by Bold Modern B in a 16-point size. The blinker is again in the Fonts box.

- Type **B** twice (to choose Bold Modern B).
- Press Tab (to move to the Sizes box).
- Press Up Arrow as many times as necessary to get the number 16 in reverse video. Press Enter.

Viewing the Title and Subtitle Fonts

Before you can see the title and subtitle fonts on screen, you must tell Works to show them.

- Press Alt and type **OS** (Options/Show Printer Fonts).
- Hold down Shift and press F10 (to draw the chart). Things are really looking up! When you're ready to continue, press Escape to return to the spreadsheet.

Creating a Border

A neat and trim border around the chart can surely add to its eye appeal.

- Press Alt and type **OB** (Options/Show Border).

Now look at all you accomplished in such a short time.

- Hold down Shift and press F10. Neat. When you're ready, press Escape to return to the spreadsheet.

Naming the Pie Chart

Works assigns chart names for you: Chart1, Chart2, Chart3, and so on. Since you can have as many as eight charts stored with each spreadsheet, plain-vanilla names are less than helpful. You need something more descriptive—and what better name for a budget pie chart than BUDGET PIE.

- Press Alt and type **VC** (View/Charts). This brings up the `Charts` dialog box with the blinker on *Chart1*.
- Hold down Alt and type **N** (to move to `Name`).
- Type **BUDGET PIE** and press Enter.

The deed is quickly done and Works replaces `Chart1` with `BUDGET PIE` in the charts list. Press Escape to return to the spreadsheet.

To see BUDGET PIE in the Chart menu, press Alt and type **V**. Now press Escape to return to the spreadsheet.

Printing the Pie Chart

If you have a color monitor and a printer that prints in black-and-white, you can get a better idea of what the printed chart will look like by turning off your screen colors. Use the Options menu's Format For B&W command.

You're all set to print the pie chart, so turn on your printer.

- Press Alt and type **PP** (Print/Print). The settings in the `Print` dialog box (1 copy, most of the others dimmed) are fine, so press Enter.

The percentage indicator at the left of the status line keeps track of how much of the chart has been processed. And here comes your chart in all its pristine glory.

Saving the Pie Chart

Now store the chart on disk with the spreadsheet.

- Press Alt and type **FS** (File/Save).

Creating a Bar Chart

This bar chart has two Y-series, one for each year. Bar and line charts can depict as many as six Y-series.

The advertising budget spreadsheet compares media allocations for a two-year period. You were able to depict only one year's numbers in the pie chart. Now create the bar chart shown in Figure 7-2, which depicts both years.

You can get a head start by copying the pie chart, and then modifying it.

Chart elements (Menu/Command):
A Title (Data/Titles)
B Title font (Format/Title Font)
C Subtitle (Data/Titles)
D Subtitle font (Format/Other Font)
E Border (Options/Border)
F Bar format (Format/Bar)
G Y-Axis
H Y-Axis title (Data/Titles)
I 1st Y-Series (Data/1st Y-Series)
J 2nd Y-Series (Data/2nd Y-Series)
K Gridline (Options/Y-Axis)
L Data point
M Category name
N X-Axis
O Legend (Data/Legends)

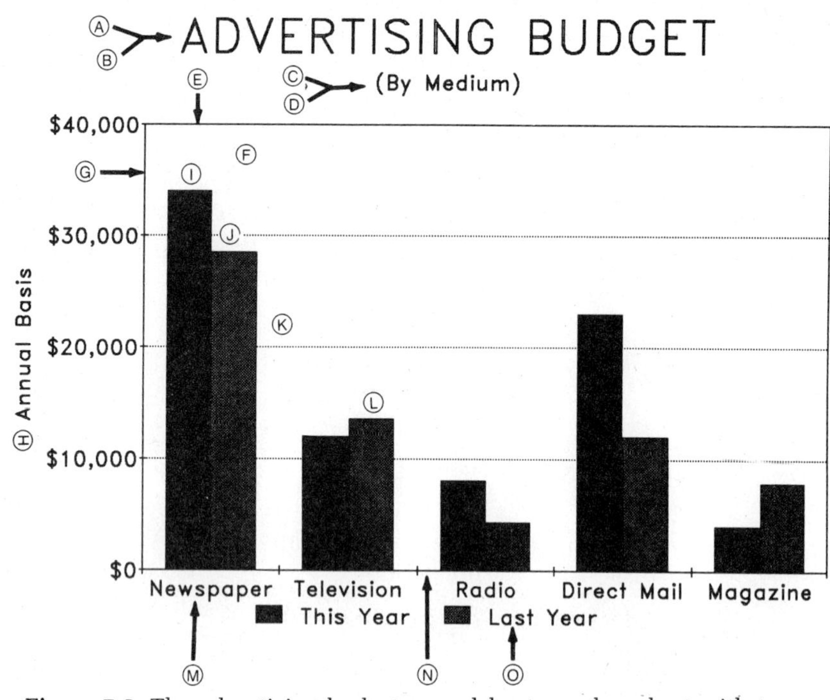

Figure 7-2. The advertising budget spreadsheet as a bar chart with two Y-series. Each bar is a data point

Duplicating an Existing Chart

When you duplicate the pie chart, you retain these custom elements: title, subtitle, title and subtitle fonts, border, and first Y-series (slices in the pie, soon to be bars in the bar chart). You're still in the chart screen.

- Press Alt and type **VC** (View/Charts). Works displays the `Charts` dialog box with the blinker on BUDGET PIE.

  Now copy BUDGET PIE under the name BUDGET BAR.

- Hold down Alt and type **N** (to move to `Name`).
- Type **BUDGET BAR**.
- Hold down Alt and type **C** (to choose `Copy`).

You now have two identical pie charts, one called BUDGET PIE and the other BUDGET BAR. Press Escape to return to the spreadsheet.

Selecting a Bar Chart Format

In the View command, Works puts a marker before the active chart.

BUDGET BAR is the active chart, so have Works transform it into a bar chart.

- Press Alt and type **TB** (Format/Bar).
- To draw the bar chart, hold down Shift and press F10. Nice.

You can now see the titles, border, and Y-series (shown before as pie slices, here as dark bars). Press Escape to return to the spreadsheet.

You need to create these new elements in the bar chart: second Y-series (lighter bars shown in Figure 7-2), gridlines, Y-axis title along the left margin, and legends below the category names.

Defining a Second Y-Series

Define the second Y-series, which is derived from the cells in Column D. Place the cursor on D5.

- Press F8 (to extend the selection).
- Move the cursor to D9 (to select D5 through D9).
- Press Alt and type **D2** (Data/2nd Y-Series).

Adding Gridlines

Y-axis gridlines run horizontally from the left Y-axis, while X-axis gridlines run vertically from the X-axis. Both gridline settings are toggles. Selecting them once turns on the gridlines. Selecting them again turns them off.

Gridlines make a chart easier to read and interpret. Let's show vertical gridlines on the bar chart.

- Press Alt and type **OY** (Options/Y-Axis). Works brings up the `Y-Axis` dialog box.
- Hold down Alt and type **G** (to turn on `Grid Lines`). Press Enter.

Now have Works draw the chart showing the second Y-series and gridlines.

- Hold down Shift and press F10.

When you're ready, press Escape to leave the chart view.

Changing and Adding Titles

This chart reflects a 2-year period, so change the chart subtitle.

- Press Alt and type **DT** (Data/Titles). Works brings up the Titles dialog box showing the title and subtitle you created for the pie chart.
- Hold down Alt and type **S** (to move to Subtitle).
- Type **(By Medium)** and press Tab twice (to move to Y-axis). Now create a title to identify the amounts along the Y-axis.
- Type **Annual Basis** and press Enter.

Adding Legends

To enter text in legends, either type the text in the Legends *dialog box or type a cell location containing the text.*

Before you view the chart again, create the legends that identify the Y-series. You can save typing time by using a title already on the spreadsheet. All you need do is enter the cell location of the title in the Legends dialog box.

- Press Alt and type **DL** (Data/Legends). Works brings up the Legends dialog box with the blinker on *1st Y*.
- Hold down Alt and type **L** (to move to Legend). The title that you want—*This Year*—is in B3.
- Type **B3** and press Enter.

Now do the same for the other title in the legend.

- Press Down Arrow (to move to 2nd Y).
- Hold down Alt and type **L** (to move to Legend). The title Last Year is in D3.
- Type **D3** and press Enter.

Press Escape to return to the spreadsheet. Now redraw the chart.

- Hold down Shift and press F10.

When you've seen enough for now, press Escape to return to the spreadsheet.

Printing Your Bar Chart

If you have a color monitor and a printer that prints in black-and-white, you can get an idea of the printed result before printing by turning off your screen colors. Use the Options menu's Format For B&W command.

Your chart is complete and you can print it. Be sure your printer is still turned on.

- Press Alt and type **PP** (Print/Print). Press Enter.

As it did when you printed the pie chart, the percentage indicator on the status line shows how much of the bar chart has already been processed. When it reaches 100%, the chart rolls off the printer.

Saving the Bar Chart

Now store the bar chart on disk with the spreadsheet.

- Press Alt and type **FS** (File/Save).

You now have two charts associated with the advertising budget spreadsheet. In the next chapter, you'll explore the chart menus and take a leisurely tour of other Works charts.

Exploring the Chart Menus

Charts have a happy knack of presenting facts in forms that are easy to interpret, understand, and remember. Properly executed, they can help get your points across better than a sea of numbers.

The Works menus are packed with easy-to-use commands that can sharpen the visual impact of your charts, and, as a consequence, your presentations and reports. You've worked with many of these commands in the chart workout. In this chapter, you'll find out more about the familiar ones and get to know the new ones.

A font is a family of letters, numbers, and symbols in the same design. Fonts are usually available in different sizes, referred to as points or pitches.

Fonts have an important bearing on the visual impact of your charts, and Works offers many choices. The fonts mentioned in the following discussion are supplied by Works. Any printer supported by Works that can print charts can print those fonts. Feel free to experiment until you get the effect you want.

The File Menu

The commands in the chart's File menu—Create New File, Open Existing File, Save, Save As, Close, File Management, Run Other Programs, Convert, and Exit Works—are the same and work the same as those in the spreadsheet's File menu. Refer to Chapter 6 for details on these commands.

As with everything else you do, it's a good idea to store your developing chart on disk every 15 minutes or so.

The Print Menu

The commands in the Print menu let you customize the appearance of the printed chart, specify the number of copies to print, and tell Works where to print them.

Print...

The active chart is the one shown in the View command's Charts list with a marker before it.

The Print command prints the active chart. You can specify how many copies (Works proposes 1) and whether to print the chart to the disk instead of the printer. If you installed a plotter during Works setup, you can turn on the Slow pen speed check box to improve plotting quality. If you didn't install a plotter, Works dims this check box to show that it's not available. Most dot matrix and laser printers do a good job of printing charts. For presentation prints or overhead transparencies, you're likely to want a plotter.

Page Setup & Margins

The Page Setup & Margins command lets you specify margins, chart size, paper size, and chart orientation on the printed page. Chart orientation can be portrait (across the width) or landscape (down the length) of the paper.

The advertising budget bar chart you printed in the last chapter (refer to Figure 7-2) has the standard landscape orientation. Figure 8-1 shows the same chart printed with a portrait orientation. Certain modifications were needed to fit a long chart into a narrower width and to freshen up the result.

Y-Axis Scale To trim the width of the numbers on the Y-axis, I overtyped each 5-digit number on the spreadsheet with its first 2 digits, and then gave them the General format.

X-Axis Categories To avoid truncated titles on the X-axis, I shortened two of the category names—Television to TV and Direct Mail to Dir Mail.

Margins To provide more stretching room, I reduced the left margin from 1 inch to .5 inch (Print/Page Setup & Margins).

Chart Size — To accommodate the new orientation, I changed the chart size from 9 by 6 inches to 5 by 7.5 inches (Print/Page Setup & Margins). This was a matter of playing around with different sizes until everything looked right.

Titles — To give it a new look, I changed the main title font to 38-point Bold Roman B (Format/Title Font) and made the Y-axis title 14-point Modern C (Format/Other Font), changing it to read *Thousands of Dollars*.

Gridlines — To enhance the overall effect, I added vertical gridlines (Options/X-Axis).

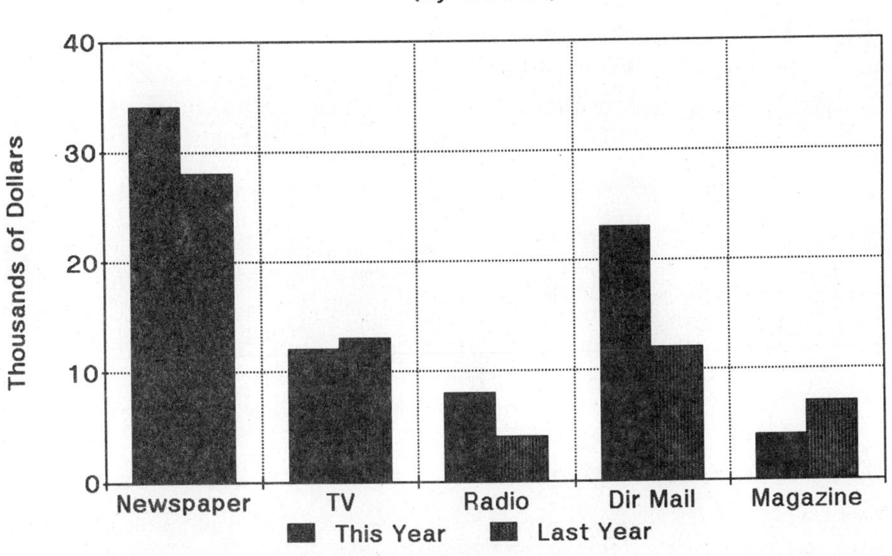

Figure 8-1. The advertising budget bar chart in a portrait orientation with two-way gridlines

Preview...

The Preview command lets you see how your chart lays out on paper before you actually print it. You can then decide if you need to change any print or display settings. You can print directly from Preview by typing **P**.

Printer Setup...

If the selected printer doesn't have enough memory to print a large chart in high resolution, use lower resolution instead. Chances are, the result will be highly acceptable.

If you specified more than one printer during the Works setup steps, the Printer Setup command lets you choose which printer to use to print your chart. If you specified one printer only, Works uses that printer. The `Graphics` box offers a choice of printing resolutions (fineness of line) expressed in dots per inch (dpi).

This command also lets you change page feed from continuous to manual, which is useful when you want to feed single sheets to the printer. It also gives you the choice of which communication port to connect to your printer.

If you want to add or replace printer drivers, be aware that drivers on the Works Setup disk are stored in compressed form (.CPR extension). To use these drivers, you must go through the Works setup steps so Works can decompress the driver. Drivers stored on the Supplemental Printer disks have a .PRD extension. You can simply copy these drivers directly into the Works subdirectory.

The Data Menu

The Data menu lets you designate numbers as Y-series and category labels as X-series, and you can create other identifiers such as titles and legends.

Y-Series

A Y-series consists of data points plotted from the Y-axis of a chart. Each number in a designated range of cells on a spreadsheet is a data point. Works then shows all of the designated data points as slices in a pie chart, bars in a bar chart, or markers in a line or hi-lo-close chart. Works can chart as many as six Y-series. The Y-Series commands (1st, 2nd, 3rd, 4th, 5th, and 6th) let you tell Works which range of cells belongs in which Y-series.

X-Series

The X-Series command lets you create category labels along the X-axis of a bar or line chart or the slices in a pie chart. As with a

Y-series, Works gathers this information from the designated range of cells on your spreadsheet.

Series...

The Series command lets you delete information in a Y-series or an X-series. With a Y-series, Works deletes every data point in the series. With an X-series, Works deletes the category labels along the X-axis, or, in a pie chart, the labels (but not the percentages) for each slice. You can also use the Series command to go to one of the series shown in the list box.

Titles...

Titles and subtitles can display up to 38 characters, depending on font size. If your title resembles a cell location, type quotation marks (") first, before typing the text.

The Titles command lets you enter the text for a main title, subtitle, and axis titles. You can either type a title into the appropriate field or enter the location of the cell containing the title.

The main title appears at the top of the chart with the subtitle directly below it. The axis titles appear on the X-axis and the left and right Y-axes (if you have a right Y-axis). Works centers each title in its respective position.

Legends...

Legends are labels that identify each Y-series in a chart. With the Legends command, you can show the name of the Y-series and the marker, line, or pattern used in formatting that series. Legends appear at the bottom of the chart unless you hide them by turning off the Show Legends command in the Options menu.

You can have up to 19 characters in each legend, depending on the number of legends. The more legends, the fewer characters in each. To delete a legend, delete its name in the **Legend** field. Use the Delete key.

Data Labels...

The Data Labels command labels the data points (bars or lines) in a Y-series, using words or numbers from a range of spreadsheet cells. You can select the Y-series you want to label from the list in the Series box. In this command, you can also delete data labels and go to the range holding the labels for the selected Y-series.

The Format Menu

The Format menu lists eight common chart types. Works initially plots your spreadsheet information as a bar chart. When you select any of the other chart types, Works immediately replots in the new format. Here's a description of each chart type and how you can use it to portray your spreadsheet facts to their best advantage.

Pie

A pie chart shows the numbers in one Y-series as slices in a pie. Each slice represents a data point in the Y-series. Works calculates the percentage contribution of each slice to the whole and sizes it accordingly.

Figure 8-2 shows an exploded version of the budget pie chart in Figure 7-1 with a new allocation for bulletin board advertising (the electronic kind). In the budget spreadsheet (please refer to Figure 5-1), I inserted a row between Radio and Direct Mail and entered BBS in A8 and 3800 in B8. The insertion was within the range of cells defined as the Y-series, so Works recalculated the percentages and adjusted the size of the slices.

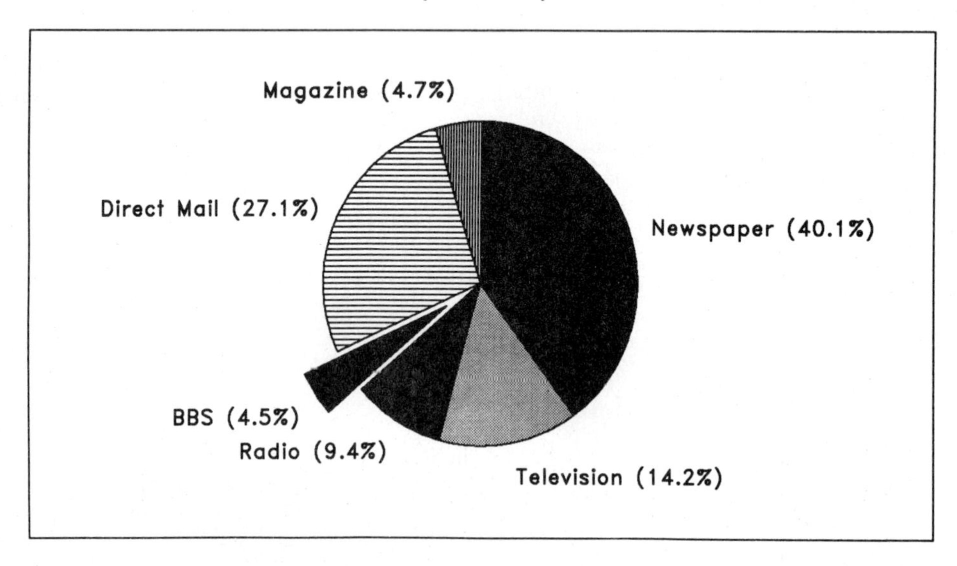

Figure 8-2. The exploded version of the budget pie chart with an allocation for bulletin board advertising and a new pattern arrangement

The exploded effect was created in the Format menu's Data Format command. Works reduced the size of the pie and exploded (separated) the selected slice from the rest of the pie. You can explode as many slices as you want, even every slice. Switching the patterns of the slices (also in the Data Format command) adds a bit of variety. The Newspaper allocation is now in Dense, Television is in Sparse, and the newcomer BBS is in Solid.

Bar

You can mix bars and lines in a bar chart by converting a bar into a line in the Options menu's Mixed Line & Bar command.

A bar chart shows the numbers in each Y-series as bars perpendicular to the X-axis. Each bar represents a data point measured and plotted from the Y-axis. Works sizes each bar relative to the total of all the bars in that Y-series. You can have up to six Y-series in a bar chart, which makes it easy to compare increases and decreases over a period of time.

The bar chart in Figure 8-3 depicts the same information as the one in Figure 7-2 and your printout. Here, it shows dollar amounts—called *data labels*—above the bars and no gridlines. Each bar duo is called a *category*. Therefore, this chart has a newspaper category, a television category, a radio category, and so on.

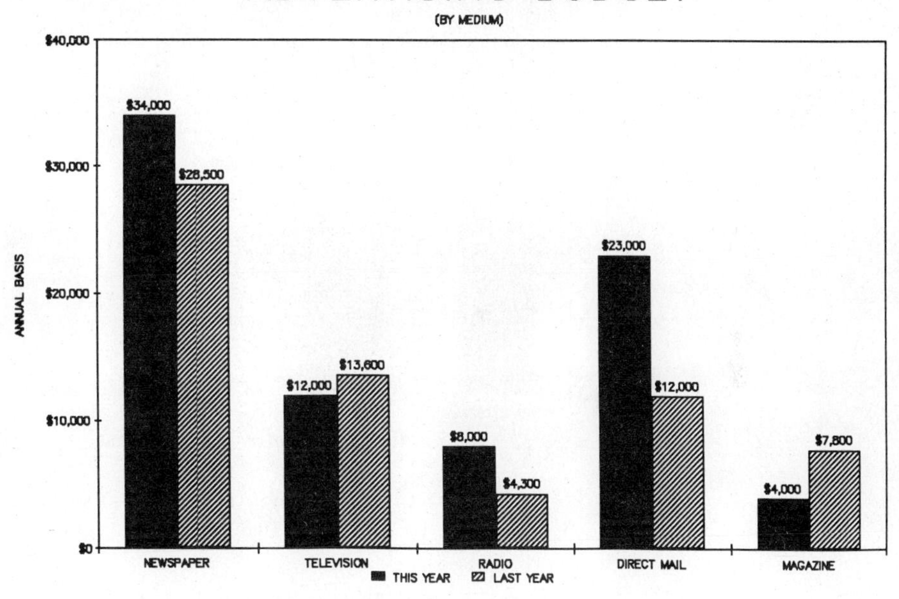

Figure 8-3. The budget bar chart showing data labels (dollar amounts above the bars)

To prevent the data labels from bumping into the bars, they appear in 8-point Modern B (Format/Other Font). The category names, now in the same small font, are made more prominent by putting them in uppercase on the spreadsheet. The main title is now in 30-point Bold Modern B to keep it in proportion. The snappy stripe in the second Y-series is courtesy of the Format menu's Data Format command.

Stacked Bar

The stacked bar chart shown in Figure 8-4 stacks bars one on top of the other, starting with the first Y-series. Each bar in the stack represents the unit contribution of each number in each Y-series. The result is the combined total of the spreadsheet numbers in each category.

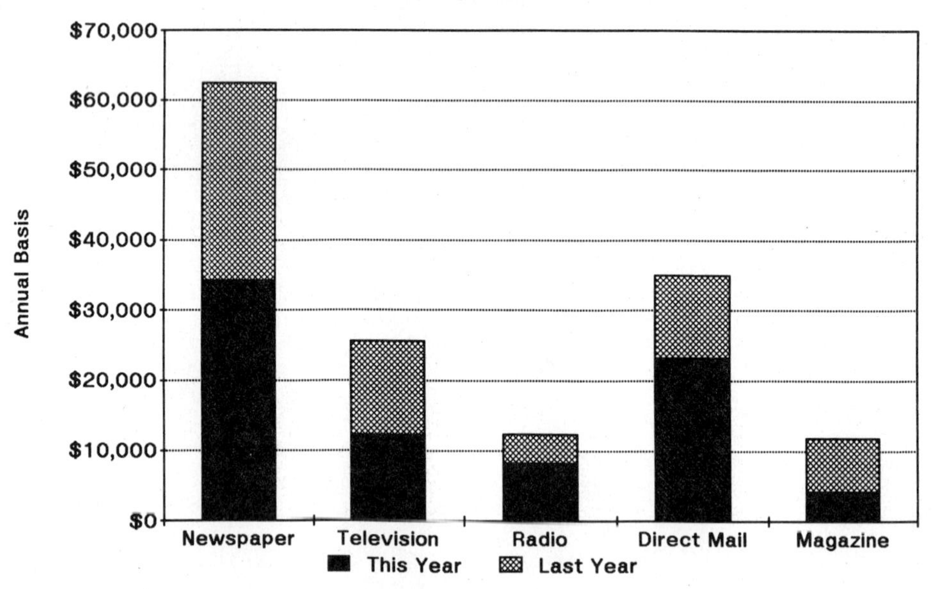

Figure 8-4. A stacked bar chart with the second Y-series stacked on top of the first

Here, the main title is in 36-point Bold Modern B, and the other titles are in 14-point Modern C. The Format menu's Data Format command produced the patterns in both series.

100% Bar

Like a stacked bar chart, the 100% bar chart shown in Figure 8-5 stacks bars one on top of the other, starting with the first Y-series.

Each bar is of equal length to show the percentage contribution of each number in a Y-series to the total in each category.

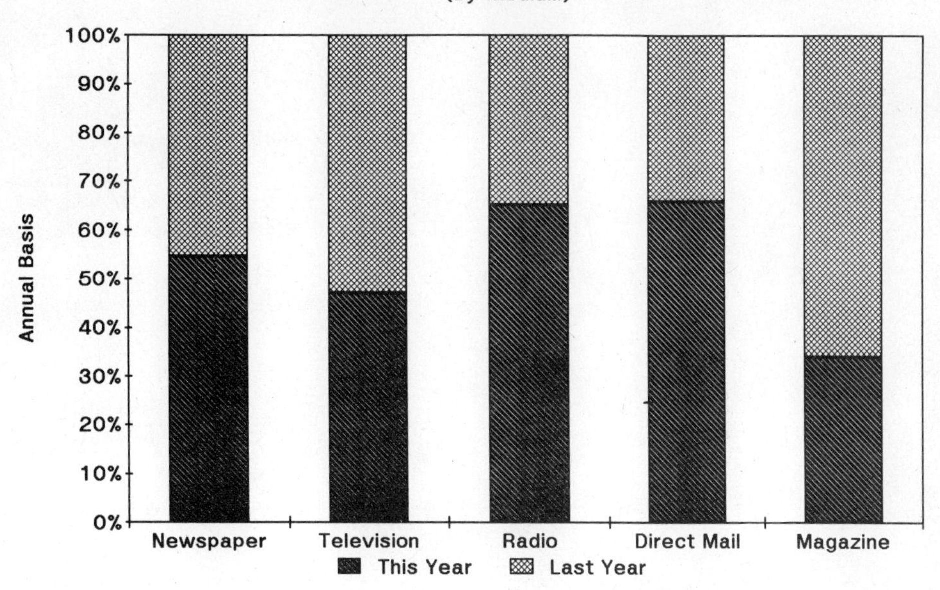

Figure 8-5. A 100% bar chart

This time, the main title font is 36-point Bold Roman B, with the other titles in 14-point Modern C. The Format menu's Data Format command produced the same patterns as those in Figure 8-4.

Line

You can create a combined line chart (standard line or area line) and bar chart in the Options menu's Mixed Line & Bar command.

A line chart shows the numbers in each Y-series as markers connected by lines. Works measures and plots each Y-series from the X-axis. Figure 8-6 shows the restaurant sales spreadsheet that provides the information for the charts in Figures 8-7 and 8-8.

The City numbers in column B constitute the first Y-series, the Suburb numbers in column C the second Y-series, and the Resort numbers in column D the third Y-series. The months in column A provide the labels for the X-axis.

In keeping with the chart's airy look, the main title appears in 30-point Bold Italic Roman B and the other titles are in 12-point Modern C. The Format menu's Data Format command produced the markers on the lines.

	A	B	C	D	E
1		DINING-OUT TRENDS			
2		(Typical Year - in 1000's)			
3	==========	==========	==========	==========	
4	Month	City	Suburb	Resort	
5	----------	----------	----------	----------	
6	Jan	$450	$375	$150	
7	Feb	$475	$350	$75	
8	Mar	$500	$400	$50	
9	Apr	$750	$47	$46	
10	May	$975	$45	$395	
11	Jun	$866	$267	$450	
12	Jul	$777	$325	$895	
13	Aug	$754	$268	$1,300	
14	Sep	$650	$86	$1,155	
15	Oct	$675	$75	$650	
16	Nov	$800	$70	$555	
17	Dec	$1,023	$240	$780	

Figure 8-6. The restaurant sales spreadsheet that provides the information for the line charts in Figures 8-7 and 8-8

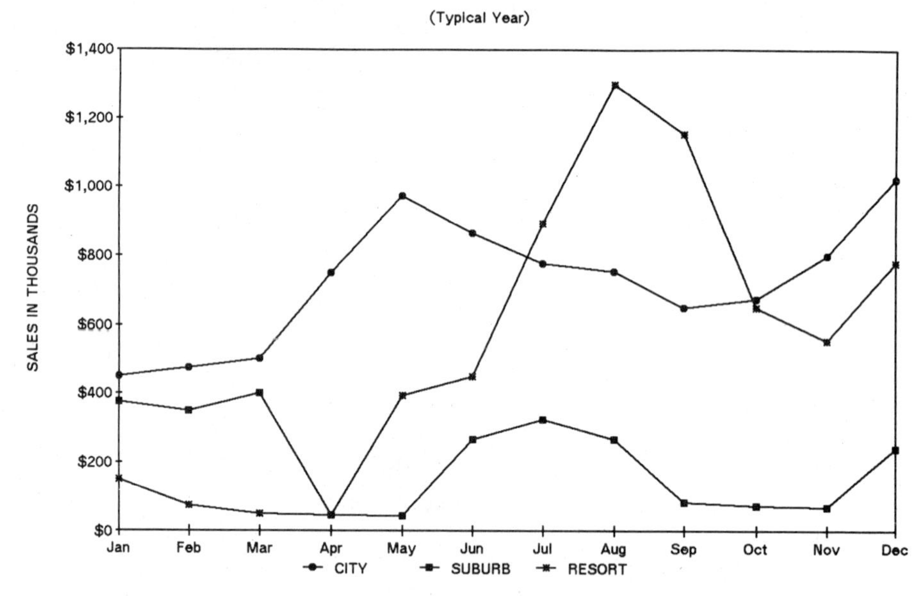

Figure 8-7. A line chart containing three Y-series that show eating-out trends in different areas during a one-year period

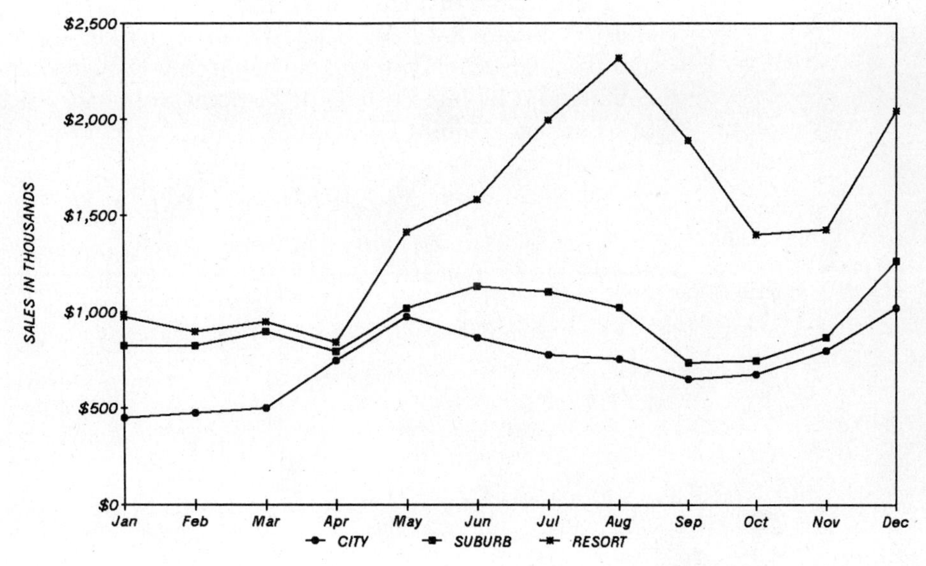

Figure 8-8. An area line (stacked line) chart that reflects the combined trend in all three areas during one year

Area Line

An area line chart, like a stacked line chart, measures and plots the first Y-series from the X-axis, and then each additional Y-series from the Y-series immediately below, instead of from the X-axis.

Figure 8-8 shows an area line chart depicting the same information as Figure 8-7. Works plots the first Y-series (City) from the X-axis, the second Y-series (Suburb) from the City series, and the third Y-series (Resort) from the Suburb series. As a result, the Resort series shows the combined total of the spreadsheet numbers in each month.

The main title is in 30-point Bold Roman Italic B, the same as in Figure 8-7. To create a different effect, the other titles are in 12-point Italic Modern C.

Hi-Lo-Close

You can connect the high markers by selecting a line style in the Patterns box of the Format menu's Data Format command.

The hi-lo-close chart shows the range between the highest and lowest value in each category. Each marker on the vertical line represents one value. This type of chart is commonly used to show the high, low, and closing prices on the stock market pages of a newspaper.

You need at least two Y-series to create it, and can include as many as six Y-series in one chart.

The chart in Figure 8-9 reflects the information in the spreadsheet in Figure 8-10. Works assigns the marker shapes for high, low, and closing, which you can change in the Format menu's Data Format command. The main title is in 34-point Bold Modern B, and the other titles are in 12-point Modern C.

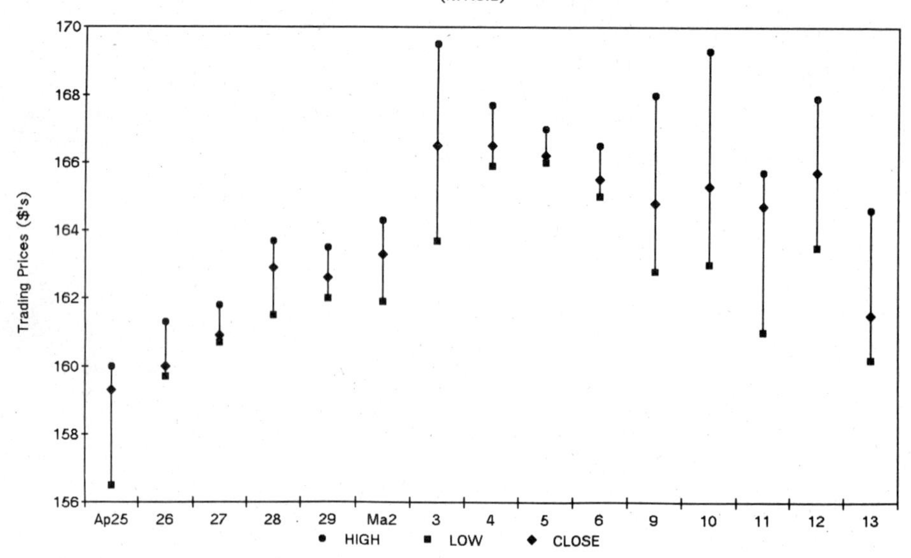

Figure 8-9. A hi-lo-close chart that graphs the market index in Figure 8-10

X-Y

An X-Y chart (also called a *scatter chart* or *scattergram*) uses pairs of spreadsheet numbers to plot points along the X-axis and Y-axis. Figure 8-11 depicts the salaries shown in Figure 8-12 as an X-Y chart.

The main title appears in 17-point Bold Modern C, and the other titles are in 12-point Modern C.

Title Font... and Other Font...

These commands let you choose the font and font size for the chart titles. Title Font handles the main title, while Other Font handles all others, including the chart subtitle, axis titles, data point labels, and legends.

	A	B	C	D	E
1		MARKET INDEX (N.Y.S.E.)			
2		TRADING PRICES			
3	==========	==========	==========	==========	
4	WEEK ENDING	HIGH	LOW	CLOSE	
5	----------	----------	----------	----------	
6	Ap25	160	156.5	159.3	
7	26	161.3	159.7	160	
8	27	161.8	160.7	160.9	
9	28	163.7	161.5	162.9	
10	29	163.5	162	162.6	
11	Ma2	164.3	161.9	163.3	
12	3	169.5	163.7	166.5	
13	4	167.7	165.9	166.5	
14	5	167	166	166.2	
15	6	166.5	165	165.5	
16	9	168	162.8	164.8	
17	10	169.3	163	165.3	
18	11	165.7	161	164.7	
19	12	167.9	163.5	165.7	
20	13	164.6	160.2	161.5	

Figure 8-10. A market index spreadsheet that provides the information for the hi-lo-close chart in Figure 8-9

	A	B	C	D
1	EMPLOYEE SALARIES			
2	==========	==========		
3	Salaries	Number of		
4	(in Thousands)	Employees		
5	----------	----------		
6	57	2		
7	55	1		
8	47	3		
9	40	6		
10	37	5		
11	30	12		
12	27	3		
13	25	15		

Figure 8-11. The employee salaries spreadsheet that provides the information for the chart in Figure 8-12

The list boxes in each command initially show the screen font and size. When you turn on the List Printer Formats command in the Options menu, Works shows the font styles and sizes for your printer.

Data Format...

Different printers provide different choices of colors, patterns, and markers.

A chart's data format consists of colors and patterns of bars and slices in bar and pie charts and line types and markers in line charts. Works assigns these data formats each time you create a chart. The Data Format command lets you format each Y-series yourself or format some

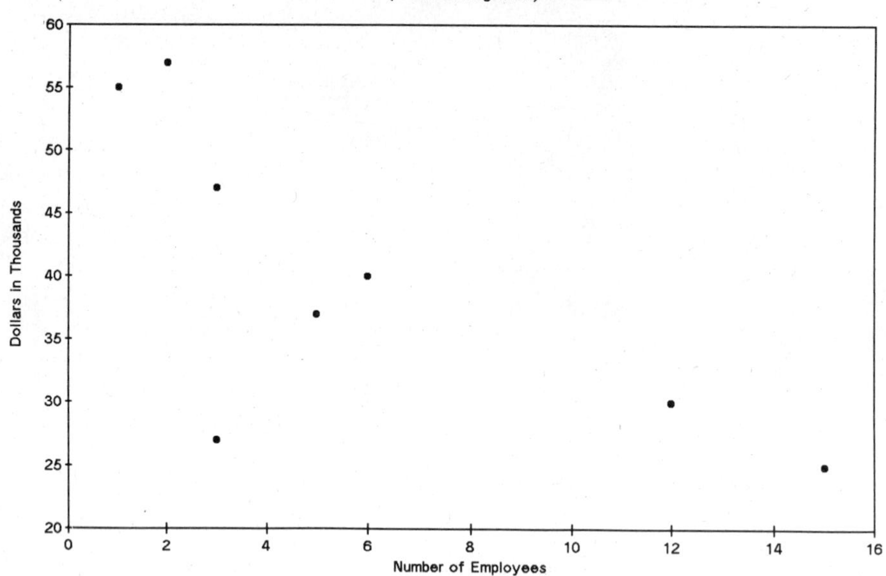

Figure 8-12. The employee salaries plotted on an X-Y chart (also known as a scatter chart)

yourself and let Works do the others. You can also explode (as shown in Figure 8-2) or unexplode slices in a pie chart when using this command.

The Options Menu

The first four commands in the Options menu—Works Settings, Calculator, Alarm Clock, and Dial This Number—are the same and work the same in every Works application.

(Please refer to the Options menu in Chapter 6 for an explanation of these commands, and to Chapter 1, "The Works Environment," for more details on the desk accessories.)

The rest of the commands are strictly art-of-the-chart. They let you expand your chart repertoire, add visual and text elements, view your chart on screen in black and white, and display the selected fonts on screen.

X-Axis...

The X-Axis command behaves differently depending on whether you're working with a bar or line chart or with an X-Y chart. In each type of chart, Works lets you turn gridlines on or off. Then divergence occurs.

If the active chart is a bar or a line chart, the X-Axis dialog box lets you specify how many category labels to skip before showing the next one—for example, you can set it to skip every other one —which prevents a mishmash of overlapping labels.

The values and intervals on a logarithmic scale are always powers of 10, such as 0.1, 1, 10, 100, 1000, and so on.

If the active chart is an X-Y chart, the X-Axis dialog box lets you define the numerical starting and ending points on the X-axis and the amount to skip between numbers (for example, count by 15's). In this command, you can switch from standard linear to logarithmic scaling. Logarithmic scaling is best used for charting Y-series with broad numerical ranges, as on spreadsheets that show exponential growth rates.

Y-Axis...

Changing the intervals on a scale can improve the appearance or change the emphasis of a chart.

The Y-Axis command, similar to the X-Axis command, lets you turn gridlines on and off, define the starting points, ending points, and intervals on the Y-axis scale, choose the type of Y-axis format (normal, stacked, 100%, or hi-lo) for bar and line charts, and switch from linear to logarithmic scaling.

Right Y-Axis...

The Right Y-Axis command lets you determine the scale and type of the right Y-Axis. If your chart doesn't have a right Y-axis, Works dims this command.

Two Y-Axes...

The Two Y-Axes command creates a second Y-axis at the right end of the chart, which lets you chart information on two different Y-scales. Figure 8-13 shows a two Y-axes chart that depicts employee productivity. The left scale charts the total annual sales for each division, while the right scale charts the sales based on the number of employees in the division.

The relative size of the bars in each category reveal some fascinating facts. The NY division leads in sales, but sales per employee is relatively low. The GA division has lower sales than the rest but utilizes its employees with greatest efficiency.

The main title appears in 36-point Bold Modern B, and the other titles are in 14-point Modern C. Figure 8-14 shows the spreadsheet that feeds the facts to this chart.

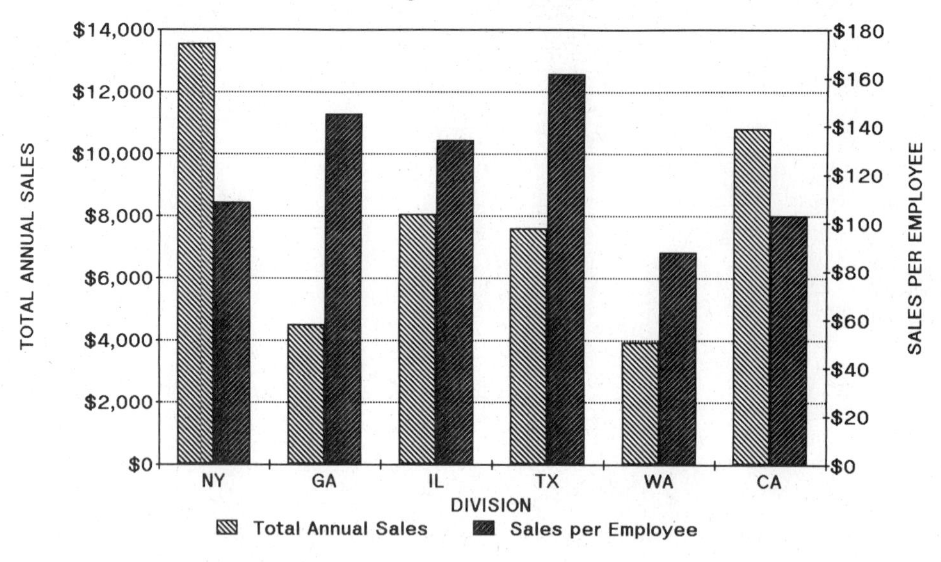

Figure 8-13. A two Y-axes bar chart that measures employee productivity

	A	B	C	D
1		SALES BY DIVISION		
2		(Figures in Thousands)		
3	============	============	============	============
4				Sales per
5	Division	Sales	Employees	Employee
6	------------	------------	------------	------------
7	NY	$13,550	125	$108
8	GA	$4,500	31	$145
9	IL	$8,050	60	$134
10	TX	$7,600	47	$162
11	WA	$3,950	45	$88
12	CA	$10,800	105	$103
13		--------	----	
14		$48,450	413	

Figure 8-14. The spreadsheet that feeds information to the employee productivity chart

Mixed Line & Bar

The Mixed Line & Bar command transforms any chart with at least two Y-series into the special format shown in Figure 8-15. You can specify which Y-series to display as bars and which Y-series to display as lines.

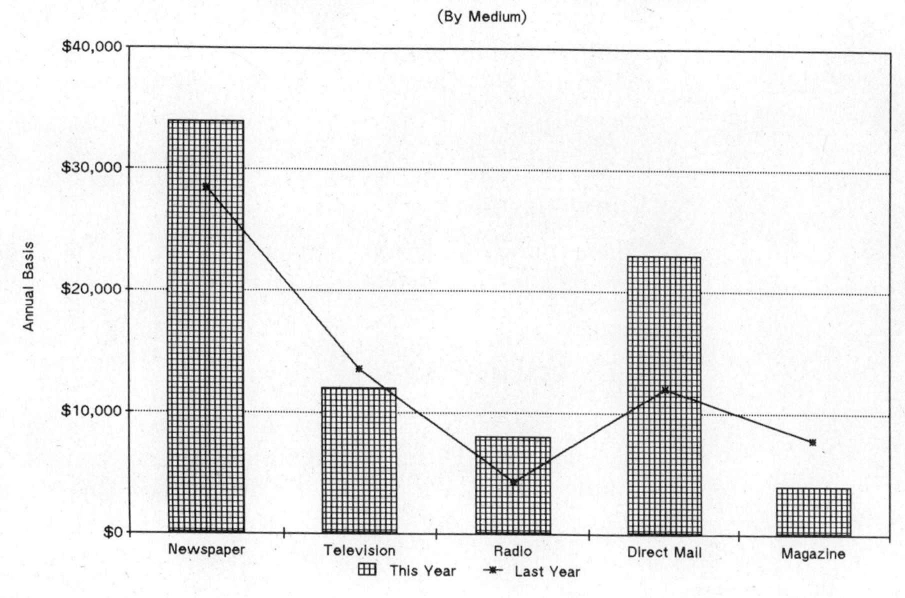

Figure 8-15. The mixed line and bar chart version of the advertising budget

The main title appears in 28-point Bold Roman B, and the other titles are in 12-point Modern C.

Format For B&W

If you're working with a color monitor but printing in black-and-white, this command can give you a good idea of how your printed chart will look before you print it. Selecting the command once turns it on, and selecting it again turns it off.

List Printer Formats

If you have more than one printer, be sure to select the printer you'll be using to print your charts before choosing this command.

You can see the formats available for your screen or printer in the list boxes in the Format menu's Data Format command. Works routinely lists the formats available for your screen, as indicated by the absence of a marker before the List Printer Formats command. When you choose the List Printer Formats command, Works marks the command name and lists the formats available for your printer.

Show Printer Fonts

Until you turn on the Show Printer Fonts command, Works displays your chart using your computer's screen fonts. When you turn on this command and select larger fonts, Works displays the chart using those fonts.

Show Legends

When you create legends, Works displays the legends. You can hide legends and turn them on again with the Show Legends command.

Show Border

Works, obviously, draws a border at the X-axis and Y-axis of every chart but pies. Turning on the Show Border command tells Works to complete the border on other sides of the chart. To turn off the border, choose the Show Border command again.

The View Menu

The commands in the chart's View menu—Spreadsheet, New Chart, Charts, and a list of existing charts—are identical to the spreadsheet's View menu.

Spreadsheet

The Spreadsheet command returns you to the spreadsheet menus. You can get there faster with the F10 shortcut key.

New Chart

After Works speed-charts a bar chart, you can replace the bar format with any of the other chart formats available in the Format or Options menus.

The New Chart command creates a new bar chart through a process called *speed charting*. If the designated information is in contiguous cells, simply select the cell ranges before starting the New Chart command, and Works speed-charts the Y-series, X-series, and legends in one step.

If the information is scattered throughout the spreadsheet, select one series that Works can speed-chart, and then select each of the other series and identify it in the Data menu's Series commands.

Charts...

The Charts command brings up a dialog box loaded with handy options that let you name, rename, delete, or copy a chart. Works names charts Chart1, Chart2, and so on. To make them easy to identify in the list of existing charts, give each chart a descriptive name.

Chart List

The only way to get into the chart screen from the spreadsheet without creating a new chart first is to type the number of a chart in the list, and then press Escape after Works displays it.

The Chart List presents a list of existing charts, each preceded by a number. When you type the number, Works displays the chart. Works then puts a mark before that number in the chart list to show that it's the active chart.

You can view the active chart by pressing Shift+F10 in the chart screen or spreadsheet screen. If you view it from the spreadsheet screen, Works returns you to the spreadsheet (not the chart screen) when you press Escape.

The Window Menu

The commands in the chart's Window menu—Move, Size, Maximize, Arrange All, and Split—are the same, and they work the same as those in the spreadsheet's Window menu. Refer to Chapter 6 for details on these commands.

The Help Menu

The commands in the chart's Help menu—Using Help Index, Getting Started, Keyboard, Mouse, and Works Tutorial—are also the same and work the same as those in the spreadsheet's Help menu. Again, please refer to Chapter 6 for details on these commands.

Where Were Those Gridlines?

Works provides a wealth of ways to get the best-looking chart on paper—so many, in fact, that you may not remember them all, or you may forget how to find the one you do remember. To give you every possible advantage, Table 8-1 maps the route to the perfect printed chart. The first column shows the destination, the second column the expressway, and the third column the exit ramp.

Table 8-1. Commands that affect the printed chart

Keyword	Menu	Command
Black-and-white screen display	Options	Format For B&W
Border	Options	Show Border
Colors	Format	Data Format
Create new chart	View	New Chart
Data labels	Data	Data Labels
Exploded pie	Format	Data Format
Format (chart type)	Format	(bold letter)
Fonts:		
Main title	Format	Title Font
Other titles	Format	Other Font
Gridlines:		
Horizontal	Options	Y-Axis
Vertical	Options	X-Axis
Height	Print	Page Setup & Margins
Legends:		
Create/delete	Data	Legends
Display/hide	Options	Show Legends
Label frequency	Options	X-Axis
Logarithmic scale:		
X-axis	Options	X-Axis
Y-axis	Options	Y-Axis
Margins	Print	Page Setup & Margins
Markers	Format	Data Format
Mixed line & bar chart	Options	Mixed Line & Bar

Keyword	Menu	Command
Orientation (landscape/portrait)	Print	Page Setup & Margins
Page length/width	Print	Page Setup & Margins
Patterns	Format	Data Format
Preview	Print	Preview
Printer fonts	Options	List Printer Formats
Printer setup	Print	Printer Setup
Right Y-axis scale	Options	Right Y-Axis
Right and left Y-axes	Options	Two Y-Axes
Title text (Main, Subtitle, Axis)	Data	Titles
Width	Print	Page Setup & Margins
X-series:		
Create	Data	X-Series
Labels delete	Data	Series
Y-axis scale:		
Minimum/maximum value	Options	Y-Axis
Normal/stacked/100%/hi-lo	Options	Y-Axis
Y-series:		
Create	Data	(number)
Delete	Data	Series

To round out this roundup of chart information, Table 8-2 provides a handy reference to the chart numbers.

Table 8-2. Useful chart numbers

Parameter	Number
Charts in each spreadsheet	1 to 8
Y-series in a chart	1 to 6
X-series in a chart	1
Maximum length of a chart title or subtitle	38 characters
Maximum length of a Y-axis title	27 characters

(*continued*)

Table 8-2. *(continued)*

Parameter	Number
Maximum length of a legend title (actual length depends on number of legends)	19 characters
Legends	1 to 6
Maximum length of a data label	9 characters
Length of a chart name in a displayed list	1 to 15 characters
Standard print settings:	
Top margin	1 inch
Left margin	1.3 inches
Chart height	9 inches
Chart width	6 inches
Page length	11 inches
Page width	8.5 inches

P A R T

three

The Database

Database Essentials

Imagine keeping track of thousands of customers and clients, addresses and appointments, inventories and investments, projects and personnel, sales and schedules, and any other information important to you. Imagine having instant access to all that information, culling only the information you want, and generating reports with lightning speed. Imagine no more flipping index cards, sifting piles of paper, or hunting for misfiled files. Impossible dream, you say? No, merely the dazzle of the database.

A database keeps facts at your fingertips.

A database is an electronic file cabinet—a place to store, scan, search, sort, and select information. Like its metal-drawer counterpart, a database can contain many records arranged in a logical way from which you can pull specific records. Unlike its drawered counterpart, it lets you arrange and rearrange information at will, based on the task at hand, scan records selected according to one or several pieces of information, and merge information from separate drawers with only a few keystrokes.

Starting with a customer database of names, addresses, and sales histories, for example, you can select customers by region, product, or amount of sales, send regional customer lists to sales managers, merge names and addresses with marketing material, send out personalized form letters and newsletters, and generate mailing labels as often as you wish—free of charge, up-to-date, and without typos.

Getting Acquainted with the Database

This chapter discusses the essential "whys" and "hows" of the Works database. It describes the activities in a database, the database screens, the kinds of information you can keep in a database, how to organize and retrieve information, and the report-generating processes.

You can get a good idea of how the database works by reading the text and referring to the illustrations. You don't have to keep Works on screen all the time. It will make it easier to have Works up and running at certain times, however, particularly while you read about the database screens.

When you're ready to work with Works, fire up your computer and follow the instructions in the section "Loading Works," in the Introduction to this book. At the Works gateway, type **ND** (Create New File/New Database) to create a new database file.

Database Definitions

A database has a vocabulary of its own, so let's start with a few definitions:

Character: A letter, number, symbol, or blank space. There are 9 characters in the words *Last Name*; 5 characters in *A-123*.

Entry: An individual piece of information, such as the last name *Smith*, or the product description *Green Widgets*.

Field: One type of information, such as the last names in the database or all of the product descriptions.

A database can have 4096 records, and each record can have as many as 256 fields.

Record: All information about a particular person or product, such as the last name, first name, address, and phone number of Paul Smith, or the description, part number, and price of a widget.

File: A collection of all records about people or products; in other words, a database.

Creating a Database

Creating a database involves three major activities: design, input, and output. These activities take place in the Form, List, Query, and

Report screens. Figure 9-1 shows the flow of activity among the screens and the keystrokes that take you from one to another.

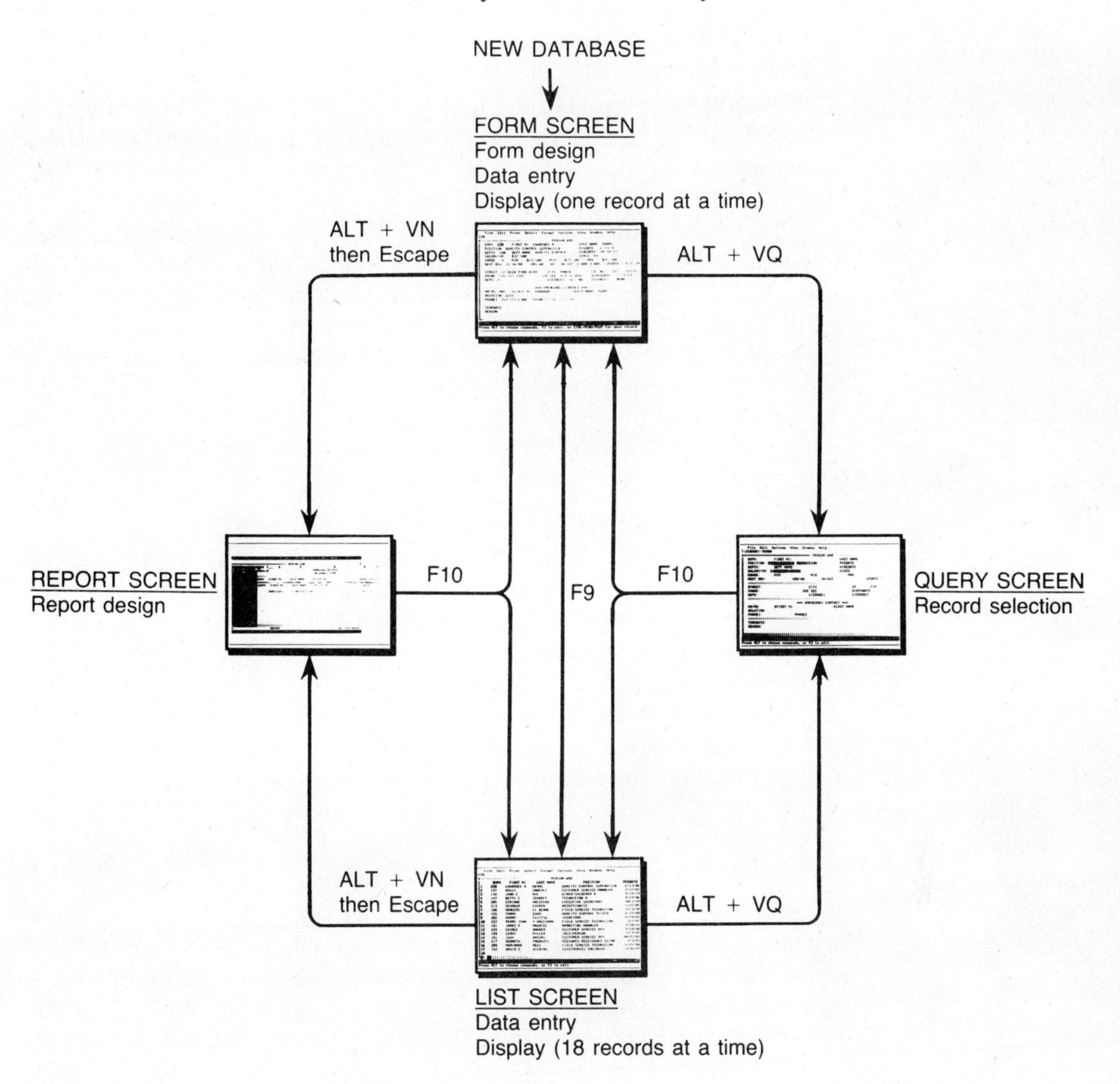

Figure 9-1. The flow of activity in the Form, List, Query, and Report screens

Database Design

Thoughtful planning is the key to successful database design. Planning involves deciding on the purpose of the database (that's basic!), the kind and quantity of information you want to store, and the types of reports you need to generate both on screen and on paper. Works is flexible and forgiving, and you can make design changes at virtually any stage, but changes do take time and many can be avoided by careful planning.

Turning your plan into reality involves creating fields to hold the information, which you can do in either the Form or List screen. Works assumes you want to start by creating a form, so the Form screen is the first to appear.

In the Form screen, you can move fields around to different positions on the form (you can even have more than one per row).

The Form and List screens share field names, entries, and other elements. The big difference is how Works lays them out on the screen. The Form screen shows field names and entries in rows down the left side of the screen; the List screen shows them in columns across the top of the screen. Pressing F9 shuttles you between the Form and List screens.

Database Input

Entering information in fields is similar to filling in the blanks on a form.

Input activities start with entering information in the fields you create. The Form screen shows one record only, while the List screen shows multiple records. Each time you fill a record in the Form screen, Works presents another. In the List screen, you can fill record after record in row after row.

Input also means keeping records current by inserting, updating, and deleting existing information. You can enter and maintain information in either the Form screen or List screen.

Database Output

The output of a database includes the screen displays and printed reports that you generate from information in the records. You can vary the content and appearance of these reports by doing such things as adding report titles, arranging records in alphabetical, numerical, or chronological order, selecting records, hiding and revealing records, and using formulas and functions to produce calculations.

The Query and Report screens come into play during these activities. In the Query screen, you can tell Works which records to display or print, while in the Report screen, you can design and customize your printed report. You access the Query screen by pressing Alt+VQ (View/Query), and you access the Report screen by pressing

Alt+VN (View/New Report) or Alt+V and a report number listed in the View menu.

Pressing F10 returns you to the screen you left (either Form or List) before bringing up the Query or Report screen.

The Form Screen

Although the Form and List screens differ in significant ways, they also have much in common. Figure 9-2 shows the Form screen, which is your first view of the database. Let's examine it closely.

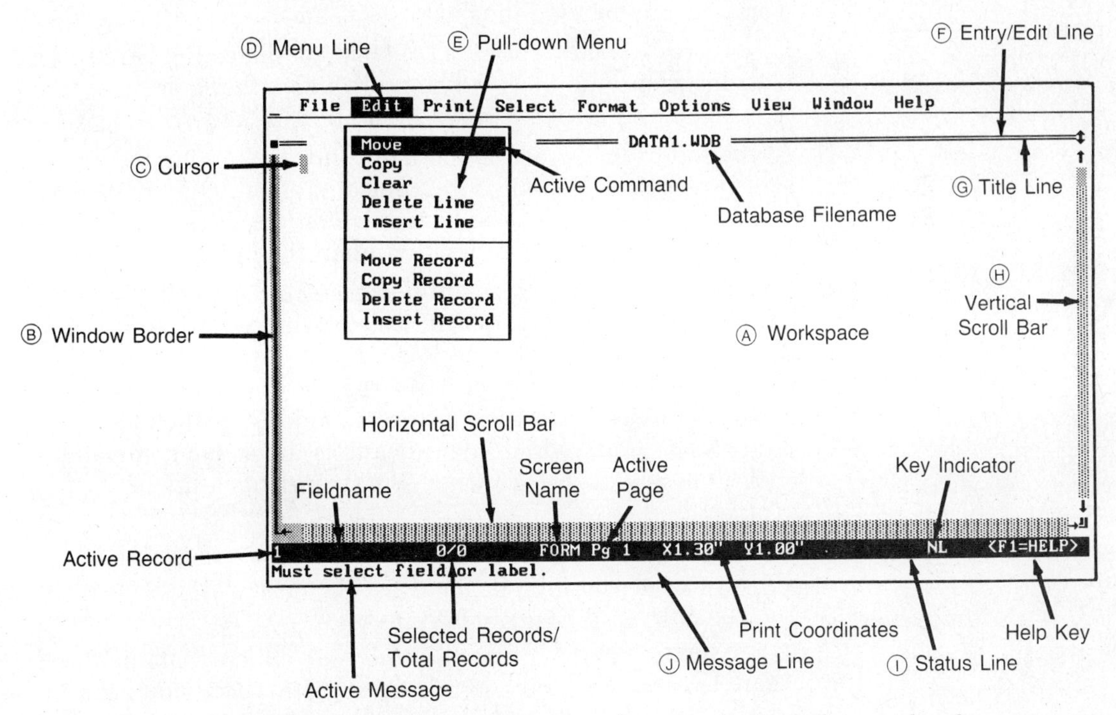

Figure 9-2. The Form screen, where you design a form and make entries in a record

A column in the Form screen is the same as a character. Therefore, 256 columns can hold 256 characters.

A. The empty area is the *workspace*. It's here that you create fields and make entries in those fields. The workspace is a window to your computer's memory, through which you can view and manage a database. As large as this area looks now, it's actually only a small portion of the whole. The entire Form screen is 256 columns wide by 95 rows long. Holding down the Page Down key accesses four more screens, each one called a page, in one long, continuous form. Pressing Ctrl+Right Arrow accesses areas to the right.

B. The vertical line at the left edge is the *window border*, which separates the window from the screen.

C. The highlight in the upper-left corner of the workspace is the *cursor*. The cursor identifies the active column— the one that can accept the field name you type. As you type more characters in the field name, the cursor widens to make more columns active. You can enter a field name anywhere in the workspace by moving the cursor to it first.

   If you have a mouse installed, the cursor shares the workspace with the mouse pointer, which looks like either a small rectangle or an arrow, depending on screen mode.

D. At the top of the screen is the *menu line* containing the Form screen menus: File, Edit, Print, Select, Format, Options, View, Window, and Help. These menus, which are the same in the List screen, let you create and maintain the database.

E. Below the menu line is a *pull-down menu* listing the Edit commands: Move, Copy, Clear, Delete Line, Insert Line, Move Record, Copy Record, Delete Record, and Insert Record. Commands tell Works to perform specific tasks. The first command—Move—appears in reverse video (light letters on a dark background), which identifies it as the active command. Each time you choose a menu, Works presents a list of commands.

F. Below the menu line is the *entry/edit line*, where Works displays what you type or the contents of the cell the cursor is on. The entry/edit line is empty now.

G. Below the entry/edit line is the *title line*, which contains the database filename. You use this filename to load, store, and otherwise keep track of a file. Until you name the new database, Works assigns the standard filename—**DATA1.WDB**.

H. At the right edge of the window is the *vertical scroll bar*; below the workspace is the *horizontal scroll bar*. Each scroll bar contains a *scroll box*. In the Form screen, the horizontal scroll box moves along the horizontal scroll bar as you move the cursor, showing the location of the cursor relative to all columns. The vertical scroll box remains stationary no matter where the cursor is located.

Mouse users can zip along to distant places in the List screen by gliding the scroll box along the horizontal or vertical scroll bar.

In the List screen, both scroll boxes move with the movement of the cursor, showing which part of the file is currently on screen. For instance, when the cursor is on record 2048, the scroll box is in the middle of the vertical scroll bar. With the cursor in the middle field, the scroll box is in the middle of the horizontal scroll bar.

I. Directly below the horizontal scroll bar is the *status line*. The left end of the status line shows the number of the active record—here, 1. With no records in a new database, Record 1 is always active when you start. The now-empty space to the right of the active record number contains the name of the field at the cursor's location.

The double zeros (0/0) show the number of records selected from all existing records—now zero out of zero. FORM is the view you're in. *Pg 1* means that this is the first page of the potential five vertical pages worth of field names.

Coordinates X5.00" and Y2.00" indicate in inches where the current entry prints on the page—vital when you're working with pre-printed forms. NL shows that the Num Lock key is on. If you turn on the Caps Lock key, the letters CL appear on the status line next to NL.

<F1=HELP> reminds keyboarders to press F1 to get help. Mouse users can click on this element to get help.

J. Below the status line is the *message line*, where Works describes the active command or prompts your next action. The Move command is active, so the message line displays Must select field or label. This means you must select something to move *before* starting this command. Sure makes sense.

Around the perimeter of the screen are click-on symbols and other mouse elements described in Chapter 1.

Designing in the Form Screen

Figure 9-3 shows a screenful of fields in a sample personnel database. Because this screen is in text mode, each field consists of a field name and a colon. If the screen is in graphics mode, Works inserts a dotted line to represent the entry area. This entry area, empty as it is here or containing a dotted line, is called a cell (as on a spreadsheet). The field name describes the contents of the cell, such as EMP# for employee number and FIRST MI for first name, middle initial.

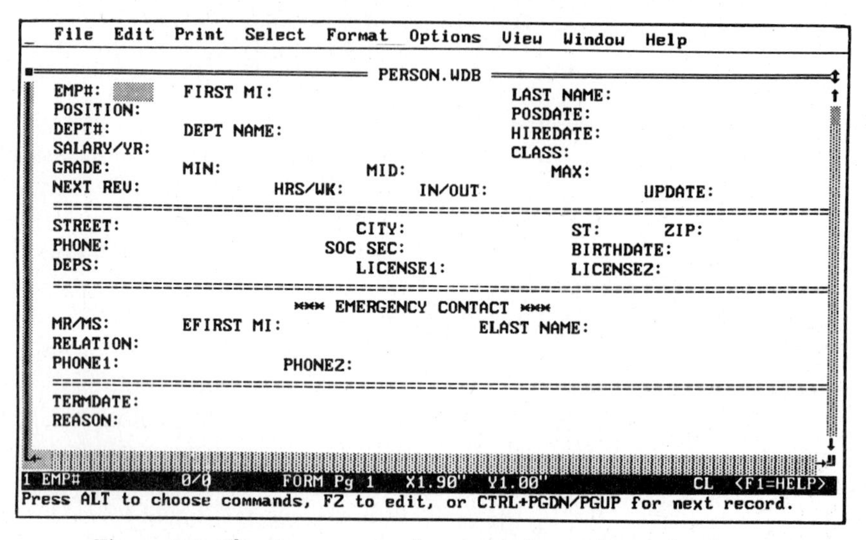

Figure 9-3. The Form screen for a sample employee database

Halfway down the screen you see *** EMERGENCY CONTACT ***. It's not followed by a colon, so this is a *label*. Labels don't hold entries. You can use labels for titles, screen name, instructions for completing the form, and the like. The long lines across the screen are also labels. They separate the screen into sections to make it easier to read.

Entering Field Names and Labels

Works gives you total freedom to position fields and labels anywhere on the form to satisfy your personal work methods, as well as your sense of design. You can stagger them from left to right, as shown in Figure 9-3, list one below the other, center them, align them on the colons, use side-by-side columns, or use any combination that makes sense to you.

It's wise to keep the most active fields at the beginning of the Form screen so you don't have to spend a lot of time tabbing past inactive fields to get to them.

To enter a field name, position the cursor, type the field name (up to 15 characters) and a colon, and press Enter. (Works then asks for the field size. More about this shortly.) The colon distinguishes a field from a label. If you omit the colon, Works accepts what you type as a label. You can enter and see these labels only in the Form screen. The List screen, which copies certain Form screen information (and vice versa) shows no sign of them.

If you want a field name longer than 15 characters, use the field's entry as the field name instead. First select the field name you want to hide. Then use the Format menu's Show Field name command to hide the field name. The entry, which can be as long as 256 characters, can then appear to be the field name, with another field name and entry to the right or below it.

You can use the same label over and over, but not the same field name. Works insists on a unique name for each field. This way, it knows which information belongs in which field. If you try to duplicate a field name, Works displays `Field name already used` and refuses to accept it. When you see this message, press either Enter or Escape. Enter lets you modify the field name, while Escape cancels the name so you can start from scratch.

Be creative in avoiding duplicate names. The database in Figure 9-3, for example, holds two first names as well as two last names. To make each field name one-of-a-kind, FIRST MI and LAST NAME contain the employee's name, and EFIRST MI and ELAST NAME contain the name of the emergency contact.

A good rule to follow when creating fields is to keep things separate. For instance, with an address, create one field for the city, another for the state, and yet another for the ZIP code. This makes it easy to sort entries in any field.

If you plan to use the database to produce form letters, you should create separate fields for courtesy titles (Mr., Ms., Prof., and the like), first names, middle initials, and last names, so that you don't end up with letters that start `Dear Prof. Donald T.` or `Dear Barbara C. Cantrell.`

The Form screen and List screen use the same field names but keep them in different layouts. Field names you create in the Form screen appear across the top of the the List screen; field names you create in the List screen appear down the left side of the Form screen.

Table 9-1 summarizes the keys that move the cursor around the Form screen and shortcut keys that let you use certain commands without going through a menu.

Table 9-1. Keystrokes in the Form screen

What You Want To Do	Keystroke	Command Equivalent
Move left one column	Left Arrow	
Move right one column	Right Arrow	
Move up one row	Up Arrow	
Move down one row	Down Arrow	
Move to beginning of row	Home	
Move to end of row	End	
Move to previous screen in record	Page Up	
Move to next screen in record	Page Down	
Move to previous record	Ctrl+Page Up	
Move to next record	Ctrl+Page Down	
Move to first record	Ctrl+Home	
Move to next empty record	Ctrl+End	
Move to contents of next field in list (with horizontal layout, Tab only)	Tab or Down Arrow	
Move to contents of previous field (with horizontal layout, Shift+Tab only)	Shift+Tab or Up Arrow	
Get help	F1	Help/Help Index
Access the tutorial	Shift+F1	Help/Works Tutorial
Enter or exit edit mode	F2	
Move information	F3	Edit/Move Field
Copy label	Shift+F3	Edit/Copy Label
Go to a specific cell	F5	Select/Go To
Repeat last search	F7	
Switch to List screen	F9	View/List
From Query screen, apply query and return to Form screen	F10	View/Form
From Report screen, return to Form screen	F10	View/Form
View active report	Shift+F10	View/Report Number

What You Want To Do	Keystroke	Command Equivalent
Erase contents of cell	Backspace then Enter	Edit/Clear Field Contents
Erase formulas in field	Equal sign then Enter	Contents
Enter current date	Ctrl + ; (semicolon)	
Enter current time	Ctrl + Shift + ; (semicolon)	

Determining the Width and Height of a Cell

The size of a field is never etched in stone, and you can easily make a cell wider, narrower, taller, or shorter in the Format menu's Field Size command.

One of the important tasks of form design is making each cell large enough to accommodate entries in the field. When you enter a field name, Works proposes to make the cell 20 characters wide and one line high. That's fine for a street address, for example, but a reason for termination or notes to yourself can often use more room, while a 3-digit employee number needs far less. Works lets you give any or every cell any width from 1 to 256 characters and any height from 1 to 256 lines.

When you create a one-line entry area, Works accepts what you type and displays only as much of the entry as the cell is wide. If you have long entries that you want to display completely, you can create an entry area more than one line high. This type of entry area is called a multiple-line cell. When you type text into a multiple-line cell, Works fills the first entry line with enough words for the field width you specify, and then wraps around to the beginning of the next entry line and continues filling there.

If the field will contain values (numbers or dates), be sure to make the cell wide enough to display any characters produced by cell formatting, such as a dollar sign, commas, decimal point, and decimal places. If a cell is too narrow to display a value completely, Works will show number signs (#######) instead of giving a misleading result.

If you design a screen with fields next to each other (as shown in Figure 9-3) or with multiple-line cells, try to make each cell the proper size as you go along. This way, you can avoid having to backtrack later if one field runs into another. If you're entering fields in a list and each field is one line high, this isn't a concern, because you can easily adjust the width and height of cells after entering all fields.

Remember to put the cursor in the entry area, not on the field name, before choosing the Format menu's Field Size command.

Effects on the List Screen

The List screen accepts only field names, alignments, and formats (how entries are displayed) from the Form screen, not any changes in cell size. When you switch to the List screen after setting up the form, you'll want to make the column size suit entries in the fields.

Even with careful planning, designing a form often means shifting fields around, inserting here and deleting there. If you insert a field in the Form screen, Works routinely places it after the last field in the List screen. So, you're likely to find a different sequence of field names in both screens.

For example, suppose you just finished entering all the fields in the form. You remember one more and insert it after the second existing field. When you get to the List screen, you find it at the end of all the fields, not where you inserted it in the Form screen.

Getting sequences in both screens to agree is a simple matter. In the List screen, select the field with Shift+F8, and then use F3 (the shortcut key for the Edit menu's Move command) to shift the field.

Designing in the List Screen

Designing a database in the List screen is different but just as easy as in the Form screen. The Form screen has a slight edge, because you can see many more fields on the screen at one time.

Entering the Field Names

Each row in the List screen is a record; each column is a field.

Figure 9-4 shows the employee database in the List screen, which is quite similar in appearance to the spreadsheet screen. The numbers down the left side are record numbers. The line directly below the entry/edit line shows the first five field names (the rest of the field names are in the off-screen columns to the right). The cells below each field name, now empty, will hold entries in those fields. Reading from left to right, the status line shows:

- the number of the record at the cursor's location (1)
- the name of the field at the cursor's location (EMP#)
- the number of records selected from total records (0/0)
- the name of the screen (LIST)
- the key turned on (NL for Num Lock)
- the help key (<F1=HELP>).

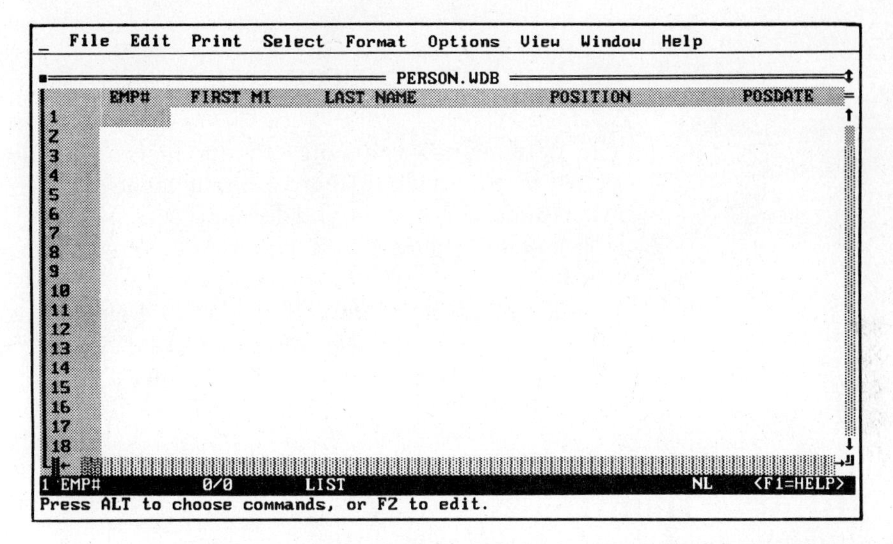

Figure 9-4. The List screen showing the first five fields in the employee database

You create a field in the List screen by naming an empty column.

To enter a field name in this screen, place the cursor on any cell in the column (or field), choose the Edit menu's Field Name command, type the field name (up to 15 characters), and press Enter. You don't type a colon after the field name.

As in the Form screen, you can't use a field name more than once. If you try to duplicate a field name, Works will again refuse to accept it. Unlike the Form screen, you can wait until you enter all field names before specifying the size of the entry cells.

The Width of the Cell

Making a column 0 characters wide hides the field and its entries.

Initially, each column in the List screen is 10 characters wide. You can make one, several, or all columns any width from 0 to 79 characters to accommodate entries in the field. A 0-character column hides both the field and its entries.

A good time to change column widths is after you make some entries. This way, you know the length of a typical entry and can adjust the column width accordingly. Timing is irrelevant. You can make columns wider or narrower at any time without disturbing anything. Be sure to keep columns wide enough to prevent field names or entries from bumping into each other.

Effects on the Form Screen

The field names you enter in the List screen appear in the Form screen in a list layout (that is, one below the other). The Form screen reflects the alignments and formats you specified in the List screen, but not any changes you made in the sequence of fields and cell width.

To get the sequence and size of fields to agree, return to the Form screen where you can use the Edit menu's Move command to rearrange the fields and the Format menu's Field Size command to adjust the cell size.

Filling a Database

You can fill records in either the Form or the List screen, regardless of which screen you used to design the database. As with field names, any entry in one screen appears in the other.

The Form screen shows every field name and entry in one record only. In this sample database, that record occupies only one screen. The record in Figure 9-5 contains the work background of Lawrence A. Adams, Quality Control Supervisor. Conveniently packaging everything in one screen means that you can see every entry in every field without scrolling around. While this works well here to demonstrate the concept, it isn't always possible (or even desirable) in every database.

If you enter long notes in a multiple-line field in the Form screen, Works lets it spread into empty columns in the List screen. Instead of using several contiguous columns for the note, you can increase the width of the column.

The List screen shows entries in as many as 18 records but only in as many fields as can fit in the screen width. Figure 9-6 shows the first five fields in Larry Adams' record, as well as 16 other records. Scrolling to the right brings other fields into view. The List screen is convenient when you're working with several records or entering new information in only one field.

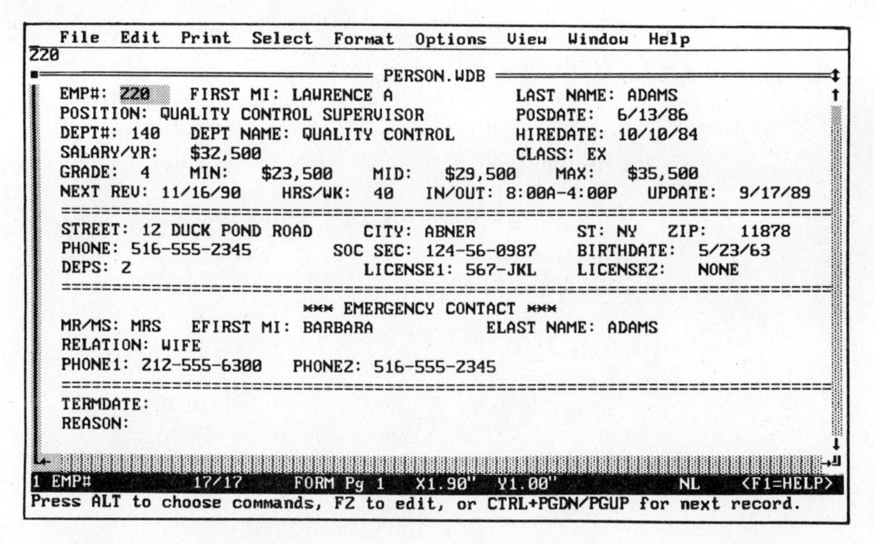

Figure 9-5. The Form screen showing all fields in one record in the employee database

File Edit Print Select Format Options View Window Help
220
PERSON.WDB

	EMP#	FIRST MI	LAST NAME	POSITION	POSDATE
1	220	LAWRENCE A	ADAMS	QUALITY CONTROL SUPERVISOR	6/13/86
2	197	HOLLY	SANCHEZ	CUSTOMER SERVICE MANAGER	2/17/81
3	134	JOHN E	RYE	WIRER/SOLDERER A	9/14/74
4	147	BETTY C	SCHRAFT	TECHNICIAN A	4/23/86
5	205	CORINNE	HALSTEAD	EXECUTIVE SECRETARY	10/1/84
6	213	SEYMOUR	COOPER	RECEPTIONIST	5/21/85
7	188	MARGERY	LE BLANC	FIELD SERVICE TECHNICIAN	11/3/78
8	155	TOMMY	CHEN	QUALITY CONTROL TESTER	6/21/88
9	202	HARRY	FUJITSU	SECRETARY	8/29/83
10	222	PERRY JOHN	O'HALLORAN	FIELD SERVICE TECHNICIAN	3/7/85
11	181	JAMES R	MAURICE	MARKETING MANAGER	4/20/81
12	229	GEORGE	DANDER	CUSTOMER SERVICE REP	9/14/88
13	199	LEROY	MILLER	SALESPERSON	12/3/82
14	191	JUDY	BROOKS	CUSTOMER SERVICE REP	10/25/82
15	217	KENNETH	PAGNOZZI	ACCOUNTS RECEIVABLE CLERK	8/3/83
16	209	MARIANNE	BELL	FIELD SERVICE TECHNICIAN	6/21/88
17	152	DAVID C	WILKINS	ELECTRONICS ENGINEER	3/16/89
18					

1 EMP# 17/17 LIST NL <F1=HELP>
Press ALT to choose commands, or F2 to edit.

Figure 9-6. The List screen showing the first five fields in the 17 records in the employee database

An entry in a cell, called the cell contents, can be text, numbers, or a formula—the same as on a spreadsheet. The way you work with text and numbers is virtually identical to the spreadsheet, so the following section summarizes the pertinent discussion in Chapter 3,

"Spreadsheet Essentials." Because working with field formulas is significantly different, this topic is covered in detail.

There's plenty of activity when you fill a database, so Tables 9-1 and 9-2 show the keys that move the cursor around each screen and the shortcut keys you can use instead of commands.

Table 9-2. Keystrokes in the List screen

What You Want To Do	Keystroke	Command Equivalent
Move left one cell	Left Arrow	
Move right one cell	Right Arrow	
Move up one cell	Up Arrow	
Move down one cell	Down Arrow	
Move left one block	Ctrl+Left Arrow	
Move right one block	Ctrl+Right Arrow	
Move up one block	Ctrl+Up Arrow	
Move down one block	Ctrl+Down Arrow	
Move left one screen	Ctrl+Page Up	
Move right one screen	Ctrl+Page Down	
Move up one screen	Page Up	
Move down one screen	Page Down	
Move to first field	Home	
Move to last field	End	
Move to beginning cell (row 1 field 1)	Ctrl+Home	
Move to ending cell in active area	Ctrl+End	
Move to next unlocked cell (protection on)	Tab	
Move to previous unlocked cell (protection on)	Shift+Tab	
Get help	F1	Help/Help Index
Access the tutorial	Shift+F1	Help/Works Tutorial
Enter or exit edit mode	F2	
Move information	F3	Edit/Move
Copy record, field, or contents of cell	Shift+F3	Edit/Copy

What You Want To Do	Keystroke	Command Equivalent
Go to specific cell	F5	Select/Go To
Go to next window pane	F6	
Go to previous window pane	Shift + F6	
Go to next window	Ctrl + F6	
Go to previous window	Ctrl + Shift + F6	
Repeat last search	F7	
Repeat last copy command (after selecting record, field, or cell)	Shift + F7	
Extend or select	F8	Select/Cells
Select field (column)	Shift + F8	Select/Field
Select record (row)	Ctrl + F8	Select/Record
Select range (also F8 and then Arrow)	Shift + Arrow	Select/Cells
Select entire database	Ctrl + Shift + F8	Select/All
Switch to Form screen	F9	View/Form
From Query screen, apply query and return to List screen	F10	Select/Apply Query
From Report screen, return to List screen	F10	View/List
View active report	Shift + F10	View/Report Number
Collapse current selection	Escape or Arrow	
Turn off extend action	Escape	
Enter current date	Ctrl + ; (semicolon)	
Enter current time	Ctrl + Shift + ; (semicolon)	
Copy contents of above cell (if formula, copies result only)	Ctrl + ' (apostrophe)	
Erase contents of cell	Backspace then Enter	Edit/Clear
Erase formulas in field	Equal sign then Enter	

In both the Form and List screens, you move from the entry area of one cell to the next by pressing the Tab key. If you overshoot, pressing Shift+Tab moves the cursor to the previous entry area. In the List screen, you can also use the arrow keys to move among the cells. If you want to stay in the cell, press Enter.

Entering Text

A cell can hold more information than you can see. The field size determines how much of the contents Works displays.

Text in a database cell can be a name, address, job title, department name, phone number, social security number, class grade, or anything else that Works can't interpret as a number or formula. Text can take these forms:

Hyphens (6-21-90) tell Works a date is text. Slashes (6/21/90) make it a value.

Maury T. Paramour
Technician
121-17-0562
1600 Pennsylvania Avenue
(516) 555-1212
#172
6-21-88
A+
D-
234 567
"1234
"==========
"June 21, 1931

Works recognizes most forms of text as text. When text looks like a value, certain techniques relieve Works' confusion. Typing quotation marks before a number ("1234) or a numerical value ("June 21, 1931) or using hyphens (6-21-88) or spaces (234 567) in a number turn the number into recognizable text.

Enter text by placing the cursor on the selected cell and typing the text, which then appears on the entry/edit line and at the cursor's location. When you finish typing, either press Enter or move the cursor to another cell, and Works enters the text in the selected cell. Works routinely aligns text in the left of the cell. You can center or right-align it with the Format menu's Style command.

In the Form screen, Works displays as much text as the cell size allows and truncates the rest. All of the text is still stored in the cell; it simply can't be displayed completely unless you make the cell entry area larger. In the List screen, however, Works lets long text spill into the next cell to the right, if that cell is empty. If the cell is not empty, it again truncates the text.

Entering Numbers

Numbers consist of numerals 0 to 9, numerals and other characters (decimal point, minus sign, dollar or percent sign, parentheses, or the letter E [for scientific notation]), and dates and times, which Works stores as numbers. Numbers can take these forms:

-456
(456)
4,567
1.75
5 7/8 or 5.875
876E-2
55%
$1.50
6/21/90
June 21, 1990

The cell's format determines the appearance of the number. Until you change it, the General commands shows numbers as precisely as possible in an integer, decimal fraction, or exponential format. You can use the Format menu to replace the General format with a Fixed, Currency (Dollar or other), Comma, Exponential, Percent, True/False, or Time/Date format. Except for True/False and Time/Date, which are different kinds of values, these formats allow 0 to 7 decimal places.

Typing format elements with the number changes the cell format as surely as using the Format command. For example, when you type a dollar sign before a number, the cell adopts the Dollar format. Typing a percent sign after a number gives the cell the Percent format.

In the List screen, you can enter a sequential series of numbers or dates by selecting the cells and then using the Edit menu's Fill Series command.

Enter numbers in the same way as text—by selecting the cell, typing the number, and either pressing Enter or moving the cursor. Works aligns a number in the right of the cell, which can cause a visual meld with left-aligned text in the neighboring cell. Changing the alignment can improve the readability of the screen. For instance, the left-aligned employee numbers in Figure 9-6 produce a good separation with the first names in the next column. Use the Format menu's Style command to left-align or center entries.

If a cell is too narrow to display a number completely, Works converts it to scientific notation. If the number is formatted or is a long date, Works displays ###### (number signs) in the cell. To show the entire entry, use the Format menu's Field Size command (Form screen) or Field Width command (List screen) to widen the cell.

Field Formulas and Common Entries

A field formula enters the same information in a designated field in every new record, which spares you the task of typing it over and over. There are two types of field formulas: *constant* and *calculation*. A constant field formula enters the same text, number, date, or time in a field. A calculation field formula enters the same formula. You can create field formulas in either the Form or List screen. Each field can have only one formula.

Common Text and Numbers

Virtually every new batch of records has entries that are common to many or all of them. If you spend a few moments scanning the records before working on them, you're bound to come up with something. For example, suppose most of your customers or clients live in Carmel, Indiana. You can create constant field formulas that automatically enter Carmel, IN, and a ZIP code in every new record.

Always precede a formula with an equal (=) sign.

Here's how it works: Let's say you've created fields to hold a city, state, and ZIP code. You enter

="**Carmel**	in the city field,
="**IN**	in the state field
=**46032**	in the ZIP field

The equal sign tells Works you're entering a formula. The quotation marks before Carmel and IN tell Works your formula consists of text. Now, when you make your very first entry in a new record, Works plunks `Carmel` in the city field, `IN` in the state field, and `46032` in the Zip field. It's as easy as that.

You can make dates and times constant using the forms =**6/21/89** and =**8:30 AM**.

Common Calculations

A calculation field formula uses numerical entries in the fields to calculate a result. Suppose you have two fields named SALES1 and SALES2 that contain the quarterly sales generated by both people on your sales staff. You create a third field named TOTAL and enter the following formula in a cell:

=SALES1+SALES2

Works then adds both sales amounts and displays the result in the TOTAL cell. You now hire two more people for your sales staff. You insert two new fields before the TOTAL column, and then change the formula (either replaced from scratch or overtyped) in the TOTAL cell to

=SUM(SALES1,SALES2,SALES3,SALES4)

When you enter amounts in the new SALES cells, the TOTAL formula adds them and displays the result. Each time you start a new record, Works enters the formula in the TOTAL cell in that record.

In addition to functions (such as SUM) and fields containing numbers (such as SALES1), calculation field formulas can contain numbers you supply as well as the operators shown in Table 9-3. Any functions available on the spreadsheet are available in the database. You'll find the functions directory in Chapter 4.

Works uses the following standard algebraic rules to calculate a calculation field formula:

- Evaluates equations as it finds them, from left to right.
- Evaluates values in the innermost set of parentheses first.
- Evaluates operators in their order of precedence. This order is discussed in Chapter 3.

Changing or Removing Field Formulas

You can enter only one field formula (constant or calculation) in a field. That formula affects every cell in that field. If you want to

Table 9-3. Database operators and special symbols

Character Typed	Operation Performed
Arithmetic Operators:	
^	Exponentiation
*	Multiplication
/	Division
+	Addition
−	Subtraction
Comparison Operators:	
=	Equal to
<>	Not equal to
<	Less than
>	Greater than
<=	Less than or equal to
>=	Greater than or equal to
Logical Operators:	
&	And
~	Not
|	Or
Other Operators and Symbols:	
:	Field name
%	Percentage
"	Start of text
=	Start of a field formula (CAUTION: When entered by itself in a cell, erases all formulas in that field)
?	Wildcard (replaces single character)
*	Wildcard (replaces multiple characters)

change a formula, simply overtype it in one cell, which again affects every cell in the field.

If a field formula doesn't apply to a particular record, overtype it with the proper entry (but not with another formula) or blank out the cell. Overtyping and blanking affect only that record, not past records or future records. To blank, place the cursor on the cell, press Back-space, and hit Enter.

To remove a field formula entirely, place the cursor on any cell in that field, type an equal sign, and hit Enter. If there's something about this process that troubles you, you're right. Because it's so easy to deliberately erase a field formula, it's clearly just as easy to wipe it out inadvertently. Caution is advised.

Speed Entering

Works has quick and painless ways besides field formulas to enter the same information without retyping. One of those methods involves copying an entire record, another "dittoing" an entry, and a third, copying an entry. The last two techniques work only in the List screen.

Copying a Record

New records sometimes contain many of the same entries. In this case, it's faster to copy a record than start from scratch. Suppose you need four records for one customer, each with the name of a different contact. Instead of typing the company name, address, and phone number four times, fill in one record.

In the List screen, select that record with Ctrl+F8, and use Shift+F3 to copy it. Then overtype one contact name with another and change any other information that doesn't apply.

Dittoing the Previous Entry

Sometimes, the same entry appears in several records but not often enough to warrant a constant field formula. In this case, you can type the entry once and then ditto it into the cells below.

Suppose you have a customer at several different locations. Instead of typing the customer name over and over, you can type it once. In your next record, when the cursor is in the customer name field, press Ctrl+' (apostrophe) and press Enter. Like magic, the name appears in that cell, too. What Works did is ditto the entry in the cell above.

Dittoing works just as well to edit information. Let's say you want to replace a company address in several contiguous cells in the same field. Type the new address in the top cell in the group, and then zip down the field while pressing Ctrl+'. You can also use this technique to blank out cells. Blank out the first one, and then ditto that empty cell.

Copying an Entry

The Edit menu's Fill Down command works in a similar way. Here, you type an entry, select as many cells as you want in a column, and then copy it into those cells. Fill Down works best when you need to fill or edit a large group of cells, while Ctrl+' is efficient when you're working with only a few cells.

Changing the Sequence of Fields

Another way to speed enter your records is to rearrange fields. Suppose you have several hundred index cards with information in this order: first name, last name, phone number, street, city, state, and ZIP code. But your fields are in this order: last name, first name, street, city, state, ZIP code, and phone number. The facts are all there, but the order is different. Instead of skipping around a record making entries or scanning the cards trying to find entries, consider matching the sequence of fields to the input documents. You can do this only in the List screen or in a Form screen where fields are in a list, not staggered across the screen.

In the Form screen, you can only move a field to an unused area. In the List screen, Works parts the columns to make room for a moved field.

A field shift in one screen isn't reflected in the other, so decide first which screen you want to work in. If you choose to work in the Form screen, place the cursor on either the field name or cell contents of the field to be moved, press F3 (the shortcut for the Move command), move the cursor to an empty location, and hit Enter.

If you're working in the List screen, place the cursor on any cell in the column to be moved and press Shift+F8 to select the column. Press F3, move the cursor to the new location (even atop an existing field), and hit Enter. Works inserts the column to the left of the cursor. Repeat as many times as needed to rearrange the fields.

After you enter everything you need from those documents and save them, either leave the fields as they are, or shift them back to their original positions. If the information in the next batch of documents is in a different order, make life simple and shift the fields again.

Entering Information in a Selected Area

If you're entering information in a group of contiguous records in the List screen, you can confine the cursor to a specific area and have Works move it part of the time. This may not sound like much, but it is. It saves your moving the cursor over and over from one end of an area to the beginning. That's a lot of keystrokes you'll never have to make.

- If you're working with fields, when the cursor reaches the bottom cell in a selected column it scoots to the top cell in the next selected column, saving you the task of doing it. This is an up and down zig-zag.
- If you're working with records, when the cursor reaches the last cell in the selected row it scoots to the first cell in the next selected row. That's a left to right zig-zag.

Your keystroke after each entry controls the direction in which the cursor moves, as shown in Table 9-4. There's only one qualification: You must select the area with the Shift+Arrow keys, not the Shift+F8 (field/column select) or Ctrl+F8 (record/row select) keys.

Table 9-4. Keys that move the cursor in a selected area

What You Want To Do	Keystroke
Move cursor down by cell to end of selected column, then to top cell in next selected column, and so on	Enter
Move cursor up by cell to top of selected column, then to bottom cell in previous selected column, and so on	Shift+Enter
Move cursor right by cell to end of selected row, then to first cell in next selected row, and so on.	Tab
Move cursor left by cell to beginning of selected row, then to last cell in previous selected row, and so on.	Shift+Tab

Keeping a Database Up-To-Date

Keeping a database current is what keeps a database valuable. The kinds of housekeeping tasks that accomplish this goal involve editing entries in a record, inserting new fields and records, and deleting obsolete fields and records.

Editing Entries in a Record

You can change something already in a cell by overtyping, editing, or clearing the cell. These activities can take place in either the Form or List screen.

Overtyping replaces whatever is in the cell with something new. Editing lets you correct those places that need correcting and leave the rest intact. You're likely to want to do this with a long or complicated entry.

To edit, place the cursor on the cell and press F2. Works displays the cell contents on the entry/edit line with the blinker after the last character. Press Backspace to erase the character before the blinker or use Left Arrow or Right Arrow to move the blinker through the entry without erasing anything. When you get to the problem place, type the new information or press Delete to delete unwanted information. Table 9-5 shows these and other editing and movement keys.

Table 9-5. Action of edit keys in all screens after F2

What You Want to Do	Keystroke
Move left one character	Left Arrow
Move right one character	Right Arrow
Move to beginning of entry/edit line	Home
Move to end of entry/edit line	End
Select character to left of blinker	Shift+Left Arrow
Select character to right of blinker	Shift+Right Arrow
Delete selected characters or only character at blinker	Delete
Delete character to left of blinker	Backspace

If you want to clear a cell, place the cursor on the cell, press Backspace, and then Enter.

Inserting New Records

You can insert records into an existing database in either the Form or List screen. It doesn't really matter where you insert them—before the first record, after the last record, or somewhere in between—because sorting will reorder the sequence of records.

Works inserts a new record above the cursor's location. So, if the cursor is on Record 4 when you insert, the newcomer becomes Record 4, and the rest of the records are renumbered.

To insert a new record within existing records, use the Edit menu's Insert Record/Field command. In the Form screen, Works brings up a ready-to-fill record immediately. In the List screen, Works gives you a choice of inserting a record or field. When you choose the Record option, Works makes room between records. You can have as many as 4096 records in each database.

If you simply must add records after the last record, press Ctrl+End in the Form screen to bring up a new record. In the List screen, press Ctrl+Home to move the cursor to the first field in the first record, press Page Down enough times to reach the last record, and finally, press Down Arrow to move one row down. Sorry, there's no easier way.

Inserting New Fields

After you use a database for a while, it's not unusual to find that you need another field for information overlooked earlier. Works makes it easy to insert fields in the Form screen or List screen.

In the Form screen, place the cursor where you want the field, type the field name followed by a colon, and hit Enter. In the List screen, place the cursor in the field to the right of the insertion, choose the Edit menu's Insert Record/Field command, and this time choose the Field option. After inserting the field, use the Field Name command in the Edit menu to name it.

Regardless of where you insert a field in the Form screen, Works places it after the last field in the List screen. The reverse is true in the List screen. Works places a field inserted in the List screen after the last field in the Form screen. Use the Edit menu's Move command to shift fields where you want them.

Deleting a Field

Database housekeeping means getting rid of outdated information, which includes obsolete fields and their entries. This activity can take place in the Form or List screen. Caution is always advisable, because deletions can be permanent. If you do delete something in error, you can rescue it from oblivion only if you have an undeleted version of the file stored on disk.

To delete a field in the Form screen, place the cursor on the field name (not the entry), press Backspace, and hit Enter. Works then asks if it's `OK to delete data in this field?` When you press Enter to confirm, the field and its entries are gone. You can delete only one field at a time.

In the List screen, place the cursor on any cell in the doomed field, choose the Edit menu's Delete Record/Field command, and then the Field option. Here, you aren't asked to confirm your intention. When you press Enter, the field is gone, and other fields close the gap. You can delete contiguous fields in one step if you use F8 to extend the selection to other fields first.

Deleting a Record

Record deletions can take place in the Form or List screen, again courtesy of the Edit menu. In the Form screen, use the Delete Record command; in the List screen, use the Delete Record/Field command and Record option.

In the Form screen, place the cursor anywhere in the doomed record before opening the Edit menu. When you select Delete Record, the whole record disappears, no questions asked, and Works displays the next record. It happens so fast, you may think it didn't happen at all.

In the List screen, place the cursor on a cell in the doomed record before opening the Edit menu and choosing the Delete Record command. You can delete contiguous records in one step if you use F8 to extend the selection to other cells first.

A neat little technique makes big record cleanups easy. When you set up query criteria (discussed shortly), you can hide all the records you want to keep, select the remaining records, and then use the Delete Record/Field command in the List screen to delete them all in one step. Because the Delete command deletes displayed records only, the hidden records remain safe and sound behind the scenes. Afterward, you can use the Select menu's Switch Hidden Records command to switch the hidden records into view.

If you have more wanted records than unwanted ones, hide the unwanted records first, and then switch them into view and delete them.

Finding and Selecting Records

Before you can change, add, or delete anything, you must find the record. There are several ways to go about this. You can:

- Step through each record in the Form screen
- Browse around the List screen
- Use the Go To command to zero in on a record
- Use the Search command to send Works looking for the record
- Set up query criteria to select records

When you have a small database and only a few records, any method, even a visual scan, will do. If you have hundreds of records, stepping through records in the Form screen or browsing around the List screen is tedious and time-consuming. So, if you're searching for a specific record, the sensible approach is to let Works do it.

The Go To and Search Commands

The Select menu's Go To and Search commands are opposite sides of the same coin. Both can get you to a specific record, but Go To requires that you know the record's exact location, while Search is willing to scout around. You can use these commands in both the Form and List screens.

Going to a Record

Pressing F5 brings up the Go To dialog box and a list of database field names. When you give Works a record number and/or field name, the cursor zips to that record or field. Unless you choose another field, the cursor lands in the same field the cursor was in when you started the search. The Go To command is most efficient when you're sure of a record number. After sorting, however, record numbers do change.

The field names in the Go To dialog box serve other useful purposes, notably getting to a hidden column so you can bring it into view. After you hide a column by reducing its width to 0 characters, you can select its field name from the Go To list, and then use the Format menu's Field Width command to widen the column. Widening it to anything greater than 0 characters brings the column into view.

Searching the Records

With Search, you simply type into the `Search` dialog box all or part of an entry you know is in the record—name, address, number, job title, or other identifying information. You then choose one of two search methods: Stop at each record containing the search information (`Next record`) or display all such records (`All records`) on screen at one time.

If you start the search in the Form screen, Works shows matching records one at a time; in the List screen, you can see all records.

In the `Next record` method, Works searches below the cursor position until it finds a record with an entry matching the search information. Each time you press F7, Works searches for the next record, cycling through the database in this way until it finds each matching record.

Here's how it works. Suppose the employee database in Figure 9-6 consists of several hundred records instead of only 17. Your task is to enter a 5 percent wage increase for every Technician. The cursor is now in the LAST NAME field of record 6. You choose the Search command and enter the word **Technician** in the dialog box. Works instantly moves the cursor to the POSITION field of record 7, which shows FIELD SERVICE TECHNICIAN. You enter a wage increase in that record, and then press F7 to repeat the search. Works moves the cursor to the POSITION field in record 10, another FIELD SERVICE TECHNICIAN. You enter a wage increase in that record. The next time you press F7, the cursor moves to record 16, another FIELD SERVICE TECHNICIAN. You get the idea.

In the `All records` method, Works finds and displays only those records that match the search information, hiding all other records.

For example, in the database in Figure 9-6, Works displays records 4, 7, 10, and 16—that is, every record containing the word TECHNICIAN in any form—TECHNICIAN A as well as FIELD SERVICE TECHNICIAN. This method is quick, and it works well when you want to perform the same operation on all displayed records. It also makes it easy to print, include in a report, or mail merge the selected records.

Using the Select menu's Show All Records command brings the hidden records into view.

Querying the Database

A query is a search for records that meet a variety of conditions.

Querying lets you select records that fit certain criteria, such as all Technicians in the database or only those Technicians earning a specific salary. Like the Search command, you can then view, print, include in a report, or use for mail merge and mailing labels only the selected records. Unlike the Search command, which lets you specify only one piece of search information, you can fine-tune selection criteria in a query to satisfy a variety of conditions.

You define the selection criteria in the Query screen, which looks just like a ready-to-fill Form screen except that it has fewer menus and the word QUERY on the status line. Figure 9-7 shows the Query screen in the employee database with two criteria filled in. You can get to the Query screen from either the Form or List screen via the View menu's Query command.

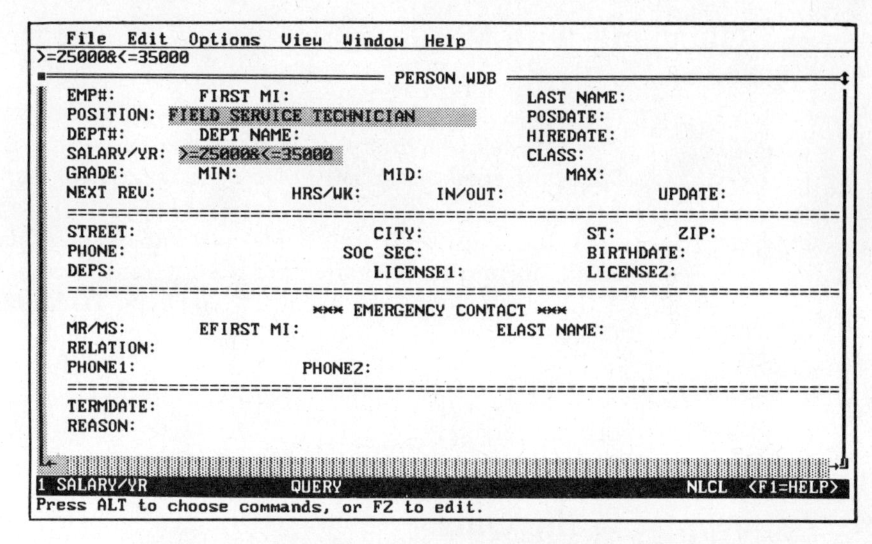

Figure 9-7. The Query screen in the employee database

Types of Selection Criteria

There are two types of selection criteria: equality and comparison. Equality criteria select records on the basis of matching information—for example, all Field Service Technicians in a company. Comparison criteria select records on the basis of information that falls within a range—for example, Field Service Technicians earning between $25,000 and $35,000 per year.

You can see both types of criteria in the shaded areas in Figure 9-7. The equality criterion, FIELD SERVICE TECHNICIAN, is in the POSITION field, and the comparison criterion, >=25000&<=35000, is in the SALARY/YR field.

You can use comparison and logical operators in one field or in several fields.

The comparison operators, **>=** (greater than or equal to) and **<=** (less than or equal to), let you query for ranges of numbers, dates, times, and text. In plain English, these criteria are meant to select records where the salary is *greater than or equal to 25000 and less than or equal to 35000*. The ampersand character (&), also known as the logical operator AND, lets you link both criteria in the query.

Refer to Table 9-3 for other comparison and logical operators you can use in your criteria.

Querying with Wildcards

Works has two wildcard symbols— the question mark (?) and asterisk (*)—that let you query a database for variations in text or spelling. Wildcard symbols substitute for characters in a specific position in queried text.

The question mark stands for single characters, and the asterisk stands for multiple characters. If you want to select only Technician A, B, or C records, for example, you type **Technician ?** in the POSITION field. If you want to select only Field Service Technician records, you type **F*T*** in the POSITION field. You can find a detailed description and other examples of the wildcard process in Chapter 12.

Applying the Query

Once you are in the Query screen, Tab to the desired cell, type the criterion, and press Enter. If you have other criteria, Tab to those cells and enter them in the same way. When you finish, press F10 (the Select/Apply Query shortcut key) to apply the criteria.

If you left the Form screen for the Query screen, Works applies the criteria and returns you to the Form screen where you can see each selected record one at a time. If you left from the List screen, Works applies the criteria and returns you to the List screen, where you can see a screenful of selected records.

Figure 9-8 shows a screenful of fields in the employee database, this one containing position titles, position dates, department numbers, department names, and annual salaries in all records.

```
 File  Edit  Print  Select  Format  Options  View  Window  Help
"QUALITY CONTROL SUPERVISOR
                                    PERSON.WDB
       POSITION                  POSDATE DEPT#     DEPT NAME        SALARY/YR
1   QUALITY CONTROL SUPERVISOR   6/13/86  140  QUALITY CONTROL      $32,500
2   CUSTOMER SERVICE MANAGER     2/17/81  120  CUSTOMER SERVICE     $37,555
3   WIRER/SOLDERER A             9/14/74  200  PRODUCTION           $18,750
4   TECHNICIAN A                 4/23/86  200  TEST                 $24,560
5   EXECUTIVE SECRETARY         10/1/84   170  ADMINISTRATION       $23,430
6   RECEPTIONIST                 5/21/85  160  ADMINISTRATION       $17,000
7   FIELD SERVICE TECHNICIAN    11/3/78   210  FIELD SERVICE        $23,500
8   QUALITY CONTROL TESTER       6/21/88  140  QUALITY CONTROL      $21,550
9   SECRETARY                    8/29/83  160  SALES                $19,680
10  FIELD SERVICE TECHNICIAN      3/7/85  210  FIELD SERVICE        $27,000
11  MARKETING MANAGER            4/20/81  100  MARKETING & SALES    $42,560
12  CUSTOMER SERVICE REP         9/14/88  120  CUSTOMER SERVICE     $24,560
13  SALESPERSON                 12/3/82   100  SALES                $32,000
14  CUSTOMER SERVICE REP       10/25/82   120  CUSTOMER SERVICE     $29,000
15  ACCOUNTS RECEIVABLE CLERK     8/3/83  160  ACCOUNTING           $18,630
16  FIELD SERVICE TECHNICIAN     6/21/88  210  FIELD SERVICE        $28,756
17  ELECTRONICS ENGINEER         3/16/89  250  ENGINEERING          $46,780
18
1 POSITION       17/17      LIST                                CL  <F1=HELP>
Press ALT to choose commands, or F2 to edit.
```

Figure 9-8. The part of the List screen that shows position titles and dates, department numbers and names, and salaries per year

If you apply only the equality criterion described in the previous example—FIELD SERVICE TECHNICIAN—Works displays records 7, 10, and 16, as shown in Figure 9-9. Note that the status line shows 3/17—3 records selected out of 17. If you apply both the equality and comparison criteria—FIELDSERVICE TECHNICIAN and >=25000<=35000—Works displays records 10 and 16, as shown in Figure 9-10. This time

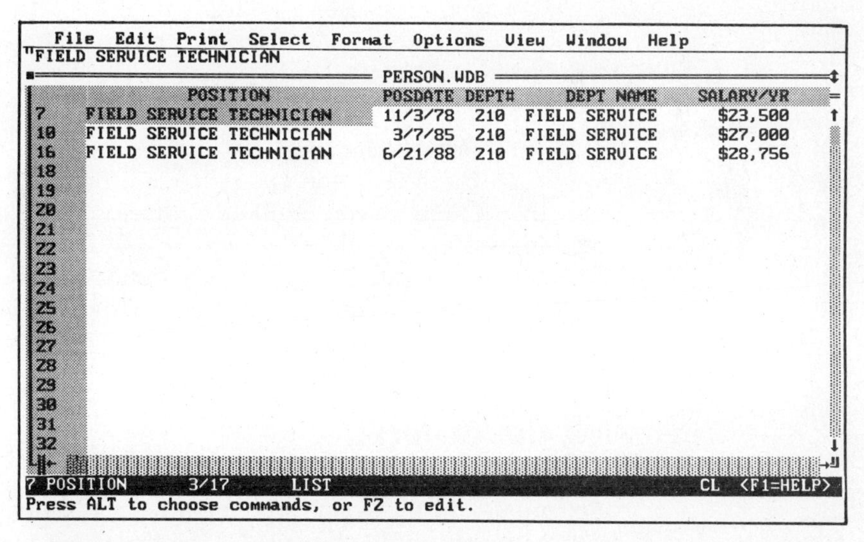

Figure 9-9. Records selected by Field Service Technician position only

the status line shows 2 records selected out of 17. In both cases, Works hides from view every other record not matching the criteria.

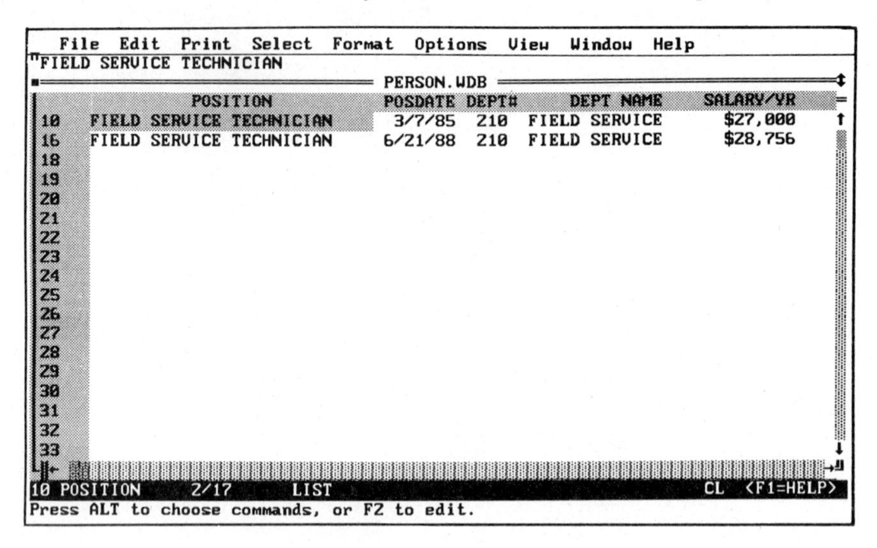

Figure 9-10. Records selected by Field Service Technician position and salary range criteria

You can bring all records into view by using the Select menu's Show All Records command or deleting all criteria.

To restore all records to view, use the Select menu's Show All Records command. Though all records are now displayed, the query criteria remain. You can apply the query again at a later time.

Changing the Criterion

You can erase a criterion that outlives its usefulness by placing the cursor on the cell in the Query screen, pressing the Backspace key, and then Enter. If you want to replace one criterion with another, simply overtype the doomed one.

To remove all criteria in one step, use the Edit menu's Delete Query command in the Query screen. This also restores all records to view.

Reversing the Criteria

Sometimes, instead of displaying all records that match the criteria, you will want to display only those that don't match.

Assume you already created a criterion to select all Technicians in the company and entered a 5 percent wage increase for each one. Management decided today to give every other employee a 7.5 percent increase. Using the Select menu's Switch Hidden Records command, you can swap hidden records (non-Technicians) with displayed ones (Technicians), and then enter the increase.

You can swap records as often as you like. When you want the hidden records to rejoin the displayed records on screen, choose the Select menu's Show All Records command.

Getting the Right Sort

Database information is always easier to use when records are arranged in a meaningful order, not randomly as you entered them. This process of arranging records is called sorting. Works can sort records alphabetically (company name, for example), numerically (ZIP code, for example), and chronologically (hire date, for example) in ascending or descending order.

Sort Fields

You can have Works sort on as many as three fields at a time. When you choose the Select menu's Sort Records command, Works brings up the dialog box shown in Figure 9-11. This is where you enter the names of sort fields and the sort order in each field: ascending (A to Z, 1 to 9, or earliest date to latest) or descending (Z to A, 9 to 1, or latest date to earliest). The Works standard is ascending order, so those boxes are already marked for you.

To get you started, Works enters the name of the first field in your database (here, EMP# from the sample employee database) in the 1st Field slot. If you want something else, you can delete or overtype this field name.

Sorting entries in one, two, or three fields at a time lets you arrange records in an increasingly precise order. Say you're using three sort fields. In the 1st Field field, you enter the name of the most important sort field, in the 2nd Field field, the second most important sort field, and in the 3rd Field field, the least important sort field. Until you change things, Works sorts records based on the field names and sequence you specified.

A phone directory is a common use of a three-way sort. The last name, first name, and middle initial are the sort fields. The last name

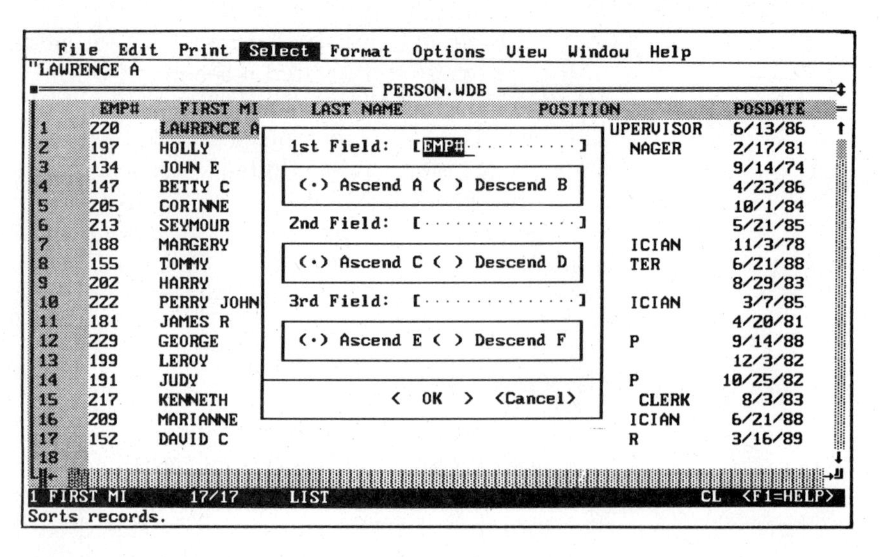

Figure 9-11. The Sort dialog box showing places for the names of three key fields and sort order

is the most important of the three, so it's the first sort field. The first name is the second most important, so it's the second sort field. The middle initial is the least important, so it's the third sort field.

In this type of database, Works sorts the records by last name in ascending order. When it finds two last names (first sort field) that are the same, it looks at the first name (second sort field) to see which goes first. If the first names are the same, it looks at the middle initial (third sort field) to see which goes first. This process continues until the entire database is sorted.

You can sort more than three fields by sorting the database twice. Specify the least important sort fields the first time and the more important fields the second time.

The Order of Sorts

With ascending order, Works sorts entries in a field in this sequence: entries with a leading space, text, NA (not available) values, numbers, ERR (error) values, and empty cells. Text includes the following characters, shown in Table 9-6 in ascending sort order from left to right:

Table 9-6. Types of characters in ascending sort order

Type of Character	Character
Special Characters	Space ! " # $ % & ' () * + , — . / :; < = > ? @ [\ ] ^ _ ' { | } ~
Alphabetic Characters	a A b B c C through z Z
Numeric Characters	0 1 2 3 4 5 6 7 8 9

Works ignores any distinction between uppercase and lowercase letters. For instance, Ruth comes after runner.

When you choose descending order, Works follows the same pattern in reverse.

Printing the Records

Works offers two ways to print records: from the List screen or from a custom report definition. Both methods use the commands in the Print menu.

The Print menu's Preview command lets you get a bird's eye view of a report before you actually print it.

When you print from the List screen and choose the Print command's `Print record and field labels` option, Works prints all records and fields. The result bears a strong resemblance to the way records appear on screen.

You can also specify the size of the margins, add a header or footer to the report, and insert page breaks to print specific pages. The word processor's merge feature, described in Chapter 13, lets you print in a format resembling the Form screen.

The fancier stuff—titles, calculations, labels, and lines—is reserved for report definitions. You'll find out how to create them in the next chapter.

About Reporting

As valuable as a database is on screen, it reaches its full potential in a printed report. Printed reports can present introductory text and statistical summaries, provide an audit trail of purged records, and preserve historic details for future reference.

Works offers a variety of ways to get a professional-looking report that not only looks good but reads well.

You can insert titles and headings in this kind of report, choose the fields you want to print, switch fields, calculate fields, change column widths, select and sort records, print totals, dates, and page numbers, and do a host of other things to tailor the report to suit your needs.

Works lets you create as many as eight different reports in a database. So, when you complete one report, you can create another that presents the records in a different way or presents different records. Works saves the reports with the database.

Report Definitions

The key to all this activity is a report definition. A report definition tells Works what kind of information to include in a report and where to print it. You can create a report definition from scratch or have Works do it for you in a process called speed reporting. Both methods take place in the Report screen.

Figure 10-1 shows the Report screen with a report definition for the employee database in Chapter 9 (refer to Figures 9-5 and 9-6 if you need refreshing). It includes columns A through F, even though you can actually see only columns A through D in one screen. If you scrolled to the right, you could see columns E and F. Both screens are joined in Figure 10-1 (a bit of author license) to show the complete report definition.

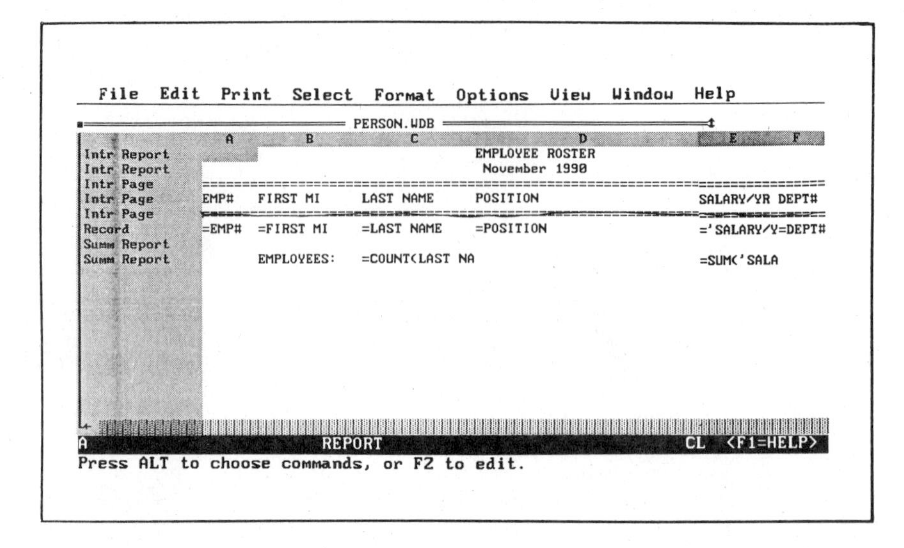

Figure 10-1. Report screen showing a custom report definition in the employee database

Figure 10-2 shows the report it produces—an employee roster that sports a page-number header (PAGE 1), report title (EMPLOYEE

Page 1

EMPLOYEE ROSTER
November 1990

EMP#	FIRST MI	LAST NAME	POSITION	SALARY/YR	DEPT#
220	LAWRENCE A	ADAMS	QUALITY CONTROL SUPERVISOR	$32,500	140
197	HOLLY	SANCHEZ	CUSTOMER SERVICE MANAGER	$37,555	120
134	JOHN E	RYE	WIRER/SOLDERER A	$18,750	200
147	BETTY C	SCHRAFT	TECHNICIAN A	$24,560	200
205	CORINNE	HALSTEAD	EXECUTIVE SECRETARY	$23,430	170
213	SEYMOUR	COOPER	RECEPTIONIST	$17,000	160
188	MARGERY	LE BLANC	FIELD SERVICE TECHNICIAN	$23,500	210
155	TOMMY	CHEN	QUALITY CONTROL TESTER	$21,550	140
202	HARRY	FUJITSU	SECRETARY	$19,680	160
222	PERRY JOHN	O'HALLORAN	FIELD SERVICE TECHNICIAN	$27,000	210
181	JAMES R	MAURICE	MARKETING MANAGER	$42,560	100
229	GEORGE	DANDER	CUSTOMER SERVICE REP	$24,560	120
199	LEROY	MILLER	SALESPERSON	$32,000	100
191	JUDY	BROOKS	CUSTOMER SERVICE REP	$29,000	120
217	KENNETH	PAGNOZZI	ACCOUNTS RECEIVABLE CLERK	$18,630	160
209	MARIANNE	BELL	FIELD SERVICE TECHNICIAN	$28,756	210
152	DAVID C	WILKINS	ELECTRONICS ENGINEER	$46,780	250
	EMPLOYEES:	17		$467,811	

Figure 10-2. Employee roster produced by the report definition in Figure 10-1

ROSTER), subtitle (November 1990), field names (EMP#, FIRST MI, and so on), long lines, records, label (EMPLOYEES:), record total (17), and salary total ($467,811).

The Report Screen

The Report screen bears a strong resemblance to the List screen. Though the named fields in the List screen are lettered columns here, it has the same menus and grid-like layout.

The workspace is divided into rows and columns to form cells. The cells hold the field names, formulas, and text that make up the report definition. The left side of the screen contains descriptors that describe the nature of each row. In this employee roster:

- Two Introductory Report (Intr Report) descriptors print the title EMPLOYEE ROSTER and subtitle November 1990 on the first page of the report.
- Three Introductory Page (Intr Page) descriptors print long lines and field names at the top of each page.
- One Record (Record) descriptor prints the entries in each record. The equal sign before each field name indicates a formula.
- Two Summary Report (Summ Report) descriptors produce a blank line and grand totals at the end of the report. Here, formulas count the last names and add the salaries. The word EMPLOYEES: in column B explains the number resulting from the count of last names.

It's easy to increase the column width to see an entire formula, but it's not worth the bother, because you'll want to reduce it before printing.

Some formulas in the Record and Summ Report rows are truncated because they occupy narrow cells. In column E, the Record formula is ='SALARY/YR'. In columns B and E, the Summ Report formulas are COUNT(LAST NAME) and =SUM('SALARY/YR'). When you place the cursor on a truncated formula, you can see it completely on the entry/edit line.

The letter A at the left end of the status line shows the location of the cursor—in this case, column A. When you store or print a report, Works replaces this letter temporarily with percentages that show how much of the database has already been processed.

Creating a Report Definition

The report definition determines the kinds of information in a report and how the information looks on paper. Starting from the View menu's New Report command, you can have Works speed report a definition or create it yourself from scratch. It's clearly easier to let Works do it, and then customize the result to suit your needs.

Speed Reporting

Pressing F10 in the Report screen returns you to the List or Form screen.

When you choose the View menu's New Report command from either the Form or List screen, Works displays the first page of a no-frills report in a List screen layout. Holding down Enter cycles you through the rest of the report until you've seen it all, at which point Works drops you into the Report screen. Pressing Escape at the first page brings you directly to the Report screen.

In the Report screen, Works displays a report definition consisting of row descriptors, text, and formulas. Figures 10-3 and 10-4 show the speed-reported result for the employee database. This report definition, in keeping with the initial report it produces on screen, is no-frills too. But it's a good start.

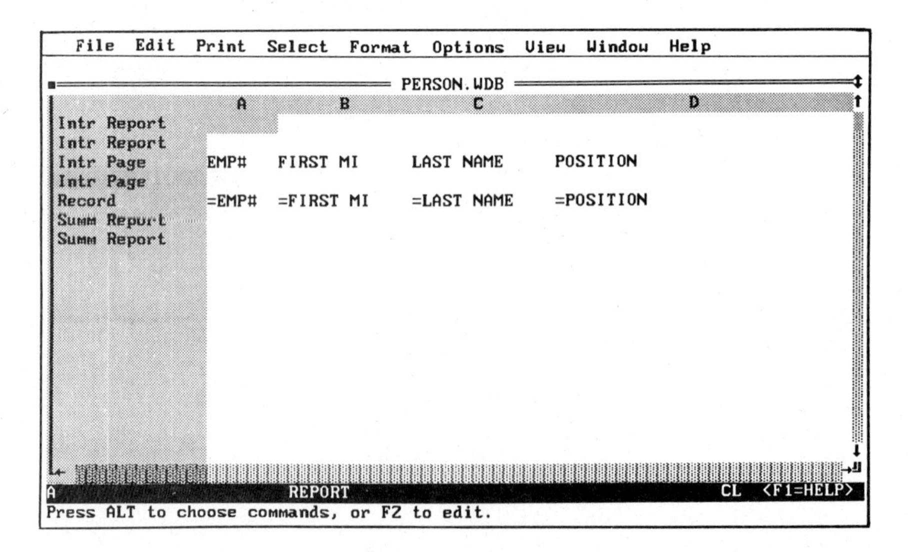

Figure 10-3. The Report screen showing columns A through D in a speed-reported report definition

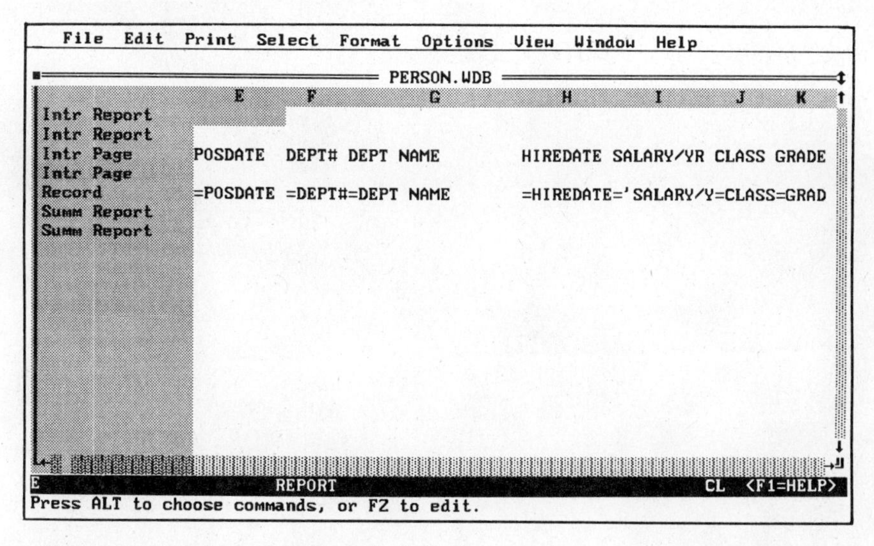

Figure 10-4. Columns E through K in the speed-reported report definition

Works copies the column widths in the database, saving you the task of redoing them, and creates a basic set of row descriptors:

- Two Introductory Report descriptors print two empty rows at the beginning of the report. You can enter titles here.
- Two Introductory Page descriptors print field names as column headings and an empty row at the top of each page.
- A Record descriptor prints once for each record. Formulas (field names with an equal sign before them) determine the fields included in the report.
- Two Summary Report descriptors produce two empty rows at the end of the report. You can enter formulas in these rows to get totals, counts, averages, and other summary results.

Customizing a Speed Report

Figure 10-5 shows the printed result of Works' initial effort at speed reporting. Yes, it is your basic bland report. No doubt about it. Tracing the path from here to the final version in Figure 10-1 can give you a good understanding of how database reporting works.

```
EMP#   FIRST MI       LAST NAME

220    LAWRENCE A     ADAMS
197    HOLLY          SANCHEZ
134    JOHN E         RYE
147    BETTY C        SCHRAFT
205    CORINNE        HALSTEAD
213    SEYMOUR        COOPER
188    MARGERY        LE BLANC
155    TOMMY          CHEN
202    HARRY          FUJITSU
222    PERRY JOHN     O'HALLORAN
181    JAMES R        MAURICE
229    GEORGE         DANDER
199    LEROY          MILLER
191    JUDY           BROOKS
217    KENNETH        PAGNOZZI
209    MARIANNE       BELL
152    DAVID C        WILKINS
```

Figure 10-5. The first page in a speed-reported employee roster before any custom tailoring

Table 10-1 shows cursor movement and shortcut keys that speed the work you want to do. Because the Report screen is so much like the List screen, many keystrokes are the same here.

Table 10-1. Cursor movement and shortcut keys in the Report screen

What You Want To Do	Keystroke	Command Equivalent
Move left one cell	Left Arrow	
Move right one cell	Right Arrow	
Move up one cell	Up Arrow	
Move down one cell	Down Arrow	
Move left one block	Ctrl+Left Arrow	
Move right one block	Ctrl+Right Arrow	
Move up one block	Ctrl+Up Arrow	
Move down one block	Ctrl+Down Arrow	
Move left one screen	Ctrl+Page Up	
Move right one screen	Ctrl+Page Down	
Move up one screen	Page Up	
Move down one screen	Page Down	
Move to first column	Home	
Move to last column	End	

What You Want To Do	Keystroke	Command Equivalent
Move to beginning cell (row 1 field 1)	Ctrl+Home	
Move to ending cell in active area	Ctrl+End	
Move to next unlocked cell (protection on)	Tab	
Move to previous unlocked cell (protection on)	Shift+Tab	
Get help	F1	Help/Help Index
Access the tutorial	Shift+F1	Help/Works Tutorial
Enter or exit edit mode	F2	
Move information	F3	Edit/Move
Copy contents of cell	Shift+F3	Edit/Copy
Repeat last copy command	Shift+F7	
Extend or select	F8	Select/Cells
Select column	Shift+F8	Select/Column
Select row	Ctrl+F8	Select/Row
Select range (also F8 then Arrow)	Shift+Arrow	Select/Cells
Select entire database	Ctrl+Shift+F8	Select/All
Return to List screen	F10	View/List
View active report	Shift+F10	View/Report Number
Collapse current selection	Escape	
Turn off extend action	Escape	
Enter current date	Ctrl+; (semicolon)	
Enter current time	Ctrl+Shift+; (semicolon)	
Erase contents of cell	Backspace then Enter	Edit/Clear

Increasing the Printing and Viewing Width

The standard margin settings—left margin at 1.3 inches and right margin at 1.2 inches—allow only a few fields to print on a page or to be viewed on screen. Seeing as much of a report as possible helps in designing it.

You can use the Print menu's Page Setup & Margins command to reduce the left and right margins to zero, and then reset the margins to the size you want after everything's finished. Figure 10-6 shows the result of zero margins.

EMP#	FIRST MI	LAST NAME	POSITION	POSDATE	DEPT#
220	LAWRENCE A	ADAMS	QUALITY CONTROL SUPERVISOR	6/13/86	140
197	HOLLY	SANCHEZ	CUSTOMER SERVICE MANAGER	2/17/81	120
134	JOHN E	RYE	WIRER/SOLDERER A	9/14/74	200
147	BETTY C	SCHRAFT	TECHNICIAN A	4/23/86	200
205	CORINNE	HALSTEAD	EXECUTIVE SECRETARY	10/1/84	170
213	SEYMOUR	COOPER	RECEPTIONIST	5/21/85	160
188	MARGERY	LE BLANC	FIELD SERVICE TECHNICIAN	11/3/78	210
155	TOMMY	CHEN	QUALITY CONTROL TESTER	6/21/88	140
202	HARRY	FUJITSU	SECRETARY	8/29/83	160
222	PERRY JOHN	O'HALLORAN	FIELD SERVICE TECHNICIAN	3/7/85	210
181	JAMES R	MAURICE	MARKETING MANAGER	4/20/81	100
229	GEORGE	DANDER	CUSTOMER SERVICE REP	9/14/88	120
199	LEROY	MILLER	SALESPERSON	12/3/82	100
191	JUDY	BROOKS	CUSTOMER SERVICE REP	10/25/82	120
217	KENNETH	PAGNOZZI	ACCOUNTS RECEIVABLE CLERK	8/3/83	160
209	MARIANNE	BELL	FIELD SERVICE TECHNICIAN	6/21/88	210
152	DAVID C	WILKINS	ELECTRONICS ENGINEER	3/16/89	250

Figure 10-6. The first page in the employee roster after an increase in print width

Each time you make a change of any kind in the report definition, you can view the result in two ways:

1. Press Shift+F10 (the shortcut for the View menu's Report command) to display as much of the active report as fits on screen.
2. Summon the Print menu's Preview command to get a bird's-eye view of the entire report, one page at a time.

Selecting and Shifting the Fields

A report can contain every field in a database or selected fields only. If you decide to include every field, Works prints as many fields as will fit across a page and continues printing on as many succeeding pages as needed to print all the fields.

Ordinarily, you'll want to rearrange and pick-and-choose only those fields that relate to the subject of the report. The key to this activity is the Edit menu's Move command, which lets you shift fields effortlessly from one place to another.

Moving affects only the sequence of fields in this particular report, not any other report or the structure of the database.

In this report, the SALARY/YR field replaces the POSDATE (position date) field. Figure 10-4 shows both fields in the Report screen. With the cursor in column I, you press Shift+F8 to select the column, press F3 (the shortcut for Move), move the cursor to column E, and press Enter. Works then inserts the entire salary field (field name, entries, and dollar format) in column E, shifting the displaced position dates and succeeding fields one column to the right.

A second move made in the same way shifts the POSDATE field to a column outside the print area, perhaps to the left of HIREDATE.

Adding a Title and Subtitle

Reports usually contain a report name and other identifying information on the first page. Works leaves two empty lines for these types of entries. You type and enter **EMPLOYEE ROSTER** as you would any other piece of text. The date subtitle `November 1990` is a slightly different story.

Unless you indicate otherwise, Works recognizes a date you type as a value and shows it in standard date format—for example, **November 1990** becomes `Nov 1990` and sits at the right edge of its cell. When you want the full version of a date (that is, November 1990) that's left-justified in its cell, tell Works the date is text by first typing quotation marks.

In this report, typing a space after the quotation marks indents the date and centers it below the title.

Inserting a Line

You can have as many row descriptors of each type as you like.

Lines above and below the field names add a professional touch to a report. You already have an empty row for this line below the field names. You need to insert another one above. These lines are meant to print at the beginning of each page, so you need an `Intr Page` row descriptor.

Works inserts lines above the cursor position. So, with the cursor in the first `Intr Page` row, you choose the Edit menu's Insert Row/Column command. Works then brings up the Row/Column dialog box with `Row` already marked. When you press Enter, Works shows the `Type` dialog box containing various types of row descriptors. When you choose `Intr Page` and hit Enter again, Works inserts an empty row for a line printed at the beginning of each page of a report.

To enter a line above the field names, start with the cursor in column A and type quotation marks to signal to Works that the next character, an equal sign, is text, not a mathematical operator. You then type enough equal signs to fill almost the full length of the entry/edit line and press Enter. In the empty row below the field names, you enter a line composed of minus signs in the same way.

Creating a Header Page Number

You can print a page header, page footer, or both on each page of a report. Page headers and footers print the same thing on each page—for instance, a report title in a header or a page number in a footer.

To make things a bit different, this report has a page number header. Header creation takes place in the Print menu's Headers & Footers command. The header that does the job in Figure 10-2 is

&RPage &P

These codes tell Works to right-align (&R) the word Page and the page number generated by the &P code. The space after Page produces the space between Page and the page number. You'll find a discussion of headers and footers and a list of special codes in Chapter 14.

Sorting the Records

Sorting presents records in a meaningful way. In this type of database, you have a choice of meaningful sorts. For instance, you can sort employees by position or department to get a slant on work groups, by position date or hire date to derive an experience factor, or by last name and first name to get a quick fix on who works where doing what.

You can sort on as many as three fields at one time.

In this report, records are sorted by last name and first name. Figure 10-7 shows the dialog box in the Select menu's Sort Records command, which now contains LAST NAME in the first (most important) field and FIRST MI in the second (second most important) field. Two sorts suffice, so the third (least important) field is empty.

You don't have to tell Works to sort. After you type in the sort fields and press Enter, Works simply does it.

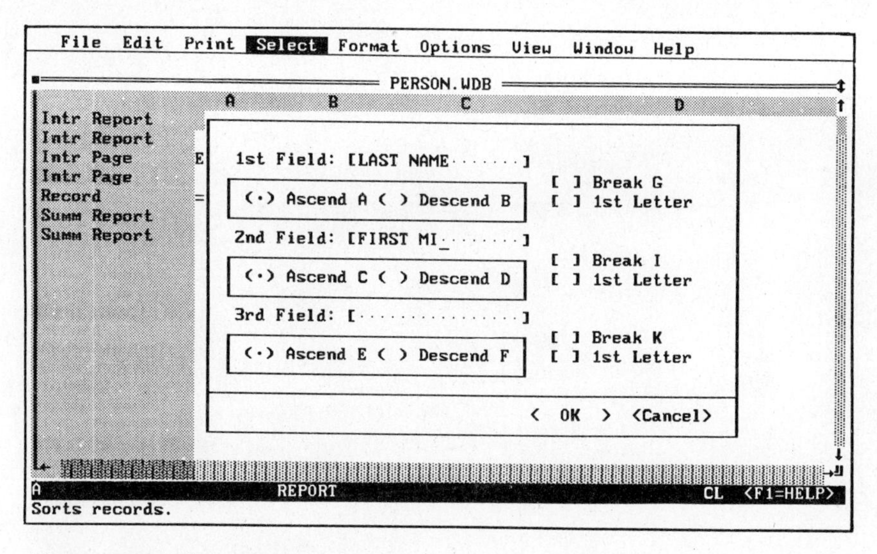

Figure 10-7. The Sort Records dialog box showing sort fields LAST NAME and FIRST MI and unused Break boxes

Inserting Formulas

Figure 10-8 shows the roster at this stage of development—well past the half-way point from speed report in Figure 10-6 to final report in Figure 10-2. Now is the time to insert formulas that make summary calculations. In this report, that means a count of last names, which shows the number of employees, and total salaries, which can show the annual payroll.

Getting these types of calculations is a function of the Edit menu's Insert Field Summary command. When you choose this command, Works presents a dialog box containing lists of fields and types of calculations. When you choose one from list A (`Fields`) and one from list B (`Statistic`), Works plunks the proper formula into the cell at the cursor's location.

You can see the two calculating formulas (COUNT and SUM) in this report in the second `Summ Report` row in Figure 10-1. The first `Summ Report` row is empty to allow a bit of breathing room between the records and calculations.

```
                                                                    Page 1

                                      EMPLOYEE ROSTER
                                       November 1990
========================================================================
EMP#   FIRST MI      LAST NAME     POSITION                    SALARY/YR DEPT#
------------------------------------------------------------------------
217    KENNETH       PAGNOZZI      ACCOUNTS RECEIVABLE CLERK   $18,630    160
                                   1
197    HOLLY         SANCHEZ       CUSTOMER SERVICE MANAGER    $37,555    120
191    JUDY          BROOKS        CUSTOMER SERVICE REP        $29,000    120
229    GEORGE        DANDER        CUSTOMER SERVICE REP        $24,560    120
                                   3
152    DAVID C       WILKINS       ELECTRONICS ENGINEER        $46,780    250
205    CORINNE       HALSTEAD      EXECUTIVE SECRETARY         $23,430    170
                                   2
209    MARIANNE      BELL          FIELD SERVICE TECHNICIAN    $28,756    210
188    MARGERY       LE BLANC      FIELD SERVICE TECHNICIAN    $23,500    210
222    PERRY JOHN    O'HALLORAN    FIELD SERVICE TECHNICIAN    $27,000    210
                                   3
181    JAMES R       MAURICE       MARKETING MANAGER           $42,560    100
                                   1
220    LAWRENCE A    ADAMS         QUALITY CONTROL SUPERVISOR  $32,500    140
155    TOMMY         CHEN          QUALITY CONTROL TESTER      $21,550    140
                                   2
213    SEYMOUR       COOPER        RECEPTIONIST                $17,000    160
                                   1
199    LEROY         MILLER        SALESPERSON                 $32,000    100
202    HARRY         FUJITSU       SECRETARY                   $19,680    160
                                   2
147    BETTY C       SCHRAFT       TECHNICIAN A                $24,560    200
                                   1
134    JOHN E        RYE           WIRER/SOLDERER A            $18,750    200
                                   1

       EMPLOYEES:    17                                        $467,811
```

Figure 10-8. The records sorted and grouped by position

Inserting a Label

A label is a piece of text you enter in a report to make things perfectly clear. In this report, the word **EMPLOYEES:** before the number 17 (the count of last names in Figure 10-1) explains the meaning of the number. A 17 alone would look very much in limbo. You enter a label in the same way as any other text.

Aligning and Formatting Entries

The metamorphosis from speed reporting to custom definition ends with aligning and formatting entries. While Works copies all original alignments and formats from the List screen, giving the salaries the dollar format, little touches here and there can enhance the final product.

Place the cursor on the element representing the item you want to align or format, and then use the Format menu's number and alignment commands. For example, in this report definition:

- The COUNT(LAST NAME) formula in column C of the Summ Report row is left-justified to make EMPLOYEES: and the number 17 appear unified. Otherwise, Works right-justifies the number, keeping it far away from the label.
- The SUM('SALARY/YR) formula in column E of the Summ Report row is formatted for Dollars to match the salaries in the cells above.
- The 'SALARY/YR and SUM('SALARY/YR) formulas are centered to give them better balance with their field name heading.

Voila, the report in Figure 10-2 emerges in all its glory.

There's no question that speed reporting gives you a headstart on a report. Sometimes, though, you may find it more efficient to create a report definition from scratch. Your experience with Works will help you decide the best route to take and under what circumstances.

More Custom Tailoring

Works has even more ways to customize the appearance of a printed report, including defining break fields, selecting records and fields, changing the column widths, changing the font size, inserting page breaks, double spacing, using statistical functions, and specifying text enhancements such as underline and boldface.

Row Descriptors

You can use any number of row descriptors in a report definition.

You know by now that row descriptors can print main titles at the beginning of a report, field names on each page, a count of records, a sum of numbers, and the records themselves. Works has row descriptors that perform other functions. Table 10-2 gives a complete list of row descriptors, what they do, how often, and where they do it.

Table 10-2. Row descriptors and what they do

Row Descriptor	What and Where It Prints
Intr Report	Introductory text at the beginning of a report
Intr Page	Introductory text at the top of each page
Intr BREAKFIELD	Text or calculation at the beginning of each group of sorted records. You can have three Intr BREAKFIELDs corresponding to the break fields specified in the Sort Records dialog box
Record	Entries in each record in the database
Summ BREAKFIELD	Subtotals at the end of each group of sorted records. You can have three Summ BREAKFIELDs corresponding to the break fields specified in the Sort Records dialog box
Summ Report	Summary of all calculations at the end of a report

Sorting and Grouping the Records

A simple sort arranges records sequentially; a sort and break splits them into groups with totals of numbers or counts of text entries at the end of each group.

Reports can show records split into groups based on sort fields and break fields. Break fields tell Works where splits should occur and let you specify breaks by first letter.

For example, if you specify a sort/break by last name and first letter, Works groups the records based on the first letter of the last name (for example, all A's in one group, all B's in the next) or, if the sort/break is by position, by position titles (for example, all Secretary's in one group, all Technician's in another).

These sort and break settings take place in the Select menu's Sort Records command. You can see these fields in Figure 10-7. The boxes next to each sort field—Break and 1st Letter—show the break choices. Works dims the 1st Letter box until you turn on the Break box. If you then turn on the 1st Letter box, too, Works inserts a break in the records when the first letter in the sort group changes.

Works saves sort field and break field settings with the report.

To give you an idea of how this looks, the report in Figure 10-8 shows the employee records sorted and split into groups by position. Visualize the Sort Records dialog box with POSITION in the 1st Field and LAST NAME in the 2nd Field. Both the Break and 1st Letter boxes in the POSITION field are turned on.

In the report definition, Works inserts a row descriptor—in this case, `Summ POSITION#`—to indicate a break field. It also enters a formula in every field (except those containing dates or times) in the `Summ POSITION#` row. These formulas add the numerical entries (employee numbers, salaries, and department numbers), count the text entries (first names, last names, and positions), and produce a number below each group.

Clearly, adding employee numbers and counting first names doesn't make much sense, so it's up to you to erase the unneeded formulas. This is a simple matter of placing the cursor on the cell and pressing Backspace and then Enter.

Double Spacing a Report

Double spacing can enhance the legibility of a report. You can get it by inserting a `Record` row descriptor above or below the one produced by speed-reporting.

You can triple-space a report by inserting two `Record` *row descriptors in the same way.*

In the Report screen, place the cursor in column A in the `Record` row and choose the Edit menu's Insert Row/Column command. Press Enter to confirm `Row`, and Works brings up the list of descriptors. You'll see `Record` in reverse video, because the cursor was in that row when you started. When you press Enter, Works inserts an empty row in the report definition. This translates into an empty line between each record.

Selecting the Records in a Report

As a matter of routine, Works prints every record in the database. When it gets to the bottom of a page, it prints any remaining records on the next page and continues onto as many pages as necessary to print all the records.

You can select records for printing by establishing query criteria in the same way that you select records for display. The query process is described in Chapter 9. In addition to querying, you can use the Select menu's Hide Record command to hide any records you don't want to print in a report. This command is available in both the Form and List screens.

Fitting in More Fields

Works routinely measures character size in points. Don't confuse points with pitch. A 12-point font is equivalent to a 10-pitch font. A 10-point font is equivalent to a 12-pitch font.

The number of fields that Works can print on a page depends on the size of the character, margins, and width of the paper. The smaller the character, the more fields that can fit. The reports in this chapter are printed in 12-point Courier, which prints 10 characters to the inch. On letter-size paper, this is the equivalent of 80 characters across. A 10-point font prints about 96 characters across.

If you can't fit all the fields you want on a page, consider using smaller characters (Format menu/Font command), reducing the margins (Print menu/Print Setup & Margins command), reducing the column widths (Format menu/Column Width command), or deleting a field (Edit menu/Delete Row/Column command).

Setting the Page Breaks

A page break tells the printer when to stop printing on one page and when to start on the next. Works calculates the page breaks for you, based on the paper length and the top and bottom margin settings in the Print menu's Page Setup & Margins command. You can use the Print menu's Insert Page Break or Delete Page Break commands to insert or delete your own page breaks.

Using Statistics in Formulas

Insert statistics in a report definition by choosing the Edit menu's Insert Field Summary command.

The Edit menu's Insert Field Summary command lets you use statistical functions that summarize numerical entries in the records. You've already seen the COUNT and SUM functions in action. Table 10-3 lists all the functions and what they do.

Table 10-3. Statistical functions and what they do

Function	What It Does
AVG	Produces average of the group
COUNT	Counts number of items in a group
MAX	Produces largest number in a group
MIN	Produces smallest number in the group
STD	Calculates standard deviation of a group
SUM	Produces total of a group
VAR	Calculates variance of a group.

Most of the time, you'll put these statistics in SUMM rows. For example, entering a statistical function in a Summ BREAKFIELD row summarizes the numbers in the preceding group of cells. In a Summ Report or Intr Row row, the function summarizes the cells in the entire report.

Emphasizing the Printing

Works lets you underline, boldface, and italicize text or numbers in a report. This is an effective way to emphasize important parts you want to be sure no one misses. You can also combine styles, such as bold and underline or bold and italic.

When you want to use these enhancements, place the cursor on the element (text or formula) and choose the Format menu's Style command. If you enhance a field element, your selection affects all entries in the field.

Printing the Report

You can choose one of two commands in the Print menu—Print or Preview—to print a report. Preview shows you a miniature version of the report before printing, while Print simply forges ahead.

Either way, Works asks how many copies to print and proposes one copy. You can now tell Works where to print the report (your printer or to a text file on disk), select which pages to print, and specify whether or not to print the records. If you choose not to print records, Works prints everything before and after the records, including the summary rows.

In the next chapter, you'll turn the concepts in this chapter into reality when you create a mailing list database, design a report definition, and print the report.

Database Workout: Customer Mailing List

One of the most common uses of a database is to compile names and addresses for mailing labels.

Databases often contain names and addresses for mailing lists and mailing labels. Figure 11-1 shows this kind of list compiled by restauranteur Antonia Chavez, owner of Chez Chavez, a trendy local restaurant. Chez Chavez recently underwent extensive renovation and expansion to the kitchen and dining rooms.

	MR/MS	FIRST MI	LAST NAME	STREET	CITY	ST	ZIP
1	Mr.	Richard	Aldrich	55 Primrose Path	Redfern	NY	11569
2	Mr. & Mrs.	Michael	Aven	4 Mockingbird Hill	Abner	NY	11878
3	Mrs.	Evelyn	Aven	21 June Lane	Aquabogue	NY	11678
4	Professor	Burt E.	Byrd	72 Golf Course	Abner	NY	11878
5	Mr.	Catto	Champagne	1234 Magpie Court	Blueport	NY	11570
6	Ms.	Jennifer	Chan	88 Cricket Court	Abner	NY	11878
7	Ms.	Justine	LeClerc	103 Circus Lane	Kensington	NY	12011
8	Mr. & Ms.	Walter	Ortiz	567 Cottage Circle	Abner	NY	11878
9	Ms.	Caroline	Pasiri	1891 Butternut Lane	Abner	NY	11878
10	Mr. & Dr.	Clinton	Powell	543 Any Place	Abner	NY	11878
11	Dr. & Mrs.	Michael	Ryan	19 Tennis Court	Aquabogue	NY	11678
12	Mr. & Ms.	John Q.	Smith	5 Red Creek Lane	Redfern	NY	11569
13	Ms.	Karen E.	Spolberg	80 Shad Row	Abner	NY	11878
14	Mr.	Corey	Thompson	37 Sandpiper Road	Blueport	NY	11570
15	Mr.	Ben	Weissman	2141 Holland Ave	Abner	NY	11878

Figure 11-1. A list of Chez Chavez customers sorted by name

Pretend you're Antonia Chavez. In your first Works database, you enter the names and addresses of your steady patrons in a database. You plan to invite these special people to a festive dinner (as your guest, of course) as a token of appreciation and to let them know Chez Chavez is again open for business.

This session is a long one loaded with goodies. It's split into two parts to give you a chance to take a break if you need one. In the first part, you enter labels and field names; adjust column widths in the

Form and List screens; create constant field formulas; enter, sort, and search records; ditto entries; query the database; select and unselect records, and print a customer list.

In the second part, you create a report definition; insert and delete row descriptors; enter a title, subtitle, and date; redefine the sorts and break field; enter and format formulas; preview the report; and print a customized report with subtotals and a grand total.

Later, in Part Six, "Works Fireworks," you merge this database with an invitation created in the word processor workout, ending up with distinctive, personalized dinner invitations and mailing labels.

Keystrokes and Other Matters

The instructions guide you each step of the way, giving keystrokes and cursor movements relating to each task. In some actions, you need to *press* the Alt key, and in others, *hold down* the Alt key. There's only a slight semantic difference between pressing and holding down a key, but it makes a big difference in the way Works works.

- When you see such instructions as *Press Alt and type TW (Format/Width)*, press and release Alt before you type the letters. Alt activates the menu line, and the letters choose a menu and a command.
- With instructions such as *Hold down Alt and type 2 (to move to 2nd Field)*, press the Alt key, and without releasing Alt, type the number. The number leads you to a field in a dialog box.

Unless the instructions say otherwise, use the Arrow keys (Left, Right, Up, and Down) to move the cursor. Keep an eye on the coordinates in the middle of the status line to be sure the cursor is at the correct place before you take the next action. If you run into a snag, press the Escape key to cancel what you're doing. Then pick up where you left off.

Part I: Creating a New Database

Load Works as described in the Introduction to this book. At the File menu, the gateway to Works, type **ND** (Create New File/Database).

Works brings up a new database screen called DATA1.WDB. This is the temporary filename Works assigns until you assign your own.

The Form screen shows every field in one record.

You're in the Form screen, as indicated by the word FORM on the status line. This is where you design the database form, create a record by filling in the form, and view the records one at a time.

The status line helps you keep track of where you are and what you're doing. Reading from left to right, here's a refresher on status line elements:

- The number 1 is the active record on screen. The empty space to its immediate right will soon contain a field name.
- 0/0 is the number of records selected from all existing records. You're just starting, so it shows no records out of no records.
- FORM is the view you're in.
- Pg 1 means that this is the first page of the potential five pages (vertical screenfuls) worth of field names.
- Coordinates X5.00" and Y2.00" indicate where the current entry (in this case, the ZIP code) appears on the printed page. Coordinates are critical when you want to position entries properly on a pre-printed form.
- NL shows that the Num Lock key is on. Press the Caps Lock key to make everything you type really stand out. The letters CL now appear on the status line beside NL.
- <F1=HELP> is a reminder that you can press F1 to get help. Mouse users can click on this element to get help.

Figure 11-2 shows labels and fields. The top four lines (three lines of text, one line of asterisks) are labels. They identify the purpose of the database. The seven lines below them are fields, distinguished from labels by the presence of a colon. The shaded area to the right of each field name represents the field width.

Now, let's make your screen look something like this one. If you make a typo, press Backspace (not an Arrow key) to back up the cursor and erase.

Entering the Labels

As you enter labels, compare your results with Figure 11-2 to be sure they're in the proper place on the screen. The cursor is in the first column in the first row.

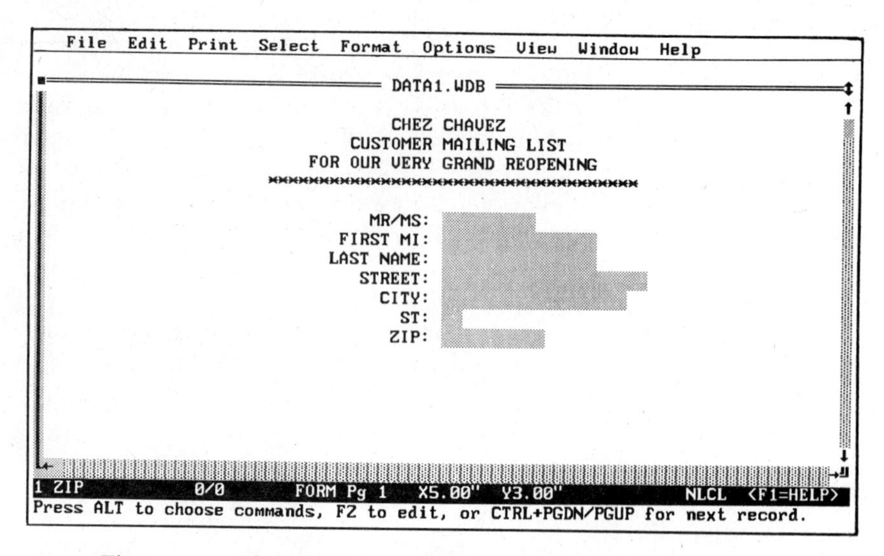
File Edit Print Select Format Options View Window Help

DATA1.WDB

CHEZ CHAVEZ
CUSTOMER MAILING LIST
FOR OUR VERY GRAND REOPENING
****

MR/MS:
FIRST MI:
LAST NAME:
STREET:
CITY:
ST:
ZIP:

1 ZIP 0/0 FORM Pg 1 X5.00" Y3.00" NLCL <F1=HELP>
Press ALT to choose commands, F2 to edit, or CTRL+PGDN/PGUP for next record.

Figure 11-2. The single record form in the mailing list database

- Press Down Arrow to move the cursor one row down, and press Right Arrow 32 times to move toward the middle of the screen. On the status line, you should see X4.50" Y1.17".
- Type **CHEZ CHAVEZ** and press Down Arrow. Press Left Arrow four times. The status line shows X4.10" Y1.33".
- Type **CUSTOMER MAILING LIST** and press Down Arrow. Press Left Arrow four times. The status line shows X3.70" Y1.50".
- Type **FOR OUR VERY GRAND REOPENING** and press Down Arrow again. Press Left Arrow four times. The status line now shows X3.30" Y1.67".
- Press the asterisk key 36 times (you'll need to Shift) and press Down Arrow twice. Press Right Arrow 10 times. The status line now shows X3.30" Y2.00".

Entering the Fields and Field Widths

Telling Works which is a label and which is a field is a simple matter of typing a colon after the field name.

Next, enter the field names and field widths. The field width allots room for entries in that field. Getting the proper width is a matter of estimating the length of a typical entry in that field. As you can see from the varying lengths of the shading in Figure 11-2, some entries need more room and others need less.

After you type a field name, Works asks for the field width and height. Though field widths in this database vary, all fields are one row high. Now press Right Arrow ten times to move the cursor to X4.30" Y2.00".

- Type **MR/MS:** (be sure to type the colon) and press Enter. Works brings up the Width dialog box, proposing 20 characters.
- Type **9** and hit Enter again. If you're working in graphics mode, Works now displays a dotted line after the field name to show the field width. If you're working in text mode, this area remains empty. Press Left Arrow three times. The cursor moves to X4.00" Y2.17".
- Type **FIRST MI:** and press Enter. The FIRST MI field holds first names and middle initials.
- Type **15** and hit Enter. Press Left Arrow once. The cursor moves to X3.90" Y2.33".
- Type **LAST NAME:** and press Enter again.
- Type **15** and hit Enter. Press Right Arrow three times. The cursor is at X4.20" Y2.50".
- Type **STREET:** and press Enter.
- Type **20** and hit Enter again. Press Right Arrow twice. The cursor is now at X4.40" Y2.67".
- Type **CITY:** and press Enter.
- Type **18** and hit Enter. Press Right Arrow twice. The cursor is at X4.60" Y2.83".
- Type **ST:** and press Enter. The ST field holds the state entries.
- Type **2** and hit Enter. Press Left Arrow. The cursor is at X4.50" Y3.00".
- Type **ZIP:** and press Enter.
- Type **10** and hit Enter again. The cursor should now be at X4.50" Y3.17".

This completes the form design. Except for the entry areas, which either show a short line or nothing, your screen should match the one in Figure 11-2. Move the cursor to the right of the ZIP field and press Up Arrow six times. The varying width of the cursor should match the shaded areas in Figure 11-2.

If all is well, continue to the next section, "Entering New Records in the Form Screen." If something's amiss, follow the instructions in "Editing in the Form Screen," below.

Editing in the Form Screen

If a field name is in the wrong place, place the cursor on the field and press F3 (the Move shortcut key). You'll see MOVE on the status line. Use the Right or Left Arrow key to move the cursor to the place where the first letter in the field name should appear, and press Enter. Works then shifts the field.

If the field width is the wrong size, place the cursor in the entry area to the right of the field name. Press Alt and type **TZ** (Format/ Field Size). Type the proper number and press Enter.

Entering New Records in the Form Screen

It's not necessary to press Enter after typing each entry. Moving the cursor to the next field enters what you typed in the active cell and saves a keystroke every time.

Figure 11-3 shows the entries in the first record in this database. If you're not already there, place the cursor in the entry area to the right of the MR/MS field (coordinates X5.00" Y2.00"). Depress the Caps Lock key so you can type in uppercase and lowercase.

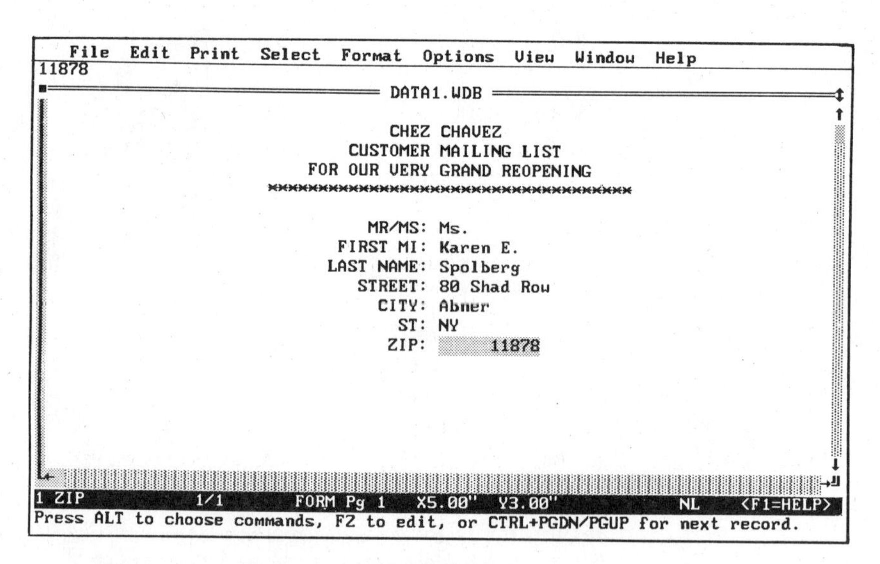

Figure 11-3. The Form screen showing entries in the first record

- Type **Ms.** and tab to the FIRST MI field. If you prefer, use Down Arrow instead of Tab to move from one field to the next.

- Type **Karen E.** and tab to the LAST NAME field.
- Type **Spolberg** and tab to the STREET field.
- Type **80 Shad Row** and tab to the CITY field.
- Type **Abner** and tab to the ST field.
- Type **NY** and tab to the ZIP field.
- Type **11878** and leave the cursor where it is.

Press Tab to jump to the first field in the second record. (As you do, Works enters the Spolberg ZIP code in its field. You'll see it shortly.) The status line now shows record 2 at the left end, and 1/1 to the right. Make the entries in this record as you did the first.

- Type **Ms.** and tab to the FIRST MI field. With the first entry, Works shows 2/2 on the status line.
- Type **Justine** and tab to the LAST NAME field.
- Type **LeClerc** and tab to the STREET field.
- Type **103 Circus Lane** and tab to the CITY field.
- Type **Kensington** and tab to the ST field.
- Type **NY** and tab to the ZIP field.
- Type **12011** and press Enter.

Now press F9 so you can check into how things you've done in the Form screen are working out in the List screen.

Exploring the List Screen

And here's the List screen. Press Ctrl+Home to move the cursor to the first entry in the first record. There are many similarities as well as differences between the Form and List screens. Here's a summary:

- Though the menus are the same, certain commands are different.
- While the Form screen can display only one record at a time, the List screen can show as many as 18.
- The current record number appears on the status line in the Form screen. In the List screen, the number appears to the left of each record.

- Field names you enter in one screen always appear in the other screen, but the layout is different. In the Form screen, Works arranges field names vertically, down the left side of the workspace; in the List screen, Works shows field names horizontally, above the workspace.
- The status line in both screens is similar, with only the Form screen's page number and coordinates missing from the List screen.

Adjusting the Field Width in the List Screen

When you can, keep as many fields on the screen while giving entries the room they need.

Works takes only the field names from the Form screen, not the field widths you entered earlier. As a result, some entries are scrunched into others. To give the screen more eye-appeal and make it easier to read, change the field widths here as well.

All fields are now 10 characters wide. The cursor is in the MR/MS field, so increase it to 11 characters.

- Press Alt and type **TW** (Format/Field Width). Works now shows the number 10, the standard field width, in the `Field Width` box.
- Type **11** (the new width in characters) and press Enter.

The FIRST MI field is fine at 10 characters, but the LAST NAME field needs to be a bit wider. Press Right Arrow twice to move the cursor to the LAST NAME field.

- Press Alt and type **TW** (Format/Field Width).
- Type **11** and press Enter.

Now move the cursor to the STREET field and increase its width to 20 characters.

- Press Alt and type **TW** (Format/Field Width).
- Type **20** and press Enter.

Continue in this way to make the CITY field 11 characters, the ST field 4 characters, and the ZIP field 6 characters.

Entering Constant Field Formulas

Constant field formulas make certain entries standard, saving you the task of typing them over and over.

Figure 11-4 shows all records in this database. As you can see, many Chez Chavez customers live in Abner and all live in New York. You can save typing time by entering constant field formulas that tell Works to enter *Abner*, *NY*, and *11878* (the Abner ZIP code) every time you create a new record. To see how this works, place the cursor in the third record's CITY field.

```
  File  Edit  Print  Select  Format  Options  View  Window  Help
"4 Mockingbird Hill
■════════════════════════════ MAILING.WDB ═════════════════════════════↕
      MR/MS         FIRST MI   LAST NAME        STREET              CITY       ST   ZIP
 1   Ms.           Karen E.   Spolberg    80 Shad Row          Abner        NY  11878
 2   Ms.           Justine    LeClerc     103 Circus Lane      Kensington   NY  12011
 3   Professor     Burt E.    Byrd        72 Golf Course       Abner        NY  11878
 4   Mr. & Ms.     Walter     Ortiz       567 Cottage Circle   Abner        NY  11878
 5   Mr. & Ms.     John Q.    Smith       5 Red Creek Lane     Redfern      NY  11569
 6   Mr.           Corey      Thompson    37 Sandpiper Road    Blueport     NY  11570
 7   Mr.           Catto      Champagne   1234 Magpie Court    Blueport     NY  11570
 8   Mr.           Ben        Weissman    2141 Holland Ave     Abner        NY  11878
 9   Dr. & Mrs.    Michael    Ryan        19 Tennis Court      Aquabogue    NY  11678
 10  Mrs.          Evelyn     Aven        21 June Lane         Aquabogue    NY  11678
 11  Ms.           Jennifer   Chan        88 Cricket Court     Abner        NY  11878
 12  Mr. & Dr.     Clinton    Powell      543 Any Place        Abner        NY  11878
 13  Ms.           Caroline   Pasiri      1891 Butternut Lane  Abner        NY  11878
 14  Mr.           Richard    Aldrich     55 Primrose Path     Redfern      NY  11569
 15  Mr. & Mrs.    Michael    Aven        4 Mockingbird Hill   Abner        NY  11878
 16
 17
 18
15 STREET        15/15      LIST                                              <F1=HELP>
Press ALT to choose commands, or F2 to edit.
```

Figure 11-4. All records in the mailing list database

- Type =“**Abner** and move the cursor to the ST (state) field.

Quotation marks tell Works that a formula is text. Though it seems as if nothing has happened, Works has accepted the field formula.

- Type =“**NY** and move the cursor to the ZIP field. Again, there is no visual response from Works.
- Type =**11878** and press Enter. You don't need quotes, because this formula is a number. You'll see all three entries in a moment.

Entering New Records in the List Screen

Turn off the Num Lock key, and then press Home to reach the third record's MR/MS field. Now fill in the other entries in the third record, as shown in Figure 11-4.

- Type **Professor** and move to the FIRST MI field. Instantly, Works plunks **Abner, NY**, and **11878**—the three entries produced by field formulas—into their cells.
- Type **Burt E.** and move to the LAST NAME field.
- Type **Byrd** and move to the STREET field.
- Type **72 Golf Course** and press Down Arrow. Hit Home to move to the MR/MS field in the second record.

Referring to Figure 11-4, enter the courtesy title, name, and street for Mr.& Mrs. Ortiz. Works will enter the city, state, and ZIP code.

Dittoing the Previous Entry

The ditto feature, available only in the List screen, lets you copy the entry in the cell above.

The Smith record has `Mr. & Ms.` in the MR/MS field, the same as the Ortiz record above it. Instead of typing **Mr. & Ms.** again, you can ditto it from the cell above.

- Hold down the Ctrl key and press the apostrophe key. You now see `Mr. & Ms.` on the entry/edit line, just as if you typed it. Press Right Arrow to move the cursor to the FIRST MI field. Works plunks the courtesy title, as well as Abner, NY, and 11878, into the cells in this record.
- Type in the name and street for the Smiths. Now pause a moment. These customers live in Redfern, so simply overtype the Abner entry with **Redfern** and the Abner ZIP code with **11569**.

Entering More Records

Using Figure 11-4 as a guide, enter the rest of the records in the same way, dittoing previous entries where possible and overtyping the results of field formulas where necessary. To get to the first field in the next record, press Down Arrow and then Home.

There's no problem with dittoing into a cell that's already filled—as in the second Blueport records and second Aquabogue records, both of which will contain Abner before you ditto into them-—because the new information replaces the old.

Saving and Naming the Database

You've finished entering the records, so this is a good time to save and name the database. Let's call it MAILING. Leave the cursor where it is.

- Press Alt and type **FA** (File/Save As). Works now brings up the `Save As` dialog box so you can type a filename, and if needed, a drive or directory. If you're saving to the current drive, simply type the filename. Otherwise, type the drive or directory before the filename, like this: **A:MAILING**.
- Type **MAILING** and press Enter. Works appends the extension `.WDB` (for Works Database).

As the file is being saved, the cell indicator at the left end of the status line shows the percentage already processed. When the record number reappears, Works is ready for your next action.

Sorting the Records

You can sort records alphabetically, numerically, and chronologically in ascending or descending order, and specify up to three sort fields.

Pretend you have hundreds of records in this database. Sorting alphabetically by last name (most important field) and first name (second most important field) will make them easier to work with. Leave the cursor where it is.

- Press Alt and type **SO** (Select/Sort Records). Unless you specify something else, Works sorts on the first field, so you now see `MR/MS` in the `1st Field` field.
- Type **LAST NAME** (to specify the first sort). Ascending order is fine.
- Hold down Alt and type **2** (to move to `2nd Field`).
- Type **FIRST NAME** (to specify the second sort). Again, ascending order is fine, so press Enter. The List screen now returns with all records fully sorted by name.

Searching the Records

It's been a busy Saturday night at Chez Chavez, and one of your regular customers left his hat and umbrella behind. You want to get in touch with him. He once mentioned living on Red... something lane. You'll know his name when you hear it. Let's try a database search. Leave the cursor where it is.

- Press Alt and type **SS** (Select/Search). Works brings up the `Search for` dialog box.
- Type **Red** (the search item). A search by `Next record` is fine, so press Enter.

If you don't find the search item immediately, you can repeat the search by pressing F7.

And the cursor jumps to Redfern, Richard Aldrich. No, that's not it. Press F7 to repeat the search.

Instantly, Works finds `5 Red Creek Crescent`. John Q. Smith. That's the name! If this database had a phone number field (which this type always does), you could be dialing now.

Querying the Database

Several months pass, and you're thinking seriously about opening another restaurant in Blueport. You want to see only the records of customers who live there. Let's query the database.

- Press Alt and type **VQ** (View/Query). Works brings up the Query screen showing all the field names. Move the cursor to the CITY entry area.
- Type **Blueport** (the query criteria) and press Enter.
- Press F10 to apply the query.

Works now displays the Catto Champagne and Corey Thompson records, the only ones in this database that match the criterion. (Of course, in a real database there'd be lots more.) On the status line, Works shows `2/15`, meaning two of the fifteen records are displayed.

Displaying All Records

Now display every record. You can do this in two ways: by telling Works to display all records or by deleting the criterion. Leave the cursor where it is and have Works display all records.

- Press Alt and type **SL** (Select/Show All Records). And here are all 15 records again.

  To keep things neat and trim, get rid of the criterion anyway.

- Press Alt and type **VQ** (View/Query). You see the Query screen again. Place the cursor in the CITY field.
- Press Backspace and hit Enter. This clears the cell. Press F10 to return to the List screen.

Preparing for Printing

In the next step, you'll print the records. To fit every field across the page, reduce the left and right margins to zero. This increases the print width to the maximum and still leaves small, respectable margins. Leave the cursor where it is.

- Press Alt and type **PM** (Print/Page Setup & Margins). You now see the `Page Setup & Margins` dialog box.
- Hold down Alt and type **E** (to move to `Left Margin`).
- Type **0** (for zero inches).
- Press Tab (to move to the `Right Margin`).
- Type **0** again. The other print settings are fine for this listing, so press Enter.

Printing the List

Assuming you specified one text printer during Works Setup, the only thing left is to tell Works to print. (If you specified more than one text printer, press Alt now, type **PS** for Print/Printer Setup, and choose your printer.) Turn on the printer so you'll be ready.

- Press Alt and type **PP** (Print/Print). You now see the `Print` dialog box.
- Hold down Alt and type **L** (to turn on `Print record and field labels`). Works enters an X in the check box. Press Enter.

The printer whirs, and here's your customer list looking like the one in Figure 11-1. Save the database again: Press Alt and type **FS** (File/Save).

In the next part of this workout, you'll create a report definition and print a custom report. If you're taking a break now, leave the cursor where it is.

- Press Alt and type **FX** (File/Exit). You're now at the DOS prompt. See you back here real soon.

Part II: Creating a Report Definition

Printing a no-frills report from the List screen works well for everyday activities. For something a bit fancier, you need a report definition.

A report definition consists of descriptors that define what each row contains, such as headings, records, and calculations. Figure 11-5 shows a report that groups and counts customers by city, while Figure 11-6 shows the report definition that produces it.

```
5/17/90                    CHEZ CHAVEZ CUSTOMERS
                                  By City

MR/MS        FIRST MI  LAST NAME  STREET              CITY        ST  ZIP

Mr. & Mrs.  Michael   Aven       4 Mockingbird Hill   Abner       NY  11878
Professor   Burt E.   Byrd       72 Golf Course       Abner       NY  11878
Ms.         Jennifer  Chan       88 Cricket Court     Abner       NY  11878
Mr. & Ms.   Walter    Ortiz      567 Cottage Circle   Abner       NY  11878
Ms.         Caroline  Pasiri     1891 Butternut Lane  Abner       NY  11878
Mr. & Dr.   Clinton   Powell     543 Any Place        Abner       NY  11878
Ms.         Karen E.  Spolberg   80 Shad Row          Abner       NY  11878
Mr.         Ben       Weissman   2141 Holland Ave     Abner       NY  11878
                                                      8
Mrs.        Evelyn    Aven       21 June Lane         Aquabogue   NY  11678
Dr. & Mrs.  Michael   Ryan       19 Tennis Court      Aquabogue   NY  11678
                                                      2
Mr.         Catto     Champagne  1234 Magpie Court    Blueport    NY  11570
Mr.         Corey     Thompson   37 Sandpiper Road    Blueport    NY  11570
                                                      2
Ms.         Justine   LeClerc    103 Circus Lane      Kensington  NY  12011
                                                      1
Mr.         Richard   Aldrich    55 Primrose Path     Redfern     NY  11569
Mr. & Ms.   John Q.   Smith      5 Red Creek Lane     Redfern     NY  11569
                                                      2
                                                      15
```

Figure 11-5. The list of restaurant customers grouped and counted by city

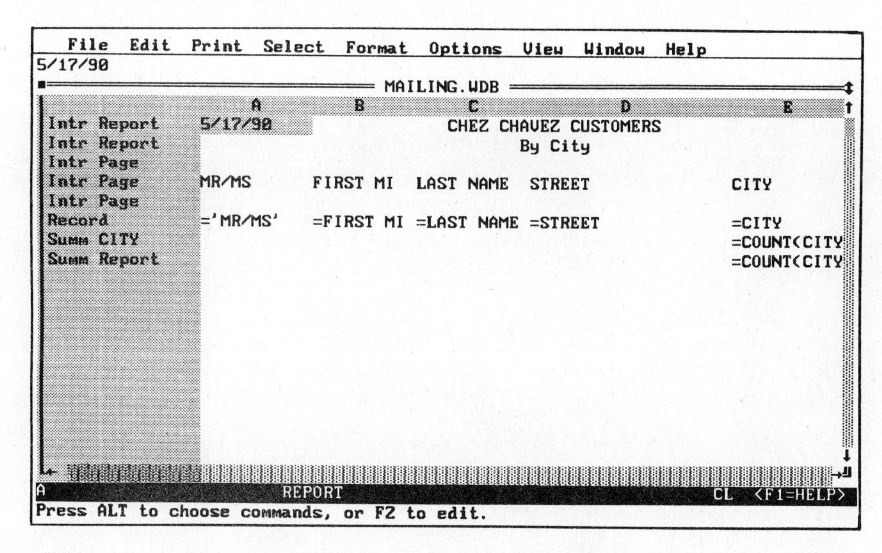

Figure 11-6. The report definition that produces the report in Figure 11-5

If You're Continuing On...

If you're continuing from Part I of this workout, you should still be in the List screen. Skip to "Speed Reporting."

If You're Starting Anew...

If you're starting anew, load the Works program again. At the File menu, type **O** (to choose `Open Existing File`). At the `Open Existing File` dialog box, press Tab to move into the `Files` list. Type **M** to jump the blinker to the first filename that starts with the letter M. If this is `MAILING.WDB`, press Enter. If the blinker is on a different filename, type **M** until you get to `MAILING.WDB` and press Enter. You should now see the MAILING records in the List screen.

Speed Reporting

Pressing Shift+F10 lets you see a report but doesn't take you into the report definition screen after you press Escape. It brings you back to the List screen instead.

You can create a report definition from scratch, entering each descriptor, piece of text, and formula, or have Works give you a headstart in a process called speed reporting. Let's have Works do it. Leave the cursor where it is.

- Press Alt and type **VN** (View/New Report).

Instantly, Works brings up the Report screen showing the first four field names and entries in the first thirteen records.

■ Press Enter three times to see the rest of the fields and records.

Press Escape to display the report definition Works created to produce this report. The result on your screen should match the one in Figure 11-7.

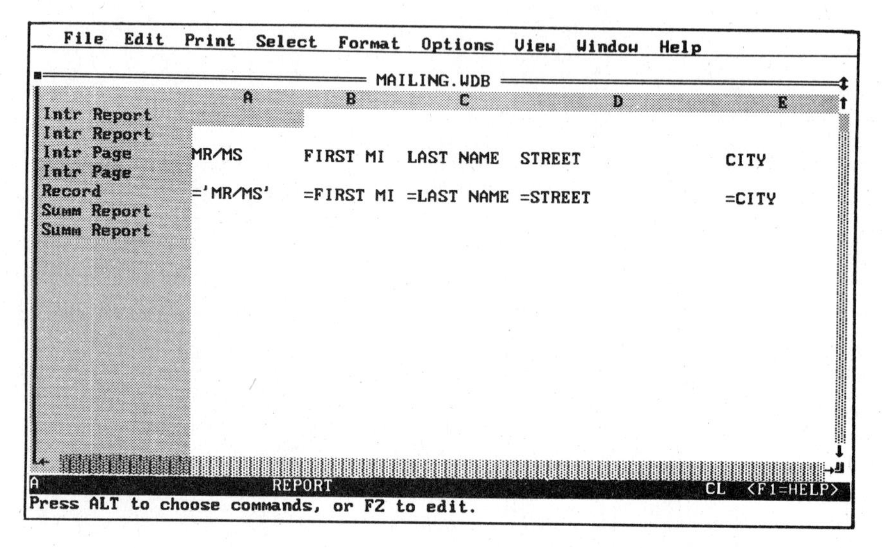

Figure 11-7. The report definition initially produced with speed reporting

Row descriptors at the left describe the kinds of information in the report:

1. Intr Report leaves two blank rows at the beginning of the report, ideal for a two-line title or a one-line title with a blank row below it.
2. Intr Page prints field names at the top of each page with a blank row below them.
3. Record prints the entries in each record.
4. Summ Report leaves two blank rows at the end of the report. You can enter summary statistics here or create groupings.

The workspace shows the text and formulas corresponding to the descriptors, with formulas preceded by an equal sign.

Customizing the Report

After Works gets you started on a report definition, you can increase the viewing width, add a report title and date, insert statistics, group records, and do many other things to get the exact result you want. The place to do this is in the report definition screen. The goal now is to get from the report definition in Figure 11-7 to the one in Figure 11-6.

Increasing the Viewing Width

Start by reducing the print margins so you can display all the fields. Leave the cursor where it is.

- Press Alt and type **PM** (Print/Page Setup & Margins).
- Hold down Alt and type **E** (to move to `Left margin`).
- Type **.7** (for 7/10 inches).
- Press Tab (to move to the `Right margin`).
- Type **.5** (for one-half inch) and press Enter.

Previewing the Report

You can see the entire report at any time by using the Preview command. Leave the cursor where it is.

- Hold down Alt and type **PV** (Print/Preview). All dialog box settings are fine, so press Enter.

Works brings up a miniature version of the report. Although every field now fits on one page, there's work to be done in other areas. Press Escape to return to the report definition.

Entering the Title and Subtitle

Enter a title and subtitle to describe the purpose of the report. Indenting before typing places them about in the center of the line. Place the cursor in the top cell in column C.

- Press the Spacebar 3 times. Type **CHEZ CHAVEZ CUSTOMERS** and press Down Arrow.
- Press the Spacebar 10 times. Type **By City** and press Enter.

Entering and Aligning a Date

Date-stamping your reports shows which one is most current. Move the cursor to the top cell in column A.

- Hold down Ctrl and press ; (the semicolon key). On the entry/edit line and in the active cell in column A, Works displays the date entered at DOS startup or the one kept by your computer's clock.
- Press Enter (to move the date into its cell).

Dates are values, so Works right-aligns it in its cell. To get a better blend with the entries in column A, left-align the date instead. Leave the cursor on the date cell.

- Press Alt and type **TS** (Format/Style).
- Type **L** (to move to `Left`) and press Enter.

Inserting an Empty Row

Now insert a blank row to separate the subtitle from the field names in the row below.

If you were creating a report definition from scratch, this is how you'd insert row descriptors.

- Press Down Arrow twice (to move to `MR/MS`).
- Press Alt and type **EI** (Edit/Insert Row/Column). Works now brings up the `Insert Row/Column` dialog box showing `Row` selected. Perfect. Press Enter.

You now see the `Type` box with Works proposing an `Intr Page` descriptor. You want the empty row only on the first page where you print.

- Move the cursor to `Intr Report` and press Enter.

Works now inserts an `Intr Report` descriptor at the left and an empty row in the workspace.

Defining the Sorts and Breaks

When you sort and define a break field, Works inserts a `fieldname` *descriptor in the report definition.*

The customer records are now sorted by last name, and then first name. It makes more marketing sense to sort them by city. You want CITY to be the most important field, LAST NAME the second most important field, and FIRST MI the least important. Further, you want Works to group the records by city, a matter of defining the break field. Figure 11-8 shows the dialog box with these settings.

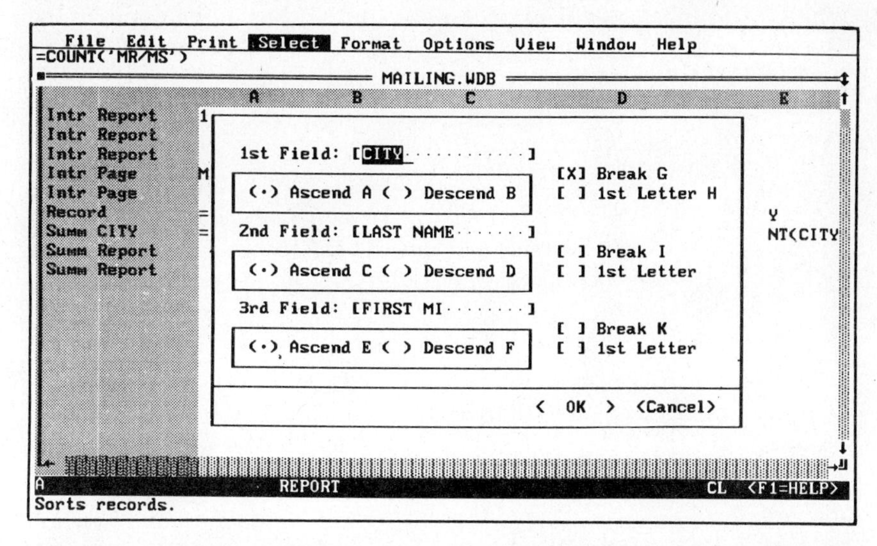

Figure 11-8. The Sort Records dialog box showing the sort and break field

Place the cursor in column A in the first `Summ Report` row.

- Press Alt and type **SO** (Select/Sort Records). Works brings up the `Sort Records` dialog box. Define the first sort.
- Type **CITY** (the first sort field). Tell Works to break only on the city entries.
- Hold down Alt and type **G** (to move to the first field `Break`). Now continue defining the other sorts.
- Hold down Alt and type **2** (to move to `2nd Field`).
- Type **LAST NAME** (the second sort field).
- Hold down Alt and type **3** (to move to `3rd Field`).
- Type **FIRST MI** (the third sort field) and press Enter.

In the report definition screen, Works now inserts `Summ CITY` at the left and a row of formulas in the workspace.

Previewing the Report

Preview the report again to see how far you've come. Leave the cursor where it is.

- Hold down Alt and type **PV** (Print/Preview). Press Enter.

This version is a vast improvement over the earlier one, but there are still a few more things to be done, especially the subtotals in every category, produced by the `Summ CITY` formulas. Press Escape to return to the report definition.

Erasing Formulas

Now erase every `Summ CITY` formula except the one in column E. Place the cursor in column A in the `Summ CITY` row.

- Press F8 (to extend the selection).
- Move the cursor to column D (to select cells A to D in the `Summ CITY` row).
- Hold down Alt and type **EE** (Edit/Clear).

Move the cursor to column F in the `Summ CITY` row.

- Press F8 (to extend the selection).
- Move the cursor to column G (to select cells F and G in the `Summ CITY` row).
- Hold down Alt and type **EE** (Edit/Clear).

Inserting Formulas

You want a total of all the records in this report, so you need a counting formula. Place the cursor in column E in the first `Summ Report` row.

*You can also type a formula (for instance, type =**COUNT(CITY)** and press Enter). Sure, it's easy this way—if you're not prone to typos.*

- Press Alt and type **ES** (Edit/Insert Field Summary). Works now brings up the `Insert Field Summary` dialog box listing field names and calculating statistics. The blinker is on `MR/MS` in the Fields list.
- Type **C** (to move to `CITY`).

- Press Tab (to move to the Statistic list).
- Type **C** (to move to COUNT) and press Enter.

And the formula magically appears.

Left-Aligning the Formulas

Works routinely right-aligns numbers. Left-aligning the subtotals and grand total generated by the formulas will bring them flush left with the city names—an aesthetic judgment call. The cursor is on the COUNT formula in the first Summ Report row.

- Press F8 (to extend the selection).
- Press Up Arrow (to select =COUNT(CITY) in the Summ CITY row).
- Press Alt and type **TS** (Format/Style). You selected more than one entry, so Works neutralizes the proposed responses in the Style box.
- Type **L** (to move to Left) and press Enter.

Deleting an Empty Row

Before previewing the report again, delete the second Summ Report row, which serves no purpose in this report definition. Place the cursor in column A in the second Summ Report row.

- Press Alt and type **ED** (Edit/Delete Row/Column).
- Press Enter (to confirm Row).

Previewing and Printing the Report

Practice, patience, and perseverance—the three P's to perfect databases.

Now preview the report again. Leave the cursor where it is.

- Hold down Alt and type **PV** (Print/Preview). Press Enter.

Your report looks mah-velous! You can print it directly from the Preview screen, so turn on your printer and type **P** (for Perfect!).

And here's the list of restaurant patrons, looking just like the one in Figure 11-5.

Saving the Report Definition

Store this report definition on disk with the database.

- Press Alt and type **FS** (File/Save).

Your database workout is over, so relax for now. Keep in mind that in Chapter 20, you'll be merging the records in this database with a dinner invitation. You'll want everything then to be exactly as it is now. If you just can't wait to do terrific things with this database, save it under another name first (File/Save As) and work with that one.

Next, you take a guided tour of the database menus.

Exploring the Database Menus

Now that you've completed the mailing list, you're eager to know more about those remarkable storage places called databases, so this chapter explores all of the database menus and commands.

Unlike the spreadsheet and word processor, which each have one screen in which to work, the database has four screens—Form, List, Query, and Report. Many commands are the same in each screen. Some commands that do about the same thing have different names, depending on the screen in which you can choose them. For instance, the Move command in the List screen works about the same as the Move Field command in the Form screen.

To help you distinguish which command works where, the name of the screen appears in parentheses next to the command name. Where no specific screen is mentioned, the discussion pertains to all database screens.

Works does its best to make maneuvering the menus in the database as easy as in other applications. Although command names vary from screen to screen, Works keeps related commands in the same menu whenever possible. An ellipsis (...) after a command name means that choosing these commands produces a dialog box where you make further choices.

And now, on to the database menus.

The File Menu

A file is a collection of related information.

Works stores your spreadsheets, documents, and databases in files. In the spreadsheet, files consist of titles, numbers, and formulas; in a document, words and numbers; and in a database, records containing names, numbers, and formulas.

The File menu is the traffic manager for files. It lets you create new files, open and close existing files, save and name files, use DOS (Disk Operating System) commands without leaving Works, run other programs from Works, and quit the Works program. All commands in the File menu are the same in every application.

Create New File...

When you open a new database file, Works brings up an empty form screen where you can design the database.

When you choose the Create New File command, Works presents the dialog box where you can open a new word processor, spreadsheet, database, or communications file.

If you've already created and saved a template file in that application (see the Save As command), Works opens the template file instead. A template file contains your standard settings.

Open Existing File...

The Open Existing File command lets you open a file you've already created. The `File to open` dialog box lists the names of all files in the current directory and provides access to other drives and directories. Double dots in the `Directories` box take you to the next higher directory.

Works lists files alphabetically within their type-Word Processor, Spreadsheet, Database, Communications, and Other Files. The fastest way to select a file from this list is to type the first letter of the filename. You can have as many as eight files open at one time, and then use the Window menu to switch quickly from one to another or show several files on screen at one time.

If you want to list the filenames of only one type of file, use the asterisk wildcard in the `File to open` box. For instance, type ***.WKS** to list only spreadsheet files, ***.WDB** for database files, ***.WPS** for word processor files, and ***.WCM** for communications files. The asterisk stands for any number of characters in the same position.

If your computer is part of a network, you can open the file as a read-only file. This allows more than one person to see the file but not make any changes.

Save and Save As...

Better saved than sorry. It takes only a fraction of a second to avoid hours of rebuilding.

The Save and Save As commands store an open file on disk. Any work you've done since you last saved the file is stored only in computer memory. If something unexpected happens (power outage, electric cord pulled out of socket, and so on), that unsaved work is lost.

The Save command saves a file to the current drive, replacing any prior version if it exists. Works doesn't ask you to confirm the replacement. It just goes ahead and does it. If you save a new file with the Save command, Works responds as if you had chosen the Save As command.

The Save As command lets you save a new file and give it a filename. If you don't type an extension, Works tacks one on, based on file type: .WPS for word processor, .WKS for spreadsheet, .WDB for database, and .WCM for communications.

If you type a drive letter and colon first (for instance, **A:FILENAME**) or drive letter and subdirectory first (for instance, **B:\WDATA\FILENAME**), you can save the file under the same filename but to a different drive or directory. When you use Save As to save to another drive or directory, Works asks you to confirm replacement of an existing file.

The Save As command is loaded with other goodies. For starters, it lets you make a backup copy of a file after you save and name it the first time. If you check the Make backup copy box, work on the file, and save your changes, Works saves the current version as the active file and the prior version as a backup file with a new extension—.BKS for spreadsheet, .BDM for database, .BPS for word processor, and .BCM for communications.

You can also use the Save As command to save a file as a text (ASCII) file with or without formatting. ASCII (which stands for American Standard Code for Information Interchange) lets you convert a file so it can be read by other spreadsheet, database, and word processor programs.

But that's not all. The Save as template check box lets you create a master file (aka template), such as a mailing list with category names, field widths, and print settings but no entries. Each time you create a new database file, Works brings up the master mailing list and awaits your entries. If you turn off the mailing list's template status, Works brings up a virgin file instead. You can also turn off or turn on template status in the Options menu's Works Settings command.

Close

Before Works closes and saves an unnamed file, it asks you to name it.

The Close command removes an open file from computer memory and clears it from the screen. When you finish working on a file or you want to open another file but already have eight files open, the Close command makes room for others.

File Management...

Your computer's disk operating system (DOS) provides commands that make working with files and functions easier. You can do such tasks as copy, delete, and rename files, create or remove a directory, copy or format a disk, and set your computer's date and time. The File Management command lets you access these DOS commands without leaving Works. When you're ready to return to Works, type **Exit** (not Works).

Run Other Programs...

The Run Other Programs command lets you launch applications programs without leaving Works. This gives you direct access to other commonly used software, as well as to DOS commands such as CHKDSK, EDLIN, and TREE, that are unavailable in the File Management command. You can choose the programs that appear on the launcher menu. As with File Management, type **Exit** (not Works) to return to Works.

Convert...

The conversion feature applies only to word processor files. Exchanging a Works database file with dBase or other database programs requires an ASCII (text) file convert.

Convert lets you convert a file created in another word processing program, such as Microsoft Word, WordPerfect, DisplayWrite, and MultiMate, to Works file format, with most (if not all) formatting intact. You can then open and use the converted file just as you would any Works document. You can also do the reverse—convert a Works file to another word processor file format. Pressing Escape during a file conversion cancels the conversion.

Exit Works...

The Exit command is a safe and sure way out of the Works program. If you just turn off the computer in midstream, everything in computer memory is lost. Instead, Works gently prods you to save each changed or new, unsaved file, giving you one last chance to rescue your work from oblivion. When you Exit, Works saves information about your work, your printer, and any changes you made in the Works Settings command in a file called WORKS.INI. It uses this information the next time you start Works.

The Edit Menu

The commands in the Edit menu in every screen let you move, copy, insert, and delete information. The Edit menu in the List screen also lets you name fields, and in the Report screen, rearrange fields.

Move (List and Report) Move Field, Move Label, and Move Record (Form)

The Move command, available in the List and Report screens, moves entire records (rows) and fields (columns), including contents and formats, to a new place in the database. Moved information disappears from its original location and reappears at its destination.

Select the record or field before moving it.

Works inserts moved records between existing records, shifting records below the insertion farther down and renumbering them. It inserts moved fields between existing fields, shifting fields to the right of the insertion further to the right.

In the Form screen, the Move Field command moves a field and its contents to a new place on the form. The Move Label command moves a label. The Move Record command moves the entire record to another place in the records, renumbering succeeding records. That's true specialization.

In both screens, the shortcut key F3 lets you move information without going through the Edit menu. During a move, Works displays the word MOVE on the status line.

Copy (List and Report) Copy Label and Copy Record (Form)

Moving the cursor to the next place you want a copy and pressing Shift+F7 repeats the last Copy command.

The Copy command in the List and Report screens copies the contents and format of single cells, as well as entire records and fields (but not field formulas), to a new location in the database and to other open Works files. Copied information remains in its original location and also appears at the destination. The Copy command parts existing records or fields to insert new information, but it replaces the contents of single cells already containing information.

In the Form screen, you'll find the Copy command dimmed, meaning it's not available. If the cursor is on a field name, Copy is unavailable, because Works won't let you duplicate an existing field name. If the cursor is on an empty cell, Copy is unavailable, because there's nothing to copy. (In this event, the Move and Clear commands are dimmed, too.) If the cursor is on a label, such as a title or instruction, Works replaces the dimmed Copy command with an undimmed Copy Label, because you can use the same label as often as you want.

The Copy Record command, available only in the Form screen, duplicates an existing record. This handy feature saves time when you need two records with basically the same entries—for instance, two contact people at the same company. You can then change only those entries that need to be changed instead of starting from scratch.

Shortcut key Shift+F3 lets you copy without going through the Edit menu. During a copy, Works displays the word COPY on the status line.

Fill Right and Fill Down (List)

The Fill Right and Fill Down commands, which appear in the List screen only, copy the content and format of a cell into contiguous cells to the right or below. Fill Right copies into cells to the right of the source cell, and Fill Down copies into cells below the source cell (in displayed records only). Select the source and destination cells before choosing these commands.

Another way to copy into a cell directly below is with the ditto feature, which is available only in the List screen. Place the cursor on the destination cell, press Ctrl+; (Ctrl+semicolon) and then Enter, and Works copies the contents and format of the cell above.

Fill Series (List)

The Fill Series command, a List screen feature, fills any number of cells with a series of numbers, dates, days, months, or years in increments of your choice. The starting value must be a number or date you enter in a cell, not a number or date generated by a formula.

You can use Fill Series to enter such things as a series of months, customer numbers, model numbers, product numbers, invoice numbers, and the like. Before opening the Edit menu and choosing the Fill Series command, type the starting number or date in a cell, and then select the cells into which you want the series to appear.

Clear (List and Report)
Clear Field Contents (Form and Query)

The Clear command (List and Report screens) and Clear Field Contents command (Form screen) clear or "erase" the contents of cells. This leaves the cell empty but the format intact. In the List screen, Clear works with a single cell, a block of cells, or rows or columns of cells.

The exceptions are field formulas, which blissfully remain in their cells even when they are being barraged by Clear. They are, however, unable to withstand the onslaught of an equal sign. Simply enter an equal sign in any cell in the field and all field formulas are gone.

The quick way to erase the contents of a single cell (even one containing a field formula) without going through the Clear command is to place the cursor on the cell, and press Backspace and then Enter.

Delete Record/Field (List)
Delete Line, Delete Label, Delete Field, and Delete Record (Form)
Delete Row/Column (Report)
Delete Query (Query)

The Delete family of commands gets rid of unwanted information. Unlike Clear, which only erases the contents of cells, Delete removes entire rows or fields. Both the contents and format are gone, and the remaining rows or fields close the gap. In the Form screen, commands change, depending on where your cursor is located when you open the Edit menu. Use Delete to remove the following kinds of information:

- In the List screen, the Delete Record/Field command lets you delete entire records and fields.

- In the Form screen, you can delete an empty row (Delete Line), a label (Delete Label), a field and its contents (Delete Field), or the displayed record (Delete Record). You must use a Delete command to delete an empty row, field, or record, but you can use Backspace and Enter to delete a label or an entry in a field. It's all too easy, so use caution.
- In the Report screen, the Delete Row/Column command deletes entire rows, including the row descriptor, and fields, including entries.
- In the Query screen, Delete Query deletes all selection criteria at one time. If you're erasing only one criterion, use Backspace and then Enter. If you're replacing one criterion with another, simply overtype.

Insert Record/Field (List)
Insert Line and Insert Record (Form)
Insert Row/Column (Report)

The Insert family of commands lets you insert empty records (rows) and fields (columns) in the List, Form, and Report screens.

In the List screen, select one or more cells before choosing the Insert Record/Field command, and Works will insert as many empty records or fields as you select. Works inserts new records between existing records, shifting records below the insertion farther down and renumbering them. Works inserts new fields between existing fields, shifting fields to the right of the insertion further to the right.

In the Form screen, you can insert anything from one line to an entire record. Both the line and record are inserted above the cursor's location.

In the Report screen, the Insert Row/Column command lets you insert an empty row into a report definition and specify the row descriptor. If you choose a Record row descriptor and leave the row empty, your report will print double-spaced. The empty row in the report definition will produce an empty line between each record.

Field Name... (List)

The Field Name command lets you name or rename a field in the List screen. There's no need to type a trailing colon after typing a field name, as you must do in the Form screen. Works copies the field name to the Form screen. You can rename a field at any time without losing data.

Insert Field Name..., Insert Field Contents..., and Insert Field Summary... (Report)

These commands, available only in the Report screen, let you rearrange data in a report definition without affecting the structure of the database.

You can insert a field name with the Insert Field Name command, insert entries in a field with the Insert Field Contents command, and insert statistical formulas with the Insert Field Summary command. In each case, Works brings up a dialog box listing the field names in the database.

Figure 12-1 shows the dialog box in the Insert Field Summary command, which lists functions you can use in formulas to produce statistical summaries in a report. These functions are: SUM (total), AVG (average), COUNT (number of items), MAX (largest number), MIN (smallest number), STD (standard deviation), and VAR (variance).

The Print Menu

The Print, Page Setup & Margins, Preview, and Printer Setup commands are the same in every Works application. In the database,

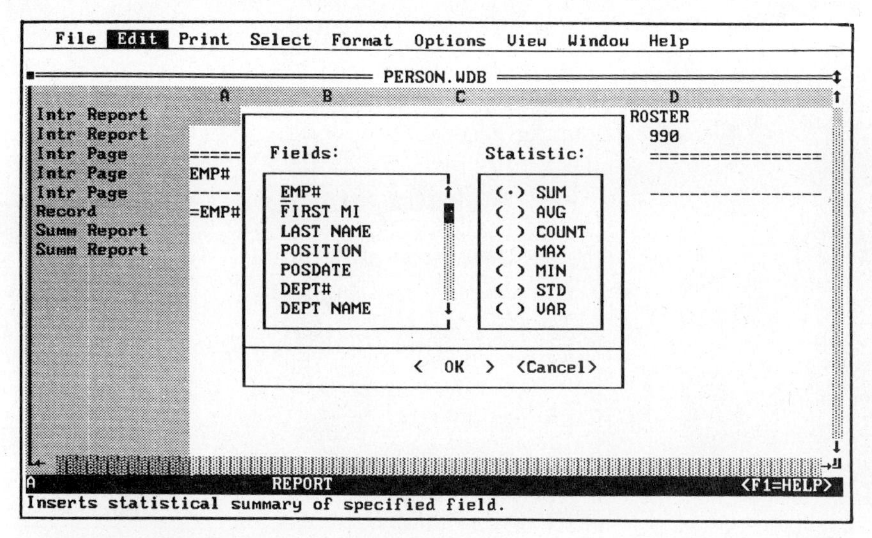

Figure 12-1. The Insert Field Summary dialog box showing fields and summary statistics

they're available in the Form, List, and Report screens. Print commands let you specify, among other things, margins, pages to print, size and style of characters, positioning, page size, page numbers, page breaks, and the content and alignment of headers and footers.

Print... (List, Form, Report)

The Print command tells Works how many copies to print, which pages to print if you're not printing every page, whether to send the report to the printer or to a disk file, and whether to print record and field labels (record numbers and field names). Works prints until a page is full or it encounters a page break, at which point it stops printing on that page and start printing on the next. Works determines page breaks based on margins and paper size.

To print certain pages only, turn on the Print specific pages box, which undims the Pages field. Type the page numbers in the Pages field. Separate single pages with commas (for instance, **2,5,8,10** tells Works to print pages 2, 5, 8, and 10) and a range of pages with a colon or dash (for instance, **7:9** or **4-6** tells Works to print pages 7, 8, and 9 and 4, 5, and 6).

The Print menu in the Form screen provides a format for forms generation. You can print forms with three different purposes: field names only for fill-in forms, entries only for preprinted forms, or both field names and entries for complete forms.

Figure 12-2 shows the Print command's dialog box, where, in addition to the usual settings for number of copies, which pages, and file destination, you can tell Works which records to print, which items to print, and how much space to leave between records.

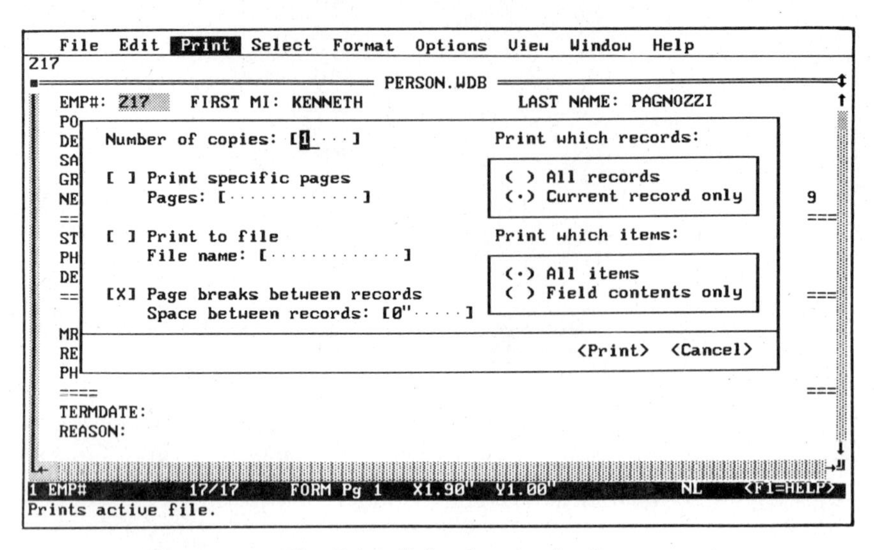

Figure 12-2. The Print dialog box in the Form screen

The Print menu in the Report screen offers to `Print all but record rows` instead of `Print record and field labels`, available in the List and Form screens. This command tells Works to print everything in a report—introductory titles, field names, and statistics—but not the records.

Page Setup & Margins... (List, Form, Report)

Header and footer margins should always be smaller than the regular top and bottom margins.

You can specify the page layout with the Page Setup & Margins command. The margin settings (`Top`, `Bottom`, `Left`, and `Right`) tell Works when to start and stop printing on a page. Header and footer margins control the distance between the top of a page and the top of a header and the bottom of a page and the bottom of a footer.

The page length setting tells the printer when to move the paper forward and begin printing on the next page. The page width setting controls the distance the print head moves across the paper, which prevents the printing from running onto the platen. Works prints as many rows as the page length and top and bottom margins allow, printing leftover rows on second and subsequent pages. It prints as many columns as the page width and the left and right margins allow, printing leftover columns on second and subsequent pages.

The page number setting tells Works what to number the first page, assuming your header or footer contains a page number code.

Preview... (List, Form, Report)

The Preview command shows on screen how your printed report will look on paper. In this miniature version, Works shows margins, headers, footers, and page breaks in their proper locations, and scales the text to show the specified size. You can print from Preview by typing **P**.

Insert Page Break and Delete Page Break (List, Form, Report)

Your page breaks take precedence over the ones Works calculates. Page breaks in one screen have no affect on any page breaks in another screen.

The Insert Page Break command lets you set a page break that tells Works when to stop printing on one sheet and start on the next. In the List screen, you can create a horizontal page break between records (rows) or a vertical page break between fields (columns). Select a cell in the record or field first. In the Form screen, you can break between rows only. Select a cell in the row first.

Works enters the symbol » at the left of the row or the top of the column where a page break occurs. The record, field, or row displaying the break symbol becomes the first row or column printed on the next page.

When a page break outlives its usefulness, the Delete Page Break command removes it. Select a cell in the row or column containing the page break symbol before choosing the Delete Page Break command.

Works dims the Delete Page Break command in the menu if you haven't used the Insert Page Break command. When the cursor is on a page break row in the Form screen, Works dims the Insert Page Break command, because you can't insert any more breaks at that location. The two commands are available in the List screen until you select both a row and field break at the same location.

Headers & Footers... (List, Form, Report)

The Headers & Footers command lets you create headers and footers on your reports. A header is text that prints at the top of each page, and a footer is text that prints at the bottom. Headers usually contain such things as a filename, page number, date, or time. Footers usually contain a page number. You can have a header, footer, both, or neither.

The standard alignment centers header and footer text. Works has special alignment codes that can left-justify or right-justify text instead. Other codes produce such things as a filename, page number, and date. You can find the header and footer codes in Chapter 14.

Headers print one-half inch from the top of the paper, while footers print one-half inch from the bottom. Change these settings in the Page Setup & Margins command if you want them to print higher or lower on the page.

You can print a header on every page except the first by checking the No header (or No footer on 1st page) box. This works well when the first page is a title page. You can turn off a header or footer by deleting the text in the Header or Footer field.

Printer Setup... (List, Form, Report)

If you specified more than one printer during the Works setup steps, the Printer Setup command lets you choose which printer to use to print your report. If you specified one printer only, Works uses that printer.

If you want to add or replace printer drivers, be aware that drivers on the Works Setup disk are stored in compressed form (.CPR extension). To use these drivers, you must go through the Works setup steps so Works can decompress the driver. Drivers stored on the Supplemental Printer disks have a .PRD extension. You can simply copy these drivers directly into the Works subdirectory.

With printers that print graphics, the Graphics list in the dialog box offers a choice of print resolutions (fineness of line) expressed in dots per inch (dpi). Works uses the resolution setting only for printing charts, not text.

This command also lets you change page feed from continuous to manual, which is useful when you want to feed single sheets to the printer. It also gives you the choice of which communication port to connect to your printer.

The Select Menu

The commands in the Select menu shown in Figure 12-3 let you select records and fields, move the cursor to a specific cell or specific information, hide or display records based on your rules, and arrange records.

Cells (List and Report)

You can select only one cell at a time in the Form screen.

The cell the cursor is on is always the selected cell. When you want to select more than one cell for your next command to work with, you can use the Cells command or simply press F8 (the extend key) and

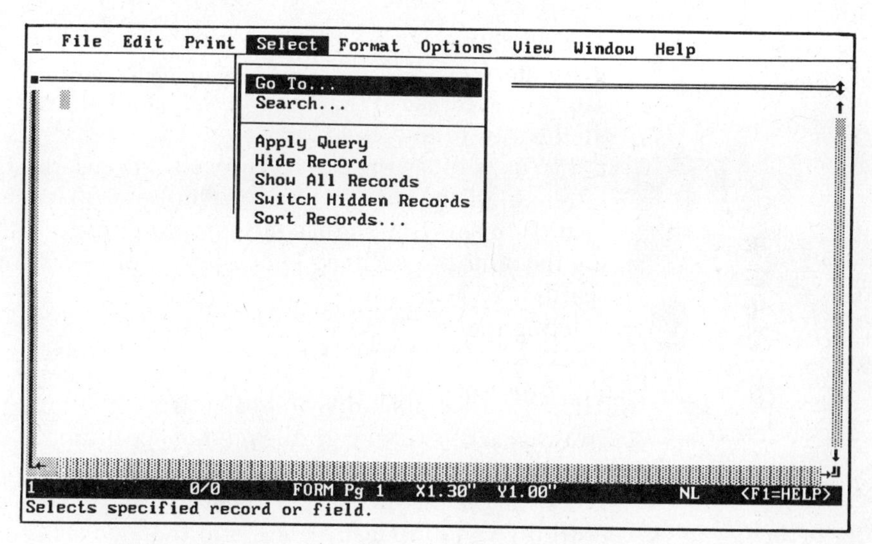

Figure 12-3. Commands in the Form screen's Select menu

move the cursor to other cells you want to include in the group. When you extend the selection in this way, Works shows EXT on the status line.

Record and Field (List)

Row and Column (Report)

The Record and Field commands in the List screen select the row or column at the cursor position. The Row and Column commands work the same in the Report screen, here selecting entries in a descriptor row or in a column.

It's faster to use Ctrl + F8 to select a record/row and Shift + F8 to select a field/column. If you want to select several rows or columns, select one row or column first, press F8 to extend the selection, and then move the cursor to the others.

All (List and Report)

The All command lets you select the entire database—for example, before copying to another file. Instead, hold down Ctrl and Shift and press F8 (Ctrl + Shift + F8).

Go To... (List and Form)

You can zero in on a specific record or field with the Go To command, but F5 is quicker. When you press F5, Works displays the Go

To dialog box with a place to type a record number and a choice of field names. Enter a record number in the `Go to` field, and Works sends the blinker to that record. Select a field name, and Works sends the blinker to that field.

You can use the Go To command to insert a field name in a field formula. All you do is type the formula up to the point where you want to insert the field name, press F5, choose the field name from the list, and press Enter. Type the rest of the formula and press Enter again.

Search... (List and Form)

If you select an area before the search (List screen only), Works searches only that area.

The Search command searches cells for the text, number, or formula you specify, starting at the cursor position. The search item can include any letter, number, punctuation mark, or special character. Works searches the current record, continues searching each record until it gets to the last record, and then cycles back to the first record and starts over again. Hidden records are ignored.

You can have Works pause each time it finds a matching record (`Next record`, the standard setting) or display all matching records on screen at one time (`All records`).

At the `Next record` setting, Works pauses with the cursor on the cell containing the search item. Pressing F7 sends it to the next occurrence. Repeatedly pressing F7 cycles the cursor through the database, stopping at each occurrence of the search item.

At the `All records` setting, Works displays only those records containing the search item, hiding all others from view. The Select menu's Show All Records command restores all records to the screen.

You can use all or part of an entry as a search item. Let's suppose you're looking for the record for Sandford, Kalabash, Gilhoolie & Co. You can tell Works to search for *Sandford*, *San*, *Kal*, *Gil*, or any other sequence of characters in the name. Uppercase and lowercase don't affect a match.

Works provides two wildcard characters—question mark (?) and asterisk (*)—to help find entries that are similar but not quite the same. Wildcards substitute for characters at the same location in the search item. The question mark stands for a single character, and the asterisk stands for any number of characters.

Here's how it works: Suppose your inventory part-numbering system uses a 4-digit number followed by a letter and the year the part went into stock. You want to find every piece of the part number *1234-* that was put into stock this year. You enter **1234-?-90**. Works locates 1234-a-90, 1234-A-90, 1234-B-90, and so on, but not 1234-A-88 or 1233-A-89.

Now suppose you want to find a customer named Smithers, not Smith or Smits. Enter **Smith*s** as the search value, and Works zeros in on the proper cell, ignoring Smith, Smits, and any other close-but-not-close-enough combination of characters.

Apply Query (List and Form)

*You can use the wildcards ? and * in a query, letting the question mark represent a single character and the asterisk represent any number of characters.*

After you create a query, the Apply Query command applies the query to the records in the database. Works then displays any records matching the query criterion and hides the others. You can apply the query faster with shortcut key F10, which exits the Query screen and returns you to the Form or List screen, (whichever you left before creating the query).

If you return to the Form screen, press F9 to enter the List screen so you can view all query-satisfying records. To restore all records to view, use the Select menu's Show All Records command, or delete the query.

Hide Record (List and Form)

You can hide one or more records at a time with the Hide Records command. Select one entry in each record before choosing the Hide Record command. Hidden records don't appear on any screen or in any printed report. They are unaffected by the Delete command unless restored to view.

In the Form screen, the only thing that gives away a hidden record is the record selection indicator on the status line. In the List screen, it's the record selection indicator plus the absence of the record number.

Show All Records (List and Form)

When you want to bring all hidden records into view—for instance, records that failed to satisfy search or query criteria —use the Show All Records command.

Switch Hidden Records (List and Form)

You can swap hidden and displayed records with the Switch Hidden Records command so that all hidden records are displayed and all displayed records are hidden.

Sort Records... (List, Form, Report)

The Sort Records command arranges records alphabetically, numerically, or chronologically in ascending or descending order. You can arrange records on up to three fields in a single sort. In the Report screen, the Sort Records command lets you define break fields to group records in a certain way in a printed report. Refer to Chapters 9 and 10 for more information on sorting.

The Format Menu

The commands in the Format menu control how Works displays text and numbers in cells and in print. Works provides standard formats that you can replace with your own in selected fields or in every field in the database. You need to format only one cell in a field for every cell in that field to be formatted. This includes the emphasis styles—bold, underline, and italic.

The dialog box that appears after you choose the Fixed, Currency, Comma, Percent, or Exponential command proposes 2 decimal places, which you can overtype with another number. Each of those formats allows 0 to 7 decimal places.

The Format menu in the List, Form, and Report screens contains the same commands. The Query screen lacks a Format menu.

General

Works initially gives numbers the General format, which shows each one as an integer (567), decimal fraction (5.67) or, if the number is too large or too small to fit into the cell, in scientific notation (5.68E+11). Negative numbers have a leading minus sign.

Fixed..., Comma..., and Percent...

The Fixed command shows numbers with a fixed number of decimal places and no commas. The Comma command embeds a comma every third place. The Percent command multiplies the number by 100 and adds a percent sign. Negative numbers in a Fixed or Percent format have a leading minus sign. Negative numbers in a Comma format are enclosed in parentheses.

Currency...

The Currency command shows numbers according to the country selected during the Works setup steps or the `Country` setting in the Options menu's Works Settings command. With `USA` selected, numbers appear with a leading dollar sign and an embedded comma every third place. Negative numbers are enclosed in parentheses.

Exponential...

The Exponential command displays numbers in scientific notation, which is handy when you need to display very large or very small numbers. For example, the number 1234567890 with 2 decimal places becomes 1.23E+09. Negative numbers have a leading minus sign.

True/False

The True/False command causes cells to display the logical values TRUE or FALSE in place of a number. A cell that contains a zero displays `FALSE`, and a cell that contains a number other than zero displays `TRUE`.

Time/Date...

The Time/Date command displays a number in date or time format. You can show a date in long or short form as month, day, and year; month and year; month and day; or month only. The long forms are Jan 31, 1991, Jan 1991, Jan 31, and Jan. The short forms are 1/31/91, 1/91, and 1/31.

You can show time in hours, minutes, and seconds or in hours and minutes, based on a 24-hour or 12-hour clock. The forms in the 12-hour version are 2:30:00 PM, 2:30 PM, and 2 PM; in the 24-hour version, 14:30:00 and 14:30.

Font...

A font is a family of characters in a distinctive design.

The Font command lists font types and sizes available on your printer. Font size, measured in points, expresses how large your printed characters will be when printed. A point is 1/72 of an inch. The larger the point size, the larger the character.

Works selects a font type and size for you, which you can easily change to something else. Proportionally spaced fonts print irregular columns, so select a nonproportional font.

Style...

The Style command aligns, enhances, locks, and unlocks entries in cells. The General (or standard) alignment left-aligns text, right-aligns numbers, and centers `ERR` (error) messages. You can left-justify, right-justify, or center these entries, as well as print them in bold, italic, underlined, or a combination of styles. Works displays enhanced entries on screen either in high intensity or as they'll appear on paper, depending on the screen mode selected (`Text` or `Graphics`) in the Works Settings command.

Left-justified text is at the left edge of the cell, while right-justified numbers and dates are at the right edge of the cell. When you right-justify text, it aligns at the right edge, just as left-justified numbers align at the right edge. This makes it easy to match text and numbers on screen and in a report. Neatness counts.

In the Form screen's dialog box, Works lets you close up spaces to the left of an entry if the entry doesn't use up the entire cell. When you print the form, the field contents print without leading spaces. You can turn on this feature in the Slide to Left check box.

It's wise to disable the lock on any oft-changed cells before turning on the Protect Data command.

The Works cell protection scheme, which allows you to lock cells to prevent accidental change, is handled in part by the Style command. The turned on Locked box in the Style command's dialog box enables the protection. You need only toggle the Protect Data command in the Options menu to lock every cell.

Field Width... (List)

Field Size... (Form)

The List screen's Field Width command lets you change the width of a field/column from the standard 10 characters to any number from 0 through 79 characters. Reducing a column to 0 characters hides it on screen and in a printed report. You can unhide hidden columns with the Select menu's Go To command.

The Form screen's Field Size command lets you change the width of a field/entry area from the standard 20 characters to any number from 1 through 256 characters. But that's only half the story. In the Form screen, you can create fields that are more than one line high—much more than one line high. In fact, you can create fields as many as 256 lines high. (Why?) This lets you display long entries, such as instructions or notes to yourself, in a cell. Works fills the first entry line with as many words as will fit, wraps around to the next line down, and continues filling there.

You can apply these List screen and Form screen sizes to every field in the database or to selected fields only.

Show Field Name (Form)

The Show Field Name command, available only in the Form screen, hides field names from view. Hiding is handy when you have several fields headed by one title and don't need a separate field name for each column. The List screen is unaffected by a field name hidden in the Form screen.

The Show Field Name command is a toggle. Choosing it once hides the field name. Choosing it again reveals the field name. Works puts a mark before the command name when it's turned on (that is, active).

The Options Menu

The first four commands in the Options menu—Works Settings, Calculator, Alarm Clock, and Dial This Number—are the same and work the same in all applications. They let you customize the window display, select settings that affect the entire Works program, and access a neat trio of desk accessories. Chapter 1, "The Works Environment," covers the desk accessories in more detail. Other commands in this menu let you provide protection from inadvertent change.

Works Settings...

Works stores your settings in the WORKS.INI file, so you need to make your changes only once.

The Works Settings command lets you change the current settings in the Works program. Many of these settings reflect your response to questions about your hardware configuration during Works setup. Works now gives you the chance to change your mind. It's here that you can:

- Select the subset of another country. Countries have different standards. Your choice can affect page size, currency symbol, and date and time format.
- Redefine the unit of measure from inches to centimeters, pitches, or points.
- Choose the screen colors. Your options depend on the capabilities of the video card selected during the Works setup steps.
- Choose the screen mode, again a function of your video card. The screen mode controls the way character styles and the mouse pointer appear on screen. In text mode, Works shows enhanced characters (bold, underline, italic) in different colors. In graphics mode, it's WYSIWYG (What You See Is What You Get), with Works showing characters on screen similar to the way they look on paper.
- Apply or deny template status. When you save a file with the File menu's Save As command and make it a template, Works turns on the check box for that application in the `Use templates`

for box. Erasing the check mark removes template status, while checking off an application applies template status. The last file opened in that application becomes the designated template.

- Specify the communications port to which your modem is connected.
- Specify whether your telephone has tone or pulse dialing.
- View your Works version and serial number.

Calculator...

The Calculator command displays a screen calculator that works a lot like a hand-held calculator. It performs simple calculations that you can transfer into a word processor, spreadsheet, or database file.

Alarm Clock...

The Alarm Clock command displays a screen where you can enter appointment dates, times, and reminders. At the appointed time, your computer beeps and displays the reminder. If your computer is turned off when the appointed time arrives, Works flashes the reminder the next time you start up.

Dial This Number

With a Hayes-compatible modem hooked up to your computer, you can have Works dial a phone number in your spreadsheet, database, or word processor file.

Protect Data (List and Form)

When protection is turned on, use Tab (clockwise) and Shift+Tab (counter-clockwise) to move the cursor to unlocked cells.

The Protect Data command, available in the List and Form screens, prevents accidental change to the contents and format of cells. Locking is in a ready state but it is not enabled until you choose the Protect Data command, which then locks every filled cell.

Before you choose the Protect Data command, select those cells whose contents you want to change regularly, and unlock them in the Format menu's Style command.

Protect Form (Form)

The Protect Form command, available only in the Form screen, prevents accidental change to the design of the form, not to the contents of any field. You can still enter and edit entries in cells. You're merely unable to change labels, field names, field locations, and field sizes.

The View Menu

The View menu, available in the Form, List, Report, and Query screens, is the transportation hub for the database screens. You can easily reach any screen—Form, List, Report, and Query—from here. Shortcut keys make the trip even faster. Figure 12-4 shows these commands.

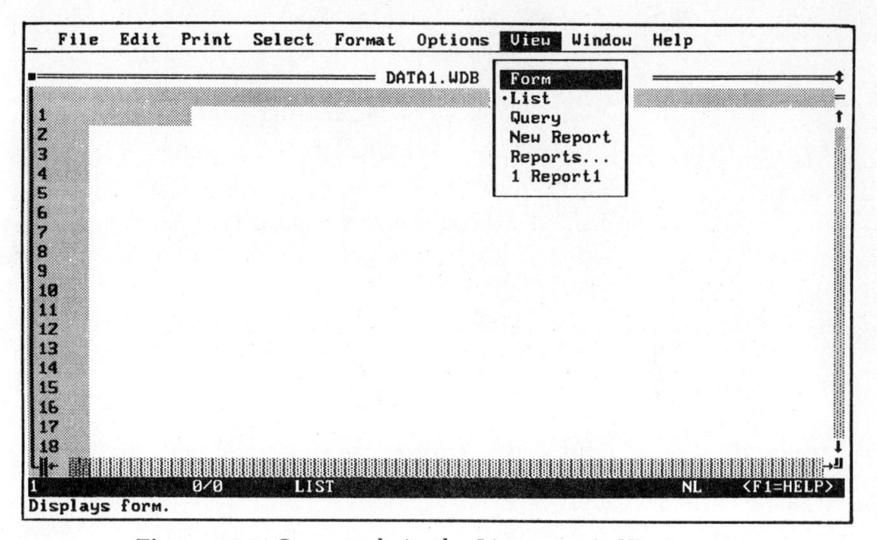

Figure 12-4. Commands in the List screen's View menu

Form, List, and Query

These commands let you shuttle between screens. Use the F9 shortcut key to switch between the Form screen and List screen. It's faster than going through the menu.

Choosing the Form command (the only screen available) takes you out of the Query screen, while at the same time applying any query you created.

From the Report screen, pressing the shortcut key F10 returns you to either the Form screen or List screen, whichever you left before reaching the Report screen. In the View menu, you can choose the screen you left, either Form or List. Works dims the other command.

New Report

The New Report command, available in all screens, tells Works to speed report or create a new report definition based on the field names and records in the database. Each database can have as many as eight report definitions.

Reports...

The Reports command brings up a dialog box containing a list of existing reports, which you can rename, delete, or copy.

It's a good idea to replace the Works standard name (Report1, Report2, and so on) with a descriptive one. This makes it easy to spot which report does what without having to view it first. Another tip: If you want to create a new report similar to an existing one, copy the existing report under another name, and then customize the new one.

Report List

Each time you create a report, Works assigns a number (1, 2, 3, and so on) and a standard name (Report1, Report2, and so on), and adds it to the Report List in the View menu.

When you type a number, Works displays the report. Works then puts a mark before that number in the report list to show that it's the active report. You can view the active report by pressing the shortcut key Shift+F10, or you can make another report active by typing its number.

The Window Menu

The Window menu appears in every database screen—Form, List, Report, and Query.

All commands in the Window menu are the same in every application. They let you view and work on as many as eight different files at a time, each in its own window. You can determine the size, position, and arrangement of the windows. The shortcut keys Ctrl+F6 switch to the next window, and Shift+Control+F6 switch to the previous window.

Chapter 1, "The Works Environment," covers the Move, Size, Maximize, and Arrange All commands in more detail.

Move

The Move command lets you move a window anywhere on screen and even off screen, as long as the upper-left corner remains on screen.

Size

The Size command lets you reduce or enlarge the size of a window.

Maximize

The Maximize command lets you increase a window you reduced with the Size command so that it fills the entire screen again.

Arrange All

The Arrange All command places open files in side-by-side windows.

Split (List)

You can create four panes in the database and spreadsheet, but you can create only two panes in the word processor.

The Split command, available only in the List screen, divides the window into panes through which you can view and work on different areas of the database. You can create two side-by-side panes, two top-and-bottom panes, or four panes, making panes the same or different sizes in each type of split.

The F6 key moves the cursor to the next pane and Shift+F6 moves the cursor to the previous pane.

Open Files

Each time you open a file, Works adds it to the list in the Window menu. If you have only one window open, you can display a file from this list by simply typing its number. That file then replaces the one that was on screen.

When you finish working on a file, close it with the File menu's Close command. The file disappears from computer memory, leaving room for the next file you want to open.

The Help Menu

When you have questions about Works, you can interrupt your work temporarily to get answers and instruction from commands in the Help menu, and then you can return to where you left off before asking for help. All commands in the Help menu are the same in every application. Chapter 1, "The Works Environment," covers the Help commands in more detail.

Using Help

This command explains how to go about getting help.

Help Index

Pressing F1 brings up a Help screen on the task you're currently engaged in. If no Help screen exists for that task, Works displays a Help Index listing all help topics. You can also view the index by choosing the Help Index command in the Help menu or by selecting the Index button in the Help screen you access with F1.

Works Tutorial

Pressing Shift+F1 presents the Works tutorial. You can also view the tutorial by choosing the Works Tutorial command or by selecting the Lesson button in the Help screen that you access with F1.

Getting Started

The Getting Started command brings up an explanation of how to use Works with the type of file (spreadsheet, database, word processor, or communications) now on screen.

Keyboard and Mouse

The Keyboard command produces a comprehensive list of keystrokes that run the Works program. The Mouse command explains how to get around with the mouse.

How Many Reports Did You Say?

The database, like every other Works application, has its share of important numbers. For instance, how many reports can you create in a database and how many fields in a record? When you need the answers to these and other "how many?" questions, you may not always remember where to find them. To help you find these answers quickly, numbers pertaining to the database are assembled in Table 12-1.

Table 12-1. Useful database numbers

<table>
<tr><th>Parameter</th><th>Number</th></tr>
<tr><td>Files open at one time</td><td>1 to 8</td></tr>
<tr><td>Length of a filename</td><td>1 to 8 characters plus 3-character extension (any character except * ? / . , ; [] + = \ : | < > space)</td></tr>
</table>

Parameter	Number
Maximum length of command in Run Other Programs dialog box	124 characters
Maximum number of ranges to print in Print dialog box	10
Maximum records per database	4096 (use depends on RAM)
Maximum fields per record	256
Length of a field name	1 to 15 characters
Maximum width of one form	256 columns (each column equiv to a character)
Maximum length of one form	95 rows (5 screenfuls)
Standard field size:	
Form screen	20 characters wide by 1 line high
List and Report screen	10 characters by 1 line high
Available field size:	
Form screen	1 to 256 characters wide by 1 to 256 lines high (to display 256 characters, turn off Show Field Name command)
List screen	0 to 79 characters wide by 0 or 1 line high (can display only 75 characters but print 79)
Maximum user characters on 80-character List screen	75 (four spaces needed for row numbers, plus one space between last digit of row number and first user-available space)
Maximum sort fields in a single sort	3
Maximum reports per database	8
Field formulas per field	1
Available window panes	2 or 4
Available decimal places	0 to 7
Built-in functions	57
Standard print settings:	
Top and bottom margins	1 inch

(continued)

Table 12-1. *(continued)*

Parameter	Number
Left margin	1.3 inches
Right margin	1.2 inches
Page length	11 inches
Page width	8.5 inches
Header and footer margins	0.5 inches

The next chapter introduces you to yet another of Works' fine facets—the word processor.

P A R T

four

The Word Processor

Word Processor Essentials

Imagine typing without worrying about typos, editing effortlessly until you get it just right, designing page layouts and changing them at will, and then printing letter-perfect copy. Imagine anything you'd ordinarily type—letters, reports, memos, speeches, specifications, manuscripts, law briefs, ad copy, even the Great American Novel—with no erasures, white-out blots, or handwritten corrections. Sound like a piece of fiction? Not at all. Merely the dazzle of the word processor.

Everything you type is faster and more efficient with a word processor. It's easy to see why. With only a few keystrokes, you can delete one word or whole chunks of text without leaving gaps behind, move and copy text from one place to another, and replace unwanted words with other words every place in a document.

Because editing is so easy, word processing encourages you to experiment, to play "what if" games with your writing. What if I switch those sentences around or replace this word? What if I try a stronger opening or delete that cumbersome closing? And you don't have to ponder the result. All you do is read the screen, and if the revision reads better, you save it. If not, you try again.

You can experiment with the way the document looks on paper—showing words in bold or italics, giving paragraphs double or triple spacing, justifying paragraphs, and producing text in different fonts and sizes, and then redoing the look if you want to without retyping anything. Once you get the hang of word processing, you'll wonder how you ever got along without it.

Getting Acquainted with the Word Processor

Word processing is a three-part process: creating (setting your words down), editing (smoothing out the rough spots), and formatting (altering the appearance for visual impact).

This chapter discusses the essential "whys" and "hows" of creating and editing. It describes the word processor screen, how to move the cursor around the screen, how to enter, move, copy, and delete text, how to find and replace text, how to check your spelling and use the thesaurus, and when to recycle what you write.

Chapter 14, coming up next, covers the essentials of formatting. Both chapters give you the solid background you need to create your first document—the invitation to a restaurant reopening—which you will learn to do in Chapter 15.

Until you create the invitation, you can get a reasonably good idea of how word processing works by reading the text and referring to the illustrations. You don't have to keep Works on screen all the time. However, it will make it easier to have Works up and running at certain times, particularly while you read about the word processor screen.

When you're ready to work with Works, fire up your computer and follow the instructions in the section "Loading Works," in the Introduction to this book. At the Works gateway, type **NW** (Create New File/New Word Processor) to create a new word processor file.

The Word Processor Screen

The word processor screen shown in Figure 13-1 is a window to your computer's memory. Memory is to a word processor what paper is to a typewriter, but this "paper" is very, very long—in fact, as long as the available storage space on your disk. When your computer's memory is filled with open files, including your document, Works stores on disk that part of your document residing in memory to give you more room to write.

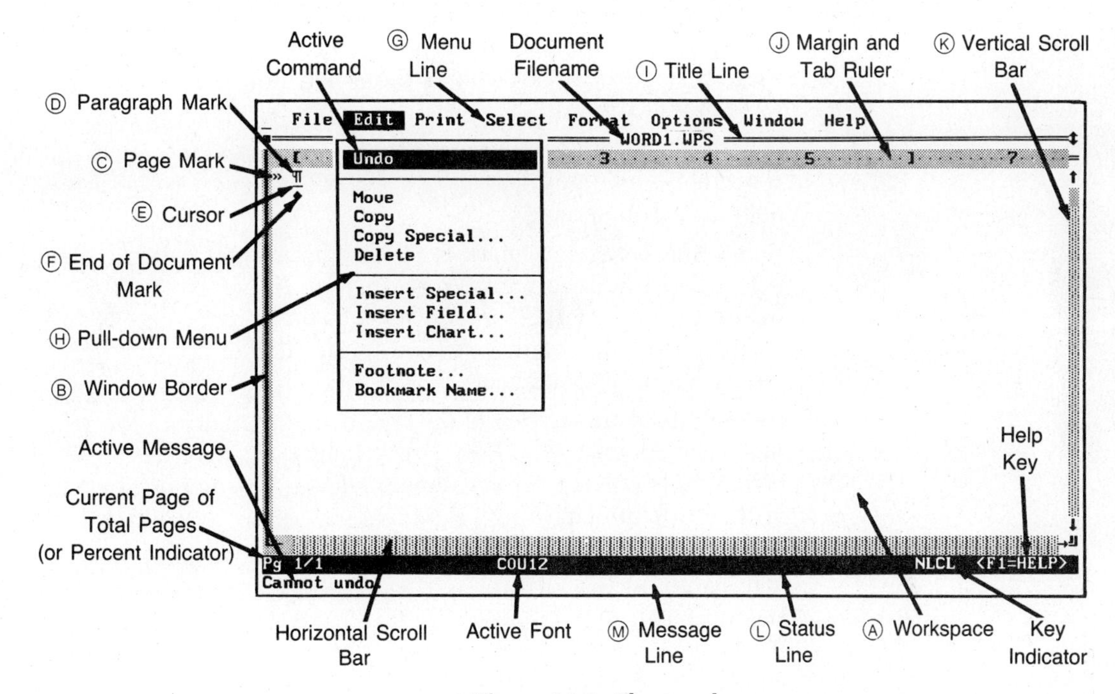

Figure 13-1. The word processor screen

The screen can show 19 lines of text, or, if you hide the ruler, 20 lines. For purposes of this discussion, think of text as any combination of letters, numbers, and symbols.

These are the elements of the word processor screen:

A. The empty area is your *workspace*. It's here that you enter, edit, and format a document. As you fill the screen with text, Works moves filled lines up to provide empty lines at the bottom and continues to provide empty lines as you type.

B. The vertical line at the left edge is the *window border*, which separates the window from the screen.

C. At the left edge of the screen is the *new page symbol* (»), which indicates the start of a new page. The new page symbol sits outside the workspace in an area called the *selection bar*. The selection bar can also display letters to distinguish a header (H) and footer (F) from the rest of the text.

D. The symbol to the right of the page mark is a *paragraph mark* (¶), which indicates the end of a paragraph. The paragraph mark has no paragraph to end right now, so it sits by itself on the line.

E. The blinking highlight below the paragraph sign is the *cursor*, which shows where your next typed character appears. In

Figure 13-1, the cursor and a pull-down menu (item F) are on the screen together—a bit of poetic license that marks their locations. You can see one or the other, not both, on the screen at the same time.

If you have a mouse installed, the cursor shares the workspace with the mouse pointer—either a small rectangle or an arrow, depending on screen mode.

F. Below the paragraph mark is the *end mark* (◆), which shows the end of the document. Works inserts whatever you type before the end mark. The end mark is an integral part of the word processor screen. You can neither delete nor move the cursor below the end mark.

G. At the top of the screen is the *menu line* containing the word processor menus: File, Edit, Print, Select, Format, Options, Window, and Help. These menus let you create, edit, and format a document.

H. Below the menu line is a *pull-down menu* listing the commands in the Edit menu: Undo, Move, Copy, Copy Special, Delete, Insert Special, Insert Field, Insert Chart, Footnote, and Bookmark Name. Commands tell Works to perform specific tasks. The first command—Undo—is in reverse video (light letters on a dark background), which identifies it as the active command. Each time you choose a menu, Works presents a list of commands.

I. Below the menu line is the *title line*, which contains the document filename. You use this filename to load, store, and otherwise keep track of a file. Until you name the new document, Works assigns the standard filename— **WORD1.WPS**. The extension **.WPS** identifies a word processor file.

J. Below the title line is the Works *ruler*, which shows the margins, tab stops, and indents for the paragraph containing the cursor. The numbers in the ruler indicate inches.

The bracket at the beginning of the ruler (at the 0-inch mark) is the left margin, which starts 1.3 inches from the left edge of the paper. The bracket at the 6-inch mark is the right margin, which starts 1.2 inches from the right edge of the paper. Tab stops are at half-inch intervals. Each time you press Tab, the cursor jumps one-half inch to the right. You can change any or all of these settings.

Mouse users can zip along to distant parts of a document by gliding the scroll box along a scroll bar.

K. At the right edge of the window is the *vertical scroll bar* that shows the location of the cursor, relative to all lines in the document. A *horizontal scroll bar* below the workspace shows the cursor's location, relative to all columns (or characters).

Each scroll bar contains a *scroll box* that moves along the scroll bar as you move the cursor, showing which part of the file is currently on screen.

L. Immediately below the horizontal scroll bar is the *status line*. The left end of the status line shows the current page number and the total number of pages in the document—at this stage, page one of one. When you save or print, Works replaces the page indicator either with percentages or page numbers, showing how much of the document has already been processed.

To the right of the page indicator is the active font indicator—now the standard Courier 12-point. The right end of the status line shows <F1=HELP>—the direct route to immediate on screen help. Keyboarders can press F1 to get help. Mouse users can click on this element to get help.

Works reserves the area between the page indicator and Help key for status reports on your activities, such as EXTEND (when you're selecting more text), MOVE (when you're moving text), or SPLIT (when you're splitting the window into panes). It also shows when certain keys are active (NL is Num Lock and CL is Caps Lock).

M. Below the status line is the *message line*, where Works describes the active command or proposes your next action. The Undo command is active, so the message line displays Cannot undo. This seemingly harsh prohibition only means that without having done anything you have nothing to undo.

Around the perimeter of the screen are click-on symbols and other mouse elements described in Chapter 1.

Modifying the Screen

The workspace has certain characteristics—a ruler and special screen characters—designed to facilitate your word processing. The ruler shows the length of lines, indents, and tab stops for the paragraph at the cursor's location. You can have different line lengths, indents, and tab stops in a document, and even vary them from paragraph to paragraph. When you move the cursor from one paragraph to the next, the ruler reflects the characteristics of that paragraph.

As you type, Works inserts special characters in the text—dots in the spaces between words, right arrows to represent tab marks, down arrows for end-of-line marks, and optional hyphens.

Figure 13-2 shows a memo in a screen displaying the ruler and special characters. (Certain empty lines lack paragraph marks—between MEMO TO and FROM, for example—because the Format menu's Indents & Spacing command, not the memo writer, inserted those lines.)

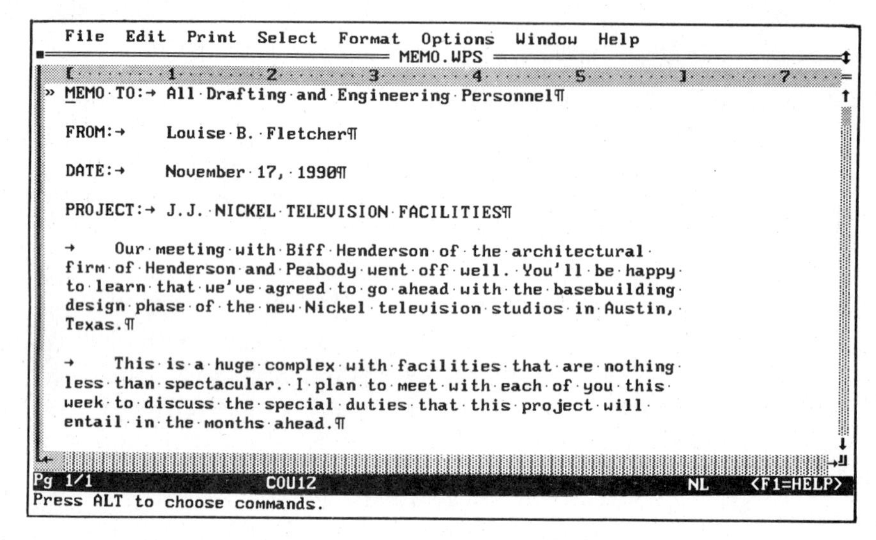

Figure 13-2. A memo in a screen displaying the special screen characters

Though the screen tends to look busy with all of these characters visible, they can clearly point up extra spaces between words, too few or too many tab stops, extra lines between paragraphs, and similar problems.

If you prefer a more serene, less cluttered look, you can use the Options menu's Show All Characters command to turn off the screen characters for good or turn them on and off at will. You can use the Options menu's Show Ruler command to turn off the ruler, which allows one more line of text to fit on screen. Figure 13-3 shows the same memo in a screen without special characters or ruler.

Creating a Document

Writing is a personal thing that no two people approach in the same way. Some writers forge ahead to a first draft, spilling out words and ideas in a steady stream, and then hone and polish, while others

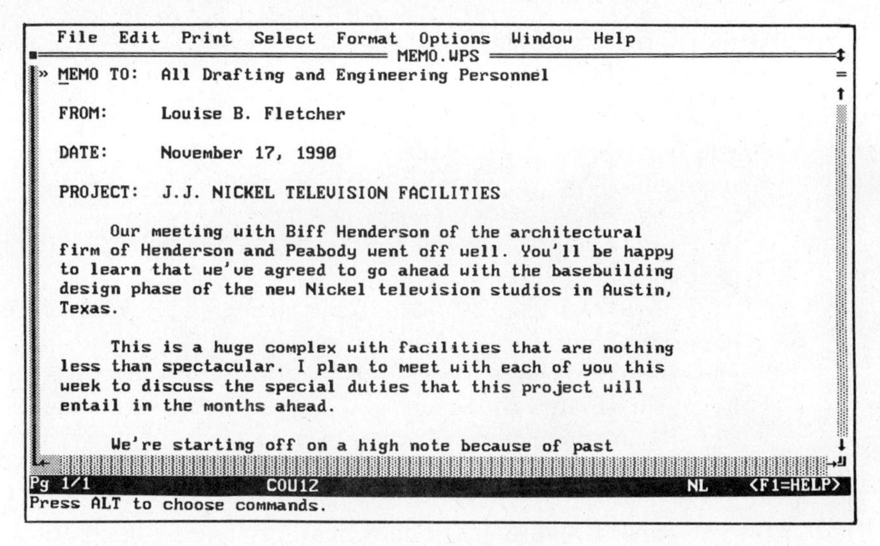

Figure 13-3. The memo screen without special screen characters or ruler

write and rewrite as they go. It doesn't matter which style is your style, because Works lets you make changes to your heart's content whenever you want to.

The Joy of Wordwrap

The first thing you notice about word processing is that you don't have to peer at the screen or listen for a "ping" to signal that you're at the right margin, as you do with a typewriter. If the word you're typing doesn't fit at the end of the line, it moves down to the beginning of the next line by itself. It's called *wordwrap.*

There are no carriage returns until you end a paragraph. Then you press Enter and the cursor skips to the beginning of the next line. If you want an empty line between paragraphs, you press Enter again to bring the cursor one line down, exactly as you do with a typewriter. An Enter also ends one-liners that don't wrap around, such as a single word, a title, or a short sentence.

If you're like most newcomers to word processing, your finger will itch to hit the Enter key at the end of each and every line. Resist it. After a short while, the itch will go away.

Getting Rid of Typing Mistakes

The next thing you notice is that your typing goes a lot faster because you don't have to worry about making mistakes. Getting rid of those inevitable typos is simply a matter of pressing Backspace, which backs up the cursor and erases the character. If you hold down Backspace, the cursor continues moving to the left, gobbling up characters as it goes.

It's just as easy to delete typos in existing text. You place your cursor on the doomed character and press Delete. Presto, it's gone, and wordwrap closes the gap that's left behind. Works has faster ways to get rid of large chunks of text, which you'll learn about shortly.

If something is missing, you simply place the cursor on the character to the right and type the character. Works separates the existing characters to make room for the newcomer.

Table 13-1 lists the actions of all of the keys that perform special functions and commands in a document.

Table 13-1. Word processor operations and the keystrokes that perform them

What You Want To Do	Keystroke	Command Equivalent
Get help	F1	Help/Help Index
Access the tutorial	Shift+F1	Help/Works Tutorial
Move information	F3	Edit/Move
Copy information	Shift+F3	Edit/Copy
Go to a specific page or bookmark	F5	Select/Go To
Jump to the next bookmark	Shift+F5	
Go to next window pane	F6	
Go to previous window pane	Shift+F6	
Go to next window	Ctrl+F6	
Go to previous window	Ctrl+Shift+F6	
Repeat last search	F7	
Repeat last copy command	Shift+F7	

What You Want To Do	Keystroke	Command Equivalent
Extend or select (repeated pressings extend selection further)	F8	
Shrink the selection (repeated pressings shrink selection further)	Shift+F8	
Collapse the selection	Escape and then Arrow	
Paginate now	F9	
Turn off the extend/ select action	Escape	
Move to next tab stop	Tab	
Move to previous tab stop	Left Arrow	
End a paragraph	Enter	
Insert page break	Ctrl+Enter	Print/Insert Page Break
Insert end-of-line mark	Shift+Enter	Edit/Insert Special
Insert optional hyphen	Ctrl+- (hyphen)	Edit/Insert Special
Insert nonbreaking hyphen	Ctrl+_ (underline)	Edit/Insert Special
Insert nonbreaking space	Ctrl+Shift+ Space	Edit/Insert Special
Enter page number placeholder	Ctrl+P	Edit/Insert Special
Enter filename placeholder	Ctrl+F	Edit/Insert Special
Enter date placeholder	Ctrl+D	Edit/Insert Special
Enter time placeholder	Ctrl+T	Edit/Insert Special
Show current date	Ctrl+; (semicolon)	Edit/Insert Special
Show current time	Ctrl+Shift+; (semicolon)	Edit/Insert Special
Delete character to left of cursor	Backspace	
Delete all selected text at cursor	Delete	Edit/Delete
Undo last editing or formatting	Alt+Backspace	Edit/Undo action

Controlling Wordwrap

A nonbreaking space looks the same on screen as an ordinary space. It's worthwhile to note its existence and any other special attributes of the file on paper.

Sometimes, you'll want to control wordwrap. Say you have Engelhardt & Co. in your text. It can look strange if Engelhardt & ends one line and Co. starts the next. You can prevent a split by using a nonbreaking space instead of an ordinary space between words.

To insert a nonbreaking space, you hold down the Ctrl (Control) and Shift keys and press the Spacebar where you would otherwise press the Spacebar alone—in this example, between Engelhardt and & and between & and Co. Because all three words can't fit at the end of the line, Works places them together on the next line.

Works lets you control hyphenated words too, so that both parts remain on one line instead of having one part of the word and the hyphen at the end of a line and the second part of the word at the beginning of the next line. The keys that perform this function are Ctrl + Shift + minus sign.

Editing shifts text around, so it makes sense to wait until you finish the document before inserting any nonbreaking spaces and hyphenation controls.

Finding the Perfect Word

The Works Thesaurus contains 300,000 synonyms for over 30,000 keywords—a veritable Roget's on disk. When you find yourself searching your mind for the perfect word to express your thoughts, Works can help.

Select a word in your text, choose the Thesaurus command in the Options menu, and Works suggests alternatives, including parts of speech, such as noun (n) or verb (v).

Figure 13-4 shows the Thesaurus dialog box with a variety of meanings for the word PROJECT and a list of suggested synonyms. Synonyms are words having the same or similar meaning as the selected word. If a synonym hits the mark, all you need to do is tab to the Synonyms list, choose that word, and hit Enter. Works instantly replaces the selected word in the text with the synonym.

You can also find synonyms of a synonym by choosing the Suggest button (Alt + S) from the Synonyms box. Works then pages through its Roget's to find other categories of synonyms to enrich your writing.

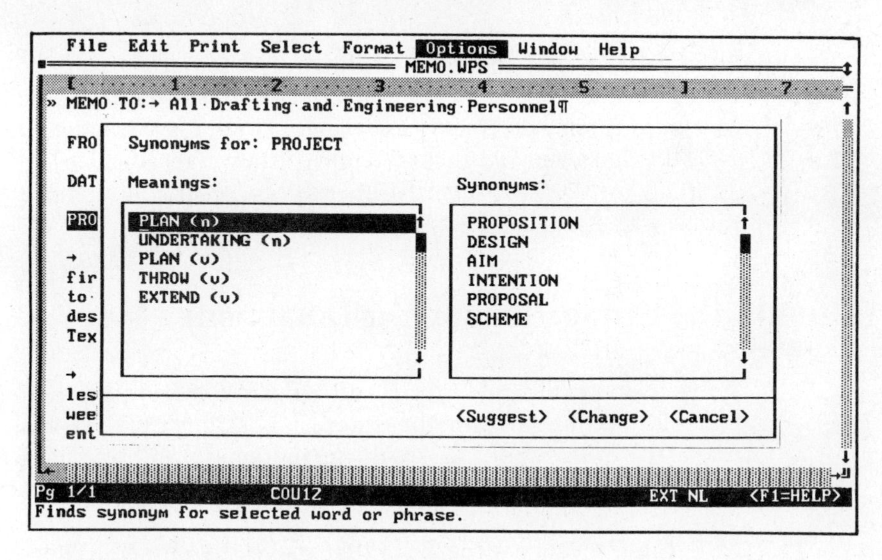

Figure 13-4. The Thesaurus dialog box, where you can find synonyms

Creating Footnotes

Footnotes contain information supporting a statement in the main text of a document—for instance, in a statistical or technical report, term paper, or thesis. They are often used for comments, explanatory notes, and references in a bibliography.

You can create footnotes using the Edit menu's Footnote command. Each time you do, Works embeds a marker in the text, which can be a number or a character, such as an asterisk. Works then opens a footnote pane where you can type footnote text. When you finish typing this text, pressing F6 moves the cursor into the document window.

If you delete a number marker, Works renumbers the remaining footnotes.

You can edit footnote text in the footnote pane as you would any word processor text. You can also move, copy, or delete the text marker. If you delete it, Works deletes the footnote text.

You can continue to work with the footnote pane open, or you can hide it with the Options menu's Show Footnotes command. Works dims this command until you create your first footnote, at which time Works turns it on for you. Show Footnotes is a toggle, so choosing it the first time closes the footnote pane, and then opens it the next time you choose it.

Works prints footnotes at the end of the document. To get some space between text and footnotes, leave several empty lines after the last line of text, or create a new page, perhaps with the title FOOTNOTES, followed by several empty lines. Pressing Ctrl+Enter (the shortcut for the Print menu's Insert Page Break command) can create a new page.

Moving the Cursor through a Document

As your document gets longer and longer, you need a way to get from one place to another in the shortest possible time. Works lets you move the cursor from as small an increment as one character to as large an increment as the entire document. A variety of keystrokes move to in-between stops by lines, words, and screenfuls.

Table 13-2 lists the keys that move the cursor. When you hold down a key, the cursor movement repeats rapidly.

Table 13-2. Keys that move the cursor in a document

What You Want To Do	Keystroke
Move left one character	Left Arrow
Move right one character	Right Arrow
Move up one line	Up Arrow
Move down one line	Down Arrow
Move left one word	Ctrl+Left Arrow
Move right one word	Ctrl+Right Arrow
Move to beginning of paragraph	Ctrl+Up Arrow
Move to end of paragraph	Ctrl+Down Arrow
Move to beginning of line	Home
Move to end of line	End
Move to beginning of screen	Ctrl+Page Up
Move to end of screen	Ctrl+Page Down
Move up one screen	Page Up
Move down one screen	Page Down
Move to beginning of document	Ctrl+Home
Move to end of document	Ctrl+End

The Select menu's Go To command zips the cursor to a specific page or bookmark in the text, saving you the time of scrolling through intervening text.

You can create bookmarks as you enter text or after you finish.

A bookmark is a specific place in the text. You can designate this place by placing the cursor there and assigning a name in the Edit menu's Bookmark Name command. When you later give Works the name, it moves the cursor to the place.

Pressing F5 brings up the Go To dialog box where you can enter a page number or select from a list of bookmark names. You can press Shift+F5 to move the cursor to the next bookmark without going through any command.

Safeguarding Your Work

The operative word in everything you do is *SAVE*. Press Alt and type **FS** (for File/Save) every 15 minutes or so to store your work on disk. That way, if something unexpected happens, you will have lost only that small portion of the document that was in computer memory at the time.

Unexpecteds include such things as shutting off the computer without going through the usual exit process (where Works gently prods you to save your changes), accidentally kicking out the power plug, or an emergency power outage.

Editing a Document

The ease of entering text is matched only by the ease of editing it. Editing means rearranging sentences, shifting paragraphs around, inserting new text, and deleting and replacing text—in other words, honing and polishing to a fine professional finish.

Selecting Text for Editing

Before you can edit, you must select the text you want to edit. You can select anything from one character to an entire document, although selecting words, sentences, and paragraphs is more common.

Works highlights the selected text.

Pressing F8 puts Works into the select/extend mode. Each subsequent press of the F8 key selects increasingly larger chunks of text:

- The first press selects the word containing the cursor.
- The second press selects the sentence containing the word.
- The third press selects the paragraph containing the sentence.
- The fourth press selects the document containing the paragraph.

After pressing F8 twice, you can select pieces of text instead of words, sentences, paragraphs, or documents. For example, placing the cursor on a word in the middle of a line and pressing the End key extends the selection to the end of the line. Or starting in the middle of a paragraph and pressing Down Arrow can select several sentences below. The same keys that move the cursor under ordinary circumstances, shown in Table 13-2, move the cursor for these special purposes.

You can shrink the selection in two ways: By pressing the Escape key and then Up Arrow (which leaves the cursor one line up), or by pressing Shift+F8 several times and then the Escape key (which shrinks in reverse order and leaves the cursor where you started).

Moving Text

You can move a word, phrase, paragraph, or several paragraphs from one location to another in the same document or to an open file without retyping anything. Moved text disappears from its current location and reappears at its destination.

All you do is select the text and press F3 (the Move shortcut key). Works now shows MOVE on the status line. Place the cursor where you want the text moved and press Enter. Works moves both the text and its character formatting to the new location and deletes it from the original location. If the selection contains a paragraph mark, Works moves the paragraph formatting, too.

Copying Text

The copy process is similar to moving, but the original stays where it is and a copy appears at another location. This location can be in the same document or another open file. When you select the text and press Shift+F3 (the copy shortcut key), Works shows COPY on the status line. Simply place the cursor where you want the text copied and press Enter. That's all there is to it.

You cannot copy in one word processor file and repeat it in another. You can, however, copy directly from one file to another.

Works copies the text and character formatting, and, if the selection contains a paragraph mark, the paragraph formatting. Writers often find they can use similar types of wording at different places in a document. If you need several copies of the same text, move the cursor to the next location and press Shift+F7 to repeat the last copy command. Then edit the text.

Replacing Selected Text

Editing often involves replacing text outright. The Options menu's Typing Replaces Selection command lets you insert new text and erase old text in one operation. Simply select the doomed text first. As soon as you start typing the new text, Works erases the old.

If you're replacing an entire paragraph, Works deletes the paragraph mark too, joining what you type with the following paragraph. You can avoid this by selecting the paragraph but unselecting the paragraph mark by hitting the Left Arrow key once. Then anything you type remains in a paragraph by itself.

Typing Replaces Selection is a toggle. Choosing it once turns it on; choosing it again turns it off.

Deleting Text

Backspace deletes the character to the left of the cursor and Delete deletes the character at the cursor.

If replacing selected text won't get rid of all unwanted text, outright deletion will. You have several ways to go about it. As you read earlier, the Backspace and Delete keys delete one character at a time.

Larger chunks of text are at the mercy of the Delete command or the Delete key. Both accomplish the same purpose, but the Delete key is faster. Simply select the text you want to delete and press the Delete key. The text disappears from the document and Works closes the gap left behind.

Recovering Deleted Text

That moment when you find you've deleted something in error can be a scary one. No need to panic. Works lets you recover deleted text with the Edit menu's Undo command or the shortcut keys

Alt+Backspace. But before you become complacent about this capability, be aware that only your last deletion can be recovered, and other caveats prevail.

You can undo the following editing and formatting actions if you do it immediately:

- All typing you did between the last command and the last time you moved the cursor.
- All commands in the Edit menu, except Bookmark Name and Undo itself.
- All commands in the format memo.
- All words changed during a spelling check by the Options menu's Check Spelling command.
- The last word replaced with the Select menu's Replace command using the `Replace button`.
- All words replaced with the Select menu's Replace command using the `Replace All` button.

Finding and Replacing Text

In a word processor loaded with neat features, one of the neatest is the ability to replace any kind of text—word, proper name, number, symbol, phrase, and even special characters such as a paragraph mark—with something else.

Here's a typical scenario: You're working on a long report and suddenly realize you've misspelled **accommodate** as **accomodate** (my personal nemesis) over and over. You could scan every line in the report, and each time you find **accomodate**, delete it and type **accommodate**. But this is the word processor age, not the Dark Age. Why would you want to do it yourself when Works can find each misspelling and replace it in a flash? (Granted, a spelling check will catch this misspelled word, too. You can do it either way.)

The search-and-replace process is handled by the Select menu's Replace command. The search can start at the cursor's location and continue to the end of the document, or it can take place within selected text. When Works finds the search text, it pauses and asks if it should replace that occurrence. When you respond yes or no, Works does as it's told. Pressing F7 continues the search to the next occurrence.

You can replace every occurrence of the search text all at once or view each one first. The standard method is to pause at each occurrence. When Works runs out of occurrences, it displays No match found. The ball game's over.

Now suppose you want to replace the word format with layout. When you choose the Replace command, Works brings up the dialog box shown in Figure 13-5.

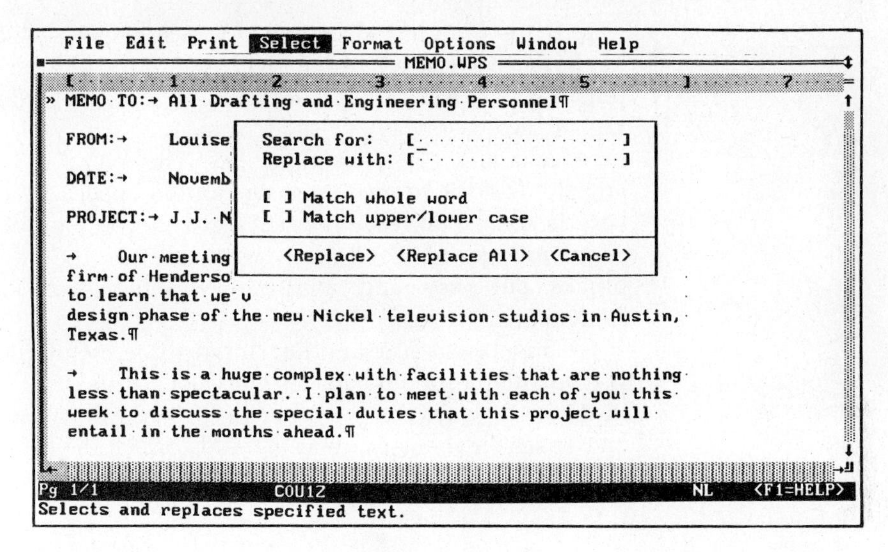

Figure 13-5. The Replace command's dialog box showing the search-and-replace choices

Wildcards can make searching easier. If you're not sure of the spelling, you can use a question mark (?) to represent a single character. For example, Thors?n *finds* Thorsen *and* Thorson.

In the Search for field, you type **format**. In the Replace with field you type **layout**. During its search, Works will obligingly find each instance of format, but it will also find any words containing format, such as information, reformat, and formatting—all of which can try your patience.

You can prevent these tiresome finds by checking the Match whole word box first. Now Works ignores words embedded in other words and only finds the whole word format in any form: format, Format, and FORMAT.

If you also check the Match upper/lower case box, Works looks for whole words that match in every way, including uppercase and lowercase. Now it finds only format, Format, or FORMAT— whichever one matches perfectly. It then replaces each occurrence with the text you specified.

The Replace command is a real time-saver when you use a long or difficult name or phrase throughout a document. Let's say you're writing a report about The Don Johnson School of Okeechobee Land Surveying. Instead of typing that name over and over, you can simply

type **[DJ]** wherever it belongs in the text, and then use the Replace All button to replace each [DJ] with the full school name. If you have several abbreviations, it can be worthwhile to enter them and their long counterparts in a glossary at the beginning of the document, so you don't forget they're there. After you replace the abbreviations, delete the glossary.

If you omit a replacement, Works deletes the searched text. Let's suppose you know you've overused the qualifier *very* (as in *very* remarkable or *very* complex). Using *very* rarely adds to anyone's writing and nearly always detracts from it. So, in the Search for field, you type **very** and press the Spacebar. The space is important, because you don't want to end up with double spaces between words when very is gone. You leave the Replace with field empty. You then get the command going. Each time you confirm the replacement, Works plucks out very and a space, which leaves succinct, seamless sentences.

This brings up another interesting technique. If you suspect you've entered double spaces between words, you can get rid of them in the same way. Simply enter two spaces in the Search for field and one space in the Replace with field, or, as in the previous example, enter one space in the Search for field and leave the Replace with field empty.

Replacing Special Characters

You can find and/or replace special characters or a combination of special and regular characters in both the Search and Replace commands. Table 13-3 lists these special characters and their corresponding codes, which you type into the Search for and Replace with fields. Pressing Shift+6 produces the caret (^) before the character.

Table 13-3. Special search and replace characters

What You Want To Find or Replace	Code
Tab mark	^t
Paragraph mark	^p
End-of-line mark	^n
Manual page break mark	^d
Nonbreaking space	^s
Optional hyphen	^-
Nonbreaking hyphen	^~

What You Want To Find or Replace	Code
Caret	^^
Question mark	^?
Any ASCII character (where # is the ASCII number)	^#
White space	^w
Any character	?

White space is any combination of consecutive spaces, tab marks, nonbreaking spaces, end-of-line marks, paragraph marks, and manual page breaks.

Finding Text

Sometimes you won't want to replace text, just find it. The Select menu's Search command searches for the text you specify, starting at the cursor position and continuing to the end of the document, or, if you have text selected, from the end of the selected text to the end of the document.

When Works finds the text, it halts the search with the cursor on the text. Pressing F7 tells Works to continue the search to the next occurrence. Works lets you know when there are no more occurrences.

Be sure to move the cursor to the beginning of the document (Ctrl+Home gets you there quickly) or wherever you want the search to begin before choosing either the Search or the Replace command.

Dealing with Change

Even when good sense says you should, you may be reluctant to edit your work. What if the original turns out to be better than the rewrite? Many people feel that way. Don't be concerned. Works has built-in safeguards, and there are other things you can do to ease your mind.

Works Techniques

Works tries in every way possible to make sure you never lose any of your precious words.

1. If you change your mind about something you've done, you can *undo* it with the Edit menu's Undo command. This reverses only your most recent editing or formatting action. If you've done other things since the change that you want to reverse, you'll have to undo it yourself.
2. If you turn on the Make backup copy check box in the File menu's Save As command, Works will keep a copy of your file in a backup subdirectory that it creates on your disk. So, you actually have two copies—the current version and the backup version. Each time you save that file, Works stores the new version on disk and replaces the backup with the last saved version.
3. Until you save a file, any editing you do resides in computer memory only. The original remains unchanged on disk. Before you close a file or quit a Works session, Works asks if you want to save the changes. You can always say no, although this means that you'll lose all changes—even the good ones. Instead, use the Save As command to store the changed file on disk under another name. This way, you'll have both the changed version and the original, unchanged version.

Word Processing Techniques

If you're still uneasy about editing, try these guaranteed-to-soothe-the-nerves word processing techniques:

1. If you're working on only a paragraph or two, use the Copy command to copy the text to a place just below the original, and edit there. Having both versions on screen can help you evaluate the merits of each. Then delete the loser.
2. If you're about to tackle a major editing job, save the document under a different filename. If something in the original turns out to be more inspired than the rewrite, you can always copy it into the new file. You can even keep several versions of the same document, each at a different stage of development.
3. Print the text before editing. If it's one screenful or less, print from screen. If you're editing more than a screenful, use the Print command to print specific pages or the entire document. That solid piece of paper is a great security blanket and a real lifesaver when you need it.

To print from screen, use Print Screen, PrtSc, Ctrl+Print, or your computer's hardcopy keystrokes.

4. Remember—you always have the latest version of the file on a backup disk (you do, don't you?). If worst comes to worst, you can reuse that file or copy the best parts of it to another file.

Checking the Spelling

After all that writing and all that editing, you want to be sure everything about your document is letter-perfect. For this, you need a spelling checker.

Clearly, you can check your spelling at any time and as often as you want, not only when you finish working on a document.

The Check Spelling command in the Options menu looks up every word in your document in a 100,000-word main dictionary to make sure everything's spelled correctly. If it finds a misspelled or otherwise unfamiliar word, the spelling checker lets you correct, ignore, or add it to your own personal dictionary. It even suggests alternate words or spellings. The spellcheck process also checks for improper hyphenation, capitalization, and double words (the the).

Figure 13-6 shows the dialog box that appears when Works finds a questionable word. Here, that word is a proper noun. You can have Works replace only this occurrence of the name or all occurrences, ignore this occurrence as well as all others, suggest alternative words or spellings, or add the name to your personal dictionary.

If you have many acronyms (words all in uppercase, such as ASCII, SMPTE, or AMA), you can check off the `Skip capitalized words` box, telling Works in no uncertain terms not to stop and question any of those words. Period.

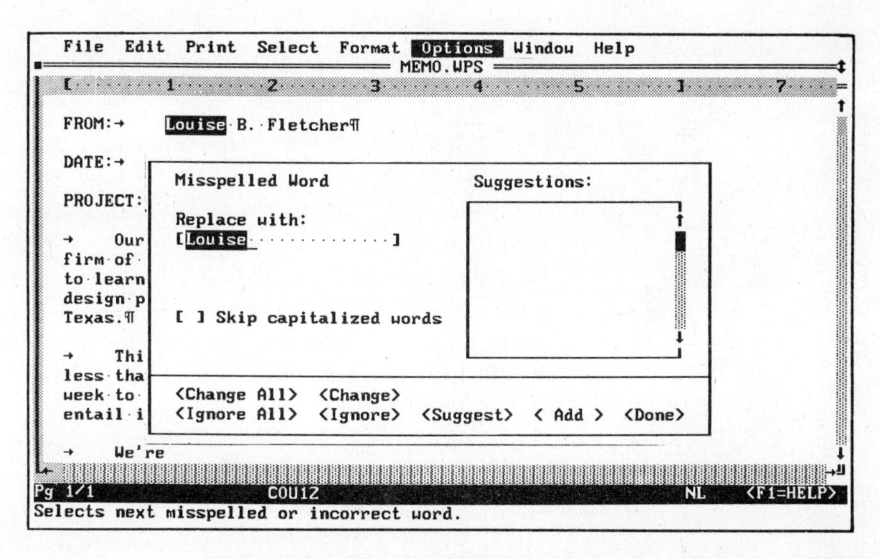

Figure 13-6. The check spelling dialog box

To begin a spell check at the beginning of a document, use the Ctrl+Home keys to move the cursor to the first word. Otherwise, Works checks spelling from the cursor's location to the end of the document, and then pauses and asks if you want to check the spelling from the start. If you want to confine the spelling check to a specific area, select the area first.

Editing the Personal Dictionary

You can see both MAIN.DIC and PERSONAL.DIC in the Open Files list in the File menu.

Works starts with one dictionary named MAIN.DIC. This dictionary cannot be added to or altered in any way. The first time you tell Works to add an unfamiliar word to the dictionary, Works creates a personal dictionary called PERSONAL.DIC and stores the word there. Every time you do a spelling check from then on, Works thumbs through both dictionaries (MAIN.DIC and PERSONAL.DIC).

You can alter the contents of PERSONAL.DIC whenever you want. Suppose you added a word to the dictionary that you now realize is misspelled. You can open PERSONAL.DIC as a word processor file and correct the spelling of that word, as well as add or delete words.

Specifically, choose the Open Existing File command in the File menu. In the `File to open` field, type **PERSONAL.DIC** and press Enter. Works now brings up a dialog box asking for the type of file you want to create, and proposes `Word processor`. That's exactly what you want. When you press Enter, Works displays the words in your personal dictionary.

Refer to an ASCII chart for the complete sequence.

You can now change the dictionary, making sure to follow one important rule: Keep everything in strict ASCII sequence—that is, words beginning with an uppercase letter in alphabetical order followed by words beginning with a lowercase letter in alphabetical order, and so on. If you enter words in non-ASCII order and save it that way, Works will refuse to recognize PERSONAL.DIC as your personal dictionary.

After you change your personal dictionary, be sure to use the Save command, not the Save As command to save it. Save As deletes the old version before writing the new one. Determined to protect you from yourself, Works refuses to delete certain important files, among them PERSONAL.DIC. So, you get nowhere.

Recycling Your Writing

Word processing makes it easy for you to work less and accomplish more. With boilerplate documents and form letters, you can use the same phrases over and over without retyping, and get a new, customized look every time.

Boilerplate Documents

Any document that contains standard information can become a boilerplate document. Suppose you write a lot of proposals. Chances are, each one covers the same ground and contains the same or similar phrases—even whole pages of text. You can design one proposal as a master, incorporating a variety of sample wordings and clauses. When proposal time rolls around, you simply save the master under another filename, delete the phrases that don't apply, and customize the rest of the document to suit the situation. You can do the same thing with other kinds of documents, such as contracts and wills.

A boilerplate-type document favored by writers can serve as a repository for inspired jottings that don't necessarily have anything to do with each other, but which you can harvest during writing dry-spells to create a document so artfully constructed that no one would guess you didn't create it from scratch.

Works Templates

If you find yourself using the same standard document every time you start up Works, you can assign that file template status. Then, each time you choose a new word processor file, Works will bring up that template, which you can change and edit to your heart's content.

If you intermix template files and empty files, using the template only a bit more often than empty files, you can turn off template status until you need it again. All of this can happen in the File menu's Save As command or the Options menu's Works settings command.

Form Letters

Form letters are boilerplate documents, in the sense that they contain the same text as all other letters of that particular ilk. The point of divergence is the personalized information inserted by Works.

Suppose you write a letter to your customers announcing a new product line. When you merge that letter with the customer names and addresses in a Works database, you can print as many letters as there are customers, each with a different name and address.

The key to merging form letters and database records is a *placeholder*. A placeholder, as its name implies, holds the place for information retrieved from a database field, such as a company name. A placeholder consists of a double left angle bracket, a field name, and a double right angle bracket—for example, **<<COMPANY NAME>>**.

The Print Form Letters command in the Print menu handles this type of merge, which is one of the Works integration features. Works prints one copy of a form letter for each visible record in the database. Both files must be open before you can merge. You'll find out more about merging in Part Six, "Works Fireworks."

An important part of word processing is determining how you want what you write to look on paper or on screen—a topic unto itself. In the next chapter, you'll learn about character and paragraph formats, pagination, and printing.

F O U R T E E N

About Formatting

Formatting is the third in the trio of essential word processing tasks, after text entry and editing. Formats determine the look of your text on screen and on paper. You can, for example, print titles in large type, show headings in bold or italic, put paragraphs in bulleted lists, increase or reduce the size of margins, and right-align a header or footer.

You can divide formatting into three major groups: character, paragraph, and document. Most of the character and paragraph formatting is handled by the Format menu shown in Figure 14-1. The

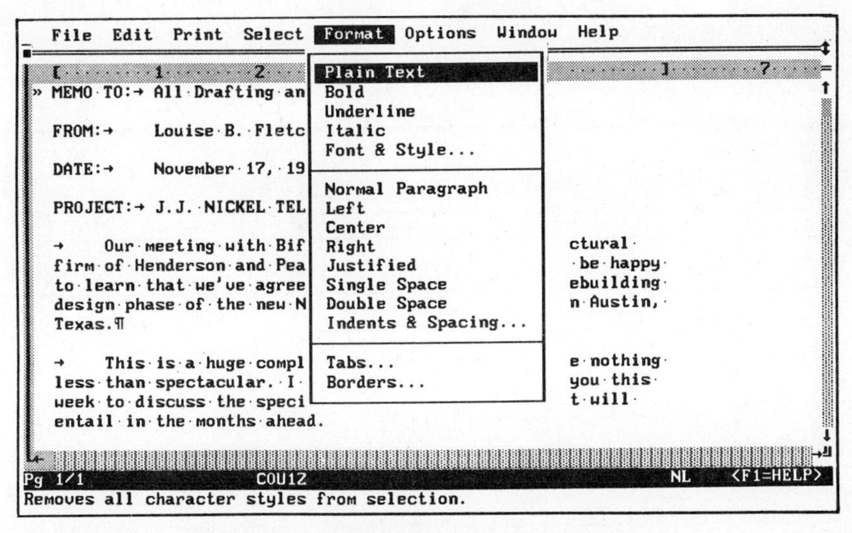

Figure 14-1. Commands in the Format menu

first group contains character formats, the second group contains paragraph formats, and the third group, other types of formats.

The most commonly used character and paragraph formats are available by using individual commands or shortcut keys, shown in Table 14-1. All of these formats are also available in either the Font & Style command (character) or the Indents & Spacing command (paragraph). Both commands allow you to apply more than one type of format at a time.

Table 14-1. Keystrokes and commands for character and paragraph formatting

Format Type	Keystroke	Command Equivalent
Character Format		
Plain text	Ctrl + Spacebar	Format/Plain Text
Bold	Ctrl + B	Format/Bold
Underline	Ctrl + U	Format/Underline
Italic	Ctrl + I	Format/Italic
Strikethrough	Ctrl + S	Format/Font & Style
Superscript	Ctrl + + (plus)	Format/Font & Style
Subscript	Ctrl + = (equal sign)	Format/Font & Style
Font type and size	None	Format/Font & Style
Paragraph Format		
Normal paragraph	Ctrl + X	Format/Normal Paragraph
Left-align	Ctrl + L	Format/Left
Center	Ctrl + C	Format/Center
Right-align	Ctrl + R	Format/Right
Justify left and right	Ctrl + J	Format/Justified
Single space	Ctrl + 1	Format/Single Space
Double space	Ctrl + 2	Format/Double Space
1-1/2 space	Ctrl + 5	Format/Indents & Spacing
Nested indent	Ctrl + N	Format/Indents & Spacing
Undo nested indent	Ctrl + M	Format/Indents & Spacing
Hanging indent	Ctrl + H	Format/Indents & Spacing
Undo hanging indent	Ctrl + G	Format/Indents & Spacing

Format Type	Keystroke	Command Equivalent
One line before paragraph	Ctrl+O (letter O)	Format/Indents & Spacing
No lines before paragraph	Ctrl+E	Format/Indents & Spacing
Lines after paragraph	None	Format/Indents & Spacing
Border	None	Format/Borders

Document formatting is involved with the overall look of a document. This requires attention to the nitty-gritty details of character and paragraph formatting, as well as a concern for the larger elements of paging and page layout.

Character Formats

Character formats are usually applied by the word, such as You or I, but there's no prohibition against applying them by character.

Formats that affect characters fall into three categories: font (type and size), style (bold, italic, underline, strikethrough, or plain), and position on a line (normal, superscript, or subscript). The same character can have more than one format—for example, a title can be both bold and underlined or be italic in a 14-point font.

Character formats show up differently on screen, depending on the screen settings in the Options menu's Works settings command. You'll learn more about this shortly.

Using the Standard Formats

Works has a standard set of character formats that produce presentable, polished prose suitable to most situations. Unless you change things, Works applies the character formats shown in Table 14-2.

Table 14-2. Works' standard character formats

Character Format	Standard Setting
Font type	Courier (or your printer's equivalent)
Font size	12-point
Style	Plain
Position on the line	Normal

Pressing Ctrl+Space restores formatted text to a plain, unadorned state.

Figure 14-2 shows these settings in the Font & Style dialog box. If you're applying more than one format, it makes sense to do it in this dialog box. If you're applying only one format, you can use the individual commands, but it's faster to use the shortcut key shown in Table 14-1. Be sure to select the text first.

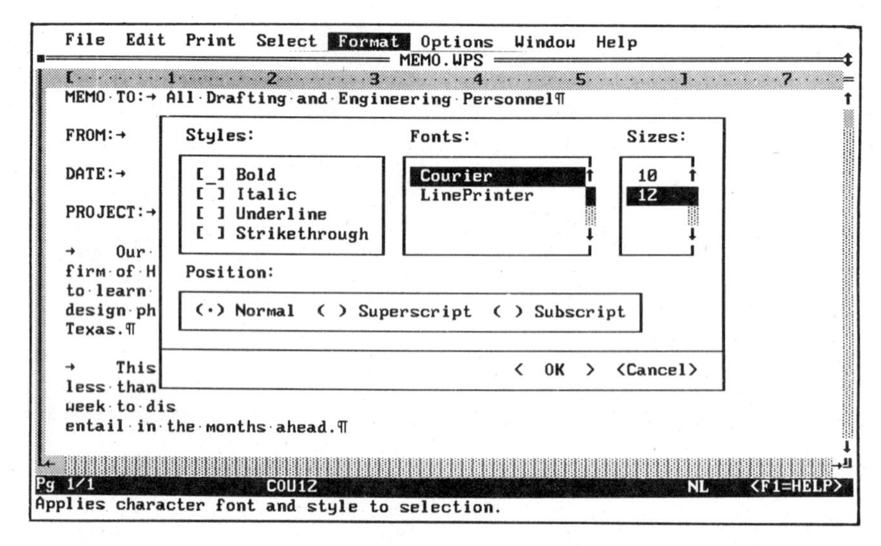

Figure 14-2. The Font & Style dialog box showing a choice of character formats

Font

A font is a family of letters, numbers, and symbols in the same design. The size of the font, which Works refers to in terms of points, affects the amount of text that can print across a page. The most commonly used sizes are 8, 10, 12, and 15 point. The larger the number, the larger the character. The larger the character, the fewer characters can fit across a page.

A point is 1/72 of an inch. Some printers specify font sizes in terms of pitch—a measure of how many characters fit into one horizontal inch of space. To convert points to pitch, divide 120 by the pitch. For instance, 10 pitch is equivalent to 12 points (120/10), while 12 pitch is equivalent to 10 points (120/12).

The style and size of fonts available to you depends on the capabilities of the printer you specified during Works setup. You can see a list of those fonts in the Font & Style dialog box.

If your printer can produce proportional spacing, some font names contain the letters *PS*. Proportional spacing gives each character only as much width as it needs and produces a denser, typeset look. Not all printers can print with proportional spacing, and results vary among those that do. Your best bet is to try it out to see what your printer can do.

If your printer's fonts aren't listed in the Font & Style dialog box, check the Printer Setup command to be sure you have the right printer selected.

Adjusting for Font Size

You can vary the font style and size in a document, giving single words, titles, or paragraphs a totally different look. Though you select a different font style for printing, Works shows the text on screen in the standard screen font.

It does, however, vary the length of text on screen based on font size. For instance, if you choose a small font, Works displays more characters on a line. Conversely, if you choose a large font, Works displays fewer characters on a line.

The Wrap For Screen command has no effect on line breaks when you print.

With a small font, the lines of text are likely to extend beyond the width of the window. With a large font, each line is bound to be short. You can control the length of lines by using the Wrap For Screen command in the Options menu. This command treats all characters as if they were 12-point fonts. It fits fewer 8-point characters on a line, for instance, just as it fits more 16-point characters on a line, based on existing margins.

Style

Style makes a character stand out from the rest of the text. *Bold* (Ctrl+B) tells the printer to strike each character more than once. This produces darker, thicker characters distinctively different from one-strike printing. Bold printing is ideal for titles, paragraph headers, and parts of text that require special emphasis.

Italics (Ctrl+I) slants characters to the right. It's useful as chapter titles or references in text. *Underline* (Ctrl+U) prints a line beneath the selected text. *Strikethrough* (Ctrl+S) prints a dashed line through each character—a technique often used in editing to show a proposed deletion.

Position on a Line

Superscript and *subscript* refer to the position of characters relative to the normal line of text. Superscript prints characters one-half line above the normal line. Subscript prints characters one-half line below.

The most common application for superscript is a footnote number, such as

`Inventories often make up 50% or more of a firm's current assets.`[4]

The most common application for subscript is a scientific expression such as:

`The formula for water is` H_2O.

To get superscript, press Ctrl + + (plus sign). To get subscript, press Ctrl + = (equal sign).

Seeing Character Formats on Screen

Works shows character formats on screen in several ways, depending on the screen settings in the Options menu's Works settings command. In Text mode with screen color 1, for instance, you can see bold, italic, or underlined characters in high intensity white. If you use Text mode with screen color 3, Works shows bold in green, italic in red, and underline in blue.

In Graphics mode, it's WYSIWYG (What You See Is What You Get). Works produces a semblance on screen of what you will get on paper. Characters formatted for bold appear as thicker characters, italicized characters slant to the right, and underlined characters have a line below them.

To make it even easier to distinguish one style from another, no matter which screen mode you use, Works puts a letter on the status line. When the cursor is on a formatted character, it shows `B` for bold, `I` for italic, `U` for underline, `S` for strikethrough, a plus sign for superscript, and an equal sign for subscript.

The mix of styles in this memo is strictly for demonstration purposes.

For example, the memo in Figure 13-2 (previous chapter) uses several styles to give you an idea of the effect. Good page design discourages overuse of enhanced characters. The subject of the memo is in bold, so Works displays it in high intensity white (or in color or with thicker lines, according to screen mode) with `B` on the status line. Other words are italicized, and still others are underlined.

Strikethrough words are due for deletion. Figure 14-3 shows the printed result.

MEMO TO: All Drafting and Engineering Personnel

FROM: Louise B. Fletcher

DATE: November 17, 1990

PROJECT: **J.J. NICKEL TELEVISION FACILITIES**

Our meeting with Biff Henderson of the architectural firm of Henderson and Peabody went off well. You'll be happy to learn that we've agreed to go ahead with the basebuilding design phase of the new Nickel television studios in Austin, Texas.

This is a *huge complex* with facilities that are nothing less than spectacular. I plan to meet with each of you this week to discuss the special duties that this project will entail in the months ahead.

We're starting off on a high note because of past experiences with this client. Our last project for them was received by all levels of management with enthusiasm ~~and applause~~.

Figure 14-3. The sample memo with various styles applied

Paragraph Formats

A paragraph can be a one-word title, a sentence, or several sentences.

The formats that affect paragraphs fall into three categories: indent (first line only, hanging, nested), alignment (left, center, right, justified), and line spacing (single, double, triple, other). Table 14-1 shows the shortcut keys for paragraph formats.

Works stores formats in the paragraph mark at the end of each paragraph. If you delete a paragraph mark, the text joins with the next paragraph, taking on the format of that paragraph.

Standard Paragraph Formats

Paragraph formats produce the traditional paragraph look. Until you change things, Works applies the paragraph formats shown in Table 14-3.

Table 14-3. Works' standard paragraph formats

Paragraph Format	Standard Setting
Left, first line, and right indents	0 inches
Line spacing	Auto (single spacing)
Space before a paragraph	0 lines
Space after a paragraph	1 line
Alignment	Left
Keep paragraph together	Off
Keep with next paragraph	Off
Tab stops	Every 0.5 inches

Figure 14-4 shows most of these settings in the Indents & Spacing dialog box.

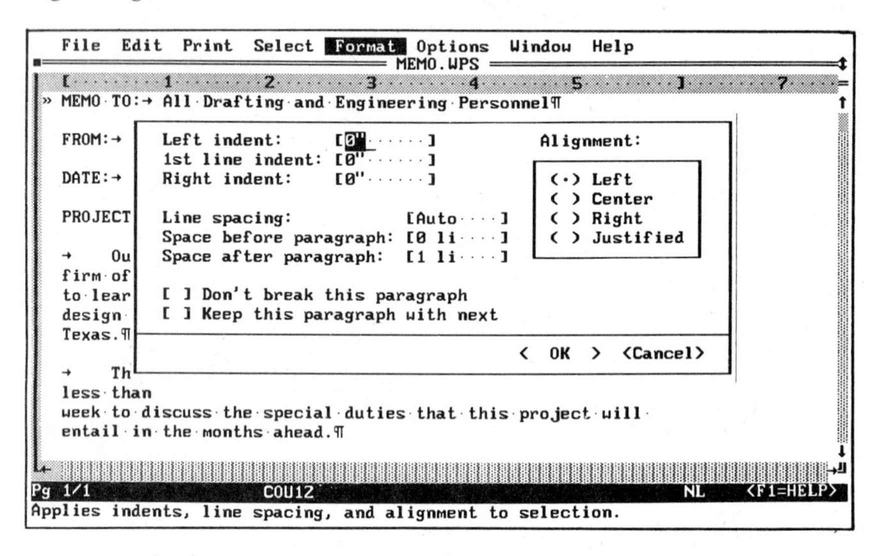

Figure 14-4. The Indents & Spacing dialog box that shows indent, spacing, and alignment settings

Indents

The lines in a paragraph can be indented from the left margin, right margin, or both margins. An indent is the distance from the margin, not from the edge of the page.

The most common type of indent starts the first line several characters from the left margin and places each succeeding line at the left margin, such as in the following paragraph from an employee handbook:

```
    If you see a potentially dangerous situation, or if
you have a suggestion concerning safety and health, please
report it to your supervisor immediately.
```

Indented paragraphs can also start with a bullet (often a lowercase "o," but other markers as well) or a number, as in these paragraphs:

```
   o  "Hot" items - merchandise that is extremely popular and in
great demand for a short period of time.

   5. Please list the kinds of equipment you're in a position to
review or recommend.
```

You can indent by pressing Tab at the start of each paragraph, but there's an easier, more pervasive way. When you enter a number in the `1st Line indent` field in the Indents & Spacing dialog box, Works moves the blinker to the indented position in the next line each time you end a paragraph. Let me make this perfectly clear: You can simply continue to type paragraphs, and Works will indent the first line of every one of them. A first-line indent of .3 inches produced the indents in the preceding examples.

You can create an indent at any time. With a new, empty document, leave the cursor on the paragraph sign in the top left corner and set the indent. Until you change things, every paragraph you type will have the same indent. With an existing paragraph, place the cursor anywhere in the paragraph before setting the indent. There's no need to select the entire paragraph first.

To undo an indent in one paragraph, press Ctrl+X with the cursor in the paragraph. To undo an indent in several succeeding paragraphs, select the paragraphs first.

Hanging Paragraphs

The hanging paragraph is the reverse of the standard indent. Here, the first line starts at the left margin, and succeeding lines wrap around one-half inch (the standard Works tab stop) from the left margin.

Like indented paragraphs, hanging paragraphs often start with a bullet or a number, which tends to disguise their hanging characteristic. These are examples of hanging paragraphs:

```
The ratio of current assets to current liabilities is known as
    the current ratio. This gives you a concise picture of the
    liquidity of the business.

o   The Berkshire Hills Choral Society is meeting in the New
    South Room. A panel of speakers will take questions on the
    musical concerns of members.

4.  Sell chapters as you complete them. It's wise not to wait
    until you complete the entire manuscript.
```

Works puts a first-line indent mark (|) in the screen ruler to show the start of the hanging paragraph.

You can make any paragraph a hanging paragraph by placing the cursor anywhere in the paragraph and pressing Ctrl+H.

When you want to create a hanging paragraph with a wraparound other than the standard one-half inch, specify the indent in the Indents & Spacing dialog box. First, type the amount in the `Left indent` box, and then type a *negative* number in the `1st Line indent` box equal to the number in the `Left indent` box. The preceding examples have a .4-inch wraparound. To produce them, you enter **.4** in the `Left indent` box and **-.4** in the `1st Line indent` box.

To restore a hanging paragraph to normal (first line indent or no indent, whichever it started with), press Ctrl+G, with the cursor in the paragraph.

Nested Paragraphs

Indenting a paragraph on both sides gives it a "nested" look. Nested paragraphs are often used to emphasize important points in a report or to distinguish text taken from other sources. The following example shows a nested paragraph in the body of a memo:

```
Their pre-employment inquiry guide covers the kinds of questions
that employment interviewers are permitted to ask job applicants
and other questions they should avoid. In the realm of age, it
states:

   Inquiries To Avoid: How old are you? What is your date of
   birth? How would you feel working for a person younger than
   you? Can you furnish proof of age in the form of a birth
   certificate?

I trust this answers the issues you raised at the meeting. Please
feel free to contact me for further clarification.
```

When you place the cursor in a nested paragraph, you can see the deeper margins in the screen ruler.

You can create a nested effect in the Indents & Spacing dialog box. Assuming the paragraphs above and below are at the normal margins, place the cursor in the paragraph and enter a number in the `Left indent` and `Right indent` fields. The middle paragraph in the preceding example has a .3-inch indent on each side.

If you want to indent from the left side only, place the cursor on the paragraph and use Works shortcut key Ctrl+N. This shifts the paragraph text one-half inch away from the left margin.

To undo the left-side indent that Works creates, press Ctrl+M with the cursor in the paragraph; to undo either the Works indent or a two-sided indent that you created, press Ctrl+X instead.

Using Borders

Nested paragraphs, as well as other types of paragraphs (such as tables and one-line titles), can assume a special importance with borders. You can create single, double, or bold line borders in the Format menu's Borders dialog box.

Borders can be added above, below, at the left, or at the right of a paragraph. You can put an outline (four-sided) border around one or more paragraphs. When bordering one paragraph only, place the cursor anywhere in the paragraph. When bordering more than one paragraph, select the paragraphs first.

If the paragraph is short, you can reduce the length of the horizontal lines by increasing the paragraph's indents.

Setting Tab Stops

Tab stops define the precise position where text starts. When you press the Tab key (which Works shows on screen as a right arrow), the cursor moves to the next tab stop, so you don't have to indent with lots of spaces.

You can accept the standard tab intervals of one-half inch, or set your own in the Format menu's Tabs command. In this command, you can also clear specific tab stops or clear every tab stop that you set. Your tab settings apply only to the document on which you're working.

With bulleted or numbered paragraphs, you need a tab stop several spaces after the bullet or number. When you type the bullet or number and press Tab, you want the cursor to move to the next tab stop, where you can type the text. Even if your paragraph numbers contain a varying number of digits—for example, 1, 52, and 107 or I, II, and VIII—a touch of the Tab key can start the text in every paragraph at the same position.

Creating Columnar Matter

When you work with columnar matter, such as tables, you want a tab stop for each column in the table so that you can press Tab to move the cursor to the next column. Again, you can accept the standard one-half inch interval between tab stops, or you can set your own.

If you use the Spacebar instead of a tab stop to move to the next column, don't be too surprised if what you see on screen is not what you get on paper. You should always use tab stops.

You're more likely to set your own tab stops in tables, because more than likely the standard half-inch interval is either too narrow to contain your information or too much of a bother to tab through in getting from one column to the next.

Table 14-4 shows a variety of alignments at a tab stop. You can align entries in each column so they are flush left (the first character is at the tab stop), flush right (the last character is at the tab stop), centered (each entry is centered on the tab stop), or lined up on the decimal point.

Table 14-4. Alignment of entries at a tab stop

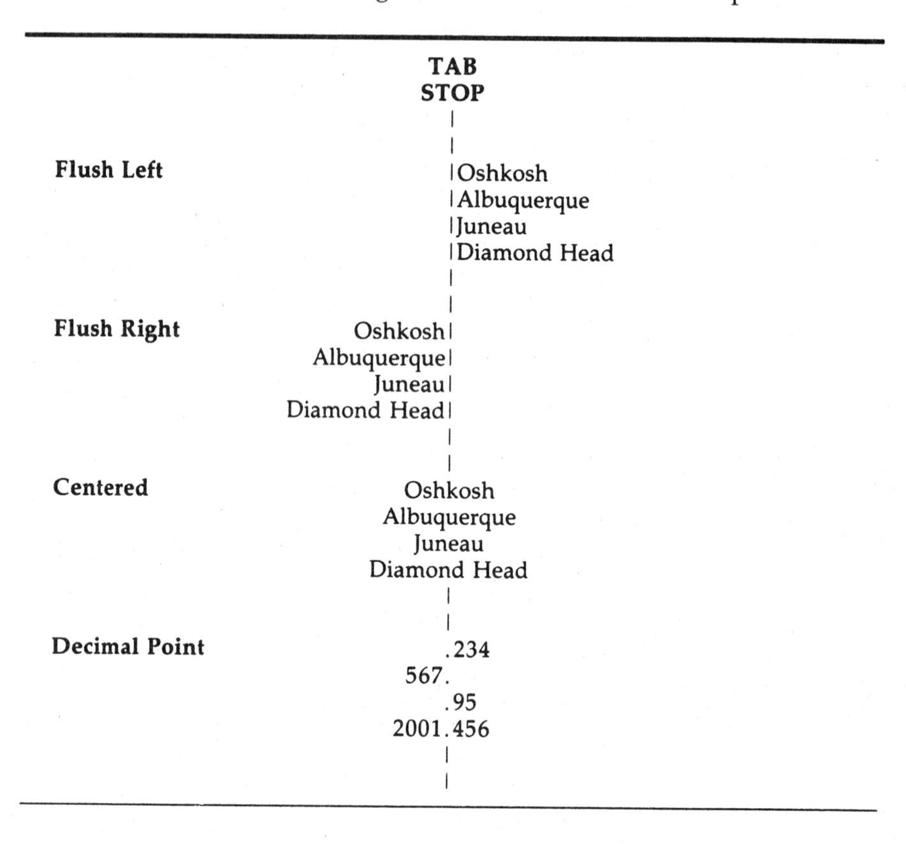

	TAB STOP
Flush Left	Oshkosh
	Albuquerque
	Juneau
	Diamond Head
Flush Right	Oshkosh
	Albuquerque
	Juneau
	Diamond Head
Centered	Oshkosh
	Albuquerque
	Juneau
	Diamond Head
Decimal Point	.234
	567.
	.95
	2001.456

Shift+Enter, the line connection keys, produce an end-of-line mark, which appears on screen as a down arrow.

Most of the time, you'll want Works to treat the table as a unit, not as individual lines. This makes it easy to copy the table or format it in one step. Pressing Shift+Enter instead of Enter alone at the end of each line connects that line to the next line you create, thus unifying the table. Pressing Enter after the last line in the table produces the normal paragraph mark and separates the table from any text that follows.

Now all you have to do to select the entire table (no matter what its size), and only that table, is hit F8 three times with the cursor in the table. Works won't let you set a first-line indent for each line in a unified table, so set a tab stop at the place where you want each line to start.

When you create special tables, such as a table of contents, Works lets you choose a leader character to fill the space between the columns. Leader characters can be dots, dashes, double dashes, or a solid line. If you prefer, you can even leave the space between the columns empty.

All actions pertaining to tabs, as well as to the selection of leader characters, take place in the Format menu's Tab command.

Justification and Alignment

Works applies alignment to an entire paragraph. The Print menu's Preview command lets you view alignment (as well as headers, margins, font sizes, and page breaks) on screen prior to printing.

Justification refers to the position of lines in a paragraph relative to the margins. Lines can be aligned at the left margin (left-justified), aligned at the right margin (right-justified), placed equidistant between the margins (centered), or aligned at both margins (justified). Works provides these alignments in the Indents & Spacing dialog box and as shortcut keys.

Left-Justified Paragraph

Works routinely places all lines in a paragraph at the left margin, which produces a right margin known as "ragged right." This is a left-justified paragraph:

```
A beginner rarely shoots a hole in one, hits a bull's
eye, or hooks a prize-winning trout. Topnotch
performance in golf, shooting, and fishing requires
knowledge, practice, and perseverance. It's the same
in business. Profit comes to those who strive for
topnotch performance.
```

Paragraphs are normally left-justified. You only need to apply left-justification to a paragraph to undo another type of alignment. Pressing Ctrl + X with the cursor in the paragraph does the trick.

Right-Justified Paragraph

Aligning paragraphs with all lines at the right margin produces a "ragged" left margin and creates an interesting effect. It looks like this:

```
A beginner rarely shoots a hole in one, hits a bull's
      eye, or hooks a prize-winning trout. Topnotch
  performance in golf, shooting, and fishing requires
 knowledge, practice, and perseverance. It's the same
    in business. Profit comes to those who strive for
                              topnotch performance.
```

Right-justification is often used for stationery letterheads and in report headers where the writer is seeking something unusual that's also pleasing to the eye. Press Ctrl + R to right-align a paragraph.

Centered Paragraph

Centering aligns each line in the paragraph at an equal distance between the left and right margins. Ordinarily, only one-line titles are centered. If you're working on something special, you can center every line in a paragraph. It looks like this:

```
A beginner rarely shoots a hole in one, hits a bull's
    eye, or hooks a prize-winning trout. Topnotch
 performance in golf, shooting, and fishing requires
knowledge, practice, and perseverance. It's the same
  in business. Profit comes to those who strive for
               topnotch performance.
```

Pressing Ctrl + C centers every line in a paragraph, just as if each line was a one-line paragraph unto itself.

Justified Paragraph

When you select justified, Works adjusts the spacing between words to produce lines of equal length. Justification gives paragraphs an even left and right margin similar to the layout used in newspapers and magazines. A short last line in the paragraph isn't justified. This is an example of a justified paragraph:

```
A beginner rarely shoots a hole in one, hits a bull's
eye, or hooks a prize-winning trout. Topnotch
performance in golf, shooting, and fishing requires
knowledge, practice, and perseverance. It's the same
in business. Profit comes to those who strive for
topnotch performance.
```

Press Ctrl+J to have Works adjust the interword spacing in a paragraph.

Alignment, like text formats, is stored in the paragraph mark at the end of each paragraph. If you delete a paragraph mark, the text joins with the next paragraph, taking on the attributes of that paragraph.

Line Spacing

You can change the line spacing as often as you want within a document. Place the cursor in the paragraph first.

Line spacing refers to the spacing between lines of text in a paragraph. Paragraphs are usually single or double spaced, but they can also be one-and-one-half spaced or triple spaced. The most typical types of line spacing are handled by commands in the Format menu and by shortcut keys. Other types of line spacing lack shortcut keys and are available only in the Indents & Spacing command.

Single and Double Spacing

When you create a document, Works makes your text single spaced. With certain documents, you want the line spacing to reflect the purpose or stage of development. For instance, you may want to double-space the draft of a report and single space the final version.

You can use Ctrl+2 to double space, which inserts a blank line between each line of text on screen. You can write between these lines on paper (making comments, for instance, or adding text) but not on screen. Pressing Ctrl+1 returns the document to single spacing.

One-and-one-half line spacing also allows room for editing. Even better, one-and-one-half line spacing can make a report easier to read than single spaced text, without having the draft-look of a double-spaced report. Pressing Ctrl+5 assigns this line spacing.

Works shows line spacing only in whole-number increments, so half-line spacing and double-spacing look the same on screen but print differently on paper.

Line Spacing Field

Like Clark Kent and Superman, the Line spacing field is mild-mannered on the outside but does spectacular things. With Auto (or number 1) in the field, Works produces the standard single spacing. When you enter other numbers, Works inserts the corresponding lines between the text: 1.5 for one-and-one-half lines (half-line spacing), 2 for two lines (double spacing), and 3 for three lines (triple spacing). But that you can do with shortcut keys.

Where it shines is when you want to leave large gaps in the text for such items as paste-in illustrations or photographs. Works can insert up to 22 empty lines between each line of text on the screen and just as many on paper. Place the cursor at the proper place, and in the dialog box, type the number of blank lines you want in the Line spacing field.

Space Before and Space After Paragraph

Each time you press Enter, Works ends that paragraph and gets ready to begin a new one on the next line. Some documents look best with a blank line between paragraphs. Works can produce these blank lines at each Enter, saving you the task of pressing Enter more than once.

Before you begin a new document, specify the number of blank lines in the Space before paragraph or Space after paragraph fields in the Indents & Spacing dialog box. For example, if you want two empty lines when you press Enter, type **2** in the field. These empty lines are truly blank and stay that way. Even with the screen characters turned on, there are no paragraph marks. In existing text, select the paragraphs, and then specify the number of blank lines.

To get one blank line at each Enter, you can use the Ctrl+O shortcut key instead of going through the command. Shortcut key Ctrl+E removes the blank line inserted with Ctrl+O. Entering a zero in the Space before paragraph or Space after paragraph fields removes all blank lines that you specified before. Select the paragraphs first.

When the Dialog Box Is Neutral

Selecting more than one paragraph to format sends mixed signals to Works, either because those paragraphs already have formats or because Works knows it's dealing with more than one unit.

To resolve any potential confusion, Works simply neutralizes (erases) the usual proposed settings in the Indents & Spacing dialog box. Instead of seeing standard entries or markers, you now have empty fields, as well as some empty boxes and others that contain a dash.

Just go ahead and pick your formats as usual. Works will either add these new formats to existing formats for every paragraph in the selection or replace one format with another where duplication exists.

Copying Formats

When you create a character or paragraph format that's something special—most often a combination of several formats—Works lets you copy the whole kit and caboodle to other characters and paragraphs, so you don't have to start from scratch.

Place your cursor on the text whose format you want to copy, and choose the Edit menu's Copy Special command. When you press Enter, COPY appears on the status line, and Works brings up a dialog box offering a choice of character or paragraph format.

Select one of these formats, move the cursor to the text to be formatted, and press Enter. Works then copies the format. Simple.

Formatting the Document

The goal in formatting is to make a document read well and look good on paper. This involves fine-tuning the page layout, controlling pagination, and making sure that printing takes place in the right way at the right place.

Works provides standard settings well suited to letters and many other types of documents. Most of the time, you don't have to change anything, unless you're either working with something special or you want more of a custom look.

Page Layout

The settings in the Print menu's Page Setup & Margins command and Header & Footer command control, for starters, the size of margins, paper size, and headers and footers. Table 14-5 shows the standard settings.

Table 14-5. Works' standard settings for page layout

Page Layout	Standard Setting
Top and bottom margins	1 inch
Left margin	1.3 inches
Right margin	1.2 inches
Page length	11 inches
Page width	8 inches
First page number	1
Header and footer margins	0.5 inches
Header and footer alignment	Center
Header or footer on first page	Off
Header or footer paragraph	Off

Margin settings tell Works how far away from the edge of the paper (top, bottom, left, or right) to start printing the text and where to stop it. When you change the size of the margins, Works rearranges the text to fit more or less on a page, recalculates the page breaks, and renumbers the pages.

Margin settings are fixed. Whatever settings you use (standard or your own) affect the entire document. You can vary them in other ways. Use indents (Format menu's Indents & Spacing command) to increase the left and right margins at certain places, and use Enters to create a deeper top margin. For example, to print the title on a title page lower than the text in the rest of the report, press Enter enough times before the title to shift it down.

The page length and page width settings tell Works the size of the paper you use to print your document. The standard setting assumes letter-size paper. You can choose any other size that fits your printer.

Headers and Footers

Headers and footers add identity and a finishing touch to a document. A header prints the same text at the top of each page, and a footer prints the same text at the bottom. Headers and footers contain such information as the title of a report, the report date, recipient's name, and page number. Figure 14-5 shows a typical header, and Figure 14-6 shows a typical footer.

```
Report to Floyd W. Harris                                    Page 1
11/22/88
```

Figure 14-5. A typical page header

```
                              - 1 -
```

Figure 14-6. A typical page footer

You can create two kinds of headers and footers—a one-liner in the Print menu's Header & Footers dialog box or a paragraph in the word processor screen. Each has its own distinct personality.

Header and Footer One-Liners

The Headers & Footers dialog box contains one field to hold header contents and another field to hold footer contents. When you enter text and special codes in either or both of these fields, Works prints the same one-line header and/or footer on each page of your document. You can see the special codes in Table 14-6.

Table 14-6. Header and footer special codes

What You Want To Do	Code
Left-align characters that follow	&L
Center characters that follow	&C
Right-align characters that follow	&R
Print filename	&F
Print page number	&P
Print current date (standard format 6/21/90)	&D
Print current time (standard format 1:30 P.M.)	&T
Print an ampersand (&) character	&&

You can include as many codes as you want in a single header or footer.

Text can be such things as Page or Report to Mr. Murphy. For instance, if you enter **Report to Prof. Murphy - &D** in the Header field, Works prints Report to Prof. Murphy - 11/22/90 at the top of the first page and all succeeding pages of the document. If you enter **Page &P** in the Footer field, works prints Page 1 at the bottom of the first page of the document, Page 2 at the bottom of the second page, and so on. Other codes can generate the filename and time.

Works routinely centers headers and footers. This may be fine for a page number footer, but headers are typically positioned at the left margin. You can use the alignment codes to specify left or right. You can even print part of a header (or footer) at the left of the line, another part in the center, and yet another part at the right.

In the Headers & Footers command, you can also tell Works to omit a header or footer on the first page. This is sound strategy when the first page is a title page. In the Print menu's Page Setup & Margins dialog box, you can change the header and footer margins.

Header and Footer Paragraphs

Header and footer paragraphs are only available in the word processor; the spreadsheet and database use the standard one-line header or footer.

The Headers & Footers command lets you create header and footer paragraphs in a document. When you check the Use header and footer paragraphs box, Works produces the header and footer display shown in Figure 14-7.

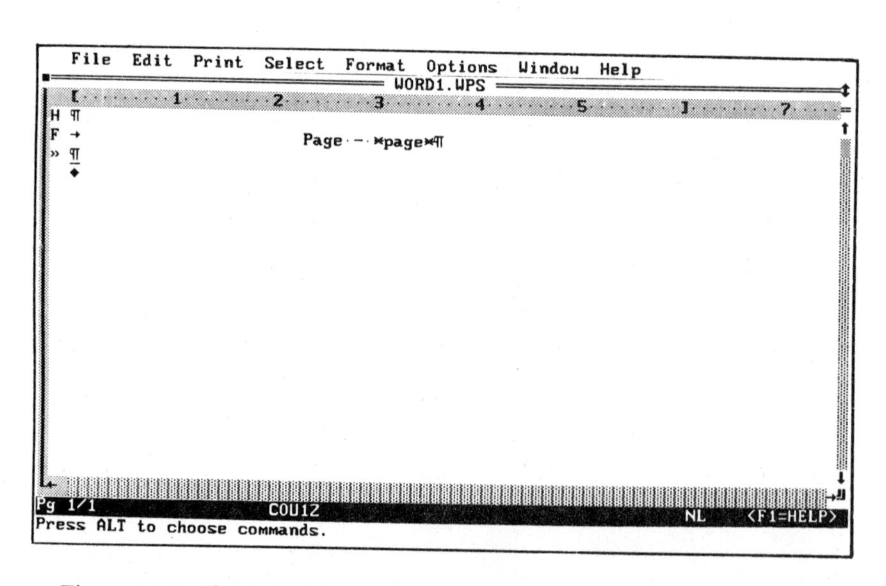

Figure 14-7. The initial header and footer display produced by Works

Letters **H** (header) and **F** (footer) in the selection bar at the left hold the place for header and footer text. The header area is empty now. The footer area is occupied by the word **Page** and a page number placeholder that prints a centered page number at the bottom of each page. You can accept this footer, replace it with something else, or delete it entirely.

The advantages to this method are clear. First, all header and footer actions take place in the word processor screen, not in the cramped quarters of a dialog box. Further, you can enter, format, and align header and footer text in the same way as any text. Best of all, you can use more than one line of text.

There are certain rules to be followed in creating a multiple-line paragraph:

1. You can use only one paragraph in the header and footer areas. The paragraph can be any length that makes sense.
2. Each line in the paragraph, with the exception of the last line, must end with an end-of-line marker (Shift+Enter).
3. The last line must end with a paragraph mark (Enter).

You can left-align, center, or right-align the text in each line or use any combination—for example, align the report title at the left margin and a page number at the right, or a date at the left, a report title in the center, and a page number at the right.

Works provides preset tab stops at the center and right of each line. You only have to type the text and press Tab to move to the next location, where you can type more text.

The standard header and footer margins leave one-half inch between the top of the page and the header and the bottom of the page and the footer. When you have several lines in a header or footer, you need to increase the header or footer margin (and maybe the top and bottom margins as well) to accommodate the additional text. You can do this in the Page Setup & Margins dialog box in the Print menu. If you forget, Works will remind you.

Placeholders

Works provides placeholders that can enter a page number, filename, date, and time anywhere in a document, including headers and footers created in the word processor screen. They accomplish the same purpose as the special codes (placeholders of another kind) you can enter in the Headers & Footers dialog box.

When Works prints the file, it replaces the placeholder with the actual information. Table 14-7 shows the keystrokes that produce the placeholders.

Table 14-7. Placeholders and the keystrokes that produce them

What You Want To Print	Keystroke	Placeholder
Page number	Ctrl + P	*page*
Filename	Ctrl + F	*filename*
Current date in M/D/Y format (11/22/90)	Ctrl + D	*date*
Current time in H:M PM format (1:07 PM)	Ctrl + T	*time*

You can include as many placeholders as you want in a header or footer paragraph.

To produce the header shown in Figure 14-5, for example, you would enter the text and placeholders shown in Figure 14-8. First, turn on the Use header & footer paragraphs box in the Headers & Footers command. Works now produces the initial layout shown in Figure 14-7 with the cursor under the bottom paragraph sign.

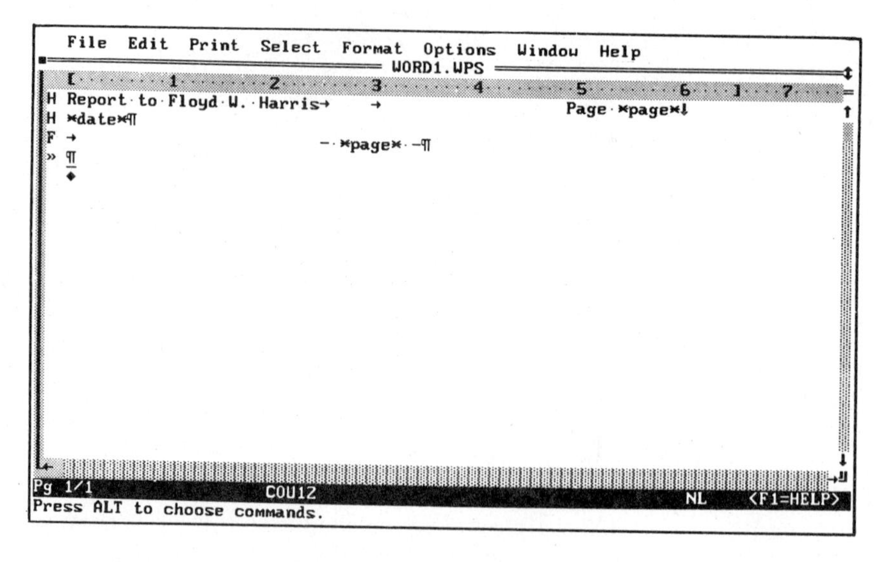

Figure 14-8. Text and placeholders that produce the header in figure 14-5

When you're ready, here's how to create the header, step by step:

- Move the cursor two rows up, to the paragraph in the Header (H) line.
- Type **Report to Floyd W. Harris**
- Press Tab twice to move to the Right tab mark. You can see R in the ruler.
- Type **Page** and a space. Works enters the word from right to left.
- Press Ctrl+P to insert a page placeholder (*page* appears).
- Press Shift+Enter to end that line and move to the next line down—a new header line that Works inserted.
- Press Ctrl+D to insert a date placeholder (*date* appears).

The header is now complete. You can create the footer in Figure 14-6 by either deleting the standard footer and entering **- *page* -** (a page placeholder with hyphens and spaces) or modifying the standard footer to look like that.

Pagination

Works counts the pages in your document, calculates page breaks, and assigns page numbers. This process is called *pagination*. Page breaks occur when you type enough text to fill a complete page, less the margins. As you type new text or delete existing text, Works recalculates the page breaks, showing the start of each page by double right-angle brackets (») at the left edge of the screen.

Works follows certain rules in determining page breaks. At least two lines of a paragraph must be on a page. The first line of a paragraph that ends up at the bottom of a previous page shifts to the top of the next page. Similarly, the last line of a paragraph that ends up at the top of a page shifts to the bottom of the previous page. This prevents awkward page breaks known as "widows" and "orphans"—short, single lines at the top or bottom of a page.

The page indicator at the left end of the status line shows the current page number and the page count. For example, 2/15 means that your cursor is in the second page of a 15 page document.

Manual Page Breaks

The idea of a manual page break is to make sure that a page starts where you want it to. This is important, for example, when you start a new section in a report.

When you press Ctrl+Enter, Works inserts a manual page break above the line of text containing the cursor, indicating its presence by drawing a line of dashes across the screen and showing the usual double right angle brackets to the left of the first line in the new page. It then recalculates the breaks for succeeding pages.

You can have as many manual page breaks as you need. To delete a manual page break, place the cursor on the dashed line and press Delete.

If we all howl loudly enough, maybe Microsoft will restore the Manual Pagination command available in Works 1.0. This command allowed you to freeze pagination—vital during editing to keep track of which page contains what text. Now, pagination simply keeps rippling along, changing the page numbers as you edit.

When you absolutely must find text by page number, insert manual page breaks on each page with Ctrl+Enter. After you finish editing, use search and replace to erase all those page breaks. Here's how: Move the cursor to the beginning of the document and choose the Select menu's Replace command. In the `Search for` field in the dialog box, enter **^d** (Shift+6 and then **d**, the manual page break character). Leave the `Replace with` field empty. Choose the `Replace All` button, and Works will whisk away every manual page break in a flash.

Keeping Paragraphs Together

Pagination sometimes separates text at inappropriate places—for instance, a paragraph heading from a paragraph or an introductory sentence from a bulleted list. You can have Works lock blocks of text to prevent page breaks within a paragraph or between paragraphs.

Within a paragraph, first select the paragraph, choose the Format menu's Indents & Spacing command, and turn on the `Don.t break this paragraph` box. To lock paragraphs, select the paragraphs, and then turn on the `Keep this paragraph with next` box.

If the page that contains the locked text now exceeds the page break limit, Works pulls over the locked paragraph or paragraphs to the next page, causing a short previous page.

If you subsequently insert or delete text, it's likely to affect pagination, and you may no longer need to lock the paragraphs. To dissolve the lock, turn off the check box in the Indents & Spacing command by choosing it again.

Previewing the Document

As you edit a document—inserting text here and deleting it there, switching paragraphs around and changing the format—you affect page layout.

You can check the impact of your efforts with the Print menu's Preview command, which displays a miniature version of the document on screen. Every word will not be easily decipherable, but you can get a good idea of the overall appearance of the page.

Printing the Document

Although you can preview your work at any time, the moment that you print the document—the first tangible proof that your words really do exist—is sweet indeed. Until that time, you may have felt you were on a magical mystery tour of menus, microchips, and memory.

You can use the standard print settings or choose your own, printing any time and as often as you wish during document development. The important thing is to be sure that Works and your printer can communicate. If you selected more than one printer during Works setup, select the printer you want to use in the Print menu's Printer Setup dialog box.

In the Print command in the Print menu, tell Works how many copies to print, specify the pages to print if you're not printing every page, whether to print to a file on disk instead of the printer, and whether to print the document in draft quality—that is, without character formats, which often speeds up the printing.

If you choose Draft Quality, you may get faster printing, but there's a down side. Among other divergences from the norm, Works refuses to print any charts inserted in a document and turns off the microspacing required by some printers for text justification. If you're getting strange results when you choose draft quality, restore normal quality (choose Draft Quality again).

If your printed document somehow misses the mark, you can return again and again to the Print menu to select new settings. Be patient and persistent. Chances are, Works has exactly the settings you want. All you need do is get them all together.

In the next chapter, you'll try your hand at creating a personalized dinner invitation that puts to work many of the word processing concepts and techniques you learned about in this chapter.

Word Processor Workout: Dinner Invitation

There's going to be a party and you're invited.

One of the interesting and unusual things you can do with a word processor is create invitations for special events. In this chapter, you'll create an invitation to you (yes, you) to attend the grand reopening dinner at Antonia Chavez' newly refurbished Chez Chavez. Figure 15-1 shows the invitation for Jonathan Q. Peters, another honored guest. Your name replaces his.

In this chapter, you enter text, check the spelling, select font style and size, apply boldface, copy a format, align the text, save your work, view the invitation on screen, and then print it. This one's fun!

Later, in the Works Fireworks section, you'll merge this invitation with the records in Antonia's customer database (the workout in Chapter 11) to produce a bunch of personalized invitations and mailing labels—all designed to get you really comfortable with more of the dazzling things Works can do.

Keystrokes and Other Matters

The instructions guide you each step of the way, giving keystrokes and cursor movements that relate to each task. In some actions, you need to *press* the Alt key, and in others, *hold down* the Alt key. There's only a slight semantic difference between pressing and holding down a key, but it makes a big difference in the way Works works.

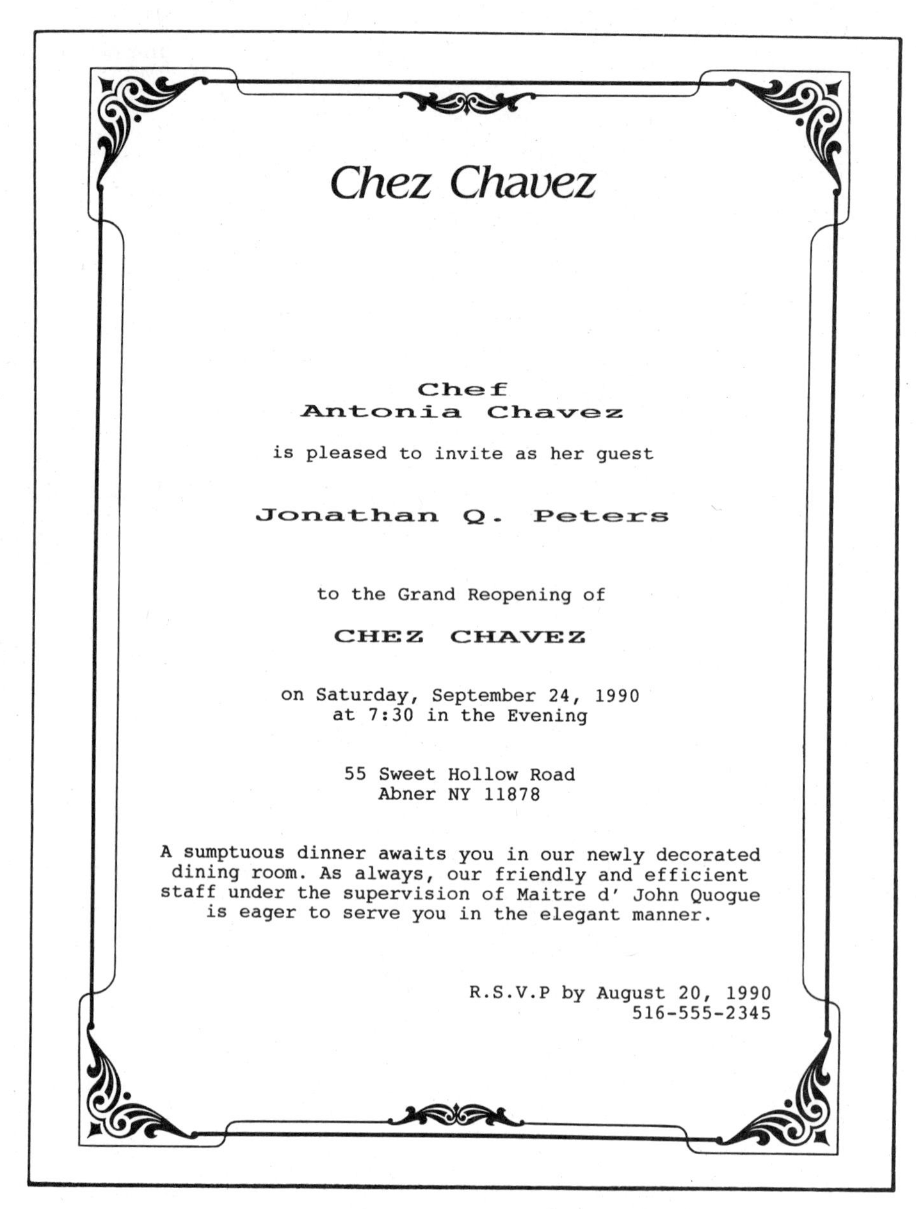
Chez Chavez

Chef
Antonia Chavez

is pleased to invite as her guest

Jonathan Q. Peters

to the Grand Reopening of

CHEZ CHAVEZ

on Saturday, September 24, 1990
at 7:30 in the Evening

55 Sweet Hollow Road
Abner NY 11878

A sumptuous dinner awaits you in our newly decorated dining room. As always, our friendly and efficient staff under the supervision of Maitre d' John Quogue is eager to serve you in the elegant manner.

R.S.V.P by August 20, 1990
516-555-2345

Figure 15-1. An invitation to dine at Chez Chavez

- When you see such instructions as *Press Alt and type OS (Options/Check Spelling)*, press and release Alt before you type the letters. Alt activates the menu line, and the letters choose a menu and a command.

- With instructions such as *Hold down Alt and type F (to enter the Fonts box)*, press the Alt key, and without releasing Alt, type the letter. The letter leads you to a field in a dialog box.

Unless the instructions say otherwise, use the Arrow keys (Left, Right, Up, and Down) to move the cursor. If you run into a snag, press the Escape key to cancel what you're doing. Then pick up where you left off.

Creating a New Document

Load Works as described in the Introduction to this book. At the File menu, the gateway to Works, type **NW** (Create New File/New Word Processor). Works brings up a new word processor screen with the standard filename `WORD1.WPS`.

The word processor screen has menus across the top, a ruler directly below, a new page symbol (») in the selection bar to the left of the window, a paragraph mark (¶) underlined by the cursor, and an end-of-document mark (◆). The cursor shows where your first typed character appears.

Entering the Text

Now let's make your screen look like the one in Figure 15-2. The paragraph marks show where to press Enter to end a paragraph or to insert blank lines between paragraphs. The tiny dots between words show where to press the Spacebar. If you make a typo, press the Backspace key (not an Arrow key) to back up the cursor and erase.

The dot between words is strictly a screen character. It doesn't appear in the printed document.

- Type **Chef** and press Enter to end the paragraph.
- Type **Antonia Chavez** and press Enter twice to end the paragraph and insert a blank line. Works inserts a dot between first and last name to show where you pressed the Spacebar.
- Type **is pleased to invite as her guest** and press Enter three times to end the paragraph and insert two blank lines.
- Type your name (in upper- and lowercase, using a middle initial if you have one) and press Enter four times.
- Type **to the Grand Reopening of** and press Enter twice.
- Type **CHEZ CHAVEZ** and press Enter three times.
- Type **on Saturday, September 24, 1990,** and press Enter.

```
» Chef¶
  Antonia·Chavez¶
  ¶
  is·pleased·to·invite·as·her·guest¶
  ¶
  ¶
  Jonathan·Q.·Peters¶
  ¶
  ¶
  ¶
  to·the·Grand·Reopening·of¶
  ¶
  CHEZ·CHAVEZ¶
  ¶
  ¶
  on·Saturday,·September·24,·1990¶
  at·7:30·in·the·Evening¶
  ¶
  ¶
  55·Sweet·Hollow·Road¶
  Abner·NY·11878¶
  ¶
  ¶
  A·sumptuous·dinner·awaits·you·in·our·newly·decorated·dining·
  room.·As·always,·our·friendly·and·efficient·staff·under·the·
  supervision·of·Maitre·d'·John·Quogue·is·eager·to·serve·you·
  in·the·elegant·manner.¶
  ¶
  ¶
  ¶
  R.S.V.P.·by·August·20,·1990¶
  516-555-2345¶
  ◆
```

Figure 15-2. The text in the invitation

- Type **at 7:30 in the Evening** and press Enter three times. Works scrolls the window down to provide empty lines for more text.
- Type **55 Sweet Hollow Road** and press Enter.
- Type **Abner NY 11878** and press Enter three times.

  Before you continue, here are two advisories on the next paragraph: 1. Type the entire paragraph without pressing Enter. Wordwrap will move any word that can't fit at the end of a line down to the beginning of the next line. 2. To be sure everyone is at the same place, press the Spacebar only once between sentences.

- Type **A sumptuous dinner awaits you in our newly decorated dining room. As always, our friendly and efficient staff under the supervision of Maitre d' John Quogue is eager to serve you in the elegant manner**. Press Enter four times.

- Type **R.S.V.P. by August 20, 1990** and press Enter.
- Type **516-555-2345** and leave the cursor where it is. This completes text entry.

Checking the Spelling

Before going any further, check the spelling. Works starts at the cursor's position, so hold down Ctrl and press Home to jump the cursor to the first word in the invitation.

The following instructions assume you haven't made any spelling errors of your own. If you have, you can take this opportunity to correct them. The screen messages and the following instructions will guide you. The instructions also assume your name isn't Antonia Chavez.

- Press Alt and type **OS** (Options/Check Spelling).

Instantly, Works brings up the dialog box claiming that Antonia is a misspelled word. Antonia is a proper name and, therefore, understandably absent from the Works dictionary. There's no point in adding it to your personal dictionary.

Replacing an entry with the same entry, as Works proposes to do in the Replace with *field, is the same as ignoring it.*

- Press Enter (to replace Antonia with Antonia). Works immediately finds Chavez, another name you don't need in your personal dictionary.
- Press Enter (to replace Chavez with Chavez). Chances are, Works now finds your first name. If it does, make that the first entry in your personal dictionary.
- Hold down Alt and type **A** (to choose Add). If Works now finds your last name, add that to the dictionary by holding down Alt and typing **A** again. Next, Works finds CHEZ.
- Press Enter (to replace CHEZ with CHEZ).

Time out. With a long document, it can be worthwhile to turn on the Skip capitalized words box. This tells Works to ignore words in uppercase only and stop at unfamiliar words with an initial cap. Therefore, Works would skip over such words as CHEZ and CHAVEZ (and ASCII and SMPTE) but stop at Abner and Quogue (and Jefferson and Lincoln). Now back to the present.

- In rapid succession, Works finds CHAVEZ, Abner, and Quogue. Press Enter for each one.

Works now informs you that the spelling check is finished. Press Enter to confirm.

Saving the Invitation

This is a good time to save the document and give it the filename INVITE. Leave the cursor where it is.

- Press Alt and type **FA** (File/Save As).

Works now brings up the `Save As` dialog box so you can type a filename, and, if needed, a drive or directory. If you're saving to the current drive, simply type the filename. Otherwise, type the drive or directory before the filename (for example, **A:INVITE**).

- Type **INVITE** and press Enter. Works assigns the extension `.WPS`, for Works Word Processor.

As the file is being saved, the indicator in the left of the status line shows the percentage already processed. When the page number reappears, Works is ready for your next action.

Printing the Text

It's always an eye opener to see what text looks like on paper in its raw, unformatted state, so turn on your printer.

- Press Alt and type **PP** (Print/Print).

You now see the `Print` dialog box. All proposed settings are fine, so press Enter. The printer whirs, and here's the invitation, looking like the one in Figure 15-2 (without paragraph marks, of course). Yawn.

Formatting the Text

Formatting can turn this ugly duckling into the swan you see in Figure 15-1. That invitation is printed in 12-point Courier except for CHEF ANTONIA CHAVEZ, your name (or Jonathan Q. Peters), and CHEZ CHAVEZ, which is printed in 24-point Courier.

Your choice of font depends on the capabilities of your printer. If you don't have either or both of these Courier fonts, choose something comparable as you go through the following format instructions.

Selecting the Printer

If you specified only one printer during Works setup, you can skip this step and go on to the next section, "Specifying the Font Style." Otherwise, leave the cursor where it is.

- Press Alt and type **PS** (Print/Printer Setup). The blinker is in the `Printers` box.
- Type the first letter of the printer name or press Down Arrow until you reach it.
- Press Tab (to reach the `Model` list). Choose the model and press Enter.

Works will list the fonts available on this printer when you choose the Format menu's Fonts & Style command.

Specifying the Font Style

If you see `COU12` on the status line, you can skip this step and go on to "Using a Larger Font and Bold." Otherwise, format the entire invitation for the Courier 12-point font. Leave the cursor where it is.

- Press Alt and type **SA** (Select/All).
- Press Alt and type **TF** (Format/Font & Style).

Works brings up the dialog box containing the style and font selections. Because you selected more than one word, Works neutralizes the settings, showing a dash in some boxes and leaving others empty. The blinker is in the `Bold` box.

- Hold down Alt and type **F** (to enter the `Fonts` box).
- Type **C** (to choose `Courier`) or type the first letter of a comparable font.
- Press Tab (to move to `Sizes`).
- Type **1** enough times to move the cursor to `12` (to choose 12-point) and press Enter.

Using a Larger Font and Bold

Printing the important elements in a bold, large font really adds pizzazz to this invitation. Press Up Arrow to collapse the selection. The cursor is below the `C` in `Chef`.

- Press F8 (to enter the selection mode).
- Press End, Down Arrow, and End again (to select `Chef Antonia Chavez`).
- Press Alt and type **TF** (Format/Font & Style).
- Type **B** (to turn on `Bold`).
- Hold down Alt and type **F** (to enter the `Fonts` box).
- Type **C** (to choose `Courier`) or type the first letter of a comparable font.
- Press Tab (to enter the `Sizes` box).
- Type **2** enough times to move the cursor to `24` (to choose 24-point) and press Enter.

Text mode shows characters in high intensity white or color. Graphics mode shows them as they look when printed (WYSIWYG).

Works returns you to the document and shows Antonia's name in high intensity white, color, or bold, depending on your screen mode. The status line shows the letter `B` for `Bold` and `COU24` (or a comparable font) for the font style and size.

Copying a Format

You can give your name the same treatment by copying the formats you gave Antonia's name. Leave the selection as it is.

- Press Alt and type **ES** (Edit/Copy Special). Works displays `COPY` on the status line.
- Press Down Arrow five times, and then press Home (to move to the first character in the name).
- Press F8 (to start the selection).
- Press End (to select the name) and hit Enter. Works displays the `Copy Special` dialog box with `Paragraph Format` the proposed response.
- You want to copy character formats, not paragraph formats, so type **C** (`Character format`) and press Enter.

Works now shows your name in high intensity white, color, or bold.

Copying a Format Again

The name of the restaurant deserves as much attention as Antonia's name and your name, so copy the formats again.

- Press Alt and type **ES** (Edit/Copy Special).
- Press Down Arrow six times, and then press Home (to move to the first character in the restaurant name).
- Press F8 (to start the selection).
- Press End (to select the name) and hit Enter.
- Type **C** (`Character format`) and press Enter.

The restaurant name is now in high intensity white, color, or bold.

Centering the Text

The next step centers all of the text, line by line, between the margins. Leave the restaurant name selected.

- Press F8 three times (to select all text).
- Hold down Ctrl and type **C** (to choose `Center`).

Works swoops down the screen, centering each line. When it stops, you can see only the last line containing the phone number. Press Ctrl+Home to jump the cursor to the first word, which also collapses the selection. Everything is now centered.

Right-Aligning the Lines

To add a bit of variety to this piece, right-align the last two lines, as shown in Figure 15-1. Hold down Ctrl and hit the End key to jump the cursor to the last paragraph mark. Now press Up Arrow to place the cursor beneath the zero in the date.

- Press F8 four times and then End (to select only the last two lines).
- Hold down Ctrl and type **R** (to choose `Right`).

Instantly, Works shifts both lines to the right. To see the finished product, press Ctrl+Home, and then hold down Down Arrow to scroll through the rest of the invitation.

Setting the Margins

You're eager to print the invitation, but have patience. A few changes in the size of the margins must be made first. Leave the cursor where it is.

- Press Alt and type **PM** (Print/Page Setup & Margins). The blinker is in the `Top margin` field. Increase the size of the top margin to make room for the restaurant logo.
- Type **2.5** (to increase the top margin).
- Hold down Alt and type **E** (to move to `Left margin`).
- Type **1.4** (to increase the left margin).
- Press Tab (to move to `Right margin`).
- Type **1.7** (to increase the right margin).

All the other print settings are fine, so press Enter. This completes the preparation.

Previewing and Printing the Invitation

To make sure all is as it should be, you can preview the invitation layout before printing. Leave the cursor where it is.

- Press Alt and type **PV** (Print/Preview).

Again, you see the Print dialog box. Everything in the box is fine, so press Enter.

Works shows a gem of an invitation, with the layout looking just like the one in Figure 15-1. You can print directly from Preview, so be sure the printer is turned on.

- Press Alt and type **PP** (Print/Print).

The printer whirs, and here's the invitation with your name on it. Quite a change from the earlier one.

- Save the document again by pressing Alt and typing **FS**.

Your word processor workout is over. Remember, this invitation merges with database information in Chapter 20. You'll want everything then exactly the same as it is now. If you can't wait to try out your ideas, save the invitation under another name (File/Save As) and work on the copy.

In the next chapter, you'll explore all of the word processor menus and commands. They're loaded with more neat features and special effects.

Exploring the Word Processor Menus

The dinner invitation you completed in Chapter 15 gave you a bit of the flavor of word processing. There's lots more to satisfy even the heartiest of appetites, so this chapter explores all the word processor menus and commands.

An ellipsis (...) after a command name means that choosing this command produces a dialog box where you make further choices.

And now, on to the word processor menus.

The File Menu

Works stores your spreadsheets, documents, and databases in files. In the spreadsheet, files consist of titles, numbers, and formulas; in a document, words and numbers; and in a database, records containing names, numbers, and formulas.

The File menu is the traffic manager for files. It lets you create new files, open and close existing files, save and name files, use DOS (Disk Operating System) commands without leaving Works, run other programs from Works, and quit the Works program. All commands in the File menu are the same in every application.

Create New File...

When you choose the Create New File command, Works presents the dialog box where you can open a new word processor, spreadsheet, database, or communications file.

If you've already created and saved a template file in that application, Works opens the template file instead. A template file contains settings that you want to use every time you open a new file.

For instance, in the word processor you can make your margins, header text, and paragraph formats standard for any document you later create. You create, edit, or replace a template file in the Save As command.

Open Existing File...

You can have as many as eight files open, and then use the Window menu to switch quickly from one file to another or show several files on screen at one time.

The Open Existing File command lets you open a file you've already created. The `File to open` dialog box lists the names of all files in the current directory and provides access to other drives and directories. Double dots in the `Directories` box take you to the next higher directory.

Works lists files alphabetically within their type—Word Processor, Spreadsheet, Database, Communications, and Other Files. The fastest way to select a file from this list is to type the first letter of the filename.

If you want to list the filenames of only one type of file, use the asterisk wildcard in the `File to open` box. For instance, type ***.WKS** to list only spreadsheet files, ***.WDB** for database files, ***.WPS** for word processor files, and ***.WCM** for communications files. The asterisk stands for any number of characters in the same position.

If your computer is part of a network, you can open the file as a read-only file. This allows more than one person to see the file but not make any changes.

Save and Save As...

The Save and Save As commands store an open file on disk. Any work you've done since you last saved the file is stored only in computer memory. If something unexpected happens (power outage, electric cord pulled out of socket, and so on), that unsaved work is lost.

The Save command saves a file to the current drive, replacing any prior version if it exists. Works doesn't ask you to confirm the replacement. It just goes ahead and does it. If you save a new file with the Save command, Works responds as if you had chosen the Save As command.

The Save As command lets you save a new file and give it a filename. If you don't type an extension, Works tacks one on based on file type: `.WPS` for word processor, `.WKS` for spreadsheet, `.WDB` for database, and `.WCM` for communications.

If you type a drive letter and colon first (for instance, **A:FILENAME**) or a drive letter and subdirectory first (for instance, **B:\WDATA\FILENAME**), you can save the file under the same filename but to a different drive or directory. When you use Save As to save to another drive or directory, Works asks you to confirm replacement of an existing file.

The Save As command is loaded with other goodies. For starters, it lets you make a backup copy of a file after you save and name it the first time. If you check the `Make backup copy` box, work on the file, and save your changes, Works saves the current version as the active file and the prior version as a backup file with a new extension—`.BKS` for spreadsheet, `.BDM` for database, `.BPS` for word processor, and `.BCM` for communications.

You can also use the Save As command to save a file as a text (ASCII) file with or without formatting. ASCII (which stands for American Standard Code for Information Interchange) lets you convert a file so it can be read by other spreadsheet, database, and word processor programs.

But that's not all. The `Save as template` check box lets you create a master file (aka template)—for instance, a memo with paragraph formats, font size, and print settings but no memo text. Each time you create a new word processor file, Works brings up a memo template awaiting your entries. If you turn off the memo's template status, Works brings up a virgin file instead. You can also turn off or turn on template status in the Options menu's Works Settings command.

Close

The Close command removes an open file from computer memory and clears it from the screen. When you finish work on a file or you want to open another file but already have eight files open, the Close command makes room for others.

File Management...

Your computer's disk operating system (DOS) provides commands that make working with files and functions easier. You can do such tasks as copy, delete, and rename files, create or remove a directory, copy or format a disk, and set your computer's date and time. The File Management command lets you access these DOS commands without leaving Works. When you're ready to return to Works, type Exit (not Works).

Run Other Programs...

The Run Other Programs command lets you launch applications programs without leaving Works. This gives you direct access to other commonly used software as well as to DOS commands, such as CHKDSK, EDLIN, and TREE, that are unavailable in the File Management command. You can choose the programs that appear on the launcher menu. As with File Management, type **Exit** (not Works) to return to Works.

Convert...

The conversion procedure is somewhat different if you're working with a floppy disk instead of a hard disk system. See the Works manual.

Convert lets you convert a file created in another word processing program, such as Microsoft Word, WordPerfect, DisplayWrite, and MultiMate, to Works file format with most (if not all) formatting intact. You can then open and use the converted file just as you would any Works document. You can also do the reverse—convert a Works file to another word processor file format. Pressing Escape during a file conversion cancels the conversion.

Exit Works...

When you Exit, Works saves information about your work, your printer, and any changes you made in the Works Settings command in a file called WORKS.INI.

The Exit command is a safe and sure way out of the Works program. If you just turn off the computer in midstream, everything in computer memory is lost. Instead, Works gently prods you to save each changed or new, unsaved file, giving you one last chance to rescue your work from oblivion.

The Edit Menu

The commands in the Edit menu let you give full reign to your creativity by moving, copying, inserting, and deleting text and other information. If you go too far, it gives you a way to undo that excess burst of enthusiasm.

Undo

The Undo command reverses your last editing or formatting action, effecting an instant rescue of changed text. Undo is a lifesaver in many situations, but it can only undo your last change.

Move

The Move command moves the selected text (words, phrases, sentences, and paragraphs) and its character format to a new location in the document. If the selection contains a paragraph mark, Works moves the paragraph format too.

Moved information disappears from its original location and reappears at its destination, shifting any existing text after the insertion further to the right and any existing text below the insertion further down. If you select text at the destination, the moved information replaces it.

Shortcut key F3 lets you move information without going through the Move command. During a move, Works displays the word MOVE on the status line.

Copy

The Copy command copies the selected text and its character format to another place in a document or to another open Works file. If the selection contains a paragraph mark, Works copies the paragraph format too.

To copy the same thing to several places, move the cursor to the next place and press Shift+F7. This repeats the last Copy command.

Copied text remains in its original location and a copy appears at its destination. If you select text at the destination, the copied text replaces it.

You can use shortcut key Shift+F3 to copy without going through the Copy command. During a copy, Works displays the word COPY on the status line.

Copy Special...

The Copy Special command copies only the character or paragraph format of the selected text (not the text itself) to other selected text in a document. During the process, Works displays the word COPY on the status line.

Delete

The Delete command gets rid of unwanted text. It's easier to select the text and simply press the Delete key. To delete characters to the left of the cursor, use the Backspace key; to delete characters at the cursor, use the Delete key. To undo the last deletion, use the Edit menu's Undo command immediately.

Insert Special...

The Insert Special command inserts special characters and codes in your document. You can see the dialog box in Figure 16-1 and, at the left, how these elements look on screen. The page break symbol (»), paragraph mark (¶), and end-of-page (◆) symbols in the figure are regular screen characters. They have nothing to do with these special characters and codes. The nonbreaking space character (fourth from the top) is invisible.

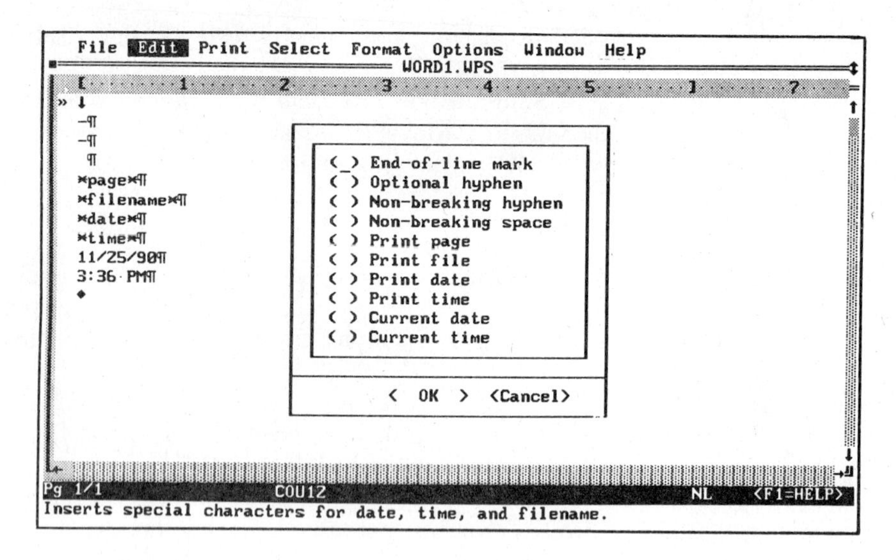

Figure 16-1. Insert Special dialog box with special characters you can insert in a document

Special characters and codes fall into three general groups:

Text placeholders hold the place for text that Works inserts when you print the document.

1. Text controllers (end-of-line mark, optional hyphen, nonbreaking hyphen, and nonbreaking space).
2. Text placeholders (print page, print filename, print date, and print time).
3. Text inserters (current date and current time).

All special characters have corresponding shortcut keys (see Table 13-1) that insert faster than the Insert Special command.

Insert Field...

The Insert Field command inserts placeholders that tell Works where to insert information retrieved from a field in the database. The dialog box lists the open database files and field names in the selected database.

When you print the document, Works replaces the placeholders with information from the database field.

Insert Chart...

The Insert Chart command brings up a dialog box listing open spreadsheet files and their charts. When you select a chart, Works inserts a placeholder in the document in this form:

chart FILENAME.EXT:CHARTNAME, where FILENAME.EXT is the name of the spreadsheet file and CHARTNAME is the name of the chart.

Place the cursor on the chart placeholder and choose the Format menu's Indents & Spacing command, and Works brings up the chart format dialog box instead of the usual paragraph format dialog box. Here you can specify chart indents, number of lines above and below the chart, chart height, and chart orientation (landscape or portrait).

You can preview the selected chart in the document by using the Print menu's Preview command. When you print the document, the chart prints. The spreadsheet file must be open at the time.

If you choose Draft Quality printing for a document with a chart placeholder, only the text prints, not the chart. Instead, Works leaves a gap in the document where the chart belongs. This is a fast way to check page layout without waiting for the chart to print each time.

Footnote...

Footnotes are often used for comments, explanatory notes, and references in a document.

The Footnote command compiles the footnotes you create to support a statement in the main text of a document. Works inserts a visible marker in the document at the footnote location and prints footnotes at the end of the document.

Bookmark Name...

The Bookmark Name command lets you name passages in your document so you can find them quickly. This makes it easy to navigate long documents. Works inserts a hidden marker in the document.

You can get to the bookmark by pressing F5 to open the Go To dialog box and selecting from the list of bookmark names.

The Print Menu

Works gives you a great deal of control over how a printed document looks. You can specify, among other things, margin sizes, pages to print, text placement on the printed page, size and style of characters, page numbers, page breaks, content and alignment of headers and footers, and which printer to use.

All of these features are great, but the shining stars of this menu are the merge commands, which let you blend files from different sources with little effort on your part.

Print...

The Print command tells Works how many copies to print, which pages to print if you're not printing every one, whether to send the document to the printer or to a disk file, and whether to print draft quality. Draft quality prints text without character formats, and, as a result, does it faster.

To print certain pages only, turn on the Print specific pages box, which undims the Pages field. Type the page numbers in the Pages field. Separate single pages with commas (for instance, **1,3,6** tells Works to print pages 1, 3, and 6) and a range of cells with a colon or dash (for instance, **8:10** or **8-10** tells Works to print pages 8, 9, and 10).

Page Setup & Margins...

Header and footer margins should always be smaller than the regular top and bottom margins.

Margins (Top, Bottom, Left, and Right) tell Works when to start and stop printing on a page. Header and footer margins control the distance between the top of a page to the top of a header and the bottom of a page to the bottom of a footer.

The page length and page width settings tell Works the size of the paper you'll be using to print your document. Works prints until a page is full or until it encounters a page break, which tells it to stop printing on that page and start on the next. It determines page breaks based on margin settings and paper size.

The page number setting tells Works what to number the first page, assuming your header or footer contains a page number code.

Preview...

The Preview command shows on screen how your document will look on paper. In this miniature version, Works shows margins, headers, footers, and page breaks in their proper locations and scales text to show the specified size. You can print from Preview by typing **P**.

Print Form Letters...

The Print Form Letters command lets you print form letters and similar types of documents using information from an open database file. First, create a document with placeholders that tell Works which information to retrieve from the database and where to print it.

Works prints one copy of the document for each displayed record in the database, replacing each placeholder with information from the database field. Before printing, make sure that only those records you want to print are displayed. You can press Escape at any time to cancel printing.

If you want to proofread the text or check the layout of your document, you can print one copy without merging. Use the Print menu's Print command, not the Print Form Letters command. Works then prints the placeholders instead of the database information.

Print Labels...

The Print Labels command prints mailing labels using information from an open database file. First, create a document with placeholders that tell Works which information to retrieve from the database and where to print it.

In the `Print Labels` dialog box, specify the name of the database and either accept or replace the proposed settings for size and spacing of labels and number of labels to print across the page.

Works prints one label for each displayed record, replacing each placeholder with information from the database field. If the field is empty, Works leaves a small gap on the label. This gap is the space between placeholders.

Choosing the `Test` box in this command tells Works to print one label only or one row of labels, so you can check the spacing and alignment.

Insert Page Break

A page break tells Works when to stop printing on one page and start on the next. It calculates the break point based on page size and margins. The Insert Page Break command lets you determine where page breaks occur, making it easy to start a new page before a new section in a report, for example. You can also use Ctrl+Enter to insert a manual page break.

Works uses the symbol (») to show a page break on screen. The line displaying the page break symbol becomes the first line on the next printed page. You can delete a page break with the Delete key.

Headers & Footers

The Headers & Footers command lets you create headers and footers in your documents. A header is text that prints at the top of each page, and a footer is text that prints at the bottom. Headers usually contain such things as a title, page number, date, or time. Footers usually contain a page number. You can have a header, footer, both, or neither.

You can create one-line headers and footers in the dialog box or turn on the `Use header and footer paragraphs` box, which lets you create header and footer paragraphs in the word processor screen.

The standard alignment centers header and footer text. Entering special alignment codes in the dialog box right-justifies or left-justifies one-liners. You can align header and footer paragraphs created in the word processor screen as you do any other text. Special codes enter the filename, page number, date, and time in a header or footer.

Headers print one-half inch from the top of the paper, while footers print one-half inch from the bottom. You can change these settings in the Page Setup & Margins command to print higher or lower on the page.

You can print a header or footer on every page but the first by checking the No header (or No footer) on 1st page box. This works well when the first page is a title page.

Chapter 14 covers headers and footers in greater detail and gives the header and footer codes.

Printer Setup...

If you specified more than one printer during the Works setup steps, the Printer Setup command lets you choose which printer to use to print your report. If you specified one printer only, Works uses that printer. Figure 16-2 shows the settings in the dialog box.

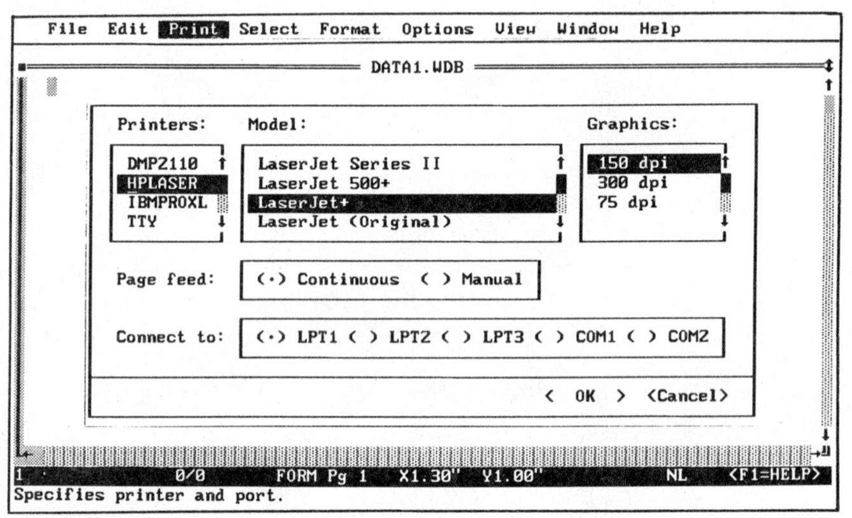

Figure 16-2. The printer setup screen where you can choose your printer, type of page feed, and communication port

With printers that print graphics, the Graphics box offers a choice of print resolutions (fineness of line) expressed in dots per inch (dpi). Works uses the resolution setting only for printing charts, not text.

This command also lets you change page feed from continuous to manual, which is useful when you want to feed single sheets to the printer. It also gives you the choice of which communication port to connect to your printer.

If you want to add or replace printer drivers, be aware that drivers on the Works Setup disk are stored in compressed form (.CPR extension). To use these drivers, you must go through the Works setup steps so Works can decompress the driver. Drivers stored on the Supplemental Printer disks have a .PRD extension. You can simply copy these drivers directly into the Works subdirectory.

The Select Menu

The commands in the Select menu let you select text you want Works to work on, move the cursor quickly to a specific page, find specific text, or find and replace text.

Text

The Text command starts text selection at the cursor's location. You can then use the arrow keys to select the rest of the text. Pressing F8 and then the arrow keys is more efficient than using this command. Press Escape to turn off the selection.

All

Using the All command instead of pressing F8 five times reduces from five to three the number of keystrokes needed to select the entire document.

Go To...

The Go To command sends the cursor to a specific place in the document, either a bookmark or a page number. Using shortcut key F5 to bring up the Go To dialog box is quicker.

Search...

The Search command searches the document for the text you specify. Text can be words, numbers, symbols, or special characters, such as tab marks and paragraph marks. The search starts at the cursor position and continues to the end of the file. If you select text first, Works limits the search to the selected area.

You can have Works search only for whole words that match the search word, ignoring words embedded in other words, and search for perfect matches, including uppercase and lowercase letters.

When Works finds the text, it halts the search. Pressing F7 continues the search to the next occurrence. When there are no more occurrences, Works lets you know with a screen message.

Replace...

The Replace command searches the document for the text you specify. When it finds the search text, it replaces it with other text. The search starts at the cursor position and continues to the end of the file. If you select text first, Works limits the search to the selected area.

You can choose to replace text one occurrence at a time or all at once. If you choose the former, each time Works finds the text, it pauses so you can review what it found and say whether or not to replace it. The search then continues without your having to press F7. If you choose the latter, Works replaces every occurrence, with no further instruction from you.

You can match whole words and case, the same as the Search command. Because Replace is a command with built-in neat tricks, Chapter 13 discusses it in detail.

The Format Menu

The commands in the Format menu control the ways in which Works displays and prints text. Text formats fall into two groups: character and paragraph, both of which are covered in Chapter 14. You have three ways to choose format commands:

1. As individual commands in the Format menu.
2. In the Format menu's Font & Style (character format) and Indents & Spacing (paragraph format) dialog boxes. Here, you can apply more than one format at a time.
3. With the shortcut keys shown in Table 14-2.

Plain Text, Bold, Underline, and Italic

You can apply all character styles with shortcut keys and restore them to plain text by pressing Ctrl + Spacebar.

These commands (plus strikethrough, superscript, and subscript) constitute the character format group. Bold causes the printer to overstrike text to produce darker, thicker characters. Underline draws a line below text. Italic slants text to the right. After you apply a style, Plain Text restores the text to standard character format.

Before applying a style to existing text, select the text with F8. If you're typing new text, select the paragraph mark at the cursor location. Any new characters you type will appear in that style.

Font & Style...

The dialog box in this command offers all character formats— bold, italic, underline, strikethrough, superscript, and subscript.

WYSIWYG (What You See Is What You Get) means that, in graphics mode, Works shows styles on screen the way they print on paper.

Strikethrough prints a dashed line through each character, which is useful during editing. Superscript positions text one-half line above normal text, while subscript positions text one-half line below. Normal restores superscript or subscript characters to the normal position on the line.

In addition, the dialog box lists the font types and sizes available on your printer.

Normal Paragraph, Left, Center, Right, Justified, Single Space, and Double Space

These commands (plus paragraph indents and other types of line spacing) constitute the paragraph format group. Left (the standard paragraph alignment) aligns all lines in the paragraph flush with the left indent. Center centers each line in the paragraph between the left and right indents. Right aligns all lines flush with the right indent. The Justified command increases the space between words so that every line, except a short last one, is flush with both the left and right indents.

The Double Space command inserts a blank line between each line of text. The Single Space command restores text given double, triple, or other spacing to single spacing.

After you apply formats, the Normal Paragraph command restores the text to standard paragraph format—left-aligned, single spaced, no space before or after, no custom tab stops, and indents set to zero.

Indents & Spacing...

The Indents & Spacing command presents the same alignment choices (Left, Center, Right, and Justified) and line spacing (single and double) available as individual commands, plus new ones dealing with paragraph indents, other kinds of line spacing, and locking devices to prevent unwanted paragraph breaks.

When you insert a chart placeholder in a document, choosing this command with the cursor on the placeholder brings up the chart dialog box instead of the paragraph dialog box. This is where you can specify indents, lines above and below the chart, chart height, and chart orientation (landscape or portrait).

Tabs...

Tab stops define the precise placement of text, particularly in columns and tables. The Tabs command clears and sets tab stops.

Standard tab stops occur at half-inch intervals, with text or numbers routinely left-aligned at each stop. You can change these intervals as well as alignment, centering or right-aligning text and aligning numbers along the decimal point. Figure 16-3 shows the dialog box where these activities take place.

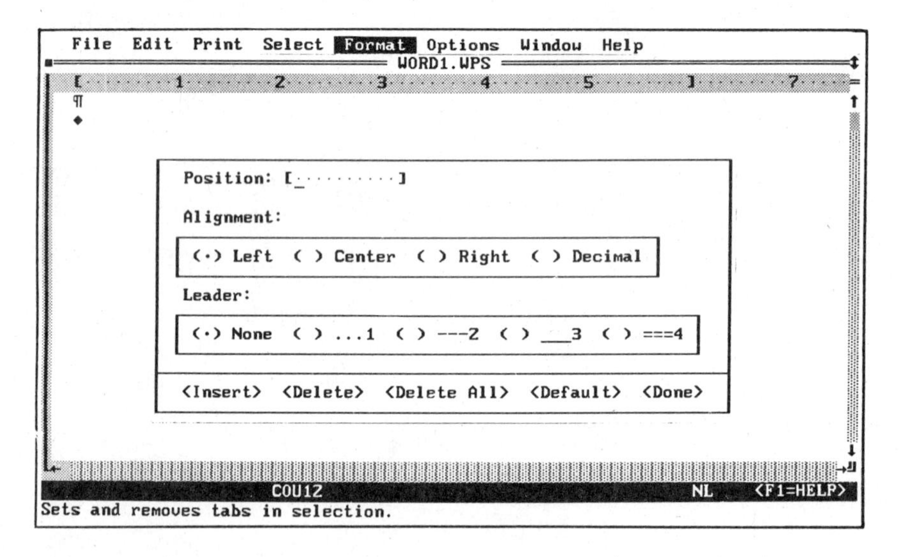

Figure 16-3. The Tabs dialog box where you can set and remove tabs and select leader characters

The most common use of leader characters is in a table of contents.

This command also gives you a choice of leader characters to fill the space between columns. Leader characters can be dots, single dashes, a solid line, or double dashes. You can also choose to have no leader characters.

Borders...

The Borders command produces boxes around your paragraphs, horizontal lines between them, or vertical lines on either side.

The Options Menu

The first four commands in the Options menu—Works Settings, Calculator, Alarm Clock, and Dial This Number—are the same and work the same in all applications. They let you customize the window display, select settings that affect the entire Works program, and access the desk accessories. Chapter 1, "The Works Environment," covers the desk accessories in more detail.

Figure 16-4 shows these and other commands that keep the ruler and special screen characters on screen, display footnotes, ignore the selected font size, replace existing text, check your spelling, suggest synonyms, and paginate the document.

A mark before Show Ruler and Show All Characters means that these commands are turned on. This is their initial condition.

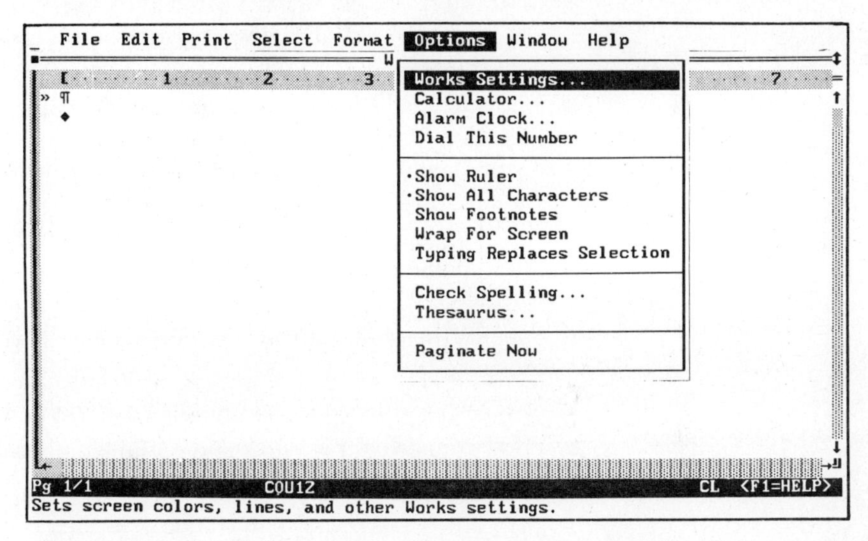

Figure 16-4. The Options menu with an array of commands vital to word processing

Works Settings...

The Works Settings command lets you change the current settings in the Works program. Many of these settings reflect your response to questions about your hardware configuration during Works setup. Works now gives you the chance to change your mind. Works stores your settings in the WORKS.INI file, so you need to make your changes only once.

It's here that you can:

- Select the subset of another country. Countries have different standards. Your choice can affect page size, currency symbol, and date and time format.
- Redefine the unit of measure from inches to centimeters, pitches, or points.
- Choose the screen colors. Your options depend on the capabilities of the video card selected during the Works setup steps.
- Choose the screen mode, again a function of your video card. The screen mode controls the way character styles and the mouse pointer appear on screen. In text mode, Works shows enhanced characters (bold, underline, italic) in different colors. In graphics mode, it's WYSIWYG (What You See Is What You Get), with Works showing characters on screen similar to the way they look on paper.
- Apply or deny template status. When you save a file in the File menu's Save As command and make it a template, Works turns on the check box for that application in the `Use templates for` box. Erasing the check mark removes template status, while checking off an application applies template status. The last file opened in that application becomes the designated template.
- Specify the communications port to which your modem is connected.
- Specify whether your telephone has tone or pulse dialing.
- View your Works version and serial number.

The designated template appears each time you open a new file in that application.

Calculator...

The Calculator command displays a screen calculator that works a lot like a hand-held calculator. It performs simple calculations that you can transfer into a word processor, spreadsheet, or database file.

Alarm Clock...

The Alarm Clock command displays a screen where you can enter appointment dates, times, and reminders. At the appointed time, your computer beeps and displays the reminder. If your computer is turned off when the appointed time arrives, Works flashes the reminder the next time you start up the computer.

Dial This Number

With a Hayes-compatible modem hooked up to your computer, you can have Works dial a phone number in your spreadsheet, database, or word processor file.

Show Ruler

Works displays a ruler at the top of the screen to show the position of margins and indents in your document and to enable you to measure such things as tab stops and the length of lines. The initial status is on. The Show Ruler command lets you turn the ruler off or on.

Show All Characters

Works displays helpful characters on screen to show where you press the Spacebar (dot), press Enter (paragraph mark), or hit Tab (right arrow). These and other special characters, including the end-of-line mark, optional hyphen, and nonbreaking hyphen, appear only on screen, not in print.

When you first start Works, the screen characters are turned on. Selecting the Show All Characters command turns them off. This command is a toggle, so the next time you select Show All Characters, the screen characters appear again.

Show Footnotes

Works displays the footnotes you create in a window pane below the text. If the footnotes are distracting, or you prefer more text on the screen, you can close the footnote pane with the Show Footnotes command. When you select this command again, Works displays the footnotes again. Works prints footnotes at the end of the document.

Wrap For Screen

The altered visual display doesn't affect the printed result. Works still prints the proper number of characters on each line.

Works fits as many characters across a line as font size permits. When you select a small font for printing (for instance, 8-point), the lines of text on screen can extend beyond the viewing area.

Turning on the Wrap For Screen command tells Works to treat any font as if it were a 12-point font. This also permits a large font, ordinarily shown by fewer characters on a line, to spread across the screen.

Typing Replaces Selection

When you turn on the Typing Replaces Selection command, any text you type replaces any text you select. If this command confuses you,

you can get the same result by selecting doomed text, pressing Delete to get rid of it, and then typing new text.

Check Spelling...

The first time you add an unfamiliar word to the dictionary, Works creates PERSONAL.DIC, the file that holds your own words.

The Check Spelling command looks up your words in the 100,000 word Works dictionary and your personal dictionary to find misspelled words. Each time it finds an unfamiliar word, it gives you the chance to make corrections and request suggestions. During the spell-check, the command also looks for improper hyphenation, capitalization, and double words (the the).

Thesaurus...

The Thesaurus command thumbs through its 300,000 word list to find synonyms for the word you select.

Paginate Now

As you type, Works calculates the page breaks and assigns page numbers in a process called pagination. In a long document, this can take time. Choosing the Paginate Now command or pressing F9 supposedly speeds up the process. It's like getting water to boil faster.

The Window Menu

All commands in the Window menu are the same in every application. They let you view and work on as many as eight different files at a time, each in its own window. You can determine the size, position, and arrangement of the windows. Shortcut keys Ctrl+F6 switch to the next window and Shift+Control+F6 switch to the previous window.

Chapter 1, "The Works Environment," covers the Move, Size, Maximize, and Arrange All commands in more detail.

Move

The Move command lets you move a window anywhere on screen (and even off screen) as long as the upper left corner remains on screen.

Size

The Size command lets you reduce or enlarge the size of a window.

Maximize

The Maximize command lets you increase a window you reduced with the Size command so it fills the entire screen again.

Arrange All

The Arrange All command places open files in side-by-side windows.

Split

The Split command divides the window into panes through which you can view and work on different areas of a document. You can create two top-and-bottom panes, making each pane the same or different size. Be sure to press Enter after you split the screen into panes.

Use the F6 key to jump the cursor to the next pane and Shift+F6 to jump to the previous pane.

Open Files

Each time you open a file, Works adds it to the list in the Window menu. If you have only one window open, you can display a file from this list by simply typing its number. That file then replaces the one that was on screen.

When you finish working on a file, close it with the File menu's Close command. The file disappears from computer memory, leaving room for the next file you want to open.

The Help Menu

When you have questions about Works, you can interrupt your work temporarily to get answers and instruction from commands in the Help menu, and then return to where you left off before asking for help. All commands in the Help menu are the same in every application. Chapter 1, "The Works Environment," covers the Help commands in more detail.

Using Help

This command explains how to go about getting help.

Help Index

Pressing F1 brings up a Help screen on the task you're currently engaged in. If no Help screen exists for that task, Works displays a

Help Index listing all help topics. You can also view the index by choosing the Help Index command in the Help menu or by selecting the Index button in the Help screen you access with F1.

Works Tutorial

Pressing Shift+F1 presents the Works tutorial. You can also view the tutorial by choosing the Works Tutorial command or by selecting the Lesson button in the Help screen that you access with F1.

Getting Started

The Getting Started command brings up an explanation of how to use Works with the type of file (spreadsheet, database, word processor, or communications) now on screen.

Keyboard and Mouse

The Keyboard command brings up a comprehensive list of keystrokes that run the Works program. The Mouse command explains how to get around with the mouse.

What's the Line Limit in a Document?

As you type new text and open more files, you fill computer memory. When memory is full, Works stores your text on disk. There's no maximum length imposed by Works on a document—only the limit imposed by the amount of available space on the disk holding your data.

When you need the answer to these and other "how many" questions, refer to Table 16-1, which contains the workaday numbers relating to the word processor.

Table 16-1. Useful word processor numbers

<table>
<tr><th>Parameter</th><th>Number</th></tr>
<tr><td>Files open at one time</td><td>1 to 8</td></tr>
<tr><td>Length of a filename</td><td>1 to 8 characters plus 3-character extension (any character except * ? / . ; [] + = B : | < > space)</td></tr>
<tr><td>Maximum length of command in Run Other Programs dialog box</td><td>124 characters</td></tr>
<tr><td>Maximum number of ranges to print in Print dialog box</td><td>10</td></tr>
</table>

Parameter	Number
Standard lines on screen	19
Maximum lines on screen (ruler off)	20
Maximum number of lines in document	Limited only by disk storage space
Maximum tab stops in one paragraph	20
Maximum length of footnote mark	10 characters
Maximum characters merged from database file to document	2,050
Maximum placeholders in document	128
Maximum characters in all placeholders in one document	1,920
Available window panes	2
Words in the Works dictionary	100,000
Synonyms in the Works thesaurus	300,000 for 30,000 key words
Maximum length of text selected for Thesaurus check	32 characters
Standard print settings:	
Top and bottom margins	1 inch
Left margin	1.3 inches
Right margin	1.2 inches
Page length	11 inches
Page width	8.5 inches
Header and footer margins	0.5 inches
Standard print label settings:	
Vertical spacing	1 inch
Horizontal spacing	3.5 inches
Labels across	1

The next chapter covers the communications capabilities of Works.

P A R T

five

Works and the Outside World

Communications Essentials

You can send anything Works can create: letters, spreadsheets, charts, databases, and reports.

Imagine exchanging information with computer users across the room, across town, across country, or across the world. Imagine sending electronic mail messages to one person or a hundred in the blink of an eye. Imagine checking the headlines, reviewing your bank account, scanning stock prices, and booking airline flights, hotel reservations, and theater tickets with only a few keystrokes at your computer. Pie-in-the-sky, you think? No, merely the dazzle of Works communications.

Communications keeps the world at your fingertips. For free (excluding phone charges), you can hook into your local computer bulletin board systems (BBS) to read messages, get the latest public domain software, and chat with friends and colleagues without uttering a word. For a fee, you can tap into commercial data banks (Dow Jones, CompuServe, and others) and their staggering array of information on such diverse topics as travel, world weather, medicine, patents, law, childhood diseases, arms control, and yes, even dating etiquette.

Getting Acquainted with Communications

This chapter discusses the essential "whys" and "hows" of the communications application. It describes the communications screen, what you need to get started, setting up your computer, and how to send and receive information.

You don't need a modem or any other special equipment right now to learn. You can get a reasonably good idea of how things work by reading the explanations and referring to the illustrations.

When you're ready to work with Works, fire up your computer and follow the instructions in "Loading Works" in the Introduction to this book. At the Works gateway, type **NC** (Create New File/New Communications) to create a new communications file.

The Communications Screen

The communications screen shown in Figure 17-1 is your window on a world of information, ideas...and just plain fun. The following paragraphs introduce you to its elements.

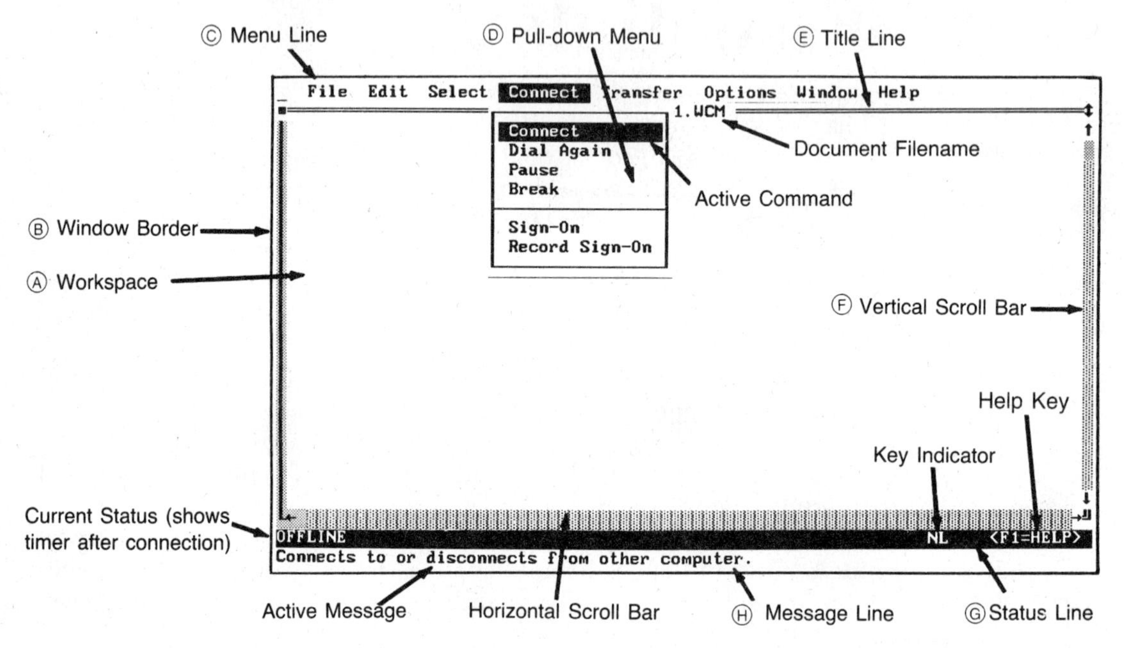

Figure 17-1. The Works communications screen

A. The empty area is your *workspace*. This is where you see text that you send or receive. Text can include phone numbers, connect messages, prompts for sign-on information, and responses to prompts. The workspace ordinarily contains a flashing underline called a *cursor* in the top left corner. The cursor shows where the next character appears. Because the Connect menu is open, the cursor is absent now. If you have a mouse installed, the cursor shares the workspace with the mouse pointer, which looks like a small rectangle or an arrow, depending on screen mode.

B. The vertical line at the left edge is the *window border*, which separates the window from the screen.

C. At the top of the screen is the *menu line* containing the communications menus: File, Edit, Select, Connect, Transfer, Options, Window, and Help. The menus let you create and maintain communications files as well as send and receive text.

D. Below the menu line is a *pull-down menu* listing the commands in the Connect menu: Connect, Dial Again, Pause, Break, Sign-On, and Record Sign-On. Commands tell Works to perform specific tasks. The first command, Connect, appears in reverse video (light letters on a dark background), which identifies it as the active command. Each time you choose a menu, Works presents a list of commands.

E. Below the menu line is the *title line*, which contains the filename (here, hidden behind the pull-down menu). You use the filename to load, store, and otherwise keep track of a file. Until you name it, Works assigns the standard filename—`COMM1.WCM`. The extension `.WCM` identifies a communications file.

F. At the right edge of the window is the *vertical scroll bar* that shows the location of the cursor relative to all lines in the file. A *horizontal scroll bar* below the workspace shows the cursor's location relative to all columns.

Mouse users can zip along to distant parts of a long file by gliding the scroll box along a scroll bar.

Each scroll bar contains a *scroll box* that moves along the scroll bar as you move the cursor, showing which part of the file is currently on screen. For example, when the scroll box is in the middle of the scroll bar, you're looking at the middle of the file.

G. Directly below the horizontal scroll bar is the *status line*. The left end of the status line shows the current status—now `OFFLINE`, which means that the computer isn't connected to any other computer. When you connect to another computer, a timer replaces the `OFFLINE` message. The right end shows F1, the key to immediate on-screen help. If your computer is connected to another computer, press Alt+F1.

Works reserves the area between `OFFLINE` and Help key for status reports on your current activity, such as *SEND* (when you're sending a file), *CAPTURE* (when you're saving text being sent to you), and certain keys (*CL* is Caps Lock and *NL* is Num Lock).

H. Below the status line is the message line where Works describes the active command or proposes your next action. The Connect command is active, so the message line displays `Connects to or disconnects from other computer.`

What You Need To Get Started

To get started in communications, you need a modem and either a telephone line or a cable connecting your computer to another computer. The other computer can be part of the vast computer network of a commercial information service, a mainframe or minicomputer, a system configured as a bulletin board, or a friend or colleague's personal computer.

Using a Modem and Phone Lines

A modem (short for *MO*dulator/*DEM*odulator) is a device that enables your computer to communicate with another computer over an ordinary telephone line. A modem converts the digital signals sent by your computer into analog sounds that phone lines can carry. When your computer receives data, it reverses the process, converting the analog sounds into digital signals that your computer can use.

Modems come in different makes, models, and capabilities. Your modem can be external (a separate unit attached with a cable to your computer's serial port) or internal (a board installed in a slot in your computer). The other end of the modem plugs into the telephone circuitry, either at the phone base or where the phone cable enters the wall. Whether external or internal, Works works only with a Hayes or Hayes-compatible modem that can respond to the Hayes command set (also called AT—or Attention— commands).

Works is all set to run at 1200 baud.

Transmission speed is measured in bits per second (bps), expressed as *baud rate*. A 300-baud modem can send or receive roughly 300 bits of information (about 30 characters) per second. At this speed, it can transmit a half-page of typewritten text in about one minute. A 1200-baud modem is four times faster (about two pages of text per minute) and a 2400-baud modem is faster still.

Virtually all modems are capable of more than one transmission speed, most commonly 300 and 1200 baud, often 2400 baud. Information services and bulletin boards usually handle transmissions at 300 or 1200 baud and beyond. High rates of transmission over phone lines can be hampered by noise interference that causes garbled transmission or loss of data. Noise notwithstanding, the trend is toward speed.

Using a Direct-Connect Cable

For close-by communication, you don't need a modem at all—you need only a cable long enough to connect two computers directly. This cable, called a *null modem*, fools the computers into thinking they have a modem between them. The computers can be any kind—microcomputers, minicomputers, mainframes, or networks. Ask your computer system manager or dealer for specific information on the hardware and software needed for this kind of setup.

Computers connected by a null modem are free from the problems of noise, garbled transmission, or loss of data that can occur when you run a modem at high baud rates over phone lines. They can, therefore, communicate cleanly at great speed.

Before You Go On-Line

If settings don't match, Works can't make the connection.

Going on-line means connecting to and communicating with another computer. The key to a successful connection is matching your communications settings to the other computer so they are totally compatible. You can find out which settings to match by checking with the person at the other computer or reading the brochures from a commercial service.

Three commands in the Options menu—Terminal, Communication, and Phone—contain these settings, with one setting in each group designated as standard. Standard settings match most communications conditions. You only need to change a setting if it differs from the other computer.

Before going on-line, you need to create a new communications file or open an existing one to store the information Works needs to communicate with other computers. These files store communications settings, phone numbers, and recorded sign-ons only.

When you save the communications file, these settings are saved. The next time you open the file, Works uses this information to connect with another computer.

The Terminal Command

The buffer is a temporary way-station for text received from another computer.

Terminal settings control how your computer displays and responds to the information it receives. Figure 17-2 shows the dialog box in this command. The proposed settings are usually correct. The only settings you may want to change on occasion are LF (line feed), Buffer, and Local echo.

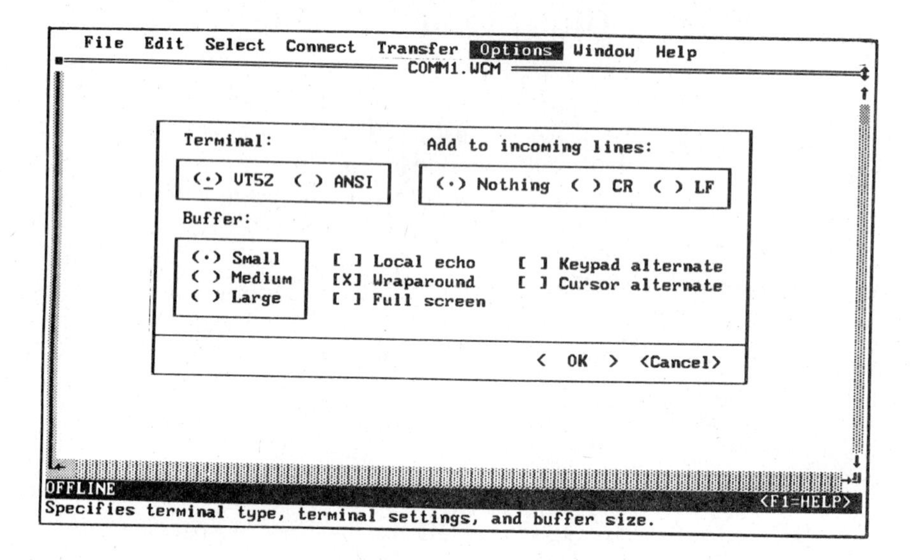

Figure 17-2. The settings in the Terminal command

Terminal

When your computer is connected to another computer via a network, it functions as a data terminal—that is, it doesn't use its own computing power. To function properly, it must emulate, or act like, a terminal known to that computer. This setting selects the terminal you want your computer to emulate.

You can have it respond to either VT52 or ANSI control sequences sent by the other computer. VT52 (similar to the Zenith Z19) is typically used for commercial information services, electronic mail services, and bulletin board systems; ANSI is equivalent to the DEC VT100 or VT220/VT240 terminals used on minis and mainframes. The Works standard is VT52.

Add to Incoming Lines

Checking the CR box inserts a carriage return character at the end of each line of text received by your computer; checking the LF box inserts a line feed character at the end of each line of text. You can check either CR or LF, but not both. If you don't check either box, Works keeps the standard Nothing.

If incoming text continually overwrites the previous line of text, check LF. Works will then insert end-of-line markers to display the text properly. If lines break and shift down in the middle of the screen, check CR. If text is double spaced, try CR or Nothing.

Buffer

Works stores incoming text temporarily in a scrollable buffer. After pausing the transmission or disconnecting from the other computer, you can review the text or copy it directly to other Works files.

Works starts you out with a 100-line (Small) buffer. You can increase the size to either 300 lines (Medium) or 750 lines (Large). The larger the buffer, the more memory you set aside for this storage. If memory is a concern, keep the buffer only as large as you absolutely need it.

If you want to save incoming text that contains more than 750 lines, you can bypass the buffer and bring it in directly to a file with the Transfer menu's Capture Text command.

Local Echo

When you check the Local echo box, you can see characters as you type them. Leaving this box empty keeps your computer in remote echo mode. This means that the other computer echoes back the characters you type.

If you see double characters after going on-line, you have the best (and worst) of both worlds—Local echo is on and the other computer is echoing back your characters. Turn off Local echo.

Wraparound

The Wraparound box causes long lines of incoming text (more than 80 characters wide) to wrap around to the beginning of the next line, so you can see them all. Wraparound is turned on as standard.

Full Screen

When checked, the Full screen option causes the menu, status, and message lines to disappear, giving you more screen area to display incoming text. Turn on `Full screen` when you're using terminal emulation. It goes into effect when you connect.

Even with the menu line turned off, you can still use the communications menus. Simply press Alt to choose a command and the menu line reappears temporarily. Turning off `Full screen` restores the screen to normal.

Keypad Alternate

When you check the Keypad alternate box, Works puts your computer into keypad alternate mode. If your computer is emulating either a VT52 or ANSI terminal and the Num Lock key is on, your keypad keys send special command sequences to the other computer instead of numbers and symbols.

Cursor Alternate

When checked, Works puts your computer into VT100 cursor key application mode. If your computer is emulating an ANSI terminal and the Num Lock key is off, your cursor movement keys sends special command sequences to the other computer instead of moving the cursor.

The Communication Command

If you alter any settings (Works or yours), be sure to save them in the communications file so you don't have to start from scratch each time.

Communications settings control the flow of text between your computer and the other computer. If you end up with garbled text or strange characters on screen after connecting, check these settings first. Figure 17-3 shows the dialog box in this command.

Baud Rate

The number in the `Baud rate` field sets the transmission speed. The higher the number, the faster the transmission. The most common settings for modems are 300, 1200, and 2400. The Works standard is 1200 baud. Use 9600 for direct cable connections.

If parts of the outgoing text are absent from your screen after you go on-line, try a lower baud rate, or use the Transfer menu's Send Text command to tell Works to pause at the end of each line.

Data Bits

The setting in the `Data bits` box controls the number of bits, which can be 7 or 8, used for each transmitted character. The Works standard is 8 data bits.

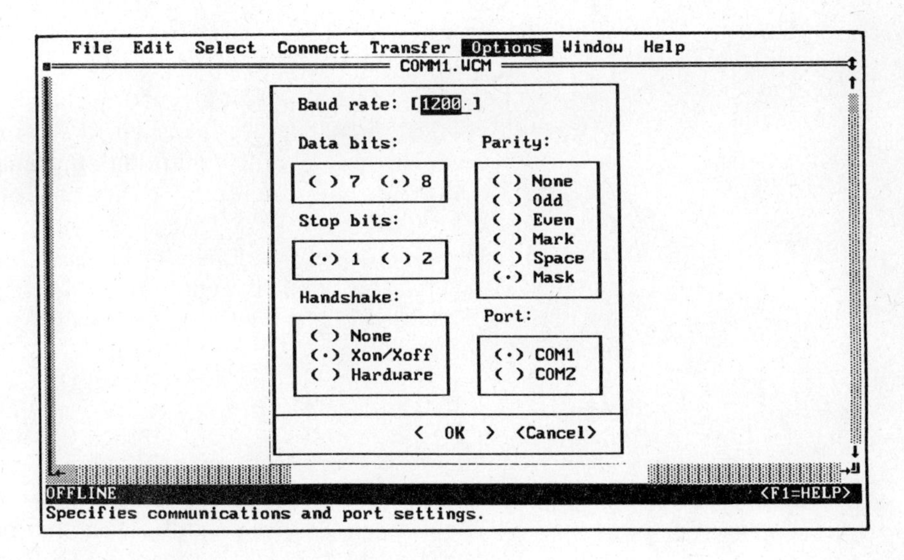

Figure 17-3. The settings in the Communication command

Stop Bits

The setting in the `Stop bits` box controls the number of bits, which can be 1 or 2, used to indicate the end of one character and the start of the next. Virtually all systems use 1 stop bit, which is the Works standard.

Handshake

The setting in the `Handshake` box permits the computer to send a Pause signal (Connect menu's Pause command) to suspend communications temporarily without data loss—for example, if data flow is too fast. When the computer is again ready to receive text, it sends a Continue signal. You have a choice of three settings:

1. `Xon/Xoff` (the Works standard) for computers that respond to software handshake signals. To pause, the computer sends an `Xoff` (short for Xmit off, or transmit off) character. To resume, it sends an Xon (Xmit on, or transmit on) character.
2. `Hardware` for computers that respond to hardware handshake signals. This is used only when you have a direct cable connection between computers.
3. `None` when the other computer doesn't use handshaking.

Parity

The Parity setting detects errors occurring during transmission of a byte (eight bits) of data. The 8th bit is set to a value of 0 or 1, which causes even or odd parity. Both computers must have the same type of parity checking or both must omit parity checks. With 8 data bits, there can be no parity.

You can select None, Odd, Even, Mark, Space, or Mask (the Works standard) to match the requirements of the other computer. Mask parity masks off the 8th bit to keep you from getting strange characters on screen.

Port

The Port setting tells Works the port that is connected to your modem or cable. Works selects COM1 initially, but you can choose COM2 instead.

If Works informs you that it can't access that port, you may have another device connected to it. Change the COM port setting.

The Phone Command

Phone settings control how and when your modem makes and receives calls and which number it calls. Figure 17-4 shows the dialog box in this command.

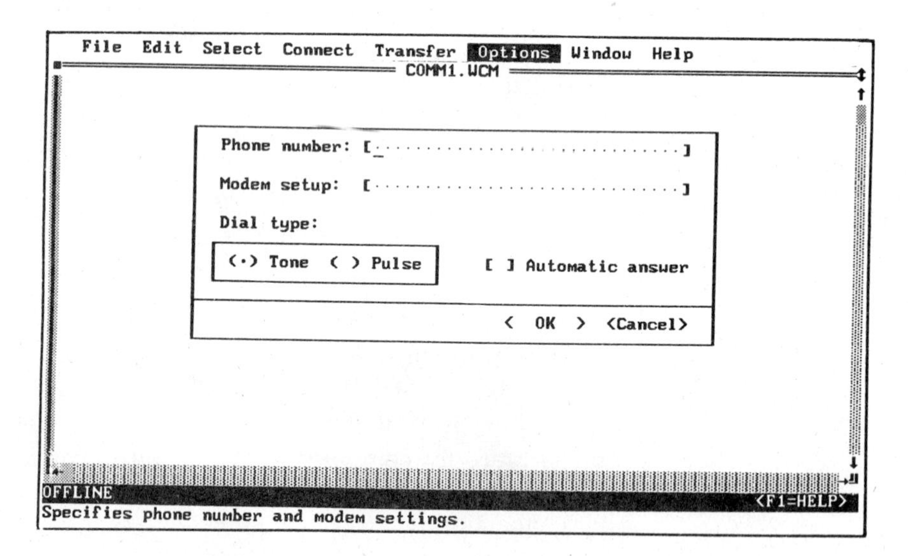

Figure 17-4. The settings in the Phone command

Phone Number

Dashes and parentheses in the phone number don't affect the dialing.

Works dials the number you enter in the `Phone number` field. Type all digits exactly as you would dial them yourself. For example, `9,1-800-555-1212` accesses an outside line (9), pauses for another dial tone (comma), and then dials the 1-800 phone number.

The entry in this field cannot exceed 38 characters. If your number is longer than 38 characters, enter it without any dashes and parentheses. If you're using a null modem (cable connection between computers), leave this field empty.

Modem Setup

The entry in the `Modem setup` field adjusts your modem before dialing the number. These settings, for example, can detect a busy signal (which throws `BUSY` on your screen) and control the speaker volume. See your modem manual for commands supported by your modem.

The entry in this field cannot exceed 38 characters. If you're using a null modem, leave this field empty.

Dial Type

The `Dial type` box sets `Tone` (push-button) dialing as standard. If you have a rotary phone, select `Pulse` dialing instead.

Automatic Answer

The `Automatic answer` box, when checked, tells your modem to answer incoming phone calls. This option becomes active after you choose the Connect Menu's Connect command. When you set the modem to answer calls, Works ignores the phone number in the Phone Number box.

Going On-Line

With the communications file open and the settings set, you're ready to connect to another computer. When you choose the Connect menu's Connect command, Works goes into action. (If you're using a direct cable connection, Works establishes a connection when you choose Connect.)

If you see **BUSY** *or* **NO CARRIER** *instead of* **CONNECT**, *Works was unable to connect to the other computer. You can have Works redial by choosing the Connect menu's Dial Again command.*

The screen now shows the instructions Works sends to the modem and the phone number you entered in the Phone number field. When the other modem answers, Works displays CONNECT and a connect-time timer replaces the OFFLINE message on the status line.

If you're connected to a bulletin board or a commercial information service, within seconds (usually) you see a short welcoming message and a request for information. This request is typically for your name or identification number (ID) and a password that allows you to log on, or connect, to the service. As protection against prying eyes, the password remains invisible even as you type.

Preliminaries over, you can now communicate on a real-time basis or send and receive files created earlier and stored on disk. Sending a file to the other computer is called *uploading*; receiving a file from the other computer is called *downloading*.

If you're setting up to receive information, you need to know two things: the settings of the other computer, so you can match them, and when to expect the call, so you don't tie up your computer needlessly.

Before the call, turn on the Automatic answer box in the Options menu's Phone command. As long as this box is turned on, Works ignores any number in the Phone number field. Then choose the Connect menu's Connect command. On the screen, Works displays OK to indicate its state or readiness. When the call comes in and the computers connect, you're on your way.

Holding a Keyboard Conversation

In a keyboard conversation, you let your fingers do the talking. As you type, Works sends each character to the other computer. The other computer echoes back what you type, displaying it on your screen.

Like a phone call conversation, this type of communication encourages a free-wheeling give and take. You can send to the other computer and receive from the other computer spontaneously.

Receiving a Saved File

With the Transfer menu's Capture Text command, your computer can capture (receive and store) text sent from another computer, receiving it either in the communications buffer, or, if the text exceeds 750 lines (the maximum buffer storage area), directly into a Works file.

When you first select this command, Works asks for a filename, which can be the name of a new file or an existing one. If you're creating a new file, add a Works extension (.WPS, .WKS, or .WDB) to the filename so you can load the file from the File menu's Open command.

If you're bringing text into an existing file, tell Works either to append the captured text to the end of that file or replace anything currently in the file with the new text. You can cancel the capture at any time by choosing the Transfer menu's End Capture Text command.

When you pause during transfer, Works puts **PAUSE** *on the message line.*

Though it is admittedly difficult without a crystal ball, try to make sure you have enough room on disk for the entire incoming file. If you run out of disk space, don't panic. Works displays an alert and simply cancels the capture. If this happens, your first action is to tell the other computer to stop sending, which you can do by choosing the Connect menu's Pause command.

To use Pause, you must have Handshake (`Xon/Xoff` or `Hardware`) turned on in the Options menu's Communication command and the other computer must be able to respond to handshaking. Xon/Xoff is standard, so Handshake is turned on unless you've changed the setting.

You can then change drives or insert another disk and choose Capture Text again. Type the filename and choose the Append option, and then choose Pause again to tell the other computer to resume sending. Since the file is sent without the XMODEM protocol, be aware that it can contain errors.

Sending a Saved File

To save time and expense (both phone and connect time if you're hooked into a commercial service), you can upload (send) an entire file already created. It transfers and echoes back as if you were typing from the keyboard, but clearly runs a good deal faster than conversational style.

Using the Transfer menu's Send Text command, you can transfer any type of file, but transfer and display only text files without special characters or formats such as bold or italics. The text in the file transfers and displays continuously until the end.

If the other computer has trouble keeping up with the data flow, you can specify a delay at the end of each line of transmitted text. The number you enter in the `Delay` field represents one-tenth of a second. For example, enter **1** and Works pauses for one-tenth of a second after sending each line.

Be aware that the text is being sent without XMODEM protocol, which affords error correction protection. If you're sending binary files or formatted Works files, use the Transfer menu's Send File command instead.

Sending an Error-Free File

The Transfer menu's Send File command makes sure the file you send (upload) arrives at its destination error free. With Send File, Works applies XMODEM protocol to detect and correct any errors that may occur during transfer. The other computer must also support XMODEM protocol and be ready to receive when you send.

File Formats

When you select the name of the file to send, you can also tell Works its format:

Format Binary	The file is a formatted Works file, computer program, or any other formatted file that contains nonprintable characters. This is the standard setting.
Format Text	The file is an ASCII text file or other file that was saved unformatted—that is, with alphanumeric characters only, not with special characters.

You can also specify end-of-line characters—either CR (carriage return) or LF (line feed)—to match the type of line terminations used by the other computer. Works inserts both a carriage return and line feed as standard.

Screen Display

You can cancel the transfer at any time by pressing Escape or Enter, and then choosing OK when Works asks for confirmation.

During transfer, Works displays a Status dialog box, not the file. The status box shows how many bytes have already been sent, as well as the number of retries. If Works detects more than ten errors when sending a block of the file, it cancels the transfer. Otherwise, it simply continues error checking and sending.

The status box indicates the ebb and flow of data by alternating between SEND and WAIT. When Works completes the transfer, it displays Transfer Successful. Pressing Enter continues the communications session.

Receiving an Error-Free File

The Transfer menu's Receive File command makes sure you receive (download) an error-free file from another computer. This is comforting when you're downloading large amounts of text. The other computer must support XMODEM transfers. Before choosing Receive File, you need to tell the other computer you're ready to receive what it sends.

The process is quite similar to using the Send File command. When you enter the new filename, you can accept the standard Binary format or specify `Text` format for the file you're receiving. With `Text` format, Works converts all incoming end-of-line sequences to carriage returns and line feeds. It adds a carriage return to lines ending with only a line feed, and a line feed to lines ending with only a carriage return. This ensures that the received file is always a valid DOS text file.

During the transfer, Works displays a `Status` dialog box showing the number of bytes received, as well as retries. The status box message alternates between `RECEIVE` and `WAIT`. Upon completion, it shows `Transfer Successful`.

If more than ten errors occur when receiving a block of the file, Works cancels the transfer instead.

Copying Text Back and Forth

You can use the Edit menu's Copy command to copy text received via modem from another computer—for example, stock quotes from a commercial information service into a Works file. Works stores received text in the communications buffer and displays it on- screen, so that you can review or copy all or part of it to a spreadsheet, database, or word processor file.

If you're still connected to the other computer, be sure to choose the Connect menu's Pause command before selecting and copying the text. Otherwise, Works transmits these keystrokes to the other computer. To resume the transfer, choose the Connect menu's Pause command again.

You can also copy text stored in a Works spreadsheet, database, or word processor file to another computer—for example, a speech or a report. Copy all or part of the text to a communications file, and from there transmit via modem to another computer.

Signing Off

When you finish a communications session, all you need do to disconnect from the other computer is again choose the Connect menu's Connect command. This is the same as hanging up the phone. After disconnecting, close the communications file.

If you're disconnecting from a commercial information service, always log off the service before you disconnect. Otherwise, you may find yourself charged for the time it takes the other computer to recognize that you've disconnected.

You're not logging off with communications yet. In the next chapter, you can explore and enjoy all of the communications menus.

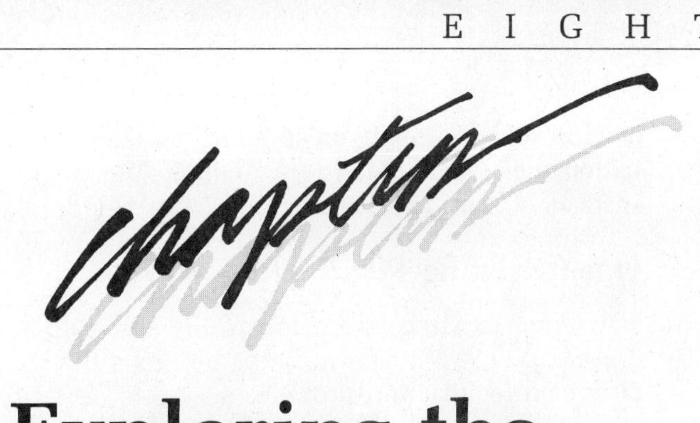

Exploring the Communications Menus

Reaching beyond your computer to the outside world is heady stuff. The mere idea of all those little bits and bytes dancing across phone lines is enough to keep you coming back for more and more.

In the last chapter, you learned about many of the features of the communications application. This chapter describes them all. An ellipsis (...) after a command name means that choosing this command produces a dialog box where you make further choices.

When you select some commands, Works puts a marker before it. These commands are toggles. Selecting them once activates them. Selecting them again deactivates them.

And now, onto the communications menus.

The File Menu

The File menu is the traffic manager for files. It lets you create new files, open and close existing files, save and name files, use DOS (Disk Operating System) commands without leaving Works, run other programs from Works, and quit the Works program. All commands in the File menu are the same in every application.

Create New File...

When you choose the Create New File command, Works presents the dialog box where you can open a new word processor, spreadsheet, database, or communications file.

If you've already created and saved a template file in that application (see the Save As command), Works opens the template file instead. A template file contains your standard settings.

Open Existing File...

The Open Existing File command lets you open a file you've already created. The `File to open` dialog box lists the names of all files in the current directory and provides access to other drives and directories. Double dots in the `Directories` box take you to the next higher directory.

Works lists files alphabetically within their type—Word Processor, Spreadsheet, Database, Communications, and Other Files. The fastest way to select a file from this list is to type the first letter of the filename. You can have as many as eight files open at a time, and then use the Window menu to switch quickly from one file to another or to show several files on screen at one time.

If you want to list the filenames of only one type of file, use the asterisk wildcard in the `File to open` box. For instance, type ***.WKS** to list only spreadsheet files, ***.WDB** for database files, ***.WPS** for word processor files, and ***.WCM** for communications files. The asterisk stands for any number of characters in the same position.

If your computer is part of a network, you can open the file as a read-only file. This allows more than one person to see the file but not make any changes.

Save and Save As...

The Save and Save As commands store an open file on disk. Any work you've done since you last saved the file is stored only in computer memory. If something unexpected happens (power outage, electric cord pulled out of socket, and so on), that unsaved work is lost.

The Save command saves a file to the current drive, replacing any prior version if it exists. Works doesn't ask you to confirm the replacement. It just goes ahead and does it. If you save a new file with the Save command, Works responds as if you had chosen the Save As command.

The Save As command lets you save a new file and give it a filename. If you don't type an extension, Works tacks one on based on file type: `.WPS` for word processor, `.WKS` for spreadsheet, `.WDB` for database, and `.WCM` for communications.

If you type a drive letter and colon first (for instance, **A:FILENAME**) or drive letter and subdirectory first (for instance, **B:\WDATA\FILENAME**), you can save the file under the same filename but to a different drive or directory. When you use Save As to save to another drive or directory, Works asks you to confirm replacement of an existing file.

The Save As command is loaded with other goodies. For starters, it lets you make a backup copy of a file after you save and name it the first time. If you check the `Make backup copy` box, work on the file, and save your changes, Works saves the current version as the active file and the prior version as a backup file with a new extension—`.BKS` for spreadsheet, `.BDM` for database, `.BPS` for word processor, and `.BCM` for communications.

You can also use the Save As command to save a file as a text (ASCII) file with or without formatting. ASCII (which stands for American Standard Code for Information Interchange) lets you convert a file so it can be read by other spreadsheet, database, and word processor programs.

But that's not all. The `Save as template` check box lets you create a master file (aka template)—for instance, a file with specific settings and phone number. Each time you create a new communications file, Works brings up that file. If you turn off the file's template status, Works brings up a virgin file instead. You can also turn off or turn on template status in the Options menu's Works Settings command.

Close

Before Works closes a changed file, it asks for permission to save it.

The Close command removes an open file from computer memory and clears it from the screen. When you finish working on a file or you want to open another file but already have eight files open, the Close command makes room for others.

File Management...

Your computer's disk operating system (DOS) provides commands that make working with files and functions easier. You can do such tasks as copy, delete, and rename files, create or remove a directory, copy or format a disk, and set your computer's date and time. The File Management command lets you access these DOS commands without leaving Works. When you're ready to return to Works, type *Exit* (not Works).

Run Other Programs...

The Run Other Programs command lets you launch applications programs without leaving Works. This gives you direct access to other commonly used software as well as to DOS commands, such as CHKDSK, EDLIN, and TREE, that are unavailable in the File Management command. You can choose the programs that appear on the launcher menu. As with File Management, type *Exit* (not Works) to return to Works.

Convert...

Convert lets you convert a file created in another word processing program, such as Microsoft Word, WordPerfect, DisplayWrite, and MultiMate, to Works file format with most, if not all, formatting intact. You can then open and use the converted file just as you would any Works document. You can also do the reverse—convert a Works file to another word processor file format. Pressing Escape during a file conversion cancels the conversion.

Exit Works...

When you Exit, Works saves in the WORKS.INI file information about your work, your printer, and any changes made with the Works Settings command.

The Exit command is a safe and sure way out of the Works program. If you just turn off the computer in midstream, everything in computer memory is lost. Instead, Works gently prods you to save each changed or new, unsaved file, giving you one last chance to rescue your work from oblivion.

The Edit Menu

The Edit menu contains one important command—Copy, which lets you transfer text between Works applications and other computers.

Copy

The Copy command copies text received from other computers to Works files and copies text stored in Works files to other computers.

When your computer receives text from another computer, Works stores it in a communications buffer temporarily and displays it on screen. You can select part or all of the text, and then copy it to a Works spreadsheet, database, or word processor file. The computer must be paused or disconnected while you are doing this. Otherwise, your keystrokes are transmitted to the other computer.

You can also copy text stored in a Works spreadsheet, database, or word processor file to a communications file and transmit it to another computer from there.

The Select Menu

The commands in the Select menu let you identify the text you want to copy from the communications buffer to a Works spreadsheet, database, or word processor file.

Text

Before selecting, use the Connect menu's Pause command to prevent your keystrokes from being transmitted to the other computer. After selecting, choose Pause again to resume.

The Text command lets you select text in the communications buffer for copying to a Works file. You can use Shift+Arrow key to select instead of going through the command. Pressing Escape undoes the selection.

All

The All command lets you select all text in the buffer for copying. Works copies the characters exactly as stored in the buffer.

The Connect Menu

The commands in the Connect menu connect and disconnect your computer and the other computer, suspend and resume transfer, break into the transfer, and let you sign on with an information service manually or automatically.

Connect

The Connect command dials the phone number in the Options menu's Phone command and establishes a connection when the other computer answers. If the computers are directly cabled via a null modem, Connect establishes a connection. When you're connected, choosing this command hangs up (disconnects from the other computer).

Dial Again

If you get a busy signal or fail to connect with the other computer, the Dial Again command redials the phone number. If you (a human) want to talk to another human (not computer to computer), use the Telephone Dialer desk accessory.

Pause

The Pause command protects your computer from a potential text overflow while you're reviewing or copying text in the buffer. If you're still connected to another computer, this command prevents the other computer from continuing to send text that can be lost.

To use Pause, you must have either `Xon/Xoff` (the Works standard) or `Hardware` turned on in the Handshake option of the Options menu's Communication command.

Break

This command sends a break signal to the other computer. Break is an attention-getting device that interrupts communications long enough for you to force the other computer to interrupt a program it is running, or to log off (discontinue communications).

Sign-On

To avoid a jumble of messages, be sure to replay the sign-on from the exact point that you started to record.

In response to prompts from the other computer (ordinarily an information service), this command plays back a recorded sign-on sequence giving identifying information, such as your name or identification number and password.

Record Sign-On

This command records a sign-on sequence and stores it in the communications file. Recorded sign-ons let you replay often repeated numbers and procedures at the touch of a button. You can also use this command to record any series of prompts and responses, not only sign-on sequences.

The maximum length of a sign-on sequence is 16,384 characters. Now aren't you glad you asked?

The Transfer Menu

The commands in the Transfer menu send and receive ASCII text and use the XMODEM error-correction protocol to make sure transferred text arrives error-free at either end of the modem.

Capture Text...

The Capture Text command stores the incoming text in a file on disk. The file can be a new or existing one. With an existing file, you have the option to add the new information to the old or replace the old with the new.

After the communications session is over, you can open the resulting file as a word processor document, edit and print it, or integrate the information with another file.

Send Text...

This command sends a text file without using the XMODEM protocol. A text file contains only ASCII characters (no formatting or special characters). This is the type of file that you get when you save a Works document as a text file in the File menu's Save As command.

Because Send Text doesn't use the XMODEM protocol, there's no guarantee the file will arrive error-free. On the plus side, you can send large amounts of text quickly. If the other computer can't process the text as quickly as you send it, you can enter a delay in the dialog box, expressed in tenths of seconds. This delay controls how long Works pauses at the end of each line of transmitted text.

Receive File...

A protocol is a set of rules two computers follow to achieve compatibility when communicating.

This command uses the XMODEM protocol to ensure error-free transmission of either text or binary files. During a transfer, Works sends the file block by block. If the receiving computer detects an error, it requests retransmission of a block. The process continues until the entire file has been sent without errors.

Works displays a status dialog box showing the number of bytes received as well as retries. The message in the status box alternates between `RECEIVE` and `WAIT`. If all goes well, it shows `Transfer Successful`.

Send File...

This command uses the XMODEM protocol to ensure error-free reception of either text or binary files. During a transfer, the other computer sends the file block by block. If Works detects an error, it requests retransmission of a block. The process continues until the entire file has been received without errors. If more than 10 errors occur while sending one block of the file, Works cancels the transfer.

Works displays a status dialog box showing the number of bytes sent, as well as retries. The message in the status box alternates between `SEND` and `WAIT`. If all goes well, it shows `Transfer Successful`.

The Options Menu

The first four commands in the Options menu—Works Settings, Calculator, Alarm Clock, and Dial This Number—are the same, and they work the same in all applications. They let you customize the window display, select settings that affect the entire Works program, and access the desk accessories. Chapter 1, "The Works Environment," covers the desk accessories in more detail.

Other commands let you adjust various communications settings to make your computer compatible with the other computer. These settings are detailed in Chapter 17.

Works Settings...

Works stores your settings in the WORKS.INI file, so you need to make your changes only once.

The Works Settings command lets you change the current settings in the Works program. Many of these settings reflect your response to questions about your hardware configuration during Works setup. Works now gives you the chance to change your mind. It's here that you can:

- Select the subset of another country. Countries have different standards. Your choice can affect page size, currency symbol, and date and time format.
- Redefine the unit of measure from inches to centimeters, pitches, or points.
- Choose the screen colors. Your options depend on the capabilities of the video card selected during the Works setup steps.
- Choose the screen mode, again a function of your video card. The screen mode controls the way character styles and the mouse pointer appear on screen. In text mode, Works shows enhanced characters (bold, underline, italic) in different colors. In graphics mode, it's WYSIWYG (what you see is what you get), with Works showing characters on screen similar to the way they look on paper.
- Increase the number of lines displayed on the screen, again depending on video card.
- Apply or deny template status. When you save a file in the File menu's Save As command and make it a template, Works turns on the check box for that application in the `Use templates for` box. Erasing the check mark removes template status, while checking off an application applies template status. The last

file opened in that application becomes the designated template.

- Specify the communications port to which your modem is connected.
- Specify whether your telephone has tone or pulse dialing.
- View your Works version and serial number.

Calculator...

The Calculator command displays a screen calculator that works a lot like a hand-held calculator. It performs simple calculations that you can transfer into a word processor, spreadsheet, or database file.

Alarm Clock...

The Alarm Clock command displays a screen where you can enter appointment dates, times, and reminders. At the appointed time, your computer beeps and displays the reminder. If your computer is turned off when the appointed time arrives, Works flashes the reminder the next time you start up.

Dial This Number

With a Hayes-compatible modem hooked up to your computer, you can have Works dial a phone number in your spreadsheet, database, or word processor file.

Terminal...

Before you change any settings, try the standard settings first. Chances are, they'll work fine.

The Terminal command contains options that control how your computer displays and responds to the text it sends and receives. These options are

- `Terminal` to emulate the `VT52` (standard) or `ANSI`.
- `CR` (carriage return) or `LF` (line feed) if lines overwrite each other or break on the screen, or the standard `Nothing`.
- `Buffer` to expand temporary buffer storage from the standard 100 lines (Small) to 300 lines (Medium) or 750 lines (Large).
- `Local echo` to see text as you type it.
- `Wraparound` to wrap around lines of text longer than the screen can otherwise display.
- `Full screen` to expand the viewing area to the entire screen sans menu, status, and message lines.

- Keypad alternate to send special command sequences to the other computer, depending on the terminal you specify.
- Cursor alternate to send special command sequences to the other computer instead of moving the cursor.

Communication...

The Communication command contains options that control the flow of information between your computer and another computer. These options are

- Baud rate to specify speed of transmission.
- Data bits, Stop bits, and Parity to set parameters that achieve compatibility between computers.
- Handshake to permit either computer to suspend and resume transmission without losing data.
- Port to tell Works where the modem is connected.

Phone...

The Phone command contains settings that control how your modem makes phone calls. You enter the phone number you're calling here, specify any modem setup instructions, select Tone or Pulse to match your type of phone, and put your computer into an automatic answer mode.

The Window Menu

Shortcut keys Ctrl+F6 switch to the next window and Shift+Control+F6 switch to the previous window.

All commands in the Window menu are the same in every application. They let you view and work on as many as eight different files at a time, each in its own window. You can determine the size, position, and arrangement of the windows.

Chapter 1, "The Works Environment," covers the Move, Size, Maximize, and Arrange All commands in more detail.

Move

The Move command lets you move a window anywhere on screen, and even off screen, as long as the upper left corner remains on screen.

Size

The Size command lets you reduce or enlarge the size of a window.

Maximize

The Maximize command lets you increase a window you reduced with the Size command so that it fills the entire screen again.

Arrange All

The Arrange All command places open files in side-by-side windows.

Split

The Split command is unavailable in the Communications application.

Open Files

Each time you open a file, Works adds it to the list in the Window menu. If you have only one window open, you can display a file from this list by simply typing its number. That file then replaces the one that was on screen.

When you finish working on a file, close it with the File menu's Close command. The file disappears from computer memory, leaving room for the next file you want to open.

The Help Menu

When you have questions about Works, you can interrupt your work temporarily to get answers and instruction from commands in the Help menu, and then return to where you left off before asking for help. All commands in the Help menu are the same in every application. Chapter 1, "The Works Environment," covers the Help commands in more detail.

Using Help

This command explains how to go about getting help.

Help Index

Pressing F1 (or Alt+F1 when your computer is connected to another computer) brings up a Help screen on the task you're currently engaged in. If no Help screen exists for that task, Works displays a Help Index listing all help topics. You can also view the index by choosing the Help Index command in the Help menu or by selecting the Index button in the Help screen you access with F1 or Alt+F1.

Works Tutorial

Pressing Shift+F1 presents the Works tutorial. You can also view the tutorial by choosing the Works Tutorial command or by selecting the Lesson button in the Help screen that you access with F1 or Alt+F1.

Getting Started

The Getting Started command brings up an explanation of how to use Works with the type of file (spreadsheet, database, word processor, or communications) now on screen.

Keyboard and Mouse

The Keyboard command brings up a comprehensive list of keystrokes that run the Works program. The Mouse command explains how to get around with the mouse.

What Are Those Settings?

Successfully navigating a complicated course of communications requires, for starters, that the computers follow the same rules and talk the same language. So, when someone at the other end of a modem says "How many baud?" or "How many bits?," you should be able to answer without too much thought or fluster.

When you need the answer to these and other "how many" questions, refer to Table 18-1, which contains the numbers that relate to the communications application.

Table 18-1. Useful communications numbers

Parameter	Number
Files open at one time	1 to 8
Length of a filename	1 to 8 characters plus 3-character extension—any character except * ? / . ; [] + = B : | < > (space)

Parameter	Number
Maximum length of command in Run Other Programs dialog box	124 characters
Maximum number of ranges to print in Print dialog box	10
Standard parameters	8 bits, 1 stop, mask parity
Standard baud rate	1200 bps
Available baud rates	300, 1200, 2400, and 9600 bps
Maximum length of sign-on	16,384 characters
Available delay at end of each line of transmitted text	0 to 60 (in tenths of seconds)
Maximum length of phone number	38 characters
Maximum modem setup string	38 characters
Retries during XMODEM transmission	up to 10 times, then cancels
Standard buffer storage	100 lines (Small)
Available buffer storage	100 lines (Small) 300 lines (Medium) 750 lines (Large)

The next chapter describes how you can get it all together with Works.

P A R T

Six

Works Fireworks

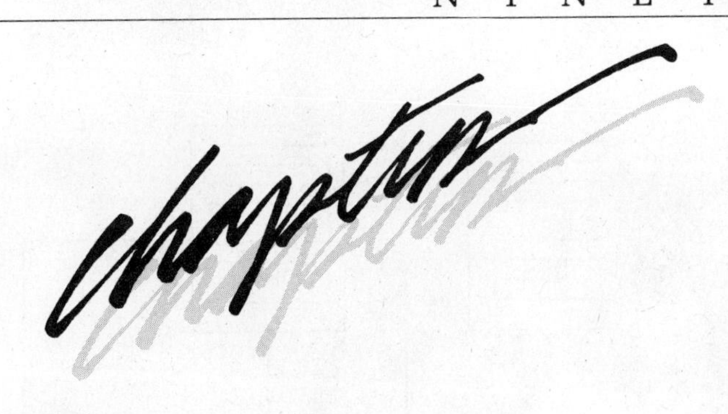

Integration Essentials

Integration lets you exchange information among spreadsheet, database, word processor, and communications files. Effortlessly.

Imagine creating something in one type of file and copying it to another, taking a piece from this one and a piece from that one, mixing and matching to your heart's content, and using information in different ways without having to type the same thing twice.

Imagine no more charts or spreadsheets stapled to the back of a memo, no more tedious typing of long columns of numbers in a report, and no more cutting text out of one document, taping it into another, and then using a copy machine to make it look like one page of information.

With Works, you can combine files electronically. It's called integration, and the process is surprisingly simple.

An Integration Example

Works integration means total compatibility, so each application interacts smoothly with the others.

Figure 19-1 shows the kinds of integration (also called merging) Works can handle. To give you an idea of how this works, suppose you want to merge a customer sales list with a marketing report, and then drop in a pie chart showing sales projections for the next six months. You have all three files open:

1. Customer sales database
2. Sales projection spreadsheet containing the pie chart
3. Marketing report created in the word processor

The marketing report is on screen.

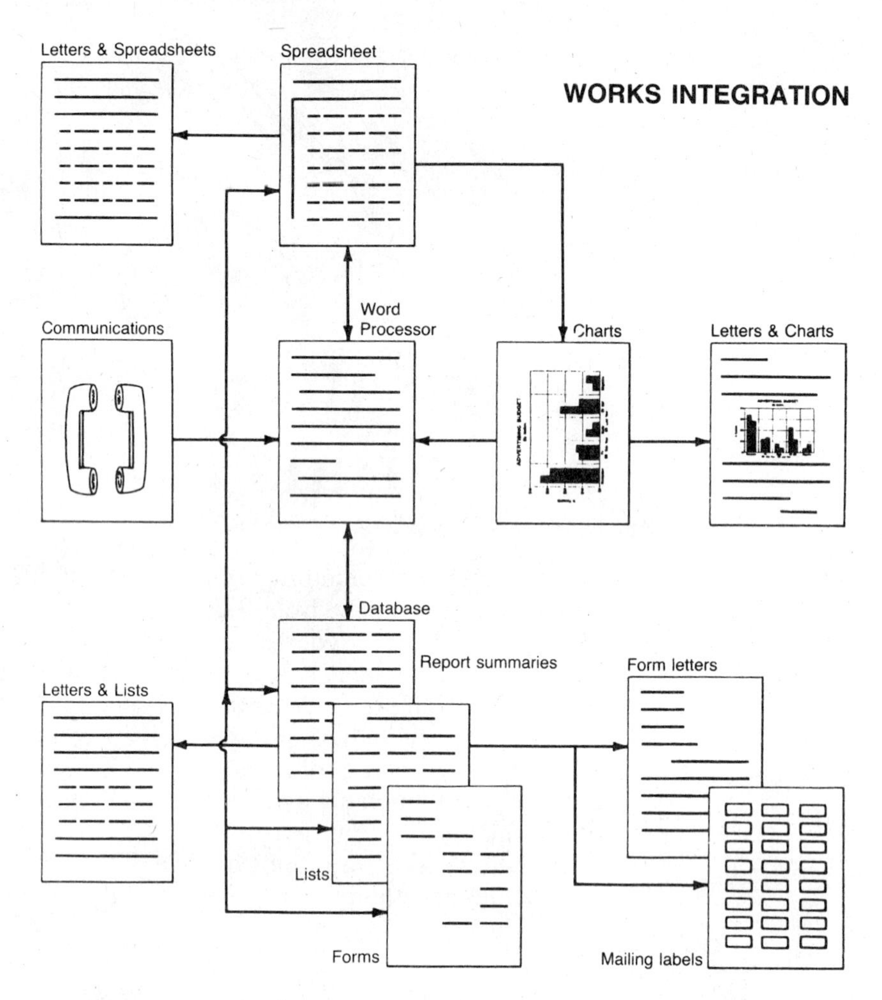

Figure 19-1. The flow of information in the Works applications

Using the Window menu, you switch to the sales database, select the customer list, and press Shift+F3 (the Copy shortcut key). Again using the Window menu, you switch back to the marketing report, place the cursor where you want the customer list to appear, and press Enter. Instantly, the list pops into the report.

You next place the cursor where you want the chart to appear, and choose the Edit menu's Insert Chart command. In the dialog box, you choose the pie chart in the sales projection spreadsheet. Instantly, Works pops a chart placeholder in the report.

After previewing the result on screen, you do a bit of editing to make sure the document is totally seamless, and then print a comprehensive report containing a customer sales list, marketing analysis, and chart of sales projections. Truly dazzling.

Integration Characteristics

Because you use text to describe a spreadsheet, database report, or chart, the word processor is the hub of integration. It provides the mortar that holds the other application bricks in place. You can copy all types of information into a word processor document, creating combinations of text, numbers, charts, and records.

Copying from the Spreadsheet or Database to the Word Processor

Anything you copy into a word processor file assumes the characteristics of a document. Works arranges information that was in spreadsheet or database cells into a table of rows and columns, inserting a tab mark between columns (or fields) and a paragraph mark at the end of each row (or record). The original character style (bold, italic, underline) and alignment (left, right, centered) of copied information is preserved, but font type and size are changed to agree with the surrounding text in the new environment.

If the copied information is too wide to fit within the document's print width, the last columns wrap around and cause a jumble at the left margin. You can correct this by editing the text or increasing the print width.

Once copied into a word processor file, a spreadsheet or database is text only, just as if you typed it from scratch. With copied formulas, Works copies only the values produced by the formulas, not the formulas themselves. This means that you can no longer calculate the text version.

There's no link between files. If you change anything on the source spreadsheet or database and want the information in the document to match, you must update the document manually.

Copying a Chart to the Word Processor

A dot matrix or laser printer lets you print a chart in the midst of text. Instead of using the Copy command to bring the chart into the document, you use the Edit menu's Insert Chart command. Works inserts a chart placeholder, not the chart itself, in the document in this form:

```
*chart FILENAME.EXT:CHARTNAME*
```

FILENAME.EXT is the name of the spreadsheet file and CHARTNAME is the name of the chart. To give you an idea of page layout and page count, Works calculates enough lines to hold the chart. You can see the chart and text on screen by using the Preview command in the Print menu.

If you need to adjust the size of the chart, do it in the Format menu's Indents & Spacing command. Be sure to place the cursor on the chart placeholder before choosing the command so that you get the chart dialog box, not the paragraph dialog box.

You can then change the settings for left and right indents (measured in inches from the current margins), number of lines separating the chart from the text above and below it, chart height, and orientation (vertical portrait or horizontal landscape).

Because of their immutable relationship, a chart always reflects any change in the source spreadsheet. If you change any number or formula, the chart changes accordingly. Because the chart is represented only by a placeholder, the printed chart always shows the latest information.

When you print a document containing a chart, the chart's spreadsheet file must be open. If you want to delete a chart, select the placeholder and then delete it.

Copying from the Word Processor to the Spreadsheet or Database

You'll sometimes want to copy information from the word processor to a spreadsheet or database file, for example, to take advantage of their extensive calculating capabilities.

Say you want to add a table of numbers in a document. After you copy the table, you can perform any arithmetic or function calculation. The columns in the table in the word processor must be separated by tab marks so that each entry can fit into its own cell on the spreadsheet. Be sure that each line ends with an end-of-line mark or a paragraph mark.

Copying Between the Spreadsheet and Database

When you copy between a spreadsheet and database, a spreadsheet column becomes a database field, a spreadsheet row becomes a database record, and vice versa. You can copy database information from the List screen only.

Incoming information replaces anything currently in the cells, so be sure to copy into an unused area and leave enough room for the copied information to fill as many cells to the right and below the cursor position in the copy as it does in the original.

If you select an area in the destination file before you complete the copy, Works fills only that area and ignores any overflow information. Works doesn't copy character formatting.

Form Letters and Mailing Labels

The potent combination of database records and a word processor document produces form letters and mailing labels. This saves you the drudgery of typing the same thing over and over and produces far more accurate results.

Creating a Form Letter

When you create a form letter, you insert placeholders in the document to match the fields in the data base containing information you want to merge. Here's how to do it:

1. Create a database containing information needed in the document or use an existing database. For instance, if you plan to merge names, titles, and addresses in a letter, the database must contain that information.
2. Create a word processor document containing the standard text that remains the same for each form letter.
3. Using the Edit menu's Insert Field command, insert placeholders in the document where you want Works to merge database information. Each placeholder holds the place for entries in one field and includes the field name enclosed in angle brackets. This works best when the database file is open.

You can format, move, copy, or delete placeholders just like any other text.

4. In the database, use the query process to select those files you want to merge.
5. With the database file open, print the document, using the Print menu's Print Form letters command. Works prints one copy for each displayed record, replacing each placeholder with the entry in the field.

To check out page layout and print settings before printing lots of form letters, use the Print menu's Print command to print only one copy. Instead of replacing placeholders with database entries, Works prints the placeholders themselves.

Creating Mailing Labels

Creating mailing labels is also a process of merging database records and a word processor document, this one containing only placeholders.

1. Create a new database or use an existing one containing information needed in the document. For instance, if your label contains names, titles, and addresses, the database must contain that information.
2. With the database file open, create a word processor document and use the Edit menu's Insert Field command to insert placeholders.
3. In the database, use the query process to select those files you want to merge.
4. With the database file open, print labels using the Print menu's Print Labels command. In the dialog box, change print settings as needed. Works then prints one copy for each displayed record, replacing each placeholder with the entry in the field.

To check out the label layout and settings before printing lots of labels, use the Print command's Test button to print only one copy. Works prints the database entries in one line of labels.

The workout in the next chapter gives you hands-on experience with a form letter of sorts (an invitation to a complimentary Chez Chavez dinner) and mailing labels.

Communications

If incoming text is longer than 750 lines, or if you prefer to bypass the buffer, you can receive the text directly into a word processor or other type of file.

You can integrate files received from other computers during a communications session in the same way as files you create yourself. Works can either capture the incoming text in the communications buffer, leaving it up to you to copy it to a Works file, or send the text directly to a Works file.

Suppose an associate sends you a memo. If the memo contains less than 750 lines of text (the buffer ceiling), you can store it in the communications buffer temporarily, copy all or part of it to a word processor file, append your reply, and return it speedily via communications.

When you copy information from the buffer to a document, first select the text, and then copy it into a Works file. Works copies the characters exactly as stored in the buffer. If your computer is still connected to the other computer, pause the incoming flow before selecting and copying. Otherwise, Works will transmit your keystrokes to the other computer.

You can copy text or tables from the buffer to a spreadsheet or database file. When you copy text, Works stores each line inside a single cell in the spreadsheet or database. When you copy a table, Works recognizes the rows and columns in the table and copies the table format into rows and columns in the spreadsheet or database.

Editing and Formatting

You can edit and format an integrated document as you would any conventional document.

Works does its best to blend the diverse pieces and parts in an integrated document perfectly. Sometimes, it's not 100 percent successful. When that occurs, you must step in and do whatever is necessary to get everything looking just right.

A common integration problem arises when the print width of a document is too narrow for an imported spreadsheet or database report. Any column that can't fit within the print width blithely wraps around to the left margin of the document. It looks like a mess.

Different problems require different solutions. In this case, the first thing you can do is delete any tab marks (small right arrows) cluttering up the imported text. Then set tab stops that make the columns narrower, format the spreadsheet or report to print in a smaller font than the rest of the text, reduce the width of the margins, or do all three.

You'll find out more about Work integration in the workout in the next chapter, as well as in Part Seven, "Putting Works to Work."

Integration Workout: Personalized Dinner Invitations and Mailing Labels

Here's how to get extra mileage out of files you created earlier.

Printing personalized dinner invitations to regular patrons of Chez Chavez is a matter of merging two files you've already created—MAILING.WDB, which contains the customer names and addresses from the database workout, and INVITE.WPS, the dinner invitation from the word processor workout. If you haven't created both files yet, now is a good time to do it.

The key to these merge activities are placeholders that hold the place in the invitation for entries in the database records. The macro you create in this chapter speeds the task of entering placeholders in the invitation.

In this session, you open existing files, record a macro, view the macro on screen, insert placeholders, hide and restore records, and save the file. When you finish, the first invitation that rolls off your printer should look like the one in Figure 20-1, sans artwork.

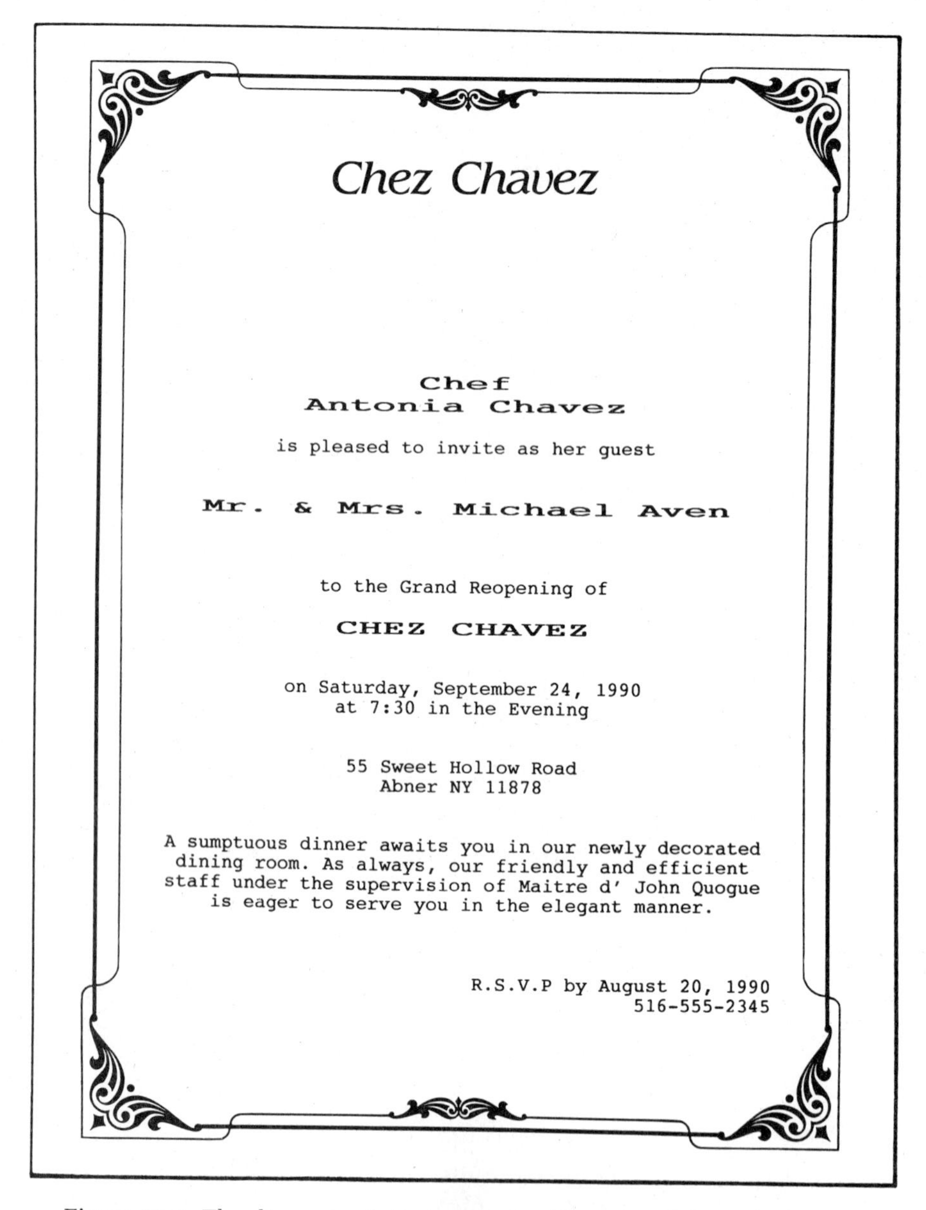

Chez Chavez

Chef
Antonia Chavez

is pleased to invite as her guest

Mr. & Mrs. Michael Aven

to the Grand Reopening of

CHEZ CHAVEZ

on Saturday, September 24, 1990
at 7:30 in the Evening

55 Sweet Hollow Road
Abner NY 11878

A sumptuous dinner awaits you in our newly decorated dining room. As always, our friendly and efficient staff under the supervision of Maitre d' John Quogue is eager to serve you in the elegant manner.

R.S.V.P by August 20, 1990
516-555-2345

Figure 20-1. The dinner invitation merged with a record from the customer database

You then copy the placeholders from the invitation to a new word processor file, reformat them, choose a font, test the settings, save the file, and then use Works integration to produce mailing labels for the invitations. Sure sounds like fun.

Keystrokes and Other Matters

The instructions guide you each step of the way, giving keystrokes and cursor movements relating to each task. As you did when you created the database and invitation, be sure to observe the distinction between pressing and holding down a key.

- With instructions such as *Press Alt and type FO (File/Open Existing File)*, press and release Alt before you type the letters.
- With *Hold down Alt and type Q (to assign the playback key)*, press the Alt key, and, without releasing Alt, type the letter.

Unless the instructions say otherwise, use the Arrow keys (Left, Right, Up, and Down) to move the cursor. If you run into a snag, press the Escape key to cancel what you're doing. Then pick up where you left off.

Printing Personalized Invitations

Before you can merge the files, MAILING.WDB and INVITE.WPS must both be open, with INVITE.WPS on the screen. Assuming you're starting anew, load Works. At the File menu, type **O** (Open Existing File) to bring up the Files dialog box.

Opening the Database File

First open MAILING.WDB.

- Press Tab (to move the blinker to the `Files` list).
- Type **M** to jump the blinker to the first filename starting with the letter M.
- If this is `MAILING.WDB`, press Enter. If the blinker is on a different filename, type **M** as many times as needed to reach `MAILING.WDB`, and press Enter.

Depending on the speed of your computer, you may see percentages at the left of the status line as Works loads the file.

The records should appear in the List screen. If they appear in the Form screen instead, press F9 to get to the List screen. Press Ctrl+Home if needed to display them all on screen.

Opening the Invitation File

Now open the INVITE.WPS file.

- Press Alt and type **FO** (File/Open Existing File). Here's the dialog box again.
- Press Tab (to move to the `Files` list).
- Type **I** as many times as needed to jump the blinker to `INVITE.WPS` and press Enter.

You now have INVITE on screen and MAILING waiting in the wings (actually, in the Window menu).

Entering the Placeholders

Figure 20-2 shows the dinner invitation with three placeholders— `<<MR/MS>>`, `<<FIRST MI>>`, and `<<LAST NAME>>`— instead of your name. These are three of the fields you created in the customer database. When you print, Works will replace these placeholders with entries in those fields.

The first task is to erase your name to make room for the placeholders. The cursor is under the `C` in `Chef`.

- Press Down Arrow six times and then press Home to place the cursor on the first character in your name. Press Delete enough times to delete your name *but not* the paragraph mark after it. The cursor should now be at the paragraph mark.

Creating a Macro To Enter Placeholders

You'll find this macro just as handy when you later insert placeholders in your own documents.

```
<begdef><ctrlq><menu>EF<xdown><tab><enddef>
```

This line contains three placeholders. Instead of inserting each one on your own, you can teach Works by doing it once, and then have a macro do it the rest of the times. This macro moves from the document screen to the Edit menu's Insert Field dialog box, where placeholders are kept. It stops at that point so you can select the placeholder you want to insert.

Chef
Antonia Chavez

is pleased to invite as her guest

«MR/MS» «FIRST MI» «LAST NAME»

to the Grand Reopening of

CHEZ CHAVEZ

on Saturday, September 24, 1990
at 7:30 in the Evening

55 Sweet Hollow Road
Abner NY 11878

A sumptuous dinner awaits you in our newly decorated dining room. As always, our friendly and efficient staff under the supervision of Maitre d' John Quogue is eager to serve you in the elegant manner.

R.S.V.P by August 20, 1990
516-555-2345

Figure 20-2. The dinner invitation with placeholders for courtesy title and name

Recording the Macro

Have Works record your keystrokes as you insert the first placeholder. Leave the cursor on the paragraph mark.

- Hold down Alt and type a slash (to activate the first macro menu).
- Press Enter (to confirm Record Macro). Works brings up the Playback dialog box asking for a playback key and macro description. Make Ctrl+Q the playback key for this macro.
- Hold down Ctrl and type **Q**.

- Press Tab (to jump to Title).
- Type **ENTER PLACEHOLDERS (DB TO WP)** and press Enter.

Works returns you to the invitation, and the word RECORD appears on the status line.

As you type, Works enters your keystrokes in MACROS.INI, the file that stores the macros.

Go slowly, following each of the next three steps carefully. If you make a typing error, correct it but don't be concerned about it. The macro will contain the error and the correction, which you can later edit out if you like.

1. Press Alt and type **EF** (Edit/Insert Field). You are now in the Insert Field dialog box with the blinker in the Databases list.
2. Press Down Arrow (to choose the MAILING.WDB filename). Works now pops the field names in the MAILING.WDB database into the Fields box.
3. Press Tab (to move to the Fields list).

This is all you want the macro to do, so tell Works to stop recording.

- Hold down Alt and type a slash (to activate the second macro menu). The blinker is at End Recording, which is in reverse video.
- Press Enter (to confirm End Recording). Press Escape to return to the invitation. RECORD now disappears from the status line and the macro is ready to run. The cursor is still on the paragraph mark.

Using the Macro

Now use the macro to move from the invitation to the Insert Field dialog box so that you can get the MR/MS placeholder. Things will happen quickly.

- Hold down Ctrl and type **Q**. Instantly, the blinker is in the Fields list. Typing the first letter of a field name is the fast way to choose it.
- Type **M** (to choose the MR/MS field) and press Enter.

Works now inserts <<MR/MS>> in the invitation, showing it in high intensity white, color, or bold, depending on your screen mode. Press the Spacebar to separate this field from the next. Now get the FIRST MI placeholder.

- Hold down Ctrl and type **Q**.
- Type **F** (to choose the FIRST MI field) and press Enter. Works inserts <<FIRST MI>> in the invitation. Press the Spacebar once. Now insert the LAST NAME placeholder in the same way.
- Hold down Ctrl and type **Q**.
- Type **L** (to choose the LAST NAME field) and press Enter. Works inserts <<LAST NAME>> in the invitation.

These placeholders are holding the place for 24-point characters, so Works wraps NAME around to the center of the line below. Except for this wraparound, your screen should look like the one in Figure 20-2.

Saving the Invitation

Now save the invitation with the placeholders in place. Leave the cursor where it is.

- Press Alt and type **FS** (File/Save).

Your placeholders are now stored safely on disk.

Viewing the Macro

Let's see what the macro looks like in your MACROS.INI file. Leave the cursor where it is.

- Press Alt and type **FO** (File/Open Existing File).
- Press Tab (to move to the Files list).
- Type **M** as many times as necessary to reach MACROS.INI, and press Enter.
- Works lets you know you can't use macros while this file is open. Press Enter to acknowledge.

Move the cursor until you have the macro title ENTER PLACEHOLDERS (DB TO WP) and the macro on screen. Your title and macro should look just like the one in Figure 20-3. Table 20-1 describes each element in the macro.

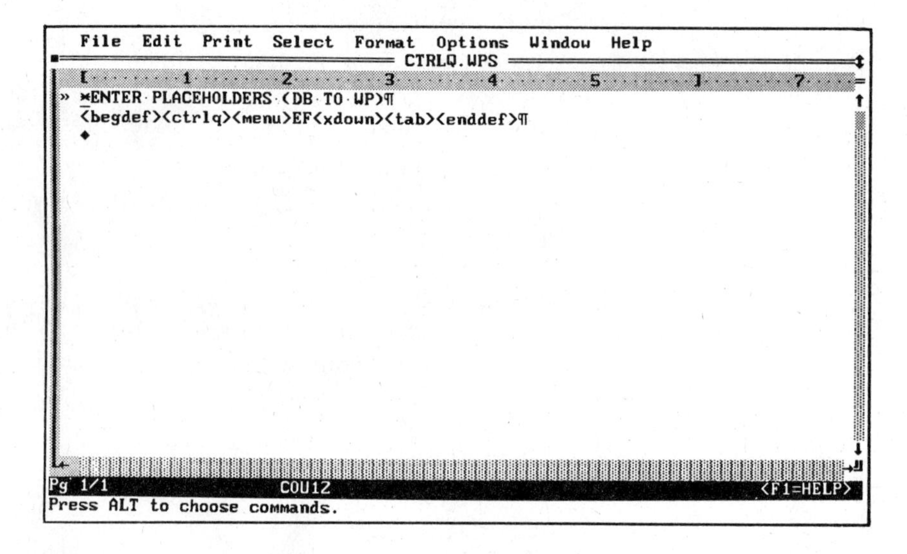

Figure 20-3. The macro that brings a placeholder from database to document

Table 20-1. Elements in the placeholder macro and what they mean

Element	Meaning
<begdef>	Beginning of the macro definition (Works generated)
<ctrlq>	Macro storage/playback key
<menu>	Alt key that activates the menu line
EF	Edit menu's Field Insert command (it doesn't matter if letters are in uppercase or lowercase)
<xdown>	Down Arrow key that chooses the database filename
<tab>	Tab key that jumps the blinker into the Fields list
<enddef>	End of the macro definition (Works generated)

Now close the MACROS.INI file.

- Press Alt and type **FC** (File/Close).

Printing the Invitations

The next step is to print the invitations. It doesn't make sense to print all 15 records right off the bat. Instead, make a test run with three records to make sure everything goes according to plan. First, display the database.

- Press Alt and type **W** (Window).
- Type the number corresponding to MAILING.WDB. And here's that familiar database.

Hiding the Records

Works prints visible records only, so a good approach is to hide all records except the first three. Place the cursor on `Mr. & Ms.` in the MR/MS column in record 4 (`Mr. & Ms. Walter Ortiz`).

- Press F8 (to extend the selection).
- Hold down Ctrl and press End (to select all records below record 4).
- Press Alt and type **SH** (Select/Hide Record).

It doesn't matter that you leave records selected while you work on other things.

Works makes all of the selected records disappear. You can tell that records are hidden by the absence of record numbers 4 to 15 along the left side of the screen.

Printing the Personalized Invitations

Now return to the invitation.

- Press Alt and type **W** (Window).
- Type the number corresponding to INVITE.WPS.

Now print an invitation for each of the three remaining records. The current print settings are fine, so there's no need to do anything except turn on your printer.

- Press Alt and type **PF** (Print/Print Form Letters). Works brings up the `Databases` dialog box showing MAILING.WDB in reverse video.
- Press Enter (to confirm the database). Works now brings up the print dialog box. All settings are fine.
- Press Enter to confirm one copy of each displayed record.

As the printer prints, Works shows the current record number on the status line. Except for the restaurant logo and frame, your first printed invitation should look like the one in Figure 20-1 for Mr. and Mrs. Michael Aven. The others should be for `Professor Burt E. Byrd` and `Ms. Jennifer Chan`.

Restoring the Hidden Records

Display the database again so you can restore the hidden records.

- Press Alt and type **W** (Window).
- Type the number corresponding to `MAILING.WDB`. The cursor should be in the MR/MS column in record 16.
- Press Alt and type **SL** (Select/Show All Records). Works instantly brings all hidden records into view. Press Up Arrow to collapse the selection.

Now return to the invitation.

- Press Alt and type **W** (Window).
- Type the number corresponding to INVITE.WPS.

If you want to practice your new-found skills, you can print all 15 records in the same way. Strictly optional.

Printing Mailing Labels for the Invitations

The process of printing mailing labels for the invitations is similar in many ways to printing the personalized invitations. All you need is a new document containing a few more placeholders for the address.

Figure 20-4 shows the mailing labels, and Figure 20-5 shows the placeholders that produce them. It's not necessary to put label paper in your printer. You can get a good idea of how things work with regular printer paper.

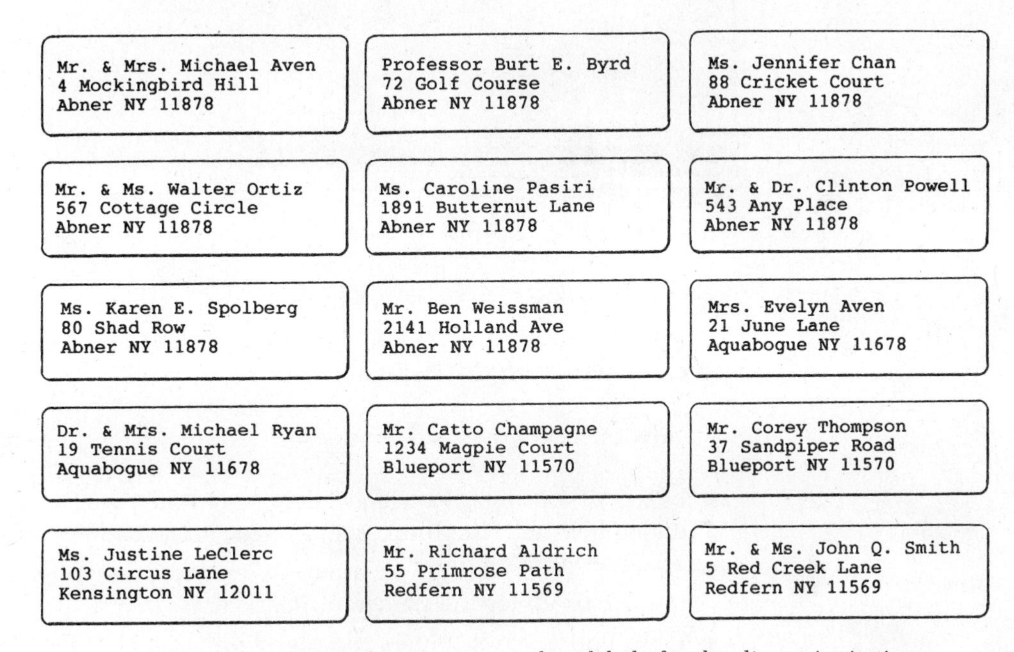

Mr. & Mrs. Michael Aven
4 Mockingbird Hill
Abner NY 11878

Professor Burt E. Byrd
72 Golf Course
Abner NY 11878

Ms. Jennifer Chan
88 Cricket Court
Abner NY 11878

Mr. & Ms. Walter Ortiz
567 Cottage Circle
Abner NY 11878

Ms. Caroline Pasiri
1891 Butternut Lane
Abner NY 11878

Mr. & Dr. Clinton Powell
543 Any Place
Abner NY 11878

Ms. Karen E. Spolberg
80 Shad Row
Abner NY 11878

Mr. Ben Weissman
2141 Holland Ave
Abner NY 11878

Mrs. Evelyn Aven
21 June Lane
Aquabogue NY 11678

Dr. & Mrs. Michael Ryan
19 Tennis Court
Aquabogue NY 11678

Mr. Catto Champagne
1234 Magpie Court
Blueport NY 11570

Mr. Corey Thompson
37 Sandpiper Road
Blueport NY 11570

Ms. Justine LeClerc
103 Circus Lane
Kensington NY 12011

Mr. Richard Aldrich
55 Primrose Path
Redfern NY 11569

Mr. & Ms. John Q. Smith
5 Red Creek Lane
Redfern NY 11569

Figure 20-4. Three-across mailing labels for the dinner invitations

Copying the Placeholders to a New Document

Copying the placeholders from the invitation to a new document can give you ahead start. INVITE.WPS is on your screen. Place the cursor on any character in the placeholders.

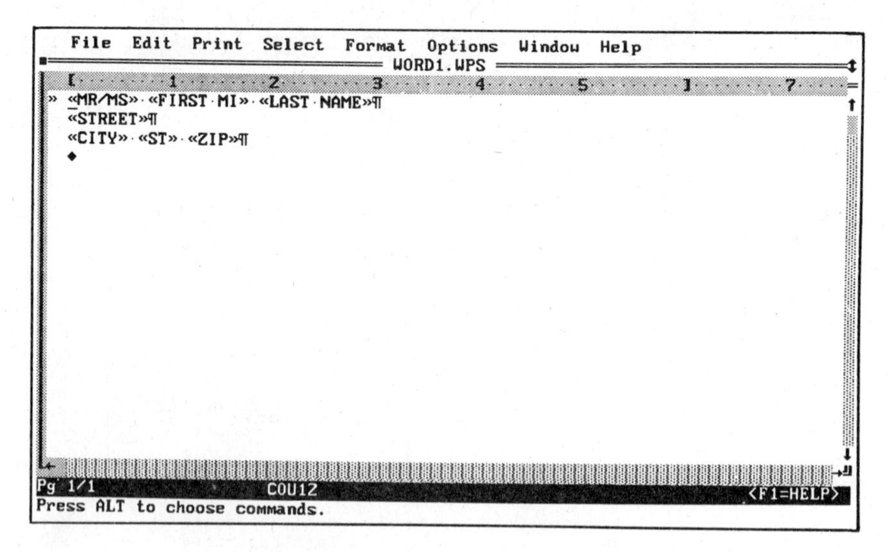

Figure 20-5. The placeholders that generate the mailing labels

- Press F8 three times (to select the placeholders).
- Hold down Shift and press F3 (to enter the Copy mode). You can see `COPY` on the status line.

  Now open a new word processor file to hold the placeholders.

- Press Alt and type **FN** (File/Create New File). You now see the dialog box with the blinker at `New Word Processor`.
- Type **W**. Works brings up a new Word Processor screen with the cursor under the paragraph mark.
- Press Enter. Works enters the placeholders and their format: Bold style, centered alignment, and large, 24-point font.

Reformatting the Placeholders

Left-align the placeholders and eliminate the bold. Your cursor is on the first character in the placeholders.

- Hold down Ctrl and type **X** (to shift the placeholders to the left).
- Press F8 three times (to select the placeholders).

- Hold down Ctrl and press Spacebar (to return the placeholders to plain text).

Leave the font size as is for now.

Using the Macro To Enter More Placeholders

Now use the placeholder macro to enter the other placeholders. Press Down Arrow, which collapses the selection and moves the cursor to the paragraph mark on the next line.

- Hold down Ctrl and type **Q**. The blinker moves quickly to the `Fields` list.
- Type **S** (to choose the `STREET` field) and press Enter. Works inserts **<<STREET>>** in the line below the name placeholders. Press Enter to move one line down.
- Hold down Ctrl and type **Q** again.
- Type **C** (to choose the `CITY` field) and press Enter. Works inserts **<<CITY>>** in the line below the street placeholder. Press the Spacebar to insert a space.
- Hold down Ctrl and type **Q** again.
- Type **S** twice (to choose the `ST` field) and press Enter. Works inserts **<<ST>>** after **<<CITY>>**. Press the Spacebar.
- Hold down Ctrl and type **Q** again.
- Type **Z** (to choose the `ZIP` field) and press Enter. Works inserts **<<ZIP>>** after **<<ST>>**.

Your placeholders are all in place and should look like the ones in Figure 20-5.

Choosing the Font

Now format the placeholders to print the labels in Courier 12-point to match the font in the invitation. (If this font isn't available on your printer, choose the same font you used for the invitation.) Even if your status line shows `COU12`, do this step anyway to make sure the name placeholders are in the proper font size. Leave the cursor where it is.

- Press F8 four times (to select all placeholders).
- Press Alt and type **TF** (Format/Font & Style). You've selected multiple elements, so Works shows neutral settings in the dialog box.
- Hold down Alt and type **F** (to move into the `Fonts` list).
- Type **C** (to choose `Courier`).
- Press Tab (to move into the `Sizes` list).
- Type **1** enough times to move the blinker to `12` (to choose 12-point) and press Enter. Press Up Arrow to collapse the selection.

Saving the Label File

This is a good time to save the file and name it LABELS. Leave the cursor where it is.

- Press Alt and type **FA** (File/Save As).

Works brings up the dialog box so you can type a filename, and, if needed, a drive or directory. If you're saving to the current drive, simply type the filename. Otherwise, type the drive or directory before the filename—for example, **A:LABELS**.

Defining the Label Layout

Settings in the Print menu's Page Labels and Page Setup & Margins commands control the label layout. First set the spacing in the Print Labels dialog box.

A `Horizontal` setting of 3.58 inches with these margins works well for two-across labels.

You want to fit three labels across 8.5-inch wide paper, less left and right margins of .5 and .25 inches, respectively. This leaves a page width of 7.75 inches, which works out to about 2.58 horizontal inches per label.

- Press Alt and type **PL** (Print/Print Labels). The dialog box appears with `MAILING.WDB` already selected. With standard labels one inch in height (actually 15/16 inches with 1/16 inch between labels), the `Vertical` setting of one inch is fine.
- Hold down Alt and type **H** (to move to `Horizontal`).

- Type **2.58** (the number of inches between labels).
- Press Tab (to move to across page).
- Type **3** (the number of labels across).

Before printing every label, it's a good idea to try a test run with only one row. You can do this by choosing the Test box at the bottom of the dialog box.

- Hold down Alt and type **T** (to choose Test).

These settings work fine on my printer, but printers behave differently. Yours may require smaller or larger margins to position the text properly on the label. Experiment.

Works accepts your settings and now brings up the dialog box in the Page Setup & Margins command. You want to change a few settings here, too. The blinker is in the Top margin field.

- Press Tab twice (to move to Left margin).
- Type **.5** and press Tab (to move to Right margin).
- Type **.25** and press Tab (to move to Header margin).
- Type **0** and press Tab (to move to Footer margin).
- Type **0** and press Enter.

You're now greeted by yet another dialog box, this one with the number of copies. All settings are fine. Be sure the printer is turned on.

- Press Enter to confirm one copy, and start the printing.

After a few seconds, the first three labels roll off the printer. Works now asks if you want to print all labels or reprint the test labels.

- You want to print all labels this time, so press Enter.

Works starts again and prints a label for each record in the database. Your result should match the one in Figure 20-4.

Now save the completed mailing label format. Leave the cursor where it is.

- Press Alt and type **FS** (File/Save).

About Mailing Labels

Labels come in a wide variety of shapes and sizes. The most common are pressure sensitive and mounted on form feed paper one, two, or three labels across. You can print three across on most standard carriage printers (80-column).

The mailing labels you're most likely to use on letter envelopes come in two standard heights: 1-inch and 1-inches (actually 15/16-inch and $1\frac{7}{16}$-inch, respectively, with 1/16-inch between labels). At 6 lines to the inch, you can print 6 lines of text on 1-inch labels and 9 lines of text on $1\frac{1}{2}$-inch labels. For really nice looking labels, try to print only 4 lines on 1-inch labels and 6 lines on $1\frac{1}{2}$-inch labels, leaving one empty line at the top and bottom of each label.

Getting the proper left margin is a matter of testing various settings to see how the printing lays out on the label. Experiment on regular formfeed paper to find the most attractive result before using the more expensive label paper.

When you work with labels, avoid rolling the printer platen back and forth. Those labels do have a way of peeling off and sticking to hard-to-reach places below the platen.

Okay. You now know a lot about Works applications, but there's still a lot more to know. In the next section, you'll find hands-on chapters loaded with tips, tricks, and techniques— all designed to expand your skills with the spreadsheet, database, and word processor.

P A R T

seven

Putting Works to Work

T W E N T Y - O N E

Quarterly Income Statement

The income statement is also known as a profit-and-loss statement.

An income statement summarizes the activities of a business during a specific period of time. It lists sales (what came in), cost of goods sold and operating expenses (what went out), operating income (how much was left), and net income (how much remained after payment of taxes and interest). Income statements can reflect business activities for any period—annually, quarterly, monthly, and even weekly.

Figure 21-1 shows a quarterly income statement. You make the entries in the first three quarters—but not all by yourself. You have an interactive macro to help. Your macro sidekick moves the cursor to cells needing a number, waits for your input from the keyboard, and then moves to the next cell and waits for the next number. It does this over and over until you enter all relevant numbers for that quarter.

	A	B	C	D	E	F
1		QUARTERLY	INCOME STATEMENT			QINCOME
2	=========================	==========	==========	==========	==========	==========
3		1st Qtr	2nd Qtr	3rd Qtr	4th Qtr	YTD
4		--------	--------	--------	--------	--------
5	Sales	167,500	210,000	287,250		664,750
6	Cost of Goods Sold	58,625	73,500	79,625		211,750
7		--------	--------	--------	--------	--------
8	Gross Profit	108,875	136,500	207,625	0	453,000
9						
10	Operating Expenses:					
11	Selling Expense	16,450	19,395	26,800		62,645
12	General & Admin	15,725	16,000	17,750		49,475
13	Depreciation	5,835	5,835	5,945		17,615
14	Interest Expense	3,280	3,390	3,545		10,215
15		--------	--------	--------	--------	--------
16	Total Op Expenses	41,290	44,620	54,040	0	139,950
17						
18	Profit Before Taxes	67,585	91,880	153,585	0	313,050
19	Taxes	5,945	7,360	16,170		29,475
20						
21	Net Profit	61,640	84,520	137,415	0	283,575

Figure 21-1. The completed quarterly income statement spreadsheet

In this chapter, you change column widths, enter lines, enter and format titles and numbers, create and copy formulas, record and run a macro with a variable input pause, view the macro in the MACROS.INI file, learn how to edit a macro, define the page layout, and preview and print the spreadsheet. Lots of good stuff.

Keystrokes and Other Matters

The instructions guide you each step of the way, giving keystrokes and cursor movements relating to each task. Please observe the distinction between pressing and holding down a key.

- With instructions such as *Press Alt and type TW (Format/Width)*, press and release Alt before you type the letters.
- With *Hold down Alt and type C (to move to Center)*, press the Alt key and, without releasing Alt, type the letter.

If you hit a snag, press Escape to cancel what you're doing. Then pick up where you left off.

Unless the instructions say otherwise, use the Arrow keys (Left, Right, Up, and Down) to move the cursor. Keep an eye on the cell indicator in the left side of the status line to be sure the cursor is on the correct cell before you take the next action.

Creating a New Spreadsheet

Load Works as described in the Introduction to this book. At the File menu, type **NS** (Create New File/Spreadsheet), bringing up the spreadsheet screen. Now let's make your spreadsheet look like the one in Figure 21-2.

Adjusting the Column Widths

Making the columns wider gives the titles room to stretch.

To give the titles the room they need, make column A wider. Your cursor is on A1.

- Press Alt and type **TW** (Format/Width). Works displays the `Width` showing the current width of column A—10 characters.
- Type **20** (the new width) and press Enter.

Columns B through 4 can stay at the standard 10 characters.

	A	B	C	D	E	F
1		QUARTERLY	INCOME	STATEMENT		QINCOME
2	====================	==========	==========	==========	==========	==========
3		1st Qtr	2nd Qtr	3rd Qtr	4th Qtr	YTD
4		--------	--------	--------	--------	--------
5	Sales	167500	210000			
6	Cost of Goods Sold	58625	73500			
7		--------	--------	--------	--------	--------
8	Gross Profit					
9						
10	Operating Expenses:					
11	Selling Expense	16450	19395			
12	General & Admin	15725	16000			
13	Depreciation	5835	5835			
14	Interest Expense	3280	3390			
15		--------	--------	--------	--------	--------
16	Total Op Expenses					
17						
18	Profit Before Taxes					
19	Taxes	5945	7360			
20						
21	Net Profit					

Figure 21-2. Titles, lines, and numbers in the quarterly income statement spreadsheet

Entering the Lines

Use an equal sign to enter a double line in A2. Typing quotation marks before the equal sign tells Works the sign is text, not a value. Place the cursor on A2.

- Type quotation marks and 20 equal signs (the width of the cell). Move the cursor to B2, and Works enters the line in its cell.

Now enter a line in B2, which is 10 characters wide. The cursor is on B2.

- Type quotation marks and 10 equal signs. Move the cursor to B4.

Let's now use a minus sign to enter the short line in B4. This line starts one character from the left of the cell and stops one character from the right. This prevents it from overhanging the numbers. The cursor is on B4.

- Type quotation marks and press the Spacebar.
- Type 8 minus signs and press Enter.

When you have many lines on a spreadsheet, the Copy commands lets you enter them with the least effort. Start by copying the line from B4 to B7. Leave the cursor on B4.

- Hold down Shift and press F3 (to enter the Copy mode). You now see COPY on the status line.
- Move the cursor to B7 and press Enter.

Works lets you repeat the last Copy command, as long as you do it immediately. Move the cursor to B15.

- Hold down Shift and press F7.

Now that you have all the lines needed in column B (B2, B4, B7, and B15), you can use Copy Right to enter them in columns C, D, E, and F. Leave the cursor on B15.

- Press F8 (to extend the selection).
- Press Page Up, and then Right Arrow four times (to select B1 through F15).
- Press Alt and type **ER** (Edit/Fill Right).

Entering the Titles and Numbers

Next, enter the titles and numbers shown in Figure 21-2. You don't have to press Enter after typing a title. Simply move the cursor to the next cell that needs a title, and Works enters the title you just typed in its cell. If you make a typo, press Backspace (not an Arrow key) to back up the cursor and erase. Place the cursor on B1, which also collapses the selection.

As you type, this long title appears on the entry/edit line and also at the cursor's location, gliding by in its cell.

- Type **QUARTERLY INCOME STATEMENT** and move the cursor to F1. When you do, Works enters the title in B1, allowing it to spill into C1 and D1.

Enter a filename directly on the spreadsheet and you don't have to rely on memory to find it in the Open Files list.

This spreadsheet doesn't have a header, so it's a good idea to enter a filename to identify it.

- Type **QINCOME** and move the cursor to F3.
- Type **YTD** and move the cursor to E3.
- Type **4th Qtr** and move the cursor to D3.

- Type **3rd Qtr** and move the cursor to C3.
- Type **2nd Qtr** and move the cursor to B3.
- Type **1st Qtr** and move the cursor to A5.

Using Figure 21-2 as a guide, enter the rest of the text and numbers in this sequence:

- Titles in column A from rows 5 through 21. Indent these titles in a stair-step fashion: Press the Spacebar twice before `Gross Profit` (A8), `Total Op Expenses` (A16), and `Net Profit` (A21), all of which show totals. Press the Spacebar once before titles that fall under a general title—for example, `Selling Expense` (A11) under `Operating Expenses:` (A10).
- Move the cursor to B5 and enter the numbers in column B.
- Move the cursor to C5 and enter the numbers in column C. After `7360` in C19, press Enter.

Aligning the Titles

The next step is to align the titles, starting with the spreadsheet filename. Place the cursor on F1.

- Press Alt and type **TS** (Format/Style). Here's the `Style` dialog box.
- Type **R** (to move to `Right`) and press Enter.

Now center all titles in row 3. Place the cursor on F3.

- Hold down Ctrl and press F8 (to select row 3).

When you select more than one cell to work on, Works neutralizes the dialog box—that is, proposes nothing. Option boxes are empty and check boxes contain a dash.

- Press Alt and type **TS** (Format/Style). You've selected more than one cell, so Works shows the `Style` dialog box with empty option boxes in the alignment group and check boxes containing a dash in the style group.
- Type **C** (to move to `Center`) and press Enter.

Formatting the Numbers

Now have Works embed commas in the numbers that are large enough, which makes them easier to read. It doesn't matter if you include text in this step.

- Press Ctrl+Shift+F8 (to select the entire spreadsheet).
- Press Alt and type **TC** (Format/Comma). Works proposes 2 decimal places, but there's no need for any decimal places.
- Type **0** and press Enter. Press Down Arrow to collapse the selection.

Saving the Spreadsheet

Now save the spreadsheet and give it the filename QINCOME.

- Press Alt and type **FA** (File/Save As).

Works brings up the Save as dialog box so you can type a filename, and, if needed, a drive or directory. If you're saving to the current drive, simply type the filename. Otherwise, type the drive or directory before the filename (for example, **A:QINCOME**).

- Type **QINCOME** and press Enter. Works appends the extension .WKS (for Worksheet) and saves the file.

As the file is being saved, the cell indicator on the status line shows the percentage already processed. When the cell location reappears, Works is ready for your next action.

Entering the Formulas

Works makes it possible to enter the same formula in contiguous cells at the same time. There's no need to enter a formula in one cell, and then copy it to the others.

Formulas are mathematical equations that use numbers on the spreadsheet and other elements to produce new numbers. Figure 21-3 shows the locations of the formulas on the income statement. You'll be entering formulas in the unshaded cells containing zero, and you'll copy them to the shaded cells at the same time.

First read the explanation of how the formula works, and then follow the step-by-step instructions. Keep an eye on the status line to make sure the cursor is on the correct cell before taking your next action. If you run into a snag, press Escape and start again.

	A	B	C	D	E	F
1		QUARTERLY	INCOME	STATEMENT		QINCOME
2	========	========	========	========	========	========
3		1st Qtr	2nd Qtr	3rd Qtr	4th Qtr	YTD
4		--------	--------	--------	--------	--------
5	Sales					0 (5)
6	Cost of Goods Sold					0
7		--------	--------	--------	--------	--------
8	Gross Profit	0 (1)	0	0	0	0
9						
10	Operating Expenses:					
11	Selling Expense					0
12	General & Admin					0
13	Depreciation					0
14	Interest Expense					0
15		--------	--------	--------	--------	--------
16	Total Op Expenses	0 (2)	0	0	0	0
17						
18	Profit Before Taxes	0 (3)	0	0	0	0
19	Taxes					0
20						
21	Net Profit	0 (4)	0	0	0	0

Figure 21-3. Formula locations in the quarterly income statement spreadsheet

Formula 1: Gross Profit =B5-B6

Formula 1 subtracts cost of goods sold (B6) from sales (B5) to produce the gross profit in B8. Both cell references are relative, so you can enter Formula 1 in B8, C8, D8, and E8 simultaneously. Place the cursor on B8.

- Press F8 (to extend the selection). You can see EXT on the status line.
- Press End (to select B8 through F8).
- Type an equal sign and move the cursor to B5.
- Type a minus sign (the cursor jumps back to B8) and move the cursor to B6. You should now see =B5-B6 on the entry/edit line and in B8.
- Hold down Ctrl and press Enter. Works enters the formula in all five cells.

Except for F8, which contains a zero on your screen, your results should match the spreadsheet in Figure 21-4. As you enter each of the other formulas, compare your results with the figure.

	A	B	C	D	E	F
1		QUARTERLY	INCOME STATEMENT			QINCOME
2	========================	==========	==========	==========	==========	==========
3		1st Qtr	2nd Qtr	3rd Qtr	4th Qtr	YTD
4		--------	--------	--------	--------	--------
5	Sales	167,500	210,000			377,500
6	Cost of Goods Sold	58,625	73,500			132,125
7		--------	--------	--------	--------	--------
8	Gross Profit	108,875	136,500	0	0	245,375
9						
10	Operating Expenses:					
11	Selling Expense	16,450	19,395			35,845
12	General & Admin	15,725	16,000			31,725
13	Depreciation	5,835	5,835			11,670
14	Interest Expense	3,280	3,390			6,670
15		--------	--------	--------	--------	--------
16	Total Op Expenses	41,290	44,620	0	0	85,910
17						
18	Profit Before Taxes	67,585	91,880	0	0	159,465
19	Taxes	5,945	7,360			13,305
20						
21	Net Profit	61,640	84,520	0	0	146,160

Figure 21-4. Formula results on the quarterly income statement spreadsheet

Formula 2: Total Operating Expenses =SUM(B10:B15)

Formula 2 adds operating expenses (B11 through B14) to produce the total in B16. The formula includes blank cell B10 and the line in B15. In this way, you can later insert rows anywhere between rows 10 and 15, and Works will adjust the formula to include the new expenses. Again, both cell references are relative, so you can enter the same formula in the other cells in the row simultaneously. Place the cursor on B16.

- Press F8 (to extend the selection).
- Press End (to select B16 through F16).
- Type =**SUM(** and move the cursor to the line in B15.
- Press F8 (to extend the selection) and move the cursor to empty cell B10. You now see `=SUM(B10:B15` on the status line and some of the formula in B16.
- Type a close parenthesis. The cursor jumps back to B16.
- Hold down Ctrl and press Enter.

Formula 3: Profit Before Taxes =B8-B16

Formula 3 subtracts total operating expenses (B16) from gross profit (B8) to produce the profit before taxes in B18. Both cell references are relative, so you can again enter the formula in the other cells at the same time. Place the cursor on B18.

- Press F8 (to extend the selection).
- Press End (to select B18 through F18).
- Type an equal sign and move the cursor to B8.
- Type a minus sign (the cursor jumps back to B18) and move the cursor to B16. You should now see =B8-B16 on the entry/edit line and in B18.
- Hold down Ctrl and press Enter.

Formula 4: Net Profit =B18-B19

Formula 4 subtracts taxes (B19) from profit before taxes (B18) to produce the net profit in B21. Both cell references are relative. Place the cursor on B21.

- Press F8 (to extend the selection).
- Press End (to select B21 through F21).
- Type an equal sign and move the cursor to B18.
- Type a minus sign (the cursor jumps back to B21) and move the cursor to B19. You should now see =B18-B19 on the entry/edit line and in B21.
- Hold down Ctrl and press Enter.

Formula 5: Year-To-Date Sales =SUM(B5:E5)

Formula 5 adds sales in each quarter (B5 through E5) to produce the year-to-date sales in F5. Because both cell references are relative, it can perform the same calculation for the cost-of-goods-sold entries. Place the cursor on F5.

- Press F8 (to extend the selection).
- Press Down Arrow (to select F5 and F6).
- Type =**SUM(** and move the cursor to E5.
- Press F8 (to extend the selection).
- Move the cursor to B5. You now see `B5:E5` on the status line.
- Type a close parenthesis (the cursor jumps back to F5).
- Hold down Ctrl and press Enter. The Gross Profit formula in F8 now has something to work with, so it produces the result shown in Figure 21-4. Press Down Arrow to collapse the selection.

Copying Formula 5

Other cells in column F need Formula 5. Instead of creating it again from scratch, copy from F5. Leave the cursor on F6.

- Hold down Shift and press F3 (to access the Copy mode again).
- Move the cursor to F11 and press Enter. You now have a calculation there, too.
- Press F8 (to extend the selection).
- Move the cursor to F14 (to select F11 to F14).
- Press Alt and type **EF** (Edit/Fill Down).
- Press Down Arrow (to collapse the selection).
- Hold down Shift and press F3 (to access the Copy mode once more).
- Move the cursor to F19 and press Enter.

This completes the formulas. Your screen should now entirely agree with the spreadsheet in Figure 21-4. Press Alt and type **FS** (File/Save) to store the spreadsheet on disk.

Creating a Moving Macro That Pauses for Variable Input

```
<begdef><ctrla><menu>SG<vfld><enter>
<vfld><xdown><vfld><xdown><xdown><xdown><xdown><xdown><vfld>
<xdown><vfld><xdown><vfld><xdown><vfld><xdown><xdown><xdown>
<xdown><xdown><vfld><xup><xup><xup><xup><xup><xup><xup><xup>
<xup><xup><xup><xup><xup><xup><enddef>
```

Pretend this spreadsheet is loaded with numbers that you update often. The macro you're about to create makes entering these numbers easy, because it stops only at cells that need a new number and scoots past the others. The macro consists mainly of variable input fields (vfld) and cursor movements (xdown and xup). You can see it in a screen shot in Figure 21-5.

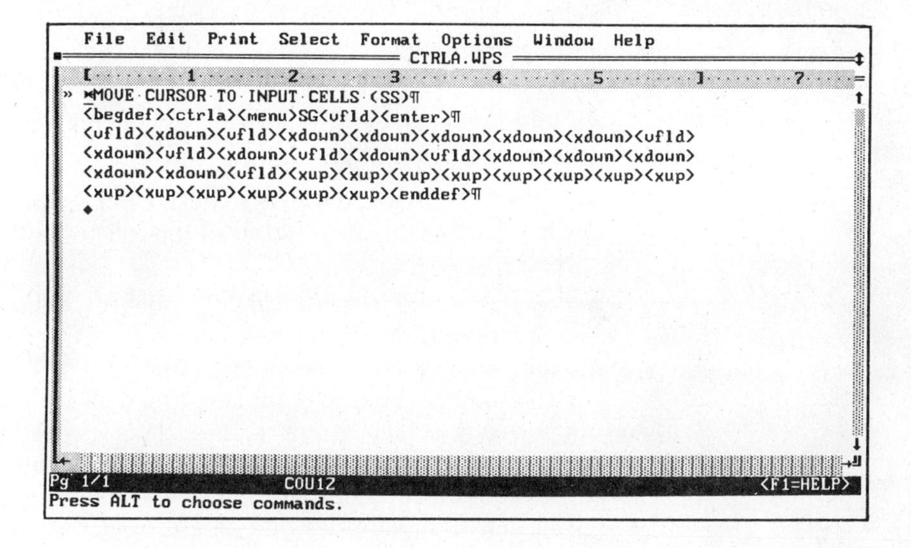

Figure 21-5. The variable input macro shown in a word processor file

First, the macro chooses the Select menu's Go To command. It then pauses to let you type a starting cell location. The <vfld> element tells the macro to accept any number of characters—for example, B5 as well as B55 or B555.

The cursor then moves to the starting cell you specified and pauses again, this time waiting for you to type a number, which can also be any length. When you type that number and press Enter, the cursor moves down one cell and pauses, so that you can type another number. When you type this number and press Enter, the cursor moves down five cells.

And so the macro continues, pausing at each cell that needs a number. After you type the last number in a column and press Enter, the cursor scoots up to the starting input cell in the column and stops.

Recording the Macro

The easy way to enter this macro is to record it as you hit the keys. Then you can see each action as it happens. Leave the cursor where it is.

- Hold down Alt and type a slash (to activate the first macro menu).
- Press Enter (to confirm Record Macro). Works brings up the Playback dialog box asking for a playback key and macro description. Make Ctrl + A the playback key for this macro.
- Hold down Ctrl and type **A** (to assign the Playback key).
- Press Tab (to jump to Title).
- Type **MOVE CURSOR TO INPUT CELLS (SS)** (Works shifts the early part of the description to the left to make room for the rest).
- Press Enter (to return to the spreadsheet). The word RECORD now appears on the message line.

Macros often zip by so quickly that you don't see either an error or its correction.

Recording is about to start. Don't be concerned about any typing errors you may make. Simply correct them as best you can and continue entering the macro. The macro will record the errors and corrections, which you can later edit out if you like.

Column B already has numbers in its cells. To make the macro easier to record, you'll use column B as the prototype. Here goes.

1. Press Alt and type **SG** (Select/Go To). Works brings up the Go to dialog box.
2. Hold down Alt and type / (to activate the second macro menu).
3. Type **V** (Variable Input) and press Enter. This inserts a pause so that you can type a cell location.
4. Type **B5** and press Enter twice: once to confirm the cell location and again to confirm the variable input. The macro won't record the cell location, only the variable pause. The cursor moves to B5, which contains 167,500.

5. Hold down Alt and type / (to activate the second macro menu again).
6. Type **V** (Variable Input) and press Enter twice: once to confirm the nonentry (you see word VARINPUT [variable input] on the message line) and again to end the variable input pause. You now see RECORD again on the message line.

When you create a variable input pause in a macro, Works has no interest in counting characters. Instead of typing a sample entry and pressing Enter to confirm the entry, and then pressing Enter again to end the variable input pause, simply press Enter twice.

7. Press Down Arrow to move the cursor to B6.
8. Hold down Alt and type / (to activate the second macro menu).
9. Type **V** (Variable Input) and press Enter twice.
10. Press Down Arrow five times to move the cursor to B11.
11. Hold down Alt and type / (to activate the second macro menu).
12. Type **V** (Variable Input) and press Enter twice.
13. Press Down Arrow to move the cursor to B12.
14. Hold down Alt and type / (to activate the second macro menu).
15. Type **V** (Variable Input) and press Enter twice.
16. Press Down Arrow to move the cursor to B13.
17. Hold down Alt and type / (to activate the second macro menu).
18. Type **V** (Variable Input) and press Enter twice.
19. Press Down Arrow to move the cursor to B14.
20. Hold down Alt and type / (to activate the second macro menu).
21. Type **V** (Variable Input) and press Enter twice.
22. Press Down Arrow five times to move the cursor to B19.
23. Hold down Alt and type / (to activate the second macro menu).
24. Type **V** (Variable Input) and press Enter twice.
25. Press Up Arrow 14 times to move the cursor to B5.

This is all you want the macro to do, so have Works stop recording.

- Hold down Alt and type a slash (to activate the second macro menu). The blinker is at End Recording, which is in reverse video.
- Press Enter (to confirm End Recording).

Viewing the Macro

Before running the macro, make sure it's totally correct. Leave the cursor where it is and bring up the MACROS.INI file, where Works stored this macro.

Works disables the macros feature while the MACROS.INI file is open.

- Press Alt and type **FO** (File/Open Existing File).
- Press Tab (to move to the `Files` list).
- Type **M** as many times as necessary to reach `MACROS.INI`, and press Enter.
- Works advises that you cannot use macros while this file is open. Acknowledge by pressing Enter.

Works now brings up the MACROS.INI file, where all your macros are stored. Find the one that has `<ctrla>` as its second element. Table 21-1 shows what element means.

Table 21-1. Elements in the moving macro and what they mean

Element	Meaning
`<begdef>`	Beginning of the macro definition (Works generated)
`<ctrla>`	Macro storage/playback key
`<menu>`	Alt key that activates the menu line
SG	Select menu's Go To command (it doesn't matter if letters are in uppercase or lowercase)
`<xdown>`	Down Arrow key that moves the cursor to next cell down
`<vfld>`	Variable-input field that pauses the macro so that you can type a number
`<xup>`	Up Arrow key that moves the cursor to next cell up
`<enddef>`	End of the macro definition (Works generated)

Now compare each element in your macro (uppercase or lowercase doesn't matter—`sg` is just as good as `SG`) with the one in Figure 21-5. If something is awry, skip to the next section, "Editing the Macro." If everything agrees, close MACROS.INI.

- Press Alt and type **FC** (File/Close).

You now have the spreadsheet back on screen. With MACROS.INI closed, Works enables the macros feature.

Editing the Macro

Use the Right and Left Arrow keys to move the cursor to the problem. Type a missing element, or use Delete to delete an offending element. Works doesn't save an edited macro automatically the way it does a recorded macro, so when you're finished, hold down Alt and type **FS** (File/Save). Now press Alt and type **FC** (File/Close) to close the file and return to the spreadsheet.

Running the Macro

Here's the fun part—pressing the magic button that gets the macro going. For practice, run the macro in column C, overtyping the numbers already there. Leave the cursor where it is.

- Hold down Ctrl and type **A** (to start the macro). Works brings up the `Go to` dialog box. You can now see `PLAYBACK` on the message line.
- Type **C5** (the starting cell) and press Enter. The cursor goes to C5.
- Type **210000** (the number already in the cell, but without a comma) and press Enter. The cursor moves down one cell.
- Type **73500** and press Enter again. The cursor jumps to C11.
- Type **19395** and press Enter again. The cursor moves to C12.

Continue in this way, typing the number already in the cell and pressing Enter until you type the last number in C19, at which point the cursor zips up to C5.

Now for the real thing—using the macro to enter the numbers in column D from scratch. Leave the cursor where it is.

- Hold down Ctrl and type **A** (to start the macro again).
- In the `Go to` box, type **D5** (the starting cell) and press Enter.
- Type **287250** (again, no comma) and press Enter. The cursor moves down one cell.
- Type **79625** and press Enter. The cursor jumps to D11.

Using Figure 21-1 as a guide, type the rest of the numbers in column D as you did in column C, pressing Return after each one. When you're finished, the cursor should be in D5, and your spreadsheet should look like the one in Figure 21-1. Press Alt and type **FS** to save it. Wasn't that fun?

Defining the Page Layout

The next step is to print the income statement, which is 75 characters wide, including the 5 characters that Works uses for row numbers and a space. The statement prints in 12-point type on one sheet of 8-by-11-inch paper. You need only change the left and right margins to allow the entire spreadsheet to print on one page. Leave the cursor where it is.

- Press Alt and type **PM** (Print/Page Setup & Margins). Here's the Page Setup & Margins dialog box, where you specify margins and other settings.
- Hold down Alt and type **E** (to move to Left margin).
- Type **.5** (the new left margin setting) and press Tab (to move to Right margin).
- Type **.5** (the new right margin setting). Press Enter.

Now save the spreadsheet with the margin settings: Leave the cursor where it is. Press Alt and type **FS** (File/Save).

Previewing and Printing the Spreadsheet

Before printing, it's a good idea to get an advance look at the spreadsheet on screen.

Make all your settings now and you can go directly from preview to printing. No need to even see the Print *dialog box.*

- Press Alt and type **PV** (Print/Preview). Works brings up the Preview dialog box, which has the same settings as the Print dialog box. Works proposes one copy, which is fine.
- Hold down Alt and type **L** (to turn on Print row and column labels), and press Enter.

Works goes to work producing a miniature spreadsheet on screen. Looks fine, so print directly from the Preview screen. Turn on the printer and type **P**.

The printer whirs, and here's your spreadsheet looking the same as the completed one in Figure 21-1.

The spreadsheet in the next chapter is quite different from this one. It lets you compare car purchases and features a powerful loan amortization program.

TWENTY-TWO

Car Loan Comparison Spreadsheet

Comparing loans can help you decide on the best deal.

For many people, borrowing money is a fact of life, whether the money is needed for personal purchases, such as a car or home, or for business reasons, such as getting a business started or keeping a business going. The spreadsheet shown in Figure 22-1 applies the loan concept to a car purchase, comparing and contrasting car deals for the fictional Sonesta and the equally fictional Madrigal.

In this chapter, you change column widths, enter lines, titles, and numbers, emphasize text and numbers with boldface, format numbers, name cells, create loan and other formulas, copy a formula, list cell names and locations on the spreadsheet, define the page layout, create a filename header, preview and print the spreadsheet, and print the formulas. All in all, a busy, productive session.

Keystrokes and Other Matters

The instructions guide you each step of the way, giving keystrokes and cursor movements relating to each task. Please observe the distinction between pressing and holding down a key.

- With instructions such as *Press Alt and type TW (Format/ Width)*, press and release Alt before you type the letters.
- With *Hold down Alt and type C (to move to Center)*, press the Alt key and, without releasing Alt, type the letter.

CARLOAN.WKS

	A	B	C	D
1	11/28/90	**CAR LOAN CALCULATOR**		
2	=========================	==================	==================	==================
3		Sonesta (1)	Madrigal (2)	Diff (2-1)
4		------------	------------	------------
5	Price of Car	10,844.00	13,553.00	2,709.00
6	Rustproofing	250.00	269.00	19.00
7	Sales Tax (8%)	887.52	1,105.76	218.24
8	Registration/Other Fees	35.00	36.50	1.50
9	NYS Inspection	8.00	8.00	0.00
10		------------	------------	------------
11	Total Cost	12,024.52	14,972.26	2,947.74
12	Deposit	50.00	50.00	0.00
13	Down Payment	1,500.00	1,500.00	0.00
14	Amount Financed	10,474.52	13,422.26	2,947.74
15				
16	Annual Interest Rate (%)	7.9	13.9	6.0
17	Term in Years	3	5	2
18	Term in Months	36	60	24
19				
20	**Monthly Loan Payment**	327.75	311.62	(16.13)
21	Annual Loan Payment	3,933.00	3,739.41	(193.60)
22	Total Loan Payment	11,799.01	18,697.03	6,898.01
23	Total Interest Charge	1,324.49	5,274.77	3,950.27
24				
25				
26				
27	COST1	B4:B10		
28	COST2	C4:C10		
29	PRINCIPAL1	B14:B14		
30	PRINCIPAL2	C14:C14		
31	RATE1	B16:B16		
32	RATE2	C16:C16		
33	TERM1	B18:B18		
34	TERM2	C18:C18		

Figure 22-1. The completed car loan comparison spreadsheet

If you hit a snag, press Escape to cancel what you're doing. Then pick up where you left off.

Unless the instructions say otherwise, use the Arrow keys (Left, Right, Up, and Down) to move the cursor. Keep an eye on the cell indicator in the left side of the status line to be sure the cursor is on the correct cell before you take the next action.

Creating a New Spreadsheet

Load Works as described in the Introduction to this book. At the File menu, type **NS** (Create New File/Spreadsheet), bringing up the spreadsheet screen. Now let's make your spreadsheet look like the one in Figure 22-2.

```
             A                          B               C               D
1                                  CAR LOAN CALCULATOR
2    ========================================================================
3                                  Sonesta (1)     Madrigal (2)    Diff (2-1)
4                                  ------------    ------------    ------------
5    Price of Car                        10844           13553
6     Rustproofing                         250             269
7     Sales Tax (8%)
8     Registration/Other Fees               35            36.5
9     NYS Inspection                         8               8
10                                 ------------    ------------    ------------
11   Total Cost
12    Deposit                               50              50
13    Down Payment                        1500            1500
14   Amount Financed
15
16   Annual Interest Rate (%)              7.9            13.9
17   Term in Years                           3               5
18   Term in Months
19
20   Monthly Loan Payment
21   Annual Loan Payment
22   Total Loan Payment
23   Total Interest Charge
```

Figure 22-2. Titles, lines, and numbers in the car loan comparison spreadsheet

Adjusting the Column Widths

The standard width of the columns is 10 characters. The titles in column A can use more room, so make that column wider. Your cursor is on A1.

- Press Alt and type **TW** (Format/Width). Works displays the `Width` box showing the current width of column A—10 characters.
- Type **25** (the new width) and press Enter.

The numbers and titles in columns B, C, and D can also use more room, so make these columns a uniform 15-character width, all in one step. Place the cursor on B1.

The status line displays various status messages. Now it shows **EXT**, *meaning you're in the Extend mode.*

- Press F8 (to extend the selection).
- Press Right Arrow twice (to select B1, C1, and D1). The cell indicator on the status line now shows `B1:D1`.
- Press Alt and type **TW** (Format/Width).
- Type **15** and press Enter.

Entering the Lines

Next, use an equal sign to put a double line across row 2. Typing quotation marks first signals Works that the equal sign is text, not a value. Place the cursor on A2.

- Type quotation marks and 25 equal signs (the width of the cell).

After the last equal sign, move the cursor to B2, and Works enters the line in its cell. Now continue the line into B2, C2, and D2. The cursor is on B2.

- Press F8 (to extend the selection again).
- Press End (to select B2, C2, and D2).
- Type quotation marks and 15 equal signs.
- Hold down Ctrl and press Enter.

Pressing Ctrl + Enter instead of Enter after you type into one cell in an extended area tells Works to enter what you typed into each selected cell.

Use a minus sign to enter the shorter lines in row 4. To prevent it from forming a continuous line, indent the line two characters and stop it one character shy of the full column width. Place the cursor on B4.

- Press F8 (to extend the selection).
- Press End (to select B4 through D4).
- Press Spacebar twice and type 12 minus signs. Works recognizes the space character as the start of text, so you don't need to type quotation marks before these minus signs.
- Hold down Ctrl and press Enter.

Row 10 needs the same kind of lines, so copy them from row 4. Leave the cells in row 4 selected.

- Hold down Shift and press F3 (to access the Copy mode). Works removes the selection from C4 and D4.
- Move the cursor to B10 and press Enter.

Entering the Titles and Numbers

Next, enter the titles and numbers shown in Figure 22-2. Don't bother to press Enter after each typing title. Simply move the cursor to the next cell that needs a title and Works enters the title you just typed in its cell. If you make a typo, press Backspace (not an Arrow key) to back up the cursor and erase. Place the cursor on B1.

- Type **CAR LOAN CALCULATOR** and move the cursor to B3. Works enters the long spreadsheet title in its cell, letting it spill into C1.
- Type **Sonesta (1)** and move the cursor to C3.
- Type **Madrigal (2)** and move the cursor to D3.
- Type **Diff (2-1)** (meaning the difference between the amount in column 2 minus the amount in column 1) and move the cursor to A5.

Using Figure 22-2 as your guide, enter the rest of the text and numbers. To indent a title under a general heading (for example, `Rustproofing` in A6 under `Price of Car` in A5), press the Spacebar once before typing. After typing a title or number, move the cursor to the next cell. After the last entry, press Enter.

Formatting the Titles

Using boldface makes items of importance stand out from the rest of the entries. Boldface can be just as effective in the spreadsheet as in the more typical application, a word processor document.

The next step is to center the titles in row 3 and show them in boldface so they look like the ones in Figure 22-1. Place the cursor on C3.

- Hold down Ctrl and press F8 (to select row 3).
- Press Alt and type **TS** (Format/Style). Here's the `Style` dialog box. The responses are neutralized (some boxes empty, others containing a dash) because you selected more than one cell.
- Type **C** (to move to `Center`).
- Press Tab (to move to the Styles boxes). The blinker is in the Bold check box.
- Hold down Alt and type **B** (to choose `Bold`) and press Enter.

You can select either Text or Graphics as the screen mode. With Text, you get high intensity; with Graphics, the style you specified (bold, italics, or underline).

Works now shows the title in high intensity or in bold, depending on the screen mode. Have Works print those all-important monthly loan payments in bold, too. Place the cursor on C20.

- Hold down Ctrl and press F8 (to select row 20).
- Press Alt and type **TS** (Format/Style).
- Hold down Alt and type **B** (to move to `Bold`). Press Enter.

Formatting the Numbers

Most of the numbers are dollar amounts. Dollar signs can clutter a spreadsheet, so format the numbers for commas instead. Place the cursor on B5.

- Press F8 (to extend the selection).
- Move the cursor to B14, and then press End (to select B5 through D14).
- Press Alt and type **TC** (Format/Comma). Works proposes two decimal places, which is fine, so press Enter.

Repeat these steps to format the loan amounts to show commas. Place the cursor on B20.

- Press F8 (to extend the selection).
- Move the cursor to B23, and press End (to select B20 through D23).
- Press Alt and type **TC** (Format/Comma). Press Enter to accept two decimal places.

Saving the Spreadsheet

Now save the spreadsheet and give it the filename CARLOAN. Leave everything as is.

- Press Alt and type **FA** (File/Save As).

Works brings up the Save as dialog box so you can type a filename, and, if needed, a drive or directory. If you're saving to the current drive, simply type the filename. Otherwise, type the drive or directory before the filename, for example, **A:CARLOAN**

- Type **CARLOAN** and press Enter. Works appends the extension .WKS (for Worksheet).

As the file is being saved, the cell indicator on the status line shows the percentage already processed. When the cell location reappears, Works is ready for your next action.

Naming the Cells

When you give cells plain English names, you can use these names instead of cell locations in your formulas. This makes the formulas easy to enter, and even better, easy to understand.

Before you enter the formulas that do your calculations, give the Sonesta cells (B4 through B10) the name of COST1. If you later need more rows for more items, you can insert them anywhere between rows 4 and 11, and Works will include the newcomers in the group of named cells. Place the cursor on the line in B4.

- Press F8 (to extend the selection).
- Move the cursor to the line in B10 (to select B4 through B10).
- Press Alt and type **EN** (Edit/Name). Works proposes a dashed line (the closest text) in the `Name` box. This clearly won't do.
- Type **COST1** and press Enter.

Now name the Madrigal cells COST2. Place the cursor on C4.

- Press F8 (to extend the selection).
- Move the cursor to C10 (to select C4 through C10).
- Press Alt and type **EN** (Edit/Name). You can now see the COST1 name and cell locations in the NAME dialog box. Again, Works proposes a dashed line.
- Type **COST2** and press Enter.

Next, name the cells that will contain the Sonesta amount financed (B14). The monthly loan payment formula you'll soon enter in B20 needs this amount to do its calculations. Place the cursor on B14.

- Press Alt and type **EN** (Edit/Name). Works proposes to name the cell `Amount Financed` (the title in A14), a perfectly reasonable name. For reasons that will become clear when you enter the formulas, name the cell PRINCIPAL1 instead.
- Type **PRINCIPAL1** and press Enter. Move the cursor to B16, another cell to name.
- Press Alt and type **EN** (Edit/Name).
- Type **RATE1** and press Enter. Move the cursor to B18.
- Press Alt and type **EN** (Edit/Name). The `Names` list is really starting to fill out.
- Type **TERM1** and press Enter.

Now name the cells needed by the monthly loan payment formula in C20. Place the cursor on C14.

- Press Alt and type **EN** (Edit/Name).
- Type **PRINCIPAL2** and press Enter. Move the cursor to C16.
- Press Alt and type **EN** (Edit/Name).
- Type **RATE2** and press Enter. Move the cursor to C18.
- Press Alt and type **EN** (Edit/Name).
- Type **TERM2** and press Enter. You've named all the cells that need to be named. The next step is to enter the formulas that use these names.

Entering the Formulas

Formulas are mathematical equations that use numbers on the spreadsheet and other elements to produce new numbers. Figure 22-3 shows the locations of the formulas in the car loan spreadsheet. You enter the formulas in the unshaded cells in column B and copy them to the shaded cells in column C at the same time. With Formula 9, you copy to the cells below.

First read the explanation of how the formula works, and then follow the step-by-step instructions. Keep an eye on the status line to make sure the cursor is on the correct cell before taking your next action. If you run into a snag, press Escape and start again. After each formula, your result should match the one in Figure 22-1.

Formula 1: Sales Tax of 8 Percent =(B5+B6)*0.08

Formula 1 adds the price of the car (B5) and rustproofing (B6), calculates an 8 percent sales tax on the total, and enters the result in B7. You can later edit the formula to work with the sales tax rate for your area. Place the cursor on B7.

- Press F8 (to extend the selection).
- Press Right Arrow (to select B7 and C7).
- Type an equal sign and an open parenthesis.

	A	B	C	D
1	11/28/90	CAR LOAN CALCULATOR		
2	==========	==========	==========	==========
3		Sonesta (1)	Madrigal (2)	Diff (2-1)
4		------------	------------	------------
5	Price of Car			⑨ 0.00
6	Rustproofing			0.00
7	Sales Tax (8%)	0.00 ①	0.00	0.00
8	Registration/Other Fees			0.00
9	NYS Inspection			0.00
10		------------	------------	------------
11	Total Cost	0.00 ②	0.00	0.00
12	Deposit			0.00
13	Down Payment			0.00
14	Amount Financed	0.00 ③	0.00	0.00
15				
16	Annual Interest Rate (%)			0.0
17	Term in Years			0
18	Term in Months	0 ④	0	0
19				
20	**Monthly Loan Payment**	⑤ **ERR**	**ERR**	**ERR**
21	Annual Loan Payment	ERR ⑥	ERR	ERR
22	Total Loan Payment	⑦ ERR	ERR	ERR
23	Total Interest Charge	ERR ⑧	ERR	ERR

Figure 22-3. Formula locations in the car loan comparison spreadsheet

- Move the cursor to B5 and type a plus sign.
- Move the cursor to B6 and type a close parenthesis.
- Type an asterisk (the multiplication operator).
- Type **.08** (you should now see `=(B5+B6)*.08` on the entry/edit line and in B7).
- Hold down Ctrl and press Enter. Compare your results with Figure 22-1.

Formula 2: Total Cost =SUM(COST1)

Formula 2 adds entries in B4 through B10 (the cells named COST1) to produce the total cost of the car in B11. Place the cursor on B11.

- Press F8 (to extend the selection).
- Press Right Arrow (to select B11 and C11).
- Type the entire formula:

  =SUM(COST1)
- Hold down Ctrl and press Enter.

Formula 3: Amount Financed =B11-B12-B13

Formula 3 subtracts the deposit (B12) and down payment (B13) from the total cost of the car (B11) to produce the amount financed in B14. Place the cursor on B14.

- Press F8 (to extend the selection).
- Press Right Arrow (to select B14 and C14).
- Type an equal sign and move the cursor to B11.
- Type a minus sign and move the cursor to B12.
- Type a minus sign and move the cursor to B13.
- Hold down Ctrl and press Enter.

Formula 4: Term in Months =B17*12

Formula 4 multiplies the term in years (B17) by 12 to produce the term in months in B18. Place the cursor on B18.

- Press F8 (to extend the selection).
- Press Right Arrow (to select B18 and C18).
- Type an equal sign and move the cursor to B17.
- Type an asterisk and the number 12.
- Hold down Ctrl and press Enter.

Formula 5: Monthly Loan Payment =PMT(PRINCIPAL1,RATE1/100/12,TERM1)

The PMT function is one of Works' calculating shortcuts. When you identify the principal, rate, and term of a loan, PMT figures out the periodic payment. Be sure to keep time elements in a formula on an equal basis.

Formula 5 calculates the monthly loan payment in B20. The formula uses the PMT (payment) function, whose syntax is *PMT(PRINCIPAL,RATE,TERM)*. This is why you named the cells as you did—so the formula would resemble the function. To get a monthly rate, Formula 5 converts the annual interest rate in B16 (the cell named RATE1) to a percentage and divides it by 12, which appears as RATE1/100/12. Place the cursor on B20.

- Press F8 (to extend the selection).
- Press Right Arrow (to select B20 and C20).
- Type the entire formula:

  =PMT(PRINCIPAL1,RATE1/100/12,TERM1)
- Hold down Ctrl and press Enter.

Now press Right Arrow and look at the entry/edit line. Works was smart enough to use the names in column C as cell references for the formula in C20, so you see:

```
=PMT(PRINCIPAL2,RATE2/100/12,TERM2)
```

Formula 6: Annual Loan Payment =B20*12

Formula 6 multiplies the monthly loan payment (B20) by 12 to produce the annual loan payment in B21. Place the cursor on B21.

- Press F8 (to extend the selection).
- Press Right Arrow (to select B21 and C21).
- Type an equal sign and move the cursor to B20.
- Type an asterisk and the number 12.
- Hold down Ctrl and press Enter.

Formula 7: Total Loan Payment =B21*B17

Formula 7 multiplies the annual loan payment (B21) by term in years (B17) and enters the total loan payment in B22. Place the cursor on B22.

- Press F8 (to extend the selection).
- Press Right Arrow (to select B22 and C22).
- Type an equal sign and move the cursor to B21.
- Type an asterisk and move the cursor to B17.
- Hold down Ctrl and press Enter.

Formula 8: Total Interest Charge =B22-PRINCIPAL1

Formula 8 subtracts the amount financed in B14 (the cell named PRINCIPAL1) from the total loan payment (B22) to produce the total interest charge in B23. Place the cursor on B23.

- Press F8 (to extend the selection).
- Press Right Arrow (to select B23 and C23).
- Type an equal sign and move the cursor to B22.
- Type a minus sign and type **PRINCIPAL1**.
- Hold down Ctrl and press Enter.

Formula 9: Difference between Car Deals =C5-B5

Formula 9 subtracts the price of the Sonesta from the price of the Madrigal and enters the difference in D5. Place the cursor on D5.

- Press F8 (to extend the selection).
- Move the cursor to D9 (to select D5 through D9).
- Type an equal sign and move the cursor to C5.
- Type a minus sign and move the cursor to B5.
- Hold down Ctrl and press Enter.

Now press Escape to collapse the selection.

Copying Formula 9

Sometimes it's more efficient to copy a formula into many contiguous cells (even into cells that don't need it) than to repeat the copy steps over and over. You can then erase the unneeded formulas.

Other cells in column D need Formula 9. Instead of creating each one from scratch, copy from D5. Leave the cursor on D5.

- Hold down Shift and press F3 (to access the Copy mode).
- Move the cursor to D11 and press Enter.

Now copy Formula 9 down its column so that it calculates the difference between the other items in columns C and D. Leave the cursor on D11.

- Press F8 (to extend the selection).
- Move the cursor to D23 (to select D11 to D23).
- Press Alt and type **EF** (Edit/Fill Down). Press Escape to collapse the selection.

Now, all you have to do is erase the formulas in D15 and D19: Place the cursor on D15, and press Backspace and Enter. Now place the cursor on D19 and press Backspace and Enter.

Formula 10: Today's Date =NOW( )

The NOW function can enter today's date in a cell on the spreadsheet. Works updates the date each time the spreadsheet recalculates.

Formula 10 is the NOW function, which enters the serial number of the date you typed at the DOS prompt when you turned on your computer or the date kept by your computer's clock, if you have one. Hold down Ctrl and press Home to jump the cursor to A1.

- Type =**NOW( )** and press Enter.

Works shows the serial number for the date. To see it as a date, choose the Time/Date format. Leave the cursor on A1.

- Press Alt and type **TT** (Format/Time/Date). Works brings up the `Time/Date` dialog box with an array of offerings.
- Type **M** (to choose `Month, Day, Year`) and press Enter.

The date that appears is a value, so Works right-aligns it. Left-align it so it's flush with the other entries in column A. Leave the cursor on A1.

- Press Alt and type **TS** (Format/Style).
- Type **L** (to move to `Left`) and press Enter.

Now save the spreadsheet with all the formulas: Press Alt and type **FS** (File/Save).

Listing the Cell Names

Works lets you list cell names on a spreadsheet to document your actions. Ordinarily, the best place to list these names is in an out-of-the-way location where you can exclude them from the print area. In this spreadsheet, list the names on the same page as the spreadsheet so you can see them easily. Place the cursor on A27.

- Press Alt and type **EN** (Edit/Name).
- Hold down Alt and type **L** (for List).

Instantly, Works plunks all the cell names and cell locations into rows 27 through 34. Alphabetically of course.

Defining the Page Layout

This spreadsheet is 75 characters wide, including the 5 characters Works uses for row numbers and a space. It prints in 12-point type on one sheet of 8-1/2-by-11-inch paper.

Setting the Margins

Making the left and right margins smaller lets the entire spreadsheet print on one page. Leave the cursor where it is.

- Press Alt and type **PM** (Print/Page Setup & Margins). Here's the Page Setup & Margins dialog box where margins settings are made.
- Hold down Alt and type **E** (to move to Left Margin).
- Type **.5** (the new left margin setting) and press Tab (to move to Right margin).
- Type **.5** (the new right margin setting). Press Enter.

Creating a Filename Header

Now create a header that prints only the spreadsheet filename. This makes it easy to identify the spreadsheet in the Works Files directory.

- Press Alt and type **PH** (Print/Headers & Footers). You now see the Headers & Footers dialog box with the blinker in the Header field.

- Type **&L&F**. These codes tell Works to left-align (&L) the filename (&F). Press Enter.

(Printing is close at hand. If you specified more than one printer, press Alt now, type **PS** (Print/Printer Setup), and choose your printer.)

Save the spreadsheet one more time: Leave the cursor where it is. Press Alt and type **FS** (File/Save).

Previewing and Printing the Spreadsheet

Now it's time to print. Before you do, sneak a peak at the spreadsheet to make sure everything is as it should be.

- Press Alt and type **PV** (Print/Preview). Works brings up the `Preview` dialog box, which has the same settings as the `Print` dialog box. Works proposes one copy, which is fine.
- You plan to print directly from Preview, so hold down Alt, type **L** (to turn on `Print row and column labels`), and press Enter.

Works goes to work producing a miniature spreadsheet on screen. Beautiful, so turn on the printer and type **P** to print.

The printer whirs, and here's your spreadsheet, looking the same as the completed one in Figure 22-1.

Printing the Formulas

A formula printout can be a real lifesaver if something on disk goes haywire and you have to recreate the spreadsheet from scratch.

Works can print the formulas just as easily as the spreadsheet. Before you can print them, you must display them.

- Press Alt and type **OF** (Options/Show Formulas).

Move the cursor around the screen and you can see formulas, unformatted titles and numbers, and the list of cell names. Even though Works doubled the cell width before showing the formulas, some cells are still too narrow to display them completely. Later, when you want to view or print your own formulas, you can increase the cell width accordingly.

Now print the formulas in the same way that you printed the spreadsheet. They need three pages to print completely. Figure 22-4 shows the second page.

```
CARLOAN.WKS

                    B                                     C
1   CAR LOAN CALCULATOR
2   ===============                  ===============
3   Sonesta (1)                      Madrigal (2)
4     ------------                     ------------
5   10844                            13553
6   250                              269
7   =(B5+B6)*0.08                    =(C5+C6)*0.08
8   35                               36.5
9   8                                8
10    ------------                     ------------
11  =SUM(COST1)                      =SUM(COST2)
12  50                               50
13  1500                             1500
14  =B11-B12-B13                     =C11-C12-C13
15
16  7.9                              13.9
17  3                                5
18  =B17*12                          =C17*12
19
20  =PMT(PRINCIPAL1,RATE1/100/12,T=PMT(PRINCIPAL2,RATE2/100/12,T
21  =B20*12                          =C20*12
22  =B21*B17                         =C21*C17
23  =B22-PRINCIPAL1                  =C22-PRINCIPAL2
24
25
26
27  B4:B10
28  C4:C10
29  B14:B14
30  C14:C14
31  B16:B16
32  C16:C16
33  B18:B18
34  C18:C18
```

Figure 22-4. The second page of the car loan spreadsheet formula printout

- Press Alt and type **PP** (Print/Print).

Now restore the spreadsheet to the screen. Leave the cursor where it is.

- Press Alt and type **OF** (Options/Show Formulas).

You can now enter your own numbers in the car loan calculator. Safe driving!

The next chapter takes you in a new direction—to a tax spreadsheet filled with lookup tables and lookup formulas.

TWENTY-THREE

Tax Lookup Spreadsheet

Here's a way to rough out your tax exposure.

One of the best things about spreadsheets is the way they let you preview coming events. A case in point: income taxes. With all the changes in the tax laws, you may find it difficult to gauge just where you stand. The spreadsheet shown in Figure 23-1 lets you rough out the impact of taxes for 1990, giving you a chance to plan the right moves to reduce Uncle Sam's bite. It works just as well for several people—family, friends, or clients—as it does for one person.

```
                  A                  B              C              D
1                             INCOME TAX 1990                   TAXLOOK
2    ============================================================
3                                 Filing      Est Taxable    Income Tax
4    Client Name                  Status        Income     Before Credits
5    ------------------------------------------------------------
6    Betty & Bob Boop               2          $43,140         $8,056
7    John Swensen                   1          $17,850         $2,678
8    Thelma & Dick Tracy            2          $35,500         $5,917
9    Garfield C. Catt               1          $10,000         $1,500
10   Mary Worth                     1         $105,650        $29,582
11   Harry & Edna Tortelli          2          $54,750        $11,307
12   (Your Name)                    1          $50,000        $11,844
13   ============================================================
14   TABLE 1 - SINGLE FILER
15           Taxable Income:     Base Tax:          Plus:
16                        0              0            15%
17                   18,550          2,783            28%
18                   44,900         10,161            33%
19                   93,130         26,076            28%
20
21   TABLE 2 - MARRIED FILING JOINTLY
22           Taxable Income:     Base Tax:          Plus:
23                        0              0            15%
24                   30,950          4,643            28%
25                   74,850         16,935            33%
26                  155,320         43,490            28%
```

Figure 23-1. The completed tax lookup spreadsheet

The spreadsheet features two lookup tables and powerful lookup formulas that pick and choose the correct information from the tables based on family status and income. Though complete in itself, this spreadsheet is also a module that you can drop into a comprehensive tax calculation spreadsheet where you can itemize income, adjustments, and credits.

In this chapter, you change column widths, enter and copy lines, enter and format text and numbers, create lookup tables, name cells, create a formula that combines the If and Lookup functions, learn how to edit a formula, explore a nested If formula, hide and unhide columns, define the page layout, and preview and print the spreadsheet. This is a good session loaded with techniques you need to know.

Keystrokes and Other Matters

The instructions guide you each step of the way, giving keystrokes and cursor movements relating to each task. Please observe the distinction between pressing and holding down a key.

- With instructions such as *Press Alt and type TW (Format/ Width)*, press and release Alt before you type the letters.
- With *Hold down Alt and type C (to move to Center)*, press the Alt key and, without releasing Alt, type the letter.

If you hit a snag, press Escape to cancel what you're doing. Then pick up where you left off.

Unless the instructions say otherwise, use the Arrow keys (Left, Right, Up, and Down) to move the cursor. Keep an eye on the cell indicator in the left side of the status line to be sure the cursor is on the correct cell before you take the next action.

Creating a New Spreadsheet

Load Works as described in the Introduction to this book. At the File menu, type **NS** (Create New File/Spreadsheet), bringing up the spreadsheet screen. Now let's make your spreadsheet look like the one in Figure 23-2.

	A	B	C	D
1		INCOME TAX 1990		TAXLOOK
2	========================	================	================	================
3		Filing	Est Taxable	Income Tax
4	Client Name	Status	Income	Before Credits
5	------------------------	----------------	----------------	----------------
6	Betty & Bob Boop	2	43140	
7	John Swensen	1	17850	
8	Thelma & Dick Tracy	2	35500	
9	Garfield C. Catt	1	10000	
10	Mary Worth	1	105650	
11	Harry & Edna Tortelli	2	54750	
12	(Your Name)	1	50000	
13	========================	================	================	================
14	TABLE 1 - SINGLE FILER			
15	Taxable Income:	Base Tax:	Plus:	
16	0	0	15%	
17	18550	2783	28%	
18	44900	10161	33%	Single
19	93130	26076	28%	
20				
21	TABLE 2 - MARRIED FILING JOINTLY			
22	Taxable Income:	Base Tax:	Plus:	
23	0	0	15%	
24	30950	4643	28%	Married
25	74850	16935	33%	
26	155320	43490	28%	

Figure 23-2. Text, lines, numbers, and lookup tables in the tax lookup spreadsheet

Adjusting the Column Widths

Make column A wider to give the client names the room they need. Your cursor is on A1.

- Press Alt and type **TW** (Format/Width). Works displays the `Width` box showing the current width of column A—10 characters.
- Type **23** (the new width) and press Enter.

The numbers and titles in columns B, C, and D can use more room too, so widen them to 14 characters each. Place the cursor on B1.

- Press F8 (to extend the selection).
- Press Right Arrow twice (to select B1, C1, and D1). The cell indicator on the status line now shows the range `B1:D1`.

- Press Alt and type **TW** (Format/Width).
- Type **14** and press Enter.

Entering the Lines

Next, use an equal sign to enter a double line across row 2. Typing quotation marks first tells Works that the equal sign is text, not a value. Place the cursor on A2.

You don't have to press Enter after typing an entry, even a line. Moving the cursor to the next cell that needs an entry serves the same purpose and saves a keystroke every time.

- Type quotation marks and 23 equal signs (the width of the cell). Move the cursor to B2, and Works enters the line in A2.

Now enter the line in cells B2, C2, and D2, which are 14 characters wide. You can fill all three cells at the same time by pressing Ctrl+Enter instead of Enter alone. Your cursor is on B2.

- Press F8 (to extend the selection).
- Press End (to select B2 through D2).
- Type quotation marks and 14 equal signs.
- Hold down Ctrl and press Enter. All three cells now contain equal signs.

Row 13 needs the same kind of line. All you need to do is copy it from row 2. Leave the cursor on B2.

- Hold down Ctrl and press F8 (to select row 2).
- Hold down Shift and press F3 (to activate the Copy mode). The selection seems to have collapsed, but don't be concerned.
- Move the cursor to B13 and press Enter.

In the same way, use a minus sign to enter a line across row 5. Place the cursor on A5.

- Type quotation marks and 23 minus signs. Move the cursor to B5.
- Press F8 (to extend the selection).
- Press End (to select B5 through D5).
- Type quotation marks and 14 minus signs.
- Hold down Ctrl and press Enter.

Entering the Text and Numbers

If you make a typo while typing text or numbers, press Backspace (not an Arrow key) to back up the cursor and erase.

The next step is to enter the client names and other text shown in Figure 23-2. Place the cursor on B1.

- Type **INCOME TAX 1990** and move the cursor to D1. When you move the cursor, Works enters the title in its cell.
- Type **TAXLOOK** (the spreadsheet filename) and move the cursor to A4. If you don't create a header that prints the filename, it makes good sense to enter the filename on the spreadsheet. This way, you can spot it easily in the Works `Files` list.
- Type **Client Name** and move the cursor to A6.
- Type **Betty & Bob Boop** and move the cursor to A7.
- Type **John Swensen** and move the cursor to A8.
- Type **Thelma & Dick Tracy** and move the cursor to A9.

Using Figure 23-2 as a guide, enter the rest of the names, titles, and numbers in this sequence:

- Names in A9 through A11. To keep things interesting, enter your name in A12.
- Move the cursor to B3. Enter the titles in rows 3 and 4 in columns B, C, and D.
- Move the cursor to B6. Enter the numbers in rows 6 through 12 in column B. In B12, enter your own information.
- Move the cursor to C6. Enter the numbers in rows 6 through 12 in column C. In C12, enter your own information.
- Move the cursor to A14. Enter all titles and numbers in TABLE 1 from rows 14 through 19. The alignment of the titles and numbers may be a bit confusing. Just bear in mind that Works left-justifies text and right-justifies numbers. In Table 1, for instance, enter **Taxable Income** in A15 and **0** in B15.

Tables 1 and 2 are quite similar. Instead of starting from scratch, you can copy the entire block of text and numbers, and then overtype entries that are different. First use F8 to select Table 1, and then enter the Copy mode with Shift+F3. If you feel up to it, do it that way and ignore the next step.

- Move the cursor to A21. Enter all titles and numbers in TABLE 2 from rows 21 through 26. Press Enter after the last entry.

Aligning the Titles and Numbers

The next step is to align the titles and numbers so they look like the ones in Figure 23-1. Right-align the spreadsheet filename first. Place the cursor on D1.

- Press Alt and type **TS** (Format/Style). Here's the `Style` dialog box.
- Type **R** (to move to `Right`) and press Enter. Instantly the filename shifts to the right.

Now center all titles in rows 3 and 4, except `Client Name`. Place the cursor on D3.

- Press F8 (to extend the selection).
- Press Left Arrow twice, and then press Down Arrow (to select B3 through D4).
- Press Alt and type **TS** (Format/Style).
- Type **C** (to move to `Center`) and press Enter.

Next, center the numbers that show the filing status so they align better with the title above them. Place the cursor on B6.

- Press F8 (to extend the selection).
- Press Down Arrow six times (to select B6 through B12).
- Press Alt and type **TS** (Format/Style).
- Type **C** (to move to `Center`) and press Enter. That's better.

Now right-align the titles in row 15 so they're more connected with the numbers below them. Place the cursor on B15.

- Hold down Ctrl and press F8 (to select row 15).
- Press Alt and type **TS** (Format/Style).
- Type **R** (to move to `Right`) and press Enter.

And finally, right-align the titles in row 22. Place the cursor on B22.

- Hold down Ctrl and press F8 (to select row 22).
- Press Alt and type **TS** (Format/Style).
- Type **R** (to move to `Right`) and press Enter.

Formatting the Numbers

Large numbers are easier to read with commas embedded in every third place. You can get commas by using either the Dollar or Comma format.

Format the cells in column C that contain estimated taxable income and those in column D that will soon contain estimated income tax to show dollar amounts. Place the cursor on C6.

- Press F8 (to extend the selection).
- Press Down Arrow six times and then End (to select C6 through D12).
- Press Alt and type **TU** (Format/Currency). The two decimal places that Works proposes aren't necessary on this spreadsheet.
- Type **0** and press Enter.

Now format the taxable income and base tax numbers in Tables 1 and 2 to show their amounts only with commas, not dollar signs. It doesn't matter that you include text and empty cells in the group. Place the cursor on A16.

- Press F8 (to extend the selection).
- Press Down Arrow ten times, and then press Right Arrow (to select A16 through B26).
- Press Alt and type **TC** (Format/Comma). Works again proposes two decimal places.
- Type **0** and press Enter. This completes the formatting. Press Escape to collapse the selection.

Naming the Lookup Tables

The lookup tables contain tax schedules needed by a formula that you'll soon enter. The easiest way to work with each table is to name it. Table 1 contains the schedule for a single filer, so name it SINGLE. Leave the cursor on A16.

- Press F8 (to extend the selection).
- Press Down Arrow three times, and then press Right Arrow twice (to select A16 through C19).

- Press Alt and type **EN** (Edit/Name). Works proposes to name the table `Taxable income` (the title in A15). That won't do at all.
- Type **SINGLE** and press Enter.

The other table contains the schedule for married taxpayers filing jointly, so name it MARRIED. Place the cursor on A23.

- Press F8 (to extend the selection).
- Press Down Arrow three times, and then press Right Arrow twice (to select A23 through C26).
- Press Alt and type **EN** (Edit/Name). Works again proposes to name the table `Taxable income` (the title in A22).
- Type **MARRIED** and press Enter.

You'll find out more about these tables when you create the formulas. Press Escape to collapse the selection.

Saving the Spreadsheet

This is a good time to save the spreadsheet and give it the filename TAXLOOK. Leave the cursor on A23.

- Press Alt and type **FA** (File/Save As).

Works brings up the `Save as` dialog box so you can type a filename, and, if needed, a drive or directory. If you're saving to the current drive, simply type the filename. Otherwise, type the drive or directory before the filename, for example A:TAXLOOK.

- Type **TAXLOOK** and press Enter. Works appends the extension `.WKS` (for Worksheet).

As the file is being saved, the cell indicator on the status line shows the percentage already processed. When the cell location reappears, Works is ready for your next action.

Entering the Formula

Formulas are mathematical equations that use numbers on the spreadsheet and other elements to produce new numbers. This spreadsheet contains one formula entered in several cells. The unshaded cell in Figure 23-3 shows the location of this formula, and the unshaded cells below it, its copies.

To get a clear understanding of the If and Lookup functions, read the entire explanation of how the formula works, and then follow the step-by-step instructions. Keep an eye on the status line to make sure the cursor is on the correct cell before taking your next action.

When Works lets you enter a formula that you know is wrong, press F2 to place it on the entry/edit line, and then make your corrections.

If you run into a snag, either press Escape or Enter. If you press Escape, you must start this l-o-ng formula from scratch. If you press Enter (the better way) Works will likely flash an error message on screen. Press Enter again, and Works gives you a chance to edit the formula. Use Backspace to erase characters before the blinker or use Left Arrow to move past characters without erasing anything. Then type in missing characters or delete offending ones. Continue where you left off.

A few final words: After you enter the Edit mode in this way, you can no longer use the cursor to capture C6. Type C6 into the formula instead. This will make sense when you read the formula description.

```
               A                      B              C              D
1                              INCOME TAX 1990                   TAXLOOK
2    ====================================================================
3                                  Filing      Est Taxable     Income Tax
4    Client Name                   Status         Income    Before Credits
5    --------------------------------------------------------------------
6    Betty & Bob Boop                                                  $0
7    John Swensen                                                      $0
8    Thelma & Dick Tracy                                               $0
9    Garfield C. Catt                                                  $0
10   Mary Worth                                                        $0
11   Harry & Edna Tortelli                                             $0
12   (Your Name)                                                       $0
13   ====================================================================
14   TABLE 1 - SINGLE FILER
15           Taxable Income:       Base Tax:           Plus:
16                         0               0             15%
17                    18,550           2,783             28%
18                    44,900          10,161             33%
19                    93,130          26,076             28%
20
21   TABLE 2 - MARRIED FILING JOINTLY
22           Taxable Income:       Base Tax:           Plus:
23                         0               0             15%
24                    30,950           4,643             28%
25                    74,850          16,935             33%
26                   155,320          43,490             28%
```

Figure 23-3. Formula locations in the tax lookup spreadsheet

Formula 1: Income Tax Before Credits
=IF(B6=1,VLOOKUP(C6,$SINGLE,1)+VLOOKUP(C6,$SINGLE,2) *(C6-VLOOKUP(C6,$SINGLE,0),VLOOKUP(C6,$MARRIED,1) +VLOOKUP(C6,$MARRIED,2)*(C6-VLOOKUP(C6,$MARRIED,0)))

Formula 1 uses the If function to decide on one of two possible answers. In D6, the cell in which you enter it initially, it looks at the filing status in B6. If B6 contains 1, it uses the information in Table 1, the lookup table named SINGLE, to calculate the answer. If B6 contains 2, the formula uses the information in Table 2, the lookup table named MARRIED, to calculate the answer.

The VLOOKUP (vertical lookup) function tells the formula to search the table from top to bottom until it finds the number and then move to the right by the number of columns indicated to get the entry.

Formula 1 behaves the same, regardless of which table it works with. In D6, it searches column A in the table for the largest number less than or equal to the amount in C6. It then goes one column to the right to pick up the corresponding base tax from the table in column B, which it adds to the next calculation produced by the formula.

In the next calculation, the formula again looks up the amount in C6. This time, it moves two columns to the right to pick up the corresponding percentage, which it multiplies by the amount in C6 less the taxable income already accounted for. The result is the base tax plus a percentage of the excess income between levels in the table in column A.

Formula 1 can perform the same calculations in D7 through D12, which have the same relative layout as D6. Each cell containing taxable income is a relative cell reference and each lookup table is an absolute reference, which you define as such by entering a dollar sign ($) before the table name in the formula. Now go for it. Place the cursor on D6.

An alternate and oftimes faster way to enter named cells in formulas is to press F5 to bring up the **Go to** *dialog box, tab into the* **Names** *list, and choose the name. If the named reference is absolute, as it is here, pressing F4 inserts the dollar sign before the name.*

- Press F8 (to extend the selection).
- Press Down Arrow six times (to select D6 through D12).
- Type an equal sign. Type **IF(** and move the cursor to B6.
- Type every character in the following formula EXCEPT each occurrence of `C6`. To insert C6 in the formula, simply move the cursor to C6 (it's easier than typing), and then continue typing the formula. Every once in a while pause to check what you've already done, paying particular attention to commas and

parentheses. When your formula fills the entry/edit line, Works moves it to the left to make room for more characters. Take your time. There's no need to rush anything.

=1,VLOOKUP(C6,$SINGLE,1)+VLOOKUP(C6,$SINGLE,2) *(C6-VLOOKUP(C6,$SINGLE,0)),VLOOKUP(C6,$MARRIED,1) +VLOOKUP(C6,$MARRIED,2)*(C6-VLOOKUP(C6, $MARRIED,0)))

- Now that you've finished the formula, hold down Ctrl and press Enter.

The formula now produces the estimated income tax for yourself and each client/friend/relative.

Correcting the Formula

If, when you press Enter, Works brings up an ERROR message, press Enter (not Escape) to keep the formula in plain view on the entry/edit line. Check each character carefully, using the error message as a clue to the problem.

Right Arrow and Left Arrow move the blinker through the formula without erasing anything. Home and End jump the blinker to the beginning and end of the formula. When you get to the problem, type a missing character or press Delete to delete a character. After correcting the problem, hold down Ctrl and press Enter again.

Exploring a Nested If Formula

The tax laws define other taxpayer categories, including heads of households and married persons filing singly, with corresponding tax schedules. You can create separate lookup tables for more schedules as easily as you did the others, and then modify the If/Lookup formula accordingly. No, you don't have to do it now. Just read.

Figure 23-4 shows a third table—Table 3, named HEAD—for heads of households.

You're now faced with a novel situation. A standard If formula can handle two possibilities. The one you just created works beautifully with either single or married taxpayers. Here, you have three possibilities—single, married, or head of household. This calls for a "nested" formula—that is, one If formula contained in another.

	A	B	C	D
1		INCOME TAX 1990		TAXLOOK
2	====================	====================	====================	====================
3		Filing	Est Taxable	Income Tax
4	Client Name	Status	Income	Before Credits
5	--------------------	--------------------	--------------------	--------------------
6	Betty & Bob Boop	2	$43,140	$8,056
7	John Swensen	1	$17,850	$2,678
8	Thelma & Dick Tracy	2	$35,500	$5,917
9	Garfield C. Catt	1	$10,000	$1,500
10	Mary Worth	3	$105,650	$28,425
11	Harry & Edna Tortelli	2	$54,750	$11,307
12	(Your Name)	1	$50,000	$11,844
13	====================	====================	====================	====================
14	TABLE 1 - SINGLE FILER			
15	Taxable Income:	Base Tax:	Plus:	
16	0	0	15%	
17	18,550	2,783	28%	
18	44,900	10,161	33%	
19	93,130	26,076	28%	
20				
21	TABLE 2 - MARRIED FILING JOINTLY			
22	Taxable Income:	Base Tax:	Plus:	
23	0	0	15%	
24	30,950	4,643	28%	
25	74,850	16,935	33%	
26	155,320	43,490	28%	
27				
28	TABLE 3 - HEAD OF HOUSEHOLD			
29	Taxable income:	Base tax:	Plus:	
30	0	0	15%	
31	24,850	3,728	28%	Head
32	64,200	14,746	33%	
33	128,810	36,087	28%	

Figure 23-4. The income tax spreadsheet with a third schedule for heads of households

Entered in D6, the nested formula looks like this:

=IF(B6=1,VLOOKUP(C6,$SINGLE,1)+VLOOKUP(C6,$SINGLE,2)*(C6-VLOOKUP(C6,$SINGLE,0)),IF(B6=2,VLOOKUP(C6,$MARRIED,1)+VLOOKUP(C6,$MARRIED,2)*(C6-VLOOKUP(C6, $MARRIED,0)), VLOOKUP(C6,$HEAD,1)+VLOOKUP(C6,$HEAD,2)*(C6-VLOOKUP(C6,$HEAD,0))))

As before, the formula looks at the filing status in B6. If B6 contains 1, the formula uses Table 1 (SINGLE) to calculate the answer. If the number isn't 1, it goes to the nested If formula. If B6 contains 2, it uses Table 2 (MARRIED) to calculate the answer. If B6 contains neither 1 nor 2, the formula uses Table 3 (HEAD) to calculate the answer.

You can nest a series of If formulas in the same way to calculate more possibilities. Nesting truly unleashes the power of If formulas. At your pleasure, enter Table 3 and the nested If formula. You'll find yourself doing things you never dreamed were possible.

Hiding and Unhiding Columns

A good technique to know in working with a spreadsheet that contains confidential information, such as this one, is how to hide columns. Column C has income information, so it's a good candidate for putting under wraps. Place the cursor on C6 (actually, any cell in column C will do).

- Press Alt and type **TW** (Format/Width). Works shows that column C is currently 14 characters wide.
- Type **0** (for zero width) and press Enter.

Works keeps hidden columns hidden when printing a spreadsheet report. So, if you omit row and column labels, anyone looking at the report will never know it's there.

Presto, both column and cursor disappear. The only thing that gives the hidden column away is the absence of the letter C among the column letters. Press Right Arrow to flush the cursor into the open.

Displaying column B again is a two-step process that involves sending the cursor to the hidden column via the Go To command and then widening the column with the Width command.

- Press F5 (the shortcut key that brings up the Go to dialog box).
- Type C1 (or any cell location in column C) and press Enter.

And the cursor disappears again. Because you sent it to C1 and C1 is hidden, the cursor is hidden, too. Now widen column C so you can see both the column and the cursor.

- Press Alt and type **TW** (Format/Width).
- Type 14 (to restore column C to its former width) and press Enter.

And column C reappears.

Defining the Page Layout

This spreadsheet is 70 characters wide, including the 5 characters Works needs for row numbers and a space. It prints in 12-point type on one sheet of 8 1/2-by-11-inch paper. Reducing the standard left and right margins allows the entire spreadsheet to print on one page. Leave the cursor where it is.

- Press Alt and type **PM** (Print/Page Setup & Margins). Here's the Page Setup & Margins dialog box where margin settings are made.
- Hold down Alt and type **E** (to move to Left Margin).
- Type **.7** (the new left margin setting) and press Tab (to move to Right Margin).
- Type **.8** (the new right margin setting) and press Enter.

Printing is close at hand. If you specified more than one printer, press Alt now, type **PS** (Print/Printer Setup), and choose your printer.

Now save the spreadsheet with the margin settings: Leave the cursor where it is. Press Alt and type **FS** (File/Save).

Previewing and Printing the Spreadsheet

Before printing, take a preview peak at how your spreadsheet will look on paper.

- Press Alt and type **PV** (Print/Preview). Works brings up the Preview dialog box and proposes to print one copy. You plan to print directly from the Preview screen, so this is fine.
- Hold down Alt, type **L** (to turn on Print row and column labels), and press Enter.

Works produces a miniature version of the tax lookup spreadsheet on screen. It looks exactly right, so turn on the printer and type **P** to print.

The printer whirs, and here's your spreadsheet looking the same as the completed one in Figure 23-1.

Next, you tackle an investments database, using many of Works' most elegant features.

T W E N T Y - F O U R

Investments Database

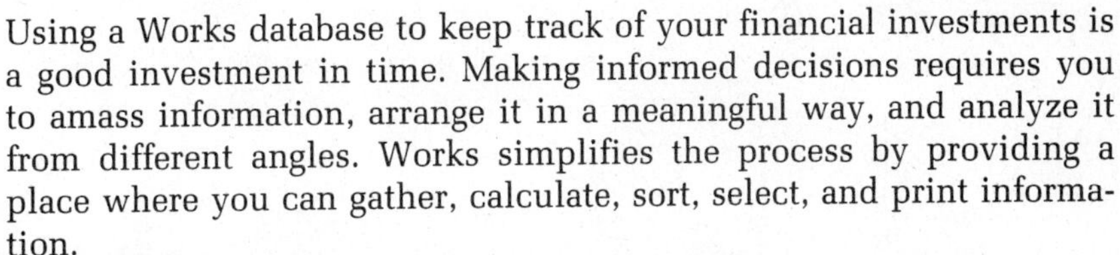

This database is a starting point for others you'll create with your own unique blend of fields, entries, and formulas.

Using a Works database to keep track of your financial investments is a good investment in time. Making informed decisions requires you to amass information, arrange it in a meaningful way, and analyze it from different angles. Works simplifies the process by providing a place where you can gather, calculate, sort, select, and print information.

Keeping track of investments you already own is only a few steps away from keeping track of investments you want to own.

In this session, you design a database for a portfolio of fictional stocks. You create fields, format cells, enter records, enter formulas in both the Form and the List screens, work with dates, and protect and unprotect cells.

You then define the printed report, in the process increasing printing width, changing the font size, entering a title and subtitle, creating a header, entering summary formulas, double-spacing the records, formatting and aligning entries, querying the database, which hides some records, and finally displaying all records. Busy, busy. The reports in Figures 24-1, 24-7, and 24-8 are the fruits of these labors.

Keystrokes and Other Matters

The instructions guide you each step of the way, giving keystrokes and cursor movements relating to each task. Please observe the distinction between pressing and holding down a key.

9/13/90 2:17 PM

MY INVESTMENT PORTFOLIO
All Records

INVESTMENT	EXCH	SHARES	OPRICE	OTOTAL	CPRICE	CTOTAL	$CHANGE	%CHANGE
COMPUTERS UNLIMITED	OTC	1000	2.25	2250.00	4.00	4000.00	1750.00	77.8%
MERLIN FUND	AMEX	200	13.75	2750.00	36.50	7300.00	4550.00	165.5%
SILVER DOLLAR STORES	NYSE	200	23.00	4600.00	18.00	3600.00	-1000.00	-21.7%
ABRACADABRA, INC	OTC	500	12.57	6285.00	9.50	4750.00	-1535.00	-24.4%
ZIP ELECTRONICS	NYSE	100	26.83	2683.00	28.18	2818.00	135.00	5.0%
5				18568.00		22468.00	3900.00	40.4%

Figure 24-1. Report 1: List of all investments showing the status of each and the overall financial picture

- With instructions such as *Press Alt and type TS (Format/Style)*, press and release Alt before you type the letters.
- With *Hold down Alt and type K (to move to Locked)*, press the Alt key and, without releasing Alt, type the letter.

Unless the instructions say otherwise, use the Arrow keys (Left, Right, Up, and Down) to move the cursor. Keep an eye on the coordinates in the middle of the status line to be sure the cursor is at the correct place before you take the next action. If you run into a snag, press the Escape key to cancel what you're doing. Then pick up where you left off.

Creating a New Database

Load Works as described in the Introduction to this book. At the File menu, type **ND** (Create New File/Database), bringing up the database Form screen.

Figure 24-2 shows fourteen fields in a form arranged for eye appeal and easy input. These fields hold the investment name, stock exchange, symbol, number of shares, original price paid for these shares, original total price, current price, current total value, dollar and percent change between the original total price and current total value, commission, purchase date, today's date, and the number of months you've held the stock.

Creating the Fields

Give each field a unique name so Works can distinguish entries in one field from entries in another.

Now let's make your screen look like the one in Figure 24-2. Press the Caps Lock key so you can type field names in uppercase. If you make a typo, press Backspace (not an Arrow key) to back up the cursor and erase.

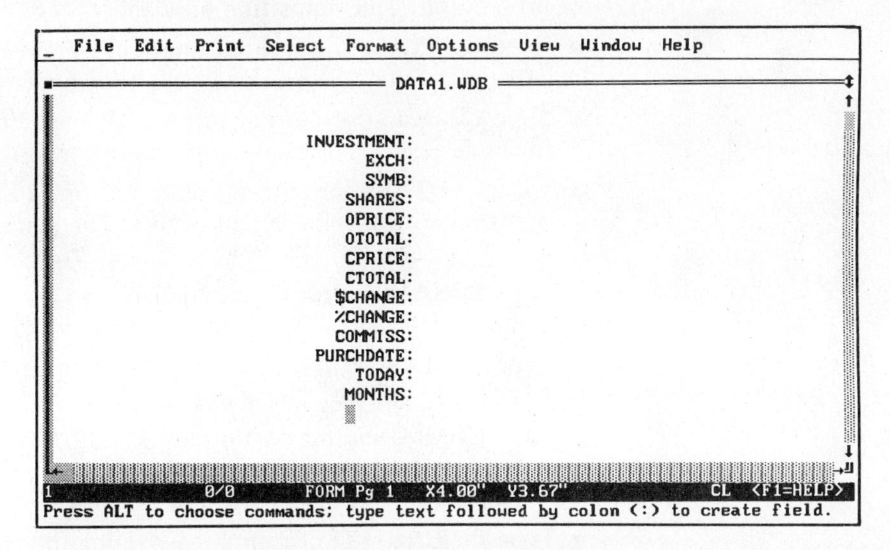

Figure 24-2. The fields in the investments database

The cursor is in the first column in the first row (coordinates X1.30" Y1.00").

- Press Down Arrow twice to move the cursor to X1.30" Y1.33".
- Press Right Arrow 23 times to move the cursor to X3.60" Y1.33".
- Type **INVESTMENT:** (be sure to type a colon after each field name) and press Enter. Works now brings up the Field Size dialog box proposing 20 characters.
- Type **22** (the length of a typical entry in the Investment field) and press Enter. You now see either a dotted line after the INVESTMENT field name or nothing. Press Right Arrow six times. The status line shows X4.20" Y1.50".
- Type **EXCH:** (for exchange) and press Enter. The width of every field from here on is 10 characters. Type **10** and press Enter. The status line shows X4.20" Y1.67".

If you're working in Text mode, the entry area after the field name stays empty; if you're working in Graphics mode, Works enters a dotted line. You can switch from one screen mode to another in the Options menu's Works Settings command.

- Type **SYMB:** (for symbol) and press Enter. Type **10** and press Enter again. Press Left Arrow twice. The status line shows X4.00" Y1.83".
- Type **SHARES:** and hit Enter. Type **10** and hit Enter again. The status line shows X4.00" Y2.00".
- Type **OPRICE:** (for original price) and press Enter. Type **10** and press Enter. The status line now shows X4.00" Y2.17".
- Type **OTOTAL:** (for original total) and press Enter. Type **10** and press Enter again. The status line shows X4.00" Y2.33".
- Type **CPRICE:** (for current price) and press Enter. Type **10** and hit Enter again. The status line now shows X4.00" Y2.50".
- Type **CTOTAL:** (for current total) and press Enter. Type **10** and press Enter again. Press Left Arrow. The status line now shows X3.90" Y2.67".
- Type **$CHANGE:** (for dollar change) and press Enter. Type **10** and hit Enter again. The status line shows X3.90" Y2.83".
- Type **%CHANGE:** (for percent change) and press Enter. Type **10** and press Enter. The status line shows X3.90" Y3.00".
- Type **COMMISS:** (for commission) and press Enter. Type **10** and press Enter again. Press Left Arrow twice. The status line shows X3.70" Y3.17".
- Type **PURCHDATE:** (for purchase date) and press Enter. Type **10** and press Enter again. Press Right Arrow four times. The status line shows X4.10" Y3.33".
- Type **TODAY:** and press Enter. Type **10** and press Enter. Press Left Arrow. The status line shows X4.00" Y3.50".
- Type **MONTHS:** and press Enter. Type **10** and press Enter. The status line now shows X4.00" Y3.67". Leave the cursor where it is.

This completes the form. Your screen (with or without visible field entry lines) should match the one in Figure 24-2. If all is well, continue to *Working in the Form screen.*

All field names align on the colon. If you need to correct any alignment, place the cursor on the field name and press F3 (the Move shortcut key). The cursor now highlights both the field name and entry area and you can see MOVE on the status line. Use the Right or Left Arrow key to move the cursor to the place where the first letter in the field name should appear. Press Enter and Works shifts the field.

Working in the Form Screen

Figure 24-3 shows the Form screen with entries in the first record. Callouts describe the cell formats:

- The text entries in the exchange and symbol fields, normally left-aligned, are right-aligned to prevent an unsightly jog with the number entries in the cells below.
- The original price, original total, current price, current total, and dollar change fields are formatted to show a Fixed number with two decimal places.
- The percent of change entry is in a Percent format with one decimal place.
- Typing a date in the purchase date field changes the cell format, so nothing further is needed there. Today's date, however, gets the short form of the `Month, day, year` format.
- The months field is formatted to show a Fixed number with one decimal place.

The circled numbers in the figure indicate fields containing formulas.

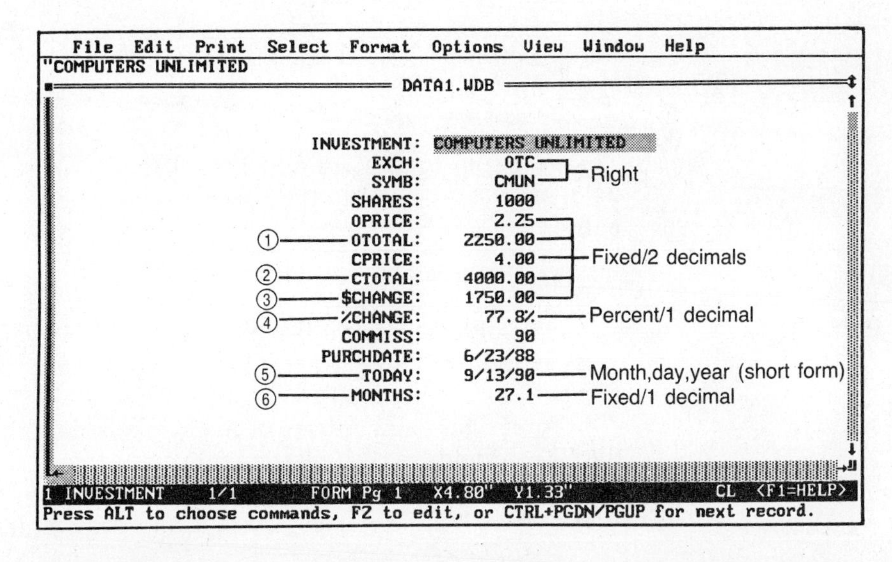

Figure 24-3. Entries in the first record showing text alignments and number formats. Circled numbers show locations of field formulas.

Filling in the First Record

Now enter the text and numbers in the first record, skipping over fields that will soon contain formulas. Use Up Arrow to move the cursor to the INVESTMENT field name (coordinates X3.60" Y1.33"). Press Right Arrow to move the cursor to the INVESTMENT entry area (X4.80" Y1.33").

- Type **COMPUTERS UNLIMITED** and press Down Arrow (to move to EXCH).
- Type **OTC** (for over-the-counter) and press Down Arrow (to move to SYMB).
- Type **CMUN** and press Down Arrow (to move to SHARES).
- Type **1000** and press Down Arrow (to move to OPRICE).
- Type **2.25** and press Down Arrow twice (to move to CPRICE).
- Type **4** and press Down Arrow four times (to move to COMMISS).
- Type **90** and press Down Arrow (to move to PURCHDATE).
- Type **6/23/88** and press Enter.

These are the only fields you need to fill in each record. The formulas will fill the others.

Formatting the Entries

The next step is to align and format the fields to agree with Figure 24-3. Move the cursor to the EXCH field, so you can right-align these entries.

- Press Alt and type **TS** (Format/Style). Works brings up the Style dialog box with your choice of alignment and styles.
- Type **R** (to move to Right) and press Enter.

Now right-align entries in the symbols field. Move the cursor to the SYMB field.

- Press Alt and type **TS**. Type **R** and press Enter.

Move the cursor to the OPRICE field. Format this field to show a fixed number with two decimal places.

- Press Alt and type **TX** (Format/Fixed). Works brings up the `Number of decimals` dialog box proposing two decimal places. This is fine, so press Enter.

Move the cursor to the empty OTOTAL field. On your own and in the same way, format this field to show a fixed number with two decimal places. Repeat the process in the CPRICE, CTOTAL, and $CHANGE fields. The CTOTAL and $CHANGE fields are empty now.

Next, move the cursor to the empty %CHANGE field and give it a Percent format with one decimal place.

- Press Alt and type **TP** (Format/Percent). Works again brings up the `Number of decimals` dialog box. This time you want only one decimal place, so type **1** and press Enter.

Next, move the cursor to the empty TODAY field, which gets the short form of a month/day/year format.

- Press Alt and type **TT** (Format/Time/Date). Type **M** to choose `Month, day, year`. Works now chooses `Short` for you, so press Enter.

And finally, move the cursor to the empty MONTHS field, which gets a Fixed format with 1 decimal place.

- Press Alt and type **TX** (Format/Fixed).
- Type **1** and press Enter.

Saving the Database

You want to be sure nothing happens to your work, so save the database under the filename INVEST. Leave the cursor where it is.

- Press Alt and type **FA** (File/Save As).

Works brings up the `Save file as` dialog box so you can type a filename and, if needed, a drive or directory. If you're saving to the current drive, simply type the filename. Otherwise, type the drive or directory before the filename, for example, A:INVEST.

- Type **INVEST** and press Enter.

Works appends the extension .WDB (for Works Database) and saves the file. The cell indicator at the left end of the status line shows the percentage already processed. When the record number reappears, Works is ready for your next action.

Entering a Formula

When you enter a formula in a field, Works enters that formula in the same field in every record you create from then on.

Formulas use numbers in the database to produce new numbers—for example, multiplying the original price per share by the number of shares produces the total cost of a stock (excluding commissions or other fees). As with virtually everything you've done so far—creating fields, aligning text, and formatting numbers—you can enter formulas in either the Form screen or List screen. While the result is the same, the method is quite different.

In both screens, you can press F5 (the Go To shortcut) and choose field names from the list, but that's time-consuming.

In the Form screen, you need to type every field name in the formula, while in the List screen you can simply move the cursor to the field and Works enters the field name for you. Working in the List screen is clearly easier and more accurate.

To get the flavor of each method, you'll create the first formula in the Form screen and then switch to the List screen to create the rest.

Formula 1: Original Total Price =SHARES*OPRICE

Formula 1 multiplies the number of shares (SHARES) by the original price (OPRICE) to produce the original total price (OTOTAL). Place the cursor in the OTOTAL field.

- Type =**SHARES*OPRICE**

As you type, Works shows the formula on the entry/edit line and at the cursor's location.

- When you finish typing, press Enter.

Works calculates a result of 2250.00.

Working in the List Screen

Now press F9 so you can view your work from the List screen. The List screen contains the same field names as the Form screen. Here, they lay out horizontally with the entries below. The numbers down the left side are record numbers. Move the cursor to the right and you can see other field names and entries in the first record, Computers Unlimited.

Adjusting the Field Width

Works carries over the field names, text alignments, and number formats from one screen to the other. Cell widths are independent of each other, so you need to widen the column that holds the investment names. Hold down Ctrl and press Home to jump the cursor to the first field in the first record.

- Press Alt and type **TW** (Format/Field Width). In the `Field Width` box, Works shows the number 10, the standard field width in the List screen.
- Type **22** (the new field width in characters) and press Enter.

To get a better-looking screen, reduce the width of the exchange, symbol, and shares fields. Move the cursor to the EXCH field.

- Press F8 (to extend the selection).
- Press Right Arrow twice (to select EXCH, SYMB, and SHARES).
- Press Alt and type **TW** (Format/Field Width). Works again shows the number 10 in the `Field Width` box.
- Type **7** (the new width in characters) and press Enter.

In the same way reduce the width of the following fields:

Field Name	Field Width
OPRICE	8
CPRICE	8
%CHANGE	8
COMMISS	8
MONTHS	7

Entering More Formulas

Now create the rest of the formulas using the quicker method possible in the List screen.

Formula 2: Current Total Value =SHARES*CPRICE

Formula 2 multiplies the number of shares (SHARES) by the current price (CPRICE) to produce the current total value (CTOTAL). Place the cursor in the CTOTAL field in the first record.

Each time you type a character (asterisk, minus sign, and the like), the cursor returns to the formula cell so you can move the cursor to the next field.

- Type an equal sign and move the cursor to the SHARES field now off-screen to the left. You can see `=SHARES` on the entry/edit line.
- Type an asterisk and move the cursor to the CPRICE field.
- You should now see `=SHARES*CPRICE` on the entry/edit line, so press Enter.

Works enters the formula, calculates the answer, and displays `4000.00` in the CTOTAL field. Each time you fill a new record, this formula calculates the current total value based on the number of shares and current price in that record.

Formula 3: Dollar Change =CTOTAL-OTOTAL

Formula 3 subtracts the original total price (OTOTAL) from the current total value (CTOTAL) to show the change in dollars ($CHANGE). Place the cursor in the $CHANGE field.

- Type an equal sign and move the cursor to the CTOTAL field.
- Type a minus sign and move the cursor to the OTOTAL field.

You should now see `=CTOTAL-OTOTAL` on the entry/edit line. Press Enter. The formula result, `1750.00`, appears in the cell.

Formula 4: Percentage of Change ='$CHANGE'/OTOTAL

When a field name combines a value and text (here, $ and CHANGE), Works encloses it in apostrophes.

Formula 4 divides the dollar change ($CHANGE) by the original total price (OTOTAL) to produce the percentage of change (%CHANGE). Place the cursor in the %CHANGE field.

- Type an equal sign and move the cursor to the $CHANGE field.
- Type a slash (division operator) and move the cursor to the OTOTAL field. You should now see `='$CHANGE'/OTOTAL` on the entry/edit line. Press Enter. Works displays `77.8%` in the formula cell.

Formula 5: Today's Date =NOW()

If today's date happens to be 9/13/90, follow the instructions anyway. It's good practice.

Formula 5 uses the NOW function to enter the date you typed at the DOS prompt at startup or the one kept by your computer's clock/calendar. You can get your date to match the one in Figure 24-3 without leaving Works. Leave the cursor in the %CHANGE field.

- Press Alt and type **FF** (File/File Management). Works brings up a list of actions you can take. The one you want is at the bottom.
- Type **S** (to move to `Set Date & Time`) and press Enter. Works now displays the current date and time.
- Type **9/13/90** and press Enter. Press Escape to return to the database.

Works recognizes dates in the slash format (9/13/90) as values, and dates in the hyphen format (9-13-90) as text. If you want to use dates in calculations, give them the slash format.

Now enter Formula 5. Place the cursor in the TODAY field.

- Type =**NOW()** and press Enter. Works looks up the date in the computer calendar and plunks `9/13/90` into the cell. Each time you load the database, Works will match the date to the calendar.

If you change the DOS date with the file already open, Works won't update the date. You don't have to close and reload the file to get the new date. With the cursor in the TODAY field, use the Edit menu's Clear command to clear the cell and Works will replace the old date with the new.

Formula 6: Months Held =(TODAY-PURCHDATE)/30

Formula 6 subtracts the purchase date (PURCHDATE) from today's date (TODAY) and then divides the result by 30 to get the number of months you've held on to the stock (MONTHS). The parentheses around TODAY-PURCHDATE tell Works to calculate this element first before dividing by 30. Place the cursor in the MONTHS field.

- Type an equal sign and an open parenthesis. Move the cursor to the TODAY field.
- Type a minus sign (-) and move the cursor to the PURCHDATE field.
- Type a close parenthesis, a slash, and the number 30.

You should now see `=(TODAY-PURCHDATE)/30` on the entry/edit line. Press Enter and Works displays `27.1` in the cell.

When Works calculates elapsed time, it's actually working with serial numbers representing the dates, not the dates themselves. For example, purchase date 6/23/88 is serial number 32317 and today's date 9/13/90 is 33129. Number 32317 subtracted from 33129 and divided by 30 produces 27.1 in the formatted cell.

Protecting the Formulas

On some computer keyboards, you must turn off the Num Lock key before you can use the Home key in the numbers keypad to move Home (that is, to the first field). Many keyboards have a second Home key that functions independently.

You'll soon fill more records. When you do, you want to avoid typing into any cells containing formulas. The best way to do this is to protect those cells against change. First remove the protection readiness from fields containing entries you'll change regularly. Press Home to move to the first field.

- Press F8 (to extend the selection).
- Move the cursor to the OPRICE field.

Ctrl+Home always gets you to the first field in the first record, no matter if the Num Lock key is on or off.

- Press Alt and type **TS** (Format/Style). In the Style dialog box, Works shows the Locked box neutralized (it contains a dash) because you selected more than one field.
- Hold down Alt and type **K** (to move to Locked). This turns on the lock. You want to turn it off.
- Hold down Alt, type **K** again, and the box is empty. Press Enter.

Move the cursor to the CPRICE field, another field in which you make entries.

- Press Alt and type **TS** (Format/Style). This time the Locked) box is turned on, as you see it when you select only one cell first.
- Hold down Alt, type **K**, and press Enter.

And finally, move the cursor to the COMMISS field, where you also make entries.

- Press F8 (to extend the selection).
- Move the cursor to the PURCHDATE field.
- Press Alt and type **TS** (Format/Style).
- Hold down Alt and type **K** twice (once to turn on the lock, the second time to turn it off). Press Enter.

All entry cells are available to you regardless of whether any other cells are locked or not. Now enable the lock on the other cells. Leave the cursor where it is.

- Press Alt and type **OP** (Options/Protect Data).

Works will now prevent you from overtyping a formula if you stray into any forbidden cells.

Works prevents change to the contents as well as the format of locked cells. Be sure to format any soon-to-be-locked cells before locking them. If you forget, toggle the Options menu's Protect Data command, which unlocks the cells.

Entering More Records

Table 24-1 shows the other records in this database. Press Home to move to the first field, and press Down Arrow to move to the second record.

Referring to the table, enter each piece of information in the second record, typing an entry and pressing Right Arrow to move to the next field. After the first entry in each record, Works will enter the formulas in that record. Continue to other records, filling them in the same way.

After the last entry (3/25/90) in Record 5, press Enter. When you finish, your screens should look like the ones in Figure 24-4.

Table 24-1. Records in the investments database

Field Name	Record 2	Record 3
INVESTMENT	MERLIN FUND	SILVER DOLLAR STORES
EXCH	AMEX	NYSE
SYMB	MMF	SILV
SHARES	200	200
OPRICE	13.75	23
OTOTAL	(formula)	(formula)
CPRICE	36.5	18
CTOTAL	(formula)	(formula)
$CHANGE	(formula)	(formula)
%CHANGE	(formula)	(formula)
COMMISS	83	138
PURCHDATE	2/28/87	6/21/89
TODAY	(formula)	(formula)
MONTHS	(formula)	(formula)
Field Name	**Record 4**	**Record 5**
INVESTMENT	ABRACADABRA, INC.	ZIP ELECTRONICS
EXCH	OTC	NYSE
SYMB	ABRA	ZIPE
SHARES	500	100
OPRICE	12.57	26.83
OTOTAL	(formula)	(formula)
CPRICE	9.5	28.18
CTOTAL	(formula)	(formula)
$CHANGE	(formula)	(formula)

Field Name	Record 4	Record 5
%CHANGE	(formula)	(formula)
COMMISS	189	80
PURCHDATE	5/23/88	3/25/90
TODAY	(formula)	(formula)
MONTHS	(formula)	(formula)

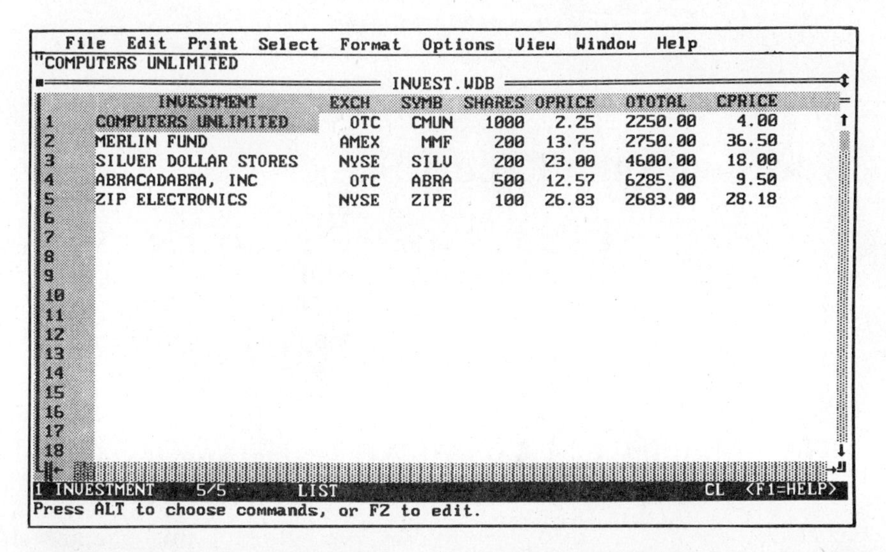

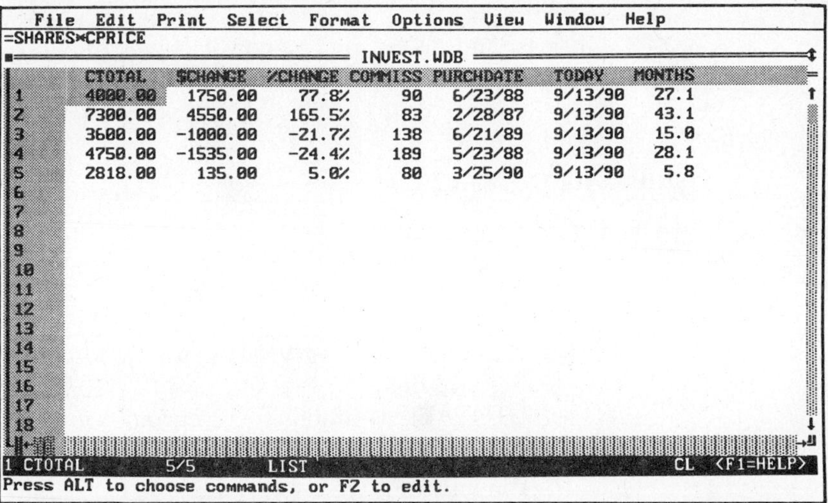

Figure 24-4. The List screens showing all records in the investments database

Saving the Database

Now save the database again with all the formulas and filled records. Leave the cursor where it is.

- Press Alt and type **FS** (File/Save).

When the record number reappears in the left of the status line, Works is ready for your next action.

Working in the Report Screen

You can use records in a database to print a variety of reports that present information in different ways or present different information. The starting point is a report definition that defines what each row contains—for example, headings, records, or formulas.

Report 1: A List of All Investments

Figure 24-1 at the beginning of this chapter shows one of these reports. It lists the exchanges, number of shares, original and current prices, and dollar and percent changes of every stock.

Speed Reporting

You can get a head start by having Works speed-report a report definition. Leave the cursor where it is.

- Press Alt and type **VN** (View/New Report). Works displays the first six fields in the database (INVESTMENT through OTOTAL), as much as the current view/print width allows.
- Press Escape. Works now drops you into the Report screen shown in Figure 24-5.

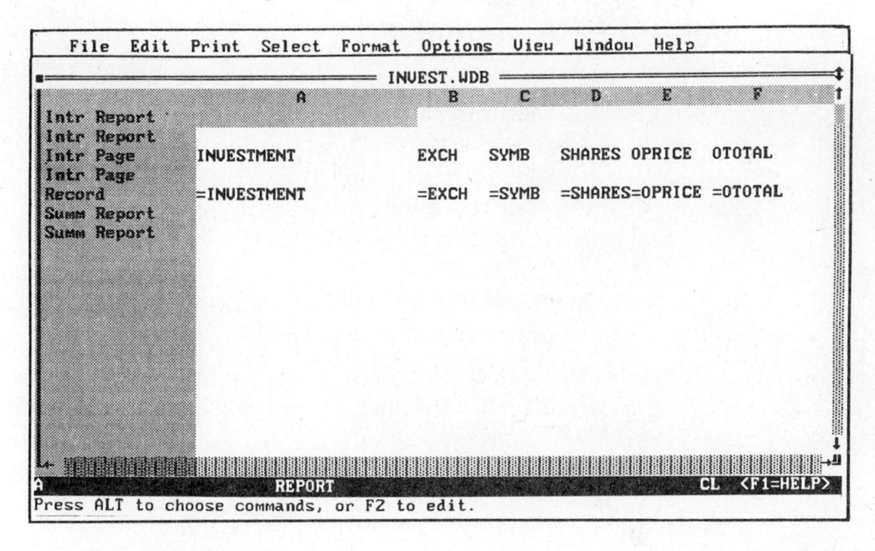

Figure 24-5. The first six columns in the report definition produced with speed reporting

The screen shows the first six field names and field name formulas, each preceded by an equal sign, representing entries in the records. Spend a few moments moving the cursor around the screen to see what Works hath wrought. Here's more about what this speed-reported definition contains:

- The same column widths, field names, and field formats as the List screen.
- Two Intr Report descriptors that leave empty lines at the beginning of the report. You can enter a title and subtitle here.
- Two Intr Page descriptors that print field names at the top of each page with an empty row below them.
- One Record descriptor that prints the entries in each record starting below the empty Intr Page row.
- Two Summ Report descriptors that leave empty lines for statistical summaries at the end of the report. You can print totals, averages, or counts here. Not bad. Not bad at all.

Deleting Unwanted Fields

You want only nine of the fourteen fields included in this report (as shown in Figure 24-1), so delete the others (SYMB, COMMISS, PURCHDATE, TODAY, and MONTHS). These deletions affect this report only—not the database and not any other report. Place the cursor in column C—the SYMB field.

- Press Alt and type **ED** (Edit/Delete Row/Column). Works presents a choice of `Row` or `Column`.
- Type **C** (to choose `Column`) and press Enter. Works zaps the SYMB field and closes the gap.

Press Right Arrow seven times to move the cursor to the COMMISS field.

- Press F8 (to extend the selection).
- Move the cursor to column M (to select COMMISS through MONTHS).
- Press Alt and type **ED** (Edit/Delete).
- Type **C** and press Enter.

This leaves the nine fields you want to print in this report.

Previewing the Report

Before continuing with this definition, preview the report on screen. Leave the cursor where it is.

- Press Alt and type **PV** (Print/Preview). Works brings up the `Number of copies` dialog box proposing one copy. This is fine, so press Enter. And here are the first five fields in the database in a teeny version of the report. There's work to be done.
- Press Escape (to cancel). You're back in the Report screen.

Increasing the Viewing Width

Reducing the size of the standard print margins lets you see and print more of the report. Leave the cursor where it is.

- Press Alt and type **PM** (Print/Page Setup & Margins).
- Hold down Alt and type **E** (to move to `Left margin`).
- Type **0** (for zero inches).
- Press Tab (to move to `Right margin`).
- Type **0** (for zero inches) and press Enter.

Now preview the report again.

- Press Alt, type **PV**, and press Enter. This time, Works displays the first seven fields in the database. That's more like it but not quite enough.
- Press Page Down (to see the rest of the report).
- Press Escape (to return to the Report screen).

Changing the Font Size

The fact that the report prints on two pages with only two fields on the second page is a good indicator that reducing the font size can fit everything on one page.

The standard font size is 12-point Courier. Your choice of fonts depends on the capabilities of your printer. In this example, choose a 10-point Courier font or something comparable. If you don't have Courier or a comparable font, simply skip this step and let the report print in the standard font with two columns on a second page. It's no big deal. Leave the cursor where it is.

- Press Alt and type **TF** (Format/Font). Works brings up the `Font` dialog box with font names on the left and font sizes on the right.
- If this is Courier, press Tab to move to the `Sizes` box. Otherwise, type **C** as many times as needed to move the blinker to Courier, then press Tab.
- Move the cursor to 10 and press Enter.

Now preview the report again.

- Press Alt, type **PV**, and press Enter. I think we've got it!
- Press Escape (to return to the Report screen).

Creating a Header

A header containing the date and time can show the currency of the report. Leave the cursor where it is.

- Press Alt and type **PH** (Print/Headers & Footers). The blinker is in the `Header` field.
- Type **&R&D &T** and press Enter. You've just told Works to print and right-align the current date and time. Preview the report again.
- Press Alt, type **PV**, and press Enter. The report is so small that it may be a bit difficult to see the header clearly. Patience. You'll see it in print soon enough. For now, press Escape.

Entering a Report Title, Subtitle, and Line

You're in the Report screen again. Up to now you've done a good deal of behind-the-scenes work on the definition for the report in Figure 24-1. Figure 24-6 shows its visible side.

To identify the subject of this report, move the cursor to column C (SHARES) in the top `Intr Report` row and enter a title.

- Press Spacebar three times (to indent) and type **MY INVESTMENT PORTFOLIO** and press Enter.

Now move the cursor to column D (OPRICE), one row below the title, so you can enter a subtitle.

- Press Spacebar twice (to center the subtitle under the title).
- Type **All Records** and press Enter.

Now move the cursor to column A (INVESTMENT) in the second `Intr Page` row, so you can enter a long line.

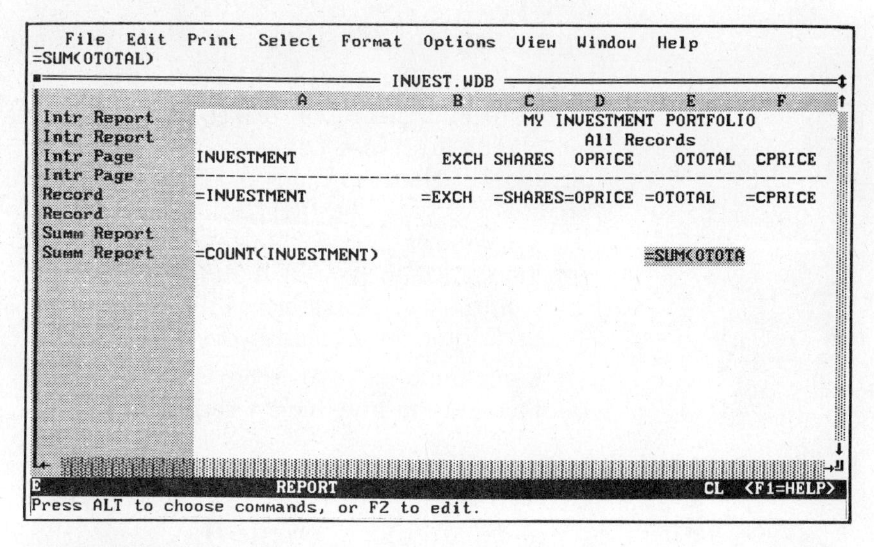

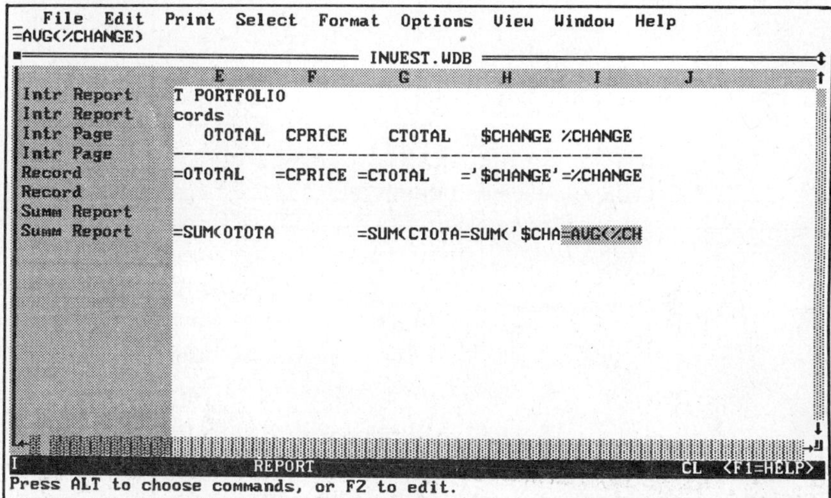

Figure 24-6. The report definition that produces the report in Figure 24-1

Quotation marks tell Works the next character is text, even though it looks, smells, and feels like a value.

- Type quotation marks, then hold down the minus sign key until the sign reaches the end of the entry/edit line. Without pressing Enter (only an extra keystroke), move the cursor to column I (%CHANGE). Type quotation marks again, type 8 minus signs, and press Enter.

Double-Spacing the Report

If you want to triple-space a report, enter two Record *row descriptors.*

Double-spacing this report makes it more readable and pleasing to the eye. All you do is insert another Record row descriptor below the existing one. Hit Home to move the cursor to column A (INVESTMENT). Place the cursor in the first Summ Report row.

- Press Alt and type **EI** (Edit/Insert Row/Column). Press Enter to confirm Row. Works brings up the Type list showing row descriptors available to you.
- Move the blinker to Record and press Enter. In the section at the left, you now have a second Record row descriptor.

Entering the Summary Formulas

Adding summary statistics makes this report more valuable. Five formulas can do the trick: One to count the number of records, three others to produce totals (original dollar amount, current dollar value, and difference between the two), and a fifth to calculate the average change in percentage. (You can see them in Figure 24-6.) Move the cursor to column A (INVESTMENT) in the second Summ Report row.

- Press Alt and type **ES** (Edit/Insert Field Summary). Works brings up the Insert Field Summary dialog box with a list of fields and statistics. The blinker is at INVESTMENT.
- Press Down Arrow (to choose INVESTMENT).
- Press Tab (to move to the Statistic list).
- Type **C** (to move to COUNT) and press Enter. You can now see =COUNT(INVESTMENT) in the cell.

Now move the cursor to column E (OTOTAL) in the second Summ Report row.

- Press Alt and type **ES** (Edit/Insert Field Summary).
- Type **O** twice (to choose OTOTAL). SUM is already selected in the Statistic box.
- Press Enter. You now see =SUM(OTOTA in the cell. The formula is longer than the cell width can display completely, so Works truncates it.

Next, move the cursor to column G (CTOTAL) in the second Summ Report row.

- Press Alt and type **ES**.
- Type **C** twice (to choose CTOTAL) and press Enter. =SUM(CTOTA appears in the cell.

Next, move the cursor to column H ($CHANGE) in the second Summ Report row.

- Press Alt and type **ES**.
- Move the blinker to $CHANGE and press Enter. Works displays =SUM('$CHA in the cell.

And finally, move the cursor to column I (%CHANGE) in the second Summ Report row.

- Press Alt and type **ES**.
- Move the blinker to %CHANGE.
- Press Tab (to jump into the Statistic box).
- Type **A** (to move to AVG) and press Enter. Works displays =AVG(%CH in the cell.

Your report definition should now look like the one in Figure 24-6. Now preview the report again.

- Press Alt, type **PV**, and press Enter. Yep. Looking good. Press Escape.

Formatting the Formula and Other Cells

Arranging records alphabetically, numerically, or chronologically also adds to the completeness of a report.

The quality that separates a so-so report from a polished piece is attention to detail, such as format and alignment. To match the format in entries above them, give the three totals formulas a Fixed format with two decimal places. Move the cursor to column E in the Summ Report row (atop =SUM(OTOTA).

- Press F8 (to extend the selection).
- Move the cursor to column H (to select the other two SUM formulas). It doesn't matter that the empty cell is in the group.

- Press Alt and type **TX** (Format/Fixed). Works proposes two decimal places, exactly what you want.
- Press Enter.

Now give the average formula a Percent format. Move the cursor to column I in the `Summ Report` row (atop `=AVG(%CH)`).

- Press Alt and type **TP** (Format/Percent). Works proposes two decimal places. You want only one.
- Type **1** and press Enter.

Next, left justify the counting formula to keep the count from appearing in limbo at the right edge of the cell. Press Home to move the cursor to column A in the `Summ Report` row (atop `=COUNT INVESTMENT`).

- Press Alt and type **TS** (Format/Style). Works brings up the `Alignment` box.
- Type **L** (to move to `Left`) and press Enter.

And finally, right-justify the field names to get a better alignment with the entries below them. Move the cursor to column B atop `EXCH` in the first `Intr Page` row.

- Press F8 (to extend the selection).
- Press End (to select all field names to column I).
- Press Alt and type **TS** (Format/Style). Here's the `Alignment` box again.
- Type **R** (to move to `Right`) and press Enter.

Leave the cursor where it is and preview the report with all these changes.

- Press Alt, type **PV**, and press Enter. Things are surely shaping up nicely. Press Escape to return to the Report screen.

Redoing the Margins and Page Orientation

Zero margins print the report too far to the left. Increasing the left margin produces a better balance on the printed page. Leave the cursor where it is.

- Press Alt and type **PM** (Print/Page Setup & Margins).
- Hold down Alt and type **E** (to move to `Left margin`).
- Type **.5** (for one-half inch) and press Enter.

Now preview the report one more time.

- Press Alt, type **PV**, and press Enter. This one looks like a go!

Printing Report 1

The report definition is complete in every respect and it's time to print, so turn on the printer. You can print directly from the Preview screen.

- Type **P**.

And here's the list of investments, looking just like the one in Figure 24-1. Now store this report on disk with the database:

- Press Alt and type **FS** (File/Save).

Report 2: Investments Losing Money

Well, it hasn't been a terribly good day on Wall Street. Now that you've updated your records, you want a report of only those stocks currently losing money. To select these stocks, simply query the database.

- Press Alt and type **VQ** (View/Query). Works brings up the Query screen (a reasonable facsimile of the Form screen) with all field names. Move the cursor to the `$CHANGE` field.
- Type **<0** (less than zero, the query criteria) and press Enter.
- Press F10 to apply the query, which returns you to the Report screen.

To see this query in action, preview the report.

- Press Alt, type **PV**, and press Enter.

Works now displays a report showing SILVER DOLLAR STORES and ABRACADABRA, INC., the only records matching the query criterion. (If you think it's difficult to see, you're not alone.)

- Press Escape.

Changing the Subtitle

Before printing this report, change the subtitle to reflect its new contents. Move the cursor to the current subtitle in column D.

- Press Spacebar twice (to center the new subtitle under the title).
- Type **Losers Only** and press Enter.

Print this report as you did Report 1, this time from the Report screen. Be sure your printer is turned on.

- Press Alt and type **PP** (Print/Print). At the `Number of copies` box, press Enter. The printer whirs, producing a report that looks like the one in Figure 24-7.

9/13/90 2:25 PM

MY INVESTMENT PORTFOLIO
Losers Only

INVESTMENT	EXCH	SHARES	OPRICE	OTOTAL	CPRICE	CTOTAL	$CHANGE	%CHANGE
SILVER DOLLAR STORES	NYSE	200	23.00	4600.00	18.00	3600.00	-1000.00	-21.7%
ABRACADABRA, INC	OTC	500	12.57	6285.00	9.50	4750.00	-1535.00	-24.4%
2				10885.00		8350.00	-2535.00	-23.1%

Figure 24-7. Records of losing investments

Report 3: Investments Breaking Even or Making Money

You can get the same result by using the Select menu's Switch Hidden Records command in the List or Form screen. Unfortunately, this command is not available in the Report screen.

Things are not always as dark as they seem. Now you want a report of stocks currently at breakeven or profit. You can query the database again, reversing the criterion.

- Press Alt and type **VQ** (View/Query). Works brings up the Query screen again. Move the cursor to the $CHANGE field.
- Type >=**0** (greater than or equal to zero) and press Enter.
- Press F10 to apply the query, which returns you to the Report screen.

Changing the Subtitle Again

Change the subtitle again to reflect the nature of this report. The cursor is on the subtitle cell in column D.

- Press Spacebar once (to center the new subtitle under the title).
- Type **Winners Only** and press Enter.

Print this report in the same way. Be sure your printer is turned on.

- Press Alt, type **PP**, and press Enter.

Works now spotlights the winners—COMPUTERS UNLIMITED, MERLIN FUND, and ZIP ELECTRONICS. Your report should look like the one in Figure 24-8.

									9/13/90 2:29 PM
			MY INVESTMENT PORTFOLIO						
			Winners Only						
INVESTMENT	EXCH	SHARES	OPRICE	OTOTAL	CPRICE	CTOTAL	$CHANGE	%CHANGE	
COMPUTERS UNLIMITED	OTC	1000	2.25	2250.00	4.00	4000.00	1750.00	77.8%	
MERLIN FUND	AMEX	200	13.75	2750.00	36.50	7300.00	4550.00	165.5%	
ZIP ELECTRONICS	NYSE	100	26.83	2683.00	28.18	2818.00	135.00	5.0%	
3				7683.00		14118.00	6435.00	82.8%	

Figure 24-8. Records of investments at breakeven or profit

Displaying All Records

You can also display all records by returning to the List screen and using the Select menu's Show All Records command.

You can display all records again by deleting the criterion or by closing the file without saving it. For practice, delete the criterion. Leave the cursor where it is.

- Press Alt and type **VQ** (View/Query). Here's the Query screen again. With the cursor on the criterion in the $CHANGE field:
- Press Backspace and hit Enter.

This clears the cell. Press F10 to return to the Report screen. Press F10 again to return to the List screen. As you can see, all fields are intact, despite the fact that you deleted many of them in the report definition. And all the records are back again.

You haven't saved the database since you created the first criterion, so the original subtitle of the report (All Records) is intact for another day. You can close the file with no concern.

The employee handbook in the most chapter lets you practice entering, editing, and formatting text.

TWENTY-FIVE

Two Pages in an Employee Handbook

Here's your chance to practice many of the most important techniques of word processing.

A handbook that clearly spells out a company's personnel policies provides one of the best ways to communicate with employees. Some states, in fact, require that employers convey such information in writing to employees. There's no "correct" design or approach. The only requirements are that the information be correct, clearly written, and easy to read.

Figures 25-1 and 25-2 show two handbook pages dealing with vacation and tuition assistance. The page layout is designed to print on letter-size pages that can be reproduced on a copy machine, stapled, and distributed to employees at minimal cost. The vacation sketch is typical of illustrations that pepper this kind of handbook.

In this chapter you enter text, create a two-column table, indent paragraphs, set tab stops, apply boldface and underlining, select font size, create bulleted paragraphs, edit the text, check the spelling, and more. Then, to top it all off, you create a table of contents for the handbook. This is truly a soup-to-nuts session.

Keystrokes and Other Matters

The instructions guide you each step of the way, giving keystrokes and cursor movements that relate to each task. As always, observe the difference between *pressing* the Alt key and *holding down* the Alt key.

ABOUT YOUR BENEFITS

PAID VACATION

As a regular employee, you are eligible for a paid vacation each year. The vacation year begins on July 1st and ends on June 30th. You earn vacation based on length of service. The vacation schedule is:

Length of Service As of June 30	Paid Vacation As of July 1
Less than 1 month	0 days
1 month less than 3 months	1 day
3 months less than 6 months	3 days
6 months less than 9 months	6 days
9 months less than 1 year	9 days
1 year less than 5 years	10 days
5 years less than 10 years	15 days
10 years or more	20 days

For example, Karen E. starts work on September 1st and is employed ten full months by June 30th of the following year. As of July 1st of that year, she's eligible for nine days of paid vacation.

David C. starts work on February 15th and is employed four full months by June 30th of the same year. As of July 1st of that year, he's eligible for three days of paid vacation.

When the next vacation year begins, both employees will be eligible for ten days of paid vacation.

The plant is customarily closed for two weeks during the summer. You are expected to take your vacation during this period. The date of the shutdown will be announced as early as possible.

You'll receive your vacation pay on the last workday before the shutdown. Your paycheck will include only those days for which you're eligible to be paid. Vacation pay is based on the number of hours in your regular workday, to a maximum of eight hours.

- 12 -

Figure 25-1. One page in an employee handbook

Employees eligible for more than two weeks of vacation may request that it be scheduled at any time during the year. Each request is considered in light of production requirements. Please notify the Payroll Department at least two weeks in advance if you want your paycheck before leaving.

There is no carry-over of vacation from year to year, and borrowing against future vacation is not permitted.

Tuition Assistance

Expanding your educational background can make you more proficient in your work and prepare you for greater responsibility with our company. We will reimburse 75% of tuition costs - including registration fees, course costs, laboratory fees, and required textbooks - to a maximum of $2,500 per year if you meet the following qualifications:

o You are a regular full-time employee with at least one year of continuous service.

o You have a satisfactory work and attendance record.

o You are studying at an accredited institution.

o You complete the course with a satisfactory grade (C or better, or pass if Pass/Fail).

o You are on the active payroll when reimbursement is due.

- 13 -

Figure 25-2. The next page in an employee handbook

- When you see such instructions as *Press Alt and type FA (File/Save As)*, press and release Alt before you type the letters.
- With instructions such as *Hold down Alt and type S (to choose Suggest)*, press the Alt key and, without releasing Alt, type the letter.

Unless the instructions say otherwise, use the Arrow keys (Left, Right, Up, and Down) to move the cursor. If you run into a snag, press the Escape key to cancel what you're doing. Then pick up where you left off.

Creating a New Document

Load Works as described in the Introduction to this book. At the File menu, type **NW** (Create New File/New Word Processor). Works brings up a new word processor screen with the standard filename WORD1.WPS. The cursor blinking in the top left corner shows where your first typed character will appear.

If you turned off the screen characters (paragraph marks, tab marks, and others), you can turn them on again by pressing Alt and typing **OA** *(Options/Show All Characters).*

Figures 25-3 and 25-4 show the text before formatting. With wordwrap, a word that won't fit at the end of a line moves down by itself to the beginning of the next line. You need only press Enter to end a paragraph or to insert a blank line between paragraphs. These places are indicated by a paragraph mark (¶).

The right arrow between columns in the vacation schedule and after the bullet in the bulleted paragraphs are tab marks. They show where to press the Tab key. Don't be concerned about those jagged columns. When you format the page, things will assume their rightful form. The down arrows at the end of each line in the table are end-of-line marks. They make the table a solid unit. The tiny dots between words show where to press the Spacebar.

Entering the Text

Now let's make your screen look like the one in Figure 25-3. For those who never make mistakes, the text contains three misspelled words: vacaton in the first paragraph, requirments in the second from last paragraph, and carryover (which should be hyphenated) in the last paragraph. Please type them that way. If you mistype anything else, use Backspace (not an arrow key) to back up the cursor and erase.

```
» ABOUT·YOUR·BENEFITS¶
  ¶
  ¶
  PAID·VACATION¶
  ¶
  As·a·regular·employee,·you·are·eligible·for·a·paid·vacaton·
  each·year.·The·vacation·year·begins·on·July·1st·and·ends·on·
  June·30th.·You·earn·vacation·based·on·length·of·service.·The·
  vacation·schedule·is:¶
  ¶
  Length·of·Service→  Paid·Vacation↓
  ··As·of·June·30→     ·As·of·July·1↓
  ↓
  Less·than·1·month→  0·days↓
  1·month·less·than·3·months→    1·day↓
  3·months·less·than·6·months→  3·days↓
  6·months·less·than·9·months→  6·days↓
  9·months·less·than·1·year→     9·days↓
  1·year·less·than·5·years→10·days↓
  5·years·less·than·10·years→    15·days↓
  10·years·or·more→    25·days¶
  ¶
  For·example,·Karen·E.·starts·work·on·September·1st·and·is·
  employed·10·full·months·by·June·30th·of·the·following·year.·
  As·of·July·1st·of·that·year,·she's·eligible·for·nine·days·of·
  paid·vacation.·David·C.·starts·work·on·February·15th·and·is·
  employed·4·full·months·by·June·30th·of·the·same·year.·As·of·
  July·1st·of·that·year,·he's·eligible·for·three·days·of·paid·
  vacation.·When·the·next·vacation·year·begins,·they'll·both·
  be·eligible·for·ten·days·of·paid·vacation.¶
  ¶
  The·plant·is·customarily·closed·for·two·weeks·during·the·
  summer.·The·date·of·the·shutdown·will·be·announced·as·early·
  as·possible.¶
  ¶
  Vacation·pay·is·based·on·the·number·of·hours·in·your·regular·
  workday,·to·a·maximum·of·eight·hours.·You'll·receive·your·
  vacation·pay·on·the·last·workday·before·the·shutdown.·Your·
  paycheck·will·include·only·those·days·for·which·you're·
  eligible·to·be·paid.¶
  ¶
  If·you're·eligible·for·more·than·two·weeks·vacation,·you·can·
  request·that·it·be·scheduled·at·any·time·during·the·vacation·
  year.·We·will·consider·each·request·in·light·of·production·
  requirments.·You·must·notify·the·Payroll·Department·at·least·
  two·weeks·in·advance·if·you'd·like·your·vacation·pay·before·
  leaving·on·vacation.¶
  ¶
  There·is·no·carryover·of·vacation·from·year·to·year,·and·
  borrowing·against·future·vacation·is·not·permitted.¶
  ¶
  ¶
  ¶
  ◆
```

Figure 25-3. The text in the employee handbook before formatting

```
» TUITION·ASSISTANCE¶
¶
Expanding·your·educational·background·can·make·you·more·
proficient·in·your·work·and·prepare·you·for·greater·
responsibility·with·our·company.·We·will·reimburse·75%·of·
tuition·costs·--·including·registration·fees,·course·costs,·
laboratory·fees,·and·required·textbooks·--·to·a·maximum·of·
$2,500·per·year·if·you·meet·the·following·requirements:¶
¶
o→    You·are·a·regular·full-time·employee·with·at·least·one·
year·of·continuous·service.¶
¶
o→    You·have·a·satisfactory·work·and·attendance·record.¶
¶
o→    You·are·studying·at·an·accredited·institution.¶
¶
o→    You·complete·the·course·with·a·satisfactory·grade·(C·or·
better,·or·Pass·if·Pass/Fail).¶
¶
o→    You·are·on·the·active·payroll·when·reimbursement·is·
due.¶
◆
```

Figure 25-4. The rest of the text before formatting

So that everyone's at the same place, press the Spacebar only once between sentences. Now enter the text.

- Type **ABOUT YOUR BENEFITS** and press Enter three times to end the paragraph and insert two blank lines. Works enters a dot between words where you press the Spacebar.
- Type **PAID VACATION** and press Enter twice to end the paragraph and insert a blank line.
- Referring to Figure 25-3, type the entire paragraph that starts with **As a regular employee, you are eligible for a paid vacaton...** (remember to misspell *vacaton*). After you finish, press Enter twice to end the paragraph and insert a blank line.

Entering the Table

Keeping as many lines together in a table as possible makes it easier to format the table later on.

Now for the table. It doesn't matter if you set indents and tab stops before or after entering the text. For now, concentrate on entering text. At the end of certain lines, you'll press Shift+Enter instead of pressing Enter alone. This tells Works to treat these lines as a unit instead of individually.

- Type **Length of Service** and press Tab. Type **Paid Vacation** and press Shift+Enter.

- Press the Spacebar twice (to indent the next words a bit). Type **As of June 30** and press Tab. Press the Spacebar once (again, to indent). Type **As of July 1** and press Enter twice to end the paragraph and insert a blank line.
- Type **Less than 1 month** and press Tab. Type **0 days** and press Shift+Enter.
- Type **1 month less than 3 months** and press Tab. Type **1 day** and press Shift+Enter.
- Type **3 months less than 6 months** and press Tab. Type **3 days** and press Shift+Enter.

Using Figure 25-3 as a guide, continue entering the rest of the table. Be sure to press Shift+Enter to insert a down arrow at the end of a line and Enter alone for a paragraph mark. After you type **25 days** in the last line, press Enter twice.

Entering More Text

You are now ready to enter more text.

- Type the entire paragraph starting with **For example, Karen E. starts work on September 1st....** As you type, Works shifts the text up to make room for more text. When you finish the paragraph, press Enter twice.
- Type the entire paragraph starting with **The plant is customarily closed for two weeks....** After you finish, press Enter twice.
- Type the entire paragraph starting with **Vacation pay is based on the number of hours....** After you finish, press Enter twice.
- Type the entire paragraph starting with **If you're eligible for more than two weeks vacation....** Remember to misspell **requirments**. Again, Works shifts the text up. After you finish, press Enter twice.
- Type the entire paragraph starting with **There is no carryover of vacation from year to year,....** Be sure to type **carryover** as one word. After you finish, press Enter four times. Works again shifts the text up.

This completes the text covering paid vacations. Figure 25-4 contains the tuition assistance text and includes bulleted paragraphs.

- Type **TUITION ASSISTANCE** and press Enter twice to end the paragraph and insert a blank line.
- Referring to Figure 25-4, type the entire paragraph starting with **Expanding your educational background can make you...** After you finish, press Enter twice to end the paragraph and insert a blank line.

Entering the Bulleted Paragraphs

Next, enter the bulleted paragraphs:

- Type a bullet (a lowercase "o") and press Tab. Type **You are a regular full-time employee with at least one year of continuous service.** and press Enter twice.
- Type a bullet and press Tab. Type **You have a satisfactory work and attendance record.** and press Enter twice.
- Type a bullet and press Tab. Type **You are studying at an accredited institution.** and press Enter twice.
- Type a bullet and press Tab. Type **You complete the course with a satisfactory grade (C or better, or Pass if Pass/Fail.** and press Enter twice.
- Type a bullet and press Tab. Type **You are on the active payroll when reimbursement is due.** and leave the cursor where it is.

You've entered the text for both pages in the handbook. Scan the screen to be sure everything is as it should be. You should see right angle brackets (») showing the start of a new page one line below `Tuition Assistance`. Check also to be sure you have only one dot—that is, one space—between words.

Saving the Document

Now save the document and give it the filename HANDBK. Leave the cursor where it is.

- Press Alt and type **FA** (File/Save As).

Works brings up the dialog box where you can type a filename and, if needed, a drive or directory. If you're saving to the current drive, simply type the filename. Otherwise, type the drive or directory before the filename, for example, A:HANDBK.

■ Type **HANDBK** and press Enter. Works assigns the extension .WPS (for Word Processor).

As the file is saved, the indicator in the left side of the status line shows the percentage already processed. When the page number reappears, Works is ready for your next action.

Previewing the Document in its Raw Form

Seeing how things look before formatting can be an eye-opening experience. Works lets you view the page layout at any time, so leave the cursor where it is.

■ Press Alt and type **PV** (Print/Preview). The settings in the dialog box are fine, so press Enter.

Works displays the tuition assistance text. Press Page Up to see the previous page. Looking good so far, but there's still work to be done. Press Escape to return to the document.

Editing the Document

Figure 25-5 shows places where you need to insert, delete, shift, and replace text—also known as editing. To get around the screen, use the Home and End keys to move the cursor to the beginning or end of a line, and the Arrow keys (Left, Right, Up, and Down) to move from character to character and line to line. Hold down the Arrow key to move the cursor rapidly.

Inserting and Deleting

That number of vacation days after ten years is a bit generous—clearly a typographical error. Place the cursor under the number 5 in the last line of the table. Type **0** and press Delete to delete 5.

In the paragraph following the table, place the cursor under the number 1 in 10. Type **ten** and press Delete twice to delete 10.

Splitting a Paragraph, Inserting, and Deleting

In the same paragraph, place the cursor under the dot in the space before David. This long paragraph will be easier to read split into several paragraphs. Press Enter twice to create a new paragraph and a blank line. Press Delete to delete the space before David.

In the new paragraph, place the cursor under the number 4 following the word employed. Type **four** and press Delete to delete 4.

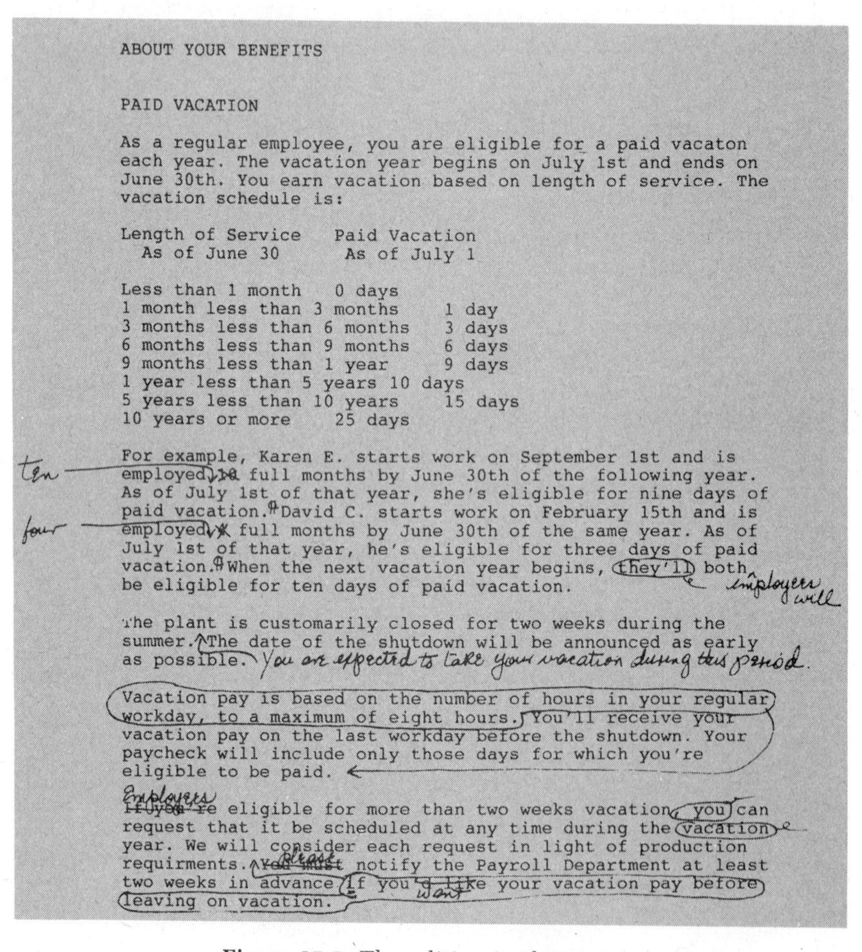

ABOUT YOUR BENEFITS

PAID VACATION

As a regular employee, you are eligible for a paid vacaton each year. The vacation year begins on July 1st and ends on June 30th. You earn vacation based on length of service. The vacation schedule is:

Length of Service As of June 30	Paid Vacation As of July 1
Less than 1 month	0 days
1 month less than 3 months	1 day
3 months less than 6 months	3 days
6 months less than 9 months	6 days
9 months less than 1 year	9 days
1 year less than 5 years	10 days
5 years less than 10 years	15 days
10 years or more	25 days

For example, Karen E. starts work on September 1st and is employed 10 full months by June 30th of the following year. As of July 1st of that year, she's eligible for nine days of paid vacation. David C. starts work on February 15th and is employed 4 full months by June 30th of the same year. As of July 1st of that year, he's eligible for three days of paid vacation. When the next vacation year begins, they'll both be eligible for ten days of paid vacation.

The plant is customarily closed for two weeks during the summer. The date of the shutdown will be announced as early as possible.

Vacation pay is based on the number of hours in your regular workday, to a maximum of eight hours. You'll receive your vacation pay on the last workday before the shutdown. Your paycheck will include only those days for which you're eligible to be paid.

If you're eligible for more than two weeks vacation, you can request that it be scheduled at any time during the vacation year. We will consider each request in light of production requirments. You must notify the Payroll Department at least two weeks in advance if you'd like your vacation pay before leaving on vacation.

Figure 25-5. The editing in the text

In the same paragraph, place the cursor under the dot after the period following vacation. Press Enter twice to create a new paragraph starting with When. Press Delete to delete the space before When.

In the new paragraph, move the cursor to the t in they'll. Press Delete 8 times to delete they'll. Move the cursor to the b in be. Type **employees will** and press the Spacebar.

More Inserting

In the next paragraph (The plant is customarily closed...), place the cursor under the period after summer. Type **You are expected to take your vacation during this period.** and press the Spacebar.

Moving and Patching

Move the cursor to the first sentence in the next paragraph (Vacation pay...). Press F8 three times to select the first sentence. Now press F3 (the Move shortcut key). Press Down Arrow three times to move the cursor under the paragraph mark. Press Enter. Works now plops the sentence into the place before the paragraph mark. Press Spacebar to insert a space before Vacation. To tidy up the move, move the cursor to the space before the paragraph mark and press Delete to delete the space.

More Inserting and Deleting

In the next paragraph, place the cursor on the I in If and press Delete nine times to delete If you're. Type **Employees** and move the cursor to the comma after vacation in that sentence. Press Delete five times to delete the comma and you.

At the end of that same sentence, place the cursor under the v in vacation. Press F8 twice to select vacation, and then press Delete to delete it.

Moving Part of a Sentence

In the last sentence in the same paragraph, place the cursor under i in if and press F8 to extend the selection. Press End to select the text to the end of the line, Down Arrow to select the text to the end of the sentence, and then Left Arrow to unselect the paragraph mark. Press F3 to enter the Move mode. Move the cursor to the Y in You at the beginning of the sentence and press Enter.

Patching and Editing

Now patch and edit the sentence. (You can see the result in Figure 25-2.) The cursor is under the i in if. Type I and press Delete. Move the cursor to the apostrophe in You'd. Press Delete seven times, and then press the Spacebar and type **want**.

Move the cursor to the period after vacation in that sentence. Type a comma, press the Spacebar, and press Delete nine times. Type **Please** and move the cursor one line down to the space before the paragraph mark. Type a period and press Delete to delete the space. You now have a seamless sentence.

You've completed the editing. Compare your text with Figures 25-1 and 25-2 to be sure everything reads the same.

Checking the Spelling

Works checks the spelling from the cursor's location to the end of the document. If you start anywhere but at the beginning, Works reaches the end of the document and offers to check from the beginning to the point it started.

This is a good time to check the spelling. You want Works to check the entire document, so hold down Ctrl and press Home to jump the cursor to the first character.

- Press Alt and type **OS** (Options/Check Spelling). Works instantly finds vacaton. Now see what it can do to correct it.
- Hold down Alt and type **S** (to choose Suggest). Works proposes three words in the Suggestions box. It likes vacation best, so it puts it into reverse video and shows it in the Replace with field. Perfect. Press Enter to accept the suggestion. If you look quickly you can see the correction in the text.
- Works now comes up with Karen, a proper name. You want to move past the name, not add it to your personal dictionary. Because Works shows the name in the Replace with field, simply press Enter. In essence, you've replaced Karen with Karen.
- It now finds David, so press Enter again.

- Next is `requirments`. Again, have Works suggest a word. Hold down Alt and type **S**. Sure enough, Works is right again. Press Enter to accept the suggestion.
- Now Works stops at `carryover`. Hold down Alt and type **S** to request a suggestion. Works admits that it has `No suggestions.` Press Enter to acknowledge, and Works moves the blinker to the `Replace with` field.
- You look up carryover in your conventional dictionary and see that it's not misspelled but it should be hyphenated.
- Press Right Arrow once, and then press Left Arrow five times (to move the blinker to the `o` in `carryover`).
- Type a hyphen and press Enter (to choose `Change`). Again, you can see the correction in the text.

Works finishes the spelling check with no further pauses. Press Enter to confirm the ending message.

Now store the file on disk by pressing Alt and typing **FS** (File/Save).

Formatting the Document

The next task is to format this unkempt text so it ends up the polished prose shown in Figures 25-1 and 25-2.

Setting the Indents in the Vacation Table

Indents control how far away text starts from the left margin.

The vacation schedule has two indents. One indent shifts the headings and the last line (`10 years or more`) .5 inches from the left margin. The other indent shifts the lines in between .6 inches from the left margin. Different indents are needed to align the single-digit numbers (1, 3, 6, 9, 1, 5) and the headings and double-digit number (10) properly.

Parts of the table are constructed as a unit, which makes it faster to work with those lines. Place the cursor under the `L` in `Length of Service`.

- Press F8 (to extend the selection).
- Press F8 three times (to select the heading lines).
- Press Alt and type **TA** (Format/Indents & Spacing). Works brings up the dialog box with the blinker in the `Left indent` field.

- Type **.5** (the indent in inches) and press Enter. Works instantly shifts the heading lines one-half inch from the left margin and shifts the left bracket in the ruler at the top of the screen.

Now set the second indent one character farther in. Press Down Arrow twice to collapse the selection and place the cursor under the first end-of-line arrow.

- Press F8 (to extend the selection).
- Press F8 twice, and then press Down Arrow twice (to select the lines from `0 days` to `15 days`).
- Press Alt and type **TA** (Format/Indents & Spacing). Because you selected more than one element, Works shows the dialog box with empty fields and dashes in check boxes.
- Type **.6** (the new `Left indent`) and press Enter.

And finally, indent the last line in the table. Press Down Arrow to collapse the selection and place the cursor under the paragraph mark at the end of the last line.

- Press F8 (to extend the selection).
- Press Home (to select the last line).
- Press Alt and type **TA** (Format/Indents & Spacing).
- Type **.5** and press Enter.

The table indents are completed. Press Up Arrow to collapse the selection.

Setting the Tab Stops

Tab stops position text precisely, which is particularly critical with a table.

As you can see in Figure 25-1, the second column in the vacation schedule needs three different tab stops: one for headings, another for single-digit days from 0 to 9, and a third for double-digit days from 10 to 20. Although there's nothing to prevent you from using spaces (that is, pressing the Spacebar lots of times) to accommodate these differences, it's not worth the extra effort.

The tab stops for the right column are set at 4, 4.2, and 4.3 inches. Four inches is a standard setting, so why set it again? Good question. Standard tab stops, which you cannot delete, occur at half-inch intervals. This means that you must Tab several times in each line to get past those intervals. When you set your own tab stops, clever Works ignores standard tab stops to the left of those you set.

First set tab stops for the heading lines. Place the cursor anywhere in the heading lines.

- Press F8 (to extend the selection).
- Press F8 three times (to select the heading lines).
- Press Alt and type **TT** (Format/Tabs). The Tabs dialog box appears.
- Type **4** (the first tab stop) and press Enter.
- Press Escape. Works instantly shifts the headings in the second column to the right. You can see the letter `L` (for `Left` tab) at the 4-inch mark in the ruler.

Press Down Arrow twice, which collapses the selection and moves the cursor under the arrow at the end of the first line in the schedule. Now set the tab stop for the first five lines in the table.

- Press F8 (to extend the selection).
- Press F8 three times (to select lines from `0 days` to `9 days`).
- Press Alt and type **TT** (Format/Tabs).
- Type **4.3** (the next tab stop) and press Enter.
- Press Escape. Works shifts the entries in the column to their proper place under the headings. The ruler now shows `L` at the 4.3-inch mark.

Press Down Arrow to collapse the selection. This lands the cursor under the paragraph mark after `10 days`. Now for the last three lines.

- Press F8 (to extend the selection).
- Press Down Arrow twice (to select the lines from 10 to 20 days). The paragraph mark holds the formats for the 10 day line.
- Press Alt and type **TT** (Format/Tabs).
- Type **4.2** (the last tab stop) and press Enter.
- Press Escape. Works shifts the entries in the column and shows `L` at the 4.2-inch mark in the ruler. Press Down Arrow to collapse the selection.

Nesting the Paragraphs

The nested indent shortcut key, Ctrl+N, indents paragraphs only from the left side.

Nesting the three paragraphs below the table indents them at both sides and sets them off from the rest of the text. Place the cursor in the paragraph that starts with `For example, Karen...`.

- Press F8 (to extend the selection).
- Press F8 three times (to select the first paragraph).
- Press Down Arrow six times (to select the three paragraphs, even though the third is only partially selected).
- Press Alt and type **TA** (Format/Indents & Spacing). The blinker is in the `Left indent` field.
- Type **.3** (the `Left indent`) and press Tab twice (to move to `Right indent`).
- Type **.3** and press Enter. Works reduces the width of the paragraphs. Press Down Arrow to collapse the selection.

Creating a Custom Format for Bulleted Paragraphs

Bulleted paragraphs are hanging paragraphs. The bullet tends to disguise the paragraph's true nature.

Now format the bulleted paragraphs in the tuition reimbursement section. The standard setting (shortcut key Ctrl+H) aligns the bullet and first line of text at the left margin and wraps around all other text in the paragraph to the standard tab stop.

Instead, create a custom format to put the bullet and the first line of text .3 inches from the margin and all other text .6 inches from the margin.

Press the Page Down key enough times to bring all the bulleted paragraphs into view. Place the cursor under the paragraph mark at the end of the first bulleted paragraph.

- Press F8 (to extend the selection).
- Press Down Arrow nine times (to select all bulleted paragraphs).
- Press Alt and type **TA** (Format/Indents & Spacing).
- Type **.6** (the `Left indent`) and press Tab (to move to `1st line indent`).
- Type **-.3** (the `1st line indent`) and press Enter. Works shifts the paragraphs to the right and wraps around the second lines. Press Up Arrow to collapse the selection.

Choosing the Font Style

The handbook text prints in a font called Courier in a 12-point size. Now for a few ifs:

1. If you see COU12 on your status line, your document was created in Courier 12-point. You can skip this step and go on to *Enhancing the Main Title*.
2. If you see something else on the status line—most likely PIC12—your document was created in Pica 12-point. Continue with this step to format for Courier.
3. If 12-point Courier isn't available on your printer, choose something comparable or simply skip this step and let the pages print in the standard font.

Leave the cursor where it is and select the entire document.

- Press Alt and type **SA** (Select/All).
- Press Alt and type **TF** (Format/Font & Style). The dialog box appears.
- Hold down Alt and type **F** (to move into the Fonts box).
- Type **C** (to choose Courier).
- Press Tab (to move into the Sizes box).
- Type **1** enough times to put 12 in reverse video and press Enter. You should now see COU12 on the status line.

Giving the Main Title a Larger Font

A large main title really perks up the text. This handbook uses a 24-point Courier. If this font isn't available on your printer, choose something comparable. Hold down Ctrl and press Home, which collapses the selection and jumps the cursor to the beginning of the document.

- Press F8 three times (to select ABOUT YOUR BENEFITS).
- Press Alt and type **TF** (Format/Font & Style). The dialog box appears.
- Hold down Alt and type **F** (to move into the Fonts box).
- Type **C** (to choose Courier) or type the first letter of another font.

- Press Tab (to move into the `Sizes` box).
- Type **2** enough times to put **24** (or the number of another large size) into reverse video, and press Enter.

Things still look the same on screen. You'll see the large characters on screen when you preview the pages again. Patience.

Boldfacing and Centering the Main Title

Now boldface the title to make it really stand out. Leave the selection as it is.

- Hold down Ctrl and type **B** (the shortcut key for `Bold`).

Works shows the title in high intensity white, color, or in bold, depending on screen mode (`Text` or `Graphics`). In any case, Works displays the letter `B` on the status line.

And finally, center the title.

- Hold down Ctrl and type **C** (the shortcut key for `Center`).

Boldfacing the Other Headings

Other headings can use the boldface treatment. Place the cursor under the paragraph mark at the end of `PAID VACATION`.

- Press F8 three times.
- Press Ctrl and type **B**.

Headings in a table can be underlined too. If that's your plan, create the headings as separate, unlinked lines. This way, you can underline the text only, ignoring the gap between columns.

Next, boldface the headings in the vacation schedule. Place the cursor anywhere in the headings.

- Press F8 four times.
- Press Ctrl and type **B**. Press Escape to collapse the selection.

And finally, boldface the tuition assistance heading. Press Page Down enough times to reach `TUITION ASSISTANCE`. Place the cursor anywhere in that heading.

- Press F8 three times.
- Press Ctrl and type **B**.

Justifying the Text

When you justify text, Works adjusts the spacing between words to produce lines of equal length and a smooth right margin. In this document, you want to justify all of the text except the headings and table. Justification does strange things to tables connected in this fashion. Place the cursor on the paragraph mark immediately below the vacation schedule.

- Press F8 then Ctrl+End (to select from that point to the end of the document).
- Hold down Ctrl and type **J** (the shortcut key for justified). Press Ctrl+Home to reach the beginning of the document.
- Place the cursor in the first paragraph and press Ctrl+J. Spend a few moments browsing around to see the effect of justification.

Making Room for the Illustration

You need to allow room for that perky illustration on the second page. Press Page Down twice, then move the cursor to the paragraph mark after the paragraph starting with `Employees eligible...`.

- Press Enter eleven times.

Works recalculates the page breaks and shows the new page mark (») to the left of the third paragraph mark in the illustration space.

Creating a Footer

Works routinely centers headers and footers. You can change the alignment with special alignment codes.

Now create a footer to print centered page numbers in this form: - 12 - at the bottom of each page. Leave the cursor where it is.

- Press Alt and type **PH** (Print/Headers & Footers). Works brings up the dialog box with the blinker in the `Header` field.
- Press Tab (to move to the `Footer` field).
- Type **- &P -** and press Enter.

Previewing the Document Again

This is the fun part—seeing how all your work lays out on the page. Leave the cursor where it is.

- Press Alt and type **PV** (Print/Preview). Press Enter.

In most respects, a thing of beauty. Press Page Down to see the next page. Now press Escape to return to the document.

Preparing To Print

Margin settings tell Works where to start and stop printing on the page.

Several settings, notably margin sizes and footer sizes, need to be made before you can print the pages.

Setting the Margins

The margins settings balance the text on the printed page. Leave the cursor where it is.

- Press Alt and type **PM** (Print/Page Setup & Margins). Here's the dialog box with the blinker in the `Top margin` field.
- Type **1.3** (the new `Top margin`) and press Tab (to move to `Bottom margin`).
- Type **2** (the new `Bottom margin`) and press Tab (to move to `Left margin`).

- Type **1.4** (the new Left margin) and press Tab (to move to Right margin).
- Type **1.4** (the new Right margin). You need a margin setting for the page number footer, so press Tab twice (to move to Footer margin).
- Type **1.5** (the new Footer margin).

Setting the First Page Number

Now pretend that these pages are somewhere in the middle of the employee handbook, say pages 12 and 13. Tell Works which page number to print in the footer.

- Hold down Alt and type **1** (to move to 1st page number).
- Type **12** and press Enter.

You're back in the document and the new page indicator should now be at the first line of the paragraph starting Employees eligible for more.

Previewing and Printing the Pages

One last preview look and then it's printing time, so turn on the printer.

- Press Alt and type **PV** (Print/Preview). These settings are still fine, so just press Enter. Yeah, that's a winner. Press Page Up or Page Down to see the other page.
- You can print directly from preview, so press P.

The printer whirs, producing justified text and stylish headings. When it stops, your pages should look like those in Figures 25-1 and 25-2 (without the illustration, of course). Press Alt and type **FS** (File/Save) to store the file on disk.

Creating a Contents Page for the Handbook

No handbook is complete without a table of contents. Figure 25-6 shows this kind of page, and Figure 25-7 shows the screen as you work on it. Creating a contents page involves working with techniques you already know from the handbook pages and learning new ones. The following instructions take you step by step through the new stuff and summarize the others.

Assuming you're continuing from the handbook, bring up a new word processor screen.

- Press Alt and type **FN** (File/Create New File).
- Type **W** (to choose `New Word Processor`). And here's a clean screen.

Entering the Text

To get the flavor of the process, start by typing only the first six lines of the contents page. Leave the cursor where it is.

- Type **CONTENTS** and press Enter three times.
- Type **President's Message** and press enter twice.
- Type **OUR POLICIES AND PRACTICES** and pause a moment.

Setting a Tab Stop and Inserting Leader Characters

Before you can continue, you need to create a model for this line and all other lines containing a page number. This involves setting a tab stop for page numbers, telling Works how to align them, and inserting leader characters in the space between topics and page numbers. This all takes place in the Tabs command.

When you set your own tab stop, Works ignores all standard tab stops to the left of the one you set.

- Press F8 twice (to select `OUR POLICIES AND PRACTICES`).
- Press Alt and type **TT** (Format/Tabs). Here's that familiar dialog box with the blinker in the `Position` field. You want a tab stop 5 inches from the left margin. This is where you'll type the page numbers.

CONTENTS

Figure 25-6. The table of contents in an employee handbook

- Type **5.5** and press Tab (to move into the `Alignment` box). You want page numbers right-aligned.
- Type **R** (to move to `Right`). And finally, tell Works to use dots as leader characters.
- Press Tab (to move into the `Leader` box).
- Type **1** (to choose the dots). Press Enter and press Escape.

Now press Right Arrow to collapse the selection, which lands the cursor at the paragraph mark after PRACTICES. Hang on, 'cause here comes the fun part.

- Press Tab. Instantly, Works insert dots to the tab stop.
- Type **2** (the page number). Page numbers are right-aligned, so Works shifts the number to the left. Press Enter twice.

Setting Another Tab Stop

With all standard tab stops gone, you now need a tab stop to start the topics a few characters from the left margin. Leave the cursor where it is.

- Press Alt and type **TT** (Format/Tabs).
- Type **.3** and press Enter. Press Escape.

Entering More Text

Now continue entering other topics.

- Press Tab to move to the first tab stop.
- Type **Attendance** and press Tab.
- Type **2** and press Enter.
- Press Tab. Type **Bad Weather Closings** and press Tab again.
- Type **10** and press Enter.
- Press Tab. Type **Bulletin Boards** and press Tab.
- Type **5** and press Enter.
- Press Tab. Type **Disciplinary Procedure** and press Tab.
- Type **9** and press Enter.

You get the idea. Using Figure 25-7 as a guide, continue in this way entering as many more lines as you like. Use the preview feature (Print/Preview) as you go along.

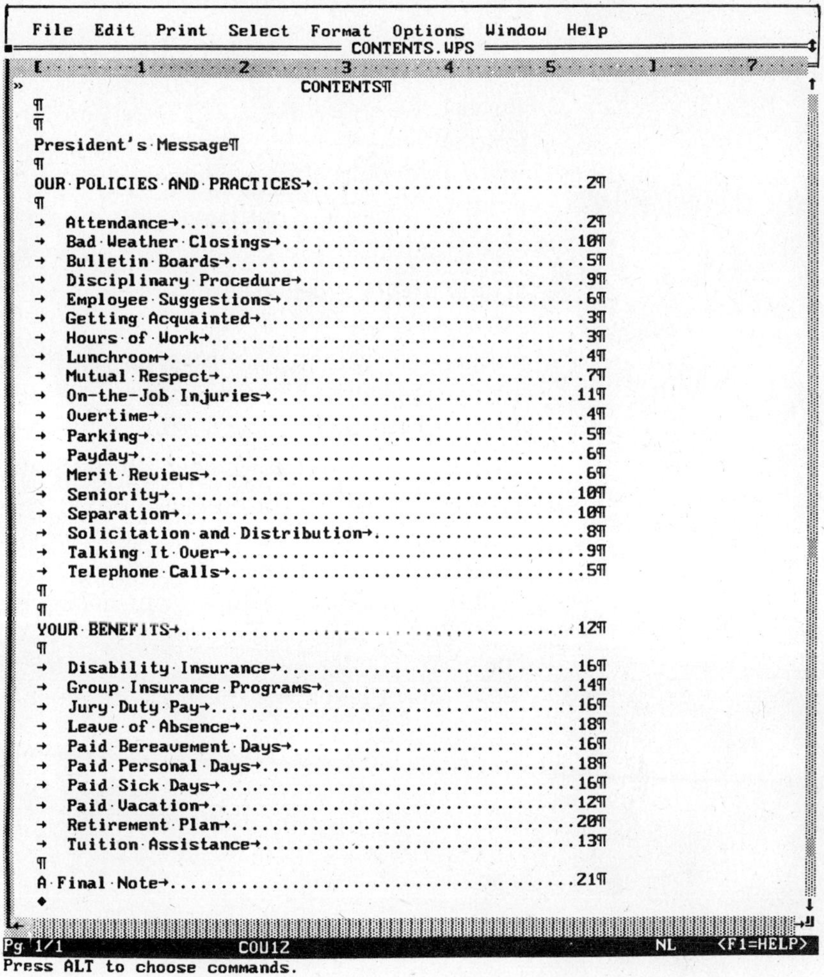

```
File  Edit  Print  Select  Format  Options  Window  Help
                         CONTENTS.WPS
                         CONTENTS¶
¶
¶
President's·Message¶
¶
OUR·POLICIES·AND·PRACTICES→...........................2¶
¶
→  Attendance→........................................2¶
→  Bad·Weather·Closings→..............................10¶
→  Bulletin·Boards→...................................5¶
→  Disciplinary·Procedure→............................9¶
→  Employee·Suggestions→..............................6¶
→  Getting·Acquainted→................................3¶
→  Hours·of·Work→.....................................3¶
→  Lunchroom→.........................................4¶
→  Mutual·Respect→....................................7¶
→  On-the-Job·Injuries→...............................11¶
→  Overtime→..........................................4¶
→  Parking→...........................................5¶
→  Payday→............................................6¶
→  Merit·Reviews→.....................................6¶
→  Seniority→.........................................10¶
→  Separation→........................................10¶
→  Solicitation·and·Distribution→.....................8¶
→  Talking·It·Over→...................................9¶
→  Telephone·Calls→...................................5¶
¶
¶
YOUR·BENEFITS→........................................12¶
¶
→  Disability·Insurance→..............................16¶
→  Group·Insurance·Programs→..........................14¶
→  Jury·Duty·Pay→.....................................16¶
→  Leave·of·Absence→..................................18¶
→  Paid·Bereavement·Days→.............................16¶
→  Paid·Personal·Days→................................18¶
→  Paid·Sick·Days→....................................16¶
→  Paid·Vacation→.....................................12¶
→  Retirement·Plan→...................................20¶
→  Tuition·Assistance→................................13¶
¶
A·Final·Note→.........................................21¶
◆
Pg 1/1            COU12                         NL    <F1=HELP>
Press ALT to choose commands.
```

Figure 25-7. The screen characters in the contents page

Matching Your Results to the Figure

To match your results with those in Figure 25-6, you need to do some of the things you did in the handbook pages.

1. Check the spelling in the page (Options/Check Spelling)
2. Format the entire document for a Courier 12-pitch font (Format/Font & Style). Press F8 four times to select all of the text before choosing the command.
3. Increase the size of CONTENTS to 24-point Courier (Format/Font & Style). Select it before choosing the command.
4. With CONTENTS selected, use Ctrl+B to boldface and Ctrl+C to center.
5. Boldface OUR POLICIES AND PRACTICES and YOUR BENEFITS, including leader characters and page number. Select each heading first, then use Ctrl+B.
6. Set a top margin of 1.5 inches (Print/Print Setup & Margins).
7. Save and name the file (File/Save As).

Use the techniques you already know and you should have no trouble at all. The Print menu's Print command prints the contents page.

The next chapter keeps you in the word processing groove as you create a form letter that merges with database records.

Personalized Form Letter

Individually typed letters that look like they're going to no one but the recipient command more attention than impersonal form letters.

Form letters that say the same thing but go to different people are the backbone of business correspondence. These letters can, for example, carry your sales pitch to prospective customers and clients, request information from suppliers, respond to requests for information, and tell job applicants if they've gotten the job.

Gone are the days when you must either type letter after letter with just about the same information or duplicate a letter on a copy machine and fill in the blanks (the personalized stuff) on a typewriter, only to end up with something that looks like junk mail. With Works, you can print as many form letters as you like, with each one looking like an original.

Pretend you're Bill Conroy, President of Blue Book Publishing. Your hot new product is a series of regional restaurant guides given away by local businesses to customers and clients.

In this session, you develop a database of potential buyers of the restaurant guides. Working in both the List and Form screens, you create fields, enter and sort records, edit entries, and save the database. You then write a marketing letter, using placeholders to reserve places for entries in the database. You enter and format text, set indents, change line spacing after each paragraph, check spelling, select the font, define the page layout, and save the letter. You also find out how to get around a few Works quirks.

Two hard-working macros automate the repetitive activities. In addition to recording and running them, you view and modify them in MACROS.INI. In a fireworks finale, you merge both files to produce the personalized form letter shown in Figure 26-1. When you print, the shaded lines will contain entries culled from the database.

BLUE BOOK PUBLISHING, INC.
7353 Madison Avenue
New York, New York 10019

September 29, 1990

Mr. James Wappinger, President
The Wappinger Group, Inc.
540 West 58th Street
New York NY 10019-0000

Dear Mr. Wappinger:

Thank you for inquiring about the Little Blue Book of Restaurants, which describes hundreds of interesting restaurants in the New York area. We are pleased to enclose a copy for your review.

The embossed square on the front cover is reserved for the name and logo of The Wappinger Group, Inc., which we will imprint free of charge if you purchase in quantity. Please see our enclosed price list for details.

The Little Blue Book fits easily into pocket or purse. We are sure you will find it to be a well-regarded gift that excites clients and customers and keeps your company's name before them.

If you have any questions, please call our toll-free number 1-800-555-0987. We look forward to hearing from you.

Cordially,

William C. Conroy

William C. Conroy
President and Publisher

The Biggest Little Blue Books in the World

Figure 26-1. The personalized form letter with database entries in the shaded areas

This session's a long one split into two parts so you can take a break in the middle if you want to. Before you can start it, though, you need to complete the integration workout in Chapter 20. The macro you create there and store under Ctrl+Q enters more placeholders here. If you haven't created that file yet, get crackin', and then come on back.

Keystrokes and Other Matters

The instructions guide you each step of the way, giving keystrokes and cursor movements relating to each task. As always, please observe the distinction between pressing and holding down a key.

- With instructions such as *Press Alt and type TW (Format/Width)*, press and release Alt before you type the letters.
- With *Hold down Alt and type 2 (to move to 2nd Field)*, press the Alt key and, without releasing Alt, type the number.

Unless the instructions say otherwise, use the Arrow keys (Left, Right, Up, and Down) to move the cursor. If you hit a snag, press the Escape key to cancel what you're doing. Then pick up where you left off.

Creating a New Database

Assuming you're starting anew, load Works. At the File menu, type **ND** (Create New File/New Database), bringing up a new database screen. You're now in the Form screen, as indicated by the word `FORM` on the status line.

The first task is to create the fields shown in Table 26-1. Press the Caps Lock key so you can type field names in uppercase, which makes them really standout. If you make a typo, press Backspace (not an Arrow key) to back up the cursor and erase.

Creating the Fields

The fields in this database are similar to the ones in the Customer database in Chapter 11. You entered those fields in the Form screen. For practice, enter these in the List screen. Press F9 now to move to

Table 26-1. Field names and field widths in this database

Field Name	Field Width List Screen	Field Width Form Screen
MR/MS	5	9
FIRST	8	15
MI	3	2
LAST NAME	11	18
TITLE	19	20
COMPANY	27	30
STREET	24	22
CITY	15	16
ST	4	2
ZIP	10	10

the List screen, where you see LIST on the status line. The cursor is in the first row (record) in the first column (field).

- Press Alt and type **EN** (Edit/Field Name). Works brings up the Name dialog box.
- Type **MR/MS** and press Enter. Press Right Arrow to move the cursor to the next column.
- Again, press Alt and type **EN** (Edit/Name).
- Type **FIRST** and press Enter. Press Right Arrow.
- Type **MI** (for Middle Initial) and press Enter. Press Right Arrow.

It's always a good idea to keep each type of entry—even a middle initial—in a separate field. This way, when you write a friendly form letter, you don't end up with Dear Carolyn L.. But there's a problem. Suppose you create a label or form letter with placeholders for first name, middle initial, and last name (as you'll do shortly) but some records lack a middle initial. Instead of closing up the space between first and last names, Works leaves a gap, which can look rather strange. This is a classic Hobson's Choice. Either omit an MI placeholder, which makes the name incomplete, or combine first name and last name in the same field, which prevents you from using that field in a letter salutation.

- Press Alt and type **EN** (Edit/Name).
- Type **LAST NAME** and press Enter. Press Right Arrow.
- Press Alt and type **EN** (Edit/Name).

Using Table 26-1 as a guide, continue in this way entering the rest of the field names. When you finish, press Home to jump the cursor to the first field.

Creating a Looping Macro To Set Variable Column Widths

```
<begdef><ctrlw><menu>TW<vfld><enter>
<xright><pause0:00:02.0><ctrlw><enddef>
```

Each column is now 10 characters wide. The next step is to widen or reduce them, as shown in Table 26-1, to accommodate their entries. Setting column widths is a repetitive activity well suited to a macro.

The macro you're about to create pauses in its run to ask for the width of the column at the cursor's location. After you type a number, it moves to the next column to the right and asks for the width of that column, continuing in this way until you tell it to stop.

You need a variable-input (not fixed-input) field because each column can be either 1 or 2 digits wide—for instance, 3 characters or 33 characters.

The pause for your input is caused by a variable-input field (vfld), which lets you type any number of keystrokes each time. Tacking the macro's keyname to the end of the macro produces a continuous loop. Each time the macro reaches the end of its run, it starts again from the beginning.

Some computers run so fast that it's difficult to stop the looping at exactly the right time. Therefore, the macro contains a 2-second timed pause that gives you the chance to press Escape. All this will make perfect sense in a moment.

Recording the Macro

As usual, recording your keystrokes is the easiest way to create this pausing, looping macro. Your cursor is now in the MR/MS column.

- Hold down Alt and type / (to activate the first macro menu).

- Press Enter (to confirm Record Macro). Works brings up the Playback dialog box asking for a playback key and macro description. Assign this macro to Ctrl+W.
- Hold down Ctrl and type **W**. Works shows <ctrlw> in the Playback key field.
- Press Tab (to jump to Title). This macro can be used in both the database List screen and the spreadsheet screen, so use this information in the title.
- Type **SET VARIABLE COLUMN WIDTHS (DB OR SS)** (as you type, the earlier characters move to the left to make room for more characters) and press Enter.

Works returns you to the List screen and RECORD appears on the message line.

Works now starts recording your keystrokes. If you make a typing error, correct it and don't be concerned. The macro will record the error and the correction, which you can later edit out if you like. The numbered steps produce the macro.

Use the MR/MS field as the macro prototype, setting it to a width of 5 characters. Your cursor is still in the MR/MS column.

1. Press Alt and type **TW** (Format/Field Width). In the Width dialog box, Works proposes 10 characters, the standard field width.
2. Hold down Alt and type / (to activate the second macro menu).
3. Type **V** (Variable Input) to insert a variable-input field, and press Enter.
4. Type **5** and press Enter twice, once to confirm the variable input and the other to execute the Field Width command.
5. Press Right Arrow (to move the cursor to the next column). Now insert the timed pause.
6. Hold down Alt and type / (to activate the second macro menu).
7. Type **P** (Pause) and press Enter. Works brings up the dialog box asking for the length of the pause.
8. Type **2.** (2 seconds) and press Enter. Now have the macro loop around to the beginning by inserting its own playback key.
9. Hold down Ctrl and type **W**. Works wants you to know you've created a looping macro.
10. Press Enter to acknowledge. Recording stops and RECORD disappears from the status line.

Although Works asks for the length of the pause in this form `hh:mm:ss.t`*, you can use* `s.`*, the shortcut for seconds.*

Viewing the Macro

The macro is safely stored in MACROS.INI, along with all other macros you've created so far. To make sure nothing's amiss, view it before running it. Leave the cursor where it is.

- Press Alt and type **FO** (File/Open Existing File).
- Press Tab (to move to the `Files` list).
- Type **M** as many times as necessary to reach `MACROS.INI`, and press Enter.
- Works lets you know you can't use macros while this file is open. Press Enter to acknowledge.

Move the cursor until you see the macro title `SET VARIABLE COLUMN WIDTHS (DB OR SS)` and the macro. Your title and macro should look just like the one in Figure 26-2, here shown by itself in a word processor file. Table 26-2 describes what each element means.

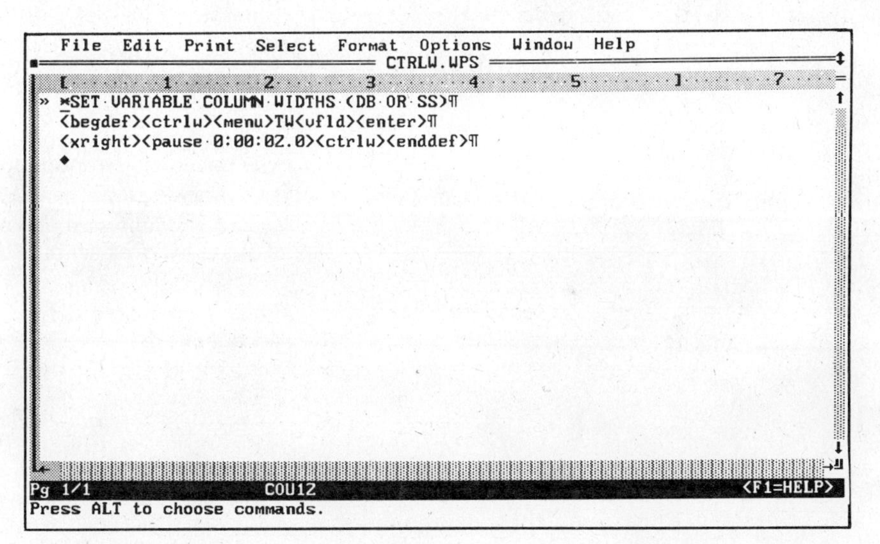

Figure 26-2. The looping macro that changes the field widths in the List screen

If everything's all right, close the MACROS.INI file.

- Press Alt and type **FC** (File/Close).

If something's amiss, solve the problem in one of two ways: If it's serious, simply reenter the macro from scratch. When Works informs you that the key already has a macro, press Enter and continue from there.

If it's not all that serious, edit the macro so it looks exactly like the one in 26-2. Then press Alt and type **FC** to close the edited file. Press Enter to tell Works to save the changes.

Table 26-2. Elements in the looping macro and what they mean

Element	Meaning
<begdef>	Beginning of the macro definition (Works generated)
<ctrlw>	Macro storage/playback key
<menu>	Alt key activates the menu line
TW	Format menu's Field Width command (it doesn't matter if letters are in uppercase or lowercase)
<vfld>	Variable-input field that waits for you to type the column width
<enter>	Enter confirms the width number you type
<xright>	Right Arrow key moves cursor one column to the right
<pause 0:00:02.0>	Two-second pause, during which time you can stop the looping action
<ctrlw>	Macro storage/playback key. When the macro encounters its own playback key, it starts all over again. This causes the looping action.
<enddef>	End of the macro definition (Works generated)

Running the Looping Macro

Now put this pausing, looping macro through its paces. The cursor is in the FIRST field.

The idea is to make columns wide enough to avoid truncating entries, yet still keep as many columns on screen at one time as possible.

- Hold down Ctrl and type **W**. Instantly, the `Width` dialog box appears with Works proposing 10 characters.
- Type **8** (the new width in characters) and press Enter. The macro reduces the width of the FIRST column, moves the

Within these two opposing camps, there's always room for compromise. If the compromise doesn't work, you can change the field width at any time.

cursor to the MI column, and pauses for two seconds to give you the chance to stop the action. You haven't stopped it, so it opens the dialog box and awaits your input for the MI column.

- Type **3** and press Enter. The macro goes through its routine again, reducing the MI column width, moving the cursor to the LAST NAME column, and pausing again. It now opens the dialog box and awaits your input for the LAST NAME column.
- Type **11** and press Enter. Again the macro changes the column width, moves to TITLE and pauses. Dialog box open, it awaits your input for the TITLE column.

Referring to Table 26-1, change the width of all other fields but ZIP, which remains at the standard 10-character width.

At the final pause, press Alt+/ (not Escape, not Pause, not Break) to stop the macro's looping action.

After you type the width of the ST field and press Enter, quickly hold down Alt and type / to stop the macro's looping action. (The computer beeps in acknowledgment.) If your fingers aren't quite fast enough that time and the dialog box appears, simply press Enter to confirm the proposed width, and then press Alt+/.

Now press Home to move the cursor to the first column.

Setting the Field Widths in the Form Screen

In the Form screen, a field consists of height as well as width, altogether known as the ***field size****. The standard height is 1 line, but you can have as many as 256 lines if this makes sense.*

Now press F9 so you can see the fields in the Form screen. The List and Form screens display the same information differently, so the fields you entered one after the other in the List screen appear one below the other in the Form screen, as shown in Figure 26-3. Here, the standard field width is 20 characters.

Hold down Tab to cycle the cursor through the fields. Field names carry-over from screen to screen, but not field widths. Even though you changed the widths in the List screen, the cursor is a uniform 20-character width here.

Modifying the Macro for the Form Screen

As you did in the List screen, you want to adjust field widths to give entries the room they need. The fast approach is to modify the looping macro you created a few moments ago so it chooses the proper command—Field Size instead of Field Width—and moves the cursor

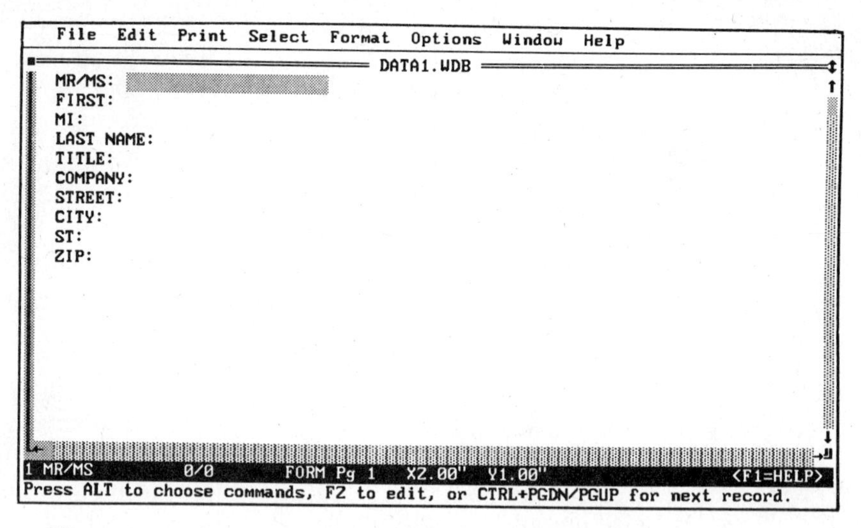

Figure 26-3. The Form screen containing the fields created in the List screen

in the proper direction—down instead of to the right. As you did before, open the MACROS.INI file.

- Press Alt and type **FO** (File/Open Existing File).
- Press Tab (to move to the `Files` list).
- Type **M** as many times as necessary to reach `MACROS.INI`, and press Enter.
- Yes, yes, you know you can't use macros while this file is open. Press Enter to acknowledge.

Move the cursor until you see the macro title `SET VARIABLE COLUMN WIDTHS (DB OR SS)` and the macro. Now place the cursor on the `W` in `TW`.

- Type **Z** (for `Field Size`) and press Delete (to delete the `W`). Now place the cursor on the `x` in the element «`xright`».
- Press Delete six times (to delete «`xright`»).
- Type **«tab»** (to insert the Tab keyname). Now close the MACROS.INI file.
- Press Alt and type **FC** (File/Close).
- Works asks if you want to save the changes. You do indeed, so press Enter.

Running the Modified Macro

You're back in the Form screen with the cursor in the MR/MS field. Now run the macro, specifying the field widths shown in Table 26-1. Space isn't much of a consideration here in the Form screen, so you can afford to be generous.

- Press Ctrl and type **W**. In the dialog box, Works proposes the standard field width, 20 characters and a standard height of one line. Though widths vary, one line is constant.
- Type **9** (the new width in characters) and press Enter. The macro narrows the MR/MS field, moves the cursor down to the FIRST MI field, pauses so you can stop the looping if you want to, and then brings up the dialog box again awaiting your input for the FIRST MI field.
- Type **15** and press Enter. The macro moves the cursor down to the MI field and displays the dialog box again.
- Type **2** and press Enter. The macro moves the cursor down to the LAST NAME field and displays the dialog box yet another time.
- Type **18** and press Enter. The macro moves the cursor down to the TITLE field and again awaits your input.

When you want to keep the number in the dialog box (either the standard width or any other width you entered earlier), simply press Enter to confirm the existing entry. There's no need to stop the macro, move the cursor past this field, and then start the macro again.

Now, referring to Table 26-1, adjust the other field widths (except TITLE, which remains at 20 characters) in the same way. After you type **10** in the ZIP field, press Alt+/ immediately to halt the looping action.

Your cursor is now in the MR/MS field of the second record. The first record is empty, so hold down Shift+Tab until you see the number 1 in the left of the status line.

Later, at your leisure, you can edit this macro to restore the List screen elements (command letter and Right Arrow key) or, better yet, copy the entire macro (including title) to another place in the MACROS.INI file and edit the copy. You will then have one macro for the List screen and another for the Form screen.

Saving the Database

This is a good time to save the database, so leave the cursor where it is.

- Press Alt and type **FA** (File/Save As).

Works brings up the dialog box where you can type a filename and, if needed, a drive or directory. If you're saving to the current drive, simply type the filename. Otherwise, type the drive or directory before the filename, for example A:FORMDB.

- Type **FORMDB** (for Form DataBase) and press Enter. Works appends the extension .WDB to the filename.

Entering Records in the Form Screen

The next step is to put something in the database, namely records. To keep things neat and trim, this database contains only the six records shown in Table 26-3.

Table 26-3. The six records in the form letter database

Field Name	Record 1	Record 2
MR/MS	Mr.	Ms.
FIRST	George	Nancy
MI		G.
LAST NAME	Akahoshi	Harmon
TITLE	Vice President	General Manager
COMPANY	Smart Hardware Company	Cumberland Computer, Inc.
STREET	7234 North Beach	456 Clermont Street
CITY	San Francisco	Carmel
ST	CA	IN
ZIP	94106-9715	46032-1234

Field Name	Record 3	Record 4
MR/MS	Mr.	Dr.
FIRST	James	Warren
MI	T.	
LAST NAME	T. Wappinger	Fenton
TITLE	President	Sr. Vice President
COMPANY	The Wappinger Group, Inc.	Fenton Computer Consultants
STREET	540 West 58th Street	444 El Centro
CITY	New York	Dallas
ST	NY	TX
ZIP	10019	75242

Field Name	Record 5	Record 6
MR/MS	Dr.	Ms.
FIRST	Delta R.	Audrey
MI	R.	
LAST NAME	Cooper	Bailey
TITLE	President	Vice President
COMPANY	Delta Cooper & Associates	World of Travel, Inc.
STREET	234 Harper Drive	60 Nighmute Street
CITY	Detroit	Napaskiak
ST	MI	AK
ZIP	48244-5678	99559

In the Form screen, pressing Tab moves you to the next field, Shift+Tab to the previous field.

Press Ctrl+Home to make sure you're in the MR/MS field in the first record. Now fill in the record. Remember, if you make a typo, press Backspace (not an Arrow key) to erase it.

- Type **Mr.** and press Tab to enter what you typed and move to the FIRST field.
- Type **George** and press Tab twice (the second time to move past the MI field).
- Type **Akahoshi** and press Tab.
- Type **Vice President** and press Tab.
- Type **Smart Hardware Company** and press Tab.

Referring to Table 26-3, enter the rest of the information in the Akahoshi record. After you type the ZIP code and press Tab, Works brings up a spanking new record. You can see the new record number at the left end of the status line.

Fill in the other five records in the same way. Yes, you can replace entries in any record with your information, such as your own name. The end result won't match the figures, but that doesn't really matter. You'll still have the concept.

When you finish, your cursor should be in the first field of an empty record, and the status line should show 7 (the active record) and 6/6 (six records selected out of six). The first number is the empty record on screen; the other number reflects completed records only.

Viewing the Records in the List Screen

You can get a different perspective by viewing the records in the List screen. Press F9, and then Ctrl+Home to bring all records into view. Now move the cursor to the right so you see the entries in the rest of the fields.

Sorting the Records

Pretend you have hundreds of records in this database. Arranging them in ZIP code order makes it easy to bundle the letters and take advantage of bulk mailing rates. Leave the cursor where it is.

- Press Alt and type **SO** (Select/Sort). Works proposes to sort on MR/MS, the first field in the database.
- Type **ZIP** (the sort field name). Ascending order is fine, so press Enter.

In a flash, Works sorts the records. Press End and you can see the ZIP field. Hold the phone. Bit of a problem here. Because the lengths of the ZIP codes vary (some have 5 digits, others 9), Works arranges the longer codes before the shorter ones, keeping entries in numerical order by group but out of order overall.

Editing the Entries

The solution is to make the ZIP codes uniform length. You can do this in one of two ways—either delete the 4-character extension where it exists or, recognizing that ZIP+4 is here to stay, add a

4-character extension. If you don't know the extension, simply enter four zeros. Here's how to edit the entries to append those zeros.

- Move the cursor to the New York ZIP code (10019 in the fourth record).
- Press F2 (to place the ZIP code on the entry/edit line).
- Type **-0000** and press Down Arrow to enter the edited entry and move the cursor one cell down.

Now edit the Texas ZIP code in the same way, and then edit the Alaska ZIP code. When you finish, all ZIP codes should be in ZIP+4 form.

Sorting the Records Again

Now sort the records again.

- Press Alt and type **SO** (Select/Sort). This time, Works proposes to sort on ZIP, the field you entered earlier.
- Press Enter.

That's more like it. Move the cursor around the records, which should now look like the ones in Figure 26-4.

Saving the Database

Now save all the work you've done in the database.

- Type **FS** (File/Save).

As the file is being saved, the indicator in the left side of the status line shows the percentage already processed. When the record number reappears, Works is ready for your next action.

If you need a break, now's the time to take it. Press Alt and type **FX** (File/Exit) to leave Works and get to the DOS prompt. When you're ready to start again, load Works. Then, at the File menu, type **O** (Open Existing File) and press Tab to move the blinker to the Files list. Type **F** as many times as needed to reach FORMDB.WDB and press Enter. The database is back on screen.

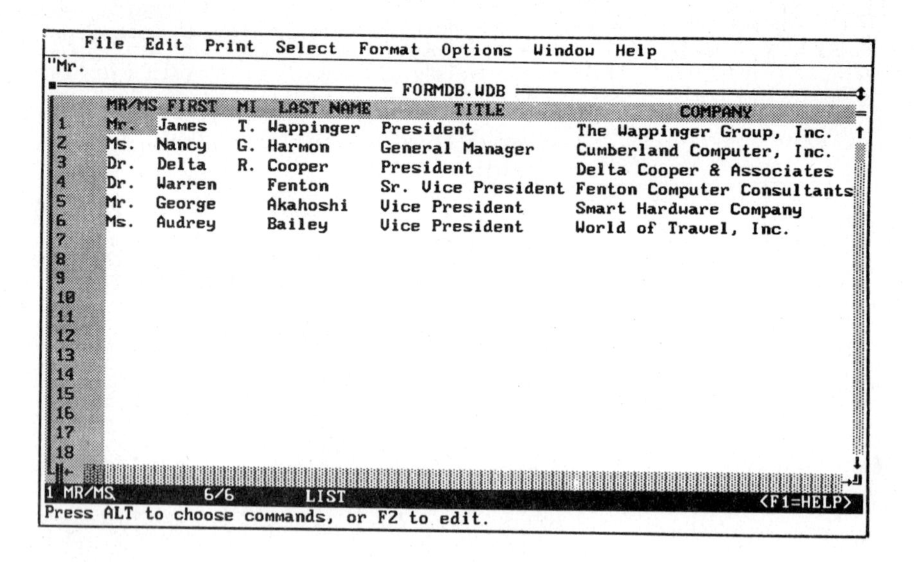

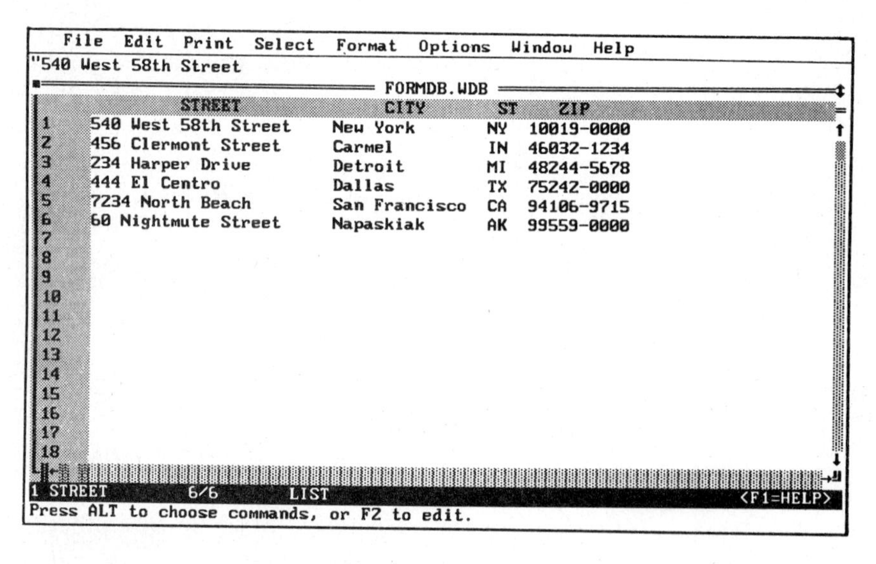

Figure 26-4. The database records arranged by ZIP code in the List screen

Part II: Creating a Form Letter

Seeing the screen characters (paragraph marks, tab marks, and spacing dots) will make it easier to work with this letter. If you need to turn them on, press Alt and type **OL** *(Options/Show All Characters).*

You're about to create the document shown in Figure 26-5. Right arrows show where you press Tab, paragraph marks where you press Enter, and tiny dots where you press the Spacebar between words. The unshaded areas contain placeholders that hold the place for entries in the database. When you print the letter, Works replaces those placeholders with database entries.

```
» →    →    →    →    →    →    →    September·29,·1990¶
¶
¶
¶
«MR/MS»·«FIRST»·«LAST·NAME»,·«TITLE»¶
«COMPANY»¶
«STREET»¶
«CITY»·«ST»·«ZIP»¶
¶
Dear·«MR/MS»·«LAST·NAME»:¶
¶
   Thank·you·for·inquiring·about·the·Little·Blue·Book·of·
Restaurants,·which·describes·hundreds·of·interesting·
restaurants·in·the·«CITY»·area.·We·are·pleased·to·enclose·a·
copy·for·your·review.¶

   The·embossed·square·on·the·front·cover·is·reserved·for·
the·name·and·logo·of·«COMPANY»,·which·we·will·imprint·free·
of·charge·if·you·purchase·in·quantity.·Please·see·our·
enclosed·price·list·for·details.¶

   The·Little·Blue·Book·fits·easily·into·pocket·or·purse.·We·
are·sure·you·will·find·it·to·be·a·well-regarded·gift·that·
excites·clients·and·customers·and·keeps·your·company's·name·
before·them.¶

   If·you·have·any·questions,·please·call·our·toll-free·
number·1-800-555-0987.·We·look·forward·to·hearing·from·you.¶

→    →    →    →    →    →    →    Cordially,¶
¶
¶
¶
¶
¶
→    →    →    →    →    →    →    William·C.·Conroy¶
→    →    →    →    →    →    →    President·and·Publisher¶
◆
```

Figure 26-5. The form letter showing the placeholders for database information

Entering the Date

Now type the date in the letter. The cursor is at the paragraph sign. If you make a typo, press Backspace to back up the cursor.

- Press Tab seven times. The standard tab stops are at half-inch intervals, so the cursor moves 3 inches from the left margin.
- Type **September 29, 1990** and press Enter four times to end the paragraph and insert four blank lines.

Entering the Placeholders

Now tell Works which entries you want printed in this letter and where. Use the macro you stored under Ctrl+Q in Chapter 20 to make inserting these placeholders quick and easy.

- Hold down Ctrl and type **Q** to activate the macro. In a flash, Works brings up the `Insert Field` dialog box, chooses `FORMDB.WDB` (you can see it in reverse video), and moves the blinker to the `Fields` list.
- Type **M** (to choose the MR/MS field) and press Enter. Works inserts `«MR/MS»` on the first line.
- Press the Spacebar (to insert a space between placeholders). Now enter the FIRST field placeholder.
- Press Ctrl+Q and type **F** (to choose FIRST). Press Enter, then the Spacebar. Not everyone in this database has a middle initial, so you'll skip the MI placeholder to avoid a gap between first name and last name, as explained earlier. Now enter the LAST NAME placeholder.
- Press Ctrl+Q and type **L** (to choose LAST NAME). Press Enter, type a comma, and press the Spacebar.
- Press Ctrl+Q and type **T** (to choose TITLE). Press Enter, and then press the Spacebar. Press Enter to end the paragraph.
- Press Ctrl+Q and type **C** (to choose COMPANY). Press Enter twice, once to confirm COMPANY and the other to end the paragraph.

Referring to Figure 26-5, enter the STREET, CITY, ST, and ZIP placeholders in the same way.

Entering the Salutation

The next step is to enter the salutation and its placeholders. To get to the proper place from the ZIP placeholder, press Down Arrow twice.

- Type **Dear** and press the Spacebar.
- Hold down Ctrl and type **Q**.
- Type **M** (to choose the MR/MS field) and press Enter. Press the Spacebar.
- Hold down Ctrl and type **Q** again.
- Type **L** (to choose the LAST NAME field) and press Enter. Type a colon.

You now have two MR/MS placeholders in the letter. No problem. You can insert the same fields in a document as often as you want.

Now press Enter twice to end the paragraph and insert a blank line.

Setting a First Line Indent

Works lets you set a first line indent, which saves you the bother of tabbing in at the beginning of each paragraph. Leave the cursor on the paragraph sign.

- Press Alt and type **TA** (Format/Indents & Spacing). Works brings up the dialog box with all of the paragraph settings.
- Press Tab (to move to the `1st line indent` field, now showing `0"`).
- Type **.3** (the indent from the left margin). Works will insert the inches mark for you, so there's no need to type it. Don't press Enter yet.

Choosing the Line Spacing Between Paragraphs

You can also specify the number of blank lines between paragraphs when you press Enter. This relieves you of yet another extra step. You're still in the dialog box.

- Hold down Alt and type **A** (to move to the `Space after paragraph` field, which now shows `0 Li`).
- Type **1** (the number of lines after each paragraph). Works will insert `Li` (lines) for you, so you don't have to type it.

Press Enter to confirm both settings. Works returns you to the document and indents the paragraph mark.

Entering the Text

Now enter the text shown in Figure 26-5. As you doubtlessly know, wordwrap causes any word that can't fit at the end of the line to move down by itself to the beginning of the next line. You don't have to press Enter except to end a paragraph or insert a blank line. To be sure your results agree with the figure, press the Spacebar only once between sentences.

Each of the first two paragraphs contains a placeholder. Read all the instructions carefully. Take your time and be sure you understand everything before you put finger to keyboard.

- Using Figure 26-5 as a guide, type the paragraph starting **Thank you for inquiring about the Little Blue Book of Restaurants....** When you get to the CITY placeholder, press the Spacebar. Now hold down Ctrl and type **Q** to start the macro. Type **C** twice to move to the CITY placeholder, and press Enter. Press the Spacebar and type the rest of the paragraph. After you finish, press Enter only once. This ends the paragraph and inserts a blank line.
- Type the paragraph starting with **The embossed square on the front cover is reserved for the name...** When you get to the COMPANY placeholder, press the Spacebar; then hold down Ctrl and type **Q**. Type **C** and press Enter to enter the COMPANY placeholder. Type a comma, press the Spacebar again, and type the rest of the paragraph. After you finish, press Enter only once.
- Type the entire paragraph starting **The Little Blue Book fits easily into pocket or purse....** After you finish, press Enter once.
- Type the entire paragraph starting with **If you have any questions, please call....** After you finish, press Enter once. The cursor is now on the paragraph mark two lines below the paragraph.

Turning Off the Paragraph Formats

You don't need indents or an extra line between paragraphs any more, so turn off the setting. Leave the cursor at the paragraph sign.

- Press Ctrl + X (shortcut for Normal Paragraph). It's as easy as that.

Saving the File

Now save this file under the name FORMLET. Leave the cursor where it is.

- Press Alt and type **FA** (File/Save As).

Works brings up the **Save As** dialog box so you can type the new filename and, if needed, a drive or directory. If you're saving to the current drive, simply type the filename. Otherwise, type the drive or directory before the filename, for example A:FORMLET.

- Type **FORMLET** and press Enter. Works appends the extension .WP5 to the filename.

Creating a Cordial Closing Macro

```
<begdef><ctrlz><tab><tab><tab><tab><tab><tab><tab>Cordially,
<enter>
<enter>
<enter>
<enter>
<enter>
<tab><tab><tab><tab><tab><tab><tab>William C. Conroy<enter>
<tab><tab><tab><tab><tab><tab><tab>President and Publisher<enddef>
```

Whether you're writing a form letter or one-of-a-kind correspondence, letters always end with a cordial closing and your name. This is another repetitive action where a macro can save you keystrokes.

The macro you're about to create tabs to the middle of the page, drops in the cordial part of the closing, skips a few lines, tabs some more, and drops in a name and title. You can later edit the macro to replace Bill Conroy's name with your own.

Recording the Macro

As usual, the fast way to create a macro is to record it. Leave the cursor on the paragraph mark below the last paragraph.

- Hold down Alt and type / (to activate the first macro menu).
- Press Enter (to confirm Record Macro). Works brings up the Playback dialog box asking for a playback key and macro description. Store this macro under Ctrl+Z.
- Hold down Ctrl and type **Z**. Works shows <ctrlz> in the Playback key field.
- Press Tab (to jump to Title).
- Type **ENTER CORDIAL CLOSING (WP)** and press Enter.

Works returns you to the letter and RECORD appears on the message line. Works is ready to record your keystrokes, including any errors and corrections. You can edit them out later. The numbered steps produce the macro.

1. Press Tab seven times (to move the cursor 3 inches from the left margin, the same as the date at the beginning).
2. Type **Cordially,** and press Enter six times, once to end the paragraph and the others to leave enough blank lines for a signature.
3. Press Tab seven times. Type **William C. Conroy** and press Enter.
4. Press Tab seven times. Type **President and Publisher** and leave the cursor where it is.

This is all you want the macro to do, so stop recording.

- Hold down Alt and type / (to activate the second macro menu).
- Press Enter (to confirm End Recording). Recording stops and RECORD disappears from the status line.

Viewing the Macro

The macro is stored in MACROS.INI with all of the other macros you already created. Before running it, view it. Leave the cursor where it is.

- Press Alt and type **FO** (File/Open Existing File).
- Press Tab (to move to the `Files` list).
- Type **M** as many times as necessary to reach `MACROS.INI`, and press Enter.
- Works lets you know you can't use macros while this file is open. Press Enter to acknowledge.

Move the cursor until you see the macro title `ENTER CORDIAL CLOSING (WP)` and the macro. Your title and macro should look just like the one in Figure 26-2, here shown by itself in a word processor file. Table 26-4 describes what each element means.

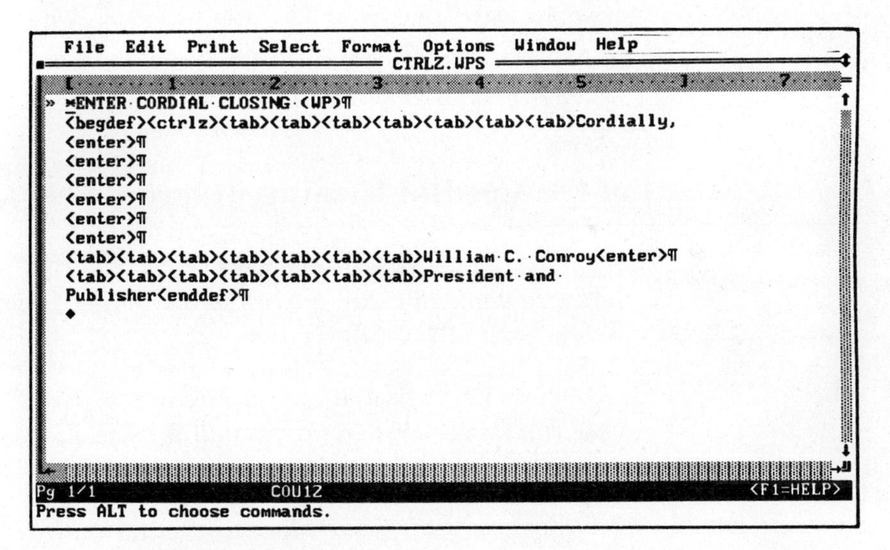

Figure 26-6. The macro that enters a cordial closing in a letter

If everything's fine, close the MACROS.INI file.

- Press Alt and type **FC** (File/Close).

If something's amiss, solve the problem in one of two ways: If it's serious, reenter the macro from scratch. When Works informs you that the key already has a macro, just press Enter and continue from there.

Later, you can delete Bill Conroy's name in the MACROS.INI file and replace it with your own.

If the problem's not all that serious, edit the macro so it looks exactly like the one in 26-2. Then press Alt and type **FC** to close the edited file. Press Enter to tell Works it should save the changes.

Table 26-4. Elements in the cordial closing macro and what they mean

Element	Meaning
`<begdef>`	Beginning of the macro definition (Works generated)
`<ctrlz>`	Macro storage/playback key
`<tab>`	Tab key moves the cursor to next tab stop
`text`	Text in the cordial closing
`<enter>`	Enter ends the paragraph
`<enddef>`	End of the macro definition (Works generated)

Running the Cordial Closing Macro

Before running the macro, delete the closing you just created in the letter, so you don't end up with two closings. Move the cursor to the first arrow in the `Cordially` line.

- Press F8 (to extend the selection).
- Hold down Ctrl and press End (to select everything from the cursor to the end).
- Press Delete.

Now unleash that energetic macro.

- Hold down Ctrl and type **Z** (to start the macro).

As you watch, Works tabs over, types out some letters, moves down a few lines, and types some more, exactly the way you did before. Nice.

Checking the Spelling

Works starts a spelling check at the cursor's location. If that's not the beginning of the document, it checks to the end, then asks for permission to start at the top.

Before going on, check the spelling. If you find spelling errors of your own, follow the screen messages to correct them. Leave the cursor where it is—but not at the beginning of the letter.

- Press Alt and type **OS** (Options/Check Spelling).

Works thumbs feverishly through its own and your personal dictionary, checking every word. Now it either brings up a message box proclaiming the end of the document—in which case, press Enter to start from the beginning—or it brings up a dialog box claiming `William` is a misspelled word. Unless your name is William, this isn't a word you expect to use regularly.

- Press Enter (to replace `William` with William, in essence ignoring it).
- Works immediately finds `Conroy`, another name you can ignore. Press Enter again.
- Works now informs you that the spelling check is finished. Press Enter to acknowledge.

Defining the Page Layout

The Works standard settings are meant for letters like this, so you only need to make a few preparations before you can print.

Choosing the Font

This letter deserves to be printed in a fine typewriter-type font, and 12-point Courier is a long-recognized standard. If your printer doesn't provide this font, simply skip this step and let the letter print in the standard font (typically 12-point Pica). Leave the cursor where it is.

- Press F8 four times (to select the entire letter).
- Press Alt and type **TF** (Format/Font & Style). The dialog box appears.

- Hold down Alt and type **F** (to move to the `Fonts` list).
- Type **C** (to choose `Courier`).
- Press Tab (to move into the `Sizes` list).
- Type **1** enough times to move the blinker to **12** and press Enter. Press Up Arrow to collapse the selection.

Setting the Top Margin and Saving the Letter

Now increase the top margin to make room for a letterhead. Leave the cursor where it is.

- Press Alt and type **PM** (Print/Page Setup & Margins). The blinker is in the `Top margin` field.
- Type **2.8** (the new top margin) and press Enter.

The letter is complete, so save it again. Leave the cursor where it is.

- Press Alt and type **FS** (File/Save).

Merging and Printing the Letter

This is the moment when all your work pays off. You're about to merge the database and form letter, so turn on your printer. Merging and printing take place simultaneously.

- Press Alt and type **PF** (Print/Print Form Letters). In the `Databases` dialog box, Works proposes to merge with `FORMDB.WDB`, the only open database.
- This is exactly what you want, so press Enter.
- Press Enter again (to confirm the number of copies and other settings in the Print dialog box).

Here come six perfectly-typed, original letters off your printer, one after the other, with each one containing its own distinctive information. The first letter should look like the one in Figure 26-1 (sans letterhead, of course).

You learn another type of integration in the next chapter when you merge a memo and spreadsheet chart.

TWENTY-SEVEN

Merging a Memo and Chart

This chapter, the last one in this book, gives new meaning to the phrase "going out in style."

Merging information created in one Works application with information created in another is where Works truly shines. Many of these merges are invisible—for instance, a form letter or a mailing label that takes information from a database or a document that combines pieces of other documents. On the surface, there's little to show the diversity of sources.

Charts are a different story. Pop one into a report, letter, or memo, and you know you've merged two alien entities. And beautifully, too.

In this session, you create a short memo—entering text, checking spelling, and selecting a font—and you then save and print it. You then modify an existing spreadsheet and its associated chart to show numbers, titles, and gridlines more appropriate to the memo.

In a final burst of Works activity, you merge both files to produce the seamless document shown in Figure 27-1. Believe it or not, this one's duck soup.

Before you can start cooking, you need to create the budget spreadsheet (ADBUDGET.WKS) and bar chart (BUDGET BAR) in Chapter 7.

Keystrokes and Other Matters

The instructions guide you each step of the way, giving keystrokes and cursor movements relating to each task. Please observe the distinction between pressing and holding down a key.

FROM: Jane Pickett, National Advertising Director

DATE: October 15, 1990

SUBJECT: PROPOSED ADVERTISING BUDGET - NEW FISCAL YEAR

Our market research has determined that we should redirect our advertising dollars into those areas where sales impact has been the greatest and reduce our commitment where our return on advertising dollars has been less cost effective.

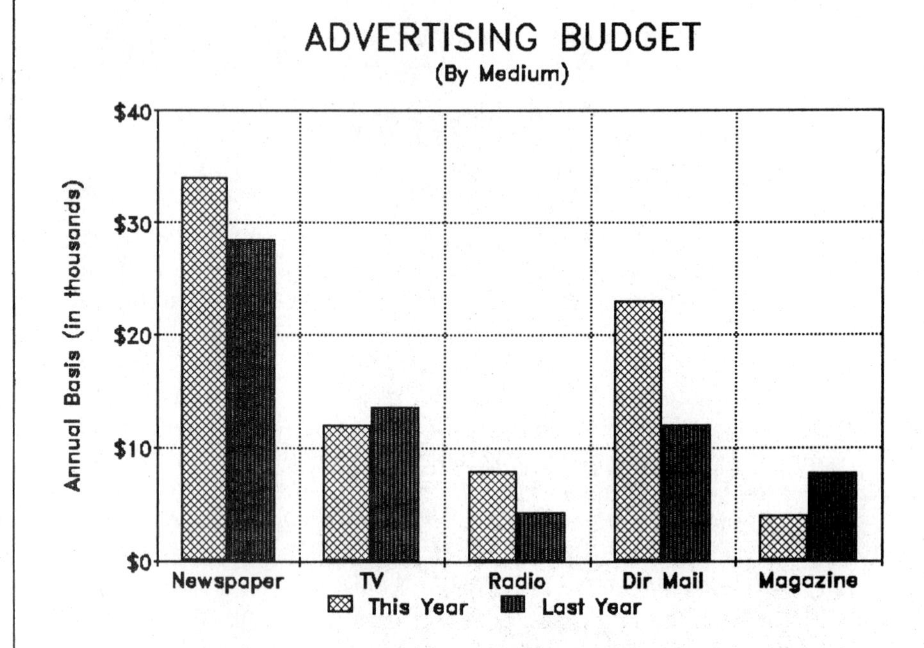

As the chart graphically represents, we are proposing increases in the areas of newspaper, radio, and direct mail advertising, and decreases in our programs for television and magazine.

Figure 27-1. A memo and bar chart integrated into a seamless document

- With instructions such as *Press Alt and type OA (Options/ Show All Characters)*, press and release Alt before you type the letters.
- With *Hold down Alt and type F (to move to Footer)*, press the Alt key and, without releasing Alt, type the letter.

Unless the instructions say otherwise, use the Arrow keys (Left, Right, Up, and Down) to move the cursor. If you hit a snag, press the Escape key to cancel what you're doing. Then pick up where you left off.

Creating the Memo

Assuming you're starting up again, load the Works program. At the File menu, type **NW** (Create New File/New Word Processor), bringing up a new word processor screen. The cursor is in the top left corner.

Seeing the screen characters (paragraph marks, tab arrows, and space dots) lets you match your screen to the figures. If you can see a paragraph mark at the cursor's location, they're turned on (the standard condition), so skip to "Entering the Text." Otherwise, press Alt and type **OA** (Options/Show All Characters) to turn them on.

Entering the Text

Figure 27-2 shows the text in the memo. Wordwrap causes a word that won't fit at the end of a line to move down by itself to the beginning of the next line. You need only press Enter to end a paragraph or to insert a blank line between paragraphs. These places are indicated by a paragraph mark (¶). The arrows facing right show where you press Tab. The tab stops occur at the standard one-half inch intervals. Tiny dots between words show where you press the Spacebar.

```
» TO:→ →     Dick·Chalmers,·Chief·Operating·Officer¶
  ¶
  FROM:→     Jane·Pickett,·National·Advertising·Director¶
  ¶
  DATE:→     October·15,·1990¶
  ¶
  SUBJECT:→  PROPOSED·ADVERTISING·BUDGET·-·NEW·FISCAL·YEAR¶
  ¶
  ¶
  Our·market·research·has·determined·that·we·should·redirect·
  our·advertising·dollars·into·those·areas·where·sales·impact·
  has·been·the·greatest·and·reduce·our·commitment·where·our·
  return·on·advertising·dollars·has·been·less·cost·effective.¶
  ¶
  As·the·chart·graphically·represents,·we·are·proposing·
  increases·in·the·areas·of·newspaper,·radio,·and·direct·mail·
  advertising,·and·decreases·in·our·programs·for·television·
  and·magazine.¶
  ◆
```

Figure 27-2. The text in the memo

Now enter the text, pressing the Spacebar only once between sentences. If you mistype anything, use Backspace to back up the cursor and erase. The cursor is at the paragraph sign.

- Type **TO:** and press Tab twice (to move to the one-inch tab stop).
- Type **Dick Chalmers, Chief Operating Officer** and press Enter twice, ending the paragraph and inserting a blank line. Works enters a dot between words where you press the Spacebar.
- Type **FROM:** and press Tab.
- Type **Jane Pickett, National Advertising Director** and press Enter twice.
- Type **DATE:** and press Tab.
- Type **October 15, 1990** and press Enter twice.
- Type **SUBJECT:** and press Tab.
- Type **PROPOSED ADVERTISING BUDGET - NEW FISCAL YEAR** and press Enter three times to end the paragraph and insert two blank lines.
- Referring to Figure 27-2, type the entire paragraph starting **Our market research has determined that....** When you finish, press Enter twice to end the paragraph and insert a blank line.
- Referring again to Figure 27-2, type the entire paragraph starting **As the chart graphically represents, we are proposing....**

This completes text entry. Scan the screen to be sure things are exactly as they should be with regard to tabs, paragraph marks, and dots between words.

Checking the Spelling

You can start a spellcheck anywhere. If you start anywhere but the beginning, Works checks to the end of the document, then asks for permission to start again from the beginning.

- Press Alt and type **OS** (Options/Check Spelling).

Works finds `Chalmers`, a proper name. You want to skip over `Chalmers`, not correct its spelling or add it to your personal dictionary.

- Press Enter (to simply replace `Chalmers` with Chalmers).
- Works now finds `Jane`. Press Enter again.
- Works finds `Pickett`, so press Enter one more time.

If Works now finds something you mistyped, follow the screen instructions to correct it. Otherwise, Works informs you that the spelling check is finished. Press Enter to acknowledge.

Selecting the Font

This memo prints in 12-point Courier. If the status line shows `COU12`, skip this step and go on to "Previewing and Printing the Memo." If it shows something else, continue on.

If 12-point Courier isn't available on your printer, choose something comparable or simply skip this step and let the text print in the standard font (typically, 12-point Pica). Leave the cursor where it is.

- Press F8 five times (to select the entire memo).
- Press Alt and type **TF** (Format/Font & Style). The dialog box appears.
- Hold down Alt and type **F** (to move to the `Fonts` list).
- Type **C** as many times as needed to choose `Courier`.
- Press Tab (to move to the `Sizes` list).
- Type **1** enough times to move to `12` and press Enter. Press Up Arrow to collapse the selection.

Previewing and Printing the Memo

To be sure all is as it should be, view the memo on screen.

- Press Alt and type **PV** (Print/Preview). The Print dialog box appears. All of these settings are fine.
- Press Enter again. Works now shows how the memo lays out on the printed page. To see it actually on the printed page, turn on your printer.
- Type **P** (to print).

The printer whirs and produces the memo shown in Figure 27-2 (without screen characters, of course). After printing, Works returns you to the memo.

Increasing the Top Margin

To give the memo better balance, increase the top margin. Leave the cursor where it is.

- Press Alt and type **PM** (Print/Page Setup & Margins). The dialog box appears with the blinker in the `Top margin` field.
- Type **1.5** (to choose a new top margin) and press Enter.

Saving and Naming the Memo

Now save the memo and give it the filename ADMEMO. Leave the cursor where it is.

- Press Alt and type **FA** (File/Save As).

Works brings up the Save As dialog box so you can type a filename and, if needed, a drive or directory. If you're saving to the current drive, simply type the filename. Otherwise, type the drive or directory before the filename, for example, A:ADMEMO.

- Type **ADMEMO** and press Enter. Works tacks on the extension .WP5 (for word processor).

  As the file is being saved, the indicator in the left side of the status line shows the percentage already processed. When the page number reappears, Works is ready for your next action.

Working with the Spreadsheet and Chart

The advertising budget you created in the workout in Chapter 7 presents the budget as a pie chart and a bar chart. Load the budget now.

- Press Alt and type **FO** (File/Open Existing File). The dialog box appears.
- Press Tab (to move the blinker to the `Files` list).
- Type **A** as many times as needed to reach `ADBUDGET.WKS`, and press Enter. You now have the advertising budget on the screen.

Saving the Budget Under Another Name

When you save a file under another name, you end up with two identical files. You can then modify one and leave the other intact.

Presenting the chart to best advantage requires that you modify the budget ever so slightly. Before you do that, save the budget under the filename CHMEMO (for CHart MEMO). Leave the cursor where it is.

- Press Alt and type **FA** (File/Save As). The dialog box appears.
- Type **CHMEMO** (do you need a drive letter first?) and press Enter. Works tacks on `.WPS` at the end.

Modifying the Budget Spreadsheet

Sharing the page with a memo gives the chart far less room than when it occupies an entire page by itself. You can take certain space-saving actions to relieve the crowding. Figure 27-3 shows the affected areas.

ADBUDGET-page 2 6/21/90 1:30 PM

	A	B	C	D	E
1		COMPARATIVE ADVERTISING BUDGET			
2	========	========	========	========	========
3	Medium	This Year	% Total	Last Year	% Total
4	--------	--------	--------	--------	--------
5	Newspaper	$34	42.0%	$29	43.1%
6	TV	$12	14.8%	$14	20.5%
7	Radio	$8	9.9%	$4	6.5%
8	Dir Mail	$23	28.4%	$12	18.1%
9	Magazine	$4	4.9%	$8	11.8%
10		--------	--------	--------	--------
11	Total Budget	$81	100.0%	$66	100.0%

Figure 27-3. The budget spreadsheet showing modified elements

Changing the Titles and Numbers

Abbreviating the titles `Television` and `Direct Mail` keep category names from truncating. Place the cursor on A6.

- Type **TV** and move the cursor to A8.
- Type **Dir Mail** and press Enter.

Reducing the number of characters in the Y-axis numbers allows more room for the chart itself. You can do this by omitting commas and thousands places in the budget's dollar amounts. (You'll soon insert a Y-axis title explaining that these numbers are in thousands.) Place the cursor on B5.

When cells are formatted for dollars, any plain number you enter in the cell appears as a dollar amount. If you type a date or a number with a percent sign, for instance, you change the cell format.

- Type **34** (no dollar sign) and move the cursor to B6.
- Type **12** (no dollar sign) and move the cursor to B7.
- Referring to Figure 27-3, type (without dollar signs) the rest of the numbers in column B and column D in rows 5 through 9 only. The numbers in row 11 are generated by formulas.

Works shows the decimal numbers you type in column D as integers ($29, $14, $4, $12, and $8) but stores them as decimals. This keeps the percentages in column E the same as before and causes the chart amounts to be correspondingly correct.

Preparing the Bar Chart

The next step is to modify the chart, so bring it on screen. Leave the cursor where it is.

- Press Alt and type **V** (View). You can now see the chart list containing BUDGET BAR and BUDGET PIE.
- Type the number of BUDGET BAR. Works now displays the bar chart.
- Press Escape (to enter the chart screen).

You can now see the chart menus and CHART on the status line.

Modifying the Data Titles and Gridlines

The Y-axis title is now Annual Basis. Change it to precisely describe the budgetary amounts. Leave the cursor where it is.

- Press Alt and type **DT** (Data/Titles). Works brings up the dialog box containing the titles you entered when you first created the charts. The chart title and subtitle are fine. Replace Annual Basis with In Thousands.

- Press Tab three times (to move to Y-axis).
- Press Right Arrow (to move the blinker after the word Basis.
- Press the Spacebar and type **(in thousands)**. As you type, Works hides the earlier text under the left bracket to make room for more text. Press Enter.

This chart already contains horizontal gridlines. Adding vertical gridlines can also add a bit of flair.

- Press Alt and type **OX** (Options/X-Axis).
- Press the Spacebar (to turn on the Grid Lines box) and press Enter.

Choosing the Title Font

A chart inserted in a memo needs smaller titles than a chart printed on its own page. For the main title, this chart uses Bold Modern B in 18 point. If this font isn't available on your printer, choose something similar. Leave the cursor where it is.

- Press Alt and type **TF** (Format/Title Font). Works brings up the dialog box with the blinker in the Fonts list.
- Type **B** enough times to reach Bold Modern B.
- Press Tab (to move to the Sizes list).
- Press the Up or Down Arrow key enough times to reach **18** and press Enter.

Choosing the Other Font

The chart prints the other titles in 10-point Bold Modern B. Again, choose something similar if this font isn't available.

- Press Alt and type **TO** (Format/Other Font). Here's the font dialog box again with the blinker in the Fonts list.
- Type **B** enough times to reach Bold Modern B.
- Press Tab (to move to the Sizes list).
- Press the Up or Down Arrow key enough times to move to **10** and press Enter.

Choosing a Bar Pattern

You can get some really great-looking charts by using different patterns. Even changing only one pattern creates an entirely new effect.

The standard setting prints the first Y-series in somber black and the second Y-series in dark grey. Lighten things up a bit by printing the first Y-series in a pattern. Leave the cursor where it is.

- Press Alt and type **TD** (Format/Data Format). The dialog box that appears has selections for series, colors, and patterns. The blinker is on `1stY` in the `Series` list.
- Hold down Alt and type `P` (to move to the `Patterns` list).
- Type **X** to reach the pattern `XX`, and press Escape to return to the spreadsheet.

This completes the preparations. Hold down Shift and press F10 to view the final version of the chart on screen. Now press Escape to return to the spreadsheet.

Saving the Changes

Now save the modifications to the spreadsheet and chart. Leave the cursor where it is.

- Press Alt and type **FS** (File/Save).

Integrating the Memo and Chart

The final steps quickly and easily integrate the memo and chart. First, switch to the memo. Leave the cursor where it is.

- Press Alt and type **W** (Window).
- Type the number of `ADMEMO.WPS` and press Enter. Works displays the memo.

Now enter a placeholder to hold the place for the chart. Place the cursor at the paragraph mark separating the two paragraphs.

- Press Alt and type **EI** (Edit/Insert Chart). Works brings up the dialog box with the blinker at `CHMEMO.WKS` in the `Spreadsheets` list.

- Press Up Arrow (to choose CHMEMO.WKS).
- Press Tab (to move to the Charts list).
- Type **B** enough times to reach BUDGET BAR, and press Enter.

Works plunks the placeholder *chart CHMEMO.WKS:BUDGET BAR* between the paragraphs, inserting a blank line before and after it. Your screen should look like the one in Figure 27-4.

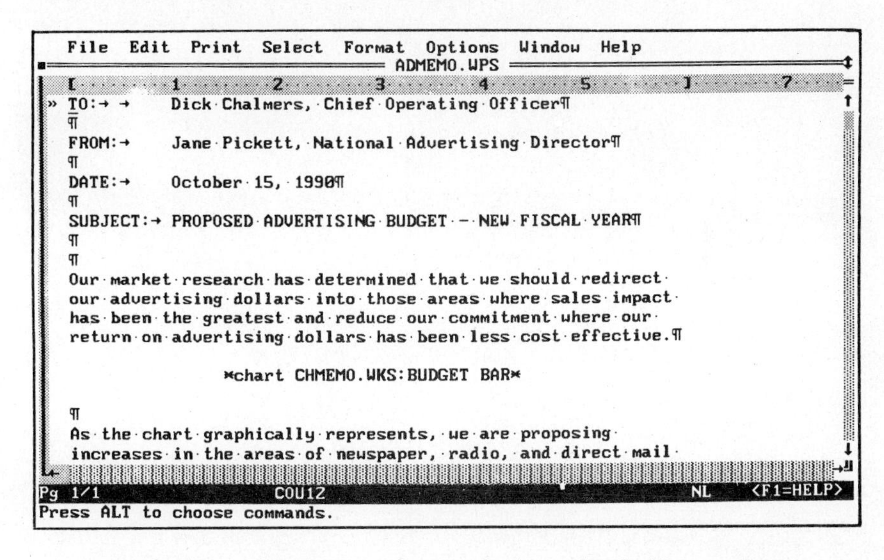

Figure 27-4. The memo screen with chart placeholder in place

Previewing and Printing the Memo

This is the big moment when all your work comes alive, first on screen, and then on paper. Be sure your printer is turned on. Leave the cursor where it is.

- Press Alt and type **PV** (Print/Preview).
- At the dialog box, press Enter.

All the pieces fall into place. Works gives the chart a portrait orientation, reduces its size to conform to the dimensions of the memo, and displays a perfect, polished document.

- Type P (to print the document). Your result should match the one shown in Figure 27-1.

Like I said at the beginning, duck soup. Save the document by pressing Alt and typing **FS**.

This is the last of the hands-on chapters. Except for the glossary, you're at the end of the book. As you move forward on your own with Works, you have every reason to feel confident in your ability to handle the program.

Glossary

Absolute cell reference In a formula, a cell reference that remains unchanged when the formula is copied. A dollar sign ($) before the cell name or cell location makes the cell absolute. For example, in `=DDB($COST,$SALVAGE,$LIFE,A13)`, the cells named `COST`, `SALVAGE`, and `LIFE` are absolute references, and cell A13 is a relative reference. The dollar sign ($) before a cell name or location makes the cell absolute. No matter where you copy this formula, it will continue to refer to the `COST`, `SALVAGE`, and `LIFE` cells. Compare *Relative cell reference.*

Active The area in a file that accepts the action you take. The area is made active by the presence of the cursor or blinker.

Argument Variables that a spreadsheet or database function works with, enclosed in parentheses after the function name. A variable can be a number, cell location containing a number, or a formula. In the argument, a comma separates one variable from the next.

Arithmetic operator A symbol that tells Works the kind of arithmetic calculation to perform with the values in a formula. These symbols are ^ (exponentiation), + (addition), – (subtraction), * (multiplication), and / (division).

Arrow keys The cluster of keys, typically in the right of the keyboard, with an arrow on each keytop. Arrow keys move the cursor in the direction of the arrow—Up, Down, Left, and Right. Also called direction or movement keys.

ASCII Acronym for American Standard Code for Information Interchange. ASCII (pronounced *ASK-ee*) is an information code that allows data devices to communicate with each other in the only way they can—with numbers. The ASCII set consists of letters, numbers, and other characters assigned to numbers 0 to 255. The ASCII code for uppercase A, for example, is 97. When you save a Works file with the Save As command's Text option, the result is an ASCII file—a text file without formatting.

Asynchronous transmission A method of data transmission that sends characters at irregular intervals. Each character is preceded by a start bit and followed by a stop bit. Compare *Synchronous transmission.*

Axis A line in a line or bar chart along which values are measured or to which positions are referred. The X-axis is a horizontal line and the Y-axis is a vertical line.

Bar In a bar chart, a rectangular-shaped element representing a data point.

Bar chart A chart that uses bars to represent numbers in a Y-series. A stacked bar chart stacks bars one on top of another, with each bar in the stack representing the unit contribution of each number in each Y-series. The result is the combined total of spreadsheet numbers within each category. A 100% bar chart shows the percentage contribution of each number in a Y-series to the grand total for each category.

Batch file A list of DOS commands that DOS executes one after the other at your command.

Baud Rate A measure of data transmission speed expressed as bits per second, or bps. For example, 300 baud roughly equals 300 bps or about 30 characters per second. Modems commonly operate at 300, 1200, or 2400 bps, though some zip along at 9600 bps. The higher the baud rate, the faster the transmission.

Binary The number system used by a computer. The only numbers in the binary number system are 0 and 1, which can be arranged in 8-bit sequences to produce 256 permutations. For example, 01000001 represents an uppercase A and 00110000 represents the number 1.

Bit A combination of the words BInary and digiT. A bit is the smallest unit of information in a binary system. It can be on or off, with 1 defined as on and 0 designed as off.

Blinker A Works cursor that operates in the menus and dialog boxes, dubbed a blinker merely to distinguish it from the cursor that operates in the workspace.

Block A group of contiguous cells filled with information. The Ctrl+Arrow keys jump the cursor to the first or last cell in a block, depending on the location of the cursor. When Works runs out of blocks, pressing Ctrl+Arrow jumps the cursor to the farthest cell in the direction of the arrow—Ctrl+Down Arrow to row 4096, Ctrl+Up Arrow to row 1, Ctrl+Right Arrow to column IV, and Ctrl+Left Arrow to column A.

Bookmark In the word processor, named text that allows you to move quickly to different parts of a document.

Break In a database report, a separation of records into groups based on sort fields. Works groups records whenever the content changes. You can create a break whenever the first letter changes, or you can choose no breaks.

Buffer An area of computer memory used for temporary storage of data received from another computer during a communications session.

Bug A software defect (shudder) that prevents a program from behaving exactly as it should.

Button An area in a Works dialog box that, among other actions, lets mouse users carry out or cancel a command.

Byte A group of 8 bits (0s and 1s) that can be arranged in 256 different ways. The computer translates each byte into a letter, number, or other information.

Carriage return An ASCII character that causes a printer or display device to place the next character at the left margin.

Category A group of data points from different series that share a position on the X-axis of a chart. Suppose your bar chart contains three Y-series and uses months as labels on the X-axis. The cluster of three bars at the January position is a category.

Cell On a spreadsheet, a box formed by the intersection of a column and a row, such as cell A1. In a database, a box formed by the intersection of a field (column) and record (row).

Character A letter, number, symbol, or blank space. There are 9 characters in the words LAST NAME, 5 characters in A-123.

Chart A graphic depiction of the numbers in a spreadsheet.

Circular reference On a spreadsheet, a formula that refers to its own cell or formulas that depend on each other for values. In the first instance, for example, a formula in G12 contains a reference to cell G12. In the second instance, a formula in B10 refers to the formula in C10 which, in turn, refers to the formula in B10, thus setting up a circular pattern. Both situations cause Works to display `CIRC` (circular) on the status line.

Command An instruction to Works to perform a specific task. Each Works menu contains a list of commands.

Communications Computers talking to each other by modem and phone line, thus enabling you, for instance, to access commercial data banks, receive and transmit Works files, transact business with your bank, even buy merchandise from the convenience of your home or office. Also referred to as telecommunications, to communicate at a distance.

Communications parameters Settings that control the flow of information between computers. The Works standard is 8 data bits, 1 stop bit, mask parity.

Criterion In a database, a logical rule (equality or comparison) used in queries. Equality criteria select records on the basis of matching information, for example, companies with 100 employees. Comparison criteria select records on the basis of information in a range—for example, companies with between 100 and 250 employees. See *Query*.

Cursor A moveable highlight that shows where your next action takes place. In a Works spreadsheet, the cursor is a horizontal rectangle; in a database, a vertical rectangle; and in a document, a blinking underscore. Arrow keys as well as other keys move the cursor. Also called a pointer.

Database A program with entries organized in cells, fields, and records. You can select database information for display or printing.

Data bits The length in bits of each transmitted character, which can be 7 bits with odd or even parity or 8 bits with no parity. The Works standard is 8 data bits.

Data point A point on a chart representing one number in a Y-series (range) on your spreadsheet. Data points can be shown as rectangular bars, pie slices, markers connected by horizontal-type lines, or markers connected by vertical (hi-lo-close) lines, depending on chart type.

Date stamp The date and/or time entered into a file by your computer, based on your input at DOS startup or your computer's calendar/clock.

Default A preset selection or response meant to be Works' "best guess" of what you want to do next. You can replace a Works default with your own. Works saves the change with the file.

Dialog box A box where you give Works further information about a command. An ellipsis (...) after a command name in the menu indicates the existence of a dialog box.

Direction keys See *Arrow Keys.*

DOS Disk Operating System. A program loaded by your computer at startup. DOS tells the computer how to do such tasks as store, retrieve, and delete files, read keystrokes, and send information to the monitor and the printer.

Download To receive a file from another computer via a modem and phone line. Compare *Upload.*

End-of-line character A character that tells the printer that the preceding text is a complete line and can now be printed.

Entry One piece of information in a spreadsheet or database cell—for example, a formula or a company name.

Field In a database, a group of cells containing the same type of information, such as company names. A field consists of a field name describing the entry and the cells containing the entries.

Field formula In a database, an element that enters information in cells automatically when you start a new record. Field formulas can be constant or equation. A constant field formula enters text, number, date, or time, while an equation field formula enters a formula.

File A collection of related entries stored on disk under a filename. A Works file can be, for example, a spreadsheet budget, a database mailing list, or a word processor memo.

Fixed-input field An interactive element in a macro that causes the macro to pause during its run, at which time you can type a fixed number of characters. In the macro, it appears as `<vfld>`. Compare *Variable-input field.*

Floppy disk A transportable recording and playback device used to store computer programs and data. The disk consists of a flat, circular platter coated with magnetic material and encased in a flexible plastic jacket. Available in 5.25-inch and 8-inch size. Compare *Minidisk* and *Hard disk.*

Font A family of letters, numbers, and symbols in the same design. The style and size of fonts Works makes available to you depends on the capabilities of your printer.

Footer Text that appears at the bottom of each page of a document (for example, a page number). Compare *Header.*

Footnote A reference to support a statement in a document. Works assigns numbers or markers to your footnotes, then prints them at the end of the document.

Format The way Works displays information on screen and on paper—for instance, numbers with dollar signs, titles in bold, or double-spaced paragraphs.

Formula An expression that produces a new value from existing values. Formulas can consist of numbers, cell locations containing numbers, cell names, operators, and functions. For example, the formula `=C5+C9` adds the values in C5 and C9. If you change a value, the formulas related to that value produce new results.

Full duplex In communications, data traveling between two computers in two directions at the same time (similar to talking on a telephone).

Function A shortcut built into the spreadsheet and database applications to calculate values, retrieve information from cells, and select from several possible answers.

Gridlines Lines in a chart that run parallel, perpendicular, or in both directions relative to the X-axis.

Half duplex In communications, data traveling between two computers in only one direction at a time (similar to a CB radio). Alternating the transmission flow allows data to travel in the opposite direction.

Handshake See *XON/XOFF*.

Hard disk A fixed recording and playback device used for storing large amounts of computer programs and data. The hard disk is a rigid disk of magnetic or magnetically-coated material rotating in a sealed housing. Compare *Floppy disk* and *Minidisk*.

Header Text that appears at the top of each page of a document (for example, a date and the recipient's name). Compare *Footer*.

Hi-lo-close chart A chart that uses markers on a vertical line to represent the highest and lowest values in a category. This chart resembles the stock market charts appearing in newspapers.

Host computer A computer accessed by your computer for the exchange of information, typically a BBS (bulletin board) or commercial data bank (CompuServe, Dow Jones, and others).

Integrated software A program that provides different but totally compatible applications, thus permitting an easy interchange of information. Works is integrated software.

Interface The distinctive look of a program—for instance, the design of the Works screen with its pull-down menus and dialog boxes.

Justify To modify the spacing between characters or words in a paragraph to make the lines of equal length and produce smooth left and right margins.

Keyname The unique name and form of keystrokes in a macro definition. For example, Enter is <enter>, Alt is <menu>, and Up Arrow is <xup>.

Leader characters Characters that fill the space between columns—for example, in a table of contents between the topics at the left and page numbers at the right. Leader characters can be dots, single dashes, a solid line, or double dashes. You can also choose to have no leader characters.

Legends Labels that identify the Y-series in a chart. Works displays legends at the bottom of the chart.

Line A horizontally oriented line in a line chart or a vertical line in a hi-lo-close chart. Markers in each line represent the data points.

Line chart A chart that shows the Y-series as markers connected by lines. Each Y-series is plotted from the X-axis. An area line chart combines Y-series, measuring and plotting each data point based on the data point immediately below, not from the X-axis. Like the stacked bar chart, the topmost line shows the grand total.

Line feed An ASCII character that causes a printer or display device to advance to the next line.

Looping macro A macro that starts again from the beginning when it reaches the end of its run. Appending the macro's playback key to the end of the macro produces the looping action. You can stop the looping by pressing Alt+/.

Macro A series of stored keystrokes that tells Works to perform certain tasks in a particular sequence. These tasks can be played back by hitting one or two keys.

Margin The distance between the edge of the paper and printed text.

Marker A symbol showing the location of a data point on a line chart or hi-lo-close chart. Markers can be dots, plus signs, asterisks, or o's.

Menu A list of commands that perform various types of tasks, such as File, Edit, Format, and Window. The names of Works menus are virtually the same in each application and some contain the same commands. The tasks in other menus can differ significantly.

Menu line The top line of the screen where Works displays the menus in an application.

Minidisk A transportable recording and playback device used to store computer programs and data. The disk consists of a flat, circular platter coated with magnetic material and encased in a hard plastic jacket about 3.5-inches square. Compare *Floppy disk* and *Hard disk*.

Modem Short for MOdulator/DEModulator. A device that enables your computer to communicate with other computers over ordinary telephone lines. A modem converts the digital signals sent by your computer into analog sounds that phone lines can carry. When your computer receives data, it reverses the process, converting the analog sounds into digital signals that your computer can use.

Movement keys See *Arrow Keys*.

Network A group of independently-controlled computers linked with each other to share information and other resources.

Null modem A device that allows two computers to exchange information without actually using a modem. The null modem consists of two connectors wired together in such a way as to make their computers think a real modem exists between them.

Parity An error detection process that sets the eighth bit of a character to a value of 0 or 1, making the total number of 1s in the character even (even parity) or odd (odd parity). Both computers must have the same type of parity checking or both must omit parity checks. With 8 data bits, there can be no parity. The Works standard is Mask parity, which masks off the 8th bit to keep you from getting strange characters on screen.

Pie chart A chart that shows the numbers in one Y-series as slices in a pie. Each slice represents a data point in the Y-series. Works calculates the relative size of each slice and shows it as a percentage of the whole pie.

Pitch The size of a printed character measured by the number of characters per inch that print along a horizontal line. For instance, if 12 characters print along one horizontal inch, each character is a 12-pitch character.

Pixel See *Resolution*.

Placeholder An element in a word processor file that holds the place for information you want Works to insert at printing. Placeholders take these forms: `<<LAST NAME>>`, which extracts information from the LAST NAME field in a database, `*page*`, which prints a page number; and `*chartFILENAME.EXT: CHARTNAME*`, which prints the specified chart (`CHARTNAME`) from the specified spreadsheet (`FILENAME.EXT`).

Point A unit of measure that describes the size of characters in a font. Each point is 1/72 inch high. Therefore, a 72-point font has characters that are 1-inch high and a 12-point font, 1/6-inch high.

Port A hardware channel through which your computer sends and receives information.

Preview A Works feature that lets you view the contents and layout of an entire page before printing.

Proportional spacing During printing, the process of spacing characters to account for different widths. Each character—skinny i or chubby w—gets only the room it needs, unlike standard spacing, which gives each character the same amount of room. Proportional spacing can give text a typeset look.

Protocol A set of rules two computers follow when sending and receiving data to achieve total compatibility. In Works communications, refers specifically to XMODEM, an error-checking and correction routine that ensures file transfer without errors.

Pull-down menu A menu that, when selected, drops down into the screen and displays its commands.

Query Logical rules or criteria that tell Works which database records to display or hide. A means of selecting records.

RAM Random Access Memory. A computer's temporary memory, which stores the data and programs you're working on. You can read and modify information stored in RAM. Information remains in RAM only as long as the computer stays on. Compare *ROM*.

Range A group of contiguous cells referred to by a common name, such as SALES, or by cell locations separated by a colon, such as A6:B11. The colon is the range operator.

Rapid-movement keys Keys that move the cursor rapidly, such as Ctrl+Home, Ctrl+End, Home, End, Page Up, Page Down, and so on.

Record A collection of related information in a database. For example, a record can show the name, contact person, title, address, city, state, ZIP code, and line of business of a company.

Relative cell reference In a formula, a cell reference that changes, depending on where a formula is copied. Assume you enter formula `=SUM(B4:B13)` in B15. Because there's no dollar sign ($) to make them absolute, cells B4 to B13 are relative. If you copy this formula to C15, it will add the information in C4 to C13, the cells relative to the formula's new location. Compare *Absolute cell reference.*

Report definition Instructions that determine the content and layout of a printed database report.

Resolution The fineness of line on a screen. Computer images (characters and graphics) are made up of tiny dots. Each dot is called a pixel (picture element). Resolution is the total number of dots on the screen. The more dots, the higher the resolution and the better the picture.

ROM Read-Only Memory. A computer's permanent memory built into semiconductor chips on the internal boards. ROM stores programs needed to operate the computer. You can read information stored in ROM, but you cannot modify it. Since ROM memory is permanent, it isn't lost when power to the computer is turned off. Compare *RAM.*

Row descriptors Instructions that determine what each row in a database report contains and where to print it.

Scale A series of number markers along a line with consistent intervals between them. Used in charting.

Scroll bar A screen element that shows the location of the cursor relative to the rest of the file. Works has a vertical and a horizontal scroll bar. Each scroll bar contains a scroll box that moves along the scroll bar as you move the cursor. Mouse users can scroll quickly to distant places in the file by gliding the scroll box along the scroll bar.

Scroll box See *Scroll bar.*

Selection bar The left edge of the word processor screen where Works shows elements in a document, such as letters `H` or `F` for a header or footer and right angle brackets for a page break.

Shortcut key A keystroke that permits you to choose a command without going through a menu.

Slice A data point in a pie chart.

Sort In a database, the process of arranging records alphabetically, numerically, or chronologically by field. Sorting can take place in ascending (A to Z, 1 to 9, earliest date to latest) or descending order (Z to A, 9 to 1, latest date to earliest).

Spreadsheet A program that organizes text and values into columns and rows. Also called a worksheet.

Stop bits The number of bits—either 1 or 2—used to indicate the end of each transmitted character. The Works standard is 1 stop bit.

Style In the Works word processor, attributes that make a printed character stand out from the rest of the text—for instance, bold, italic, or underline.

Subscript character A character that prints one-half line below the normal line.

Superscript character A character that prints one-half line above the normal line.

Synchronous transmission A method of data transmission that uses a clocking signal to send characters at regular, timed intervals. Compare *Asynchronous transmission*.

Template A designated master file in any Works application (spreadsheet, database, word processor, communications) containing standard settings and information you want Works to use when you ask for a new file.

Upload To send a file to another computer via modem and phone line. Compare *Download*.

Value A numerical entry, which can be a number, a formula yielding a number, or a cell location or cell name containing a number or formula.

Variable-input field An interactive element in a macro that causes the macro to pause during its run, at which time you can type a variable number of characters. In the macro, it appears as **<ffld>**. Compare *Fixed-input field*.

Wildcard A symbol that replaces one or more characters in text during a search or query. The question mark (?) replaces a single character and the asterisk (*) replaces multiple characters.

Word processor A program that lets you use your computer to write, format, edit, save, and print text easily.

Wordwrap In the word processor, a process that causes a word that doesn't fit at the end of a line to move down automatically to the start of the next line. This saves you the task of pressing Enter at the end of each line.

WYSIWYG An acronym for What You See Is What You Get. What you see on the screen in the way of character size and style (bold, underlined, italic, and so on) is what you get when the page prints. Your system needs graphics capability to show size and style on screen.

X-axis and Y-axis The horizontal and vertical fixed lines, respectively, in a line or bar chart.

XMODEM A protocol for transferring blocks of information with a high degree of accuracy via modem. See *Protocol*.

XON/XOFF A protocol that controls the flow of data during communications. If the flow is too fast, the computer sends an XOFF (pause) signal that suspends transmission temporarily without losing data. When the computer is again ready to receive, it sends an XON (continue) signal. Also called a software handshake.

X-series The data points or labels along the X-axis of a chart.

X-Y chart A chart that plots spreadsheet numbers from the X-axis as well as the Y-axis. Also called a scatter chart or scattergram.

Y-series The data points plotted on the Y-axis of a chart. Data points derive from the numbers in a range of cells on a spreadsheet. A Y-series can appear as markers, bars, vertical (hi-low-close) lines, or pie slices, depending on the type of chart you choose.

Index

A

B

C

D

G

H

I

J–K

L

M

N

O

P

Q–R

S

T

U–V

W

X–Y